The Early Antigonids

Coinage, Money, and the Economy

Katerina Panagopoulou

THE AMERICAN NUMISMATIC SOCIETY
NEW YORK
2020

ISSN 051-7404-x
ISBN 978-0-89722-355-3

Library of Congress Cataloging-in-Publication Data

Names: Panagopoulou, Katerina, author.
Title: The early Antigonids : coinage, money, and the economy / Katerina Panagopoulou.
Description: New York : The American Numismatic Society, 2019. | Includes bibliographical references and index. | Summary: "A systematic analysis of the precious metal coinages in the name of 'king Antigonos'. traditionally assigned to the Macedonian king Antigonos Gonatas (283/277-239 BC). Chronological and hoard evidence suggest that they may belong to both Antigonos Gonatas and Antigonos Doson. The iconography reflects the main threads of Antigonid foreign policy"-- Provided by publisher.
Identifiers: LCCN 2019018738 | ISBN 9780897223553
Subjects: LCSH: Antigonus II, King of Macedonia, 278/7 B.C.-239 B.C. | Demetrius II, King of Macedonia, 239 B.C.-229 B.C. | Antigonus III, King of Macedonia, 229 B.C.-221 B.C. | Coins, Greek--Macedonia. | Kings and rulers in numismatics--Macedonia. | Portrait sculpture in numismatics--Macedonia. | Money--Macedonia. | Macedonia--Antiquities. | Macedonia--Economic conditions. | Greece--Economic conditions--To 146 B.C. | Macedonia--History--To 168 B.C. | Greece--History--To 146 B.C.
Classification: LCC CJ546 .P36 2019 | DDC 737.4938/1--dc23
LC record available at https://lccn.loc.gov/2019018738

MATRI CARISSIMAE
PATRIS IN MEMORIAM

Contents

Preface

It is a great pleasure for me to see the publication of Katerina Panagopoulou's numismatic corpus of the Macedonian royal coinage issued after Alexander the Great. I was the external examiner of her PhD thesis, from which the book has been expanded and developed and have followed her work with great interest since. The monograph will be a landmark study of the Antigonid dynasty and its coinage because of the way she successfully weaves together numismatic, archaeological, epigraphical, historical and literary evidence into a coherent narrative. On many points she clarifies and advances scholarly understanding of the Antigonid coinage. In particular, she has resolved some problems of dating and attribution of coins between the long-lived third-century Macedonian king Antigonos Gonatas and his successors, including Antigonos Doson. Her careful reading of the coin iconography illuminates many political and identity issues that the Macedonian kings had to face in relation to their control of mainland Greece and the Aegean. For instance, she demonstrates convincingly that two key coin types, one with the head of Pan in a Makedonian shield on the front side of the coin and a standing Athena on the reverse and another with a head of Poseidon on the front side and with an Apollo bearing a bow and seated on a prow of a ship on the reverse, were long lived Macedonian royal types, started under Antigonos Gonatas but continued through to the successor of Antigonos Doson, Philip V. She also makes important arguments about the scale of the Macedonian coin issues in this period, noting a disparity between the size of issues and the actual needs of a large state. She concludes reasonably that the Macedonian state made up some of the shortfall from other precious metal coinages using the Attic standard, but also emphasizes the point that the Macedonian issues were to a considerable extent politically motivated. The period and the coins presented here have been somewhat neglected in the past. Katerina has brought both into much sharper focus and it is to be hoped that her book will stimulate renewed interest and debate about this fascinating era in Greek history and numismatics.

Cambridge, 15 November 2014

† Harold B. Mattingly

Preface

The present monograph brings the early Antigonid precious metal coinages to the attention of the numismatic world nearly twenty years after the completion of my doctoral dissertation. The compilation of this monograph was started at University College London in September 1994, under the supervision of Professors M. H. Crawford, Katerini Liampi (then at the Research Center for Greek and Roman Antiquity, Hellenic National Research Foundation, currently at the University of Ioannina) and K. Buraselis (University of Athens), from whose comments I have benefited throughout this task. Since 1996, Dr. A. Burnett (Department of Coins and Medals, British Museum) has co-mentored the thesis, constantly encouraging and stimulating its writing. The publication of this project was already suggested in the viva by the external examiner of the thesis, the late Professor Harold Mattingly, ex-President of the Royal Numismatic Society, to whose bright spirit and kindness, and, not least, to his setting an ideal example for perseverance and discipline, I am indebted in more ways than he might have imagined. His Preface to this book, presumably one of his last letters, was sent to me for inclusion some years ago, when publication seemed to be imminent; it is a great pity that he did not get to see the volume. Richard Ashton and Kostas Buraselis have become my stalwart supporters in turning the thesis into a book: their knowledgeable and thorough comments, discipline and encouragement have been invaluable throughout, while the core of the manuscript owes much to the former's meticulous editing. Andy Meadows mediated the eventual transfer of the volume from the Royal Numismatic Society to the American Numismatic Society's Numismatic Studies monograph series and generously offered me insightful information on hoard material. Oliver Hoover re-edited the final draft with scrupulous attention to detail and eliminated errors, while Andrew Reinhard supervised the final stages of the monograph's journey to the press. I am enormously grateful to them all.

My initial ambition to compile a corpus of the bronze coins as well as the gold and silver had to be abandoned because of the sheer abundance of the material. Inevitably conclusions from the study of the precious metal coinage in the name "of King Antigonos" do not fully reflect monetary production in Makedonia during the second and third quarters of the third century. It is also likely that the conclusions concerning the silver coinage will require revision when the bronze is fully studied. On the other hand, it is reassuring that the thrust of my remarks and arguments remain intact in the final version of the book, despite the remarkable increase in coin numbers through five major auction updates. In regard to practical matters, my auction catalogues were arranged by numismatic experts, whenever possible. Coins that have appeared in sales catalogues after July 2014 have not been taken into account: in the course of this protracted publication process, I eventually realised that the impact of any added material on the statistics beyond that point would have been minimal. The same end date holds for bibliographical additions.

Financial support for the thesis was provided by the Hellenic Scholarship Foundation (1994–1998), and its writing-up was further sponsored by the Alexander Onassis Foundation (1998–1999). The collection of material at the early stages of the dissertation was considerably enhanced by the prompt response of the Keepers of all the museum and bank collections and of those directors and archaeologists of Greek Ephoreiai of antiquities and Italian Soprintendenzae who gave me permission to see, make notes and include material in my doctoral dissertation.

To all of them I owe my deepest thanks. Furthermore, the University College London Graduate School financed my visit to numismatic collections at Berlin, Heidelberg, the Vatican and Leiden, for the collection of material, and a 1998 Royal Numismatic Society M. J. Price Travelling Fund enabled me to inspect coins in Paris, Brussels and through Greek museums. After that, through a British School at Athens / Foundation of the Hellenic World Postdoctoral Fellowship in 2002–2003 at the Ashmolean Museum, Oxford I was able to update the auction material and work on the manuscript in an environment that was ideal for studying numismatics. A Stanley Seeger Visiting Research Fellowship at the Program in Hellenic Studies, at Princeton University, in 2002 made possible a close inspection of the material available at the American Numismatic Society in New York, and a renewed tenure of the same fellowship in 2018 turned out to be critical in finalizing the publication process.

University College London, the Institute of Classical Studies and the British Museum have provided an appropriate academic environment for the core systematic work on this project. The—nearly endless—research through past sales catalogues, which was started at the Department of Coins and Medals at the British Museum for the thesis and was pursued at the Ashmolean Museum, Oxford in 2002-2003, under the auspices of Henry Kim and Chris Howgego, was completed at the private library of BCD in Athens: I am most grateful to him and, not least, to his secretary, Ms Patricia Felch, for having so adequately accommodated my quest for new specimens through the rare, old, and most recent auction catalogues, until electronic resources simplified this task considerably. Occasionally the Research Center for Greek and Roman Antiquity at Athens (then KERA, currently IERA/Institute of Historical Research) also hosted my project. I would like to thank the ex-director, Professor M. B. Hatzopoulos, both for having granted me permission to use the Center's research facilities and archives and for reading and commenting on the final draft of the historical chapters for the thesis. I also owe a lot to substantial discussions with Professors C. Boehringer, J. K. Davies and G. Le Rider, as well as with Makis Aperghis, Yannis Touratsoglou, Henry Kim, Andy Meadows, Constantin Marinescu, Christina Mitsopoulou, Christos Gatzolis, Graham Oliver, Paschalis Paschidis, Ilya Prokopov, Selene Psoma, and Yiannis Stoyas. Catharine Lorber kindly shared with me photographs of the hoards of "Seleucus III," 2002, "Achaeus," 2002 and "Antiochus III," 2005 before they went to press, while Christof Boehringer's record of Antigonid coins added the specimens which appear in the relevant appendix (9.7), as they came too late to be integrated into the main corpus and into the statistics. It is worth recording that Makis Aperghis prompted me to employ statistics on my sample and offered substantial feedback on my results before this became common practice in the field. Christof Boehringer, Gary Reger, Jack Kroll, Andy Meadows, Makis Aperghis, Benet Salway, Eva Parisinou-Nicklaus, Michael Metcalfe, Graham Oliver, Selene Psoma and Giorgos Tsiotas have commented on drafts of parts of my work at various stages, have improved its style and eliminated errors. I am most indebted to the following librarians: Colin Annis, of the Institute of Classical Studies, and library staff; Antony Holms, ex-librarian of the Royal Numismatic Society, for his help with practical issues and for his encouragement; Penny Wilson Zarganis and Sandra Pepelasis, and Maria Tourna, respectively of the British and the American Schools of Classical Studies at Athens, and not least, Patricia Felch, secretary of the BCD library, for their ever-lasting patience with my numerous requests. My younger sister, Athena, a graphics designer, undertook and brought to a graceful end the setup and arrangement of the plates and map and put up both with several changes in their design and with my obsession with (the as yet unattained) perfection. Peter van Alfen, Alexandros Andreou, Amelia Dowler, Sophia Diamantopoulou, Kallia Lempidaki, Stamatoula Makrypodi, Julien Olivier, Giorgos Papaioannou, Kostas Pilos, Vassiliki Stefanaki and Nikos Sougles are also thanked most cordially for providing information, photos of specimens, or assistance with technical matters. Some photos from auction catalogues were made by Pantelis Magoulas. Needless to say, any remaining errors are my own responsibility.

The accomplishment of this project would not have been possible without a band of strongly supportive colleagues and friends. In addition to those mentioned above, I am grateful to Elena Isayev, Christy Constantakopoulou, Photini Balla, Elpida Kaimaki, Yannis Papadatos, Jennifer Cargill-Thompson, Dee Murphy, Lina Georgiou, Anne Alwis, Athanassios Efstathiou, Charalampos Papageorgiou, Maria Stamatopoulou, Bill Stancomb, Spiros Pilos,Ulrike Peter, Giorgos T. and Ian Whalley, whose stimulation has been invaluable at critical moments during the processing of the manuscript; and to many more I may be forgetting at the moment. Not least, Polymnia Athanassiadi and John Avgerinos are thanked for having always been there. Finally, it is my love of music that has preserved my sanity during the interminable progress of this volume through to press: I would like to thank, among others, the Greek music radio channel "pepper fm", which helped me stay in tune with real life in the last stages of the project and to go through five auction catalogue updates.

I have reserved the final mention for my parents. My father, Themistokles, an economist and lawyer himself, instilled in me the virtues of systematic and tedious work, was the first to teach me how to think, and inspired me to focus on economic history. My thesis was dedicated to his memory, yet it would be unfair not to mention how enormously I have benefited from my mother's full support and συμπάθεια throughout the numerous pathways towards finishing this endeavour. It is for this reason that I dedicate this monograph to them both.

Katerina Panagopoulou

Athens / Rethymno, University of Crete, June 2019

Abbreviations

I. Ancient Literary Sources

Aelian. *Takt.*	Aelianus, *Taktika*, ed. H. Köchly and W. Rustow, Griechische Kriegsschriftsteller (Osnabrück: Biblio, 1855).
App. *Illyr.*	Appian, *Historia Romana*, ed. P. Viereck and A. G. Roos, vols. I–II, Loeb Classical Library (Cambridge, Mass.: Harvard University Press,1939); rev. E. Gabba, 1962.
Arist. *Oik.*	Aristote, *Économique*, ed. B. A. van Groningen and A. Wartelle (Paris: Belles Lettres, 1968).
Asklepiod. *Takt.*	Asclépiodote, *Traité de Tactique*, ed. L. Poznanski, Paris: Belles Lettres, 1992.
Athen.	Athenaeus, *Deipnosophistae*, ed. G. Kaibel, vols. 1–3 (Leipzig: Teubner, 1886–1890).
Cicero, *De Div.*	Cicero, *De Divinatione*, ed. T. E. Page, E. Cappa and W. H. D. Rouse, trans. W. A. Falconer, Loeb Classical Library (Cambridge, Mass.: Harvard University Press, 1923).
Diod.	Diodorus Siculus, *Bibliotheca Historica*, ed. F. Vogel and C. T. Fischer, vols. 1–6 (Leipzig: Teubner, 1886–1890).
Diog. Laert.	Diogenes Laertius, *Vitae Philosophorum*, ed. H. S. Long, vols. I–II (Oxford: Clarendon Press, 1964).
Euseb.	*Eusebi Chronicorum Libri duo*, ed. A. Schoene (Berlin: Weidmann, 1866–1875).
FGH	F. Jacoby, *Die Fragmente der griechischen Historiker* (Berlin: Weidmann, 1923–1958).
Frontin.	Sextus Julius Frontinus, *Strategematon*, ed. G. Gunderman (Leipzig: Teubner, 1888).
Hdt.	Herodoti *Historiae*, ed. K. Hude, vols. I–II, Oxford Classical Texts (Oxford: Oxford University Press, 1926–1927).
Just.	Marcus Junian(i)us Justinus, *Epitoma Historiarum Philippicarum Pompei Trogi*, ed. Otto Seel (Leipzig: Tebner, 1972).
Kallim.	Callimachus, ed. R. Pfeiffer, vols. I–II (Oxford: Oxford University Press, 1949–1953).
Liv.	Titus Livius, *Ab urbe condita liberi*, ed. W. Weissenborn and M. Müller, vols. I–IV (Stuttgart: Teubner, 1966).
Lucian, *Macrob.*	Luciani *Opera*, ed. M. H. Macleod, vol. 1 (Oxford: Oxford University Press, 1972).
Paus.	Pausanias, *Descriptio Graeciae*, ed. W. Jones, Loeb Classical Library (Cambridge, Mass.: Harvard University Press, 1918–1935).
Plb.	Polybius, *Historiae*, ed. L. Dindorf and T. Büttner-Wobst, vols. I–V (Stuttgart: Teubner, 1962–1963).

Plut. *Mor.*	Plutarch, *Moralia*, ed. C. Hubert et al., vols. 1–7, Leipzig 1925–1978.
Plut.	Plutarch, from the *Vitae Parallelae*, ed. K. Ziegler, vols. I–III (Leipzig: Teubner, 1969): biographies of Aemilius Paulus (*Aem.*), Agis (*Agis*), Aratus (*Arat.*), Cleomenes (*Cleom.*), Demetrius (*Dem.*), Pelopidas (*Pelop.*), Philopoemen (*Philop.*), Pyrrhus (*Pyrrh.*).
Polyaen. *Strat.*	Polyaenus, *Strategemata*, ed. E. Woelfflin et al. (Stuttgart: Teubner, 1970).
Sextus Empiricus, *Adversus Mathematicos*	*Adversus Mathematicos*, ed. H. Mutschmann, Leipzig, 1912; rev. J. Mau and K. Janacek (Leipzig: Teubner, 1954).
Str.	Strabo, *Geographica*, ed. H. L. Jones, vols. I–VIII, Loeb Classical Library (Cambridge, Mass.: Harvard University Press, 1917).
Suida	*Suidae Lexicon*, ed. A. Adler, vols. I–IV (Leipzig: Teubner, 1855).
Tacit. *Ann.*	Cornelius Tacitus, *Annales*, I.1, ed. St. Borszsak (Leipzig: Teubner, 1990); vol. I.2, ed. K. Wellesley (Leipzig: Teubner, 1986).
Xenophon, *HG*	Xenophon, *Historia Graeca*, ed. C. Marchant, vols. 1–2 (Oxford: Oxford University Press, 1900).

II. Epigraphic Publications

Blümel, *Knidos*	W. Blümel, *Die Inschriften von Knidos*, Inschriften griechischer Städte aus Kleinasien, Teil I (Bonn: Österreichische Akademie der Wissenschaften, 1992).
Dürrbach, *Délos*	F. Dürrbach, *Choix d' inscriptions de Délos*, Paris 1921–1923.
FD III	*Fouilles de Delphes*, Épigraphie Grecque, vol. III, fasc. 1–4 (Paris: De Boccard, 1909).
Hatzopoulos, *Actes de Vente*	see Secondary Literature.
Hatzopoulos, *Institutions*	see: ibid.
Hatzopoulos, *Institutions* II	see: ibid.
Helly, *Gonnoi* II	B. Helly, *Gonnoi*, vol. II (Amsterdam: Hakkert, 1973).
IG	*Inscriptiones Graecae Consilio et Auctoritate Academiae Litterarum Borussicae* Editae, vols. I–XV, Berlin: De Gruyter, 1873) (editio altera, 1913).
IG II[2]	*Inscriptiones Attikae Euclidis anno posteriores*, ed. J. Kirchner, fasc. 1–4 (Berling: De Gruyter, 1913–1940).
I.Kaunos	C. Marek, *Die Inschriften von Kaunos* (Vestigia 55; Munich, 2006).
Meiggs-Lewis, *GHI*[2]	R. Meiggs and D. Lewis, *A Selection of Greek Historical Inscriptions to the End of the Fifth Century B.C.* (Oxford/New York: Clarendon/Oxford University Press, 1988).
OGIS	W. Dittenberger (ed.), *Orientis Graeci Inscriptiones Selectae*: *Supplementum Sylloges Inscriptionum Graecarum* (Hildesheim: Olms, 1960).
SEG	H. W. Pleket and R. S. Stroud et al. (eds.), *Supplementum Epigraphicum Graecum* (Alphen aan den Rijn: Sjthoff & Noordhoff, 1923).

Syll^{3}	W. Dittenberger, *Sylloge Inscriptionum Graecorum*, vols. 1–4 (Leipzig: Herzel, 1960).
Staatsvertr./Staatsv.	H. Bengtson, *Die Staatsverträge des Altertums*, Kommission für alte Geschichte und Epigraphik des Deutschen Archäologischen Instituts (Munich: C. H. Beck, 1975).

III. Papyrological Publications

P. Cairo Zeno	*Catalogue général des antiquités égyptiennes du Musée de Caire: Zenon Papyri*, ed. C. C. Edgar, vols. 1–4 (Cairo: Institut français d' archéologie orientale 1925–1931.
P. Haun.	*Papyri Graecae Haunienses* I, ed. T. Larsen (Copenhagen: Munksgaard, 1942).

IV. Numismatic Publications

1) Principal Published Numismatic Collections

BMC Macedonia	B. V. Head, *Catalogue of Coins in the British Museum*, Macedonia, London: Trustees of the British Museum, 1879).
Davis	Hyla Troxell, *The Norman Davis Collection*, Greek Coins in North American Collections (New York: American Numismatic Society, 1969).
Dewing	Leo Mildenberg and Silvia Hurter (eds.), *The Arthur S. Dewing Collection of Greek Coins, Ancient Coins in North American Collections* (New York: American Numismatic Society, 1985).
EH I	Faucher, T., A. Meadows and C. Lorber (eds.), *Egyptian Hoards* I, *The Ptolemies* (Cairo: Institut français d' archéologie orientale, 2017).
Grose, *McClean*	S. W. Grose, *Fitzwilliam Museum. Catalogue of the McClean Collection of Greek Coins*, 2. *The Greek Mainland, The Aegean Islands, Crete* (Cambridge: Cambridge University Press, 1926).
Houghton, *Seleucid Empire*	A. Houghton, *Coins from the Seleucid Empire from the Collection of Arthur Houghton* (New York: American Numismatic Society, 1983).
Jameson	R. Jameson, *Monnaies Grecques Antiques*, vol. Ib, Macédoine (Chicago: Ares, 1980) (= Paris, 1913–1932).
Jenkins	G. K. Jenkins, *Ancient Greek Coins*, second ed., Coins in History (London: Seaby, 1990).
MacDonald, *Hunterian*	G. MacDonald, *Catalogue of Greek Coins in the Hunterian Museum*, 1. *Italy, Sicily, Macedon, Thrace, and Thessaly* (Glasgow: J. Maclehose & Sons, 1899–1905).
Pozzi	S. Boutin, *Catalogue des monnaies grecques antiques de la collection Pozzi*, vols. I–II, Maastricht 1979; idem, *Catalogue des monnaies grecques antiques de l' ancienne collection Pozzi, Monnaies frappes en Europe*, vols. I–II (Monaco: Le Louis d' Or, 1992); *Monnaies grecques antiques provenant de la collection de feu le Prof. S. Pozzi* (Monaco: Louis d' Or, 1992).

Rutter, *Edinburgh*	N. K. Rutter (ed.), *A Catalogue of ancient Greek coins in the Royal Scottish Museum, Edinburgh* (Edinburgh: Edinburgh Royal Scottish Museum, 1979).
Sartiges	*Collection du Vicompte de Sartiges, Séries Grecque et Romaine en 1910, ainsi que des acquisitions depuis cette date* (Paris: A. Longuet, 1910).
SNG	*Sylloge Nummorum Graecorum.*
SNG Aarhus	(Danish Series B) *SNG Aarhus University*, Denmark 1986; see also: *SNG Fabricius.*
SNG Alpha Bank	*SNG Greece II, The Alpha Bank Collection, Macedonia I, Alexander–Perseus* (Athens: Alpha Bank, 2000).
SNG Ashmolean	*SNG* [Great Britain] 5, *Ashmolean Museum Oxford, Macedonia III* (Oxford: Oxford University Press, 1976).
SNG Blackburn	*SNG* [Great Britain] 8, *The Hart Collection, Blackburn Museum* (Oxford: Oxford University Press / Spink & Son Ltd., 1989).
SNG BYB	*SNG The Burton Y. Berry Collection*, 1. *Macedonia to Attika* (New York: American Numismatic Society, 1961).
SNG Cop	(Danish Series A) *SNG The Royal Collection of Coins and Medals, Danish National Museum, Macedonia* 3: *Philip III–Philip VI, Macedonia under the Romans, Kings of Paionia*, ed. by H. E. Mathiesen (Copenhagen: Nationalmuseet, 1943).
SNG Delepierre	*SNG Bibliothèque Nationale, Cabinet des Médailles, Collection Jean et Marie Delepierre* (Paris: Bibliothèque nationale de France, 1983).
SNG Deutschland	*SNG Deutschland, Münzsammlung der Universität Tübingen*, 2. Heft, Taurische Chersones–Korkyra (Berlin: Mann, 1982).
SNG Evelpidis	*SNG Rena Evelpidis*, Athènes, IIe partie: Macédoine, Thessalie, Illyrie, Corcyre, Épire (Louvain: Institut supérieur d'archéologie et d'histoire de l'art de l'université catholique de Louvain, 1975).
SNG Fabricius	(Danish Series A+B) *SNG The Fabricius Collection-Aarhus University and Royal Collection of Coins and Medals* (Copenhagen: Nationalmuseet, 1987).
SNG Fitzwilliam	*SNG* [Great Britain] 4, *Fitzwilliam Museum: Leake and General Collections, Macedonia–Acarnania* (London: Oxford University Press, 1951). See also: Grose, *McClean.*
SNG Klagenfurt	*SNG Samml. Dreer/Klagenfurt für Kärnten*, III. Teil, *Thrakien–Makedonien–Päonien* (Klagenfurt: Geschichtsverein für Kärnten, 1990).
SNG Lewis	*SNG* [Great Britain] 6, vol. 3, *The Lewis Collection, Corpus Christi College* (London: Oxford University Press, 1972).
SNG Lockett	*SNG* [Great Britain] 3, *The Lockett Collection*, vol. 3 (London: Oxford University Press, 1938).
SNG Manchester	*SNG* [Great Britain] 7, *Manchester University Museum, The Raby and Güterboek Collections* (London: Oxford University Press, 1986).

SNG Milano	*SNG* [Italia], *Milano, Civiche Raccolte Numismatiche*, Vol. VI. Macedonia–Thracia, 1. Macedonia greca–Paeonia–missioni di area celtica, a cura di Novella Vismara (Milan: Comune di Milano, Settore Cultura, Civiche Raccolte Numismatiche, 1999).
SNG München	*SNG Deutschland, Staatliche Münzsammlung München*, 10/11. Heft, Makedonien: Könige Nr. 1–1228 (Munich: Prestel, 2001).
SNG Newnham Davis	*SNG* [Great Britain] I.2, *The Newnham Davis Coins in the Wilson Collection of Classical and Eastern Antiquities, Marishal College, Aberdeen* (London: Oxford University Press, 1936).
SNG Saroglos	S. Psoma and I. Touratsoglou, *SNG Greece 4, Numismatic Museum, Athens, The Petros Z. Saroglos Collection, Use-Loan by the Club of the Officers of the Armed Forces*, vol. I: *Macedonia* (Athens: Academy of Athens, 2005).
SNG Sweden II	*SNG Sweden II: The Collection of the Royal Cabinet, National Museum of Monetary History Stockholm*, part 2 (Stockholm: Almqvist & Wiksell International, 1980).
SNG Wulfing	K. Herbert, *The John Max Wulfing Collection in Washington University*, Ancient Coins in North American collections (New York: American Numismatic Society, 1979).
Weber	L. Forrer, *Descriptive Catalogue of the Collection of Greek Coins formed by Sir Hermann Weber*, vols. 1–13 (London: Spink & Son., 1922–1929).
Winterthur	H. J. Bloesch, *Griechische Münzen im Winterthur*, vol. 1, *Spanien, Gallien, Italien, Moesien, Dakien, Sarmatien, Thrakien, Makedonien, Hellas, Inseln* (Winterthur: Münzkabinett Winterthur, 1987).

II) Publications of Hoards

CH	*Coin Hoards.*
IGCH	M. Thompson, O. Mørkholm, and C. M. Kraay, *An Inventory of Greek Coin Hoards* (New York: American Numismatic Society, 1973).

III) Sale Catalogues

Aes Rude	Aes Rude, S. A. Chiasso, Lugano.
Ahlström	B. Ahlström, Stockholm.
Albuquerque	Cabinet Numismatique Françoise Albuquerque, Paris.
Amphora	Amphora (D. Hendin), New York.
ANA	American Numismatic Association, Cleveland, Ohio.
Antiqua	Antiqua (S. L.Rubinger), Woodland Hills, CA.
Antiquarius	Antiquarius (Bob Loosley), Russell, New Zealand.
Aretusa	Numismatica Aretusa, S. A., Lugano.
Argenor	Argenor Numismatique, S.A., Paris.
Ariadne	Ariadne Galleries, Inc., New York.
Athena	Athena, Münzen der Antike, GMBH (C.Ceylan), Munich.

Auch-en-Gascogne	Auch-en-Gascogne, Hotel des Ventes aux Enchères publiques, Auch/France.
Auctiones	Auctiones S.A., Basel (MMAG).
Aufhäuser	Bankhaus Aufhäuser, Munich.
Aufleger, Verzeichnis	O. Aufleger, *Verzeichnis griechischer Münzen meist aus dem kgl. Münzkabinett zu München* (München 1883).
Aurea	Aurea Numismatika, Prague.
Aureo	Aureo Subasta Numismatica, Barcelona.
Aureo & Calicó	Aureo & Calicó, Barcelona.
Baldwin	Baldwin, London.
Baldwin-Markov-M&M	Baldwin's Auctions Ltd.—D. Markov—M&M Numismatics Ltd., The New York Sale, New York.
Ball	Robert Ball Nachf., Berlin.
Baranowsky	M. Baranowsky, Milan.
Barré	G. Barré, Rennes.
Barthold-Baudey	R. Barthold, J. Baudey & M. Pesce, A. Poinsignon, Paris.
Barthold-Poplavsky	R. Barthold and G. de Poplavsky, Paris.
Bauer	G. J.Bauer, Rochester, New York.
Bayerische Vereinsbank	Bayerische Vereinsbank, Munich..
Beckenbauer	E. Beckenbauer, Munich.
Berk	H. J. Berk, Chicago, Illinois.
BerlMC	Berliner Münz-Cabinet GmbH, Berlin.
Blançon	G. Blançon Münzhandlung, Hannover.
Bonhams	Bonhams, London; see: Vecchi & Bonhams.
Bourgey	Étienne Bourgey, Émile Bourgey, and Sabine Bourgey-Louis, Paris.
BPB	J. C. Baudey and M. Pesce—R. Barthold, Lyon.
BPN-CB	Banque Populaire du Nord—Crédit de la Bourse, Paris.
Braunschweiger	Braunschweiger Münzverkehr, Braunschweig.
Burgan	Claude Burgan, Paris.
Button	E. Button, Frankfurter Münzhandlung, Frankfurt.
Cahn	A. E. Cahn, Frankfurt am Main.
Calico	X. and F. Calico, Barcelona.
Canessa	C. and E. Canessa, Naples.
Cederlind	T. Cederlind, Portland, Oregon.
Christie's	Christie's/Christie, Manson & Woods Ltd., London.
Ciani	L. Ciani, Paris.
Ciani-Vinchon	P. Ciani—J. Vinchon & Cie, Paris.
CNA	Classical Numismatic Actions Ltd. (Victor England), Quarryville/Beverly Hills; see: CNG.
CNG	Classical Numismatic Group (Victor England), Lancaster, Pennsylvania/London.
Coin Galleries	Coin Galleries, New York.
CGB	www.cgb.fr (E-sales).
CGF	Comptoir Général Financier, Paris.

CB	Crédit de la Bourse, Paris.
Cummings	J. Cummings, Lincolnshire.
Davisson	Allan Davisson Ltd., Gold Spring, MN.
Dombrowski	H. Dombrowski Münzhandlung, Münster-Angelmodde.
Dorau	Gernot Dorau, Berlin.
Dorotheum	Dorotheum, Vienna.
Egger	Brüder Egger, Vienna.
Elsen	J. Elsen, Brussels.
Emporium	Emporium, Hamburg.
Feuardent	Feuardent Frères (Félix Bienaimé Feuardent), Paris.
Feuardent-Leman	M. Feuardent and Henri Leman, Paris.
Florange-Ciani	J. Florange and L. Ciani, Paris.
Forestier & Lambert	F. B. Forestier and S. Lambert, Millon and Associés, Paris.
FM	Frankfurter Münzhandlung (Anders Ringberg), Frankfurt.
France Numismatique	France Numismatique, Mulhouse.
Freeman-Sear	Freeman & Sear, Los Angeles, CA.
Frey	Helga & P. R. Blaser-Frey, Freiburg im Breigsau.
Gadoury, Monte Carlo	France Numismatique-Antika 1-Mint State SAM—Victor Gadoury, Monte Carlo.
Galata	Galata Coins Ltd., Sacra Moneta, Wolverhampton, UK.
Galerie Numismatique (Drouot)	Galerie Numismatique (Drouot) S.A.R.L., Paris.
Gans	Numismatic Fine Arts (E. Gans), New York.
G+H	Münzhandlung Gradl & Hinterland, Nürnberg.
Gemini	Gemini Numismatic Auctions. LLC, New York.
Glendining	Glendining & Co., London.
GMG	Gallerie des Monnaies, Geneva.
Goldberg	Ira and Larry Goldberg Coins and Collectibles Inc., Los Angeles, CA.
Gorny	D. M. Gorny (Gieβener Münzhandlung), Munich.
[Gorny & Mosch	D. M. Gorny & Mosch (Gieβener Münzhandlung), Munich; see: Gorny].
Grabow	Ludwig Grabow, Rostock.
Grigoli	Numismatica Grigoli, Suzzara, Italy.
Grün	H. Grün, Heidelberger Münzhandlung, Heidelberg.
Grunow	Grunow Münzengallerie Münzen und Ausgrabungen, Berlin.
Habelt	P. Habelt, Berlin.
Hamburger	Leo Hamburger, Frankfurt am Main.
Hariga	M. Hariga, Brussels.
Helbing	Otto Helbing, Munich.
Helios	Helios Numismatik, Munich.
Henzen	Münzhandel G.Henzen, Amerongen.
Hess Lucerne	Adolf Hess Nachf., Lucerne.
Hess Frankfurt	Adolf Hess Nachf., Frankfurt am Main.
Hess-Dietrich	A. Hess and E. Dietrich, Auktion Tigurina, Zürich.
Hess-Divo	A. Hess and J.-P. Divo, AG, Zürich.

Hess-Leu	A. Hess-Bank Leu AG, Luzern.
Hesperia Art	Hesperia Art Bulletin (George Allan), Philadelphia.
HWCA	Heritage World Coin Auctions, Dallas, Texas.
G.Hirsch	Gerhard Hirsch, Munich.
J.Hirsch	Jacob Hirsch, Munich.
Hoffmann	J.H.Hoffmann, Paris.
Høiland	T.Høiland Møntauktion, Copenhagen.
Huston	S. M. Huston, San Francisco.
InAsta	InAsta, Dogana, Rep. San Marino.
Jacquier	Paul-Francis Jacquier, Kehl am Rhein.
JNFA	Journal of Numismatic Fine Arts (J. L. Malter), Encino, CA.
Johnson	I. Johnson, Manchester.
Kastner	Gitta Kastner, Munich.
KMK	Kölner Münzkabinett, Köln.
Knobloch	Frederick S. Knobloch, New York.
Knopek	Hans-Jürgen Knopek, Köln.
Kovacs	Frank Kovacs, San Francisco.
Kreisberg-Schulman	A. Kreisberg and M. F. Schulman, New York.
Kress	Karl Kress Münzhandlung, Munich.
Kricheldorf	H. H. Kricheldorf, Stuttgart.
Kritt	B. Kritt, Burtonsville, MD.
Kroh	Dennis Kroh, Empire Coins, Holy Hill, Florida.
KuMü	Kunst und Münzen AG (M. Olivari and M. Rossi), Lugano.
Künker	F. R. Künker Münzhandlung, Osnabrück.
Kurpfälzische	MünzhandlungKurpfälzische Münzhandlung, Mannheim.
Lanz	Numismatik Hubert Lanz, Munich .
Lanz Graz	Hermann Lanz, Graz.
Lee	M. G. Lee (comm. Priseur), Cairo [Coll. Zogheb].
Lepczyk	J. Lepczyk, Lansing, MI.
Leu	Leu Numismatik AG, Zürich.
Leu-Spink	Bank Leu-Spink & Son, Zürich.
Ljubljana	Stadt Ljubljana, 3. Auktion der antiken Münzen, Slovenia/Ljubljana.
Malter	J. L. Malter, Encino, CA.
Markov	Dmitry Markov Coins and Medals, New York.
Martin	C. J. Martin Coins Ltd., London.
Malloy	Alex Malloy, Inc., South Salem, New York.
McCarthy	McCarthy, H. Vincent, Ancient Coins, Southampton/UK.
Mc Sorley & Adams	C. Mc Sorley and Ch. Adams, Closter, NJ.
Meister & Sonntag	Auktionhaus Meister und Sonntag, Stuttgart.
Merzbacher	E. Merzbacher, Munich.
Mey	J. De Mey, Brussels.
MGM	Münzgalerie München und Joker KG, München.
Millon	Millon & Associés, Paris.
M&M	M & M Numismatics, Ltd., Washington, DC.

MMAG	Münzen und Medaillen A. G. (H. A. Cahn, E. B. Cahn, P. Strauss, and H.Voegtli), Basel.
Monetarium	see: SKA Monetarium.
Morgenthau	J. C. Morgenthau & Co. Inc., W. Raymond and J. C. MacAllister, New York.
Morton & Eden	Morton & Eden. In Association with Sotheby's, London.
Müller	H.-W. Müller, Solingen.
Miller	D. Miller, Coins & Classical Antiquities Inc., Hertfordshire, UK.
Münzhlg. Basel	Münzhandlung Basel (H.A. Cahn), Basel.
Myers	Robert A. Myers, New York.
Myers & Adams	Robert A. Myers & Ch. Adams, New York .
Münzzentrum	Münzzentrum (Albrecht and Hoffmann GMBH/Heinz-W. Müller), Köln/Solingen.
Mygind	Sydney Mygind, London.
NA	Numismatic Auction Ltd., New York.
NAC	Numismatica Ars Classica (R. Russo and I. Vecchi), Zürich/London.
Naville	Naville et Cie., Geneva Ars Classica, Geneva/Luzern.
Negrini	R.Negrini, Milano.
NERCA	New England Rare Coin Auctions, Boston, MA.
NFA	Numismatic Fine Arts, (Bruce McNall), Los Angeles, California.
Nicola	L. de Nicola, Rome.
NNCC	New Netherlands Coin Company Inc., New York.
Nomisma	Nomisma, Paris.
Numifrance	Numifrance, Paris.
Numismatica	Numismatica, Vienna.
Numismatica Genevensis	Numismatica Genevensis SA, Geneva.
Nomos	Nomos AG, Zürich, Switzerland.
Nummus et Ars	Nummus et Ars (A.Luise), Venice.
Oldenburg	H. G. Oldenburg, Kiel/Hamburg.
Parsy	T.Parsy, Paris.
Pegasi	Pegasi Numismatics, Historia Numismatica, Ann Arbor, MI.
Pecunem	Pecunem (Gitbud & Naumann), Munich (e-sale).
Peiresc	Cabinet Numismatique Peiresc, La Garde.
Peus	Dr. Busso Peus Nachf., Frankfurt am Main.
Platt	Clement Platt, Paris.
Phillips	W. C. Phillips, New York.
Phoenix	Phoenix Coincraft (publ.), London.
Pilarz	H. Pilarz, Köln am Rhein.
Piollet-Sabatier	Mme L. Piollet-Sabatier, Paris.
Pliego	Pliego Numismatica y Collezionismo, S. L., Seville.
Plumier	G. Plumier, Cabinet Numismatique, Paris.
PMV	PMV, Inc., Daytona Beach, FL.
Poindessault	B. Poindessault, Paris.
Poindessault-Védrines	B. Poindessault-Josianne Védrines, Paris.

Poinsignon-Pesce	A. Poinsignon and M. Pesce, Strasbourg.
Ponterio	Ponterio & Associates, Inc., San Diego, CA.
Provadalieff	M. D. Provadalieff, Paris.
Rasmussen	Arne Bruun Rasmussen, Copenhagen.
Ratto	Rodolfo Ratto, Genova/Lugano/Milan.
Rauch	Hans-Dieter Rauch, Vienna.
Raymond	W. Raymond, New York.
Raymond & MacAllister	see: Morgenthau.
RCCA-Superior	Rare Coin Company of America, Chicago-Superior Stamp & Coin Company, Beverly Hills.
Ritter	Münzhandlung Ritter, Düsseldorf.
Roma	Roma Numismatics Ltd, London (Auctions and E-sales).
Rollin-Feuardent	Ch. Rollin- F.B. Feuardent, Paris.
Rooke	H. Rooke Galleries, New York.
Rosenberg	S. Rosenberg, Frankfurt am Main.
Ryder	Dean M. Ryder, Madison, WI.
Saive	Philippe Saive Numismatique, Metz.
Salton & Schlessinger	Salton & Schlessinger. New York.
Sambon	A. Sambon, Paris/J. Sambon, Florence.
Santamaria	P. & P. Santamaria, Rome.
SB	Schweizerischer Bankverein, Zürich.
Schimmer	R. Schimmer Nürnberger Münzauktionen, Nürnberg.
Schlessinger	F. Schlessinger, Berlin/Amsterdam.
Schulman	J. Schulman/L. Schulman, Amsterdam.
Schulman New York	H. Schulman, New York.
Schulten	Münzhandlung Schulten & Co., GmbH, Köln.
Senger	Tempelhöfer Münzenhaus (Matthias Senger), Berlin.
Serrure	R. Serrure, Paris.
Shore	F. B. Shore, Schwenksville, PA (also: *The Parthian*).
SKA Bern	Schweizerische Kreditanstalt Bern, Numismatische Abteilung, Bern.
SKA Monetarium	Schweizerische Kreditsanstalt, Monetarium, Zürich.
Sotheby	Sotheby, Wilkinson & Hodge (1924) or Sotheby & Co. (1969), London.
Spink	Spink & Son Ltd., London.
Spink-GMG	Spink & Son Ltd. and Galerie des Monnaies Geneva.
Spink New York	Spink & Son Ltd., New York.
Spink-Taisei	Spink & Son, London and Taisei, Singapore.
Spink Z	Spink & Son Ltd., Zürich.
Spink Z–Taisei Z	Spink & Son, Zürich–Taisei, Zürich.
Stack's	Stack's (J.B.Stack – M.B.Stack), New York
Sternberg	Frank Sternberg, AG, Zürich.
Superior	Superior Stamp & Coin Company, Superior Galleries, Los Angeles, California.
The Parthian	see: Shore.

Tellmann	Afint Tellmann, Vaduz, Liechtenstein.
Thieme	C. G. Thieme, Leipzig.
Thirion	Dominique Thirion, Brussels.
Tietjen	Tietjen & Co., Hamburg.
Tigurina	see: Hess-Dietrich.
Tkalec	Münzauktion Tkalec AG, Zürich.
Toderi	Dr. G. Toderi, Numismatica, Florence.
Tradart	Tradart (M.Bendenoun), Geneva – Brussels.
UBS	UBS AG, Zürich.
Vecchi	Italo Vecchi Ltd., London.
Vecchi & Bonhams	see: Vecchi & Sons (Bonhams), London.
Vecchi & Sons	V. C. Vecchi & Sons, London.
Védrines	J. Védrines, Paris.
Victor England	Victor England, Quarryville, Pennsylvania/New York; see: CNG.
Vico	J. Vico, Madrid–Barcelona.
Vigne	Jean-Bruno Vigne, Paris.
Vinchon	J. Vinchon, Monte-Carlo, Paris.
Waddell	Ed. J. Waddell Ltd., Gaithesburg, MD.
Walla	Dr. F. Walla, Vienna.
Weil	A. Weil, Paris.
Westfälische	Westfälische Auktionsgesellschaft, Auktionsgesellschaft Arnsberg/Dortmund.
Whitford	C. A.Whitford Numismatic Auctions, Dearborn, MI.
Winkel	W. Winkel, Bielefeld.
Wolframm	V. Wolframm, Teutoburgerr Müünzauktion, Borgholzhausen.
Zschiesche & Köder	Zschiesche & Köder, Leipzig.

IV) Numismatic Collections

ABNC	Athens, Alpha Bank Numismatic Collection.
ANS	New York, American Numismatic Society.
ANM	Athens, Numismatic Museum.
Ashmolean	Oxford, Ashmolean Museum.
Berlin	Berlin, Staatliche Museen, Münzkabinet.
Blackburn	Blackburn Museum & Art Galleries. See: Principal Published Numismatic Collections.
BNF	Paris, Bibliothèque Nationale de France.
BM	London, British Museum, Department of Coins and Medals.
Brussels	Brussels, Cabinet des Médailles Bibliothèque Royale Albert Ier.
Cardiff	Cardiff, National Museum of Wales.
Edinburgh	Edinburgh, Royal Museum of Scotland. See: Principal Published Numismatic Collections (Rutter, *Edinburgh*).
Fitzwilliam	Cambridge, Fitzwilliam Museum, Department of Coins and Medals.
Glasgow	Glasgow, Glasgow University, Hunterian Museum.
Göttingen	Göttingen, Archäologisches Institut der Universität.

Hungary, Mayar	Hungary, Mayar Nemzeti Museum, Hungarian National Museum.
Nemzeti Israel, Eretz	Israel, Eretz Museum.
Kavala	Kavala, Archaeological Museum.
Leiden	Koninklijk Penningkabinet, Rijksmuseum, Leiden (collection formerly in The Hague).
LJ	Austria, Landesmuseum Johanneum.
Madrid	Madrid, Museo Arqueologico Nacional, Gabineto Numismatico.
Manchester	The Manchester Museum, The University of Manchester.
Marseille	Marseille, Cabinet des Monnaies et des Médailles.
Milan	Milan, Museo Archeologico, Collezione del Commune e del Gabineto Numismatico di Brera, Castello Sforzesco.
Munich	Munich, Staatliche Museen, Staatliche Münzsammlung.
Neuchâtel	Neuchâtel, Cabinet de Numismatique, Musée d' Art et d' Histoire.
Private Collection PR	Private Collection P. R. F.
Private Collection LC	Private Collection L. C.
Royal Ontario Museum	Toronto, Royal Ontario Museum.
Salzburg	Salzburger Museum Carolinoaugusteum.
Stuttgart	Stuttgart, Würtenbergisches Landesmuseum.
Vienna	Vienna, Kunsthistorisches Museum.
Vienna 2	Vienna, Institut für Numismatik der Universität, National Museum of Wales.
Warsaw	Poland, Warsaw, Museum Nadorowe w Warszawie.
Zürich	Zürich, Schweizerisches Landesmuseum, Sammlung der Zentralbibliothek.

V. JOURNALS

AA	*Archäologischer Anzeiger* (Berlin: de Gruyter).
AAA	*Ἀρχαιολογικά Ἀνάλεκτα ἐξ Ἀθηνῶν.*
ΑΔ	*Ἀρχαιολογικόν Δελτίον τοῦ Ὑπουργείου τῶν Ἐκκλησιαστικῶν καὶ τῆς Δημοσίας Ἐκπαιδεύσεως*, vols. 16–, (Athens: Hestia).
AE	Ἀρχαιολογική Ἐφημερίς: περιοδικόν τῆς ἐν Ἀθήναις Ἀρχαιολογικῆς Ἑταιρείας (Athens).
AJA	*American Journal of Archaeology* (New York: Archaeological Institute of America).
AJN	*American Journal of Numismatics*, American Numismatic Society, New York.
AJPh	American Journal of Philology (Baltimore: The Johns Hopkins Press).
AncW	*The Ancient World*, Chicago: Ares.
AnnArch de Syrie	*Annales Archéologiques de Syrie: Revue d' archéologie et d' histoire syriennes* (Damascus: Al-Taracki).
Antike Kunst	*Antike Kunst*, ed. by Vereinigung der Freunde antiker Kunst in

	Basel, Olten: Urs Graf-Verlag.
AM	See: *MDAI* (Ath).
ANSMN	*American Numismatic Society Museum Notes* (New York: American Numismatic Society).
ANS NNM	*American Numismatic Society Numismatic Notes and Monographs* (New York: American Numismatic Society).
ANS NS	*American Numismatic Society Numismatic Studies* (New York: American Numismatic Society).
Ἀρχαιογνωσία	*Ἀρχαιογνωσία* (Athens: University of Athens).
BCH	*Bulletin de Correspondance Hellénique* (Paris: De Boccard).
BMCR	*Bryn Mawr Classical Review* (Bryn Mawr: Bryn Mawr College, Pa.)
CJ	*The Classical Journal* (Athens, Ga.: University of Georgia).
CQ	*The Classical Quarterly* (Oxford University Press).
CW	*The Classical World* (Pittsburgh: Duquesne University).
Hesperia	*Hesperia: Journal of the American School of Classical Studies at Athens* (Athens: American School of Classical Studies).
Historia	*Historia: Zeitschrift für Alte Geschichte* (Wiesbaden: Steiner).
HSCP	*Harvard Studies in Classical Philology* (Cambridge, Mass./ London: Harvard University Press).
IJR	*Israel Numismatic Research* (Jerusalem: Israel Numismatic Society).
JDAI	*Jahrbuch des Deutschen Archäologischen Instituts* (Berlin: De Gruyter).
JHS	*Journal of Hellenic Studies* (London: Society for the Promotion of Classical Studies).
JIAN	*Journal International d' Archéologie Numismatique* (Athens).
JNFA	see: Sale Catalogues.
JNG	*Jahrbuch für Numismatik und Geldgeschichte* (Kallmünz: Lassleben).
JRA	*Journal of Roman Archaeology* (Ann Arbor, Mich.: University of Michigan, Department of Classical Studies).
Kadmos	*Kadmos: Zeitschrift für vor- und frühgriechische Epigraphik* (Berlin: De Gruyter).
Klio	*Klio: Beiträge zur alten Geschichte* (Berlin: Akademie Verlag).
MDAI (Ath)	*Mitteilungen des Deutschen Archäologischen Instituts* (Athen. Abt.). (Berlin: Mann).
MH	*Museum Helveticum: Revue suisse pour l' étude de l' Antiquité classique* (Basel: Schwabe).
NAC	*Numismatica e antichità classiche: Quaderni Ticinesi* (Lugano: Arti graf. Gaggini-Bizzozero.
NC	*Numismatic Chronicle* (London: Royal Numismatic Society).
NCirc	*Numismatic Circular* (London: Spink).
Nomisma	*Nomisma*, Association des Cheminôts Numismats (Paris).
NZ	*Numismatische Zeitschrift* (Vienna: Num. Gesellschaft).

OAth	*Opuscula Atheniensia*: Acta Inst. Ath. regni Sueciae, Åström, Lund (Athens).
Phoenix	*The Phoenix*: *The Journal of the Classical Association of Canada* (Toronto: University of Toronto Press).
RBN	*Revue Belge de Numismatique et de Sigillographie* (Brussels: Société Royale de Numismatique et de Belgique).
REA	*Revue des Études Anciennes*, Annales de la Faculté des Lettres de Bordeaux (Bordeaux).
REG	*Revue des Études Grecques* (Paris: Les Belles Lettres).
RN	*Révue Numismatique* (Paris: Société Française de Numismatique, Center National de la Recherche Scientifique).
SAN	*Journal of the Society for Ancient Numismatics*, Santa Monica, Calif.).
SCI	*Scripta Classica Israelica*: Yearbook of the Israel Society for the Promotion of Classical Studies (Jerusalem: Academon).
SM	*Schweizer Münzblätter* (*Schweizerische Numismatische Gesellschaft*) (Bern: Société Suisse de Numismatique).
SNR	Schweizerische Numismatische Rundschau (Bern: Société Suisse de Numismatique).
ZfN	*Zeitschrift für Numismatik* (Berlin).
ZPE	*Zeitschrift für Papyrologie und Epigraphik* (Bonn).

VI. Secondry Literature

Adams-Borza, *Macedonian*	W. L. Adams and E. N. Borza (eds.), *Philip II, Alexander the Great Heritage and the Makedonian Heritage* (Lanham: University Press of America, 1982).
Aleshire, *Asklepieion*	Sara B. Aleshire, *The Athenian Asklepieion. The People, their Dedications and their Inventories* (Amsterdam: Gieben, 1989).
Ameling et al., *Schenkungen*	W. Ameling, K. Bringmann, and H. von Steuben (eds.), *Schenkungen Hellenistischer Kherrscher in griechischen Städte und Heiligtümer,* Teil I (Berlin: Akademie Verlag, 1995).
AMNG	F. Imhoof-Blumer and T. Wiegand (eds.), *Die Antiken Münzen Nordgriechenlands*, 3 vols. (Berlin: Akademie der Wissenschaften, 1898–1935).
Aperghis, *SRE*	G. G. Aperghis, *The Seleukid Royal Economy* (Cambridge: University Press, 2004).
Archibald et al., *HellEc* I	Z. Archibald, J. K. Davies, V. Gabrielsen, and G. Oliver (eds.), *Hellenistic Economies* (London: Routledge, 2001).
Archibald et al., *MMM*	Z. Archibald, J. K. Davies, V. Gabrielsen (eds.), *Making, Moving and Managing: The New World of Ancient Economies, 323–31 BC* (Oxford: Oxbow, 2005).
Archibald et al., *EHS*	Z. Archibald, et al. *The Economies of Hellenistic Societies, Third to First Centuries BC* (Oxford: University Press, 2011).
Archibald, *Northern Aegean*	Z. Archibald, *Ancient Economies of the Northern Aegean, Fifth to First Centuries BC* (Oxford: University Press, 2013).

Andronikos, *Vergina*	M. Andronikos, *Vergina, The Royal Tombs and the Ancient City* (Athens: Ekdotike Athenon, 1984).
Ashton, *Colossus*	R. H. J. Ashton, "Rhodian Coinage and the Colossus," *RN*[6] 30 (1988), 75–90.
Ashton, Review	R. H. J. Ashton, Review of Y. Touratsoglou, *Disjecta Membra, Two Hellenistic Hoards from Greece*, *NCirc* 2 (1996), 9–10.
Ashton, *Rhodes*	R. Ashton, "The Coinage of Rhodes 408–c. 190 BC," in A. Meadows and K. Shipton, *Money and its Uses in the Ancient Greek World* (Oxford: Oxford University Press, 2001), 79–115.
Archaia Makedonia	*Ἀρχαία Μακεδονία, Ἀνακοινώσεις Διεθνῶν Συμποσίων*, vols. 1–5, *Θεσσαλονίκη: Ἵδρυμα Μελετῶν Χερσονήσου τοῦ Αἵμου*: vol. I (Thessaloniki, 1971); vol. IV (Thessaloniki, 1986).
Babelon, *Mélanges*	E. Babelon, *Mélanges Numismatiques*, vols. 3–4 (Paris: A. Numismatiques Dieudonné, 1900–1912).
Bagnall, *Administration*	R. S. Bagnall, *The Administration of the Ptolemaic Possessions Outside Egypt* (Leiden: E. J. Brill, 1976).
Baumann, *Pflanzenbilder*	H. Baumann, *Pflanzenbilder auf griechischen Münzen* (Munich: Hirmer, 2000).
Bell, *Sardis*	H. W. Bell, *Sardis*, XI: *Coins*, Part 1 (1910–4) (Leiden: E. J. Brill, 1916).
Bellinger, *Essays*	A. R. Bellinger, *Essays on the Coinage of Alexander the Great* (New York: American Numismatic Society, 1963).
Beloch, *GG*	K. J. Beloch, *Griechische Geschichte*, 4 vols. (Strasbourg/Berlin: Teubner, 1912–1927).
Billows, *Antigonus*	R. A. Billows, *Antigonus the One-Eyed and the Creation of the Hellenistic State*, (Berkeley/London: University of California Press, 1990).
Bilde et al., *Aspects of Hellenistic Kingship*	Per Bilde et al. (eds.), *Aspects of Hellenistic Kingship*, Studies in Hellenistic Civilization 7 (Aarhus: Aarhus University Press, 1996).
Bilde et al., *Center and Periphery*	Per Bilde et al. (eds.), *Center and Periphery in the Hellenistic World*, Studies in Hellenistic Civilization 4 (Aarhus: Aarhus University Press, 1993).
Billows, *Kings and Colonists*	R. A. Billows, *Kings and Colonists, Aspects of Macedonian Imperialism* (Leiden: E. J. Brill, 1994).
Blümel, *Knidos*	W. Blümel, *Die Inschriften von Knidos*, Inschriften Griechischer Städte aus Kleinasien, Teil I (Bonn: Österreichische Akademie der Wissenschaften, 1992).
Boehringer, *Chronologie*	Chr. Boehringer, *Zur Chronologie Mittelhellenistischen Münzserien, 220–160 v. Chr.* (Berlin: De Gruyter, 1972).
Boehinger, *Hierax*	Chr. Boehringer, "Antiochos Hierax am Hellespont," in M. Price et al. (eds.), *Essays Carson-Jenkins*, 37–47.
Borgeaud, *Pan*	Ph. Borgeaud, *The Cult of Pan in Ancient Greece*, trans. Kathleen Atlass and J. Redfield (Chicago: University Press, 1988).

Borza, *In the shadow of Olympus*	E. N. Borza, *In the Shadow of Olympus: The Emergence of Macedon* (Princeton: Princeton University Press, 1990).
Bresson, *Coinage and Money*	A. Bresson, "Coinage and Money in the Hellenistic Age," in Archibald et al., *MMM*, 44–72.
Bresson et al., *Approches*	A. Bresson, P. Briant, and F. Burkhalter (eds.), *Approches de l' économie hellénistique [4e rencontre de l' économie antique, Saint-Bertrand-des-Comminges (06–07 Mai 2004)* (Saint-Bertrand-des-Comminges/Paris: Musée archéologique de Saint-Bertrand-des Comminges/De Boccard, 2006).
Brown, *Royal Portraits*	B. R. Brown, *Royal Portraits in Sculpture and Coins, Pyrrhos and the Successors of Alexander the Great*, Hermeneutics of Art, vol. 5 (New York: P. Lang, 1995).
Bruneau, *Délos*	Ph. Bruneau, *Recherches sur les cultes de Délos à l' époque hellénistique et à l' époque impériale*, BÉFAR 217 (Paris: De Boccard, 1970).
Bulloch et al., *Images and Ideologies*	A. Bulloch et al., *Images and Ideologies: Self-Definition in the the Hellenistic World* (Berkeley: University of California Press, 1993).
Buraselis, *HM*	K. Buraselis, *Das Hellenistische Makedonien und die Ägäis, For schungen zur Politik des Kassandros und der drei ersten Antigoniden im Ägäischen Meer und in Westkleinasien. Münchner Beiträge zur Papyrusforschung und Antiken Rechtsgeschichte*, Heft 73 (Munich: Beck, 1982).
Burnett, *CRW*	A. Burnett, *Coinage of the Roman World* (London: Seaby, 1987).
CAH VII.1[2]	F. W. Walbank, A. E. Austin, M. W. Fredricksen, and R. M. Ogilvie (eds.), *The Cambridge Ancient History*, 2nd ed., vol. VII.1 (Cambridge: Cambridge University Press, 1984).
Callataÿ, *Axes*	F. de Callataÿ, *Les monnaies grecques et l' orientation des axes*, Glaux 12 (Milan: Ennerre, 1996).
Callataÿ, *Guerres Mithridatiques*	F. de Callataÿ, *L' histoire des guerres Mithridatiques vue par les monnaies, Publications d' Histoire de l' Art* (Louvain-la-Neuve: Departement d' Archéologie et d' Histoire de l' Art, Séminaire de Numismatique Marcel Hoc, 1997).
Callataÿ, *QMS*	F. de Callataÿ, *Quantifying Monetary Supplies in Greco-Roman Times* (Bari: Edipuglia, 2011).
Callataÿ, *Recueil*	F. de Callataÿ, *Recueil quantitatif sur les émissions monétaires hellénistiques* (Wetteren: Éditions Numismatique Romaine, 1997).
Callataÿ, Review	F. de Callataÿ, Review of Y. Touratsoglou, *Disjecta Membra. Two New Hellenistic Hoards from Greece*, *RBN* 142 (1996): 296–9.
Carradice, *Domitian*	I. Carradice, *Coinage and Finances in the Reign of Domitian AD 81–96* (Oxford: BAR, 1983).

Casson, *Ships and Seamanship*	L. Casson, *Ships and Seamanship in the Ancient World* (Baltimore/London: Johns Hopkins University Press, 1995).
Corolla Numismatica	F. Hill (ed.), *Corolla Numismatica: Numismatic essays in honour of B. V. Head* (London/New York: H. Frowde, 1906).
Coulton, *Stoa*	J. J. Coulton, *The Architectural Development of the Greek Stoa* (Oxford: Clarendon Press, 1976).
Courby, *Délos*	F. Courby, *Délos* V (Paris: Fontemoing, 1912).
Cox, *Gordion*	D. M. Cox, *A Third Century Hoard of Tetradrachms from Gordion* (Philadelpheia: The University Museum, University of Pennsylvania, 1953).
Crampa, *ILabraunda*	J. Crampa, *Labraunda. Swedish Excavations and Researches* III.1. *The Greek Inscriptions,* Part I: 1–12 (Lund: Berlingska Boktryckeriet, 1969)*;* III.2. *The Greek Inscriptions,* Part 2: 13–133 (Stockholm: C. W. K. Gleerup, 1972).
Crawford, *RRC*	M. H. Crawford, *Roman Republican Coinage* (Cambridge: University Press, 1975).
Crawford, *Coinage and Money*	M. H. Crawford, *Coinage and Money under the Roman Republic, Italy and the Mediterranean Economy* (London: Methuen, 1985).
Cunliffe, *Celts*	B. Cunliffe, *The Ancient Celts* (Oxford: University Press, 1997).
Davesne-Le Rider, *Meydancıkkale*	A. Davesne and G. Le Rider, *Le trésor de Meydancıkkale (CilicieTrachée, 1980),* 2 vols. (Paris: Éditions Recherche sur les Civilisations, 1989).
Dignas, *Economy of the Sacred*	Dignas, B., *Economy of the Sacred in Hellenistic and Roman Asia Roman Asia Minor,* Oxford Classical Monographs (Oxford/New York: Oxford University Press, 2002).
Dintsis, *Helme*	P. Dintsis, *Hellenistische Helme* (Rome: G. Bretschneider, 1986).
Doyen, *Étalons*	Ch. Doyen, *Études de métrologie grecque,* vol. II, *Étalons d' argent et du bronze en Grèce hellénistique (*Louvain-la-Neuve: Association Professeur Marcel Hoc, 2012).
Duyrat, *Arados* F.	Duyrat, *Arados hellénistique. Étude historique et monétaire* (Beirut: Institut Français du Proche-Orient, 2005).
Duyrat, *WAW*	Duyrat, F., *Wealth and Warfare. The Archaeology of Money in Ancient Syria*, Numismatic Studies 34 (New York: American Nu mismatic Society, 2016).
Eadie-Ober, *Essays Starr*	J. Eadie and J. Ober (eds.), *The Craft of the Ancient Historian: Essays in Honor of Chester G. Starr* (Langham, Maryland: University Press of America, 1985).
Eggebrecht et al. (eds.), *Albanien*	A. Eggebrecht et al. (eds.), *Albanien: Schätze aus dem Land der Skipetaren* (Mainz am Rhein: Philipp von Zabern, 1988).
Errington, *Macedonia*	R. M. Errington, *A History of Macedonia*, trans. Catherine Errington (Berkeley: University of California Press, 1990).
Erskine, *Companion*	A. Erskine (ed.), *A Companion to the Hellenistic World* (Oxford: Blackwell, 2003).

Ehrhardt, *Studies*	Chr. Ehrhardt, *Studies in the Reigns of Demetrius II and Antigonos Doson* (diss.), 2 vols. (Buffalo, 1975).
Ellis, *Philip II*	J. R. Ellis, *Philip II and Macedonian Imperialism* (London, 1976).
Essays Carson-Jenkins	see: Price et al., *Essays Carson-Jenkins*.
Essays Robinson	see: Kraay-Jenkins, *Essays Robinson*.
Études Le Rider	E. Papaefthymiou, F. de Callataÿ, and F. Queyrel (eds.), *G. Le Rider, Études d' histoire monétaire et financière du monde grec. Écrits 1958–1998*, 3 vols. (Athens: Hellenic Numismatic Society, 1999).
Faranguna, *Aspetti*	M. Faranguna, "Aspetti administrativi e finanziari della monarchia macedone tra IVe III secolo a.C.," *Athenaeum* 86 (1998), 349–95.
Fellmann, *AG*	W. Fellmann, *Antigonos Gonatas, König der Makedonen, und die Griechische Staaten* (diss.) (Würzburg, 1930).
Festschrift Mildenberg	A. Houghton, S. Hurter, P. Erhartt Mottahedeh, and J. Ayer Scott (eds.), *Festschrift für Leo Mildenberg* (Wetteren: Editions NR, 1984).
Fischer-Bossert, *Tarentum*	W. Fischer-Bossert, *Chronologie der Didrachmenprägung von Tarent, 510–280 v. Chr.* (Berlin/New York: de Gruyter, 1999).
Flacelière, *Aitoliens*	R. Flacelière, *Les Aitoliens à Delphes: contribution à l' histoire de la Grèce centrale au IIIe siècle av. J.-C.* (Paris: de Boccard, 1937).
Flament, *Athènes*	C. Flament, *Le monnayage en argent d' Athènes de l' époque archaÏque à l' époque hellénistique (c. 550–c. 40 av. J.-C.)* (Louvain-la-Neuve: Association Professeur Marcel Hoc, 2007).
Florilegium Numismaticum	H. Nilsson (ed.), *Florilegium Numismaticum, Studia in honorem U. Westermark Edita* (Stockholm: Svenska Numismatiska Föreningen, 1992).
Franke-Hirmer, *GM*	P. R. Franke and M. Hirmer, *Die Griechische Münze* (Munich: Hirmer Verlag, 1964).
Fraser, *Pausanias*	J. G. Fraser, *Pausanias' Description of Greece*, vol. 5 (London, 1897).
Fraser, *Ptol. Alex.*	P. Fraser, *Ptolemaic Alexandria*, 3 vols. (Oxford: Clarendon Press, 1972).
Frölich, *Darstellungen*	B. Fröhlich, *Die statuarischen Darstellungen hellenistischer Herrscher* (Hamburg: Kovač, 1998).
Gabbert, *AG*	J. J. Gabbert, *Antigonus II Gonatas, A Political Biography* (London/New York: Routledge, 1997).
Gabbert, *Greek Hegemony*	J. J. Gabbert, *The Greek Hegemony of Antigonos II Gonatas (r. 283–239 B.C.)*, (Diss.) (University of Cincinnati 1982).
Gabbert, *Response*	J. J. Gabbert, Response to G. Reger's Review, *BMCR* 11 (1998), 14.
Gaebler, *AMNG*	H. Gaebler, *Die Antiken Münzen Nordgriechenlands*, Band III. *Makedonia und Paionia* (Berlin: de Gruyter, 1935).
Garnsey-Whittaker, *Imperialism*	P. Garnsey and C. R. Whittaker (eds.), *Imperialism in the Ancient World* (Cambridge: University Press, 1978).

Garoufalias, *Pyrrhus*	P. Garoufalias, *Pyrrhus, King of Epirus* (London: Stacey International, 1979).
Gatzolis, *Κυκλοφορία*	Chr. Gatzolis, *Η κυκλοφορία του χάλκινου νομίσματος στη Μακεδονία (5ος–1ος αι. π.Χ.)*, PhD Diss. (Thessalonike: Aristoteleio University, 2010).
Griffith, *Mercenaries*	G. T. Griffith, *The Mercenaries of the Hellenistic World* (Chicago: Ares, 1984).
Guimier-Sorbets et al., *RCN*	A.-M. Guimier-Sorbets, M. B. Hatzopoulos, and Y. Morizot, (eds.), *Rois, cités, nécropoles, institutions, rites et monuments en Macédoine*, Actes des Colloques de Nanterre (Décembre 2002) et d' Athènes (Janvier 2004) (Paris: De Boccard, 2006).
Habicht, *Athen*	Chr. Habicht, *Athen in hellenistischer Zeit: gesammelte Aufsätze* (München: C. H. Beck, 1994).
Habicht, *Athens*	Chr. Habicht, *Athens from Alexander to Antony*, trans. Deborah Lucas Schneider (Cambridge, Mass./London: Harvard University Press, 1997).
Habicht, *Gottmenschentum*	Chr. Habicht, *Gottmenschentum und griechische Städte*, Zetemata 14 (Munich: Beck 1970).
Habicht, *HL Monarchies*	Chr. Habicht, *The Hellenistic Monarchies, Selected Papers* (Ann Arbor: University of Michigan Press, 2006).
Habicht, *Pausanias*	Chr. Habicht, *Pausanias' Guide to Greece*, 2nd ed. (Berkeley: University of California Press, 1998).
Habicht, *Studien*	Chr. Habicht, *Studien zur Geschichte Athens in hellenistischer Zeit* (Göttingen: Vanderhoek & Ruprecht, 1982).
Habicht, *Unters.*	Chr. Habicht, *Untersuchungen zur politischen Geschichte Athens im 3. Jahrhundert v. Chr.* (Munich: Beck, 1979).
Hackens, *Antidorum Peremans*	T. Hackens, "À propos de la circulation monétaire dans le le Peloponnèse au IIIe siècle av. J.-C.," in *Antidorum W. Peremans sexagenario ab alumnis oblatum*, studia Hellenistica 16 (Louvain: Publications Universitaires, 1968), 69–75.
Hammond, *Epirus*	N. G. L. Hammond, *Epirus* (Oxford: Oxford University Press, 1967).
Hammond, *Macedonia* I	N. G. L. Hammond, *A History of Macedonia* I (Oxford: Oxford University Press, 1972).
Hammond-Griffith, *Macedonia* II	N. G. L. Hammond and G. T. Griffith, *A History of Macedonia* II (Oxford: University Press, 1979).
Hammond-Walbank, *Macedonia* III	N. G. L. Hammond and F. W. Walbank, *A History of Macedonia* III (Oxford: Oxford University Press, 1988).
Hammond, *State*	N. G. L. Hammond, *The Macedonian State* (Oxford: Oxford University Press, 1989).
Hannestad, *Celts*	L. Hannestad, "Greeks and Celts: The Creation of a Myth," in Per Bilde et al., *Center and Periphery*, 15–38.
Hatzopoulos, *Actes de Vente*	M. B. Hatzopoulos, *Actes de Vente d' Amphipolis*, Meletemata 14 (Athens: Center de recherches de l' antiquité grecque et romaine, 1991).

Hatzopoulos, *Institutions*	M. B. Hatzopoulos, *Macedonian Institutions under the Kings* I, *A Historical and Epigraphical Study*, Meletemata 22 (Athens: Centre de recherches de l' antiquité grecque et romaine, 1996).
Hatzopoulos, *Institutions* II	M. B. Hatzopoulos, *Macedonian Institutions under the Kings* II, Epigraphic Appendix, Meletemata 22 (Athens: Center de recherches de l' antiquité grecque et romaine, 1996).
Hatzopoulos-Loukopoulou, *Philip of Macedon*	M. B. Hatzopoulos and L. Loukopoulou, *Philip of Macedon* Athens: Ekdotike Athenon, 1980).
Hazzard, *Ptolemaic Coins*	R. A. Hazzard, *Ptolemaic Coins, An Introduction for Collectors* (Toronto: Kirk & Bentley, 1995).
Hazzard, *Imagination*	R. A. Hazzard, *Imagination of a Monarchy. Studies in Ptolemaic Propaganda* (Toronto: University of Toronto Press, 2000).
Head, *HN*[2]	B. V. Head, *Historia Numorum: A Manual of Greek Numismatics*, 2nd edition (Oxford: Clarendon Press, 1911).
Heinen, *Unters.*	H. Heinen, *Untersuchungen zur politischen Geschichte Athens im 3. Jahrhundert v. Chr.* (Munich: Beck, 1979).
Himmelmann, *Herrscher und Athlet*	N. Himmelmann, *Herrscher und Athlet. Die Bronzen von Quirinal. Austellungskatalog Bonn* (Milan: Olivetti, 1989).
Hornblower, *Hieronymus*	J. Hornblower, *Hieronymus of Cardia* (Oxford: Oxford University Press, 1981).
Howgego, *Ancient History from Coins*	Chr. Howgego, *Ancient History from Coins* (London: Routledge, 1995).
Howgego, *GIC*	Chr. Howgego, *Greek Imperial Countermarks: Studies in the Provincial Coinage of the Roman Empire* (London: Royal Numismatic Society, 1985).
Images and Ideologies	see: Bulloch et al., *Images and Ideologies.*
Imhoof-Blumer, *Akarnanien*	F. Imhoof-Blumer, "Die Münzen Akarnaniens," *NZ* 10 (1878), 1 ff.
INC Berne Proc.	T. Hackens and R. Weiler (eds.), *Actes de 9e Congrès international de numismatique, Berne, Septembre 1979, 1. Numismatique antique*, IAPN Special Publ. 6 (Louvain-la-Neuve: IAPN, 1982).
Kalléris, *Macédoniens*	I. Kalléris, *Les anciens Macédoniens, étude linguistique et historique*, 2 vols. (Athens: Institut Français d'Athènes, 1954–1967).
Karametrou–Menteside, *Βόιον*	G. Karametrou–Menteside, Βόιον- *Νότια Ορεστίς Αρχαιο-, λογική Έρευνα και Ιστορική Τοπογραφία* (Thessalonike, 1999).
Kraay, *Archaic and Classical Greek Coins*	C. Kraay, *Archaic and Classical Greek Coins* (London: Methuen, 1976).
Kraay-Jenkins, *Essays Robinson*	C. M. Kraay and G. K. Jenkins (eds.), *Essays in Greek Coinage presented to Stanley Robinson* (Oxford: Clarendon Press, 1968).
Kraay-Mørkholm Essays	see: Le Rider et al., *Kraay-Mørkholm Essays.*
Kremydi-Sicilianou, *Tauropolos*	S. Kremydi and Sicilianou, "The Tauropolos Tetradrachms of of the First Macedonian Meris: Provenance, Iconography and Dating," in *Κερμάτια Φιλίας. Τιμητικός Τόμος για τον Ιωάννη Τουράτσογλου*, vol. 1 (Athens: Numismatic Museum, 2009), 191–201

Kroll, *Agora*	J. Kroll, *The Athenian Agora,* XXVI: *The Greek Coins* (Princeton: American School of Classical Studies at Athens, 1993).
Lane Fox (ed.), *CAM*	R. J. Lane Fox (ed.), *Brill's Companion to Ancient Macedon: Studies in the Archaeology and History of Macedon, 650 BC–AD 300* (Leiden/Boston: Brill, 2011).
Larsen, *GFS*	J. A. O. Larsen, *Greek Federal States: Their Institutions and History* (Oxford: Clarendon Press, 1968).
Launey, *Armées*	M. Launey, *Recherches sur les armées hellénistiques*, 2 vols. (Paris: De Boccard, 1949–1950).
Le Bohec, *AD*	S. Le Bohec, *Antigone Dôsôn, roi de Macédoine* (Nancy: Presses Universitaires de France, 1993).
Le Rider, *Alexandre*	G. Le Rider, *Alexandre le Grand, monnaie, finances et politique* (Paris: Presses Universitaires de France, 2003).
Le Rider, *Écrits*	G. Le Rider, *Études d' Histoire Monétaire et financière du monde grec. Écrits 1958–1998*, ed. E. Papaefthymiou, F. de Callataÿ, and F. Queyrel, 3 vols. (Athens: Hellenic Numismatic Society, 1999).
Le Rider (et al.), *Kraay-Mørkholm Essays*	G. Le Rider (et al.), *Kraay-Mørkholm Essays: Numismatic Studies in Memory of C. M. Kraay and O. Mørkholm*, Numismatica Lovaniensia 10 (Louvain-la-Neuve: Institut Supérieur d' Archéologie et d' Histoire de l' Art, Séminaire de Numismatique Marcel Hoc, 1989).
Le Rider, *Monnayage et Finances*	G. Le Rider, *Monnayage et finances de Philippe II: un état de la question* (Athens/Paris: Center de Recherches de l' Antiquité Grecque et Romaine/Fondation Nationale de la Recherche Scientifique, 1996).
Le Rider, *Philippe II*	G. Le Rider, *Le Monnayage d' argent et d' or de Philippe II frappé en Macédoine de 359 et 294* (Paris: Bourgey, 1977).
Le Rider, *Potidée*	G. Le Rider, "Trésors de statères d' or trouvés à Potidée en 1984 et à Skioné en 1985," *RN* 33 (1991), 89–96.
Le Rider, *Tétradrachmes attalides*	G. Le Rider, "Les tétradrachmes attalides au portrait de Philétaire," in *Florilegium Numismaticum*, 233–45 = Le Rider, *Écrits*, 627–39.
Le Rider-Callataÿ, *Séleucides*	G. Le Rider and F. de Callataÿ, *Les Séleucides et les Ptolémées: l' héritage monétaire et financier d' Alexandre le Grand* (Monaco: Rocher, 2006).
Lévêque, *Pyrrhos*	P. Lévêque, *Pyrrhos*, BÉFA Rome 185 (Paris: De Boccard, 1957).
Liampi, *Meletemata*	K. Liampi, "Der Makedonische Schild als propagandisches Mittel in der hellenistischen Zeit,"*Meletemata* 10 (1990), 157–71.
Liampi, *MS*	K. Liampi, *Der Makedonische Schild* (Athens: MDAI, 1998).
LIMC	*Lexicon Iconographicum Mythologiae Classicae* (Zurich/Munich: Artemis Verlag, 1981-).
Lorber, *CPE*	C. C. Lorber, *Coins of the Ptolemaic Empire,* Part 1. *Ptolemy I through Ptolemy IV*, Volume 1. *Precious Metal* (New York: American Numismatic Society, 2018).

Ma, *Antiochos III* — J. Ma, *Antiochos III and the Cities of Western Asia Minor* (Oxford: Oxford University Press, 2000).

Marcellesi, *Pergame* — M.-C. Marcellesi, *Pergame de la Fin du Ve au Début du Ier Siècle av. J.-C., Pratiques Monétaires et Histoire*, Studi Ellenistici 26 (Pisa/Roma: F. Serra, 2012).

Marinescu, *Lysimachi* — C. A. Marinescu, *Making and Spending Money Along the Bosporus: The Lysimachi Coinages Minted By Byzantium and Chalcedon and their Socio-Cultural Context*, PhD diss. (New York: Columbia University, 1996).

Martin, *Sovereignty* — T. R. Martin, *Sovereignty and Coinage in Classical Greece* (Princeton: Princeton University Press, 1985).

Mathisen, *Administrative Organization* I — R. W. Mathisen, "The Administrative Organization of Amphipolis in Early Antigonid Macedonia (c. 280–270 B.C.)," *SAN* 14.1 (1983), 10–12, 18.

Mathisen, *Administrative Organization* II — R. W. Mathisen, "The Administrative Organization of Amphipolis in Early Antigonid Macedonia (c. 280–270 B.C.)," *SAN* 14.2 (1983), 24–27.

Mathisen, *Administrative Organization* III — R. W. Mathisen, "The Administrative Organization of Amphipolis in Early Antigonid Macedonia (c. 280–270 B.C.),"*SAN* 14.3 (1983), 44–46.

Mathisen, *Pan Heads and Poseidon Heads* — R. W. Mathisen, "Pan Heads and Poseidon Heads: Two Third- and Second-Century Macedonian Tetradrachm Types," *SAN* 16 (1985), 29–35.

Mathisen, *Silver Coinages* — R. W. Mathisen, "Antigonus Gonatas and the Silver Coinages of Macedonia *circa* 280–270 B.C.," *ANSMN* 26 (1981): 79–124.

Merker, *Silver Coinage* — I. L. Merker, "The Silver Coinage of Antigonos Gonatas and Antigonos Doson," *ANSMN* 9 (1960): 39–52.

Merker, *Studies* — I. L. Merker, *Studies in Sea-Power in the Eastern Mediterranean in the Century following the Death of Alexander*, PhD diss. (Princeton: Princeton University, 1958).

Meadows-Shipton, *Money and Its Uses* — A. Meadows and K. Shipton (eds.), *Money and Its Uses in the Ancient Greek World* (Oxford: University Press, 2001).

Mettout, *Persée* — S. Mettout, *Le monnayage de Persée, dernier roi des Madédoniens (179–168 av. J.-C.)*, Mémoire de maitrise préparé sous la direction de A. Laronde, Juin 1986.

Mionnet, *Description* I — T. E. Mionnet, *Description des médailles antiques grecques et romaines* I (Paris: Testu, 1806).

Mionnet, *Description*, Suppl. — T. E. Mionnet, *Description de médailles antiques grecques et romaines*, Supplément 1–9 (Paris: Testu, 1819–1837).

Mørkholm, *EHC* — O. Mørkholm, *Early Hellenistic Coinage: From the Accession of Alexander to the Peace of Apamea (336–188 B.C.)*, ed. P. Grierson and U. Westermark (Cambridge/New York: Cambridge University Press, 1991).

Nachtergael, *Galates* — G. Nachtergael, *Les Galates en Grèce et les Sôtéria de Delphes: recherches d' histoire et d' épigraphie hellénistiques* (Brussels: Palais des Académies, 1977).

Newell, *DP*	E. T. Newell, *The Coinages of Demetrius Poliorcetes* (London: Oxford University Press, 1927).
Newell, *ESM*	E. T. Newell, *The Coinage of the Eastern Seleucid Mints, from Seleucus I to Antiochus III* (New York: American Numismatic Society, 1938).
Newell, *WSM*	E. T. Newell, *The Coinage of the Western Seleucid Mints from Seleucus I to Antiochus III*, ANS NS 4 (New York: American Numismatic Society, 1941).
Nicolet-Pierre–Kroll, *Athenian Tetradrachm Coinage*	H. Nicolet-Pierre and J. Kroll, "Athenian Tetradrachm Coinage of the Third Century B.C.," *AJN* 2 (1990), 1–35.
Olcay-Seyrig, *Mektepini*	N. Olcay and H. Seyrig, *Le trésor de Mektepini en Phrygie* (Paris: IAPO, 1965).
Opus mixtum	*Opus mixtum: Essays in Ancient Art and Society*, Acta Instituti Romani Regni Sueciae (Stockholm: P. Å. Förlag, 1994).
Osborne, *Naturalisation* II	M. J. Osborne, *Naturalisation in Athens*, vol. II (Brussels: Paleis der Academiën, 1981–1983).
Panagopoulou, *Antigonids*	K. Panagopoulou, "The Antigonids: Patterns of a Royal Economy," in Archibald et al., *HellEc* I, 313–62.
Panagopoulou, *Debates*	K. Panagopoulou, "Cross-Reading Images: Iconographic 'Debates' between Antigonids and Ptolemies During the Third and Second Centuries BC," *Eulimene* 6–7 (2005–2006), 163–181.
Paschides, *Ποσειδώνες και Αντίγονοι*	P. Paschides, "Ποσειδώνες και Αντίγονοι. Παρατηρήσεις στη νομισματική μαρτυρία για τη ναυτική δύναμη του Αντιγόνου Γονατά και του Δώσωνα," *Αρχαιογνωσία* 9 (1998): 233–57.
Picard, *Chalcis*	O. Picard, *Chalcis et la confédération eubéenne: étude de numismatique et d' histoire*, IVe-Ier siècle (Athens/Paris: École française d' Athènes/De Boccard, 1979).
Préaux, *Monde Hellénistique*	C. Préaux, *Le monde hellénistique: la Grèce et l' Orient (323–146 av. J.-C.)* (Paris: Presses Universitaires de France, 1978).
Price, *Alexander*	M. J. Price, *The Coinage in the Name of Alexander the Great and Philip Arrhidaeus* (London/Zurich: British Museum/Swiss Numismatic Society, 1991).
Price et al., *Essays Carson-Jenkins*	M. J. Price, A. Burnett, and R. Bland (eds.), *Essays in Honour of Robert Carson and Kenneth Jenkins* (London: Spink, 1993).
Pritchett, *Greek State at War*	W. K. Pritchett, *The Greek State at War* III (Berkeley/London: University of California Press, 1979).
Psôma, *Olynthe*	S. Psôma, *Olynthe et les Chalcidiens de Thrace, Études de Numismatique et d' Histoire* (Stuttgart: Steiner, 2001).
Psoma–Karadima–Terzopoulou, *Maroneia*	S. Psoma, Ch. Karadima, and D. Terzopoulou, *The Coins from Coins from Maroneia and the Classical City at Molyvoti. A Contribution to the History of Aegean Thrace*, Meletemata 62 (Athens: De Boccard, 2008).
Reger, *Kos*	G. Reger, "The Date of the Battle of Kos," *AJAH* 10 (1985 [1993]), 155–177.

Reger, *Delos*	G. Reger, *Regionalism and Change in the Economy of Independent Delos, 314–167 B.C.* (Berkeley: University of California Press, 1994).
Regling, *Priene*	K. Regling, *Die Münzen von Priene* (Berlin: H. Schoetz, 1927).
Rice, *Procession*	E. E. Rice, *The Grand Procession of Ptolemy Philadelphus* (Oxford: University Press, 1983).
Ripollès, *X4 Hoard*	P. P. Ripollès, "The X4 Hoard (Spain): Unveiling the Presence of Greek Coinages during the Second Punic War," *INR* 3 (2008), 51–64.
Ritter, *Bildkontakte*	S. Ritter, S., *Bildkontakte. Götter und Heroen in der Bildsprache griechischer Münzen des 4. Jahrhunderts v. Chr.* (Berlin: Reimer, 2002).
Ritter, *Sternsymbolik*	H. W. Ritter, "Zur Sternsymbolik im Antigonidischen und Argeadischen Makedonien," *Ἀρχαιογνωσία* 2 (1981), 159–205.
Roisman-Worthington, *CAM*	J. Roisman, and I. Worthington (eds.), *A Companion to Ancient Macedonia* (Chichester/Malden: Wiley-Blackwell, 2010).
Rostovtzeff, *SEHHRW*	M. Rostovtzeff, *The Social and Economic History of the Hellenistic and Roman World*, 2nd impression revised by P. Fraser, 3 vols. (Oxford: Oxford University Press, 1953).
SC I	A. Houghton and C. Lorber, *Seleucid Coins, A Comprehensive Catalogue*, Part I: *Seleucus I through Antiochus III*, 2 vols. (New York/Lancaster, Penn.: American Numismatic Society/Classical Numismatic Group, 2002).
SC II	A. Houghton, C. Lorber, and O. Hoover, *Seleucid Coins, A Comprehensive Catalogue*, Part II: *Seleucus IV through Antiochus XII*, 2 vols. (New York/Lancaster, Penn.: American Numismatic Society/Classical Numismatic Group, 2008).
Scholten, *Politics of Plunder*	J. B. Scholten, *The Politics of Plunder, Aitolians and their Koinon in the Early Hellenistic Era, 279–217 B.C.* (Berkeley: University of California Press, 2000).
Seltman, *Athens*	C. T. Seltman, *Athens: Its History and Coinage before the Persian Invasion* (Cambridge: Cambridge University Press, 1924).
Seyrig, *Trésors*	H. Seyrig, *Trésors du Levant anciens et nouveaux*, Institut Français d' archéologie de Beyrouth, Bibliothèque archéologique et historique 94, Trésors monétaires seleucides 2 (Paris: P. Geuthner, 1973).
Shipley, *GWA*	G. Shipley, *The Greek World after Alexander, 323–30 B.C.* (London/New York: Routledge, 2000).
Smith, *HRP*	R. R. R. Smith, *Hellenistic Royal Portraits*, Oxford/New York: Clarendon Press/Oxford University Press, 1988).
Starr, *Athenian Coinage*	C. G. Starr, *Athenian Coinage 480–449 BC* (Oxford: Oxford University Press, 1970).
Strack-Münzer, *Thrakien*	M. L. Strack and F. Münzer, *Die antiken Münzen von Thrakien* (Berlin: G. Reimer, 1912).

Studies Grierson	C. N. L. Brooke et al. (eds.), *Studies in Numismatic Method presented to Philip Grierson* (Cambridge: Cambridge University Press, 1983).
Svenson, *Darstellungen*	D. Svenson, *Darstellungen Hellenistischer Könige mit Götterattributen*, Archäologische Studien vol. 10 (Frankfurt am Main: P. Lang, 1995).
Svoronos, *Athènes*	J. N. Svoronos, *Les monnaies d' Athènes* (Munich: Bruckmann, 1923–1926).
Tarn, *AG*	W. W. Tarn, *Antigonus Gonatas* (Oxford: Clarendon Press, 1913).
TCMAA	M. Amandry and G. Le Rider, *Trésors et circulation monétaire en Anatolie antique* (Paris: Bibliothèque nationale de France, 1994).
Thomas, *Ptolemaios IV*	R. Thomas, *Eine Postume Statuette Ptolemaios' IV. Und ihr historischer Kontext*, Trierer Winckelmannsprogramme, Heft 18 (Mainz am Rhein: von Zabern, 2002).
Thompson, *Drachm Mints* I	M. Thompson, *Alexander's Drachm Mints* I: *Sardes and Miletus*, ANS NS 16 (New York: American Numismatic Society, 1983).
Thompson, *Drachm Mints* II	M. Thompson, *Alexander's Drachm Mints* II: *Lampsacus and Abydus*, ANS NS 19 (New York: American Numismatic Society, 1991).
Touratsoglou, *DM*	Y. Touratsoglou, *Disjecta Membra.* Δύο νέοι ελληνιστικοί 'θησαυροί'από τον Ελλαδικό χώρο = *Disjecta Membra. Two New Hellenistic Hoards from Greece*, trans. Marion Tzamali (Athens: Hellenic Numismatic Society, 1993).
Touratsoglou, *Circulation*	Y. Touratsoglou, *Η Νομισματική Κυκλοφορία στην Αρχαία Μακεδονία (περ. 200 π.Χ.–268–286 μ.Χ.): η μαρτυρία των θησαυρών'* = *The Coin Circulation in Ancient Macedonia (ca. 200 BC–268-286 AD): The Hoard Evidence* (Athens: Hellenic Numismatic Society, 1993).
Touratsoglou, *Contribution*	Y. Touratsoglou, Συμβολή στην Οικονομική Ιστορία του Βασιλείου της Αρχαίας Μακεδονίας (6ος–3ος αι. π.Χ.) = *A Contribution to the Economic History of the Kingdom of Ancient Macedonia (6th–3rd Century BC)*, KERMA 2 (Athens: Society for the Study of Numismatics and Economic History, 2010.
Tracy-Palagia, *Macedonians in Athens*	S. Tracy and O. Palagia (eds.), *The Macedonians in Athens, 322–229 B.C., Proceedings of an International Conference held at the University of Athens, May 24–26, 2001* (Oxford: Oxbow, 2003).
Travaux Le Rider	M. Amandry and S. Hurter (eds.), *Travaux de numismatique grecque offerts à Georges Le Rider* (London: Spink, 1999).
Troxell, *Studies*	H. A. Troxell, *Studies in the Macedonian Coinage of Alexander the Great*, Numismatic Studies 21 (New York: The American Numismatic Society, 1997).
Tsangari, *Confédération Étolienne*	D. Tsangari, *Corpus des monnaies d' or, d' argent et de bronze de la confédération Étolienne* (Athens: Helicon Interactive, 2007).

Urban, *Wachstum und Krise*	R. Urban, *Wachstum und Krise des Achäischen Bundes: Quellenstudien zur Entwicklung des Bundes von 280 bis 222 v. Chr.* (Wiesbaden: F. Steiner, 1979).
Varoucha, *Epitymbion*	I. Varoucha, "Πτολεμαϊκά νομίσματα στην κυρίως Ελλάδα," in *Epitymbion Christou Tsounta*, (Athens: No Publisher, 1941), 670–672.
Villaronga, *Denario Romano*	*L.* Villaronga, "El denario romano pesado en los tesoros de la peninsula Ibérica," *Scienze dell' Antichità, Storia—Archeologia—Anthropologia* 11 (2001–2003), 557–565.
Waddington, *Recueil*	W. Waddington, E. Babelon, and Th. Reinach, *Recueil général des monnaies grecques d' Asie Mineure* (Paris, Leroux, 1904–1912).
Wallace, *Euboian League*	W. P. Wallace,*The Euboian League and its coinage*, ANS NNM 134 (New York: American Numismatic Society, 1956).
Wartenberg, *After Marathon*	U. Wartenberg, *After Marathon: War, Society and Money in Fifth-Century Greece* (London: British Museum Press, 1995).
Westermark, *Philetairos*	U. Westermark, *Das Bildnis des Philetairos von Pergamon. Corpus der Münzprägung*, Acta Universitaties Stockholmiensis, Stockholm Studies in Classical Archaeology 1 (Stockholm: Almquist & Wiksell, 1961).
Wilamowitz-Moellendorf, *Hellenistische Dichtung* II	U. von Wilamowitz-Moellendorf, *Hellenistische Dichtung in der Zeit des Kallimachus*, vol. II (Berlin: Weidmann, 1924).
Will, *HPMH*	Ed. Will, *Histoire Politique du Monde Hellénistique (323 av. J.-C.)*, 2 vols. (Nancy: Presses Universitaires, 1979–1982).
Χαρακτήρ	*Χαρακτήρ: Αφιέρωμα στη Μάντω Οικονομίδου* (Athens: Έκδοση του Ταμείου Αρχαιολογικών Πόρων και Απαλλοτριώσεων, 1996).
Zimi, *Silver Plate*	E. Zimi, *Late Classical and Hellenistic Silver Plate from Macedonia* (Oxford: University Press, 2011).

Figures, Tables, Plates, and Map

I. Figures and Tables

II. Plates

58. Ancient imitations, Nos. 13–17.
59. Modern imitations, Nos. 1–12.
60. Modern imitations, Nos. 13–20 / Modern 20-drachma coin of the Democracy Series (1930s, Bank of Greece Numismatic Collection).
61. Comparanda, Nos. 1–14.
    - No. 1: Gold with types of Philip II: Lanz Auction 168 (Jun. 1994), lot 124.
    - No. 2: Posthumous Alexander tetradrachm, later Makedonian issue: Price, *Alexander*, no. 630.
    - No. 3: Alexander tetradrachm from Mesembria: Price, *Alexander,* no. 1005.
    - No. 4: Areus I: Grunauer–von Hoerschelmann, *Lakedaemonier*, pl. I.1
        - No. 5: Mørkholm, *EHC*, pl. 29, no. 438.
        - No. 6: Mørkholm, ibid., pl. 29, no. 439.
        - No. 7: Mørkholm, ibid., pl. 40, no. 602.
        - No. 8: Mørkholm, ibid., pl. 40, no. 603.
        - No. 9: Kos: J. Kroll, "The Late Hellenistic Tetrobols at Kos," *ANSMN* (1964), 81–117, pl. 19.17.
        - No. 10: Kos: Kroll, ibid., pl. 20.19.
        - No. 11: Kos: Kroll, ibid., pl. 23.4.
        - No. 12: Antigonid bronze, Herakles/horseman: *SNG Cop.* 1214.
        - No. 13: Antigonid bronze, Athena/Pan: ibid., 1207.
        - No. 14: Antigonid bronze, shield/crested helmet: ibid., 1223.
62. (a) Shield from Dodona: Liampi, *MS*, S2, pl. I.2.
    (b) Shield from Vegora: Liampi, *MS*, pl. I.3.
    (c) Comparison of obverse of Pan head tetradrachms (Period III) with the shield from the inscription from Gonnoi: Liampi, *MS*, S11, pl. 6.1.
63. Chr. Habicht, "Epigraphische Zeugnisse zur Geschichte Thessaliens unter der Makedonischen Herrschaft," *Archaia Makedonia* I (Thessaloniki, 1970), 265–79, pl. LXXV.

III. Map

64. Pan head–Poseidon head tetradrachms: Hoard Distribution.

οἷς γὰρ
οὐ πέλαγος, οὐκ ὄρος, οὐκ ἀοίκητος ἐρημία πέρας ἐστὶ
πλεονεξίας,
οὐδ' οἱ διαιροῦντες Εὐρώπην καὶ Ἀσίαν τέρμονες ὁρίζουσι
τὰς ἐπιθυμίας,
πῶς ἄν ἁπτόμενοι καὶ ψαύοντες ἀλλήλων ἀτρεμοῖεν ἐν τοῖς παροῦσι
μὴ ἀδικοῦντες...
ἀλλὰ πολεμοῦσι μὲν ἀεί,
τὸ ἐπιβουλεύειν καὶ φθονεῖν ἔμφυτον ἔχοντες,
δυεῖν δὲ ὀνομάτων, *ὥσπερ*
νομισμάτων,
πολέμου καὶ εἰρήνης,
τῷ παρατυχόντι χρῶνται πρὸς τὸ
συμφέρον…

Plut. *Pyrrh.* 12.3

For how those men
to whose rapacity neither sea nor mountain nor uninhabitable desert sets a limit,
men to whose inordinate desires the boundaries which separate Europe and Asia put no stop,
can remain content with what they have and do one another wrong when they are in close touch,
it is impossible to say.
Nay, they are perpetually at war,
because plots and jealousies are parts of their natures,
and they treat the two terms,
war and peace, like
current coins,
using whichever happens to be for their
advantage…

(trans. B. Perrin, *The Loeb Classical Library*)

1.0

Introduction

1.1 Aims and Methodology

This systematic analysis of the gold and silver coinages of "King Antigonos" is intended to explore the nature of the Antigonid cash economy during the second and the third quarter of the third century BC.

My principal aim in reconstructing the precious metal coinage of "King Antigonos" is to comprehend the way in which the mints concerned functioned and to identify the major issues of the period. This helps us to answer questions such as, whether or not production was continuous; on which occasions/for which purposes the mints operated; where and why the coins produced circulated and what their value at the time was; finally, whether these issues outlasted their initiator, Antigonos Gonatas. The macroeconomic profile of Antigonid Makedonia during this period will be completed by an attempt to quantify and to contextualize these Antigonid silver issues. Explanations other than military for the production of this coinage will be explored and the chronology and the role of those silver coins issued posthumously in the name of Alexander that are currently assigned to the early reign of Gonatas will be reconsidered. Finally, the geographical distribution of these Antigonid issues will be reassessed. A more detailed analysis of the nature of the regional economy will require the systematic study of the Antigonid bronze coinage, which has been excluded from this study.

The numismatic evidence shows that, rather than belonging to a single ruler, the two individual types in the name of "King Antigonos" represent a dynastic coinage extending from Antigonos Gonatas to Antigonos Doson. The continuation of Gonatas' silver coin types by his successors demonstrates a strong sense of dynastic continuity in the Antigonid dynasty, comparable to that observed in the Ptolemaic and Seleukid royal families.[1] However, it is as difficult to distinguish between the issues of the two homonyms, Gonatas and Doson, as it is to disentangle the two monarchs in contemporary epigraphical documentation.[2]

The numismatic evidence does not elucidate certain key issues, such as the ways in which Gonatas financed his army until his nomination in Makedonia, the process of his establishment in Makedonia and Greece, or the ratio between military and other expenditure of the state throughout this period. But the numismatic iconography reveals the main line of Antigonid international policy, and also allows us to define the function of the Antigonid issues within the market dominated by the Attic weight standard.

1.2 ANTIGONID MAKEDONIA, 277–221 BC

The Makedonian precious metal issues in the name of "King Antigonos" postdate the rise of Antigonos Gonatas to the throne and the establishment of the Antigonid royal dynasty in Makedonia. The transition from the old royal dynasty of the Temenids/Argeads to that of the Antigonids had not been smooth, as the death of Alexander had rendered Makedonia a bone of contention among various pretenders, not necessarily related to the Temenid dynasty. The interregnum that followed the assassination of Ptolemy Keraunos during a Celtic invasion in 279 BC, was ended only with the ascent of Antigonos Gonatas to the Makedonian throne.[3]

Antigonos, the son of Demetrios Poliorketes, had already come onto the political stage in 288 BC, when he was assigned his father's possessions in Greece. He was nominated king after his father's death (284/3 BC), although he was not in control of a kingdom.[4] The beginning of his reign in Makedonia was placed in 277/6 BC by Tarn, who related it to Gonatas' decisive victory over the Celts at Lysimacheia (277 BC),[5] but a date between 277/6 and 274/3 BC is perhaps more

1. *Contra* R. Fleischer, "Hellenistic Royal Iconography on Coins," in Per Bilde et al., *Aspects of Hellenistic Kingship*, 28–39, who excludes the Antigonids from this practice.

2. See, for instance, Chr. Habicht, "Divine honours for king Antigonus Gonatas in Athens," *SCI* 15 (1986) 131–134 = idem, *HL Monarchies*, 285–284; K. Buraselis, Παρατηρήσεις στὶς συνθῆκες τοῦ βασιλιᾶ Ἀντιγόνου μέ τήν Ἐλεύθερνα καὶ τὴν Ἱεράπυτνα (*Staatsv*. III 501, 502), *AE* (1981) 114–126; G. Reger, "The political history of the Kyklades, 260–200 BC," *Historia* 43 (1994) 32–69.

3. A full historical account in Tarn, *AG*, 167–168; Will, *HPMH* I^2, 103–110; E. Will, "From the Apogee of Lysimachus to the Establishment of Antigonus Gonatas (287–276)," in *CAH* VII^2, 110–117; F. W. Walbank, "The Years of Chaos (285–277/6 BC)," in Hammond and Walbank, *Macedonia* III, 239–258; Errington, *Macedonia*, 154–161.; J. B. Scholten, "Macedon and the Mainland," in Erskine, *Companion*, 134–158; Shipley, *GWA*, 108–120. On the Celtic invasions in Macedonia and Thrace, see K. Dimitrov, "Celts, Greeks and Thracians in Thrace during the Third Century BC. Interactions in History and Culture," in *In search of Celtic Tylis in Thrace (III c. BC), Proceedings of the Interdisciplinary Colloquium Arranged by the National Archaeological Institute and Museum at Sofia and the Welsch Department, Aberystwyth University held at the National Archaeological Institute and Museum, Sofia, 8 May 2010*, ed. L. Vagalinski (Sofia: National Archaeological Institute and Museum, 2010), 51–66. To the known evidence of the Celtic presence in Thrace J. Bouzek has recently added a hoard in a third century BC oinochoe with 434 drachmae of Alexander III, Lysimachos and other early Hellenistic successors, 115 tetradrachms of Philip II, Alexander III, Demetrios Poliorketes, Seleukos I, 3 gold staters of Alexander III: J.Bouzek, *Pistiros* III, 64 & pl. 18; Archibald, *Northern Aegean*, 204.

4. Eus. 1.237 (Schoene); Jacoby, *FGH* 260 F 3.12; Eus. 1.238 (Schoene); Lucian, *Macrob*. 11. M. Chambers, "The first regnal year of Antigonos Gonatas," *AJPh* 75 (1954), 392; N. G. L. Hammond, "Appendix 2: The Chronology of the Years 281–276 B.C.," in Hammond and Walbank, *Macedonia* III, 581–583; Errington, *Macedonia*, 162–204.

5. Diog. Laert. 2.141; P. Trog. *Prol*. 25; Apollodoros (*Philol*. 71, p. 226); Just. 25.1–2; Paus. 1.16.2; *Syll*^{3} 398, l. 1–6 (decree of Kos). Tarn, *AG*, 165–166, n. 99, 104; Gabbert, *AG*, 27. On Gonatas' activities in the East, see R. W. Mathisen, "The Activities of Antigonos Gonatas 280–77 BC and Memnon of Heracleia, *Concerning Heracleia*," *AncW* 1 (1978), 74. On his conflict with Antiochos I, see P. Trog. *Prol*. 27; Memnon, *FGH* 434, F 10; Just. 24.1.1; *OGIS* 219; Diog. Laert. 4.39; *OGIS* 748; Buraselis, *HM*, 112–115.

likely.[6] At any rate, Gonatas' position was firmly established only after he repelled the attack of Pyrrhos, on the latter's return from Italy (274–273/2 BC).[7] By making Pella his capital and by cultivating the Makedonian traditions of the Temenid era, Antigonos apparently attached priority to the consolidation of the Makedonian state before laying claim to any area south of Makedonia.[8]

Control of Makedonia provided the Antigonids with a regular source of wealth from taxation, the Makedonian mines and the region's forests (chapter 7). It required, though, the effective orchestration of diverse institutions, villages, *poleis, sympolities* and *ethne*.[9] The king's authority was mediated by the Makedonian royal family, the members of the aristocratic families, the Makedonian people (Μακεδόνες of cities, tribes) and/or koinon.[10] Since Amyntas III at least, the Makedonian poleis, in particular, were subject to the king as executive arm of the state.[11] Under Gonatas, the recognition in 243 BC of the Asklepieia at Kos by the cities of Philippoi, Amphipolis, Kassandreia and Pella according to the king's will suggests that the institutions of these poleis were at least influenced by the Makedonian king (chapter 4).[12]

The systematic organization of the state administration aimed at the long-term convergence of regional differences within and beyond the Makedonian borders through a combination of military, political and diplomatic methods with the least expenditure of resources or effort and with the maximum results.[13] With very few exceptions, it is not obvious that Gonatas consistently interfered with the internal affairs of Greek cities, although strategically located garrisons ensured Antigonid hegemony throughout the mainland.[14] Gonatas exercised his control either by the appointment of the most important magistrates or by the nomination by the commander of the local

6. Tarn's date is based on the fact that Gonatas was king of Makedonia during the 125th Olympiad and on the alleged Athenian sacrifices to Gonatas at Athens under Polyeuktos in 275/4 BC. This date contradicts, however, the literary tradition that Gonatas held the royal title for forty-four years (Medios in Lucian, *Macrob.* 11; Euseb. 1.237), on the one hand, and that he reigned in Greece ten years before he reigned in Makedonia (Euseb. ibid.), on the other. Tarn reconciles the divergent information by suggesting that Gonatas acquired the royal title after the death of his father in 284/3 BC. He places, though, Gonatas' ten-year rule in Greece between 287/6, when Poliorketes crossed to Asia, and 277/6 BC (*AG*, 112, n. 3). As the archonship of Polyeuktos (and hence the official sacrifices of Athens to Gonatas) has shifted from 275/4 (Tarn) to 250/49 or to 247/6 (D. Knoepfler, "Les relations des cités eubéennes avec Antigone Gonatas et la chronologie delphique au début de l'époque étolienne," *BCH* 119 [1995], 158–159), the alleged beginning of Gonatas' reign in Makedonia in 277/6 BC requires revision. It is worth noting that the causal relationship between the battle of Lysimacheia and Gonatas' rise to the Makedonian throne (Diog. Laert. 2.141–142) need not imply that the two events were close in time. Gonatas' rule in Makedonia was firmly established only after the death of Pyrrhos.

7. Plut. *Pyrrh.* 26; Just. 25.3.5–8; Paus. 1.13.2–3; Diod. 22.11–12. Will, *HPMH* I², 212–219; F. W. Walbank, "Macedonia and Greece", *CAH* VII², 221–224; F. W. Walbank, "Antigonus Gonatas: the early years (276–261 BC)," in Hammond and Walbank, *Macedonia* III, 259–267; Gabbert, *AG*, 29–32; Hammond, *State*, 302–307; Errington, *Macedonia*, 163–165; J. B. Scholten, "Macedon and the Mainland," in Erskine, *Companion*, 133–145; Shipley, *GWA*, 116–128.

8. M. Andronikos, "Βεργίνα. Οἱ βασιλικοί τάφοι τῆς Μεγάλης Τούμπας / Vergina. The Royal Graves in the Great Tumulus," *AAA* 10 (1977), 1–72; Tarn, *AG*, 175–222; Will, *HPMH* I², 216–219; F. W. Walbank, "Antigonus Gonatas: The Early Years," in Hammond and Walbank, *Macedonia* III, 267–276. On his policy *vis-à-vis* mainland Greece, see Gabbert, *Greek Hegemony*, 247–259; eadem, *AG*, 33–44; Shipley, *GWA*, 124–128.

9. Hatzopoulos, *Institutions*, 77–216.

10. R. M. Errington, "The Nature of the Macedonian State under the Monarchy," *Chiron* 8 (1978) 77–134; cf. Ed. Levy, "La monarchie Macédonienne et le mythe d'une royauté démocratique," *Ktema* 3 (1978), 201–255; Gabbert, *Greek Hegemony*, 36–43; Le Bohec, *AD*, 239–253; Hatzopoulos, *Institutions*, 219–230, 487–496.

11. Xenophon, *HG*, V.2.12. On royal control over Makedonian poleis at least since Amyntas III, see Hammond, *State*, 386 ff.; Hatzopoulos, *Institutions*, 204–213; A. Giovannini, "Le statut des cités de Macédoine sous les Antigonides," *Archaia Makedonia* II (Thessaloniki, 1977), 465–479.

12. Hatzopoulos, *Institutions*, 139–149; *Institutions* II, nos. 36, 41, 47, 58.

13. Gabbert, *Greek Hegemony*, 247–278. Hammond, *State*, 307–315.

14. The presence of the largest Makedonian garrison and of the most important garrison commander at Korinth, in particular, is due to the fact that Korinth was the cornerstone of Gonatas' policy in Greece. For the Makedonian garrisons in Peiraeus and Attika, see Gabbert, *Greek Hegemony*, 107–139.

Makedonian garrison of preferred individuals; alternatively, magistrates favorable to his authority were appointed "voluntarily" by the members of the poleis. The diversity in the nomenclature of the military commanders, who were regarded as the king's representatives in the cities, suggests that the principle of Antigonid "Greek hegemony" as established by Gonatas in practice depended primarily on "his subtle political control of the eastern Peloponnese, the Isthmos of Korinth, Attika and Northern Euboia. To this was added the formal state-to-state diplomatic influence in the Peloponnese and Aitolia."[15] This loose control over Greek political entities, echoing the policy adopted by Philip II after the fall of Olynthos (348 BC),[16] may have been upset by the Chremonidean War and was resumed only after 250 BC, but it had certainly yielded results by the time of Doson.[17] Polybios' description of the establishment of "tyrannies" by Gonatas in peninsular Greece may be regarded as the Greek "interpretation" of the resumption of this policy of gaining control over the *poleis* of Greece.[18]

Secure control over mainland Greece was a springboard for the adoption by the Antigonids of a progressively more active international policy *vis-à-vis* the Seleukids in the east and the Ptolemies in the south. Modifications in the equilibrium among these three powers often had a direct impact on events in the interior of each kingdom. The establishment of friendly relations with Antiochos I after the peace of 278 BC, for instance, restricted Gonatas' scope for expansion south of Makedonia[19] and made the potential cooperation of the Antigonid and Seleukid kings a considerable threat to Ptolemy II. At the same time, instability in mainland Greece was often instigated by rival kings, in order to distract the Makedonian kings from international events. For example, the Chremonidean War between Gonatas and the cities of Southern Greece, was presumably instigated by Ptolemy II (chapter 2).[20] Similarly, the encouragement of revolts and political unrest in southern Greece by the Ptolemies, along with tensions between the Achaian and the Aitolian Confederacies, as well as between each of these and the Antigonids, shifted the interest of Gonatas and of his successors away from areas vital to the Ptolemaic kingdom. The two critical naval victories of Gonatas over the Ptolemies, at Kos[21] and Andros (246/5 BC),[22] and the expedition of Antigonos Doson in Karia are inextricably bound with the settlement of affairs in mainland Greece in favor of the Antigonids. The engagement of Gonatas in Southern Greece after Andros certainly allowed Ptolemy III to establish his control over the Aegean.[23]

15. Gabbert, *Greek Hegemony*, 256–257.

16. G. T. Griffith, "The Olynthian War (352–348 B.C.)—The Peace of 346 B.C.," in Hammond-Griffith, *Macedonia* II, 325–327; Hammond, *State*, 160–165, 177–187.

17. Gabbert, *Greek Hegemony*, 77–80. Her suggestion, however, that Gonatas, unlike Doson, neglected the internal organisation of Makedonia and Thessaly because he had competent regents for his successor, Demetrios II, is not convincing. Cf. Le Bohec, *AD*, 363–403, 480–483.

18. Plb. 2.41.10; 9.29.6. Cf. J. B. Scholten, "Macedon and the Mainland," in Erskine, *Companion*, 145–148.

19. However, tensions between the two were not avoided later. In fact, the separate peace of Gonatas with Kos and the expulsion of Stratonike by Demetrios II have been assumed to have had an impact on the relations between Seleukids and Antigonids: Beloch, *GG*, IV.1, 566; Buraselis, *HM*, 117, n. 32.

20. Gabbert, *Greek Hegemony*, 171–172.

21. Athen. 5.209e; 8.334a = *FGH* 81 F 1; Plut. *Pelop.* 2.4, *Mor.* 545b, 183c; cf. Heinen, *Unters.* 191–192. The suggested dates for the battle off Kos range between 262/1 and 255 BC: F. W. Walbank, "Sea-power and the Antigonids," in Adams and Borza, *Macedonian Heritage*, 218–220; Buraselis, *HM*, 146–151; F. W. Walbank, "Antigonus Gonatas: The Naval Situation (261–251 B.C.)," in Hammond and Walbank, *Macedonia* III, 291–293; N. G. L. Hammond, "Appendix 4: The Battles of Cos and Andros," ibid., 595–600. Reger, *Kos*, 155–177. Cf. chapters 2.4.2, 3.

22. Trog. *Prol.* 27; Plut. *Pelop.* 2; Plut. *Mor.* 183c, 545b; possibly, Athen. 593a–b; *P. Haun.* 6. F. W. Walbank, "Antigonus Gonatas: The Naval Situation (261–251 B.C.)," in Hammond and Walbank, *Macedonia* III, 291–293; N. G. L. Hammond, "Appendix 4: The Battles of Cos and Andros,'" ibid., 587–295, with earlier bibliography. Further bibliography and discussion in chapters 2.4.3, 5.

23. Buraselis, *HM*, 270–271.

During the second and the third quarter of the third century BC, cash was obviously required for the finance of the navy and of the troops engaged in all these military activities. At the same time, Gonatas established major building programmes, both in Makedonia and at Delos,[24] made dedications to Apollo (including that of his flagship after the battle of Kos) and established religious foundations at Delos in 253 and 245 BC.[25] All these activities would have required coinage, to which we shall now turn.

24. The covering over of the royal tombs at Vergina/Makedonia has been assigned by Andronikos to Gonatas: Plut. *Pyrrh.* 26.7; Andronikos, *Vergina*, 59–79. On Gonatas' dedications at Delos and on the construction of the Antigonid portico, see Tarn, *AG*, 389–390, n. 61; Courby, *Délos*, 13–45; Coulton, *Stoa*, 59–60, 231; J. Tréheux, "Sur le Neorion à Délos," *CRAI* (1987), 168–184; Buraselis, *HM*, 141–149; Smith, *HRP*, 24–25; *EAD;* F. W. Walbank, "Antigonus Gonatas: The Naval Situation (261–251 B.C.)," in Hammond and Walbank, *Macedonia* III, 292; Ameling et al., *Schenkungen*, 190–196; N. G. L. Hammond, "Appendix 4: The Battles of Cos and Andros," ibid., 595–596, with earlier bibliography. For the date of the portico at Delos, see Nachtergael, *Galates*, 164 ff.

25. W. W. Tarn, "The Dedicated Ship of Antigonos Gonatas," *JHS* 30 (1910) 209–222; Buraselis, *HM*, 141–155; Bruneau, *Délos*, 557–64; N. G. L. Hammond, "Appendix 4: The Battles of Cos and Andros," in Hammond and Walbank, *Macedonia* III, 592–594; Fellmann, *AG*, 82.

2.0–5.0
Catalogue and Commentary: Gold and Silver Issues of "King Antigonos"

All the gold and silver issues discussed here carry on the reverse the simple legend ΒΑΣΙΛΕΩΣ ΑΝΤΙΓΟΝΟΥ reflecting the least developed of the formulae employed by the Antigonids in their royal correspondence.[1] The royal title, adopted by Kassander for his bronze and by Poliorketes for his silver and bronze Makedonian issues, was used by Antigonos after the death of his father in 283 BC.

The gold and silver coin types in the name of "King Antigonos" are:

1. Transitional Alexander Types, Gold and Silver, with the Legend "of King Antigonos"

1.1 Gold Staters:

O: Head of Athena r. in crested Korinthian helmet, decorated with coiled snake.
R: Nike standing l. holding aphlaston in outstretched r. hand, and mast (*stylis*) in l. hand. Legend ΒΑΣΙΛΕΩΣ ΑΝΤΙΓΟΝΟΥ.

1.2 Silver Tetradrachms:

O: Beardless head of Herakles r.
R: Zeus Aetophoros seated on stool-throne l., holding eagle on outstretched r. hand and scepter in l. Legend ΒΑΣΙΛΕΩΣ ΑΝΤΙΓΟΝΟΥ.

1. R. M. Errington, "Macedonian 'Royal Style' and its Historical Significance," *JHS* 94 (1974), 30–31, 37. The king was presented as βασιλεὺς Ἀντίγονος when confusion with other kings was unlikely. For an analysis of Antigonos' titulature, see Le Bohec, *AD*, 205–206.

1.3 Silver Drachmae:

O: Head of Herakles r. in lion's scalp. Dotted border.
R: ΑΝΤΙΓΟΝΟΥ r., ΒΑΣΙΛΕΩΣ l. Zeus seated l. on throne, holding eagle with r. hand, scepter with l. hand. Letters regular. Dotted border.

2. Personal Types: Silver.

2.1 Pan Head Tetradrachms ("Pans"):

O: Head of Pan l., in center of Makedonian shield.
R: Archaizing Athena l., brandishing a thunderbolt. Legend ΒΑΣΙΛΕΩΣ ΑΝΤΙΓΟΝΟΥ.

2.2 Pan Head Tetradrachms ("Pans"):

O: Head of Pan l., in center of Makedonian shield.
R: Archaizing Athena r., brandishing a thunderbolt. Legend ΒΑΣΙΛΕΩΣ ΑΝΤΙΓΟΝΟΥ.

2.3 Pan Head Drachmae:

O: Head of Pan l., in center of Makedonian shield.
R: Archaizing Athena l./r., brandishing a thunderbolt. Legend ΒΑΣΙΛΕΩΣ ΑΝΤΙΓΟΝΟΥ.

2.4 Poseidon Head Tetradrachms ("Poseidons"):

O: Head of Poseidon r., in wreath of marine plants. Dotted border.
R: Apollo holding brow (with string up) with his uplifted r. hand, seated l. with crossed legs on prow. Legend ΒΑΣΙΛΕΩΣ ΑΝΤΙΓΟΝΟΥ.

2.5 Zeus Head Tetradrachm ("Zeus"):

O: Head of Zeus laureate r.
R: Apollo holding brow (with string up) with his uplifted r. hand, seated l. with crossed legs on prow. Legend ΒΑΣΙΛΕΩΣ ΑΝΤΙΓΟΝΟΥ.

2.6 Zeus Head Fractional Denominations:

Drachmae, Pentobols

O: Head of Zeus r., in wreath of marine plants.
R: Athena brandishing thunderbolt l. Her shield held upright, but without *aegis* and gorgoneion. In field l., winged helmet; r., monogram.

The material in the catalogue is arranged by reverse die symbols and monograms, numbered consecutively. Abbreviations of museum collections and auction catalogues may be found in the related list, while those common in numismatic monographs, i.e. "O" for "Obverse," "R" for "Reverse," "mon." for "monogram," "l." for "to the left" and "r." for "to the right," have been employed in addition to those generally in use in Classical studies. Unless otherwise stated, an image of the first specimen in the coin list of every die combination appears on the plates. The coins in every die combination have also been die linked and are listed accordingly. Auction catalogues have been arranged by numismatic expert, wherever possible. Research on auction catalogues was ended at the end of July 2009; since then, only those coins that have appeared on www.coinarchives.com web page before July 10, 2014, have been integrated. Sales catalogues after that date have not been considered. Records of weights from auction catalogues are generally noted in brackets with the specimens related; in the cases of divergence, the lowest weight is retained, assuming some loss of weight as a result of a cleaning process. The die-axes of the coins which I have personally examined have been provided, and the die-axes recorded in listings, published and unpublished, have also been reproduced. With regard to the classification of the issues, it is worth noting that obverses linking two or more groups of the same period are considered only with the first group and that the number of obverses in the other groups is represented in brackets, as follows: [number of obverse dies/obverse dies linked to previous groups].

For ease of identification, a conventional numbering system has been adopted for elements of the Pan head type. "Star/crescents" ("units") and the spaces between them are numbered (1–7), as are the rays on each star (1–16) for the numbers of rays on each star. Our numbering starts from the first "star/crescent," space, or "star"/"ray" after 12 h and continues clockwise (Fig. 2.1).

All die combinations (first specimens) are illustrated, otherwise a symbol (°) is inserted.

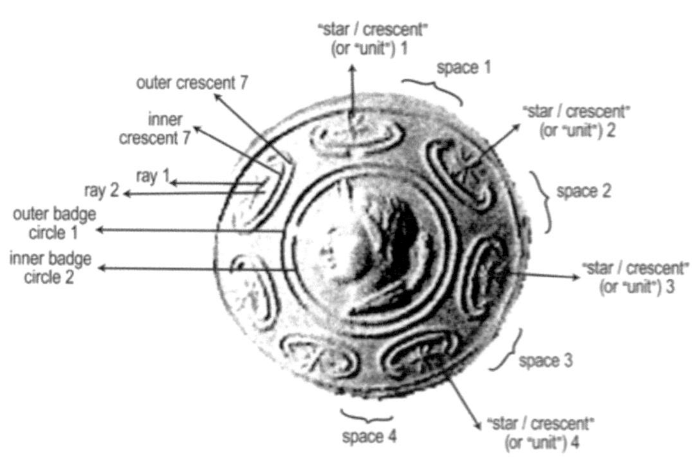

Figure 2.1. Pan head tetradrachms: conventional numbering of "star/crescents," "spaces," "rays."

I shall divide the gold and silver coin types in the name of king Antigonos into four periods, which are summarized in Table 2.2:

Table 2.2. Classification of types by period

Period	AV Alexander staters	AR Alexander tetradrachms	AR Alexander drachmae	AR Pan Head tetradrachms	AR Pan Head tetradrachms (Athena r.)	AR Pan Head drachmae (Athena l.)	AR Poseidon Head tetradrachms	AR Zeus Head tetradrachms	AR Zeus Head drachmae	AR Zeus Head pentobols
I	X	X	X	X	X	X				
II				X						
III				X	X		X			
IV				X			X	X	X	X

This classification has been determined by the fact that the Pan head and the Poseidon head tetradrachms, which form the backbone of the Antigonid issues, may be divided into four distinct sections, which are not die-linked with each other. The tentative dates that I propose for each period (which will be explained in chapters below) are as follows:

I. c. 274/3–260/55 BC; i.e., from Gonatas' firm establishment in Makedonia after the death of Pyrrhos until the capitulation of Athens and the naval conflict between the Makedonians and the Ptolemies off Kos.

II. c. 252–246/5 BC; i.e., from the revolt of Alexander, tyrant of Korinth until Gonatas' second naval victory over the Ptolemies off Andros.

III. c. 246/5–229 BC; i.e., from Gonatas' victory off Andros to the death of his successor, Demetrios II.

IV. c. 229–221 BC; i.e., during the reign of Antigonos Doson.

Key to Abbreviations in the Catalogue

Catalogue		**Coin Condition**	
FPC	Fixed Price Catalogue	B	Broken
FPL	Fixed Price List	C	Chipped
L	List/Liste	Cr	Crystallized
BBS	Buy or Bid Sale	P	Pierced

Note on the Diagrams of Die Links: Reverse numbers with different monograms, with which an Obverse is die linked, are quoted in the brackets to the right of the Reverse number, the first time the Obverse is quoted. Different colors indicate different monograms, as shown in the key at the bottom of every page. Unless otherwise stated, all die combinations carry a crested helmet symbol left.

2.0

Period I: The Chremonidean War and the Battle off Kos (271/268–260/255 BC)

"Plain Style"

The death of Pyrrhos and the establishment of Gonatas on the Makedonian throne inaugurated a critical period in both Central Greek and international politics in the 260s:[1] a coalition between Sparta, her kings and their allies on the one hand, and Athens and her allies, on the other, for all time (ἐς τὸν ἅπαντα χρόνον), announced by the Chremonidean Decree, led to the Chremonidean War (cf. Chapters 1.2, 6.4.2).[2] This allegedly defensive treaty between Athens and Sparta has

1. On the death of Pyrrhos, see Plut. *Pyrrh.* 34. Cf. Lévêque, *Pyrrhos*, 622–631; Garoufalias, *Pyrrhus*, 124–141; Hammond, *Epirus*, 557–588.

2. The dates and duration of the Chremonidean War are controversial. 268/7 and 265/4 BC have been suggested as possible dates for the archonship of Peithidemos, during whose office the Chremonidean decree was voted in Athens. Habicht, Heinen and Osborne opt for the first date: Habicht, *Unters.*, 95 ff.; Osborne, *Naturalisation* II, 165–166, n. 750. Cf. S. V. Tracy, "A fragmentary inscription from the Agora praising Ephebes," *Hesperia* 59 (1990), 543–547, esp. 545. For the policy of the Lakedaimonians, see P. Cloché, 'La politique extérieure de Lacédémoine depuis la mort d' Agis III jusqu' à celle d' Acrotatos, fils d' Areus Ier (suite et fin)," *REA* 48 (1946), 39–60; Hammond and Walbank, *Macedonia* III, 278–280; Green, *Alexander to Actium*, 147–148. On the other hand, Janice J. Gabbert reverted to Meritt's date of Peithidemos to 265/4 BC: Gabbert, *Greek Hegemony*, 163–164; eadem, "The Anarchic Dating of the Chremonidean War," *CJ* 82 (1986), 230–235; eadem, *AG*, 46–48, n. 43; eadem, *Response*, 34. Cf. B.D. Meritt, *The Athenian Year* (Berkeley, 1961), 223; idem, "Mid-Third Century Athenian Archons," *Hesperia* 50 (1981), 78–99, reconstructed by Aleshire, *Asklepieion*, 250 (inventory V, l. 5), 293–301. Reviewing Gabbert's book on Gonatas, Reger redates the beginning of the war to the summer 268 BC, on the basis of the important decree of Epichares and of the revolt of Eretria by 268 BC: Reger, *Review*, 17. n. 18–19, with further bibliography. The archonship of Antipatros is dated with greater certainty to 262/1 BC (Apollodorus, *FGH* 244, F 44 (fragment of Philodemos, *Περὶ τῶν Στωικῶν*); Paus. 3.6.6; Polyaen. 4.6.20). J. D. Morgan's announced revision of the third-century Athenian calendar is likely to revive this discussion: "The Calendar and the Chronology of Athens," *AJA* 100 (1996), 395. For recent revisions of the Chremonidean War, see J. L. O'Neil, "A Re-examination of the Chremonidean War". In P. McKechnie and Ph. Guillaume (eds.), *Ptolemy II Philadelphus and his World*, Mnemosyne Supplements: History and Archaeology of Classical Antiquity, 300 (Leiden, 2008), 65–89; J. B. Scholten, "Macedon and the Mainland," in Erskine, *Companion*, 145–148; cf. G. Hölbl, *A History of the Ptolemaic Empire* (London/New York: Routledge, 2001), 40–43.

been regarded as complementary to two unilateral treaties between each of the cities and Ptolemy II, which established firmly a triple alliance between Ptolemy II, Athens, Sparta, and their respective allies. The instigation of this alliance by the main rival of Gonatas for control of the Aegean, Ptolemy II Philadelphos, may be presumed rather than proved, but the enemy implied in the decree can only be Antigonos Gonatas.[3]

The reconstruction of the Chremonidean War is rendered difficult by the fragmentary nature of the documentation. At a certain point, Gonatas may have invaded Attika with a land army, followed by ships (Paus. 1.1.1, 3.6.4; cf. Chapter 6.4.2).[4] As a consequence of the Chremonidean Decree, Patroklos and his fleet came to aid the Athenians (Paus. 1.1; 1.7; 3.6.4); he was followed by the arrivals of Areus and the Lakedaimonians πανδημεί (Paus. 3.6.1; Just. 26.2.1).[5] The reluctance of both the Peloponnesian and the Ptolemaic forces to confront Gonatas in a pitched battle resulted in the retreat of the Lakedaimonian and Ptolemaic troops, and inaugurated the second phase of the war, in which diplomacy played a major role.[6] A mutiny of the Celtic mercenaries of Gonatas at Megara and the revolt of Alexander the Molossian in Epeiros, for instance, were meant to distract Gonatas from the Attic chora. Upon his arrival at Athens, he "invested Athens and prevented the Athenian reinforcements from entering the city."[7] While the Aitolians sent an embassy to Euboia, presumably in order to turn the Euboians against Gonatas, Alexander the Molossian invaded Makedonia.[8] These events, however, only postponed the final capitulation of Athens until autumn 261 BC, on condition, as Pausanias argues, that a garrison would be placed at the Mouseion.[9]

The capitulation of Athens may have been preceded or followed by one of the two known naval conflicts between the Antigonid and the Ptolemaic fleets during this period, near Leucolla off Kos. The battle of Kos has been redated recently to 262/1 BC (rather than between 260 and 254 BC), by G. Reger, who suggested that the Chremonidean War marked the end of an aggressive Ptolemaic policy in Greece.[10] At the same time, Gonatas established a link to the Aegean policy of his ancestors, Antigonos Monophthalmos and Demetrios Poliorketes, through this naval victory. The dedi-

3. Heinen, *Unters.*, 119, 133–139; F. Walbank, "Antigonus Gonatas: the early years," in Hammond and Walbank, *Macedonia* III, 267–80.

4. Heinen, *Unters.*, 170–171, 191.

5. Heinen, *Unters.*, 177–179.

6. Just. 26.2.7, P. Trog. *Prol.* 26, on the causal relationship between the failure of the Celtic mutiny and the retreat of the Lakedaimonians; Paus. 3.6.5–6, on Patroklos' encouragement to Areus to attack Gonatas first, promising that he would then follow with an attack on the other side: Just. 26.2.8, on the retreat of Patroklos.

7. Paus. 3.6.5: περικαθημένου δὲ Ἀντιγόνου τὰς Ἀθήνας καὶ τῆς εἰσόδου τῆς ἐς τὴν πόλιν τὰ Ἀθηναίων συμμαχικά εἴργοντος...

8. Paus. 3.6.5.

9. Paus. 3.6.6; Polyaen. 4.6.20. The archaeological evidence admittedly plays a significant role in our knowledge of this period; see, for instance, J. MacCredie, *Fortified Military Camps in Attika*, Hesperia Supplement 11 (Princeton: ASCSA, 1966). C. A. Lagos, "A Hoard of the Chremonidean War," *NC* 156 (1996), 272–278, pl. 48. To the existing hoards from Attika during this period one may add *CH* IV, 32, a hoard comprising twenty Ptolemaic coins found "near Sounion" (in fact, at Sounion). Information on this find is on file at the British Museum. On the Ptolemaic coinage around the Aegean, see, for instance, K. Chryssanthaki, "Les monnaies lagides en Égée," in F. Duyrat and O. Picard (eds.), *L'exception égyptienne? Production et échanges monétaires en Égypte hellénistique et romaine, Actes du colloque d' Alexandrie, 13–15. Avril 2002* (Études Alexandrines, 10; Cairo), 159–175.

10. Plut. *Mor.* 676D–E. G. Reger, "The Date of the Battle of Kos," *AJAH* 10 (1993 [1985]), 155–177, esp. 157, emends Buraselis' date of the battle, c. 255 BC, to 262/1 BC: Buraselis, *HM*, 141–144, 146–151, 162. One might note that Plutarch would not have confused two naval battles, Kos and that of Andros, unless they belonged to the same historical chapter. Secondly, the decline of the Ptolemies' interests in the Aegean after their defeat off Kos and the capitulation of Athens would deprive the battle of Andros of an appropriate context, leaving as well the revolts or the maintenance of the Makedonian garrison at the Mouseion unjustified.

cation of the portico of his ancestors at Delos may have been part of his celebration of this naval battle, whose impact is reflected in the divine honors paid to the Makedonian king by the demes of Ios, Kos and Rhamnous in c. 255 BC.[11]

*** *** ***

The transition from the Alexander types to the personal silver types of Antigonos Gonatas takes place during this first period of mint activity. The Antigonid silver issues start with a small group of transitional silver tetradrachms retaining the Alexander types, which can be dated only approximately between c. 274 and 255 BC. Monograms comprising various combinations of the letters E and K occur left, between the legend and the figure of Zeus, or beneath the throne of Zeus (cf. Chapter 6.2.4, fig. 6.6). These are combined with a few gold staters with the legend "of Antigonos" (see Chapter 6.4.1).

An innovation in the 260s was the introduction of a new type carrying the king's legend (Chapter 6.4.2). The new series begins with the head of a young Pan in profile view in the center of a large Makedonian shield with elliptical star/crescents. The schematic head of Pan on all the obverses of this period clearly belongs to the "plain style" that reigned in the coin portraiture of the Epigonoi from the 270s onwards. Shallow, elongated curves are combined with reduced, simplified and compact forms; the eyes are natural and the face is rendered in soft and curvilinear forms, which result in a fine and relatively unemotional characterization.[12]

The near frontality and extreme simplicity of the archaizing Athena on the reverse echo the Severe style of the Classical Age. There is much emphasis on the composition of verticals and horizontals, and the folds of the drapery are flat and nearly linear. The noble simplicity of the face on the obverse and the solid stance of the archaizing Athena on the reverse may be regarded as effective expressions of the general tendency towards tradition-quoting idealization, just as an Alexander head in the Classicistic style was deliberately chosen in 317/6 BC to go with the archaizing Athena on the silver tetradrachms of Ptolemy I.[13] The fixed type of Athena and the regular, generally similar, letter forms in the legend suggest the chronological proximity of the groups struck during the first period, even though the few reverse links do not confirm an intense minting activity.

Through the progression from eight-rayed to six-rayed stars, from tall to short and crude Athenas, from larger to smaller Makedonian helmets, the specimens of this category may be distinguished into fifty rather loosely defined groups, with very few reverse links. The vast majority of those with Athena left, forty-five out of fifty, belong to the "helmet series," with a crested Makedonian helmet left on the reverse. Their division into groups is facilitated by the monogram which occurs r. on the reverse; the crested helmet is combined with nine monograms altogether in this period.

11. *IG* XII Supplement 168 (Ios); B. Petrakos, "Ανασκαφή Ραμνούντος," *ΠΑΕ* (1989 [1992]), 31–34, no. 15, l. 2–10 = *SEG* 41, 75 (Rhamnous). Habicht, *Gottmenschentum*, 65–73 (Ios); idem, *Studien*, 15–17; idem, *Athen*, 155–156; idem, "Divine honors for King Antigonos Gonatas in Athens," *SCI* 15 (1996), 131–134; I. Kralli, "The date and context of divine honours for Antigonos Gonatas—A Suggestion," in S. Tracy and O. Palagia, *The Macedonians in Athens*, 61–66; Mikalson, *Religion*, 160; S. V. Tracy, "Antigonos Gonatas, King of Athens," in S. Tracy and O. Palagia, *The Macedonians in Athens*, 61–66. There may be some circularity in the dating of the Ios and Kos decrees so closely to 255 BC. On the portico dedicated by Gonatas at Delos, see B. Schmidt-Dounas, "Der dorische Fries der Stoa des Antigonos Gonatas auf Delos," in *MDAI(A)*, 109 (1994), 227–242. C. Tarditi, "Architettura come propaganda. Esame dell'attività edilizia degli Antigonidi in Grecia e nuove proposte di attribuzione," *Aevum Antiquum* 3 (1990), 43–74.

12. Brown, *Royal Portraits*, 36–37.

13. Brown, *Royal Portraits*, 26, 38; 48, figs. 11a–b, 12a–b.

The crested Makedonian helmet vanishes from the reverse of the last four groups of Pans. A monogram already known from the Helmet series, [monogram], [monogram] or [monogram], is transferred from right to left, and its original place is left blank.

The early silver tetradrachms with the king's individual types end with a special issue, carrying Athena right on the reverse and different control marks on either side: a *desmos* left and a monogram r. The three monograms of this issue are different from those of the Helmet series. The only fraction of this issue, a silver drachma with the same types as the tetradrachms with a crested helmet left and [monogram] right on the reverse, is stylistically similar to Group 13 of the silver tetradrachms.

*** *** ***

All the coins of "King Antigonos" during this period were struck on the Attic weight standard, as follows:

1. Gold staters:

8.65–8.61 g	1
8.60–8.56 g	4
8.55–8.51 g	1

2. Silver tetradrachms with Alexander types:

17.05–17.01 g	4
16.90–16.86 g	1
16.70–16.66 g	1
16.30–16.26 g	1
16.10–16.06 g	1
15.35–15.31 g	1

3. Silver drachmae with Alexander types:

4.15–4.11 g	1

4. Pan head tetradrachms: Weight table, Fig. 3c. The numbers above the columns represent the groups as they are in the catalogue below. Chipped, broken and pierced coins have been excluded from the figures.

5. Pan head drachmae:

4.05–4.01 g	1

The sample is small, but the weight standard aimed at seems to be around 8.60–8.56 g for the gold staters and c. 17.05–17.01 g for the silver tetradrachms with Alexander types. The weights of the far more numerous Pan tetradrachms show considerable variation, but produce a rough peak of around 17.15–17.01 g. The Pans are thus slightly heavier than the transitional Alexander tetradrachms. Many coins are significantly below this level, presumably due to long use. Unlike the posthumous Alexanders, most of which were struck off-center, the Pans of the first period are generally well-centered. The high artistic quality of the tetradrachms from this period explains the large number of pierced coins.[14] Most of the pierced tetradrachms come from Group 25, whose engraving quality is exceptionally high.

Many specimens from this period have been found in hoards (Figs. 2.3a–b), all but two from the "helmet series." The exceptions are specimen no. 170a from Thesprotia, 1992, the only coin without a crested helmet and with Monogram ⋈ left found in a hoard context, and that with Athen aright from the North of Larissa, 1985, hoard (no. 181e, *desmos*—ꟸ), (Fig. 3b, 8n and 16, respectively). The Thesprotia, 1992, Gordion, 1961, Mektepini, 1956 and S. Asia Minor, 1963 hoards are of little use for determining when the Pans were introduced, for they were buried much later. Even so, the poor state of the Pan tetradrachm from Verge ("Perge"), 1955, presumably a "savings" hoard, indicates, for one thing, that the first Pans had been long in circulation by the time the hoard was buried. Similarly, Eretria, 1937, is the only hoard with a very worn coin from the first group, but it cannot establish a firm chronological peg due to its late burial. Of the two specimens from this period coming from this hoard, specimen no. 2a from Group 1, with monogram ⋈, is poorly preserved and not cleaned. The obverse of no. 160a is in comparatively good condition. These specimens are more worn than the Pans of the "realistic portrait" style, with which they occur (Chapter 6.3).

Even though the hoards do not permit us to determine the introduction date of the Pans, they shed light on the relative chronology of certain groups. Group 3, for instance, including the specimen from Verge ("Perge"), 1955, no. 14a, is obverse linked with Groups 16, 24 and 34. Moreover, the good condition of the illustrated Pans from Period I from the hoard found at Scotussa before 1989 suggests the chronological proximity of groups 5 and 19, with O09. Groups 6, 7, 19, 38 and 39, with O10 and O11, must also be chronologically close; the pieces from Scotussa, (pre-)1989, in Groups 7 and 19 are more worn. A relatively early date is also speculated for Group 12, with Pans from Phayttos, c. 1956, and from Scotussa, (pre-)1989. Groups 12, 23, 31 and 41 are obverse linked via O17. The obverses of Group 38, a specimen of which occurs in the Eretria, 1937 hoard, dated to c. 245 BC, must also be early.

Current hoard evidence shows that the specimens from the first period are those with the longest and widest circulation. The presence of such specimens in Gordion, 1961, S. Asia Minor, 1963, and in Syria, 1970, from the last decade of the third century, and in Mektepini, 1956, from the early second century, contrasts with the absence of mid-third century hoards with Pans in Asia Minor (Chapter 7.2). The specimen from Gordion, 1961 is very worn. The two Pans from South Asia Minor, 1963, are in good condition and the only illustrated Pan from this period from South Asia Minor, 1970, is more worn than its later counterparts. The wide circulation of the early Pans is also confirmed by the broken, chipped, and chisel-cut specimens that belong to this period.

14. Pierced tetradrachms (or coins with attempted piercing), nos. 1a, 103d, 104a, 105f, 134a. As piercing for decoration was common on coins, there is no need to identify these pierced coins with Pans withdrawn from the circulation pool at Athens, as does K. Lönnqvist, "Studies on the Hellenistic Coinage of Athens: The Impact of Macedonia on the Athenian Money Market in the 3rd century B.C.," in J. Frösén (ed.), *Early Hellenistic Athens, Symptoms of a Change*, (Helsinki, 1997), 119–145, esp. 125–126. See also T. Linders, "Fallen Money and Broken Crowns—or When is a Coin Not a Coin?," in *Florilegium Numismaticum*, 255–258.

Table 2.3a. Period I: Gold specimens in hoards

No.	Hoard	Cat. No.	Group no.	Obverse no.	Monogram
1a	Poteidaia, 1984	3a	1	O03	—
1b	Poteidaia, 1984	5a	1	O5	—

Table 2.3b. Period I: Silver specimens in hoards

No.	Hoard	Cat. No.	Group no.	Obverse no.	Monogram
1a	Eretria, 1937	2a	1	O01	Ⓜ
1b	Eretria, 1937	160a	38	O10	⋈
2	Verge (Perge), 1955	14a	3	O06	⊠
3a–c	Scotussa area, (pre-)1989	21b–c, 26a	5	O09	Ⓜ
3d	Scotussa area, (pre-)1989	31c	7	O11	⊠
3e	Scotussa area, (pre-)1989	50c	12	O17	HP
3f	Scotussa area, (pre-)1989	72d	17	O20	HP
3g	Scotussa area, (pre-)1989	81c	18	O09	HP
3h	Scotussa area, (pre-)1989	122c	32	O05	⋈
3i	Scotussa area, (pre-)1989	127a	32	O05	⋈
4	Enna, 1966	45a	11	O16	HP
5	Phayttos, 1956, c.	47a–b	12	O17	HP
6a	Pherai, 1937–1938	31a	7	O11	⊠?
6b	Pherai, 1937–1938	70c	17	O20	HP
6c	Pherai, 1937–1938	122b	32	O05	⋈
7	Karditsa (Palaiokastro), 1929	58b	14	O18	HP
8a	Meydancıkkale, 1980	42b	11	O16	HP
8b	Meydancıkkale, 1980	96a	21	O26	HP
9a	Thesprotia, 1992	30a	6	O10	⊠
9b	Thesprotia, 1992	31b	7	O11	⊠
9c	Thesprotia, 1992	32b	7	O11	⊠
9d	Thesprotia, 1992	57a	14	O18	HP
9e	Thesprotia, 1992	69a	17	O19	HP
9f	Thesprotia, 1992	86a	20	O22	HP
9g	Thesprotia, 1992	89b	20	O23	HP
9h	Thesprotia, 1992	95e	20	O25	HP
9i	Thesprotia, 1992	114a	30	O26	⋈
9j	Thesprotia, 1992	123a	32	O5	⋈
9k	Thesprotia, 1992	140a	35	O07	⋈
9l–m	Thesprotia, 1992	156a, 157a	38	O10	⋈
9n	Thesprotia, 1992	170a	43	O30	⋈ I.
10a	Unknown Findspot ("Seleucus III"), 2002	7b	1	O02	⊠

Table 2.3b (continued). Period I: Silver specimens in hoards

No.	Hoard	Cat. No.	Group no.	Obverse no.	Monogram
10b	Unknown Findspot ("Seleucus III"), 2002	70a	17	O20	[monogram]
10c	Unknown Findspot ("Seleucus III"), 2002	80a	19	O09	[monogram]
10d	Unknown Findspot ("Seleucus III"), 2002	91a	20	O24	[monogram]
10e	Unknown Findspot ("Seleucus III"), 2002	180a	48	O35	[monogram]
11	Gordion, 1961	25a	05	O09	[monogram]
12a	S. Asia Minor, 1963	130a	32	O05	[monogram]
13b	S. Asia Minor, 1963	132a	33	O31	[monogram]
13c	S. Asia Minor, 1963	151b	38	O09	[monogram]
14	Tell Sukas (Gabala), 1958	130b	32	O05	[monogram]
15	N. Syria, 1960	152b	38	O10	[monogram]
16	S. Asia Minor, 1970	39b	9	O14	[monogram]
17	Mektepini, 1956	72f	17	O20	[monogram]
18	North of Larissa, 1985	181e	49	O36	[monogram]

Table 2.4. Period I: Weights of Pan head tetradrachms and drachmae

Weight (g)	1	2	3	4	5	6	7	8	9	10	11	12	13	14	15	16	17	18	19	20	21	22	23	24	25	26
17.3–17.26					1																					
17.25–17.21																			1							
17.2–17.16	2		1								1		1	4				1		1					7	
17.15–17.11	3	1		2	1				6	1		1	2	7	1	1	1	1	1						18	3
17.1–17.06	7		1	3	4	1	3		5	1	2	3	4	4	1		3	2	2	5	1				12	2
17.05–17.01		1		3			3	1	1		1	3			1			2		11					3	
17.0–16.96	3				2						2	3		2	1		6	1	2	2			1		1	1
16.95–16.91	1		1		2	1						1		1			1			5			1			
16.9–16.86	1			1	1		1					2		1						3						
16.85–16.81								1											1					1	1	
16.8–16.76			1		1				1				1	1			2								3	
16.75–16.71	1			1			1												1				1			
16.7–16.66	2		1														1									
16.65–16.61				1	1												1									
16.6–16.56														2			1									
16.55–16.51															1											
16.50–16.46					1							1		1			1			1						
16.45–16.41																									1	
16.40–16.36				1			1	1	1					1												
16.35–16.31																										
16.3–16.26																										
16.25–16.21					1																					
16.2–16.16							1													1						
16.15–16.11				1	1																					
16.10–16.06									1																	
16.05–16.01																										
15.35–15.31																										
12.5–12.01																										
4.5–4.01																										
Unknown Weight	3		1	2	4		3		2		4	4	1	2	1	1	3	2	4	7		1			6	
Broken/Pierced	1													1												
TOTAL	24	2	6	15	20	2	13	3	17	2	10	18	9	27	6	2	20	9	12	36	1	1	3	1	52	6

Table 2.4 (continued). Period I: Weights of Pan head tetradrachms and drachmae

27	28	29	30	31	32	33	34	35	36	37	38	39	40	41	42	43	44	45	46	47	48	49	50	All 4D	All D
											1													2	
																								1	
2	1			5	1			1																28	
1	1			2	2	1	2	1			2										1	2		65	
	2				2		1	3		1	3			1		1								80	
		1		1	1			1			6				2					2		2		46	
	1						1	3			3				1				1					37	
			1		1	1	1				3								1	1				23	
1				1	4			1			1													18	
	1										2											1		8	
	1		1													1								13	
	1							1														1		8	
											2							1	1					8	
																								3	
							1																	4	
								1				1												3	
									1		1													7	
																								1	
											1													6	
																								0	
					1															1				2	
											1					1			1					4	
																								2	
																								2	
											1						1							3	
		1																						1	
											1													1	
																							1		1
			1	2	6	1	2	7		1	6	1	2		3		1					2		86	
																								2	
4	8	2	3	11	18	3	8	19	1	2	34	2	2	1	6	3	2	1	4	4	1	8	1	464	1

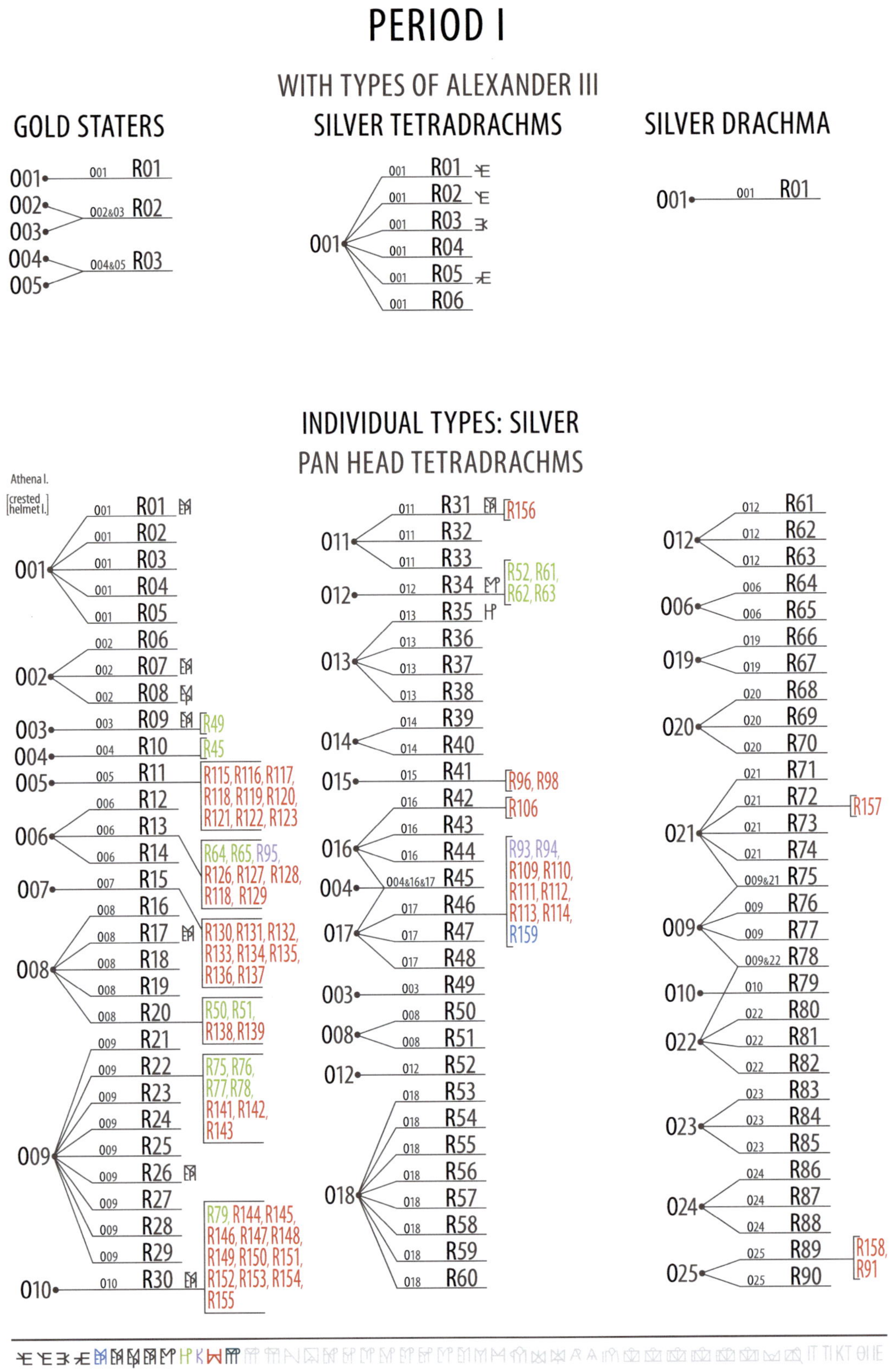

Figure 2.5a. Period I: Die links of Alexander issues and Pan head tetradrachms.

PERIOD I - PAN HEAD TETRADRACHMS

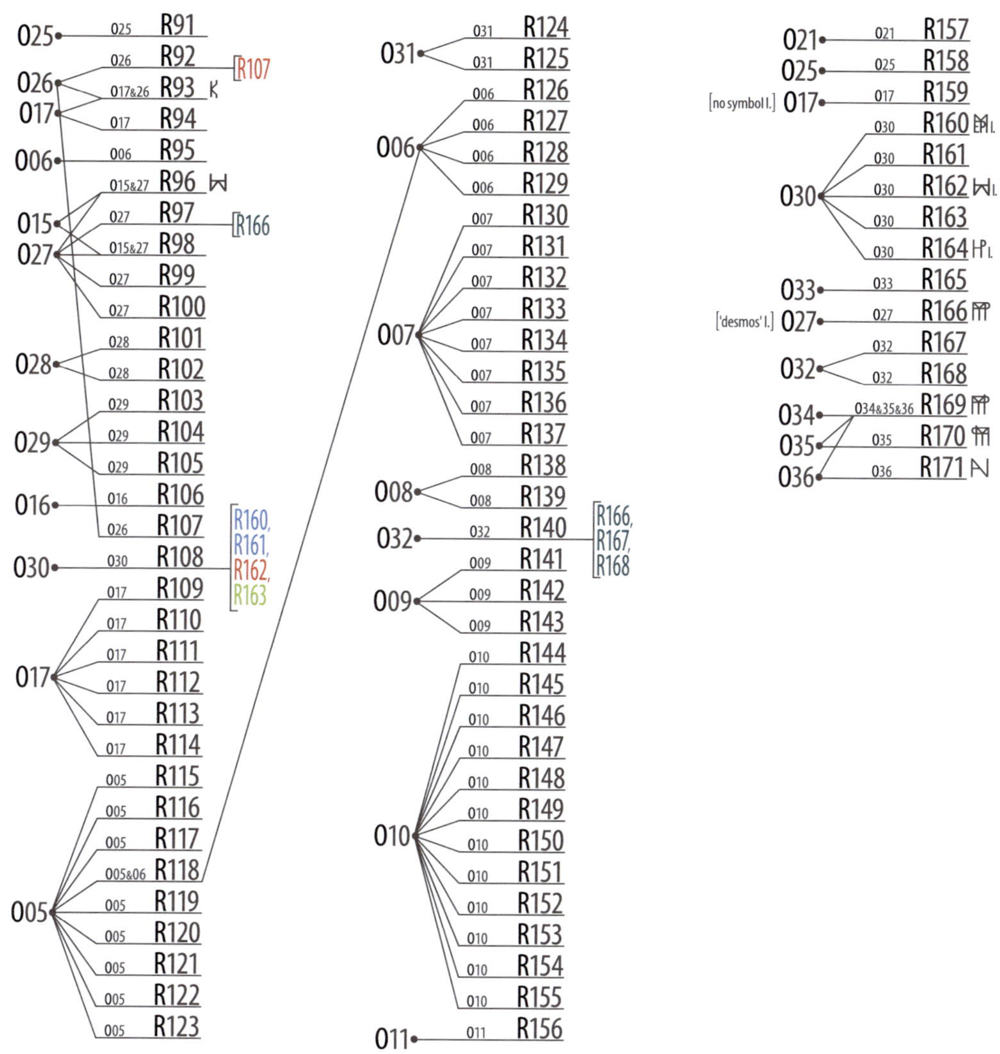

PAN HEAD DRACHMAE

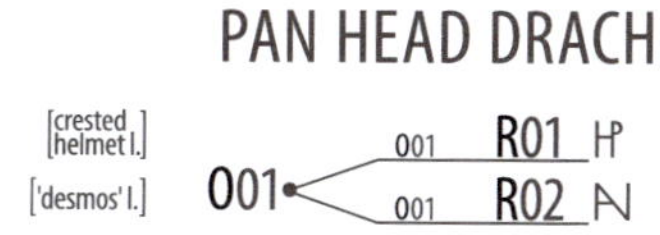

Figure 2.5b. Period I: Die links of Pan head tetradrachms and drachmae.

MINT A

2.1 GOLD STATERS WITH TYPES OF ALEXANDER III

O: Head of Athena r. in crested Korinthian helmet; in bowl, serpent wriggling r.; curved lock starts from hair, behind the ear, and hangs to front. Delicate pendent earring.
R: ΒΑΣΙΛΕΩΣ ΑΝΤΙΓΟΝΟΥ. Nike standing frontally with head to l., holding *aphlaston* with her slightly uplifted r. hand and *stylis* with her l. hand. In field l., below, wreath.

GROUP 1

Specimens: 6 Obverses: 5
Die Combinations: 5 Reverses: 3

1. O01 R01

a. De Luynes 1689 8.57 g - -
b. CNG 66 MBS (19.5.2004), 262 8.58 g - -

2. O02 R02 R (a): legend: ΒΑΣΙΛΕΩ[Σ] ΑΝΤΙΓΟΝ[ΟΥ].

a. Vienna: Gaebler, *AMNG* III.2, 179.1, pl. XXXII, 21 obv.
8.63 g - -

O: As above, but Athena without earring.

3. O03 R02

a. Paris: BNF 1326 (Mionnet, *Description*, Suppl. 3, 244, 587, XI, 1; Gaebler, *AMNG* III.2, 179.1, pl. XXXII, 21 rev.) 8.57 g - -

4. O04 R03 R: Legend farther from Nike. Wreath similar to that in no. 2.

a. Glasgow: MacDonald, *Hunterian*, 336, 1, pl. XXIII.14.3
8.54 g 9 h 15 mm

[O (a): flaw off r. end of neck.
R (a): r., break].

O: Athena without earring and without ornament above hair locks on helmet bowl.
R: As above. Wreath of different type (laurel?). Nike's *aphlaston* is replaced by a *syrinx*.

5. O05 R03

a. BM 1899-1-1-1; Price, *Alexander*, 141, 145.56215, pl. CLVIII.D; C. T. Seltman, *NC*[4] 9 (1909), 269 8.57 g 7 h -

[O (a): flaw off neck. R (a): up l., flaw from nose through to uplifted r. hand].

15. Price reports that a single gold stater in the name of Antigonos, now at the British Museum, was also in the Poteidaia, 1984 hoard (*Alexander*, 142 , pl. CLVIII.D; cf. 58), yet the only gold specimen with the types of Alexander but with the name of Antigonos which has been traced in recent sales catalogues and which might belong to this hoard is our 1b. The "Antigonos" specimen is described by Price as of different style and with a different control mark from those on its Alexander counterparts. Le Rider's publication of 148 gold staters from Poteidaia, 1984 comprises sixty-eight Makedonian posthumous Alexander staters with the name and title of Alexander: *Potidée*, 90, pl. VIII.18–23; cf. file at the British Museum. Fifty-six of the Alexander-type staters, nos. 17–18 and 19–72, belong indeed to the Makedonian groups assigned by R. W. Mathisen to the early reign of Gonatas. Cf. Mathisen, *Silver Coinages*, 95 (nos. 17–18); 89, table 5 (nos. 19–72). Cf. Chapters 6.3, 6.4.1, 7.2. Thus the fifty-six staters of "Antigonos Gonatas" in *CH* VIII (1994) 276 might be posthumous gold staters with the name and title of Alexander, but currently dated to the reign of Antigonos Gonatas. To these must

The five obverse dies and three reverse dies yield five die combinations. On the obverse, Athena's locks of hair are few, wavy, and uneven, with a diagonal lock running from the helmet through to her neck. Her less bulky helmet and her mild and natural features distinguish these gold staters from those associated with the group of posthumous Alexanders which was termed the Mu group by Mathisen due to its M-shaped monograms and a crescent;[16] the latter staters have a bulky helmet, three or four parallel spiral locks and rather heavy cheeks. The more elaborate style of the transitional staters of "King Antigonos," and the different control marks on their reverses suggest the production of these staters at a different mint or chronological moment. If these coins were not minted to cover payments to Celtic mercenaries, they may be assigned to a later date, perhaps to celebrate an event such as Gonatas' victory over the Ptolemies off Kos (cf. Chapters 6.4–6.4.1).

*** *** ***

2.2.1. Silver Tetradrachms with Types of Alexander III

O: Head of Herakles r. in lion's scalp. Dotted border.
R: ΑΝΤΙΓΟΝΟΥ r., ΒΑΣΙΛΕΩΣ l. Zeus seated l. on throne, holding eagle with r. hand, scepter with l. hand. Letters regular. Dotted border.

Group 1

Specimens: 5	Obverses: 1
Die Combinations: 2	Reverses: 2

1. O01 R01 Monogram ⱶE under throne.

a. Berlin 147 (ex Stewart's sale 1838-No 307 13-13-0); A. von Sallet, "Erwerbungen des Königlichen Münzkabinets in den Jahren 1890–1897," *ZfN* 21 (1898): 202, pl. IV.2

	16.30 g	11 h	28.5 mm
b. ANS: *ANSMN* 13 (1967), pl. V, A	15.33 g	12 h	-
c. CNA 5 (9.12.1988), 72	17.02 g	-	-

[O (a, b, c): off-center. (b–c): flaw from off nose to edge of dotted border. R (c): flaw in exergue].
(b), particularly worn, flan rather thin because of long use. Specimen broken on O: 2–5 h. R: the legend ΑΛΕΞΑΝ has been replaced by ΑΝΤΙΓΟΝΟΥ. Scratches on reverse, above the seated Zeus and on the letters ΒΑ, indicate long use. The scepter ends in spearhead or trident.

2. O01 R02

a. Athens: *SNG Alpha Bank* 982 [5679] (ex Gertzos coll.)

	17.04 g	7 h	24.0 mm

b. Brussels; Gaebler, *AMNG* III.2, 179.3, pl. XXXII.22

	17.06 g	9 h	-

[R (b): horizontal scratch on eagle; r., die break on first].

*** *** ***

be added the gold specimen with Alexander types but in the name of Antigonos, mentioned in *Alexander*, 58 and 142, but not recorded by Le Rider or at the British Museum files, as apparently its photos were not comprised in the Poteidaia, 1984 material sent by Price to Le Rider.

16. Mathisen, *Silver Coinages*, 81; Price, *Alexander*, 141.

O: Similar.
R: ΒΑΣΙΛΕΩΣ r., ΑΝΤΙΓΟΝΟΥ l.

GROUP 2

Specimens: 6 Obverses: [1-1]
Die Combinations: 4 Reverses: 4

3. O01 R03 R: Monogram ƎK in field l.

a. CNG Triton 9 (10–11.1.2006), 830; Leu 83 (6–7.5.2002), 203 (17.04 g, 2 h) 17.03 g 1 h -

b. Spink 119 (4.3.1997), 395; Ritter L 34 (06.1993), 322; Ritter L 19 (11.1983), 163; Sear 6784 16.09 g (c) - -

c. Henzen L 162 (31.8.2005), 81; Henzen L 154 (24.11.2004), 84 16.69 g - -

[O (b): test cut on edge (7 h). Scratch on face, across neck and chin.
R (b): scratch across foot].

4. O01 R04

a. Athens: ANM 1 16.89 g 4 h 31.5 mm

[O (a): small flaw off forehead; l., flaw alongside nose].

5. O01 R05 R: Monogram ⱻE in field l.

a. London: BMC 2, Bank Collection, 1034 (Head, *HN*, 229, fig. 140 = C. T. Seltman, "A Synopsis of the Coins of Antigonus I and Demetrius Poliorcetes," *NC* (1909), 268, pl. XX.6 = B. V. Head, *Coins of the Ancients* (London 1895), 4, pl. 31.12). 17.04 g 12 h 30.2 mm

[O (a): off-center. In field up, die break on dotted border, vertical flaw on lower lock of mane; angular flaw between two mane locks and border. Retouched on forehead; new flaw from nose upwards.
R (a): off-center].

6. O01 R06 R: l., beneath eagle, monogram ƎK erased.

a. Schlessinger 13 (Hermitage, 4.2.1935), 758 = B. M. Yakountchikoff, *Rare and Unpublished Greek Coins* (St. Petersburg, 1908), no. 27; Hyla A. Troxell, "The Peloponnesian Alexanders," *ANSMN* 17 (1971), 75, n. 68.

[O (a): development of flaw from nose upwards.
R (a): off-center.
NB: Module smaller].

All the transitional silver tetradrachms in the name of the new king came from a single obverse die, which had been combined earlier with reverses of the Monogram group of Makedonian posthumous Alexander tetradrachms.[17] These transitional Alexander tetradrachms do not occur in securely dated hoard contexts, but this obverse link, and the recutting of the obverse die on specimen 5, place them at the end of the Monogram group of posthumous Alexanders. The obverse is

17. Mathisen, *Silver Coinages*, 81, 95–96; Price, *Alexander*, 141.

characterized by Mathisen as "handsome," with "well proportioned features," whereas the reverses are "wholly different from that of the remainder of the Monogram group." The diversity in the style of Zeus and in the legend letters suggests that these tetradrachms were produced over a long time span (cf. Chapters 6.1, 6.4.1). Various combinations of the letters E and K yield monograms [monogram], [monogram], [monogram],and [monogram], the only control marks on this issue (cf. Chapter 6.2.4). Their position, initially beneath the throne and later in field l., tallies with that of the monograms on the Helmet group and on the Monogram group. This variation presumably reflects the mint organization at an early stage (cf. Chapter 6.2.4). These posthumous Alexander tetradrachms share no control marks with the Pan series.

The arrangement of the legend on the first two silver Alexander tetradrachms, with ΒΑΣΙΛΕΩΣ left and ΑΝΤΙΓΟΝΟΥ right, diverges not only from the general practice on the last four die combinations of transitional Alexanders, but also from that of the posthumous Alexanders and most Pan head tetradrachms (cf. Chapter 2.2.2). The initial arrangement of the legend ΒΑΣΙΛΕΩΣ ΑΝΤΙΓΟΝΟΥ echoes that on the early issues of Demetrios Poliorketes in Makedonia.[18] It may therefore illustrate Antigonos' attempt to follow the practice established by his father. The arrangement of the legend is also similar to that on the transitional gold staters in the name of king Antigonos and the Pan head tetradrachms with Athena right and with a *desmos* symbol left.

With the exception of the second and the last tetradrachms, the surviving specimens are off-center. Specimen 3 is test-cut at 9 h.

2.2.2 Fractional Denominations
Silver Drachmae with Types of Alexander III

O: Head of Herakles r. in lion's scalp. Dotted border.
R: ΑΝΤΙΓΟΝΟΥ r., ΒΑΣΙΛΕΩΣ l. Zeus seated l. on throne, holding eagle with r. hand, scepter with l. hand. Letters regular. Dotted border.

Group 3

Specimens: 1 Obverses: 1
Die Combinations: 1 Reverses: 1

7. O01 R01

a. Roma 7 (22–23.3.2014), 454; Gutekunst collection
4.11 g 12 h 19 mm

This unique drachma may be associated with the transitional Alexander-type tetradachms 1 and 2, with the legend ΑΝΤΙΓΟΝΟΥ right, ΒΑΣΙΛΕΩΣ left, but diverges from them in the careful engraving of the letters, in the complete absence of control marks and in important stylistic features, i.e., the unusual hanging of the drapery between the left leg of Zeus and the front leg of the stool and its peculiar folding on the main body; the feet floating above the exergue; the construction of the scepter. The carefully executed legend letters might associate this drachma with the *Athena right* Pan head tetradrachms, with a *desmos* symbol left in the field, and with the accompanying drachma (see below, Chapter 2.2.4, esp. tetradrachms no. 177–178, drachma no. 182).

The eagle's tail touches the first letter of the inscription ΒΑΣΙΛΕΩΣ in a way unparalleled on the drachma's Alexander-type tetradrachm counterparts. An assignation of this drachma to a mint in

18. The position of the legend ΔΗΜΗΤΡΙΟΥ r. was generally stable in the early issues, whereas ΒΑΣΙΛΕΩΣ was either left or below: Newell, *Poliorcetes*, 78–92.

the Peloponnese or to the time of Antigonos' homonymous predecessor, Monophthalmos, is not based on any firm evidence.[19]

2.2.3 Individual Silver Types: Pan Head Tetradrachms

2.2.3.1 Athena l.

2.2.3.1.1 Crested Helmet l.

The Helmet series, with a crested Makedonian helmet left on the reverse field, is the most prolific of the Pan head tetradrachms from this period.

Crested Makedonian Helmet l.—Monograms [monogram], [monogram], [monogram], [monogram], [monogram] r.

Monograms [monogram], [monogram], [monogram], [monogram], [monogram] are presumably variations of the same monogram.

O: Makedonian shield decorated by two concentric circles on edge. Seven embossed crescent and eight-rayed star units ("star/crescents"), arranged around a central emblem. In center, horned head of Pan l. with three-fold drapery round neck, tied in front, and *pedum* at shoulder. Drapery ends in straight line. Two concentric lines surround central emblem. Face small, *pedum* far from head, starting from between the middle and top drapery folds.

R: ΒΑΣΙΛΕΩΣ ΑΝΤΙΓΟΝΟΥ. Archaizing Athena l., in Athenian crested helmet and high-girdled *chiton*, falling in clearly delineated folds with one heavy fall in middle and with the hem ending in points. Shawl over shoulders falls in dove-tail pleats with two-pointed ends. *Aegis* across her back; thunderbolt on l. arm, poised to strike. She is striding, with l. leg advanced. She walks on tiptoe with both feet. In field l., crested helmet with high bowl (*pilos/konos*).

Group 1

Specimens: 24	Obverses: 4
Die Combinations: 10	Reverses: 10

1. O01 R01 R: Monogram [monogram] r.

a. ANS 1944.100.13836	17.08 g	6 h	-
b. G. Hirsch 175 (14–16.9.1990), 243	16.70 g	-	-

[O (a): flaws from (upper, middle, lower) *pedum*; also, on outer badge circle towards "unit" 1 l.; diagonal wear, from lower r. end of "unit" 1 towards outer badge end. Flaw between "unit" 3 and badge circle. Attempted piercing (6 h): star 7 scratched out.
R (a): signs of attempted piercing in field (11 h). Beginning of flaw between r. pleat behind ΣΙ. Monogram with upper horizontal hasta of Ε beneath l. angle of Μ. Beginning of flaw r. of l. vertical bar of second Ν].

2. O01 R02

a. ANM: Eretria, 1937 (*CH* IX (2002), 194; *IGCH* 175; Picard, *Chalcis*, 157.307, pl. XXIX). 17.08 g 5:30 h 30.0 mm

[O (a): flaws on badge and between outer badge circle and outer "crescent" 1 develop;

19. The careful letters, the absence of control marks and the engraving style may dissociate this specimen from Pella, but do not favor conclusively an assignation to an "uncertain mint in the Peloponnesos" c. 306 and 301 BC, as argued in *Roma* 7 (22–23.03.2014), 454. The peculiarities in the engraving and the absence of control marks may raise suspicion that this unique drachma is not genuine.

flaw between inner and outer badge circle, off "unit" 3; small flaw, from outer "crescent" 3 downwards.
R (a): l., flaws: between l. pleat and Γ; (signs), between l. pleat and second N; also, between l. pleat and figure.
NB: uncleaned].

3. O01 R03

a. CNG MBS 73 (13.09.2006), 167; Seaby, *Coin & Metal Bulletin* 460 (09.1956); K. L. Chapman Collection 17.11 g 9 h -
b. Coin Galleries (14.2.1973), 22 16.95 g - -
c. Grün 36 (16–18.5.2002), 30 - - -
d. Lanz 155 (10.12.2012), 115 16.72 g - -
e. Helios 7 (12.12.2011), 42 17.09 g - -

[O (a): breaks on badge area and off "units" 1 and 3 develop.
R (a): signs of flaw between l. pleat and figure.
NB: very bad photograph].

4. O01 R04

a. ANM: *SNG Saroglos* 925 17.20 g 4 h -
b. Henzen L 156 (1.2.1995), 107 16.90 g - -

[O (b): die repair on *pedum*].

5. O01 R05

a. Athens: *SNG Alpha Bank* 989 (1257) 17.13 g 6 h 3.08 g

[O (a): development of existing flaws. Large flaw on badge, from upper *pedum* through inner badge circle, to outer "crescent" 2. Sign of die break on outer badge circle, off "unit" 2.
R (a): similar archaizing Athena l.; shield closer to chest; hair lock shorter. R., flaws: from upper thunderbolt to edge, above ΩΣ, from each foot to edge].

6. O02 R06

a. Peus 280 (30–31.10.1972), 99 17.13 g - -
b. Salton & Schlessinger MBS 19 (17.2.1953), 33; Schlessinger 13 (1935), 776 17.00 g - -
c. Rauch L (1993), 83 16.97 g - -
d. Pecunem 9 (3.11.2013), 139 17.20 g - 31 mm
e. Lanz 153 (12.12.2011), 196 17.06 g - -

[O (a): six-rayed stars, except nos. 3 and 6 (seven-rayed); signs of flaw l., between "unit" 2 and badge circle; also, between lower r. end of "unit" 3 and badge. (b): flaws from "unit" 5 through head to "unit" 2; diagonal, wavy flaws: from "unit" 6 to middle of neck, from hair to "units" 2 and 3 and between head and *pedum*. Also, between badge edge and either side of "unit" 3; on r. end of "unit" 4; finally, on space 4.
R (a–b): diagonal flaw from upper l. bar of N to shield and from between shield and pleat to *chiton*; flaw r. of vertical *hasta* of Γ; between figure and shawl pleat].

7. O02 RO07 R: Monogram ΕΜ r.

a. Edinburgh, ED55.1923.819: Rutter, Edinburgh 55; FM 132 (30–31.05.1989), 35 (17.08 g); SB 41 (10–12.9.1996), 44 (17.07 g) 17.10 g 4 h 32 mm
b. Unknown Findspot ("Seleucus III" Hoard), 2002: *CH* X (2010), 272; A. Houghton—C. Lorber—O. Hoover, *SC* II.2, 142–150, Lot F, "Late Report of a Fragment," no. 58
\- - -
c. NAC 72 (16.05.2013), 350 17.07 g - -
d. Gorny & Mosch 204 (5.3.2012), 1306 16.97 g - -
e. Gorny & Mosch 200 (10.10.2011), 1464 17.09 g - -

[O (a): flaws starting diagonally from "unit" 5 through to nose and chin; also, between "unit" 2 and badge edge; on spaces 3 and 7. Flaw on badge, from drapery knob downwards, through to outer badge circle. Between *pedum* and head, countermark: star.
R (a): l., flaws: diagonally from *chiton* to l. pleat, from l. pleat to upper r. crest. Monogram with upper horizontal *hasta* of E starting from l. angle of M].

8. O02 R08 R: Monogram ΕΜ r.

a. Pegasi 4 (25.9.2000), 136 16.69 g - -

9. O03 R09 R: Monogram ΕΜ r.

a. Nicola L 9 (9.1974), 74 - - -

[O (a): flaws on all spaces. Flaw from "unit" 1 to l. horn and on inner badge circle, l. of l. horn; diagonal flaw up r., from inner badge circle towards upper *pedum*.
R (a): l., dot up l. of O; flaw from O to l. crest].

10. O04 R10

a. BM E. H., p. 295, no. 3 16.76 g (b) 10 h 31.2 mm

[O (a): broken on edge (6 h). All stars six-rayed. In center, between hair and badge circles, worn.
R (a): in field, above shield, dots: beginning of flaw].

*** *** ***

O: Six-rayed stars, but no. 5 with seven rays. Diagonal hair locks from crown of head downwards.
R: Athena tall, shield of medium size. Characters small. Few girdles on *chiton*.

GROUP 2

Specimens: 2 Obverses: 1
Die Combinations: 1 Reverses: 1

11. O05 R11 Monogram ΕΜ r.

a. Kurpfälzische Münzhandlung 18 (1980), 38; Helbing L 16 (1934), 221 (17.10 g); Helbing 70 (1932), 593 (17.10 g); Helbing 31 (1930), 206; R. Ratto (8.2.1928), 318
17.05 g - 32 mm
b. CNG Triton 15 (03.01.2012), 1142 17.11 g 3 h 30.0 mm

[O (a): flaws between: "unit" 1 and outer badge circle, "unit" 2 and badge r. Signs of flaw on spaces 6–7. Start of flaw up l., between inner and outer crescent 6. Flaw is development of that on no. 4. Diagonal flaw from *pedum* towards inner badge circle. Flaw between horns. R (a): l., dot off Y; r., horizontal flaw above upper horizontal bar of monogram; worn on lower *chiton*].

*** *** ***

O: Six-rayed stars with prominent center, star 2 with seven rays. Horns attached. Hair linear, flowing downwards. Face flat, nose and chin pointed, neck higher. *Pedum* emerges from middle fold of drapery, which projects and is split into two. End of drapery slightly curved.
R: Similar.

Group 3

Specimens: 6	Obverses: 2
Die Combinations: 4	Reverses: 4

12. O06 R12 R: Monogram [monogram] r.

a. Gorny 48 (2.4.1990), 261; NFA (coll. Szego), (4.12.1989), 460 (16.77 g)
16.68 g - -

[O (a): flaws on all spaces. Vertical flaws on either side of *pedum* and on badge area, from off nose downwards.

R (a): l., flaw between Y and r. foot; also, diagonally from below r. bar of N towards border; horizontal and vertical flaws on exergue. Monogram with upper horizontal hasta of E beneath l. angle of M].

13. O06 R13

a. Leiden, Coll. van Rede, 4756 16.79 g 8 h -

[O (a): development of existing flaws. Flaw on “unit” 7, between star and crescents. Flaw from end of pointed nose downwards.
R (a): l., dot between Athena and l. shawl end].

14. O06 R14

a. ANM: Verge (“Perge”), 1955: *IGCH* 455, no. 589; Varoucha, *BCH* 81 (1957), 497, pl. 9
17.18 g 2 h 29 mm
b. Peus 280 (1972), 100 17.08 g - -
c. Vinchon (20–22.5.1959), 456; Caron Sale No. 179 (2.1926), Paris
16.95 g - -

[O (a): very worn. Development of existing flaws.
R (a): up l., worn].

O: Six-rayed stars, but no. 6 with eight rays. Horns diverge, drapery ends in straight line.
R: Athena taller, many folds on *chiton*. Shield held as high as upper arm.

15. O07 R15

a. Galata (2.1979), 11 - - -

[O (a): flaw beneath chin; flaws on spaces 1–2, 5, 7.
R (a): l., flaw from A through to *chiton*; dot beside Y. In field up r., flaw on r. vertical monogram bar].

O: Similar, star 2 with 7 rays. Hair rendered in lines, *anastole* short. Eyebrows, chin, Adam's apple prominent. Three-fold drapery, *pedum* emerges from between middle and upper fold.
R: Similar.

Group 4

Specimens: 15 Obverses: 1
Die Combinations: 5 Reverses: 5

16. O08 R16

a. Auctiones 3 (4–5.12.1973), 148	17.13 g	-	-

[O (a): flaw on badge, off eye; second flaw from *pedum*; also, between "units" 2–4 and outer circle.
R (a): l., flaw between l. shawl and *chiton*; also, above shield; dot beneath TI. Monogram with upper horizontal *hasta* of E on the same level as l. angle of M].

17. O08 R17 R: Monogram r.

a. Münzzentrum L 20 (1975), 19; Münzzentrum L 19 (6.1974), 22	16.65 g	-	-
b. Superior, Chicago International Fair (30.5–1.6.1980), 2114	16.11 g	-	-

[O (a): drapery with three folds ending in curve, middle fold prominent. Flaws on spaces 1–3, 7. In badge, up l., flaw.
R (a): flaw between head and inner badge circle; also r., from top of Λ to border; horizontal flaw from r. foot through Σ to border; worn. Monogram with horizontal line connecting both angles of M].

18. O08 R18 R: Legend hastily engraved. Athena short, holds thunderbolt with lotus-tipped ends; shield diagonal. Helmet with small bowl and high crest with thin ends. Monogram r.

a. Private collection PRF1	17.05 g	-	-
b. Schulman L 204 (12.1973), 28	17.09 g	-	-
c. Gorny & Mosch 125 (13–14.10.2003), 1255; Elsen 44 (17.04.1996), 90	17.09 g	-	-
d. Lanz 28 (7.5.1984), 205	17.03 g	-	-
e. NFA 22 (01.06.1989), 268	16.37 g	5 h	-
f. NAC 64 (17.05.2012), 792	17.14 g	-	-

[O (a): worn on spaces 3, 5–6. Flaw from "unit" 1 to outer badge circle. (b): on *pedum*, countermark].

19. O08 R19

a. Aureo & Calicó 258 (20.03.2014), 1049	16.87 g	-	-

20. O08 R20

a. Berk 38 (13.8.1985), 112 - - -
b. Barthold-Baudey MBS (17.10.1985), vol. 1, 30
- - -
c. Gemini 11 (12.1.2014), 68 (Philip Davis Collection)
17.09 g 7 h -
d. Pilartz 11 (24–26.03.1966), 122 17.02 g - -
e. Emporium 67 (10.05.2012), 42 16.75 g - -

[O (a): flaws on badge circles, off "unit" 2 and from knob through to "unit" 5. Also, r., from lower *pedum* to inner badge circle.
R (a): flaw up l; from shield through Athena and monogram to Σ]

*** *** ***

O: All stars six-rayed, no. 4 eight-rayed. Horns r. and diverge; *pedum* farther from head; *nebris* ends in curve. Neck high, Adam's apple prominent.
R: Similar.

Group 5

Specimens: 20 Obverses: 1
Die Combinations: 9 Reverses: 9

21. O09 R21

a. BM 1896-7-3-192; : Sotheby (15–23.6.1896) 818
17.06 g 8 h 33.2 mm
b. Scotussa area, (pre-)1989 (*CH* VIII (1994) 283, pl. 34.6)
- - -
c. Scotussa area, (pre-) 1989 (*CH* VIII (1994) 283, pl. 34.2)
- - -

[O (a–b): flaw from chin downwards; also, on spaces 3, 7; between "unit" 3 and badge edge, "unit" 4 and badge edge. Horizontal flaw between star 1 and badge. (b): development of existing flaws, new ones on spaces 1–2, 6, "unit" 2 and badge circles. Flaw r. of neck and at upper *pedum*.
R (a–b): flaw between l. bar of Λ and monogram. (b): l., flaws on A, N, T; flaw extending horizontal monogram bar].

22. O09 R22

a. Kölner 58 (1993), 29 (16.91 g); Kölner 51 (1990), 81 (16.79 g)
16.79 g - -
b. Pegasi 12 (3.5.2005), 125; CNG MBS 67 (22.9.2004), 461 (16.88 g)
16.87 g - -
c. *SNG Sweden* II, 1139 16.21 g - -
d. NA, Ancient Coins 1 (13.12.1982), 68 17.11 g - -

[O (a): flaws on all spaces; also, between r. end of "units" 1–4 and badge edge.
R (a): l., horizontal flaws: between N and shield; r., and on top of monogram].

23. O09 R23

a. Grunow L 30 (8.1993), 297; Grunow L 27 (02.1993), 148
- - -

24. O09 R24

a. NFA (27.6.1986), 215 16.96 g - -
b. Gorny 101 (6.3.2000), 203 17.10 g - -
c. Gorny 97 (11.10.1999), 235 17.06 g - -

[O (a): l., vertical flaw slightly expands; horizontal flaws on all spaces; flaw from "unit" 2 through to upper head and eyebrows, to up r. end of "unit" 6.
R (a): up l., diagonal flaw between border and r. diagonal bar of A].

25. O09 R25

a. Gordion, 1961: *IGCH* 1405 (D. H. Cox, "Gordion hoards III, V and VII," *ANSMN* (1966), no. 40.41) 16.50 g 9 h -

R (a): l., diagonal flaw from field l., through IΓ and r. end of pleat to l. foot. Horizontal flaws from r. through ΣI to figure and from between letters Λ and E to pleat end. Test cut on *chiton*].

26. O09 R26 Monogram [monogram] r.

a. Scotussa area, (pre-)1989: *CH* VIII (1994), 283, pl. 34.7
- - -
b. Superior (1.6.1988), (Moreira part 1), 1483; Superior (12.1987), 301
16.63 g - -
c. CNG 28 (8.12.1993), 72; Gorny 44 (03.04.1989), 244 (16.97 g)
16.94 g - -

[O (a): flaw on badge, up r.; flaws on all spaces and between "units" 3–4 and badge area, past hair to upper *pedum*.
R (a): very worn. Monogram with a horizontal *hasta* connecting both angles of M].

27. O09 R27

a. Cahn 66.1 (9.5.1930), 198 17.27 g - -

28. O09 R28

a. Superior (22–24.10.1979, Northwod Institute & H. D. Glady's Spear), 1431
16.11 g - -

29. O09 R29

a. Bayerische Vereinsbank 15 (9.1977), 15 16.98 g 1 h -
b. InAsta 7 (1996), 27; InAsta 4 (5–6.11.1994), 61; InAsta 1 (20–21.02.1993), 41
17.10 g - -
c. Gorny & Mosch 196 (7.3.2011), 1427 16.94 g - -

[O (a): flaws on spaces; on badge l., diagonal flaw from off eyebrows past nose to low l.; second flaw, from horns through badge circles to "unit" 6.
R (a): up l., worn].

*** *** ***

O: Similar, but hair falls in larger locks from crown of head. Drapery ends in curve, middle fold prominent.
R: Similar.

Group 6

Specimens: 2 Obverses: 1
Die Combinations: 1 Reverses: 1

30. O10 R30 R: Monogram [monogram] r.

a. ANM: Thesprotia, 1992 (*CH* IX [2002], 200 ; Touratsoglou, *DM*, no. 47)
16.92 g 6 h -
b. Kress 91 (1951), 55 17.10 g 5 h -
[O (a): on badge, flaw from off chin downwards; second flaw, between hair and *pedum*].

*** *** ***

O: All stars six-rayed. Head rendered in flat forms. Horns curved l., diverge. Hair linear, flowing from crown downwards. Neck shorter, but Adam's apple prominent.
R: Similar. The r. end of pleat very close to r. bar of Λ. Helmet with very short bowl.

Group 7

Specimens: 13 Obverses: 1
Die Combinations: 3 Reverses: 3

31. O11 R31 R: Monogram [monogram] r.

a. ANS 1944.100.13837: Pherai 1937–8 ("Larissa environs"), (*IGCH* 168), (on file at ANS) 17.05 g 12 h -
b. ANM: Thesprotia, 1992 (*CH* IX [2002], 200; Touratsoglou, *DM*, no. 46)
16.88 g 5 h -
c. Scotussa area, (pre-)1989 (*CH* VIII [1994], 283, pl. XXXIV.3)
\- - -
d. Grigoli 3 (11–12.11.1989), 22 17.10 g - -
[O (a): flaw on badge circles and from drapery knob to outer badge circle. Beginning of flaw on outer crescent 3; also, respectively between "units"1, 2, 5 and 7 and badge edge. Flaw between lower *pedum* and middle fold of drapery. Signs of flaw on edge (space 4). (b): flaw (dots), off eye].

32. O11 R32 R: Monogram [monogram] r.

a. Müller 54 (20–21.2.1987), 32; Müller 51 (14–15.02.1986), 44; Müller L 43 (1986), 11 (17.11 g); Müller 47 (28–29.4.1984), 33; Müller 44 (1983), 50; Müller 41 (18–19.03.1983), 32; Müller 36 (1982), 70 17.10 g - -
b. ANM: Thesprotia, 1992 (*CH* IX [2002], 200; Touratsoglou, *DM*, no. 48)
16.74 g 12 h -
c. Classical Galleries, *Num. Review,* L 3.5 (1962), E56; Superior (1992), 2061; Helbing 24 (1927), 2861 17.01 g - -

d. Kurpfälzische Münzhandlung 46 (9–10.6.1994), 50
16.20 g - -
e. Serrure (18.11.1911), 47; Helbing (24.10.1927), 2861
- - -

[O (a–b): flaw on outer crescent 7; that from drapery knob expands to r. edge of "unit" 5. (b): flaws on spaces 6 and 7. (d): flaw off nose.
R (a): l., diagonal flaw from border to IΓ. In field r. below monogram, monogram deleted. In exergue, flaws beneath feet].

33. O11 R33 R: Monogram [monogram] r.

a. Peus 274 (29.10.1970), 1576 17.01 g - -
b. G. Hirsch 2 (6–7.12.1979), 136 - - -
c. Lanz 125 (28.11.2005), 259 17.08 g 4 h -
d. Pegasi BBS 131 (27.7.2004), 77; Pegasi 8 (29.4.2003), 108; Pegasi BBS 124 (17.9.2001), 83; Pegasi BBS 123 (30.7.2001), 82 16.40 g - -

[O (a): horizontal flaw from "unit" 2 through head and nose to "unit" 6; flaw up r., at l. end of "unit" 6; flaw from knob to lower badge circle develops. Flaws on spaces 2–5.
R (a): very worn].

*** *** ***

O: Similar.
R: Similar.

GROUP 8

Specimens: 3 Obverses: 1
Die Combinations: 1 Reverses: 1

34. O12 R34 Monogram [monogram] r.

a. *SNG Evelpidis* 1427 16.81 g 5 h -
b. UBS 59 (29–30.1.2004), 5448 16.40 g - -
c. CNG MBS 70 (21.9.2005), 140 17.04 g 1 h -

[O (a): Development of flaws on space 3, from lower drapery through upper "unit" 4 to border, and on space 7, from l. end of "unit" to upper badge circles; also, diagonal flaw through badge circles, off space 4. Flaw develops off nose.
R (a): l., flaw on r. end of pleat].

The eight-rayed stars in the elliptical star/crescent units on the Makedonian shield in groups 1 and 3 give way to six-rayed stars in the rest of the series. Even though the style of the archaizing Athena on the reverses and the letter forms generally remain the same, stylistic variations may be observed on the obverses. The hair locks in *anastole* on the medium-sized, carefully rendered Pan heads of the first two groups, for instance, are reminiscent of the coin portraits of Alexander as Apollo or as a young beardless hero. They are replaced by locks cut diagonally from the crown of the head towards the face on coin no. 11 from Group 2, which revert to locks flowing from the upper head downwards on the next groups. The striking similarity between the Pan heads of

Obverses 1–5 with the Pan head (three-quarters facing), in the medallion of the *mesomphalos* cup found at the Great Tumulus at Vergina (Tomb III), prompts us to place Groups 1 and 2 early in our catalogue.[20] Group 3 is distinguished by a larger head of Pan, with a higher neck. The drapery is looser and ends in a larger curve. A long neck occurs in group 4, but a shorter and thicker one characterizes group 5. A tendency to move the *pedum* away from Pan's head develops from group 3 until the end of the series, alongside a preference for smaller helmets l. in the reverse field.

Groups 8 and 9 are less skillfully designed on both obverse and reverse. The *pedum* on the obverse is at a distance from the head, the horns diverge and a different type of helmet is adopted, with an elaborate crest holder.

Twelve obverse dies and thirty-four reverse dies are used by the mint officials signing with these monograms. A large die break on the *pedum* of specimen 5 presumably explains the withdrawal of the first obverse die, and a number of flaws on O11 on specimen 33 may also account for its abandonment.

*** *** ***

Crested Helmet l.—Monogram HP r.

O: Eight-rayed stars, horns point r. *Pedum* starts from middle fold; heraldic dots at regular distances on *pedum*.
R: Athena standing on r. leg, ready to throw thunderbolt; stylized hem folds.

Group 9

Specimens: 16 Obverses: 2
Die Combinations: 6 Reverses: 6

35. O13 R35

a. Gorny 100 (20.11.1999), 136 (17.13 g); MMAG 15 (18–19.9.1985), 81
17.14 g - -
b. Athena 3 (15.5.1990), 98 17.11 g - -
c. MMAG 73 (17.10.1988), 143 17.08 g - -
d. Sotheby ("A well known collector" [Montagu]), (11–13.12.1894), 13; Lincoln
- - -

[O (a–b): flaws on spaces 2, 3, 6; near border, from space 6, connecting "units" 6-7-1. Diagonal flaws, between "unit" 6 and outer badge circle and on space 7. Flaw from r. edge of "unit" 4 to border. Flaws expand on (b). On badge, l., flaws off nose; two flaws from drapery knob, the former upwards, the latter through badge circles.
R (b): l., dot r. of Y; flaw between *chiton* and shawl; r., flaw across upper bar of Σ.
NB (d): uncleaned].

36. O13 R36

a. Coin Galleries MBS 4 (14.4.1993), 223 (17.09 g); Superior, Auction & MBS (11–12.6.1986), 994 (17.07 g) 17.09 g - -
b. G. Hirsch 159 (21–4.9.1988), 220 17.13 g - -

20. Zimi, *Silver Plate*, 217. no. 71, cf. H. Zimi, *Macedonian Silver Plate, Fourth to Second Centuries BC* (DPhil thesis, Oxford), 80, no. 44; Andronikos, *Vergina*, 212, fig. 180. See also Chapter 6.4.2.

c. Münzzentrum 72 (2–4.12.1991), 297 17.14 g - -

[O (a): expansion of flaw on space 2 to border; further die break on spaces 5 and 6. R (a): l., dot beneath O].

37. O13 R37

a. Superior (08–11.06.1981), 1544; Superior (12–14.2.1978), 2184 (16.77 g); Grose 3592 16.80 g - -

b. Elsen 107 (11.12.2010), 104 17.07 g - -

c. NAC 54 (24.3.2010), 83 (Goekoop collection) 16.10 g - -

[O (a): r., expansion of flaws, particularly on spaces 1–4. Vertical flaws, between upper *pedum* and head, lower *pedum* and drapery.
R (a): l., flaw from border to beneath r. bar of N].

38. O13 R38

a. Christie's (8.10.1991), 71 17.11 g - -

[O (a): flaw on badge, off nose; also, from knob through badge circles to "unit" 4. Flaws on either side of *pedum*.
R (a): l., flaw l. of A to lower end of l. bar and from Y diagonally to lower border].

39. O14 R39

a. *SNG Aarhus* 464 17.08 g 11 h -
b. S. Asia Minor, 1970: *CH* I (1975), 74 (or Asia Minor, 1972: *CH* I (1974), 73?)[21] - - -

c. CNG 317 (18.12.2013), 30 (E-sale) 16.39 g 9 h -

[O (a): break on spaces 3, 7. Horizontal flaw from drapery knob through badge circles. (b): flaw from nose to badge circle and from horns to "unit" 1.
R (a): break l., through N and T, past upper shield to upper border. Flaw from l. end of pleat to Y].

40. O14 R40

a. Coin Galleries (13.11.1991), 81 17.11 g - -
b. Høiland 25 (2003), F 6044; Gorny and Mosch 104 (9–10.2000), 288 (16.06 g); Elsen 48 (22.2.1997), 121 17.01 g - -

c. Spink, *The Coinex Collection* (28.09.2005), 76 17.09 g - -

[O (a): On badge, up l., curved flaw off eyes; second break between nose and badge circles; third, off hair towards upper badge circles; fourth, between *pedum* and hair. Flaws on space 2 and between "unit" 4 and badge expand.
R (a): Flaw from field l., up, past A, through figure to r. pleat. In middle, flaw develops from between O and N to l. pleat. A crude.
Struck from somewhat rotated dies, giving the impression of an undertype near the edge].

*** *** ***

21. According to note at the British Museum records, this coin belongs to the lot which was entered at the BM as *CH* I (1975), 74, but it may be *IGCH* I (1975), 73.

O: Seven- to eight-rayed stars. Horns r., slightly diverge. Linear rendering of nape-length hair, flowing downwards. Folds of drapery diagonal and regular. On neck, diagonal line between knob and cheek. Adam's apple prominent.
R: Similar. Legend letters regular.

Group 10

Specimens: 2 Obverses: 1
Die Combinations: 1 Reverses: 1

41. O15 R41

a. Berlin, Staatl. Museen, Imhoof-Blumer 17.10 g 12 h -
b. Cambridge: Grose, McClean, 3592; ex Sotheby ("A well known Collector" [Montagu]), (11–13.12.1894), 129 17.12 g 12 h 30.5 mm

[O (a–b): flaws on spaces 2 and 7; diagonal flaw on hair, from *anastole* r.; flaws on both crescent ends of "unit" 3. Die break on outer crescent of "unit" 5. In (b), flaw on outer edge of "unit" 5 and on space 7.
R (a–b): flaws developing; up l, beneath Σ, between monogram and l. foot, beneath r. foot. (a): slightly off-center].

*** *** ***

O: Stars no. 1, 2, 6 seven-rayed, no. 3 eight-rayed. Horns parallel and attached, hair locks different; drapery folds vertical. Nose pointed. *Pedum* thin.
R: Crested helmet with high bowl. Athena shorter; shield held on level of upper arm.

Group 11

Specimens: 9 Obverses: 1
Die Combinations: 3 Reverses: 4

42. O16 R42

a. Dupriez 98 (25.10.1909), 281; J. Schulman (30.3.1910), 149; Wotoch, 149
17.00 g - 31 mm
b. Silifke Museum: Meydancıkkale, 1980: *CH* X (2010), 269; *CH* VIII (1994), 308; *CH* VII (1985), 80; Davesne and Le Rider, *Meydancıkkale*, 2587 (A32)
17.06 g - -
c. Associación Numismatica Española (11–12.1961), 296
- - -

[O (a): flaws on spaces 1–2, 5–6; flaw on l. edge of "unit" 5.
R (a): r., flaw on upper lateral bar of first Σ, l., flaw on OY. (b): recut on upper diagonal bar of Σ].

43. O16 R43

a. Neuchâtel 4028 17.20 g 11 h -
b. Leu 71 (24.10.1997), 160; Kricheldorf 21 (6–7.4.1970), 63 (17.03 g)
17.10 g 11 h -

[O (a): curved flaw between l. end of "unit" 1 to inner badge circle; also, from knob towards l. end of "unit" 5.
R (a): flaw on exergue, beneath l. foot].

44. O16 R44

a. Peus 300 (1980), 99; Kroh FPL 35 (no date), 63; Plumier (05.1982), 28
17.00 g - -
b. Toderi 2 (4.1970), 124 - - -
c. Helios 8 (13.10.2012), 17 17.05 g - -

[O (a): diagonal breaks, from "unit" 7 to nose and from "unit" 6 past chin to drapery knob. Diagonal flaw from lower r. end of drapery to external badge circle.
R (a): flaw up r., across head, thunderbolt, B towards r. border].

45. O16 R45 R same as Gorny (9.3.1999), 204, Volos 148.2

a. Enna, 1966 (*CH* IX (2002), 670; *IGCH* 2232): A. Burnett, "The Enna Hoard and the Silver Coinage of the Syracusan democracy," *SNR* 62 (1983), 5–46, esp. 13.53, pl. 6.53
- - -

[O (a): in field l., die flaw from nose to inner badge circle; flaw from nose to star/crescent 5].

*** *** ***

O: Six-rayed stars, star 7 with seven rays. Horns upright, slightly diverge. Head small, hair short, locks in pear-dropped shape and arranged vertically, lower locks diagonal. Middle fold of drapery prominent. *Pedum* thin and dotted, emerging from middle fold.
R: Similar. Figure tall, with more plastic movement; large curved shield; helmet with low bowl l. Short distance between r. end of pleat and leg.

GROUP 12

Specimens: 18	Obverses: [3-2]
Die Combinations: 6	Reverses: [5-1]

46. O4 R45

a. Gorny 95 (9.3.1999), 204 17.00 g - -

47. O17 R45

a. Volos 148.2: Phayttos, c. 1956: *IGCH* 159, 2 (P. R. Franke, *JDAI* 72 (1958), 38–62, p. 48, 30, pl. 4) 17.08 g 6 h -
b. Volos 148.1: Phayttos, c. 1956: *IGCH* 159, 1 (P. R. Franke, ibid., p. 48.29, pl. 4)
17.11 g 6 h -
c. CNG Triton 5.2–4 (14–15.01.2002), 1307; R. Schonwalter Collection; Hess-Leu 36 (17–18.4.1968), 172 (17.07 g) 17.10 g - -

[O (a–b): curved flaw from "unit" 7 via outer badge circle to "unit" 1.
R (a): diagonal flaw from Λ through to shawl. Horizontal flaw beneath monogram.
(a): off-center].

48. O17 R46

a. Elsen L 142 (05.1992), 30; L 137 (11.1991), -; L 134 (5–6.1991), 33; L 133 (1991), 33; L 130 (2.1991), 19; L 122 (1–2.1990), 22 17.05 g - -
b. Kroh, Empire Coins, FPC 45 (no date), 54 17.04 g - -
c. Henzen L 176 (04.2007), 110; L 172 (10.2006), 109; L 168 (rec. 19.05.06), 111; L 159 (23.05.2005), 96; L 155 (29.12.2004), 74 17.05 g - -
d. Künker 83 (17.06.2003), 212 17.00 g - -

[O (a): Previous flaws expand. Small flaw between r. horn and inner badge circle; also, on outer badge circle, off "unit" 2; flaw on spaces 2–3, 6.
R (a): Flaw up l. from l. vertical bar of N, past shield, upwards. Second flaw off l. foot, downwards].

49. O17 R47

a. Sotheby Zürich (4–5.4.1973), 343 17.10 g 12 h 32.5 mm
b. Hesperia Art 28 (1963), 60 - - -
c. A.Weil (02.12.1981), 10; A. Weil (16.06.1980), (coll. H. Delpech), 17 16.88 g - -
d. Grün 31 (01–02.12.2000), 72; Grün 30 (06–07.10.2000), 156; Grün 29 (25–27.05.2000), 334 16.47 g - -

[R (a–b): Flaw beneath Y. (d): badly preserved].

50. O17 R48

a. Sotheby (22.5.1975), 39 - - -
b. Markov, MB Auction 11 (03–04.09.2003), 39 16.94 g - -
c. Scotussa area, (pre-)1989: *CH* VIII (1994), 283, pl. 34.8 - - -

[O (a): flaws develop, new ones on spaces 3 and 5.
R (a): vertical sign of tool l. of head, diagonal scratch between l. crest and r. foot].

51. O3 R49

a. G. Hirsch 32 (22–4.10.1962), 2353; Dorotheum L 244 (24–27.10.1961), 440 17.0 g - -
b. CNG 318 (15.01.2014), 99 (Demetrios Armounta Collection) 16.90 g 12 h 32 mm
c. Kroh FPL 34 (no date), 61 - - -

[O (a): flaws on spaces 2–5; also, between "unit" 5 and outer badge circle, "unit" 1 and outer badge circle. Recut on upper *pedum*. Central badge circles off "unit" 4 worn. Recut on "unit" 4.
R (a): l., between legend and l. pleat, worn].

*** *** ***

O: As above.
R: Similar.

GROUP 13

Specimens: 9	Obverses: [2-2]
Die Combinations: 3	Reverses: 3

52. O08 R50

a. Védrines (23.6.1993), 29	16.77 g	-	-
b. MMAG L 449 (10.1982), 6	17.10 g	-	-
c. Gorny 90 (12–13.10.1998), 213	17.08 g	-	-
d. Gorny & Mosch 199 (10.10.2011), 222; Gorny & Mosch 113 (18.10.2001), 5150; Dorau 6 (1972), 4	17.16 g	-	-
e. Gorny & Mosch 107 (2.4.2001), 130	17.15 g	-	-

[O (a–e): flaw expands on badge circles: dot off eye, l.; diagonal break from "unit" 5 through external badge circle to upper crescent of "unit" 4. (b): break on inner badge circle (2 h). R (a): flaws l. of ΑΝΤΙΓΟΝΟΥ; diagonal flaw, from vertical bar of Τ to r. end of l. pleat; curved flaw on r. foot. In exergue, small flaws].

53. O08 R51

a. Leu 30 (28.4.1982), 96	17.12 g	11 h	-
b. Malter 47 (1992), 79	17.08 g	-	-
c. Toderi L 4 (12.1971), 139	-	-	-

[O (a): additional break on spaces 2, 4–5; also, between r. end of "unit" 3 and border; horizontally, from "unit" 3 to external crescent 5, from "unit" 4 to "unit" 6. On badge, r., flaw from hair to lower *pedum*].

O: Six-rayed stars, star 3 eight-rayed. Horns dotted, upright and parallel. Head large; horizontal wrinkle on forehead. Neck shorter. Three-fold drapery.
R: Similar.

54. O12 R52

a. Dorotheum 504 (21.10.2006), 70	17.08 g	-	-

*** *** ***

O: Six-rayed stars, star 2 seven-rayed; *pedum* emerges from between middle and upper drapery fold, away from head. Hair locks in vertical arrangement from crown downwards. Small flaw on upper *pedum*.
R: Similar.

GROUP 14

Specimens: 27	Obverses: 1
Die Combinations: 8	Reverses: 8

55. O18 R53

a. Peus 348 (26–28.04.1995), 143; Peus 343 (26–28.4.1995), 123; Peus 334 (4.11.1992), 358; Vecchi & Bonhams 7 (29–30.3.1982), 119 (16.89 g); Bourgey (30.11–1.12.1967), 9
16.90 g - -
b. Pegasi BBS 123 (30.7.2001), 82 16.40 g - -
c. Auctiones 3 (4–5.12.1973), 149 17.12 g - -
d. Troxell, *Norman Davis* 95 17.14 g 12 h -

[O (a): flaws: on l. edge of "unit" 1; on space 1; off "unit" 4; between "unit" 5 and badge; between forehead and badge circle.
R (a): flaw off nose].

56. O18 R54

a. ANS 1980.109.45 17.11 g 11 h -
b. MMAG L 404 (9.1978), 3, 21; Borghesi 4 (1881)
- - -
c. NFA 27 (4–5.12.1991), 52; Sotheby (17–28.10.1993), 443
17.17 g 11 h -
d. MMAG L 452 (2.1983), 8 17.13 g - -
e. Coin Galleries (29.4.1976), 849 17.10 g - -
f. Athena 3 (1990), 99 (3 h); Athena 1 (1987), 69 (17.17 g)
17.16 g 3 h -
g. Senger 106 (17–19.11.2004), 3022 16.80 g - -

[O (a): flaw on space 1, vertical flaw from inner crescent 4 through rays 5–6 to border; small flaw on a ray of star 7.
R (a): r., flaw from A up to above Σ].

57. O18 R55

a. ANM: Thesprotia, 1992 (*CH* IX [2002], 200; Touratsoglou, *DM*, 23)
16.96 g 11 h -
b. Vico 111 (8.6.2006), 117 17.13 g - -
c. Davisson 10 (30.4.1998), 47; Kricheldorf 16 (2.7.1966), 70
17.15 g - -
d. MMAG L 404 (9.1978), 21; MMAG L 300 (5.1969), 21 (17.10 g)
17.10 g - -
e. Knopek (9.1978), 133 - (b) - -

[O (a): flaw from inner crescent of "unit" 1, l. to external badge circle; also, on space 2. Vertical flaw across rays of star 4 expands. Scratches on space 1. (c), die repair on nose].
R (a): up l., beginning of flaw off helmet. (b): flaws: l., from edge towards N; from lower l. edge towards helmet; between helmet and lower field].

58. O18 R56

a. Elsen L 114 (3.1989), 9 17.16 g - -
b. ANM: Karditsa (Palaiokastro), 1929: *CH* IX (2002), 180; *IGCH* 162, 6
16.58 g 12 h 30.5 mm
c. Künker 26 (9–11.3.1994), 107 17.14 g - -

[O (a–c): flaws on spaces 4 and 5; also, from nose l.
R (a–c): l., flaw l. of head].

59. O18 R57

a. Tkalec-Rauch (25–6.4.1989), 72; CNA 9 (1989), 49 (16.45 g)	16.47 g	-	-
b. St James's Auctions 4 (08.05.2006), 17	-	-	-

[O (a): new flaw from nose to lower badge edge. Developing break on space 1.
R (a): l., flaw between pleat's r. edge and *chiton*; also, between helmet and lower field.
Recut: Monogram [monogram] corrected to [monogram]].

60. O18 R58

a. Beckenbauer (2.1973), 27	16.978 g	-	-
b. Helios 6 (9.3.2011), 462	17.08 g	-	-

[O (a): flaws expand; new flaw from internal badge circle through "unit" 5 to border.
R (a): l., flaw continuing r. vertical bar of second N; also, on lower end of shield].

61. O18 R59

a. Negrini 23 (8.6.2006), 284; Bourgey (2–4.6.1998), 48	17.09 g	-	-
b. Pegasi 14 (11.4.2006), 76	16.59 g	-	-

[O (a–b): flaws on spaces 1–2, 5–6; two diagonal flaws from "unit" 1, one from space 1 towards center; diagonal flaw from nose to lower l. badge.
R (a–b): l., horizontal flaw beneath I].

62. O18 R60

a. Henzen L 166 (2006), 104	16.95 g	-	-
b. CNG Triton 15 (3.1.2012), 1141	17.17 g	11 h	31 mm

[O (a): flaws expand].

*** *** ***

O: Six-rayed stars, star 3 eight-rayed. Horns dotted, upright and parallel. Head large; horizontal wrinkle on forehead. Neck shorter. Three-fold drapery.
R: Athena crude; short shield, decorated with *aegis*. Few folds on central and lower *chiton*. Helmet with very small bowl.

GROUP 15

Specimens: 6	Obverses: [1-1]
Die Combinations: 3	Reverses: 3

63. O12 R61

a. Edinburgh, 1926.105: Rutter, *Edinburgh*, 54	17.05 g	12 h	31 mm
b. Sotheby (26.4.1907), 65	16.977 g	-	-

[O (a): diagonal flaw on outer badge circle, off "unit" 1; also, between external badge circle

and external crescent of "unit" 3.
R (a): l., vertical flaws following legend letters, A–Γ and N–Y].

64. O12 R62

a. BM 1852-2-22-14	17.07 g	12 h	32.5 mm
b. Berk 32 (1984), 81	-	-	-

O (a): curved flaw on space 3; also, from upper *pedum* upwards; third flaw on l. edge of "unit" 4.
R (a): l., curved flaw between shield and N].

65. O12 R63

a. SB 2 (1977), 308	17.11 g	-	-
b. Berk 152 (19.12.2006), 91	16.51 g	-	-

[O (a): r., flaw and wear on "unit" 4; l., flaw from spaces 1 and 6 through badge circles to knob of drapery.
R (a): l., vertical flaw above shield; r., horizontal flaw from B to border; second flaw starting from Λ].

*** *** ***

O: Similar.
R: Similar.

Group 16

Specimens: 2	Obverses: [1-1]
Die Combinations: 2	Reverses: 2

66. O06 R64

a. New York: ANS 1944.100.13840	17.11 g	12 h	-

[O (a): flaws on spaces 4–5, 7; between crescents of "unit" 7; also, between "unit" 2 and inner circle, no. 7 and external badge circle. On badge, flaws starting from nose: the former horizontal, from nose to circle; the second very small, diagonal; the third, towards lower badge border, l.; fourth flaw towards chin; fifth horizontal flaw, towards lower badge border. Also, curve from lower end of drapery towards badge circle; r., small flaw from middle fold of drapery towards *pedum*.
R (a): horizontal flaw between figure and r. pleat].

67. O06 R65

a. Salzburg	-	-	-

[O (a): diagonal flaw r., from inner badge circle off external crescent of "unit" 2, second flaw developing from nose downwards; diagonal flaw from middle fold of drapery towards "unit" 4.
R (a): l., flaws between legend letters and figure. Diagonal flaw from r. end of l. pleat towards lower l. vertical bar of monogram; also, between r. end of r. pleat and E].

*** *** ***

O: Similar.
R: Similar.

GROUP 17

Specimens: 20 Obverses: 2
Die Combinations: 5 Reverses: 5

68. O19 R66

a. Pegasi 14 (11.4.2006), 76 16.59 g - -

O: Similar. Drapery folds r. end in curve. Hair flows from crown.
R: Similar.

69. O19 R67

a. ANM: Thesprotia, 1992 (*CH* IX [2002], 200; Touratsoglou, *DM*, no. 22) 16.45 g 11 h -
b. *SNG Manchester* 735 - - -
c. Jenkins 735 - - -

[O (a): worn in center, l. (b): flaw between hair and *pedum*, and on space 6; *pedum* recut. R (a): flaws, from lower crest to r. arm, and on l. end of second Σ. (b): l., flaw on upper r. bar of N and r., on upper horizontal bar of last Σ].

70. O20 R68

a. Unknown Findspot ("Seleucus III," Hoard), 2002: *CH* X (2010), 272; *SC* II.2, 142–150, Lot F: "Best Coins," photos 841–2 17.06 g 11 h -
b. Christie's (14.6.1993), 20; Kroh FPL (Fall 1983), 4095 16.70 g - -
c. ANM: Pherai, 1937–1938: *IGCH* 168 (ANSMN 26 (1981), pl. 14.537) 16.62 g 11 h -
d. Peus 301 (1981), 265 17.00 g - -
e. NFA MBS (12.10.1990), 191 16.76 g - -
f. Künker 172 (8.2004), 23 (16.79 g); Künker 169 (11.2003), 28 (16.79 g); Parsy (Drouot Richelieu, Paris), (6–7.3.2003), 28 16.79 g - -

[O (a): l., start of flaw, from mouth downward. (b): l., flaw between nose and badge circles; also, r., between end of *pedum* and badge circle.
R (a): r., flaw between pleat and monogram. (d): double-struck].

71. O20 R69

a. Lanz 74 (20.11.1995), 167 16.99 g 12 h -
b. Cederlind L 105 (24.9.1996), 336; Cederlind L 103 (winter, 1996), 1659; Spink New York (7.2.1995), 2052 17.00 g - -
c. Künker 94 (27–8.9.2004), 717; NFA (17–19.09.1981), 121 (16.92 g) 16.91 g - -

[O (a–c): flaw between chin and badge circle; second, smaller flaw up, starting from off nose; flaw from "unit" 2 through badge to "unit" 3; also, on space 7.
R (a): flaw between l. end of helmet crest and Υ].

72. O20 R70

a. Christie's (28.2–1.3.1989), 1275 17.08 g - -
b. Dearborn Sale, Fine Numismatic Properties, C. A. Whitford Numismatic Auction (29.11.1993), 117 17.00 g - -
c. Ciani-Vinchon (coll. Y. E. Hindamian), (6–8.2.1956), 348 16.96 g - -
d. Scotussa area, (pre-), 1989: *CH* VIII (1994), 283, pl. 34.5 - - -
e. Ponterio, The Eighteenth Annual Chicago International Coin Fair, Public & MBA (26–27.2.1993), 149 17.00 g - -
f. Mektepini, 1956: *IGCH* 1410 (Olçay and Seyrig, *Mektepini*, no. 686) 17.07 g - -
g. Gorny & Mosch 204 (5.3.2012), 1305 17.12 g - -

[O (a): flaws on space 6 expand; flaw from nose downwards and from knob of drapery to badge circles; flaw between badge circles (2:30 h); scratch on space 3. Scratches across "unit" 7 through face and hair locks to *pedum*. (c): two flaws l., on space 6. (f): recut on nose.
R (a): large, spread letters. (c): flaw between vertical bar of Τ and upper Ι; flaw on lower l. angle of second Σ].

*** *** ***

O: Similar.
R: Similar.

Group 18

Specimens: 9	Obverses: 1
Die Combinations: 5	Reverses: 5

73. O21 R71

a. Cederlind L 109 (1997), 780 - - -

[O (a): flaws on spaces 1–3].

74. O21 R72

a. Berk BBS 148 (29.3.2006), 112; CNG, Numismatica Ars Classica, Triton 4 (05.12.2000), 178; MMAG 53 (1977), 65 (16.96 g) 16.97 g - -
b. Gorny & Mosch 200 (10.10.2011), 1468; G. Hirsch 220 (21–22.2.2002), 1239 (17.08 g) 17.06 g - -

[O (a): flaw on spaces 2–3, 5, between "unit" 1 and badge; diagonal flaw from nose to badge edge, and between *pedum* and hair.
R (a): l., flaw off second Ν and beneath second Ο; r., flaw from Σ downwards].

75. O21 R73

a. Sternberg 24 (1990), 61; Cummings (11–12.1986), G13
17.09 g - -

b. McCarthy (3.1987), 5 - - -

[O (a): new flaw l. of chin; from nose to lower badge; on badge circles off space 1.
R (a): flaw from border up l. towards nose].

76. O21 R74

a. Cahn 75 (1932), 292 17.02 g - -
b. G. Hirsch 242 (22–24.9.2005), 2001 17.05 g - -

[O (a): flaw on space 5 develops; flaw on nose and chin, from hair locks through to edge of "unit" 4.
R (a): up r., flaw on either side of thunderbolt].

77. O21 R75

a. Glasgow: MacDonald, *Hunterian*, 340.3, pl. XXIII.19
17.20 g - 30 mm
b. Gorny & Mosch 112 (17.10.2001), 4090 17.12 g - -

[O (a): flaw on space 5 expands to inner "crescent" 5 and to lower border; new flaw on space 4. R (b): double-struck.
R (a): flaw beneath l. foot].

*** *** ***

O: As above.
R: Similar.

GROUP 19

Specimens: 12 Obverses: [2-2]
Die Combinations: 5 Reverses: [5-1]

78. O09 R75

a. Gorny 20 (1–2.12.1981), 25; Sternberg 10 (1980), 74
17.00 g - -
b. Gorny & Mosch 203 (5.3.2012), 153; Gorny & Mosch 200 (10.10.2011), 1465; Gorny & Mosch 112 (2001), 4090 17.12 g - -
c. Galata L (5.1977), 6 - - -
d. Elsen 81 (11.9.2004), 91 16.73 g - -

[O (a–d): flaws on spaces 2–3.
R (a–d): flaws on and beneath exergue, l.].

79. O09 R76

a. BNF1380 17.21 g 12 h 31.0 mm
b. Bourgey (2–3.12.1993), 36; Galata L (6.1988), 22
- - -
c. Nomisma (11.5.1991), 39 16.83 g - -

[O (b): flaw between "unit" 1 and border; in center, flaw on neck.
R (b): r., flaw between E and Ω].

80. O09 R77

a. Unknown Findspot ("Seleucus III," Hoard), 2002: *CH* X (2010), 272; A. Houghton—C. Lorber—O. Hoover, *SC* II.2, 142–150, Lot F: "Before cleaning?," photos CN0979.1 = DSCN0980.1 - - -

81. O09 R78

a. BM PRK A.1, p. 88 17.06 g 12 h 32 mm
b. Berlin; C. B. Fox 17.00 g 12 h -
c. Scotussa area, (pre-), 1989; *CH* VIII (1994), 283, pl. 34.1
- - -

[O (a): flaw on lower "unit" 3; between "unit" 4 and badge. Between *pedum* and head, flaw parallel to *pedum*. (c): up, flaw from upper hair to badge.
R (b–d): r., flaw through B and thunderbolt].

O: Horns parallel and upright, drapery folds end on curve r.
R: A without horizontal bar; shield badge prominent. In field l., r. bar of N longer. Helmet away from shawl pleats.

82. O10 R79

a. Kricheldorf 4 (1957), 161 17.09 g - -

[O (a): flaws on either side of "unit" 2, between "unit" 2 and badge end; horizontal flaws, from internal badge circle to nose and mouth respectively. Horizontal flaw from internal badge circle to neck. Flaw from lower *pedum* to badge circle.
R (a): signs of flaw r. of helmet].

*** *** ***

O: Six-rayed stars, nos. 1, 3–4, 7 seven-rayed. Neck long. Curved, dotted *pedum*.
R: Large helmet with high bowl, rich crest, long cheek flaps.

Group 20

Specimens: 36	Obverses: 4
Die Combinations: 14	Reverses: [13-1]

83. O22 R78

a. *SNG Delepierre* 1064 - - -

[O (a): flaws off nose, chin and *pedum* expand.
R (a): flaw up r., through B and thunderbolt; off I and diagonally off second Σ; up l., from A to upper edge].

84. O22 R80

a. ANS 1946.89.25 17.10 g 12 h -
b. G.Hirsch 264 (25.11.2009), 223; G. Hirsch 261 (7.5.2009), 240
17.05 g - -

[O (a): flaw l. of chin; also, flaws starting from ends of drapery folds.
R (a): flaw between l. pleat ends and helmet].

85. O22 R81

a. Superior (1–2.10.2001), 1022 17.05 g - -
b. Tellmann 135 (1.2.1969), 68; Tellmann 112 (1.2.1967), 63
17.03 g - -
c. Dupriez (1904), 76 - - -

[O (a–b): flaw from nose upwards expands. Flaw off upper end of *pedum* .
R (a): sign of tooling at 12 h and 9 h. (b): sign of tooling at 12 h].

86. O22 R82
a. ANM: Thesprotia, 1992 (*CH* IX [2002], 200; Touratsoglou, *DM*, no. 20)
16.95 g 11 h -
b. Milano, B1185 (coll. Brera, n. 1185, N. Inv.: M 0.9.36659): *SNG Milano* 375
17.16 g 12 h 31.5 mm
c. ANS: *SNG BYB* 354 17.07 g 12 h -

[O (a): flaws on spaces 2–4, 6–7. In center, flaw above head and (signs), from middle fold; also, between drapery and inner badge circle, *pedum* and inner badge circle. Flaw (signs) between lower hair lock l. and knob, and between lower hair locks and upper fold of drapery. Flaw off nose. (b): l: countermark, eagle three-quarters, facing.
R (a): vertical flaw between r. end of l. pleat and helmet crest].

O: Six-rayed stars, minor repairs on stars 6 and 7. Hair linear, from crown downwards. Horizontal wrinkle on forehead.
R: Similar.

87. O23 R83

a. Platt (26–27.3.1922), 386, coll. V. Luneau - - -
b. Marseille, coll. Vernier, 390 16.99 g - -
c. BerlMC 13 (1981), 30; BerlMC 12 (4–5.12.1980), 15
16.20 g - -

[O (b): small diagonal flaw from nose to inner badge circle. (b): on badge, from border up r. towards hair; diagonal break from end of drapery towards lower border; flaw on space.
R (b): r., portion of metal flaked off in field].

88. O23 R84

a. DNW (14.3.2007), 145; CNG MBS 72 (14.6.2006), 500; R. A. Weimer collection
16.94 g 11 h -

89. O23 R85

a. NFA (3.1975), 93 16.95 g - -
b. ANM: Thesprotia, 1992 (*CH* IX [2002], 200; Touratsoglou, *DM*, no. 21)
16.46 g 11 h -

[O (b): flaws through spaces 1 and 4; also, on external badge circle, off space 2. On badge, l., diagonal flaws: from forehead to lower badge circle, from off "unit" 2 to hair. Small flaws l., r. and above *pedum*.
R (b): flaw from lower l. border past exergue downwards and in lower field, r.]

O: Six-rayed stars, a ray added to star 2. Vertical flaw on "unit" 1. Neck shorter, *pedum* starts from between upper and middle fold. Hair locks arranged towards face. Horizontal wrinkle on forehead. Two diagonal lines across neck, from lower hair to knob.
R: Similar.

90. O24 R86

a. Milan, Gab. Numismatico B1184 (coll. Brera),	16.92 g	-	-
b. G.Henzen L 175 (3.2007), 114; L 171 (7.2006), 110; 167 (3.2006), 114; L 163 (26.9.2005), 114	16.90 g	-	-
c. Kress 127 (1963), 378	17.00 g	-	-

[O (a): flaw on spaces 1, 3–4 and on nose.
R (a): flaw l., in middle; also, between helmet crest and *chiton* and between r. pleat ends].

91. O24 R87

a. Unknown Findspot ("Seleucus III," Hoard), 2002: *CH* X (2010), 272; A. Houghton—C. Lorber—O. Hoover, *SC* II.2, 142–150, lot F, "Late report of a fragment," photos 882–3, no. 46 ; CNG 90 (23.5.2012), 488	17.03 g	12 h	32 mm
b. Elsen L 113 (1.1989), 38	17.08 g	-	-

[O (a): new flaw on space 6; flaw on nose expands.
R (a): flaw in exergue, beneath r. foot].

92. O24 R88

a. Elsen L 238 (10–12.2006), 18	16.92 g	-	-
b. CNG 94 (18.9.2013), 287	16.90 g	12 h	31 mm

[O (a): flaw expands beneath nose; flaw on *pedum* expands].

O: Upper ends of "crescents" 7 converge. Flaw l. of *pedum*; *pedum* very close to badge edge.
R: Similar.

93. O25 R89

a. Brussels, de Hirsch, 117	17.07 g	11 h	31 mm
b. Copenhagen: *SNG Cop* 1200	16.86 g	10 h	-
c. Schimmer 49 (16.4.2005), ex lot 74	-	-	-
d. UBS Auction 49 (11–13.9.2000), 84	17.05 g	11 h	-

[O (a): flaws: on spaces 5–7; from *anastole* to beginning of neck; off *pedum*; diagonally, from middle drapery to external circle of central badge, off space 4.
R (c–d): progressive flaws in field r., off Λ and on exergue].

94. O25 R90

a. Shore FPL 96 (spring 2001), 33	17.05 g	-	-

95. O25 R91

a. BM 1866-12-1-1185	17.04 g	12 h	31.5 mm
b. iNumis 2 (3.11.2006), 14	17.09 g	11 h	30.5 mm
c. Raymond (25.4.1939), 39	-	-	-
d. Elsen 49 (19.4.1997), 237	17.02 g	-	-
e. ANM: Thesprotia, 1992 (*CH* IX [2002], 200; Touratsoglou, *DM*, no. 24)	17.03 g	12 h	-
f. Gorny 95 (9.3.1999), 205	17.01 g	-	-
g. Schimmer 49 (16.4.2005), 74; Emporium 12 (21–22.04.1988), 41; Emporium 10 (22–24.10.1987), 310	-	-	-
h. CNG 269 (30.11.2011), 57	17.05 g	10 h	30 mm
i. France Numismatique 21 (24.05.1982), 86	-	-	-

[O (a): double-struck. O (c–d): flaw off *pedum* expands. (e–f): countermark/wear on Pan's cheek?
R (a): recut on nose; r., flaw between r. end of pleat and legend; second flaw further, r. (f): flaw up l., from A through to head. (g): Monogram [monogram] discernible beneath Monogram [monogram]].

*** *** ***

O: Stars 6–7 with eight rays, no. 2 seven-rayed; flaw on badge l., off nose.
R: Helmet l. with small bowl, long cheek pieces and crest. Legend letters small, regular and elaborate. Monogram very close to legend. Athena more elaborate.

GROUP 21

Specimens: 1	Obverses: 1
Die Combinations: 1	Reverses: 1

96. O26 R92

a. Silifke Museum: Meydancıkkale, 1980: *CH* X (2010), 269; *CH* VIII (1994), 308; *CH* VII (1985), 80 (Davesne and Le Rider, *Meydancıkkale*, no. 2586)	17.10 g	-	-

[O (a): diagonal flaw from edge of "unit" 5 to "unit" 4; vertical flaw on space 3.
R (a): l., flaw beneath l. lateral bar of A; also, l. of r. foot, in exergue].

Coins with monogram [monogram], having twenty-one obverse dies and fifty-eight reverse dies, have a far higher output than those signed with monograms [monogram], [monogram], [monogram], [monogram]. Fourteen of the obverse dies are not combined with the previous monograms. However, the six obverses that also occur with monograms [monogram], [monogram], [monogram], [monogram], [monogram] indicate the parallel function of all the die cutters. Monogram [monogram] is recut on Monogram [monogram] on specimen 59.

The "units" with seven- to eight-rayed stars decorating the shield on groups 11–13 give way in group 14 to six-rayed stars, which henceforth become the norm. A growing preference for taller figures of Athena and for helmets with smaller bowls is observed on the reverses, though the style of the lettering generally remains the same. An Athena of crude workmanship, however, is combined with a change in the legend letters, which become larger, with a sigma with straight horizontal *hastae* and an N with vertical end even bars at the end of group 14. The heads of Pan become larger, with a *pedum* at a distance from the head, and tally with the use of wider flans; the obverse designs of nos. 39 and 40 have spread beyond the flans. Some ineptness may be observed on nos. 30, 39–40, 49, 60, and 70, which come from somewhat rotated dies. Scratches can be seen on the reverses of certain specimens (e.g., no. 50).

The last group with Monogram ΗΡ is represented by a single coin, but it deserves attention. On the obverse a rough, small head is made to fit into a small flan. The crude workmanship of the obverse is offset by the very carefully engraved letters, helmet and monogram on the reverse. This specimen is obverse-linked to Groups 22 and 30, signed with monograms ΗΡ and Ꝁ , and is stylistically similar to nos. 170–171, without a crested helmet and with Monogram ⋈ to left. The Meydancıkkale, 1980 hoard, which contained no. 81 from this catalogue, provides an approximate *terminus ante quem* around 240 BC for these groups. Rather than assuming that an issue with such an ideological importance as the Pans started with a rather crude variety,[22] one may prefer to attribute the low quality of this group to the engagement of the mint official with celebratory issues towards the end of this period.

*** *** ***

Crested Helmet l.—Monogram Ꝁ r.

O: Eight-rayed, elliptic units. Pan with short hair arranged downwards, horns turned backwards. End of neck concave. *Pedum* very thin, held upright.
R: l., helmet with long crest, high bowl and long cheek flaps.

Group 22

Specimens: 1	Obverses: [1-1]
Die Combinations: 1	Reverses: 1

97. O26 R93

a. Gorny 13 (28–9.6.1979), 84	-	-	-

[O (a): flaw: on space 1; break on external badge circle, r.; off "unit" 1; off chin. Die break on head.
R (a): signs of flaw between upper crest and l. pleat end; l., diagonally, from l. foot towards legend letters].

*** *** ***

O: As above.
R: Similar.

Group 23

Specimens: 3	Obverses: [1-1]
Die Combinations: 2	Reverses: [2-1]

98. O17 R94

a. ANS 1944.100.13842	16.74 g	2 h	-
b. Künker 83 (17.06.2003), 211	16.99 g	-	-

22. As does Mathisen: *Silver Coinages*, 111–112.

[O (a): new diagonal flaw from internal badge circle to "unit" 6; also, between l. crescent ends of "unit" 4 and border; flaws between nose and badge edge develop; new flaw off *pedum*.
R (a): l., flaw l. of Γ and on r. vertical bar of second N. R., flaw r. of both Σ, r. of Ω; recut r. of monogram; flaw further r.].

99. O17 R93

a. BM 1911-4-9-281 (Rollin) 16.95 g 5h 32.5 mm

[O (a): curved flaw between "units" 7 (inner crescent), and 1 on coins 98a–99a; diagonal flaw from up r. end of "unit" 1 diagonally to l. horn. On badge, flaw off end of drapery, towards "unit" 4 and from internal badge circle diagonally to "unit" 6. Nose pointed and worn; signs of flaw off nose and between *pedum* and badge edge.
R (a): r., flaw between pleat's r. end and *chiton*].

*** *** ***

GROUP 24

Specimens: 1	Obverses: [1-1]
Die Combinations: 1	Reverses: 1

100. O06 R95

a. Pegasi 13 (8.11.2005), 127; Spartan Numismatics BBS 41 (22.5.2005), 62 16.85 g - -

A small issue is signed by a combination of letters K and Ω, Monogram K. The obverse links among nos. 96, 97 and 114 and nos. 47–50 and 98–9, respectively, in addition to the similarity in the legend letters and in the helmet types, suggest that Groups 12 (Monogram ΗΡ), 21 (monogram ΕΡ), 23 (Monogram K), 30 (Monogram ΗΝ), and 31 (Monogram ΗΝ), are contemporary or consecutive.

*** *** ***

Crested Helmet l.—ΗΝ r.

O: Varied number of rays on each star, horns upright. Hair flows in three locks on nape, Pan's upper lip prominent, chin small, side lock curves, neck longer. Horizontal wrinkle on forehead. Diagonal folds on drapery, distance between lower drapery and inner badge circle larger. *Pedum* upright, drapery ends in straight line.

R: Similar. Archaizing Athena l., brandishing thunderbolt and walking on tiptoe with both feet, in exergue. Shawl over shoulders falls in dove-tail pleats with two-pointed ends. In field l., crested helmet with high bowl (*pilos*/*konos*).

GROUP 25

Specimens: 52	Obverses: 1
Die Combinations: 5	Reverses: 5

101. O27 R96

a. Oxford: *SNG Ashmolean* 3259 (Robinson); Glendining (2.1958), 1392; Glendining (16.7.1950), (Hall), 86 17.14 g 12 h 32 mm
b. CNG Triton 6 (14–15.1.2003), 189; Sotheby's (21–22.6.1990), 391 (Nelson Hunt Collection, Part II); S. Weintraub Collection 17.14 g - -
c. CGF (19.6.2003), 73 17.20 g 12 h 29 mm
d. Leiden 1949/70; Schulman (19.7.1970), 772 17.10 g 12 h -
e. G. Hirsch 234 (5–7.5.2004), 198 17.14 g - -
f. Cambridge: *SNG Lockett* 3, 1524 (17.10 g); Sotheby (19–21.1.1914), 143; Naville 5 (1923), 1465 (17.10 g) 17.07 g 12 h -
g. Künker 54 (7–10.3.2000), 1839; NFA (winter 1989), 461; Leu 22 (8–9.5.1979), 81 (17.12 g 12 h); Stack's (10–11.06.1970, F. S. Knobloch), 295 (17.10 g); *SNG BYB* 350; J. Hirsch 33 (1913), 669; Sotheby (24–5.6.1914), 70
17.09 g 12 h -
h. CNG Triton 3 (30.11–1.12.1999), 390; Pozzi collection, 970; Naville (14.3.1921), 970
17.12 g - -
i. Royal Ontario Museum, 9734; Freeman & Sear 2 (31.1.1996), 27
17.15 g 12 h 30.1 mm
j. Waddell (2.2000), 24 17.15 g - -
k. Gorny & Mosch 133 (11.10.2004), 152 17.16 g - -
l. H. Weber, 2163 16.97 g - 31 mm
m. A. Weil (24.05.1986), 50 (17.12 g); Jameson, 1009 (17.14 g); MMAG 4 (1935), 650 (17.10 g); Florange-Ciani (28.5.1924), 17; Ciani 99 (ex coll. Duruflé); Clement Platt, Numismatique (n.d.), 175 17.14 g - -
n. CNA 32 (1994), 119 (T. B. Lesure Collection); Santamaria (1910), 733
16.81 g - -
o. Bloesch, *Winterthur*, 161; Hess 236 (03.04.1939), 529 (17.18 g, 30 mm); Merzbacher 4 (1910), 410 (17.15 g); Gaebler, *AMNG* III.1, 186.3
17.07 g 12 h 30.1 mm
p. Hartwig (5.3.1910), 733 - - -

[O (a): beginning of small flaw from end of nose; star 2 with many rays, flaw on space 2. (f): nose, *pedum* recut.
R (a): small flaw on nose. (f): Athena flatter. (g): line between drapery and monogram].

102. O27 R97

a. Berlin; Imhoof-Blumer 17.16 g 5 h -
b. CNG Triton 10 (9–10.1.2007), 168; Freeman & Sear 5 (14.5.1999), 211; SKA FPL Monetarium 58 (spring 1992), 43 (17.16 g); SB 28 (17–19.9.1991), 90
17.15 g 7 h -
c. Paris: *SNG Delepierre* 1063 17.08 g 11 h -
d. Cambridge: *SNG Fitzwilliam* 2304; A. W. Young, 665-1936; ex Montagu 251
17.14 g 1 h 29 mm
e. J. Hirsch 26 (1910), 258 17.10 g - -
f. Zschiesche (1913), 327 - - -

g. Vinchon (27.2.1961), 121 (Lu. 1698); Bourgey (11.1957), 64

	17.13 g	-	-
h. Hess-Divo 272 (1997), 11	17.17 g	-	-
i. J. Hirsch 31 (5.1912), 276; J. Hirsch 24 (1912), 444 (17.20 g)			
	17.14 g	-	-

j. Weil (24.5.1986), 50; G. Hirsch 16 (16–19.4.1958), 80 (17.15 g); G. Hirsch 14 (10–20.9.1957), 583 (17.15 g); J. Hirsch 13 (15.5.1905), 1180 (17.12 g)

	17.12 g	-	-
k.Vinchon (24.11.1969), 118	17.08 g	-	-
l. J. Hirsch 34 (1914), 300	17.14 g	-	29.5 mm
m. NFA 6 (1979), 154	17.17 g	-	-
n. Helbing 9 (8.4.1913), 327	-	-	-
o. Egger 40 (1912), 771; J. Hirsch 14 (1905), 311	17.16 g	-	30 mm
p. Sotheby (7.1980), 28; Hess-Leu (16.4.1957), 193 (17.15 g)			
	17.05 g	-	-
q. Rauch 2012 (20.9.2012), 263	16.44 g (b)	-	-

[O (c): off-center. (g): break on lower *pedum* and on star 5. (g): recut on lower *pedum* and on star 5. (n): flaw from nose downwards and on star 7.
R (n): distance between r. end of pleat and l. leg. In field r., letter A without curves].

103. O27 R98

a. *SNG Sweden* II, 1138	17.16 g	5 h	-
b. Gans 16 (1960), 258	17.07 g	-	-
c. Ritter 65 (2004), 593	-	-	-
d. Cambridge: *SNG Fitzwilliam* 2305	16.79 g (p)	1 h	-
e. NFA 20 (1988), 682	17.10 g	-	-
f. Brussels, du Chastel	17.15 g	3 h	31 mm
g. J. Hirsch 17 (1905), 311; J. Hirsch 14 (27.11.1905), 310			
	17.14 g	-	30.5 mm
h. Numismatica Genevensis SA 7 (27.11.2012), 184			
	17.12 g	-	-
i. ANA 62 (22–26.8.1952), 2244	-	-	-
j. Kress 112 (1959), 164	-	-	-
k. Künker 158 (28.9.2009), 185	17.12 g	-	-
l. CNG 215 (29.7.2009), 74	17.07 g	7 h	-

[O (a): parallel ray added to star no. 2; flaw from nose. O (a–b): recut on side lock. (k–l): flaw on *pedum*.
R (a): horizontal bar on A hardly discernible. Athena taller. Leg discernible through folds. (b): curve joining "unit" 1 with badge; linear flaw on "unit" 5. Flaw on nose; slight difference on *pedum*].

104. O27 R99

a. BM G 0513	17.09 g (p)	3 h	32 mm

[R (a): reverse curved, change of color on obverse].

105. O27 R100

a. ANM: *SNG Saroglos* 923 17.05 g 1 h 31.0 mm
b. Leu-Spink (1987), 94; Kricheldorf 41 (1988), 98 (17.13 g); G. Hirsch 164 (29–30.12.1984), 210 (17.05 g) 17.14 g 12 h 31.0 mm
c. NFA 20 (9–10.3.1988), 681 17.05 g - -
d. Rauch 56 (1996), 82; Münzzentrum 82 (6–8.9.1995), 58 16.80 g - -
e. Cardiff Museum: Wales, 86.11H/2 16.78 g 12 h -
f. *SNG Cop* 1199 17.07 g (p), 12 h-

[O (a): stars with thinner lines. (e): flaw, two curved flaws on space 7.
R (a): r., flaw between l. end of pleat and *chiton*; also, between l. bar of monogram and *chiton*. (b): flaw up r.]

*** *** ***

O: Six-rayed stars, upper l. ray of star 3 not connected with center. Pan's dotted horns converge l. Side lock curves on lower end. Flaw on lower badge, from r. end of *pedum* to badge edge.
R: Similar.

Group 26

Specimens: 6 Obverses: 1
Die Combinations: 2 Reverses: 2

106. O28 R101

a. BM T. C., p. 107, No. 1 17.10 g 10 h 36.2 mm
b. Munich: *SNG München* 1078 17.11 g 1 h -
c. CNG Triton 6 (14–15.01.2003), 188; CNG Triton 1 (02–03.12.1997), 439 17.11 g - -

[O (a): curved flaw from ray 1 of star 1 through to upper badge circle. Concave flaw from space 6 through lower end of "unit" 7 to upper emblem. Signs of tool on space 1, worn on space 2.
R (a): r., flaw between *chiton* and monogram].

107. O28 R102

a. NFA (12.10.1988), 207 (Brauer); Coin Galleries L 1.1 (1960), A11 16.96 g - -
b. Argenor (3.5.2006), 75 17.14 g 6 h -
c. Baldwin-Markov-M&M 23 (6.1.2010), 19 17.09 g - -

[O (a): curved flaw across "unit" 1 and flaws on spaces 2, 4–5 expand; curved flaw on "unit" 7. Flaw on upper *pedum* and between its r. side and badge edge; also, from knob downwards.
R (a): up, vertical flaw from upper border to badge; l., second flaw, l. of ΓO; lower, curved flaw from r. bar of Y through r. leg to lower border].

*** *** ***

O: As above.
R: Similar.

GROUP 27

Specimens: 4 Obverses: [1-1]
Die Combinations: 2 Reverses: [2-2]

108. O15 R96

a. Kroh FPL 28 (?), H13 16.86 g - -

109. O15 R98

a. BM 1947-4-6-191 (Oman) 17.14 g 9 h 34.2 mm
b. Leu 53 (21–2.10.1991), 77; Glendining 20 (1986), (Knoepke), 170
17.17 g - -
c. ANS 1944.100.13843 17.18 g 9 h -

[O (a): flaw on space 4, on edge with badge circles; on border, on spaces 5 and 6; beginning of flaw between badge circles and unit 4. Diagonal flaw on upper badge, l. of horns. Horizontal flaw, from forehead through hair. (c): slight flaw off lower lip and chin, and off two lower folds of drapery: die slightly moved r.? Flaws on spaces 6 and 7.
R (a): l., flaw between end of l. pleat and helmet crest; a smaller one, r. of exergue. (c): recut l., between pleat and helmet crest. Flaws off r. pleat and *chiton*].

*** *** ***

O: Six-rayed stars, a ray added to no. 2. *Pedum* moves away from head.
R: Athena moderate. Shield large, held horizontally. Distance between helmet and pleat edge.

GROUP 28

Specimens: 8 Obverses: 1
Die Combinations: 3 Reverses: 3

110. O29 R103

a. CNG Triton 8 (11–12.1.2005), 186; Leu 83 (6–7.5.2002), 204; Peus 337 (1993), 118 (17.10 g); Peus 334 (1993), 359 (16.90 g); Burgan (3.7.1992), 419; Vinchon (14.5.1982), 12 (16.95 g) 17.10 g 11 h -
b. NAC AG, Auction R (17.7.2007), 1126 16.74 g - -
c. Barthold-Poplavsky (18.2.1977), 12 17.10 g - -

[O (a): flaw on spaces 1, 3, from border to badge circle l. of "unit" 4; between "unit" 5 and badge; between forehead and badge edge. Recut on nose.
R (a): l., flaw off nose; r., horizontal flaw between monogram and E].

111. O29 R104

a. Kurpfälzische Münzhandlung 48 (8–9.6.1995), 143
16.97 g - -
b. Roma 4 (28.12.2013), 207 (E-sale) 16.77 g 10 h 32 mm

c. NAC 72 (16.5.2013), 349 17.16 g - -

112. O29 R105

a. Forestier & Lambert (8.6.2007), 26; Tradart (16.11.1995), 53: enlargement of coin illustrated on p. 79; TNA 1, 68 (17.16 g) 17.14 g 11 h -
b. Albuquerque MBS 49 (1995), 6; Albuquerque MBS 45 (1994), 67: enlargement of coin illustrated; E. Bourgey (13–14.11.1980), 33; Plumier L 3 (6.1979), 27
16.84 g - -

[O (a): flaws expand on spaces 1, 4–5; new flaw between badge and chin.
R (a–b): l., flaws beneath T and IΓ; (a): l., flaw from beneath Λ and pleat end. (b): r., flaw between pleat and Σ].

*** *** ***

O: Horns parallel, pointing up r. Side locks different, lower hair longer. Two slight curves in *anastole*, no drapery fold prominent. Nose pointed. Hair locks arranged towards face. Star/crescents 5–7 closer to badge edge.
R: Similar.

Group 29

Specimens: 2 Obverses: [1-1]
Die Combinations: 1 Reverses: 1

113. O16 R106

a. J. Hirsch 13 (1905), 152; NFA 18 (1987), 124 17.03 g - -
b. Austria, Landesmuseum Joanneum, 56594 16.03 g 2 h 29 mm

[R (a): shield large and curved, monogram low in field].

*** *** ***

O: Head small, locks untidy, arranged downwards. Three-fold drapery ends in big curve. *Pedum* upright, starting from between middle and last fold.
R: Letters spread. Figure tall with stylized hem folds, thin shawl pleats and long shield, held upright. Helmet with large bowl, rich crest and long cheek pieces.

Group 30

Specimens: 3 Obverses: [2-1]
Die Combinations: 2 Reverses: 2

114. O26 R107

a. ANM: Thesprotia, 1992 (*CH* IX [2002], 200; Touratsoglou, *DM*, no 29)
16.76 g 6 h -

[O (a): flaw on "unit" 4. Diagonal flaw across *anastole*.
R (a): l., flaw between Y and helmet crest; also, from upper bar of N through pleat to crest].

115. O30 R108

a. Ahlström 28 (1983), 1913 - - -
b. CNG 289 (24.10.2012), 59 16.94 g 12 h 31 mm

[O (a): worn between "units" 2, 5 and badge, and on spaces 4–6; also, between *pedum* and head, off nose. Diagonal flaw from off "unit" 1 to hair locks. Diagonal flaw from shield downwards.
R (a): l., flaw between l. end of pleat and crest].

*** *** ***

O: As above.
R: Similar.

Group 31

Specimens: 11 Obverses: [1-1]
Die Combinations: 6 Reverses: 6

116. O17 R109

a. Schulman Amsterdam (30–31.3.1936), 62 17.20 g - -
b. Schulman New York (1.1913), 12, n. 4 - - -

[O (a): new break on space 7; worn on "unit" 5 and between "unit" 5 and badge circles. Flaws between l. horn, r. horn and "unit" 1 develop.
R (a): l., flaw between Y and helmet].

117. O17 R110

a. Gorny 56 (7.10.1991), 190 16.86 g - -
b. Berlin; C. R. Fox 17.16 g 9 h -
c. Morton & Eden (13–14.11.2002), 525; Waddell (7.2.1979), 96 (17.12 g) 17.11 g -

[O (a): flaw up l.; a ray added to star 7. Off-center. (b): horizontal flaw from "unit" 5 through to no. 6.
R: (a): vertical r. monogram bar smaller].

118. O17 R111

a. R. Ratto Colls. A. Benassy-Philippe, A. Roehrich, d' un amateur d' Amérique (9.10.1934), 110 (17.22 g); R. Ratto (24.6.1929), 257 17.18 g - -
b. Baranowsky (1931), 450 17.18 g - -
c. Ratto (9.10.1934), 110; Ratto (24.06.1929), 257; R. Ratto (13.3.1912), 650 17.15 g - -

[O (a–c): up l., flaw on space 7 through upper badge circles. (b–c): l., progressive flaws across "units" 4–6 and between "units" 3–4 and center.
R (c): r., flaw between monogram and Σ, off r. pleat; horizontal flaw from l. to r.; flaw between pleat and *chiton*].

119. O17 R112

a. Vinchon (22–24.2.1971), 80 - - -

120. O17 R113

a. Bloesch, *Winterthur*, 1619 17.19 g 5 h 31.2 mm

[O (a): flaw between "unit" 3 and badge circles.
R (a): the edge of r. pleat reaches E].

121. O17 R114

a. Lanz 16 (1979), 82 17.01 g 10 h -

[O (a): flaw between "unit" 6 and badge; also, between "units" 5 and 6.
R (a): l., diagonal flaw between Γ and O; vertical flaw between helmet crest and Υ. Horizontal flaw from l. pleat through figure to end of r. pleat].

*** *** ***

O: Stars six-rayed, a thinner ray added to star 5. Hair from upper head moves diagonally to front, arranged in two rows. Horizontal wrinkle on forehead; diagonal folds on edge of drapery. *Pedum* starts from between middle and top fold of drapery.
R: Similar.

Group 32

Specimens: 17 Obverses: [1-1]
Die Combinations: 9 Reverses: 9

122. O05 R115

a. Athens: *SNG Alpha Bank* 987 (1258) 16.86 g 8:30 h 32.0 mm
b. ANS 1944.100.13835: "Pherai," 1937–1938 (*IGCH* 168), (on file in ANS)
16.29 g 12 h -
c. Scotussa area, (pre-)1989 (*CH* VIII [1994], 283, pl. 34.9)
- - -
d. CNG 268 (16.11.2011), 62 16.93 g 7 h 31 mm

[O (a): up l., flaw between badge and internal "crescent" 1 expands to border, l. Flaw between upper head and badge circles.
R (c): legend l. starts beneath ankle].

O: Similar.
R: Letters irregular, rough, Athena crude. Shield oval-shaped, *aegis* with small dots. Legs discernible through *chiton*, middle fold shorter. Helmet bowl small, with short cheek pieces.

123. O05 R116

a. ANM: Thesprotia, 1992 (*CH* IX [2002], 200; Touratsoglou, *DM*, no. 33)
16.90 g 12 h -

[R (a): pleat edges point downwards].

124. O05 R117

a. BM E. H., p. 295, n. 2 16.86 g 1 h 34.0 mm

b. Toderi L (1981, 1983–1984), 53 - - -

[O (a): flaws: between external "crescent" 1 and badge, inner "crescent" 1 and external badge circle, l., on spaces 1, 5–7. Also, diagonal flaw between "units" 1, 4 and badge; between badge circles, up l. Hair divided by curved flaw into two rows. Flaw between *pedum* and badge circle].

125. O05 R118

a. iNumis MBS 25 (3.6.2014), 16; Peiresc (24.10.1992), 14
16.87 g 2 h 31.0 mm

126. O05 R119

a. Gorny 19 (12–14.5.1981), 28; MMAG 37 (1968), 179
17.12 g - -

[O (a): expansion of flaw from badge circles to emblem, l.; flaw lower, parallel to inner circle in field, l.
R (a): l., lateral bars on A concave. Up, sign of tooling through head].

127. O05 R120

a. Scotussa area, 1989 (*CH* VIII [1994], 283, pl. 34.4)
- - -

b. Amphora 22 (1984), 140; Amphora (D. Hendin), 18 (1981), 163
- - -

128. O05 R121

a. G. Hirsch 105 (1977), 16; Bayerische Vereinsbank 15 (09.1977), 16
17.091 g - -

b. Gorny & Mosch 203 (5.3.2012), 152 17.15 g - -

c. Grabow (9–10.7.1930), 309 17.01 g - 31 mm

[O (a–b): new flaw from off nose to lower l. emblem].

129. O05 R122

a. Peus 313 (1985), 68 17.06 g - -

b. Rauch 94 (9.4.2014), 254 17.19 g - -

[O (a): flaws around emblem expand; flaw behind *pedum* down to drapery.
R (a): r., flaw between *chiton* and lower bar of Σ].

130. O05 R123

a. S. Asia Minor, 1963: *IGCH* 1426: Boehringer, *Chronologie*, 156.19, pl. 25; MMAG L 417 (1979), 7 - - -

b. Tell Sukas (Gabala), 1958: *IGCH* 1528: P. J. Riis, "L'activité de la Mission Archéologique Danoise sur la Côté Phénicienne en 1958," *AnnArch de Syrie* 8–9 (1958–9), fig. 7A–B, esp. 125, fig. A–B; Price, *Alexander*, 414–6 - - -

[O (a), flaws between "units" 1, 2, 7 and badge; up r., horizontal flaw from "unit" 2 through head; on badge r., off nose, downwards.
R (a): l., break parallel to diagonal bar on second N and below I; also, break along border; r., between Λ and pleat].

*** *** ***

O: Stars large, six-rayed. Hair arranged in two rows, flows downwards; three locks hang from nape. *Pedum* emerges from middle fold, held upright.
R: Folds clearly delineated.

Group 33

Specimens: 3	Obverses: 1
Die Combinations: 2	Reverses: 2

131. O31 R124

a. Ponterio & Associates 41 (15.3.1990), 2367 - - -

132. O31 R125

a. Hess-Divo 283 (10.5.2000), 64; MMAG L 419 (1980), 8; possibly S. Asia Minor, 1963: *IGCH* 1426 17.11 g - -
b. CNG FPL 17.2 (1992), 19 16.93 g - -

[O (a): flaws on spaces 2, 4; horizontal flaw from border of space 6 through badge circles to level of eye. Diagonal flaw, from inner badge circle off "unit" 2 to crown of head.
R (a): l, up, beginning of flaw off A; also, beneath I; r., diagonal flaw from between main figure and pleat's l. end to upper l. angle of monogram].

*** *** ***

O: *Pedum* emerges from between middle and upper fold, moving away from head. Hair locks arranged vertically and downwards. Shield pattern different: diameter of star/crescents (0.6–0.8 mm); six-rayed stars, a ray added to nos. 1 and 2. *Pedum*: dot on upper edge, small line prominent l.
R: Athena taller, holding shield directly in front of her. The r. end of l. pleat reaches leg. A without vertical *hasta*. Fall in middle. Cheek pieces shorter.

Group 34

Specimens: 8	Obverses: [1-1]
Die Combinations: 5	Reverses: (5-1)

133. O06 R126

a. Hess-Leu 31 (1966), 264 (17.14 g); J. Hirsch 13 (1905), 1178 (17.11 g) 17.11 g - -
b. Glendining (18–20.4.1955), 290 17.13 g - -
c. Künker 94 (27–28.9.2004), 715 17.12 g - -

[O (b): flaw on "units" 2 and 6 and on space 2; flaw from star rays through to crescents of "unit" 7. Flaw from nose downwards.

R (b–c): l., horizontal flaws beneath I, Γ; also, between legend and pleat, pleat and *chiton*. Flaw beneath OY].

134. O06 R127

a. Munich: *SNG München* 1077	17.00 g (p)	7 h	-
b. Ariadne (15.9.1982), 55	16.58 g	-	-

[O (a): two flaws starting from nose].

135. O06 R128

a. *SNG Tübingen* 1188	16.93 g	5 h	-

[O (a): recut on nose.
R (a): r., flaw between foot and Σ].

136. O06 R118

a. Tkalec (19.2.2001), 65	17.07 g	-	-

[O (a): flaw up r., off unit 2. Flaw off nose; flaw from upper part of drapery, running parallel to *pedum*].

137. O06 R129

a. Ciani FPL, "Vente aux prix marqués" (no date), 97

	-	-	-

[O (a): flaw up r., off "unit" 2; also, on space 3. Repair on flaw off nose.
R (a): l., flaw on l. lateral bar of A and above A; diagonal signs from lower border l. through l. pleat to *chiton*].

*** *** ***

O: Similar. Six-rayed stars, small ray added to "units" 1–2; flaw on "unit" 5 expands; horns diverge.
R: Similar.

GROUP 35

Specimens: 19 Obverses: [2-2]
Die Combinations: 10 Reverses: 10

138. O07 R130 R: Legend letters crude, splayed Σ. Athena, helmet of different style.

a. Athens, Benaki Museum	-	-	-

[O (a): test cut on chin].

139. O07 R131

a. Superior (30.05.1995, Lewis Egnew), 7315C	-	-	-

140. O07 R132

a. ANM: Thesprotia, 1992 (*CH* IX [2002], 200; Touratsoglou, *DM*, no. 37)

	16.75 g	11 h	-

b. NYS (K. W. Güstrow collection), 11 (11.1.2006), 85; Baldwin—Markov—M&M 11 (15.1.2004), 85; M & M FPL 2 (1998), 38; MMAG 85 (1997), 59
16.99 g - -
c. Gorny & Mosch 114 (4.3.2002), 85 - - -

[O (a): flaw on spaces 1–3; flaw on "unit" 5].

141. O07 R133 R: Helmet with wide bowl and with a rich crest.

a. Malter 1 (1973), 86 17.09 g - -

142. O07 R134

a. Provadalieff, MGA (15.4.1912), 192 - - -

[O (a): beginning of diagonal die flaw on space 1].

143. O07 R135

a. G. Hirsch 30 (1962), 100 - - -
b. InAsta 10 (1999), 20 17.10 g - -

[O (a): r., flaw between *pedum* and badge circles; also, on space 4. O (b): die flaws on spaces 1 and 2; diagonal die flaw on space 6.
R (a): l., horizontal flaw between pleat and *chiton* and a vertical one, alongside l. leg; r., horizontal flaw between letter I (ΒΑΣΙΛΕΩΣ), and border].

144. O07 R136

a. Poindessault-Védrines (15.11.1991), 145 16.88 g - -
b. Glendining (13.12.1963), 227 - - -
c. Emporium 69 (4.4.2013), 47 17.10 g - -
d. CNG 238 (11.8.2010), 70 17.05 g 7 h -

[O (a): diagonal flaw on space 1, from r. end of "unit" 1 through to badge circles; between badge circles, off space 2; flaws on spaces 1, 4–5].

145. O07 R137

a. Gorny 22 (1982), 55 16.52 g - -
b. M&M Ltd, FPL 2 (4–5.1998), 38 16.99 g - -

O (a): diagonal flaw, from nose to badge circle, l.; also, from chin to lower badge circle. Expansion of existing flaws.
R (a): l., flaw between l. helmet crest and foot].

146. O08 R138

a. DNW (14.3.2007), 146 (17.17 g); CNG MBS 69 (8.6.2005), 196 (17.15 g)
17.17 g 5 h -
b. HWCA 3019 (26.4.2012), 23085 (CICF Signature Sale)
16.99 g 12 h 31 mm

[O (a): damage at l. end of "unit" 1].

147. O08 R139

a. Morgenthau (15–16.3.1938), 25 - - -

b. CNG 236 (07.07.2010), 74 17.11 g 1 h 32 mm

*** *** ***

O: Six-rayed stars, crescents semi-circular. Head crude. Hair flows in straight thick locks; upper and lower folds of drapery more prominent, *pedum* upright, emerging from lower drapery.
R: Similar. Legend letters cruder; *chiton* side folds wider.

GROUP 36

Specimens: 1 Obverses: 1
Die Combinations: 1 Reverses: 1

148. O32 R140

a. Künker 204 (12.3.2012), 231; Münzzentrum 53 (1984), 1528 (16.52 g) 16.48 g - -

*** *** ***

O: As above.
R: Similar.

GROUP 37

Specimens: 2 Obverses: [1-1]
Die Combinations: 1 Reverses: 1

149. O09 R141 R: Legend letters large, Athena crude. Helmet of different type.

a. Oxford: *SNG Ashmolean* 3258 (Oman 1947) 17.06 g 5 h 33 mm
b. ANS: Dewing 1203 (Robinson collection) - - -
[O (a): break on edge (2:30 h)].

*** *** ***

O: Horns parallel. Small distance between badge edge and drapery r.
R: Legend characters moderate in size. Athena tall. Large shield in front of Athena. Monogram lateral.

GROUP 38

Specimens: 34 Obverses: [2-2]
Die Combinations: 14 Reverses: 14

150. O09 R142

a. Glasgow: MacDonald, *Hunterian*, 340.4 17.08 g 2 h -
b. ANS: Dewing 1204; Schlessinger, 779 16.99 g 3 h -
c. HWCA 3017 (10.1.2012), 27010 16.67 g - -

[O (a): flaw between outer badge circle and "unit" 4].

151. O09 R143

a. Luynes 1698 17.05 g - -

b. S. Asia Minor, 1963: *IGCH* 1426 (Boehringer, *Chronologie*, 155–157.20, pl. 25)
- - -

[Poorly preserved.
O (a): new flaw on space 4, between outer crescent and external badge circle. Diagonal flaw on badge.
R (a): curve from top through to shield].

152. O10 R144

a. BNF 1378 17.30 g 1 h -
b. N. Syria, 1960: *IGCH* 1533 (Seyrig, *Trésors*, 14, no. 66)
- - -
c. Belgrade: V. Popovic (ed.), *Tri numizmatièka legata Univerziteta Beogradu* (Belgrade 1991), no. 23 16.24 g - 31 mm

[O (a): signs of die wear on space 1; diagonal flaw across badge circles, off "unit" 6. Recut on nose; small flaw from nose, downwards; flaw beneath *pedum*, starting from middle fold and developing alongside *pedum*.
R (a): horizontal die break on r. border].

153. O10 R145

a. Superior (30.5.1995), 7315A - - -

154. O10 R146 R: Athena crude.

a. Leiden: 3155 17.03 g 12 h -
b. ANM (Kindynis' coll.) 16.39 g 9:30 h 32.0 mm
c. Kavala 1635 (Polyzonas' coll.) 12.283 g 9 h -
d. MMAG 6 (1946), 629 - - -
e. Peus 284 (1974), 203 17.05 g - -
f. Goldberg 80 (3.6.2014), 3287 17.13 g - -
g. Kricheldorf 4 (1957), 162; Gorny 40 (1988), 1058
16.95 g - -
h. Stack's Bowers and Ponterio 182 (10.01.2014), 38 (N.Y.I.N.C. Auction Sessions A–B)
17.13 g - -

[O (a): recut on nose. Signs of horizontal flaw across internal badge circle, off "unit" 6.
R (a): r., flaw between Athena and monogram].

155. O10 R147

a. MMAG L 390 (1977), 7 16.81 g - -
b. G. Hirsch 14 (10–20.9.1957), 12 17.028 g - -
c. Kricheldorf L 27 (4.1958), 133 16.95 g - -

[O (a): beginning of new flaw, on external badge circle, off space 3. Sign of tool on upper end of "unit" 6.
R (a): l., flaws: beneath N and from r. lateral bar of Y to helmet bowl; also, beneath r. end of r. pleat].

156. O10 R148 R: ends of vertical monogram bars not connected.

a. ANM: Thesprotia, 1992 (*CH* IX [2002], 200; Touratsoglou, *DM*, no. 30)
16.50 g 1 h -

[O (a): horizontal flaw, starting from lower "unit" 7, on space 1; small diagonal flaw, from hair to lower *pedum*; small flaw beneath drapery.
R (a): *chiton* corroded: portion of surface flaked off; l., flaw continues to the l. end of helmet crest; r., flaw from upper end of A].

157. O10 R149

a. ANM: Thesprotia, 1992 (*CH* IX [2002], 200; Touratsoglou, *DM*, no. 25)
17.065 g 5 h -

b. Ritter L 75 (10.2005), 441 - - -

[O (a): flaws: from crescent 3 through to space 3; on space 4; expansion of flaw beneath *pedum*; beginning of a new one higher, off *pedum*].

158. O10 R150

a. Budapest, National Museum, no. 13, Inv. No. 23A.1912.2
16.92 g 7 h -

[R (a): shield different].

159. O10 R151

a. Myers 11 (1975), 58; Coin Galleries L 11.1-2 (1970), A 20
17.02 g - -

b. Pegasi BBS 116 (15.11.1999), 85 16.70 g - -

[O (a): flaw on space 3.
R (a): diagonal flaw between l. leg and border].

160. O10 R152 R: shield of triangular profile, helmet smaller.

a. ANM: Eretria, 1937 (*CH* IX (2002), 194; *IGCH* 175, no. 21)
17.06 g 2 h 33.5 mm

[O (a): poorly preserved; flaw beneath *pedum* ends in dot; l, signs of overstrike: trident r.
R (a): l., flaw between legend and border; higher, horizontal flaw from border to leg].

161. O10 R153

a. Pegasi BBS 95 (20.11.1995), 81 - - -

b. MMAG 17 (1988), 165 17.00 g - -

[O (a-b): flaws: on space 4 and from "unit" 7 through to space 7.
NB: very bad photograph].

162. O10 R154

a. Bayerische Vereinsbank 14 (4.1977), 12 17.028 g - -
b. Gorny 92 (21–22.11.1998), 135 16.88 g - -
c. Albuquerque MBS 21 (1990), 58 16.10 g - -

[O (a): flaw on space 6, off lower "unit" 7; also, from off "unit" 5 diagonally to badge circles.
R (a): r., flaw from middle of border towards legend].

163. O10 R155

a. G. Hirsch 68 (1970), 115; G. Hirsch 27 (1961), 759
16.81 g - -
b. Zagheb (10–11.5.1954), 157 16.98 g - -

[O (a): on badge, horizontal break and countermark on head; recut on *pedum*; die ready to break between *pedum* and "unit" 3. In field, die breaks: across star 3, on space 4, (diagonal), between "unit" 7 and head.
R (a): up l., dots].

*** *** ***

O: As above.
R: Similar.

Group 39

Specimens: 2	Obverses: [1-1]
Die Combinations: 1	Reverses: 1

164. O11 R156 R: Small helmet with short cheek pieces.

a. Poinsignon-Pesce MBS 4 (30.6.1987), 590 16.52 g - -
b. A. Weil (18.9.1986), 11 - - -

[O (a): flaws on spaces 1–2; scratch through "units" 4–5. In field l., two flaws from chin to lower l. border; r., vertical flaw from lower *pedum* through to "unit" 4.
R (a): l., flaw between l. end of pleat and foot].

*** *** ***

O: As above.
R: Similar.

Group 40

Specimens: 2	Obverses: [2-2]
Die Combinations: 2	Reverses: 2

165. O21 R157

a. SB 6 (1980), 47 - - -

[O (a): l., flaw from lower l. border and chin].

166. O25 R158

a. Parsy (7.12.2000, Collection J. L. R.), 18; CB L (3.1990), 62
- - -

[O (a): flaws: between nose and l. border; between drapery and lower badge border and from badge border to "unit" 4; flaw as upward extension of *pedum*; also, diagonal flaw between *pedum* and inner border.

R (a): l., scratches between helmet and legend letters. R., between figure and legend, monogram erased beneath Monogram Ꝁ].

Monogram ⋈ occurs on most of the Pan head tetradrachms of this period. Group 25 is the largest. The obverses of groups 25–7 are very carefully engraved and their stylistic homogeneity suggests the same hand. The elaborate constituent elements of the punches point to an early date for this group. There is also a tendency for figures of Athena on Groups 27 and 28 to be taller. The crude workmanship of the reverse dies on Group 28, with an Athena with bulging limbs, the somewhat cruder legend letters and the crested helmet with an elaborate crest holder associate these issues to Groups 8 and 38. Helmets with a higher helmet bowl, and taller Athenas, characterize the groups that follow. A different engraver appears to have cut the obverse of Group 34, but the short Athena on the reverses of specimens 133–135 suggests the proximity of these issues to the early groups carrying the same monogram. Some first signs of the engraver who continues with the reverses of Period II are detected on group 36 and on specimen 148, which only prepare us for the coinage struck in Period II. A new style is introduced with the obverses of Group 39, from which one die combination survives. The large number of die combinations suggests the exhaustive use of the respective obverse dies with a number of reverses, even though few specimens survive from this combination. Finally, flatter but heavier surfaces combine to yield the obverse of Groups 40–41, the last issues with Monogram ⋈ during this period.

The general absence of reverse links might indicate either the issue of these coins over a longer period or the cooperation of more mint officials for an urgent issue. The second alternative might be favored by the stylistic homogeneity of the legend letters in most specimens. In fact, a tendency for larger legend letters is observed on the issues with a crude Athena. A preference for wider flans tallies with a tendency for larger heads of Pan, as in Groups 33 and 35, but this need not determine the chronological sequence of the groups.

A technical mistake of the die cutters may be observed on no. 104, which, apart from being pierced, is struck in such a way that the obverse is concave and the reverse is convex. The otherwise excellent quality of the coin suggests that this mistake occurred at the earliest stages of operation of the mint, if not during the piercing of the coin. Four specimens are pierced: nos. 103d, 104a, 105f, 134a. Finally, nos. 7a (Group 1), 18b (Group 4), 86b (Group 20), 95e–f (Group 20), and 163a (Group 38), have been countermarked.

*** *** ***

2.2.3.1.2 Monogram ⋈ l.

O: Modules smaller. Six-rayed stars, nos. 1–3 with seven, no. 7 with eight rays. "Units" of smaller diameter. In center, small elaborate head; horns r.; hair locks in tear-drop shape, flowing downwards. Three-fold drapery, ending in curve. *Pedum* long, close to head.

R: Archaizing Athena, with long stylized, pleated drapery.

Group 41

Specimens: 1	Obverses: [1-1]
Die Combinations: 1	Reverses: 1

167. O17 R159

a. Gorny 76 (1996), 122 17.09 g - -

[O (a): poorly preserved. Flaws on spaces 3, 7. Curved flaw from "unit" 2 through badge to upper end of "unit" 7. In center, two flaws starting off nose, the former directed horizontally to the badge circle l., the latter towards chin.
R (a): flaw beneath I].

*** *** ***

O: As above.
R: Similar.

Group 42

Specimens: 6	Obverses: [1-1]
Die Combinations: 2	Reverses: 2

168. O30 R160

a. Hess 13 (1931), 369	16.96 g	-	-
b. Ritter L 77 (6.2006), 299; Ritter L (undated, "Ausgewählte Münzen der Antike," 2.2006?), 80; Ritter L 75 (10.2005), 441; Ritter L 74 (8.2005), 70; Ritter 72 (3.2005), 483; 71 (2.2005), 89; 70 (12.2004), 563; 69 (09.2004), 114; 65 (3.2004), 594	-	-	-
c. CNG MBS 67 (22.9.2004), 462	17.02 g	-	-
d. Winkel (21.6.1979), 1470	-	-	-

[O (a): flaws on spaces 1, 4–5. In center, flaw from upper neck through to "unit" 5. Flaw develops from *anastole* to upper head].

169. O30 R161

a. A. Page, "Collection d' un amateur parisien" (19–22.6.1933), 175	-	-	-
b. Peus 318 (1987), 1229; Kricheldorf 32 (1977), 43	17.05 g	-	-

[O (a): flaws r. and l. of "unit" 7. (b): flaws develop on spaces.
R (a): recut: l., helmet beneath monogram; r., signs of Monogram ⋈ erased. Flaw develops from upper head to eyebrows. (b): l., Monogram ΥΕ, legend erased; r., Ω erased and corrected].

*** *** ***

2.2.3.1.3 Monogram ⋈ l.

O: Similar.
R: Similar.

Group 43

Specimens: 3	Obverses: [1-1]
Die Combinations: 2	Reverses: 2

170. O30 R162

a. ANM: Thesprotia, 1992 (*CH* IX [2002], 200; Touratsoglou, *DM*, no. 7)
16.80 g 3 h -

b. Kölner Münzkabinett 38 (1985), 55 (17.08 g); Kricheldorf 9 (1961), 196 (17.075 g)
17.075 g - -

[O (a–b): flaws on spaces 1, 4–5 and from nose to lower badge edge develop. Horizontal flaw on upper hair lock.
R (a–b): l., expansion of angular flaw off monogram to Y. Off-center].

171. O30 R163

a. Dorotheum (26.5.2014), 62; Dorotheum (20.11.2013), 23; Dorotheum (22.5.2013), 67
16.24 g - -

*** *** ***

2.2.3.1.4 Monogram [monogram] l.

O: Two concentric circles on edge, six-rayed stars. Head small, horns diverge. Long *anastole*, hair flows downwards. *Pedum* dotted, close to inner badge circle. Curve between lower drapery and lower badge circle.
R: Athena short, stylized; long, stylized shawl pleats, with few folds. Shield large, decorated with *aegis*.

GROUP 44

Specimens: 2	Obverses: [2-1]
Die Combinations: 2	Reverses: 2

172. O30 R164

a. Antiquarius 29 (3.1993), 8 - - -

173. O33 R165 O: Face small. R: Legend characters smaller.

a. Kress 157 (1973), 272; Kress 137 (1966), 174 16.10 g - -

[Off-center: in exergue, r. foot beyond flan; in field r., monogram erasure].

This issue with significantly smaller modules and designs also belongs to the first period of the Pan head tetradrachms, as is suggested by the crude shape of the head and by the elliptic star/crescents. Even if the downward-pointing, flame-like hair locks on the small heads diverge from the linear hair of the first period, the drapery is curved and the *pedum* is very thin and close to the head, alongside the main inner badge circle. The transition from the eight-rayed to the six-rayed stars is also observed among specimens 167–169 and 170. These elements, and the taller figures of Athena and the style of the legend letters, suggest that these groups belong to the first period of Antigonid coin production. The engravers have succeeded in fitting the designs into considerably smaller modules, in contrast to the posthumous Alexanders, which are generally off-center (cf. above). Moreover, the reverse die of no. 168, with monogram [monogram], has been recut on a die with a Makedonian helmet l. and with Monogram [monogram] r. This places the issues with the helmet symbol before or, at least, alongside those with a monogram left in the reverse field. Finally, the obverse link between nos. 114 and 167–169, in addition to the progression of the die flaw across the *anastole* on the latter, from the upper head to the eyebrow, establish further the chronological closeness of the two issues.

In the absence of firm hoard evidence, R. W. Mathisen assigns the "Monogram l." Pans, which carry no helmet but a monogram to the left of the reverse field, to the beginning of the new type. He also explains the absence of the helmet symbol from this variety by the preoccupation of the mint official concerned with the Helmet Alexanders.[23] This suggestion presumably originates partly from his conviction that the posthumous Alexanders ceased when Gonatas' new types commenced and partly from his assumption that larger modules were eventually preferred at Amphipolis. However, as is argued elsewhere, the continuation of the Alexander types parallel to the new coinage is not impossible (see Chapters 6.2.4, 6.4.1, 6.5). Furthermore, the die study of the first period of the Pans reveals the random choice of smaller and larger flans. A preference for smaller flans for special issues, such as the *desmos* variety, may be assumed instead. Finally, the recut reverse and the obverse link between the "monogram" and the helmet issue conclusively place the "monogram" variety within or parallel to the helmet series of the Pans. The absence of the helmet symbol from this variety, its crude execution and the small flans may therefore be interpreted instead as derived from the special Athena right, *desmos* series, with which it might be regarded as contemporary.

*** *** ***

2.2.3.2 Athena r.

2.2.3.2.1 *Desmos* l.

Desmos l.—Monogram* [monogram] *r.[24]

O: Eight-rayed stars; crescents nearly semi-circular. Head diademed, *pedum* held upwards, *nebris* ties upon l. end. Two concentric circles on edge; each star bordered by two crescents.

R: ΒΑΣΙΛΕΩΣ r., ΑΝΤΙΓΟΝΟΥ l. Athena without *aegis* r., carrying thunderbolt with her uplifted r. hand and shield with her l. hand.

Group 45

Specimens: 1	Obverses: [1-1]
Die Combinations: 1	Reverses: 1

174. O27 R166

a. Florence: Svoronos, *Athènes*, pl. 21.23 16.70 g - -

[O (a): very worn, attempted piercing up r. on internal badge. Vertical flaw along hair; second flaw, from knob of drapery through to "unit" 5; third, vertically from r. end of "unit" 5 through to lower border; horizontal flaw between "unit" 5 to external badge circle.
R (a): l., flaw between O and Y].

*** *** ***

23. Mathisen, *Silver Coinages*, 111, n. 48–49.

24. An engraving of a coin with the *desmos* symbol and with monogram [monogram] on the reverse is mentioned in Gréau (1867), pl. II.1229; W. Froehmer, *Choix de monnaies anciennes* (1869), pl. IV.28.

O: Similar.
R: Similar, *desmos* smaller.

Group 46

Specimens: 4	Obverses: [1-1]
Die Combinations: 2	Reverses: 2

175. O32 R167

a. Leiden 3158 16.93 g 1 h -
b. Berlin, Imhoof-Blumer (1900); Hoffmann (11–15.11.1867), Gréau (1867), no. 1229; rev. in Gaebler, *AMNG* III.2, pl. 34.2 16.66 g 9 h -

[O (a–b): developing flaw on space 7; die breaks: across "unit" 1; between "unit" 1 and upper badge edge; from l. end of neck downwards, through to upper "unit" 4].

176. O32 R168

a. Hess-Dietrich (1988), 38 16.23 g - -
b. Rauch 89 (05.12.201), 1103 16.98 g - -

[O (a): r., flaws from "unit" 2 to badge border and from "unit" 1 through to upper head; in badge, flaws off nose].

*** *** ***

Desmos l.—Monogram r.

O: Similar.
R: Similar, *desmos* smaller.

Group 47

Specimens: 4	Obverses: 3
Die Combinations: 3	Reverses: 1

177. O34 R169

a. ANS 1944.100.13835 16.29 g 12 h -

[O (a): flaw between "unit" 2 and external badge circle; also, from nose through to "unit" 6. R (a): l., flaw between end of r. pleat and figure. The metal has been tested beneath the nose and on cheek. Rather worn].

178. O35 R169

a. Sternberg 10 (1980), 73 17.03 g - -

[O (a): flaw between "unit" 7 and external badge circle.
R (a): l., vertical flaw down to l. pleat end].

179. O36 R169

a. BM 1981-9-15-15 (Baldwin) 16.92 g 3 h 32.0 mm
b. CNG Triton 9 (10–11.1.2006), 831; Sotheby Zürich (27–8.10.1993), 442; NFA 25 (29.11.1990), 87; R. Weimer collection 17.01 g 12 h -

[O (a): flaws on spaces 1–2, 5–7. Flaw between upper "unit" 2 through to head. (b): expansion of breaks, particularly on spaces 1 and 2; new diagonal flaw on space 3.
R (a): break on r. monogram bar].

*** *** ***

Desmos l.—Monogram [monogram] r.

O: Similar.
R: Similar, *desmos* smaller.

Group 48

Specimens: 1	Obverses: [1-1]
Die Combinations: 1	Reverses: 1

180. O35 R170

a. Unknown Findspot ("Seleucus III, Hoard), 2002: *CH* X (2010), 272; A. Houghton—C. Lorber—O. Hoover, *SC* II.2, 142–150, Lot E, photos 742–3; A. Weil (17.5.2006), 22
17.11 g 12 h -

[R (a): in field r., incomplete control mark].

*** *** ***

Desmos l.—Monogram [monogram] r.

O: Similar, "units" 4 and 5 closer. Off-center.
R: ΒΑΣΙΛΕΩΣ l., ΑΝ–ΤΙΓΟΝΟΥ r. Shield smaller, held upright. Athena r., without *aegis*, shawl binds round chest and folds round arms. Dotted border.

Group 49

Specimens: 8	Obverses: [1-1]
Die Combinations: 1	Reverses: 1

181. O36 R171

a. Paris: BNF 1381A; Peus 321 (1988), 150 (16.97 g); Peus 316 (1986), 174 (16.98 g)	16.81 g	1 h	-
b. Oxford: *SNG Ashmolean* 3257	17.14 g	12 h	30 mm
c. Leiden 3157	17.11 g	12 h	-
d. *SNG Cop* 1198	17.04 g	12 h	-
e. North of Larissa, 1985: *CH* VIII (1994), 517, pl. XXXIII.26	-	-	-
f. Rauch 70.1 (14.11.2002), 57	17.05 g	-	-
g. Berlin; Löbbecke (1906)	16.73 g	12 h	-
h. Sambon FPL (1903), 232; Sambon (27–28.3.1899), 350, pl. 2.10	-	-	-

[O (a): vertical flaw on upper head of Pan].

This issue displays an important typological divergence in depicting Athena to the right. The flans are small and the artistic quality high. The control marks are different. Turning to hoards, Commerce, "Seleucus III," 2002 and North of Larissa, 1985 are too late to determine the launching date of these specimens. If Pan's features echo the age of the issuing authority, then the young Pan on obverse dies 27, 32, and 34–36 might tally with the first period of coin production, while the diademed head of Pan with mature features may belong to the third (see Chapter 4.1.2, specimens 127–131). The Makedonian shield on the obverse is more skillfully rendered, with eight-rayed stars weakly punched on the metal. The border ends in two concentric circles, and the shield is off-center. The Athena right is stylistically similar to (but more natural than), that on the early tetradrachms of Ptolemy I with the legend ΑΛΕΞΑΝΔΡΕΙΟΝ ΠΤΟΛΕΜΑΙΟΥ/ΑΛΕΞΑΝΔΡΕΙΟΝ/ΑΛΕΞΑΝΔΡΟΥ, dated to c. 314 BC.[25] Neither she nor her shield carries an *aegis*, and the gorgoneion badge on her shield on the reverse has been replaced by the head of Pan. Athena's shield breaks the legend r. on the reverse: ΑΝ–ΤΙΓΟΝΟΥ. A *desmos* on the left is combined with monograms ᛞ and ΜΡ, unknown from the main Helmet series.

The first die combination is obverse linked to the early issues of the helmet group, carrying monogram ᛞ. Most specimens are below 17.00 g, and there is great variation in the die axes.

The relationship of these coins to the main Pan/Athena left series has been the subject of considerable debate. Their careful execution suggested either an early date or a new mint, in or outside Makedonia. Their rarity and high artistic quality led F. Imhoof-Blumer to assume that they were earlier than those with Athena left and were struck immediately after the battle of Lysimacheia.[26] His view was supported by H. Gaebler, on the grounds of: (a) their thematic similarity to the bronze issues of king Antigonos Gonatas, with Athena/Pan with trophy, and (b) the substitution of the gorgoneion on Athena's shield by a head of Pan, which he relates to the alleged epiphany of the god at Lysimacheia.

Radically departing from the generally accepted Makedonian provenance of this issue, Merker suggested in 1960 a later date of production at a non-Makedonian mint. He believed that they were minted at Athens during its siege and occupation by Gonatas.[27] He noted that the obverse link between the helmet, Athena left series, and coin no. 174 in our catalogue, and the flans of the latter, proved that the Athena right is not earlier than the Athena left variety. Secondly, he pointed out that Athena right is not a mirror image of Athena left Finally, taking the crested helmet symbol to denote the main Makedonian mint and the monograms as the signatures of the die cutters in charge, he reverted to the identification by J. P. Six of the symbol on the left reverse field of the coin, then identified the *kalathos* (here *desmos*) symbol as a sign of the mint of Athens. He concluded that the *kalathos,* Athena right issue was struck for the payment of the Antigonid troops at the end of the Chremonidean War at Athens and interpreted the obverse link between coin no. 174 and the helmet group as a die transfer to the new mint (cf. Chapter 6.5).

Recent discussion, however, reassigns this variety to Makedonia. Boehringer, followed by Touratsoglou,[28] allocated it to the beginning of the main Makedonian mint, along with all the coins

25. Hazzard, *Ptolemaic Coins*, 23–24, 72–73; cf. O. Masson, "Numismatique chypriote," *RN* 33 (1991), 69–70; Mørkholm, *EHC*, 64, no. 92; cf. S. Psoma, "Alexanders after Alexander: the epigraphic evidence," in S. Kremydi and M. C. Marcellesi, *Alexanders after Alexander*, forthcoming.

26. Imhoof-Blumer, *MG*, 129.

27. This suggestion has been put forward by J. P. Six and by W. W. Tarn. The dates proposed by Six for this variety, 266–255 BC, are those accepted at the time for Gonatas' siege of Athens: J. P. Six, "Tetrachma Antigoneia," *Annuaire de numismatique* 6 (1882), 29–30; C. T. Seltman, "A Synopsis of the Coins of Antigonus I and Demetrius Poliorcetes," *NC* 9 (1909), 268; Tarn, *AG*, 174, n. 20, Merker, *Silver Coinage*, 48–49.

28. Touratsoglou, *DM*, table III, n. 1.

carrying rare symbols and monograms. Yet Boehringer finds it difficult to explain the transition from the diademed head of Pan with the personal features of Antigonos Gonatas to the undiademed head of Pan in the Athena left issue.[29] Mathisen, on the other hand, interprets the obverse link between the Helmet and the Athena right groups as a die transfer to a different Makedonian mint. On the basis of the reversed legend order on the reverses of both these specimens and the transitional posthumous Alexanders, he assumes that the Athena right variety was struck at Pella, alongside the transitional Antigonid silver Alexanders and the Monogram Group of posthumous Alexanders.

The internal evidence favors the assignation of the Athena right series to the main Makedonian mint. In the first place, there is no reason not to assign the transitional posthumous Alexanders to the main Makedonian mint. Legends had been reversed simultaneously at both mints in 291 BC, under Demetrios Poliorketes (Chapter 2.2.1, 6.5). Moreover, the impression given by the paucity of the Athena right coins, their careful execution, their absence from hoards, and the large and skillfully rendered legend letters, is that of a small special issue, with a limited circulation. The exclusive symbols and control marks of this series distinguish it from the Makedonian posthumous Alexanders and from the Pans with Athena left. However, the obverse link with the Athena left variety and the representation of an Athena left with an *aegis* on no. 128 from Period III establish a connection between the two individual Antigonid types (cf. Chapter 5.1). The obverse link with Athena left, in particular, associates the Athena right variety with the main Makedonian mint, Amphipolis. As the changes in the size of the modules have been argued not to determine the chronology of the posthumous Alexanders from Amphipolis,[30] so the small modules of the Athena right, *desmos* variety are not incompatible with a later date.

Since the introduction of Gonatas' individual coinage has been disconnected from the battle of Lysimacheia (Chapter 6.4.2), the replacement of the gorgoneion by the head of Pan on Athena's shield on the reverse and the stylistic similarity of Athena on the reverse with that on the early Ptolemaic tetradrachms require explanation. The thematic and stylistic similarity of Athena to that on the Ptolemaic tetradrachms, alongside the revival of the legends regarding Pan's critical roles in battles might identify the Athena right series as celebratory, declaring the renewal of Antigonid political claims in the Aegean against the Ptolemies. The capitulation of Athens and either of Gonatas' naval victories over the Ptolemies, off Kos and off Andros, would have offered opportune moments for striking celebratory issues. Gonatas' victory off Kos may be reflected in the ἰσοθέους τιμὰς paid to the Makedonian king by the demes of Kos, Ios and Rhamnous in the mid-250s.[31] In view, as well, of the consistent demonstration of power on the part of the Ptolemies, in the form of honorary coin issues or of penteteric processions,[32] Gonatas may have launched celebratory coin issues in gold and silver, in order to exploit this major naval victory, to reinforce his claims in the Aegean, and to gain the trust of the Greek states.

*** *** ***

29. Boehringer, *Chronologie*, 100, n. 9. Boehringer questions the existence of the coin "from Florence," mentioned by Svoronos. He suspects that it is a combination of casts from different coins, the obverse coming from a coin from Athens, of which a plaster cast survives in the cast collection from the Academy in Berlin (with code number: Athen no. 1620a), and the reverse coming from a specimen from Berlin, no. 176b in our catalogue.

I have not been able to study the specimens from the Florentine coin collection. The reverse of the coin mentioned by Svoronos is indeed identical to that illustrated in Gaebler, *AMNG* III.2, pl. 34.2, but no. 1620a from Athens is a completely different specimen. Moreover, the obverse of 105a, from Athens (Iliou Melathron Exh. I, 6 no 125 1898/99 Z, 2, room 3: "Names"), is better preserved than its Florentine counterpart, with which it is obverse linked. I am therefore hesitant to deny at present the existence of this coin.

30. Chapter 2.4, *contra* Mathisen, *Silver Coinages*, 80–81.

31. See Chapter 6.4.2.

32. See Chapters 6.4.2, 7.

2.2.4. FRACTIONAL DENOMINATIONS
SILVER DRACHMAE

2.2.4.1. ATHENA L.

Crested Helmet l.—Monogram* ꟼ *r.

O: Similar.
R: Athena with large, oval-shaped shield, decorated with *aegis*. In field r., A with curved diagonal hastae and without horizontal bar.

GROUP 50

Specimens: 1	Obverses: 1
Die Combinations: 1	Reverses: 1

182. O1 R1

a. BM, "W. Keady" 1886-11-11-1	4.02 g	1 h	19 mm

3.0
Period II:
From the Revolt of Alexander, Tyrant of Korinth, to the Battle of Andros (252/1–246 BC)

"Dramatic Style"

The second, rather small, distinct coin category consists exclusively of Pan head tetradrachms. The flans are remarkably large, and large heads, in high relief, occupy the central badge. Dramatic and dynamic profiles are drawn in energetic contrapuntal curves and are enhanced by the contrasts between light and shadow. The hair locks are tousled and rendered in full movement, the fleshy lips are somewhat parted and the eye bulges. The hair locks are stylistically reminiscent of the Hellenistic baroque style, as known from the head of the dying Gaul or from the figures of the Pergamene altar. Little space is left for the linear and upright *pedum*, which develops alongside the inner badge circle. The short and thick neck ends in a very small piece of drapery rendered in a curved line. Eight-rayed stars, rendered in high relief and confined by two-crescent units each, decorate the shield that frames the head. The figure of Athena on the reverse is taller but much less skillfully rendered. She holds a large, oval, three-dimensional shield in front of her chest and a smaller, stylized thunderbolt with her uplifted right hand. The impression of movement is more effectively given through the folds of the *chiton*, which depart from the strict forms of the previous period. A helmet with a conical bowl, a thin crest and small cheek pieces occupies the left reverse field. Large angular legend letters with splayed sigmas are also normal in the legends of this period.

The weights of most of these tetradrachms range between 16.96 g and 17.05 g (Fig. 3.1). No fractional denominations survive from this period. All coins come from unhinged dies, as is normal at the main Makedonian mint.

Twenty-nine coins from this period come from securely dated hoards, as analyzed below (Fig. 3.2). Most are too late to be of much use for dating purposes, but "Pherai," 1937–1938, Eretria, 1937 and Karditsa, 1929, are significant. Their respective burial dates of c. 250–245 BC, soon after 245 BC and 245–240 BC tally with a tentative date of this period around c. 252–246 BC. They fail, however, to establish firmly its beginning.

Only two of the recorded specimens are pierced (nos. 8a, 54a) and two are broken (12a, 53a). The surface of the metal flans is in some cases rough (nos. 12a–13a, 34a, 73–5), culminating in no. 61a, in which the metal is deformed. The same obverse is frequently combined with reverses carrying various monograms and letters. This suggests the independent cooperation of various mint officials with the principal moneyer for an urgent issue, such as that required by the military and political circumstances around the 250s.

Table 3.1. Period II: Weights of Pan head tetradrachms

Weight (g)	1	2	3	4	5	6	7	8	9	10	11	12	13	14	15	16	17	18	19	20	21	22	23	All Tetradrachms
17.3–17.26				1																				1
17.25–17.21																						1		1
17.2–17.16		2															2	1						5
17.15–17.11	1	1		1	1				2		2			1	1			1	1			1		13
17.1–17.06		2		2	1	1			1		1	1	2	2	1				3				1	18
17.05–17.01	1	3		1	1	2					2	1			1		5					1		18
17.0–16.96		2	2	1	3	2	2	1	1								1	3			1	2		21
16.95–16.91		1		2	1	2	2		1			3					1	1		1				15
16.9–16.86	1	1			2	2	1		1				1				1							10
16.85–16.81	1						1							1			2							5
16.8–16.76		2							1			1					1							5
16.75–16.71	1								1		1													3
16.7–16.66						1													1					2
16.65–16.61												1					1							2
16.6–16.56						1				1														2
16.55–16.51																					1			1
16.45–16.41				1																				1
16.40–16.36																		1						1
16.35–16.31							1															1		2
16.3–16.26																								0
16.25–16.21						2																		2
16.2–16.16									1												1			2
16.15–16.11	1																				1			2
16.10–16.06				1																				1
16.05–16.01									1															1
16.00–15.96																								
15.90–15.86																								

Table 3.1 (continued). Period II: Weights of Pan head tetradrachms

Weight (g)	1	2	3	4	5	6	7	8	9	10	11	12	13	14	15	16	17	18	19	20	21	22	23	All Tetradrachms
17.3–17.26				1																				1
15.80–15.76																								
15.75–15.71																								
15.70–15.66																	1							1
15.65–15.61																								
15.60–15.55																								
15.50–16.46																								
15.10–15.06																		1						1
14.70–14.66																		1						1
12.50–12.01											1													1
Unknown Weight		3	1	3		3	2		1	1	2	5		1	2	1	2			1	3	2		33
Broken/Pierced			1																					1
Specimens	6	17	4	13	9	16	9	1	11	2	9	12	3	5	5	1	17	9	5	2	7	8	1	172

Table 3.2. Period II: Silver specimens in hoards

No.	Hoard	Cat. No.	Group No.	Obv. No.	Monogram/Letters
1a	"Pherai," 1937–1938	26a	6	04	⋈
1b	"Pherai," 1937–1938	58a	15	03	ΕΜΡ
2a	Eretria, 1937	5b	2	02	ΗΡ
2b	Eretria, 1937	25b	6	04	⋈
3a	Karditsa (Palaiokastro), c. 1929	38c	9	09	⋈
3	Karditsa (Palaiokastro), c. 1929	73b	22	08	TI
4	Kassandreia, 1985–1987	27a	6	04	⋈
5a	Thesprotia, 1992	4a	2	01	ΗΡ
5b	Thesprotia, 1992	7a	2	02	ΗΡ
5c	Thesprotia, 1992	32a	7	05	⋈
5d	Thesprotia, 1992	34b	9	08	⋈
5e	Thesprotia, 1992	39a	9	09	⋈
5f	Thesprotia, 1992	51a	12	05	ΕΜΡ
5g	Thesprotia, 1992	64a	17	10	ΜΙ
5h–i	Thesprotia, 1992	65c–d	18	03	TI
5j	Thesprotia, 1992	67a	18	03	TI
5k	Thesprotia, 1992	71a	21	10	TI
5l	Thesprotia, 1992	74a	22	08	TI
6	Hija se Korbit, 1982	6c	2	02	ΗΡ
7a	Unknown Findspot ("Seleucus III"), 2002	6b	2	02	ΗΡ
7b	Unknown Findspot ("Seleucus III"), 2002	22b	5	06	⋈
7c	Unknown Findspot ("Seleucus III"), 2002	60a	16	03	ΕΜΡ
7d	Unknown Findspot ("Seleucus III"), 2002	68e	19	06	TI
7e	Unknown Findspot ("Seleucus III"), 2002	71c	21	10	TI
7f	Unknown Findspot ("Seleucus III"), 2002	77a	22	09	TI
8a	S. Asia Minor, 1963	42b	11	10	⋈
8b	S. Asia Minor, 1963	59a	15	03	ΕΜΡ
9	N. Syria, 1960	62a	17	10	ΜΙ
10a	Makedonia?, 1927–1928	2a	1	02	⊠
10b	Makedonia?, 1927–1928	3a	1	02	⊠
11	Mektepini, 1956	65b	18	03	TI

PERIOD II

INDIVIDUAL TYPES: SILVER
PAN HEAD TETRADRACHMS

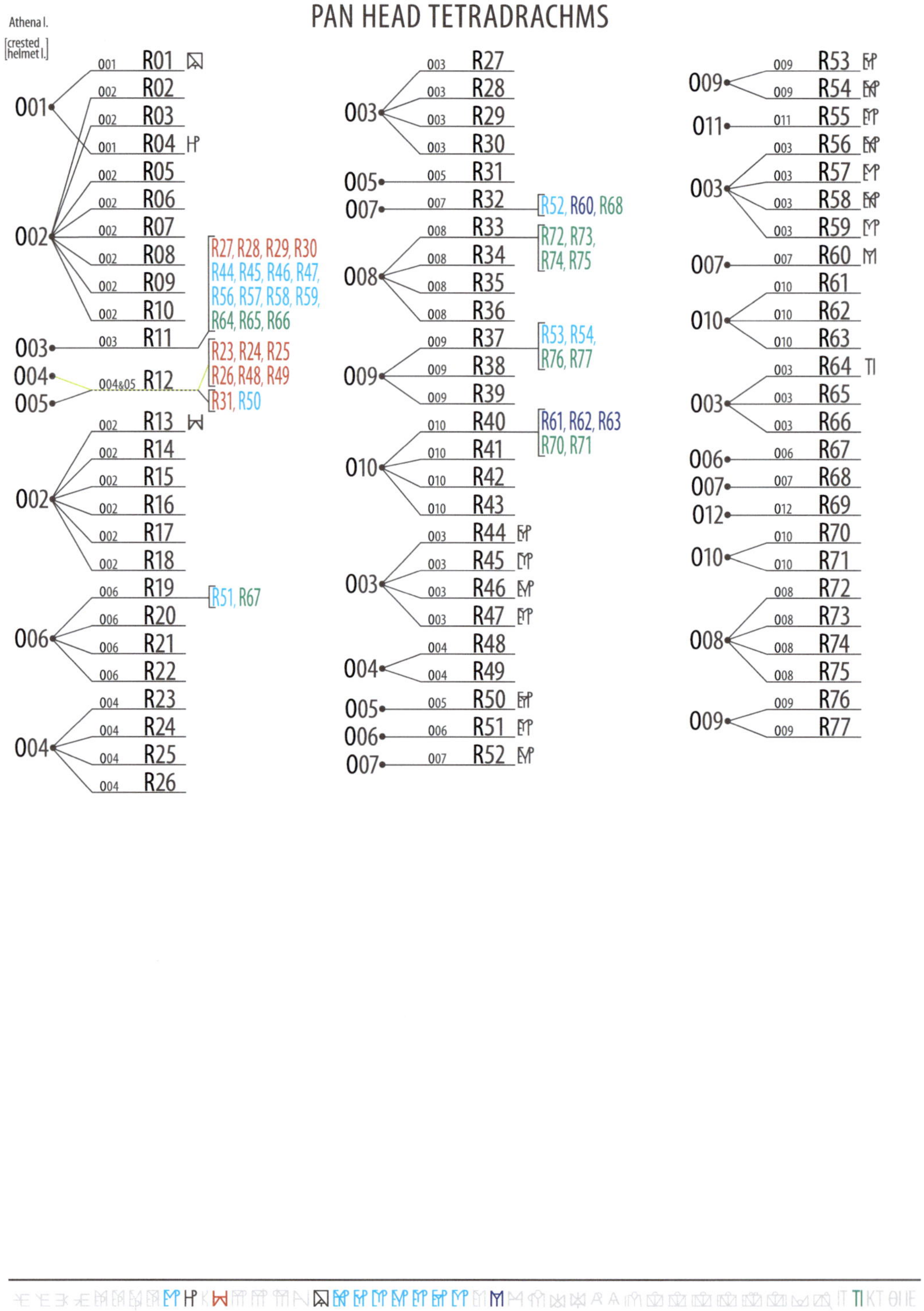

Figure 3.3. Period II: Die links of Pan head tetradrachms.

Mint A

3.1 Individual Types: Pan Head Tetradrachms

Crested Helmet l.—Monogram [monogram] r.

O: Makedonian shield with large, relief, eight-rayed star/crescents. Face with fleshy, rounded forms and wide open eyes, surrounded by hair flowing in full and various curvilinear movement from the crown of the head and hanging from the nape of the short, thick neck. Drapery small, ending in curve. *Pedum* small, upright.
R: Athena taller, chiton folds more energetic, characters smaller. Shawl pleats shorter.

Group 1

Specimens: 6	Obverses: 2
Die Combinations: 3	Reverses: 3

1. O01 R01

a. SKA Monetarium 57 (Spring 1992), 58; Superior (1988), 1482
16.85 g - -

b. Superior, Chicago International Coin Fair (1980), 2114
16.11 g - -

O: Badge larger, head tends to fill badge. Hair in tousled locks, rich in movement and contrast, flowing from crown of head to nape in two rows. Lips somewhat parted, eye open wide; two-fold drapery, *pedum* dotted and more elaborate.
R: Similar.

2. O02 R02

a. ANS 1944.100.13849 (1928/81): Makedonia? 1927–1928 (*IGCH* 469) (on file at ANS)
16.87 g 11 h -

b. Ciani-Vinchon (6–8.2.1956), 349 17.12 g - -

c. Vigne (2.1990), 18; MMAG 18 (1989), 618; Kricheldorf 21 (1970), 63 (17.03 g); Ars Classica 15 (1930), Woodward 527 17.04 g - -

[O (a): slight development of existing flaw, new flaw on space 2; worn on "unit" 4 and on badge circles. (c): development of flaws on space 2, on "units" 6–7, on space 6 and on the corresponding badge area.
R (c): l., signs of Σ beneath legend letters: overstrike].

3. O02 R03 O: Similar. R: Similar.

a. Makedonia? 1927–1928 (*IGCH* 469); Ponterio 134 (22–23.4.2005), 1381; CNG 67 (22.9.2004), 464 (16.72 g) (assigned to *IGCH* 469 in note in CNG)
16.71 g - -

The six specimens from this group come from two obverse die combinations, combining two different pairs of dies.

*** *** ***

***Crested Helmet l.—Monogram* HP r.**

O: Similar.
R: Similar.

Group 2

Specimens: 17 Obverses: [2-2]
Die Combinations: 7 Reverses: 7

4. O01 R04 O: Field flatter. Head large, in relief.

a. ANM: Thesprotia, 1992 (Touratsoglou, *DM*, no. 19)
17.01 g 11 h -

[R (a): module larger. Helmet, legend letters, Athena larger].

5. O02 R05 O: Similar. R: Shield flatter. Horizontal bar of A very small.

a. Berlin, old collection 17.09 g 9 h -
b. ANM: Eretria, 1937 (*IGCH* 175, no. 15) 17.005 g 5:30 h 31.5 mm

[O (a): die ready to break on badge circles off "unit" 7. Beginning of flaw on space 1. Horizontal flaw between "units" 3 and 4.
R (a): well preserved. In field r., beginning of flaw on lower horizontal bar of first Σ].

6. O02 R06 R: Helmet with small bowl and short cheek flaps. A with very small vertical bar.

a. Göttingen, Inv. Orig. 1988–1989; Athena 2 (1988), 100
16.93 g 11 h -
b. Unknown Findspot ("Seleucus III" Hoard), 2002: *CH* X (2010), 272; A. Houghton—C. Lorber—O. Hoover, *SC* II.2, 142–150, Lot F: "Best Coins," photos 837–838
16.98 g 1 h -
c. Hija së Korbit, 1982: *CH* VIII (1994), 299 (Shpresa Gjongecaj, "Thesari i Hijes së Korbit," *Iliria* 1 (1985), 167–193, esp. 190.282, pl. 14.282)
- - -
d. MM. Feuardent, Me. F. Lair-Dubreuil, Me. H. Baudoin (20–1.3.1925), 28
- - -
e. CNG 67 (22.09.2004), 459 17.04 g - -

[O (b): die ready to break on badge circles off "unit" 7 and on nose. (c): beginning of flaw from lower end of neck to badge circles. Signs of flaw on spaces 3–4.
R (b): portion of metal flaked off l., between Y and lower field; flaw between r. end of l. pleat and figure. R., flaw off upper horizontal bar of Σ. (c): r., flaws between pleat and monogram].

7. O02 R07 R: Ends of r. pleat longer, letters more condensed. Module larger.

a. ANM: Thesprotia, 1992 (Touratsoglou, *DM*, no. 18)
17.07 g 11 h -

[O (a): development of flaw on badge circles off "unit" 7; two flaws, respectively on spaces 4 and 6.
R (a): l., flaw between r. end of pleat and figure].

8. O02 R08

a. Madrid 6020/7-8	16.80 g (p)	11 h	30 mm
b. G. Hirsch 203 (24–26.2.1999), 187	17.13 g	-	-

[O (a): flaw from tie on lower neck through badge circles to "unit" 5. Flaw on space 3.
R (a): l., diagonal flaw from l. vertical bar of second N upwards (possibly sign of overstrike)].

9. O02 R09 R: legend spread wider in field.

a. Christie's (7.9.1989), 27; Sotheby (3.5.1984), 53	17.20 g	-	-
b. Pecunem 11 (29.12.2013) 144	17.00 g	-	32 mm
c. Künker 158 (28.9.2009) 186	17.19 g -	-	

[O (a): flaw on space 3; signs of attempted piercing on space 4. Flaw off nose. Worn on cheek.
R (a): up l., signs of attempted piercing; r., diagonal flaw between monogram and figure].

10. O02 R10

a. Lepczyk 25 (1978) 17	-	-	-
b. Berk 154 (24.5.2007) 85	16.79 g	-	-
c. Roma 2 (2.11.2013) 195	16.89 g	10 h	30.0 mm

[Very bad photograph.
O (a): flaws on all spaces. Three breaks on badge circles, off space 2, off "units" 5 and 6. Flaw on badge area, off nose.
R (a): l., diagonal flaw from r. vertical bar of A downwards].

*** *** ***

O: Double dots on either side of *pedum*.
R: Helmet smaller.

Group 3

Specimens: 4	Obverses: 3
Die Combinations: 3	Reverses: 2

11. O03 R11

a. Bourgey (18–19.11.1957) 63	17.00 g	-	-
b. Feuardent (18.6.1924) 82	-	-	-

[O (a): break on badge circles (1 h). Flaws on crescents of "units" 3 and 6. "Unit" 5 struck twice.
R (a): l., diagonal flaw from legend towards extreme edge].

12. O04 R12 O: Head smaller, *pedum* larger. R: head, upper figure smaller.

a. Schlessinger (1935), 781	17.00 g	-	32 mm

[O (a): development of flaw off "units" 1 and 2. Diagonal flaw between hair and *pedum*;

second flaw between hair and "unit" 3. Also, between *nebris* tie and "unit" 4.
R (a): r., flaw between r. pleat and chiton].

13. O05 R12 O: Similar. R: Similar.

a. Malloy MBS 59 (31.01.2001), 107; Malloy MBS 16 (1980), 55 - (b) - -

[O (a): in center, flaws above head. Diagonal flaw between hair and *pedum*. Flaws on spaces 1–2 and 5 and on "unit" 6.
R (a): l., diagonal flaw across legend and on exergue. On exergue, erasure. In field r., horizontal flaw on extreme l. end.
NB: Flan deformed].

Five different obverses are combined with reverses carrying monogram ΗΡ. The very large but elaborate and emotive heads of Pan on Group 2 give way to smaller but somewhat cruder obverses on the next group. Athena and the legend letters tend to be small, in order to fit the designs into the metal flans. The crested helmet symbol is of moderate to small size with a thin crest and short cheek flaps and with the monogram engraved on the right beneath the r. shawl pleat. The specimen from Eretria, 1937 suggests 245 BC as a *terminus ante quem* for the issue of these tetradrachms (Chapter 6.3).

*** *** ***

Crested Helmet l.—Monogram ⋈ r.

O: Similar.
R: Shield held in front of chest. Athena taller, her r. arm bent and relatively low. Legends closer to figure. Helmet beneath shawl pleats. Monogram smaller.

GROUP 4

Specimens: 13	Obverses: [1-1]
Die Combinations: 6	Reverses: 6

14. O02 R13

a. Berk 41 (1986), 103 17.15 g - -

[O (a): flaws, on space 7, from outer crescent 1 diagonally to the l.; also, on spaces 3-5. On badge, flaw from nose downwards.
R (a): l., flaw between r. helmet crest and figure].

15. O02 R14

a. J. Hirsch 30 (1911), 474 - - -

[O (a): die ready to break on badge circles off "unit" 7; flaws on spaces 4–6; "unit" 2, star 4 possibly struck twice.
R (a): l., diagonal flaw from l. helmet crest through Y to edge].

16. O02 R15

a. Lanz 117 (24.11.2003), 238; G. Hirsch 181 (22–25.2.1994), 156
16.94 g 6 h -
b. Gemini 11 (12.1.2014), 69 16.07 g 4 h -

17. O02 R16

a. NFA (12.10.1990), 625 17.00 g - -
b. G. Hirsch 175 (1992), 242 16.94 g - -

[O (a): new flaws on spaces 6–7. On badge, new flaw from nose to circles l.; flaw from neck through badge circles to "unit" 5.
R (a): up, signs of flaw above head; r., flaw off Σ].

18. O02 R17

a. Kress 143 (1961), 1416 - - -

[O (a): flaw from "unit" 7 to l. horn.
R (a): two diagonal flaws, above head and on exergue].

19. O02 R18 O: Similar.

a. Cahn 60 (1928), 460; 6 (28.1.1924 Bement), 785 (17.05 g); Rollin-Feuardent (09–11.05.1910), 344 17.30 g - -
b. Meister & Sonntag 9 (26.5.2010), 55 17.03 g - -
c. Dorotheum 500 (29–30.11.2004), 59 17.06 g - -
d. NNCC 63 (18–19.4.1972), 28 - - -
e. Berk 153 (13.3.2007), 135 16.44 g - -
f. CNG Triton 13 (5.1.2010), 114 17.09 g 10 h -

[O (a): flaw between "unit" 3 and outer badge circle; also, on space 3.
Worn between "crescents" 7 and badge circles].

*** *** ***

O: Pan with neck crossed by diagonal line, longer lower locks reach the drapery; hair arranged differently.

R: Caricature-like Athena, taller, head small. Middle fall starts from high up and falls with a number of diagonal, free and rich side folds. Thinner shawl pleats. Thunderbolt diagonal, stylized. Shield in front of chest, with badge prominent. Helmet small, with thin (nearly linear) crest and crest ends at the same level as the short and thin cheek flaps.

Group 5

Specimens: 9	Obverses: 1
Die Combinations: 4	Reverses: 4

20. O06 R19 R: Athena more elaborate. Helmet with linear crest, longer than cheek flaps. Splayed Σ.

a. ANS: *SNG BYB* 352 17.08 g 9 h -

b. Glendining (3.2.1993), 36; Glendining (7.3.1957), 37
17.01 g - -
c. Pegasi 5 (4.6.2001), 103; Pegasi BBS 118 (27.3.2000), 90 (16.96 g)
16.96 g - -
d. Elsen 74 (21.6.2003), 199 17.12 g - -

[O (a): development of flaw on spaces 1 and 2; also, from nose downwards.
R (a): l., diagonal flaw from second O downwards. R., curved flaw along edge].

21. O06 R20 O: *pedum* thinner.

a. *SNG Klagenfurt* 578 (1250) 16.897 g 1 h -

[O (a): development of flaws on spaces 1, 2 and 6. On badge, horizontal break off chin].

22. O06 R21

a. Rauch 32 (1984), 150 16.92 g - -
b. Unknown Findspot ("Seleucus III" Hoard), 2002: *CH* X (2010), 272; A. Houghton—C. Lorber—O. Hoover, *SC* II.2, 142-150, Lot F: "After Cleaning," photos 979.2–980.2, 1207–1208 16.96 g 6 h -
c. G. Hirsch 261 (7.5.2009), 238 16.86 g - -

[O (a): flaws on spaces 1, 6–7.
R (a): flaws l. and r., on either side of legends].

23. O06 R22

a. Vico (10.10.2004), 87; Vico (13.06.2002), 120; Leu 79 (2000), 522 (17.02 g)
17.00 g 3h -

*** *** ***

O: Similar.
R: Similar.

GROUP 6

Specimens: 16	Obverses: [2-2]
Die Combinations: 5	Reverses: 5

24. O04 R23

a. Poindessault (29.9.1981), 4; Bourgey (21.3.1972), 30; Platt (18–19.11.1935, coll. A. Bougon), 44; Pozzi 970 16.87 g - -
b. Schulten (5–7.10.1981), 28 17.03 g - -
c. Müller 36 (1982), 71 17.00 g - -
d. Pegasi BBS 106 (16.3.1998), 33 16.92 g - -
e. Phillips 312 (3.2005), 18 - - -

[O (a–b): developing diagonal flaw on space 7. (c): flaw between horns and upper badge circles; diagonal flaw between chin and lower badge circle.
R (c): l., diagonal flaw between legend and coin edge. Not cleaned].

25. O04 R24

a. Henzen L 160 (21.7.2005), 105 16.21 g - -
b. ANM: Eretria, 1937 (*CH* IX (2002), 194; *IGCH* 175)
17.06 g 7h -
c. CNG E-auction 326 (07.02.2014), 70 (Demetrios Armounta Collection)
16.59 g 11 h 32 mm

26. O04 R25

a. "Pherai," 1937–1938: T. R. Martin, "A Third-Century B.C. Hoard from Thessaly at the ANS (*IGCH* 168)," *ANSMN* 26 (1981), 64, pl. 13.533; *IGCH* 168
16.69 g 9 h -
b. CNG 320 (12.2.2014), 64 16.95 g 1 h 31 mm
c. St. Lowis (1.8.1979), 2402 - - -

27. O04 R26

a. Kassandreia, 1985–1957: *CH* VIII (1994), 322, pl. 39.5
- - -
b. G. Hirsch L1 (1.1987), 34 17.02 g - -
c. G. Henzen L 164 (10.2005), 111; G. Henzen L 160 (21.6.2005), 105
16.21 g - -

[O (a): diagonal flaw develops alongside horns.
NB: very bad photograph].

28. O03 R27

a. G. Hirsch 60 (1968), 86; P. G. Hirsch Miscellaneous Sales 21 (5.6.1935), 114; Helbing FPC 16 (1934), 222; Helbing 70 (9.12.1932), 592 17.00 g - 32 mm
b. Stack's (11.1.2010), 102 (Clinton Sherwood Ward collection; purchased privately from W. Donner, New York) 16.87 g - -

[O (a): development of flaw on space 1; new flaw on space 2 and on badge, from off chin towards lower badge circles and up r., above hair.
R (a): flaws on extreme l. end and beneath legend. Diagonal flaw between I and l. pleat. In field r., diagonal flaw from *aegis* to r. pleat].

*** *** ***

O: As above.
R: Similar.

Group 7

Specimens: 9 Obverses: [2-2]
Die Combinations: 4 Reverses: 4

29. O03 R28

a. Müller 38 (1982), 52 16.90 g - -
b. Platt (27.06.1925), 111 17.00 g - -

[O (a): flaw between "unit" 6 and edge and on space 6; also, from chin downwards to inner badge circle.
R (a): r., flaw between edge and legend].

30. O03 R29 R: legend letters smaller.

a. Madrid	16.98 g	8 h	-
b. DNW (14.3.2007), 147	16.34 g	3 h	-
c. Spink-Taisei 7 (2.7.1989), 172	16.94 g	-	-

[O (a): flaw on space 3 and on upper l. badge circles.
R (a): l., diagonal flaw l. of Athena's face; r., flaw across B.
NB: very bad photograph].

31. O03 R30

a. Berk 69 (1992), 74	-	-	-

[O (a): flaw on space 3 and off "unit" 7. On badge, flaw beneath chin.
R (a): flaws on outer side of both legends].

32. O05 R31

a. ANM: Thesprotia, 1992 (Touratsoglou, *DM*, no. 36)	16.85 g	1 h	-
b. G. Blançon L 10 (1991), 60	-	-	-
c. Negrini 23 (8.6.2006), 283	16.94 g	-	-

[O (a): not cleaned.
R (a): distance between l. pleat end and helmet smaller].

*** *** ***

O: Similar.
R: Similar. In field r., large and irregular legend characters become progressively smaller; splayed Σ.

GROUP 8

Specimens: 1	Obverses: 1
Die Combinations: 1	Reverses: 1

33. O07 R32

a. Stack's (10-11.6.1970 Knobloch), 194	17.00 g	-	-

[O (a): diagonal flaws on spaces 2, 3, 7. Horizontal flaw on upper *pedum*.
R (a): l., die worn between legend and face].

The progression from larger to smaller heads and modules is analogous to that in Groups 2 and 3 with Monogram ꟷ, and obverse links confirm the contemporaneity of both sets of groups. The helmet symbol is characterized by a small bowl and visor, thin and medium cheek flaps and by a long and thin crest; the length of the crest is inversely proportionate to the size of the bowl. The monogram is generally small and the diagonal bars are not firmly joined with the vertical ones.

Specimen 33 from Group 8 combines a linear, thin *pedum* with a somewhat cruder Athena and with less elaborate legend letters.

*** *** ***

O: Similar.
R: Similar.

Group 9

Specimens: 11	Obverses: 2
Die Combinations: 7	Reverses: 7

34\. O08 R33

a. BNF, H. S. 440, 1972/1340-1 17.10 g 6:30 h -
b. ANM: Thesprotia, 1992 (Touratsoglou, *DM*, no. 31)
16.76 g 1 h -

[O (a): slightly chipped on edge (11:30 h). Die ready to break on badge circles off star/crescent 2. Signs of flaw between inner and outer crescent 6].

35\. O08 R34

a. Gorny 60 (1992), 130; Peus 291 (1977), 205 (16.99 g); Bourgey (6–7.5.1971), 69; Ratto (24.6.1929), 258 16.92 g - -

[O (a): flaws: on spaces 2–3, 5–6, along badge circles off space 3, between *pedum* and hair. R (a): flaws: l., (signs) between coin edge and legend; r., (vertical) between legend and edge; on exergue, beneath l. foot].

36\. O08 R35

a. Peus 332 (1991), 175 17.15 g - -

[O (a): development of the two flaws between chin and "unit" 5 and the tie of drapery and "unit" 5 respectively.
R (a): r., two flaws, from A to field r. and from lower horizontal bar of E to beneath exergue].

37\. O08 R36

a. Kurpfälzische Münzhandlung 68 (8.6.2005), 22
16.20 g - -

[O (a): die break from nose through to outer badge circle].

38\. O09 R37 O: *Pedum* shorter, not curved.

a. Vinchon (30.6.1978), 54 - - -
b. Lanz 155 (10.12.2012), 116 17.14 g - -
c. ANM: Karditsa (Palaiokastro), 1929: *CH* IX (2002), 180, *IGCH* 162, 5
16.05 g 11 h 28 mm

[O (c): die flaw between mouth end and inner l. badge circle; also, on star-crescents 7 and 1. R (c): die flaw between shield and upper l. field; also, between l. Athena's pleat and helmet crest; also, on upper l. hasta of monogram].

39. O09 R38

a. ANM: Thesprotia, 1992 (Touratsoglou, *DM*, no. 35)

a. ANM: Thesprotia, 1992 (Touratsoglou, *DM*, no. 35)	17.00 g	1 h	-
b. CNG 264 (21.9.2011), 36	16.71 g	1 h	-

[O (a): beginning of flaw on space 2.
R (a): l., flaw from A to head].

40. O09 R39

a. G. Hirsch 242 (22–24.9.2005), 2000	16.89 g	-	-

[O (a): developing die break from nose through to outer badge circle].

*** *** ***

O: Head tends to fill most of the emblem area. Hair shape different, horns backwards. Neck ends in two-fold drapery. *Pedum* curved, developing alongside inner badge circle.
R: Similar.

Group 10

Specimens: 2	Obverses: 1
Die Combinations: 1	Reverses: 1

41. O10 R40

a. Elsen L 105 (1988), 23 (16.60 g); Elsen 8 (1987), 54 (16.60 g); Elsen MBS 7 (1987), 65	16.60 g	-	-
b. Glendining (15–17.7.1929), 293; Glendining (1–2.12.1927 C. W. Moss), 293	-	-	-

[O (a): diagonal flaw up, on badge circles. (b): flan larger. Diagonal flaw on space 1, between badge circles (12-1 h); also on internal badge circle, off "unit" 6.
R (b): flaw up, from l. *hasta* of A to above head; also, across T].

*** *** ***

O: Pan with tumbled hair locks flowing from the crown and hanging from the nape of the long, strong neck. Neck thicker, with diagonal veins. *Pedum* upright, with knobs around main area.
R: Helmet short and stylized, with medium crest very close to main bowl and at the same level as the cheek pieces, very close to l. pleat. Small head. The last three legend letters in ΒΑΣΙΛΕΩΣ progressively smaller. Monogram small, relatively high in field.

Group 11

Specimens: 9	Obverses: [1-1]
Die Combinations: 3	Reverses: 3

42. O10 R41

a. ANS 1954.203.91; Weber, 2193	17.12 g	3 h	-

b. S. Asia Minor, 1963: *IGCH* 1426 (Boehringer, *Chronologie*, 156, pl. 26.23)
\- - -
c. Gorny & Mosch 121 (10.03.2003), 98 17.11 g - -

43. O10 R42 R: helmet bowl shorter. Legend characters crude.

a. CNA 7 (4.5.1989), 56 17.05 g - -
b. Aurea Numismatika 14 (3.12.05), 157; Aurea Numismatika 10-11 (15.5.2004), 155; Lanz 14 (1978), 60 17.01 g - -
c. ANM: *SNG Saroglos* 924 12.14 g 3 h -

[O (a): horizontal flaw on spaces 1-2.
R (a): l., flaw beneath foot].

44. O10 R43

a. Sternberg 11 (1981), 82 17.07 g - -
b. Künker 93 (1991), 7; Künker 86 (1989), 161; Künker 71(1986), 286
16.73 g - -
c. Kress 138 (1967), 299a; Naville I (1921, Pozzi), 2934
\- - -

[R (a): legend letters elaborate, with serifs, close to each other; flaw between upper angles of N and shield].

In the second part of the coins signed with monogram [monogram], the heads of Pan are larger and spread through the badge of the shield, pushing the large star/crescents out of the flans. The muscles of the neck are emphasized, and the neck tends to be longer in the last issues. The *pedum* is also schematic, with a curved line developing alongside the inner badge circle.

*** *** ***

Crested Helmet l.—Monograms* [monogram], [monogram], [monogram], [monogram], [monogram] *r.

O: As above.
R: Similar.

Group 12

Specimens: 12 Obverses: [3-3]
Die Combinations: 7 Reverses: 7

45. O03 R44 Monogram [monogram] r.

a. G. Hirsch 15 (1977), 15; G. Hirsch 12 (1957), 86
\- - -

46. O03 R45 Monogram [monogram] r.

a. G. Hirsch 182 (1994), 143; G. Hirsch 179 (1993), 277
16.94 g - -
b. Piollet-Sabatier (21.2.1980), 5; Anaf (24.11.1978), 110 (16.82 g)
16.80 g - -

47. O03 R46 Monogram ΕΥΡ r.

a. Hamburger 7 (1933), 525; Naville 10 (15.6.1925), 453
17.07 g - -

48. O03 R47 Monogram ΕΥΡ r.

a. Cederlind L 102 (Fall 1995), 1182 - - -
b. Barré (1975), 10 - - -
c. CNG 308 (7.8.2013), 62 17.06 g 7 h -

49. O04 R48 Monogram ΕΥΡ r.

a. CNG MBS 67 (22.9.2004), 463 17.04 g - -

50. O04 R49 Monogram ΕΥΡ r.

a. Plumier L 3 (6.1979), 28 - - -

51. O05 R50 Monogram ΕΥΡ r.

a. ANM: Thesprotia, 1992 (Touratsoglou, *DM*, no. 51)
16.61 g 9 h -
b. Elsen L 40 (1982), 12; Elsen L 29 (1981), 6; Peus 299 (1980), 139 (16.94 g)
16.93 g - -
c. Elsen 57 (1999), 1310; Elsen L 68 (1984), 12 16.91 g - -

*** *** ***

O: As above.
R: Similar.

Group 13

Specimens: 3 Obverses: [2-2]
Die Combinations: 2 Reverses: 2

52. O06 R51 Monogram ΕΥΡ r.

a. Pegasi 104 (11.11.1997), 84; Sotheby (7.3.1996), 88 (17.09 g)
17. 07 g - -

[O (a): two horizontal flaws, on spaces 1 and 7. Dot on space 3.
R (a): l., horizontal flaws above head].

53. O07 R52 Monogram ΕΥΡ r.

a. Rauch MBS 7 (23.1.2004), 970; Rauch MBS 6 (4.10.2002), 59
17.08 g - -
b. G. Hirsch 264 (25.11.2009), 222 16.86 g - -

*** *** ***

O: As above.
R: Similar.

Group 14

Specimens: 5 Obverses: [2-1]
Die Combinations: 3 Reverses: 3

54. O09 R53 Monogram [monogram] r.

a. Stuttgart (old coll.)	16.85 g (p)	12 h	-
b. Leiden 3156	17.11 g	5 h	-
c. Gorny & Mosch 122 (10–11.3.2003), 1260	17.08 g	-	-

55. O09 R54 Monogram [monogram] r.

a. Pegasi 100 (17.02.1997), 87; Cummings Summer (1996), G57	-	-	-

56. O11 R55 Monogram [monogram] r.

a. Gorny & Mosch 146 (6.3.2006), 178	17.08 g	-	-

*** *** ***

Crested Helmet l.—Monograms [monogram], [monogram] r.

O: Similar.
R: Similar.

Group 15

Specimens: 5 Obverses: [1-1]
Die Combinations: 3 Reverses: 3

57. O03 R56 Monogram [monogram] r.

a. Kölner Münzkabinett 61 (1994), 80; Thirion L (Autumn 1992), 9 (17.07 g)	17.05 g	-	-
b. Grunow L 41 (Summer 1996), 290	17.10 g	-	-
c. PMV, Inc., 15 (7.1984), 35	-	-	-

[O (a): cheek scratched; also, flaw from end of drapery downwards. Flaws on spaces 2, 6 and 7.
R (a): flaw above shield].

58. O03 R57 Monogram [monogram] r.

a. ANS: "Pherai," 1937–1938 (T. R. Martin, "A Third-Century B.C. Hoard from Thessaly at the ANS (*IGCH* 168)," *ANSMN* 26 (1981), 64, pl. 14, 536); E. T. Newell collection	17.12 g	5 h	-

[O (a): flaws on spaces 1, 2 and 7.
R (a): flaws l. and r., between legend and coin edge. Diagonal flaw between monogram and Σ].

59. O03 R58 Monogram r.

a. Cederlind L 83 (Winter 1989), 44; S. Asia Minor, 1963: *IGCH* 1426 (Boehringer, *Chronologie*, 156, pl. 26.24) - - -

[O (a): flaws on spaces 2–3, 6–7. Also vertically, from lower chin to inner badge circle. R (a): l., flaw between upper edge and A and beneath Y. In field r., signs of overstrike: anchor].

*** *** ***

Crested Helmet l.—Monogram r.

O: (Star/crescents) similar, head smaller.
R: Similar.

GROUP 16

Specimens: 1	Obverses: [1-1]
Die Combinations: 1	Reverses: 1

60. O03 R59 Monogram r.

a. Unknown Findspot ("Seleucus III" Hoard), 2002: *CH* X (1910), 272; A. Houghton—C. Lorber—O. Hoover, *SC* II.2, 142–150, Lot B, photo 165A–166A - - -

*** *** ***

Crested Helmet l.—Monogram r.

O: Similar.
R: Similar.

GROUP 17

Specimens: 17	Obverses: [2-2]
Die Combinations: 4	Reverses: 4

61. O07 R60 R: Similar. Athena rough, shield held in front of chest. Monogram r.

a. Berlin; Löbbecke	16.87 g	11 h	-
b. G. Hirsch 298 (7.5.2014), 209	17.16 g	-	-
c. *SNG Klagenfurt* 578a	15.70 g	10 h	-

[flan deformed.
R (a): flan curved beneath l. foot; diagonal flaw on exergue].

62. O10 R61 R: Monogram r. Monogram larger.

a. N. Syria, 1960: *IGCH* 1533 (Boehringer, *Chronologie*, 69); Coin Galleries (20.11.1975), 2031 16.98 g - -

b. Henzen L 173 (11.2006), 93; Henzen L 169 (17.7.2006), 95; Henzen L 165 (17.12.2005), 96; Henzen L 161 (19.7.2005), 91; Henzen L 157 (21.3.2005), 76; Henzen L 153 (22.10.2004), 73 17.02 g - -
c. Rauch 72 (20–21.9.2003), 175 17.17 g - -
d. ANS: SNG BYB 353 16.94 g - -
e. Pegasi 54 (7.1990), 38; Pegasi 47 (Summer 1989), 32; Pegasi 42 (12.1988), 30
- - -

[O (a): three flaws, the first behind head, the second between eye and l. border, the third on badge circles, off "unit" 6].

63. O10 R62 Monogram [monogram] r.

a. Myers & Adams 6 (1973), 100 17.02 g 10 h -

[Bad photograph.
O (a): die break off "unit" 4 and on space 4; test cuts on either side of "unit" 6].

64. O10 R63 Monogram [monogram] r.

a. ANM: Thesprotia, 1992 (Touratsoglou, *DM*, no. 50)
16.63 g 11 h -
b. Müller 20 (1977), 56 16.85 g - -
c. Poinsignon 42 (1997), 607; Poinsignon 41 (1996), 572; Poinsignon 38 (1994), 608
- - -
d. Albuquerque MBS 36 (1992), 3 17.05 g - -
e. Gorny 58 (9.4.1992), 260 17.05 g - -
f. Kress 140 (1967), 63 17.05 g - -
g. MMAG 26 (1996), 130 16.81 g - -
h. G. Hirsch 293 (25.9.2013), 2230 16.79 g - -

[O (a–d): flaws: up l., along outer badge circle; on spaces 1–2 and 2–3. (d): flaw on badge, from "unit" 7 to nose. Worn on lower r. field. (e): flaw diagonally, from 1 h through to 7 h, across hair and face. Flaw on space 6. (f): scratches on rays on "unit" 3.
R (a): r., signs of monogram erasure, signs of legend letters r. of and in field l.: overstrike. (b): r., signs of monogram [monogram]. (d): monogram struck upon letters/monogram. (e): vertical flaw/sign of tooling up to elbow].

With the exception of no. 60a, the metal flans of groups 16 and 17 are somewhat smaller and the execution of the designs is rough. The deformation of the flan of no. 61 may have been caused by a metal instrument or by the insufficient heating of the metal surface when the coin was struck.

*** *** ***

Crested helmet l.—ΤΙ *r.*

O: As above.
R: Similar.

GROUP 18

Specimens: 9	Obverses: [1-1]
Die Combinations: 3	Reverses: 3

65. O03 R64

a. Schulman 254 (1971), 3038 17.12 g - -
b. Mektepini, 1956: *IGCH* 1410 (Olcay and Seyrig, *Mektepini*, 26, no. 693) 16.95 g - -
c. ANM: Thesprotia, 1992 (Touratsoglou, *DM*, no. 8) 16.99 g 12 h -
d. ANM: Thesprotia, 1992 (Touratsoglou, *DM*, no. 14) 16.36 g 11 h -
e. Gorny & Mosch 200 (10.10.2011), 1467 14.66 g - -

[O (a): beginning of diagonal flaw from l. end of "unit" 2 to outer badge circle; signs of horizontal flaw on space 7. (b): test punch on face.
R (c): recut on r. end of l. pleat?].

66. O03 R65

a. Müller 34/5 (1981), 61 15.09 g (b) - -

[O (a): development of old flaws and of that on space 2. Horizontal and diagonal flaws respectively on spaces 4 and 6.
R (a): l., flaw between Γ and end of pleat; horizontal flaws between O and N, O and Y. Up, diagonal flaw between shield and head; r. of r. foot, above and on exergue. In field r., diagonal flaw crossing thunderbolt and B; at extreme r. end, flaw r. of E].

67. O03 R66

a. ANM: Thesprotia, 1992 (Touratsoglou, *DM*, no. 15) 16.99 g 11 h -
b. MZ 123 (8-10.9.2004), 45; Künker 59 (26–28.9.2000), 130 (17.09 g) 17.20 g - -
c. Gorny & Mosch 181 (12.10.2009), 1331 17.00 g - -

[O (a): development of flaw on space 1; flaw between "unit" 7 and outer badge circle.
R (a): r., flaw between l. end of helmet crest and chiton.]

*** *** ***

O: As above.
R: Similar.

Group 19

Specimens: 5	Obverses: [1-1]
Die Combinations: 1	Reverses: 1

68. O06 R67

a. Stack's (17–18.9.1980), 82 17.09 g - -
b. Christie's (3.1990), 48 17.10 g - -
c. Wolframm 23 (25–26.2.2005), 90 17.10 g - -
d. Rauch MBS 10 (02.3.2006), 81; Rauch MBS 9 (23.9.2005), D104; Gorny & Mosch 134 (11–12.10.2004), 1282 (17.14 g) 17.13 g - -
e. Unknown Findspot ("Seleucus III" Hoard), 2002: *CH* X (2010), 272; A. Houghton—C. Lorber—O. Hoover, *SC* II.2, 142-150, Lot F: "After Cleaning," photos 1223–1224 = 985.A–982A 16.69 g 11 h -

[Edge slightly chipped (12–3 h)].
O (a): development of flaws off *pedum* and on space 2. Flaw on chin. New flaw off nose].
R (a): l., diagonal flaw l. of legend].

*** *** ***

O: Similar.
R: Similar.

Group 20

Specimens: 2	Obverses: [2-1]
Die Combinations: 2	Reverses: 2

69. O07 R68

a. Auctiones 24 (1994), 162; MMAG L 190 (1959), 12; MMAG L 195 (11–12.1959), 354 16.94 g - -

70. O12 R69

a. Ryder (06.1982), A34; Ryder (05.1982), A05 - - -

*** *** ***

O: Shield stars similar, but head rougher.
R: Shield protects chest. Helmet bowl very small, with thin crests.

Group 21

Specimens: 7	Obverses: [1-1]
Die Combinations: 2	Reverses: 2

71. O10 R70

a. ANM: Thesprotia, 1992 (Touratsoglou, *DM*, no. 13)
16.55 g 11 h -
b. G. Hirsch 203 (24–26.2.1999), 188 16.97 g - -
c. Unknown Findspot ("Seleucus III" Hoard), 2002: *CH* X (2010), 272; A. Houghton—C. Lorber—O. Hoover, *SC* II.2, 142–150, Lot F, "Late Report of a Fragment," photos 882–883, no. 51 - - -
d. Johnson 5.12 (1986), 79 - - 31 mm

72. O10 R71

a. Rauch 6 (1971), 22; Winckel (27.11.1974), 1356
16.20 g - -
b. G. Hirsch 120 (10–12.4.1980), 76 16.14 g - -
c. L. Simonetti 9.6 (12.1972–1.1973), 61
- - -

[O (b): in field, flaw on space 7; diagonal flaw from "unit" 7 through to nose].

*** *** ***

O: Nose more curved, upper side lock, drapery, *pedum* different.
R: Head small. Legend characters compact. Shield with large rim, held diagonally. Hem ends in fine folds, middle fall shorter.

GROUP 22

Specimens: 8 Obverses: [2-2]
Die Combinations: 5 Reverses: 5

73. O08 R72

a. Berlin; Löbbecke 17.12 g 12 h -
b. ANM: Karditsa (Palaiokastro), 1929 (*IGCH* 162, no. 7)
16.32 g 12 h 33.0 mm

[R (a): open].

74. O08 R73

a. ANM: Thesprotia, 1992 (Touratsoglou, *DM*, no. 9)
17.00 g 11 h -

75. O08 R74

a. Rasmussen 349 (16–18.6.1976), 136 16.98 g - -

76. O08 R75 R: letters of varied size.

a. Stack's 101 (11.1.2010), 101 (from the Estate of C. C. Vermeule); CNG 66 MBS (19.5.2004), 263 (R. Cohen collection) (17.03 g); Stack's (07–08.03.2003), 1373; Lanz 48 (1989), 198 (17.21 g 11 h); Peus 277 (1971), 89 17.02 g - -
b. MMAG 15 (1985), 82 17.21 g - -
c. Kress 135 (1966), 165 - - -

[R (a): dot on top of A. In field l., smaller crested helmet. On exergue. R (c): "units" 1–3 struck twice].

77. O09 R76

a. Unknown Findspot ("Seleucus III" Hoard), 2002: *CH* X (2010), 272; A. Houghton—C. Lorber—O. Hoover, *SC* II.2, 142-150, Lot F, "Late Report of a Fragment," photos 882–883, no. 44 - - -

*** *** ***

O: As above.
R: Similar.

Group 23

Specimens: 1	Obverses: [1-1]
Die Combinations: 1	Reverses: 1

78. O09 R77

a. BM 1955- Baldwin 4 (3.5.1995), 47 (Baldwin) 17.07 g 11 h 35 mm

The coins with the letters TI on the right started right before the transition from wide flans with large Pan heads to the smaller flans and heads. The crude execution of the obverse of no. 76, with the letters TI r. on the reverse, might suggest the issue of all three specimens at the last stages of operation of the mint during Period II, possibly during an emergency.

4.0
Period III: From the Battle of Andros to the Death of Demetrios II (246/5–229 BC)

"Portrait Style"

The new prospects created for Makedonia on the international political scene after the recovery of the Akrokorinth, Isthmos, and Euboia culminated in Gonatas' naval victory over the Ptolemaic fleet at Andros in the same year (246/early 245 BC). In fact, 246/5 BC witnessed the accomplishment of Makedonian aims both in peninsular Greece and in the Aegean: a *status quo* favorable to Gonatas was reestablished in Greece, with firm control over Korinth, Peiraeus, Chalkis, and Demetrias. Control over these naval bases presumably paved the way to the king's naval victory at Andros, which considerably restricted Ptolemaic influence in the Aegean.[1]

The wider historical context of this battle is the Third Syrian (Laodikean) War between the new kings of the Seleukid realm and Egypt, Seleukos II and Ptolemy III, during which Gonatas favored the Seleukids while defending his possessions in the Aegean (246–241 BC).[2] Ptolemy's campaign against the Hellespont and Thrace at the outset of this war is regarded by Buraselis

1. Buraselis, *HM*, 119–151, 170–179; F. W. Walbank, "Antigonus Gonatas: The Last Years," in Hammond and Walbank, *Macedonia* III, 306; Reger, *Delos*, 18–19, 23–26, 41; Paschides, *Ποσειδώνες και Αντίγονοι*, 254–245. The date suggested by Buraselis for the battle of Andros (c. 246/5 BC) might be confirmed by the stability in the prices of pitch at Delos between 246 and 169 BC: as pitch was a Macedonian monopoly, its price would have dropped or been stable when Delos was within the Antigonid realm: G. Glotz, "L'histoire de Délos d'après les prix d'une denrée," *REG* 29 (1916), 281–325; Merker, *Studies*, 76–80; G. Reger, "The price histories of some imported goods on independent Delos," in *Économie Antique, Prix et formation des prix dans les économies antiques, Entretiens d' archéologie et d' histoire* (Saint-Bertrand-des-Comminges, 1997), 53–72 = idem, in W. Scheidel and S. von Reden, *The Ancient Economy*, Edinburgh Readings on the Ancient World, (Edinburgh: University Press, 2002), 133–154; V. Chankowski, "Délos et les matériaux stratégiques. Une nouvelle lecture de la loi délienne sur la vente du bois et du charbon (*ID*, 509)," in K. Konuk (ed.), *Stephanéphoros. De l' Économie antique à l' Asie Mineure*, Mémoires 28 (Bordeaux: Ausonius, 2012), 31–51.

2. Will, *HPMH* I^2, 24861; F. W. Walbank, "Macedonia and Greece," *CAH* VII.I^2, 239–243, 248–249; J. B. Scholten, "Macedon and the Mainland, 280–221," in Erskine, *Companion*, 134–158; Shipley, *Alexander*, 120–152; W. L. Adams, "Alexander's Successors to 221 BC," in Roisman and Worthington, *CAM*, 208–224.

as the cause of the battle at Andros between the Antigonid and the Ptolemaic fleets.[3] According to Pompeius Trogus, Antigonos as commander of the Makedonian fleet defeated the Ptolemaic general Oprona.[4]

Unlike the battle of Kos, whose result did not conclusively establish either king's sovereignty over the Aegean, the second Antigonid naval victory over the Ptolemies at Andros had a major impact. This is proved not only by the lack of any effort by the Ptolemies to regain control of the Aegean, despite the recovery of Korinth by Aratos of Sikyon in 243 BC, but also by the extensive celebrations of its outcome. These included the establishment of two vase festivals at Delos, the Soteria and the Paneia.[5] The compliance of the Makedonian cities of Amphipolis, Philippoi, Kassandreia and Pella with the king's will and their recognition of the *asylia* of the priesthood of the sanctuary of Asklepios at Kos in 243 BC might also echo a rise in the king's prestige in Makedonia, as a result of this naval victory.[6]

The loss of Korinth to Aratos in 243 BC,[7] however, rendered conflict between Aratos of Sikyon and the Makedonian king inevitable. Two opposing military blocks were thus formed in Greece as, on the one hand, Ptolemy III was appointed hegemon of the Achaian Confederacy "by land and sea,"[8] and Aratos made an alliance with Sparta,[9] while on the other, Antigonos made compacts with the Aitolians to partition Achaia and with Aitolia and Epeiros to partition Akarnania.[10]

The uncontested rise of Gonatas' son to the throne after his father's death in 240/39 BC[11] suggests that Demetrios II had already been appointed coregent, following the example of Monophthalmos and Poliorketes.[12] The thrust of Gonatas' policy was maintained by his successor.

3. Buraselis, *HM*, 127, 172-3.

4. P. Trog. *Prol.* 27: *Ut Ptolomaeus Adaeum denuo captum interfecerit, et Antigonus Andro proelio navali Oprona vicerit.* Information on the naval battle is drawn from the following sources: a) Plut. *Pel.* 2: Ἀντίγονος ὁ γέρων ὅτε ναυμαχεῖν περὶ Ἄνδρον ἔμελλεν, εἰπόντος τινὸς ὡς πολὺ πλείους αἱ τῶν πολεμίων νῆες εἶεν, "ἐμέ δ' αὐτόν," ἔφη, "παρόντα πρὸς πόσας ἀντιστήσεις"; b) Plut. *Mor.* 183c: Μέλλων δὲ ναυμαχεῖν πρὸς τοὺς Πτολεμαίου στρατηγούς, εἰπόντος τοῦ κυβερνήτου πολὺ πλείονας εἶναι τὰς τῶν πολεμίων ναῦς, "ἐμὲ δέ," ἔφη, "αὐτόν παρόντα πρὸς πόσας ἀντιτάττεις"; Plut. *Mor.* 545b: καὶ Ἀντίγονος ὁ δεύτερος τἆλλα μὲν ἦν ἄτυφος καὶ μέτριος, ἐν δὲ τῇ περὶ Κῶ ναυμαχίᾳ τινὸς εἰπόντος, 'οὐχ ὁρᾷς ὅσῳ πλείους εἰσὶν αἱ πολέμιαι νῆες; "ἐμέ δέ γε αὐτὸν," εἶπεν, "πρὸς πόσας ἀντιτάττετε"; c) *P. Haun.*, 42–44; Chr. Habicht, "Bemerkungen zum *P.Haun.* 6," *ZPE* 39 (1980), 1–5. For systematic discussion of the evidence, see Buraselis, *HM*, 120–141 and F. W. Walbank, "Appendix 4: The Battles of Kos and Andros," in Hammond and Walbank, *Macedonia* III, 587–595, with earlier bibliography. For the identification of Opron, see Al. N. Oikonomides, "Opron and the Sea Battle of Andros, A Note in Ptolemaic History and Prosopography," *ZPE* 56 (1984), 151–152.

5. Buraselis, *HM*, 141 ff.; Nachtergael, *Galates*, 180, 295–414; F. W. Walbank, "Appendix 4: The Battles of Cos and Andros," in Hammond and Walbank, *Macedonia* III, 592–595; Bruneau, *Délos*, 557–64; C. Champion, "In defence of Hellas: the Antigonid Soteria and Paneia at Delos and the Aetolian Soteria at Delphi," *AJAH* 3–4 (2004–2005), 72–88; cf. Chapter 1.2.

6. Decree of Philippoi for Kos: Hatzopoulos, *Institutions* II, no. 36, l. 6–8, 9–11, 12–15 (ἐπὶ τῇ εὐνοίᾳ τῇ τε πρὸς τὸμ βασιλέα Ἀντίγονον καὶ τὴμ πόλιν τὴν Φιλίππων καὶ τοὺς ἄλλους Ἕλληνας καὶ Μακεδόνας, δοῦναι δὲ καὶ τὸ ἱερὸν τὸ ἐν Κῷι ἄσυλον, καθάπερ καὶ ὁ βασιλεὺς Ἀντίγονος προαιρεῖται…). Amphipolis: Hatzopoulos, *Institutions* II, no. 41, esp. l. 6–8, 12–14. Kassandreia: Hatzopoulos, ibid., no. 47, l. 4–7, 9–10, 12–14. Pella: Hatzopoulos, ibid., 58, l. 3–5, 12.

7. Paus. 2.8.4, 7.8.3; Index Stoic. Herc. col. xv. Plut. *Arat.* 23.5–6; Athen. 4.162d; Polyaen. 6.5. For a discussion, see F. W. Walbank, "Antigonus Gonatas: the last years," in Hammond and Walbank, "Antigonus Gonatas: the last years," in Hammond and Walbank, *Macedonia* III, 313, n. 6.

8. Urban, *Wachstum und Krise*, 52–53; Walbank, ibid., 311, n. 1.

9. Plut. *Arat.* 13–15.

10. Plb. 2.45.1; 9.34.7, 38.9; Just. 26.3.1; 28.1.1. Walbank, *Commentary*, I. 239–240. Also, F. W. Walbank, "Antigonus Gonatas: The Last Years," in Hammond and Walbank, *Macedonia* III, 311.

11 On the death of Gonatas in spring 239, see Ehrhardt, *Studies*, 140; Hammond and Walbank, *Macedonia* III, 311, n. 6.

12. Will suggests coregency with Gonatas probably beginning as early as 257/6 but definitely from 240/39 BC: *HPMH* I², 344; F. Walbank is more cautious in the absence of confirmatory evidence: "Demetrius II (239–229 BC)," in Hammond and Walbank, *Macedonia* III, 317–318; cf. J. B. Scholten, "Macedon and the Mainland," in Erskine, *Companion*, 150–153.

Demetrios II was engaged on several military fronts throughout his short reign: the Demetrian War (239–235 BC),[13] for instance, against the Achaian and the Aitolian Confederacies,[14] and the marriage of Demetrios to Phthia, princess of Epeiros,[15] were meant to counter the growth of the Aitolian and the Achaian Confederacies in mainland Greece. At the same time, he attempted to influence the Athenians by giving them command of Eleusis, Phyle, and Panakton, after his invasion of Boiotia (c. 236 BC).[16] Moreover, the renewal of hostility between Achaia and Sparta in the Peloponnese after the annexation of Megalopolis to the Achaian Confederacy and the rise of the ambitious young Kleomenes III to the Spartan throne allowed the Makedonians to regain a foothold in the area.[17] On the western front, however, their failure to provide more than indirect support to the Akarnanians' attempt to gain independence from Epeiros caused Epeiros to fall into the hands of the Achaian and Aitolian Confederacies.[18]

*** *** ***

The wide scale of Antigonid military and diplomatic activities throughout this period, both by sea and land, is reflected in the diversity of the types and in the large scale of the silver coinage. The coinage consists of tetradrachms only, Pans and Poseidons. It is during this period that the Poseidon head type was introduced (Chapters 6.4.2–3). The large numbers and the stylistic diversity of the Pan head tetradrachms make it possible that the mature portraits of Pan on certain groups are those of Demetrios II. Given Demetrios' extensive military campaigns on diverse Greek fronts, it is more than likely that he struck a precious metal coinage. The unquestioned dynastic transition from father to son after Gonatas' death renders the striking by Demetrios II of coinage in the name of his father plausible. The assignation of certain posthumous issues in the name of king Antigonos to him might then belie the alleged absence of portraiture in the name of all the successive Antigonids and reveal a deep sense of dynastic continuity in this dynasty, similar to that of the Ptolemies and the Seleukids.[19]

Certain groups of the Pan head tetradrachms, nos. 1–3 and 27–31, are stylistically more elaborate than normal. The replacement of the Macedonian helmet symbol by a trident in the left field of the reverse could suggest a naval event. The mature features of Pan, paired with the change in his drapery on the obverse, place this incident quite late in Gonatas' reign. Not least, the replacement of the *pedum* by a scepter in the second and third groups may have been meant to emphasise Gonatas' enhanced power after this event. The most plausible candidate is the battle of Andros, whose celebrations included the foundations of the Soteria and Paneia. Again, the introduction of the Poseidon head tetradrachm type may have formed part of this renewal of the political discourse regarding Antigonid naval supremacy in the Aegean (Chapter 6.4.3). The ideological burden of this second type suggests that it was struck after the naval battle, either for military payments, or in relation to the vase festivals, Paneia and Soteria. In the second case, one would assume

13. Inauguration of the war in the archonship of Lysias, 239/8: *Syll*³ 485, l. 37. For an account, see Will, *HPMH* I², 343–349; F. W. Walbank, "Demetrius II (239–229 BC)," in Hammond and Walbank, *Macedonia* III, 321–329. J. B. Scholten, "Macedon and the Mainland," in Erskine, *Companion*, 150–153; Shipley, *GWA*, 148, 151.

14. On the alliance between Aratos and Pantaleon, see Plb. 2.44.1; Plut. *Arat.* 33.1–2.

15. Just. 28.1.4. For a discussion of this marriage, see F. W. Walbank, "Demetrius II (239–229 BC)," in Hammond and Walbank, *Macedonia* III, 322–323.

16. *IG* II² 1299 = *Syll*³ 485, esp. l. 41–42, 65–66.

17. On the incorporation of Megalopolis into the Achaian Confederacy, see Plut. *Arat.* 30.3–4.

18. On Demetrios' subsidy to the king of the Illyrian Ardiaei to assist the Akarnanians against the Aitolians, see Plb. 2.2.5; App. *Ill.* 7.

19. R. Fleischer, "Hellenistic Royal Iconography on Coins," in Per Bilde et al., *Aspects of Hellenistic Kingship*, 28–39. Also see Chapter 8.0.

their periodical issue alongside these celebrations at Delos. The great similarity in the style of the obverses suggests a brief period of output.

Monograms HP, MH and AP, which occur as secondary control marks on both the Pans and the Poseidons, associate the two silver tetradrachm types (cf. Chapters 6.2.4, 6.4.3, 6.5). The presence of HP on the Poseidon head series and its disappearance from the Pans of the same period suggests the transfer of a mint official until then engaged with the minting of the Pans to the striking of the new Poseidon head tetradrachms, presumably at the same Makedonian mint; or the payment of an "end-user" with this new coinage instead of the Pans. Similarly, AP, used alongside the main monogram of a few Poseidons, establishes a connection with the X— AP tetradrachms, carrying a diademed head of Pan on the obverse (see catalogue, nos. 132–135).

The order of the Pans suggested above does not reveal any consistent development in the size of their flans, and this casts doubt on the validity of Mathisen's tentative chronological arrangement of posthumous Alexander tetradrachms on the basis of this criterion. It may, however, be argued that smaller modules were selected for the celebratory silver tetradrachm issues. Certain specimens of good quality are pierced, while others, of poorer execution, are broken. A few Poseidon head tetradrachms are also broken or pierced, and some have been cracked at the edge, as a result of the insufficient heating of the flan. Nos. 62b and 230a are test-cut.

The Pans of this period occur in fourteen different hoards, as shown below (Table 4.1a). Three of the earliest ones, Eretria, 1937, Karditsa (Palaiokastro), 1929, and Pherai, 1937–1938, come from mainland Greece and contain coins signed with monograms MH and AP (Eretria, 1937), TI (Karditsa (Palaiokastro), 1929; Pherai, 1937–1938); that from Meydancıkkale, 1980, is signed with EMP. It is worth noting that even though Macedonia?, 1927–1928, dispersed in trade, is of late date, it comprised the first coin of Period III , along with Pans of Periods II and III (see Chapter 6.3, no. 35). The Poseidons are found in fourteen hoards, mostly different from those with the Pans. The earliest hoard with a Poseidon tetradrachm (no. III.179i), Karditsa (Palaiokastro), 1929, also included four Pan tetradrachms from the first three periods, of not much worse state of wear than the Poseidon, and an Athena / Pan-erecting-trophy Antigonid bronze (*CH* IX (2002), 180, *IGCH* 162; cf. Chapter 6.3, no. 4). Apart from this hoard, Kassandreia, 1985–1987, Larissa ("Sitochoro"), 1968, and Thesprotia, 1992, are from mainland Greece and comprise specimens mostly of the later varieties. The bulk of the hoards with Poseidon tetradrachms come from Asia Minor and Syria. Finally, it is worth noting that a silver specimen of Period III, no. 245a, from Stageira, comes from an excavation context (see below).

*** *** ***

Table. 4.1a. Period III: Pan head tetradrachms in hoards

No.	Hoard	Catalogue Number	Group Number	Obverse Number	Monogram/ Letters
1	Makedonia? 1927–1928	1a	1	01	
2a	S. Asia Minor, 1963	3a	1	01	
2b	S. Asia Minor, 1963	60b	10	11	⋈
2c	S. Asia Minor, 1963	85a	16	14	KT
2d	S. Asia Minor, 1963	132a	30	20	Ʀ
3a	Unknown Findspot ("Seleucus III"), 2002	7b	3	02	⋈
3b	Unknown Findspot ("Seleucus III"), 2002	14a	4	03	⋈
3c	Unknown Findspot ("Seleucus III"), 2002	40a	8	09	⋈
3d	Unknown Findspot ("Seleucus III"), 2002	53b	10	11	⋈
3e	Unknown Findspot ("Seleucus III"), 2002	61b	10	11	⋈
3f	Unknown Findspot ("Seleucus III"), 2002	88a	18	13	Ϻ
3g–i	Unknown Findspot ("Seleucus III"), 2002	88d, f–g	18	13	Ϻ
3j	Unknown Findspot ("Seleucus III"), 2002	89c	19	13	KT
3k	Unknown Findspot ("Seleucus III"), 2002	94b	22	03	TI
3l	Unknown Findspot ("Seleucus III"), 2002	111a	25	10	TI
3m	Unknown Findspot ("Seleucus III"), 2002	120d	26	11	TI
3n	Unknown Findspot ("Seleucus III"), 2002	126b	26	11	TI
3o	Unknown Findspot ("Seleucus III"), 2002	127b	27	18	[monogram]
3p–q	Unknown Findspot ("Seleucus III"), 2002	132b–e	30	20	Ʀ
3r	Unknown Findspot ("Seleucus III"), 2002	135b	30	20	Ʀ
4a	Thesprotia, 1992	10c	4	03	⋈
4b	Thesprotia, 1992	15c	5	04	⋈
4c	Thesprotia, 1992	18a	5	04	⋈
4d	Thesprotia, 1992	30a	7	08	⋈
4e	Thesprotia, 1992	31a	7	08	⋈
4f	Thesprotia, 1992	32b	7	08	⋈
4g	Thesprotia, 1992	80a	15	13	KT
4h	Thesprotia, 1992	82a	15	13	KT
4i	Thesprotia, 1992	105a	25	10	TI
4j	Thesprotia, 1992	106a	25	10	TI
5	Mektepini, 1956	11a	4	03	⋈
6a	Eretria, 1937	39b	8	09	⋈
6b	Eretria, 1937	42a	8	09	⋈
6c	Eretria, 1937	52a	10	11	⋈
6d	Eretria, 1937	53a	10	11	⋈
6e	Eretria, 1937	54a	10	11	⋈
6f	Eretria, 1937	132d	30	20	Ʀ

Table. 4.1a (continued). Period III: Pan head tetradrachms in hoards

No.	Hoard	Catalogue Number	Group Number	Obverse Number	Monogram/ Letters
7	Meydancıkkale, 1980	62a	11	02	ΕΥΡ
8a	N. Syria, 1960	64a	12	03	ΕΥΡ
8b	N. Syria, 1960	85d	16	14	KT
8c	N. Syria, 1960	92c	22	03	TI
9a	Hija se Korbit, 1982	72b	14	12	KT
9b	Hija se Korbit, 1982	107a	25	10	TI
10a	Gordion, 1951	81c	15	13	KT
11a	Karditsa (Palaiokastro), 1929	101b	24	16	TI
12	Larissa ("Sitochoro"), 1968	110e	25	10	TI
13	Pherai, 1937–1938	125a	26	11	TI
14	S. Asia Minor ("Pisidia"), 1963	136a	31	20	-

Table 4.1b. Period III: Poseidon head tetradrachms in hoards

No.	Hoard	Catalogue Number	Group Number	Obverse Number	Monogram/ Letters
4l	Thesprotia, 1992	180a	41	29	[monogram]
4m	Thesprotia, 1992	193h	42	31	[monogram]
4n	Thesprotia, 1992	213a	44	33	[monogram]
4o	Thesprotia, 1992	235c	45	35	[monogram]
4p	Thesprotia, 1992	240a	46	37	[monogram]
5b	Mektepini, 1956	152a	35	24	[monogram] M
5c	Mektepini, 1956	188d	41	30	[monogram]
10b	Gordion, 1951	159f	37	25	[monogram]
15	Unknown Findspot ("Achaeus"), 2002	144b	33	22	[monogram] [monogram]
16a	Unknown Findspot ("Antiochus III"), 2005	147a	34	21	[monogram] ([monogram])[a]
16b	Unknown Findspot ("Antiochus III"), 2005	152a	35	24	[monogram] M
16c	Unknown Findspot ("Antiochus III"), 2005	223a	44	33	[monogram]
17	Pergamon, 1960	150c	35	24	[monogram] M
3s	Unknown Findspot ("Seleucus III"), 2002	181a	41	29	[monogram]
3t	Unknown Findspot ("Seleucus III"), 2002	186d–e	41	29	[monogram]
3u	Unknown Findspot ("Seleucus III"), 2002	194a	42	31	[monogram]
3v–w	Unknown Findspot ("Seleucus III"), 2002	195b–c	42	31	[monogram]
3x	Unknown Findspot ("Seleucus III"), 2002	230b	45	34	[monogram]
3y	Unknown Findspot ("Seleucus III"), 2002	234a	45	35	[monogram]
3z	Unknown Findspot ("Seleucus III"), 2002	238d	45	36	[monogram]
11b	Karditsa (Palaiokastro), c. 1929	179i	41	29	[monogram]
18a	Unknown Findspot, "X4"	179j	41	29	[monogram]
18b	Unknown Findspot, "X4"	205d	43	32	[monogram]
19a	Kassandreia, 1985–1987	171a	37	25	[monogram]
19b	Kassandreia, 1985–1987	191a	42	31	[monogram]
20a	Syria, 1959	186a	41	29	[monogram]
20b	Syria, 1959	195f	42	31	[monogram]
21	Unknown Findspot ("Pamphylia or Cilicia"), 2000	187f	41	29	[monogram]
12	Larissa ("Sitochoro"), 1968	213k	44	33	[monogram]
22	Oylum Höyügü, 1989	214c	44	33	[monogram]
23	Asia Minor, 1947/8	229a	45	34	[monogram]

a. Monogram [monogram] recut as [monogram].

Table 4.2. Period III: Weights of silver specimens

Weight (g)	1	2	3	4	5	6	7	8	9	10	11	12	13	14	15	16	17	18	19	20	21	22
17.80–17.76																						
17.44–17.41																						
17.40–17.36																						
17.35–17.31																						
17.3–17.26																1						
17.25–17.21																						
17.2–17.16						1			1	1					1						1	
17.15–17.11						1		1			1	3		1	1		1					
17.1–17.06			1	1		2	5	2	5	8		2	1	5	3		2			1	1	4
17.05–17.01		1	1	1	2	1	3	2	1	1		1	1	1	3	2						1
17.0–16.96	1				3	1	5	2	4	4		1	1	2	3	1	1	3	3			2
16.95–16.91					3		2	2		2				1	1			1				1
16.9–16.86	1		1	1						1			1		1		2	1				
16.85–16.81				2				1		1				1	1							1
16.8–16.76		1			1			1			1			1								
16.75–16.71						1		1														2
16.7–16.66							2	1					1									
16.65–16.61				1			1			1			1		1			1				
16.6–16.56			1				1															
16.55–16.51																			1			
16.50–16.46																						
16.45–16.41																1						
16.40–16.36														2		1		1				
16.35–16.31										2												
16.3–16.26																						
16.25–16.21																						
16.2–16.16					1					3												
16.15–16.11										1												
16.10–16.06																						
16.05–16.01																						
16.0–15.96																						
15.95–15.91																						
15.90–15.86																						
15.85–15.81																						
15.80–15.76																						
15.75–15.71													1									
15.70–15.66																						
15.60–15.56																						
15.55–15.51																						
15.35–15.31																						
15.30–15.26																						
15.15–15.11																						
15.1–15.06																						
15.05–15.01																						
15.0–14.96																						
14.95–14.90																						
14.75–14.71																						
14.3–14.26																						1
14.25–14.21																						
14.20–14.16																						
13.80–13.76																						
Unknown Weight	1		3	1	2	4	3	3	1	5				3	6	2	2			1		1
Broken/Pierced				1	1	1							1									
TOTAL	3	2	7	8	13	12	22	16	12	30	2	7	8	17	21	8	8	7	4	2	2	13

Table 4.2 (continued). Period III: Weights of Period III silver specimens

23	24	25	26	27	28	29	30	31	32	33	34	35	36	37	38	39	40	41	42	43	44	45	46	47	48	All 4D
																		1								1
		1																								1
																				1						1
																				1						1
														4						1						6
																						1			1	2
			1				1			1		1		9						5	2		1	2	3	31
1		1	4							4		3		5				2	1	15	7	5	2	4	3	66
	4	5	10			1	2	1	1	2		6	1	15		1		21	4	12	17	9	9	2	6	172
	1	4	6				1		1	1	1	2	2	12				12	7	16	5	12	5	4	5	119
1	1	10	7	1			2		1	2		2		9	1	2		12	3	8	9	10	5	7	4	134
		4	2			2								2				3	4	6	5	7	2	5	2	57
1	1		2	1						2		2		6				3	1	5	3	2	2	1	2	43
		2	1			1	1			1				4				6		4	4	1			4	36
		1	2									1		1				2			3	1			2	18
		2					1											3		2	1	3		1	2	19
		2								1		1						3		2	1	2				16
		1	1							1								2		1					2	14
										2		1		1					1	1					2	10
	1																				1	3				6
			2							2				1				1						2		8
			1																	1	2					5
	1		1																1							7
					1																					3
																		1							2	3
																						1		1		2
									1									1						1		7
																							1			2
																				1			1			2
																										0
																		1								1
												1													1	2
																										0
																						1				1
																			1							*1*
																										1
																										0
																		1								1
																			1							1
																						1				1
																				1	1					2
														1												1
														1												1
																										0
																		1								1
										1																1
																		1								1
																										1
																										0
																										0
																										0
	1	8	9				2		1	2	1	1		11			1	9	11	13	6	15	4	7	9	149
														2				4		2	1	3		1		17
3	10	41	49	2	1	4	10	1	5	22	2	21	3	84	1	3	1	90	35	98	68	77	32	38	50	975

PERIOD III

INDIVIDUAL TYPES: SILVER
PAN HEAD TETRADRACHMS

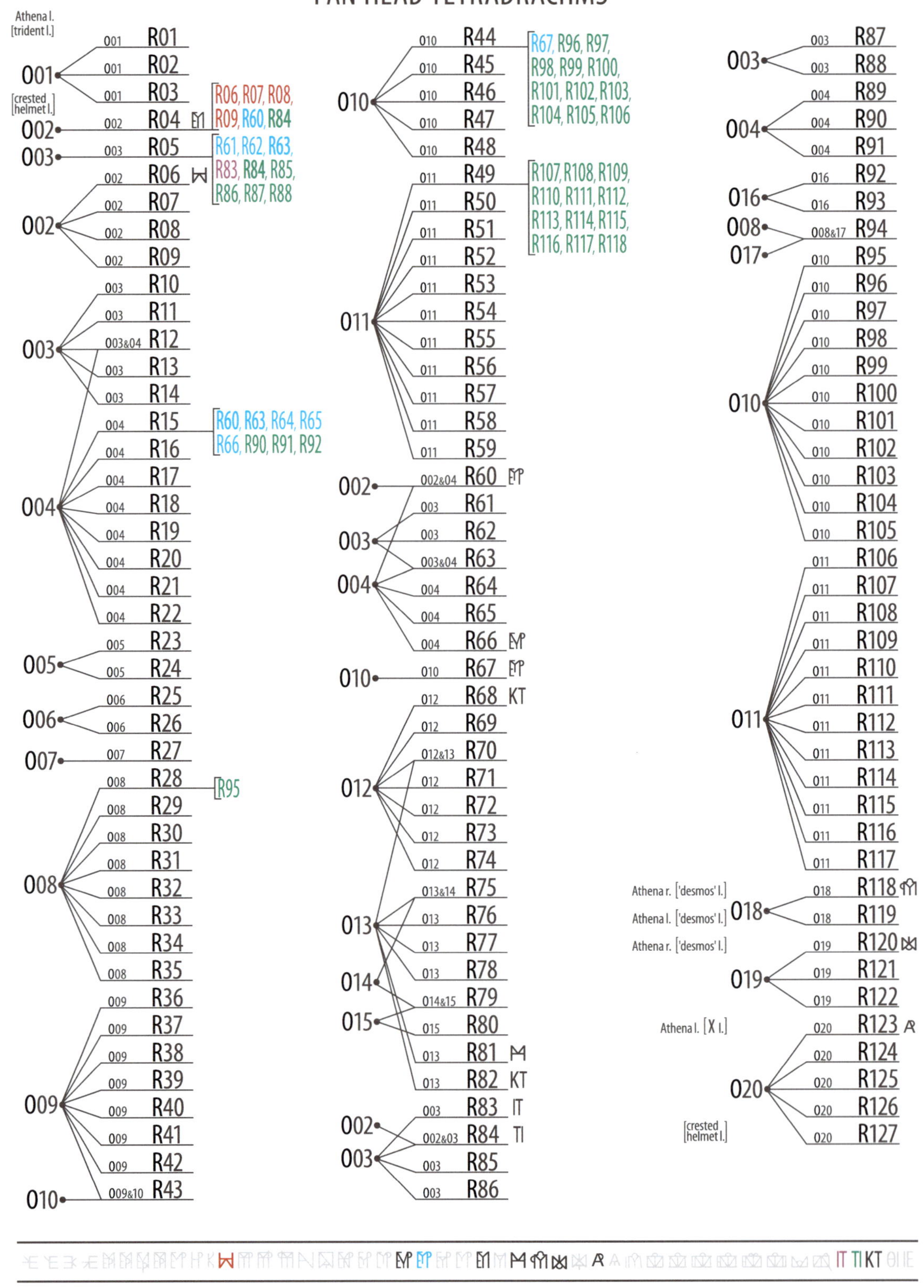

Figure 4.3. Period III: Die links of tetradrachms.

PERIOD III

POSEIDON HEAD TETRADRACHMS

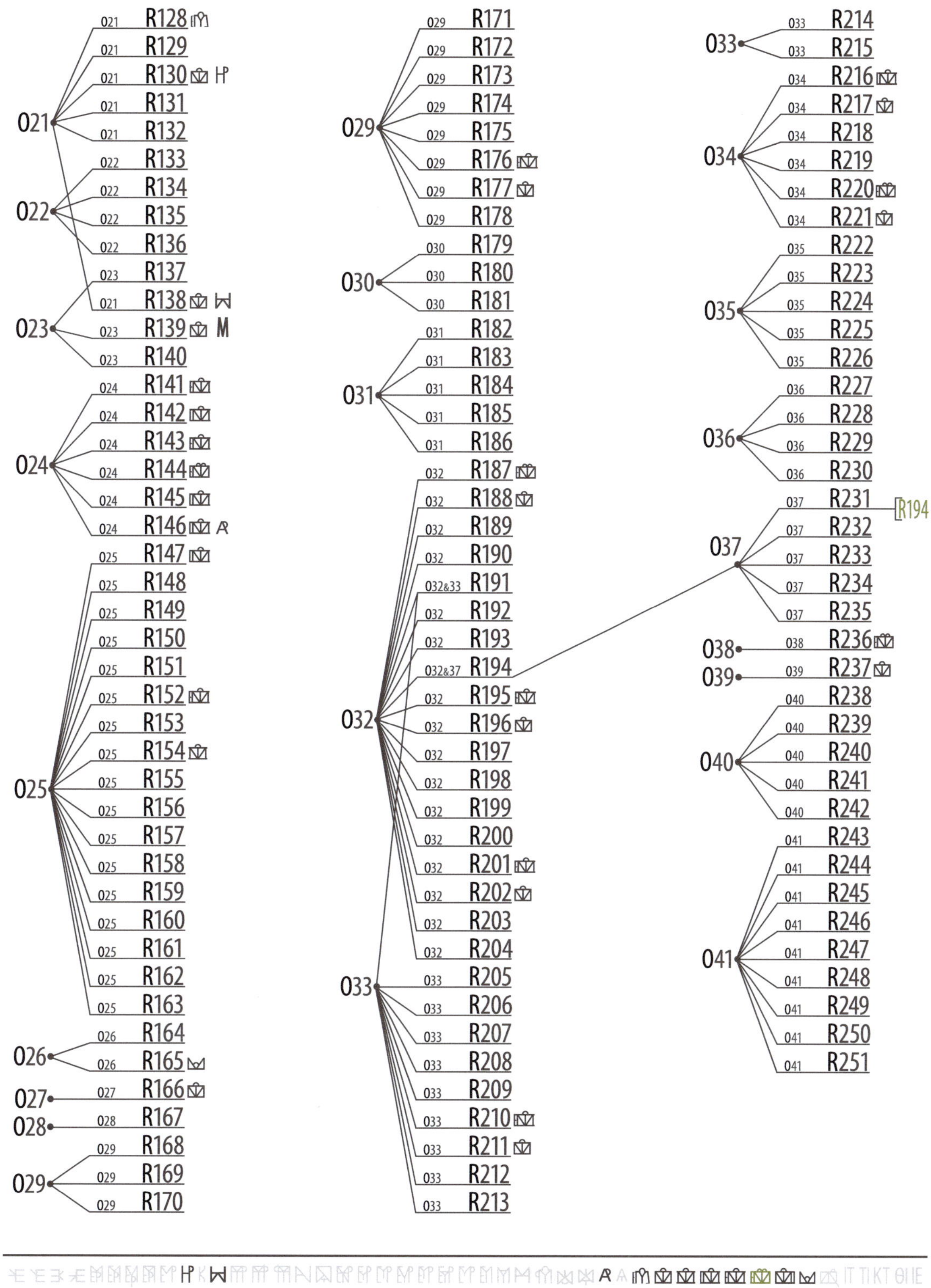

Figure 4.3 (continued). Period III: Die links of tetradrachms.

4.1 Individual Types: Pan Head Tetradrachms

Mint A

4.1.1 Athena l.

4.1.1.1 Trident l.

O: Eight-rayed stars, in high relief. Pan with bent, backward pointing horns and with tumbled locks flowing backwards and hanging from nape. Drapery folded, ending in three pleats, binding to front.

R: Hem with rich folds, the l. pleat end longer than the r. The l. end of pleat attached to leg. Head of Pan as emblem of shield, which is not particularly elaborate. Trident large, with short middle prong.

Group 1

Specimens: 3	Obverses: 1
Die Combinations: 3	Reverses: 3

1. O01 R01

a. ANS 1967.152.209: Makedonia?, 1927–1928 (*IGCH* 469)

	16.97 g	9 h	-

2. O01 R02

a. BM G10-III-109	16.89 g	5 h	30 mm

3. O01 R03

a. S. Asia Minor, 1963: *IGCH* 1426 (Boehringer, *Chronologie*, 157, pl. 26.26)

	-	-	-

A small issue with a trident left on the reverse may be placed at the beginning of this period. The heads of Pan are small and have bent horns and untidy locks; they are surrounded by eight-rayed stars in high relief and fit onto small flans. A three-fold drapery covers the majority of the neck, and is tied at the front with a knob, while the *pedum* is different from that of the previous groups.

The trident symbol left on the reverse is smaller, with a shorter handle but with a longer middle prong than that on the Poseidon head tetradrachms (cf. Chapters 5.3, 6.2.4). It need not, however, represent a new mint (cf. Chapter 2.5). The tetradrachm of this issue from S. Asia Minor, 1963, has tentatively been dated by Chr. Boehringer to c. 240 BC.[20] Even though the late burial date of S. Asia Minor, 1963, allows for an alternative production date around 225 BC for this group, its similarity in terms of style and legend letters to nos. 4 and 10–13 favors its placement at the beginning of the third period, subsequent to the battle of Andros. The distinctive control mark is compatible with a celebratory issue at the main "Makedonian" mint.

*** *** ***

4.1.1.2 Crested Helmet l.

Crested Helmet l.—Monogram [monogram] *r.*

O: Eight-rayed stars, with center prominent. Pan heads similar in shape to those of Group 1, but neater arrangement of locks. Change in direction of *pedum* (or scepter?), which is now curved, following the diagonal line of the drapery.
R: Legend letters angular. Athena in chiton with fine diagonal folds, rich in movement.

Group 2

Specimens: 2	Obverses: 2
Die Combinations: 2	Reverses: 2

4. O02 R04

a. Cambridge: *SNG Fitzwilliam* 2306 17.04 g 5 h 50 mm

[O (a): flaws: on space 3; on badge, off nose, and from lower fold upwards.
R (a): horizontal flaw, above monogram. Flaw off pleat].

5. O03 R05 O: Similar, but *pedum* upright, alongside inner badge circle.

a. Hess 251 (1982), 35; Kurpfälzische Münzhandlung 22 (1982), 27
16.80 g - -

[O (a): in center, flaw from inner circle off "unit" 2 through to hair. Also, from off nose diagonally to lower badge circle and through to "unit" 5. Flaw on space 2.
R (a): r., flaw from r. ankle to edge; lower, flaw from l. end of r. pleat through monogram to lower edge].

*** *** ***

Crested Helmet l.—Monogram [monogram] *r.*

O: *Pedum* curved (or scepter?).

Group 3

Specimens: 7	Obverses: [1-1]
Die Combinations: 4	Reverses: 4

6. O02 R06

a. Seaby 693 (1976), A393 17.09 g - -
b. NAC P (12.5.2005), 1438 16.57 g - -
c. Martin 20.1 (2.1993), G75 - - -

[O (a): flaw on spaces 2–4. Beginning of flaw on nose].

7. O02 R07

a. Peus 279 (1972), 25 17.04 g - -
b. Unknown Findspot ("Seleucus III" Hoard), 2002: *CH* X (2010), 272; A. Houghton—C. Lorber—O. Hoover, *SC* II.2, 142–150, Lot F, "After Cleaning," photos 891B–892B
16.88 g 5 h -

[O (a): flaw between crescent 7 and badge circles. In center, development of flaw from lower fold upwards; beginning of flaw between drapery and lower badge circle. (b): double-struck. R (b): r. control mark unclear].

8. O02 R08

a. Sotheby (20.5.1986), 52 - - -

[O (a): flaw on badge circles, off "unit" 2; on space 3, between badge and "unit" 5].

9. O02 R09

a. Feuardent (17–19.12.1919, Maxime Collignon), 208

- - -

[O (a): die break on badge, up r., off "units" 2 and 7 respectively; also, off chin; between "unit" 5 and badge; between "units" 3 and 4].

*** *** ***

O: Head spreads through badge, nose pointed, horns r. Two-fold drapery, from the middle of which emerges the *pedum*. Wrinkles on neck.

R: Legend letters regular. Athena short, stylized; pleats fall sheer, without many folds. L. pleat slightly longer than r. pleat. Thunderbolt stylized. Hem's middle fold shorter. Helmet with luxuriant crest, falling on either side of bowl; bowl small, with short cheek flaps.

GROUP 4

Specimens: 8	Obverses: [1-1]
Die Combinations: 5	Reverses: 5

10. O03 R10

a. BNF 1377 16.94 g (p) - -
b. MMAG 41 (1970), 92 16.90 g - -
c. ANM: Thesprotia, 1992 (Touratsoglou, *DM*, no. 38)
16.82 g 3 h -

[O (a): flaw between outer crescent 7 and edge; also, on space 1. (b): beginning of flaw on nose, flaws: on spaces 1 and 3; between outer crescent 7 and edge; on badge, between nose and inner badge circle. (c): flaw off nose and diagonally, from chin to "unit" 4.
R (a): l., small flaws between legend and coin edge. Also, diagonal flaw between monogram and r. edge, presumably as a result of piercing. (b): A without vertical bar, legend not carefully engraved. Athena crude, transparency of drapery in lower half—legs discernible. Athena on tiptoe, holding thunderbolt. Vertical lines on lower helmet; crest elaborate. (c): l., flaw l. of legend letters].

11. O03 R11

a. Mektepini, 1956: *IGCH* 1410 (Olcay and Seyrig, *Mektepini*, 690)
17.05 g - -

[O (a): l., development of flaw between nose and inner badge circle; r., from off "unit" 2 and hair; horizontal flaws on spaces 2 and 4].

12. O03 R12

a. Ahlström 51 (1995), 1622 - - -
b. Galerie Numismatique MBS 13 (21.11.1980, exp. J. Pannier), 15
17.07 g - -

[O (a): development of flaws: between nose and inner badge circle, between tie of drapery and inner badge circle. Development of flaw between outer "crescent" 3 and edge. Flaws on space 1.
R (a): l., diagonal flaw between legend and coin end and between T and l. pleat. R., diagonal flaw between lower horizontal bar of Σ and edge. Flaws on exergue.
NB: Off-center].

13. O03 R13

a. Auctiones 6 (30.9–1.10.1976), 124 16.65 g - -

[O (a): development of existing flaws. New horizontal flaw on inner badge circle, off *pedum* and between *pedum* and outer "crescent" 3. Flaws on space 3.
R (a): flaws, l. and r., between legend and edge. Up, flaws above head].

14. O03 R14

a. Unknown Findspot ("Seleucus III" Hoard), 2002: *CH* X (2010), 272; A. Houghton—C. Lorber—O. Hoover, *SC* II.2, 142–150, Lot F: "After Cleaning," photos 983.1–984.1
16.83 g 2 h -

*** *** ***

O: Similar.
R: Similar.

Group 5

Specimens: 13	Obverses: 1
Die Combinations: 6	Reverses: [6-1]

15. O04 R12 R: Shield prominent, curved. Chiton with long pleats.

a. Kress 156 (1973), 197; Kress 140 (1967), 64; Naville I (1921, Pozzi), 970
16.80 g - -
b. Göttingen, AS 168-2 16.95 g (p) 11 h -
c. ANM: Thesprotia, 1992 (Touratsoglou, *DM*, no. 39)
17.01 g 1 h -

[O (a): diagonal flaw on space 7. On badge, flaw from nose downwards.
R (a): up l., horizontal flaw from head to legend letters.
NB: Very bad photograph].

16. O04 R15 R: legend letters regular. Shield large, middle fall smaller, l. pleat slightly longer. Helmet with rich crest, lower part larger, cheek flaps small.

a. ANS 1944.100.13844 16.91 g 11 h -

b. CNG E-auction 323 (26.3.2014), 52 (Demetrios Arnounta Collection)
16.94 g 1 h 31 mm

[O (a): recut on nose. Small horizontal flaw between nose and badge circles. Diagonal flaw from beneath drapery through badge circles to "unit" 4; signs of flaw between "unit" 5 and badge circles; two flaws between "units" 5 and 6.
R (a): l., flaw beneath r. bar of first N and in between N and T; r., vertical flaw between main figure and r. pleat].

17. O04 R16

a. Vico (11.6.1998), 68; Vico (25.11.1996), 50	17.00 g	-	-

[O (a): development of flaws between "unit" 5 and badge circles and from lower drapery to "unit" 4.
R (a): up l., flaw from upper head to legend; lower, signs of flaw beneath l. crest. In field r., horizontal flaw through pleat ends to E].

18. O04 R17

a. ANM: Thesprotia, 1992 (Touratsoglou, *DM*, no. 34)	16.96 g	5 h	-
b. Button 110 (9–10.11.1964), 781	17.05 g	-	-
c. Coin Galleries (17.4.1975), 255	16.19 g	-	-
d. Malloy 61 (9.5.2001), 79	-	-	-

[O (a): development of previous flaws alongside new ones, between "unit" 2 and badge circles, and on badge circles off "unit" 3.
R (a): l., flaw between l. pleat and figure; also, beneath first O; between second O and l. helmet crest. In field r., flaw beneath Ω, and between Σ and monogram; also, from l. leg downwards].

19. O04 R18

a. Milan; Müller 8 (12.5.1973), 9	-	-	-

[O (a): on badge, flaw between chin and badge circles l. Development of flaw on space 5.
R (a): l., flaw between l. end of l. pleat and last three legend letters].

20. O04 R19

a. G. Hirsch 55 (1967), 2105	17.00 g	-	-
b. Kress 136 (1966), 225	16.95 g	-	-

[O (a): flaws on "units" 1–3; new diagonal flaw between crescent 6 and badge circles. Flaw from upper *pedum* upwards.
R (b): l. lateral bar missing on monogram].

*** *** ***

O: Eight-rayed stars, smaller in diameter than group 5, all of approximately the same size. Distance between badge circles larger; additional rays on star 6. No distance between lower badge circle and drapery edge. In center, small horned head with curls, short neck and a long side lock separating hair from face. Nose pointed, slightly curved downwards. *Pedum* attached to inner circle.
R: Middle hem fall starts from high up. Letters uniform, carefully engraved. Athena tall, transparency of drapery on second half—legs discerned, middle pleat higher. Thunderbolt, helmet small. Helmet with short lower bowl, short cheek flaps and crest at same level as cheek flaps.

Group 6

Specimens: 12	Obverses: [3-1]
Die Combinations: 7	Reverses: 7

21. O04 R20

a. Münzzentrum 66 (1989), 149 (17.10 g); Münzzentrum 62 (1987), 116 (16.70 g); Münzzentrum 39 (1988), 60; Münzzentrum 38 (12.1987), 1175; Münzzentrum L 36 (1986), 104; Münzzentrum 35 (19–20.4.1979), 104; Lanz 26 (1983), 183 (17.10 g) 17.10 g - -

[O (a): flaw between "unit" 3 and badge circle; beginning of flaw between "units" 5 and 6 and outer badge circle.
R (a): flaw from l. foot to exergue. Up r., horizontal flaw between legend and edge].

22. O04 R21

a. MMAG L 379 (1976), 16	17.04 g	-	-
b. G. Hirsch 249 (7–10.2.2004), 1325; G. Hirsch 245 (4–5.5.2006), 107; UBS 64 (24–26.1.2006), 56 (17.11 g)	17.10 g	-	-
c. Huston FPL 35 (no date), 7.4	-	-	-
d. Bourgey (4.5.1982), 9	-	-	-
e. G. Hirsch 289 (2.5.2013), 264	17.12 g	-	-

[O (a): small flaws on spaces 1, 4 and 5.
R (a): l., slightly broken on edge].

23. O04 R22

a. Dorotheum L 290 (1966), 110	15.75 g (b)	-	-

[O (a): development of flaws. Diagonal flaw from nose to "unit" 5.
R (a): r., horizontal flaw beneath N].

O: Change on spaces. One-fold drapery. *Pedum* small, dotted.
R: Rough, short Athena. Shield upright, with badge prominent. Helmet with large bowl and rich crest, long cheek flaps. On exergue. Chiton folds stylized.

24. O05 R23

a. *SNG Lewis* 539; Sotheby (2.2.1876), 21	17.16 g	3 h	-

[O (a): flaw on spaces 2, 6.
R (a): l., diagonal flaws l. and r., from upper end through chiton downwards].

25. O05 R24

a. Ponterio 141 (12–13.1.2007), 1439; UBS 49 (11–13.9.2000), 83 (16.99 g) 16.98 g 11 h -

b. Kress 122 (1962), 319 - - -

[O (a): development of flaws; break on nose.
R (a): roughly cut, legend letters smaller but regular. In field l., vertical flaw above shield; r., horizontal flaws].

26. O06 R25

a. Ponterio 128 (11.11.2003), 1065 16.72 g - -

27. O06 R26

a. Stack's (14.6.1993), lot 66; Stack's Fowler Sale (6.1969), lot 84 - - -

*** *** ***

O: Triangular head; curved, backward-pointing horns. Shawl pleats almost at same length.
R: Athena tall, helmet with very short cheek flaps.

GROUP 7

Specimens: 21	Obverses: 2
Die Combinations: 9	Reverses: 9

28. O07 R27

a. Gorny & Mosch 155 (5.3.2007), 82 17.10 g - -

29. O08 R28

a. Peus 386 (26.4.2006), 205; Button 101 (1957), 59 (16.95 g) 16.96 g - -

b. CB (1977), 6 17.05 g - -

c. Kurpfälzische Münzhandlung 68 (8.6.2005), 21 16.69 g - -

30. O08 R29

a. ANM: Thesprotia, 1992 (Touratsoglou, *DM*, no. 26) 16.68 g 9 h -

[R (a): shield larger, not upright; Athena taller, crest ends and cheek flaps at same level, distance between l. pleat and helmet smaller].

31. O08 R30

a. ANM: Thesprotia, 1992 (Touratsoglou, *DM*, no. 28) 17.06 g 9 h -

b. Hess (7.3.1935), 306; Hess 202 (1930), 2372 17.10 g - -

[O (a): signs of wear l. (a–b): flaws: off nose downwards; between chin and lower badge edge; behind hair; on space 6.
R (a): distance between helmet and pleat larger. Helmet with higher bowl. Shield small, round].

32. O08 R31

a. BM G10-III-110	17.07 g	11 h	32 mm
b. ANM: Thesprotia, 1992 (Touratsoglou, *DM*, no. 27)	17.00 g	11 h	-
c. Lanz 32 (1985), 172	16.92 g	-	-
d. Vigne (21.3.1997), 19; Vigne (6.1985), 24	16.92 g	-	-

33. O08 R32

a. Bourgey (2.12.1928), 53	-	-	-
b. Kölner Münzkabinett 85 (9–10.5.2006), 21	16.97 g	-	-

[O (a): flaw from chin to lower badge edge].

34. O08 R33

a. ANM, Iliou Melathron I.6	16.97 g	11 h	32 mm
b. Gorny 58 (1992), 259	17.05 g	-	-

[O (a): diagonal flaw from nose to "unit" 6. Flaw on space 6].

35. O08 R34

a. Aureo (15.3.2007), 1007	17.09 g	-	-
b. Sternberg L 5 (1993), 350	-	-	-

[O (a): development of flaw on space 6; new flaws, on badge, off "unit" 1 and on spaces 4 and 5.
R (a): l., scratches from edge to legend].

36. O08 R35

a. CNG 31 (1994), 154 (Dr. Frank J. Novak coll.)	16.97 g	-	-
b. Antiqua 13 (6.2005), 25; Antiqua 11 (8.11.2002), 26 (17.06 g)	17.05 g	-	-
c. Glendining (7.3.1957), 36; Glendining (2.1957), 36	16.65 g	-	-
d. Pecunem 11 (29.12.2013), 145	16.60 g	-	32 mm

[O (a–b): flaw l. (6–8 h); also, across badge circles, off "unit" 4, and on spaces.
R (a): l., flaw between r. helmet crest and chiton; r., worn].

*** *** ***

O: Seven-rayed, plastic stars. "Units" nearly semicircular, more regularly distributed around emblem. Untidy locks flow from crown. Side lock covers ear. Bulging face, chin prominent, large neck crossed by diagonal line. Two-fold drapery.

Group 8

Specimens: 16	Obverses: 1
Die Combinations: 8	Reverses: 8

37. O09 R36 R: Helmet with wide bowl, short cheek pieces and rich crest. Legend letters large, Ω large. Athena short, with rich chiton.

a. Berlin; von Knobelsdorf 16.95 g 3 h -

[O (a): die ready to break on upper *pedum* and beneath chin. Worn on space 4].

38. O09 R37 R: Athena elaborate, stylistically similar to no. 50. Crest holder high.

a. Schulman New York (14–15.12.1970, H. D. Gibbs Collection), 772
- - -

b. Rauch 6 MBS (4.10.2002), 58 17.08 g - -

[O (a): flaw from "unit" 6 to nose. Also, on spaces 3–7. Die break on badge circles, off "unit" 3.
R (a): l., flaw from edge downwards. R., horizontal break from beneath l. arm through legend letters to edge].

39. O09 R38

a. Rauch 77 (10–11.4.2006), 175; Elsen 76 (13.9.2003), 88 (17.04 g)
17.03 g - -
b. ANM: Eretria, 1937: *CH* IX (2002), 194; *IGCH* 175, 16
16.78 g (b) 2 h 31 mm
c. Roma 5 (1.02.2014), 331 16.71 g 4 h 30 mm
d. Barré (4.1973), 10 - - -
e. Coin Galleries MBS (16.6.2003), 47 17.05 g - -
f. Gorny & Mosch 215 (13.10.2013), 811 (ex Friedinger-Painter collection 1930–1950s)
17.14 g - -

[O (a–b): development of breaks at level of mouth and off nose; horizontal break on inner badge circle, off chin. Flaw from beneath drapery through to "unit" 4.
R (a–b): Middle fall starts higher, ending in middle diagonal folds. Pleats at same level. Helmet with thin crest, small bowl and short cheek flaps. Small stride. On exergue.
NB: Not cleaned].

40. O09 R39

a. Unknown Findspot ("Seleucus III" Hoard), 2002: *CH* X (2010), 272; A. Houghton—C. Lorber—O. Hoover, *SC* II.2, 142–150, Lot B, photos 168.1–9.1, CD 02760148.2–02760149.2 17.00 g 12 h -

41. O09 R40

a. Roma 7 (22.3.2014), 457 16.82 g 7 h 21 mm

42. O09 R41

a. ANM: Eretria, 1937: *CH* IX (2002), 194; *IGCH* 175, 17
16.97 g 5 h 29.5 mm
b. SQ (1986), 995; NFA 9 (1980), 183 (16.98 g); Frey (24–5.9.1954), 541
16.91 g - -
c. Gorny 92 (21–22.11.1998), 137 16.69 g - -

[O (a): development of existing flaws.
R (b): alteration at 8 h.
NB: Not cleaned].

43. O09 R42

a. Gorny & Mosch 195 (7.3.2011), 149; Auctiones 27 (10–11.12.1996), 218
17.07 g - -

[O (a): development of existing flaws. New flaws on spaces.
R (a): l., diagonal flaw from drapery to end of legend].

44. O09 R43

a. Phillips 313 (4.2005), 39 - - -

*** *** ***

O: Shield pattern similar to no. 17, horns wavy, head diademed, *pedum* decorated with dots and curved. Three-fold drapery. On badge, r., die break or *pedum* upright erased.
R: Legend letters similar to no. 10. Athena short with peculiar drapery, helmet and monogram bars small.

Group 9

Specimens: 12 Obverses: 1
Die Combinations: 6 Reverses: [6-1]

45. O10 R43

a. ANM: *SNG Saroglos* 921 17.06 g - -
b. NAC 77 (26.5.2014), 32 (privately purchased in 2001)
17.08 - -
c. Goldberg 80 (3.6.2014), 3288; Gorny & Mosch 200 (10.10.2011), 1466; Gorny & Mosch 112 (17.10.2001), 4091 16.96 g - -

46. O10 R44

a. Roma E-sale 7 (26.4.2014), 414 16.97 g 4 h 32 mm

47. O10 R45

a. Stack's 164 (6.1.2012), 176 (NYINC Auction); Coin Galleries (24.8.1970), 34
17.06 g - -
b. CNA 6 (1.3.1989), 49 16.98 g - -

[O (a): flaws on outer badge center, off "unit" 2, and between crescents of "units" 3 and 6.
R (a): l. flaw between pleat and helmet crest].

48. O10 R46

a. Numifrance (2.6.1982), 57; Sotheby (17.7.1974), 14
17.07 g - -
b. SB (Spring 1975), 144 17.08 g - -

[O (a): break between badge circles (11 h, 7 h, 8 h, 3 h).

R (a): horizontal bar of A hardly discernible; r., flaw from edge (5 h) through E and r. pleat. (b): flan larger].

49. O10 R47

a. CNG 67 MBS (22.9.2004), 460 17.03 g - -

50. O10 R48

a. Leiden 3153 17.20 g 10 h -
b. Peus 321 (1988), 150; Peus 316 (1986), 174 (16.98 g) 16.97 g - -
c. Florange-Ciani 6 (1929), 98 - - -

[O (a): on badge, horizontal flaw from hair to inner badge circle.
R (a): crest helmet ends and cheek flaps at same level, distance between l. pleat-helmet smaller. In field r., horizontal flaw across pleat].

*** *** ***

O: Head larger, nose and chin reach badge edge. *Pedum* decorated by small dots and is slightly larger.
R: Athena elaborate, small head and middle fall starting from higher up. Shield small and horizontal, with protruding center. Small helmet with medium bowl and rich crest. Pleats at same length. On exergue.

GROUP 10

Specimens: 30 Obverses: 1
Die Combinations: 11 Reverses: 11

51. O11 R49

a. MMAG L 360 (1974), 18 17.09 g - -
b. Gorny & Mosch 204 (5.3.2012), 1307; Grün 35 (9–10.11.2001), 155; Grün 31 (1–2.12.2000), 71 16.65 g - -

52. O11 R50

a. ANM: Eretria, 1937: *CH* IX (2002), 194; *IGCH* 175, 20 17.085 g 7 h 31.3 mm
b. G. Hirsch 275 (22.9.2011), 3505; G. Hirsch 120 (1980), 75 (16.01 g) 16.11 g - -
c. Schlessinger (4.2.1935), 780 17.10 g - 31 mm
d. MMAG 13 (23–4.6.1983), 169 17.09 g - -
e. Müller L 22 (6.1974), 15 - - -

[O (a): badly cleaned. On badge, flaw on neck. Die breaks on spaces 1, 3 and around space 5.
R (a): horizontal flaw through legend, pleat, figure through to r. pleat].

53. O11 R51

a. ANM: Eretria, 1937: *CH* IX (2002), 194; *IGCH* 175, no. 22 17.04 g 7 h 31.5 mm

b. Unknown Findspot ("Seleucus III" Hoard), 2002: *CH* X (2010), 272; A. Houghton—C. Lorber—O. Hoover, *SC* II.2, 142–150, Lot F, "Late Report of a Fragment," photos 882–3, no. 47 - - -

[O (a): horizontal flaw on spaces 1, 2 and 4. Development of flaws r.
R (a): l., wear between legend and shield; beginning of flaw beneath Γ; r., flaw from r. bar of monogram to Ω. In exergue, vertical flaw].

54. O11 R52 R: Athena taller.

a. ANM: Eretria, 1937: *CH* IX (2002), 194; *IGCH* 175, 19
16.98 g 10 h 31 mm
b. Riechmann 30 (1924), 468 16.36 g - -
c. Weil (with E. Bourgey) (28–29.3.1977), 55; Plumier (9.6.1976), 10
17.10 g - -

[O (a): development of flaws from head to upper badge end. Flaws on "unit" 6 and around "unit" 7.
R (a): horizontal flaw above head. In field r., horizontal flaw connecting chiton to horizontal bar of Σ].

55. O11 R53

a. Hess 224 (18.2.1936, Karl Diener Collection), 713; Bourgey (14–16.5.1914), 55
17.10 g - 29 mm
b. Rauch MBS 10 (2.3.2006), D81; Rauch 76 (17–18.10.2005), D274
17.08 g - -
c. CGB MBS 38 (30.4.2009), 130 16.85 g 12 h 30.5 mm

[O (a): flaw on spaces 2 and 4 and between "unit" 3 and central badge; horizontal flaw across "unit" 6 and badge circles.
R (a): l., diagonal flaw from l. helmet crest through to edge; r., flaw from figure through pleat and Σ].

56. O11 R54

a. Galata L (9.1979), 15; Tietjen 58 (1989), 102 16.19 g - -
b. Pegasi BBS 132 (25.1.2005), 79; Spartan Numismatics BBS 37 (7.6.2005), 73
16.16 g - -
c. G. Hirsch 261 (7.5.2009), 239 16.93 g - -

[O (a): vertical flaw from end of *pedum* to "unit" 4; also, from neck to "unit" 5 and from "unit" 7 to horns.
R (a): horizontal flaw from middle of field, l., through TI to l. pleat; r., from main figure through pleat to EΩ].

57. O11 R55

a. BPN-CB FPL (4.1987), 112; Coin Galleries FPL (Num. Rev.), 1 (1977), A98
16.33 g - -
b. Superior (2–3.6.1998, J. B. Parker), 6318 16.32 g - -

[O (a): flaws on spaces 1, 4 and 7. Horizontal flaw at level of eyes, through badge circles.

Scratches on head. (b): development of flaw between space 1 and badge circles; flaw on space 6.
R (b): l., horizontal flaws; r., diagonal flaw between r. pleat and figure].

58. O11 R56

a. Bourgey (5.1950), 59 - - -
b. Grunow L 47 (Summer 1998), 7532 16.17 g - -
c. Künker 174 (27.9.2010), 229 16.99 g - -

[O (a): two flaws starting from outer crescent 2. Between head and badge circles, small flaws. Flaws on edges of "units" 6 and 7].

59. O11 R57

a. Helbing 51 (1927), 1699 17.20 g - -
b. Baudey (7.2.1975), 10 17.00 g - -
c. Gorny & Mosch 216 (15.10.2013), 2335 16.94 g - -

[O (a): flaw off chin and diagonally from his chin to "unit" 5 (7 h).
R (a): vertical flaw from edge to upper shield; r., flaw between r. foot and legend].

60. O11 R58 R: Athena taller, middle fall starts high and disperses diagonally. O larger, r. bar of N shorter; l., flaw on r. bar of N.

a. Sotheby (15.5.1974), 25; Better 4 (Haifa) (1973), 300; Better 1 (4–6.7.1972), 7
16.99 g - -
b. S. Asia Minor, 1963: *IGCH* 1426 (Boehringer, *Chronologie*, 36, pl. 26.22)
- - -

[O (a): horizontal flaw from "unit" 6 to eye level. Second flaw from tie of drapery through badge circles to "unit" 4. Recut on nose.
R (a): up, flaw from edge above shield to A; r., horizontal flaw from edge through upper horizontal bar of Σ to lower chiton].

61. O11 R59 R: Shield flatter.

a. Athens: *SNG Alpha Bank* 986 (2335) 17.07 g 10 h 31 mm
b. Unknown Findspot ("Seleucus III" Hoard), 2002: *CH* X (2010), 272; A. Houghton—C. Lorber—O. Hoover, *SC* II.2, 142–150, Lot F "After Cleaning," photos 983.2–984.2
16.89 g 10 h -

[O (a): flaw from nose through to badge edge].

Like Group 1, the obverses of the next two groups, with monograms [monogram] and [monogram], are cut with exceptional care. The elaborate heads with short locks, neatly arranged around the head, are combined with a curved *pedum*. At the same time, on the reverses the small, crude Athenas, angular legend letters, and helmets with a small bowl and a long, thin crest at the left on the field are replaced by taller figures, regular letters and helmets with medium bowls and luxuriant crests.

From Group 4 onwards, the *pedum* develops alongside the inner badge circle. Groups 4–7 have small flans carrying small, elaborate heads of Pan with short locks. Six obverse dies are combined with various reverses, not closely interlinked with each other and carrying generally short Athenas, bell-shaped helmets and neat, large legend letters. The earlier, oval-shaped Pan heads of

Groups 2–5 may have come from the same hand as the *desmos* and X groups (see below). The Pan of Group 7 is reminiscent of the head on a shield engraved on a proxeny decree from Gonnoi. This decree, honouring Alexandros son of Admetos from Arkynia, dates from between the end of the third and the middle of the second century BC (Pl. 62c).[21]

Group 8 marks the transition from the smaller heads to larger and heavier ones. The first signs of a strong, thick and high neck already occur in O10, and they are paired with heavier surfaces on the face, but the result is smoothed by a prominent diagonal nerve across the neck. The introduction of the two-fold drapery around the neck sets the precedent for its consistent use on the silver tetradrachms of a "mature style" that follow. On the reverse, a helmet with a thin crest and with thin cheek flaps is associated with a cruder Athena, but with carefully engraved legend letters. Omega, in particular, is engraved with two dots on either side of a curve. The two specimens from Eretria, 1937 date this group around 245–240 BC.

The heads with mature features introduced with Group 9 are compatible with the attribute assigned to Gonatas after Andros, γέρων.[22] The forehead, nose and chin expand towards the inner badge circle. The head is characterized by heavy circular forms, and by a dewlap beneath the chin. The style of Athena on the reverse is natural, characterized by smaller heads and regular diagonal folds. A smaller shield is held in a nearly upright position, at the same level as her shoulder. A bell-shaped helmet to the left is also characteristic of this group. The specimens from Eretria, 1937 indicate the simultaneous production of this variety with the coins of the previous group, favoring the parallel operation of two different engravers in the same mint during this period. Of the coins coming from this hoard, numbers 39b and 42a are more worn than 52a, 53a and 54a.

*** *** ***

Crested Helmet l.—Monogram ΕΥΡ r.

O: *Pedum* curved (or scepter?).
O: Similar.

Group 11

Specimens: 2	Obverses: [1-1]
Die Combinations: 1	Reverses: 1

62. O02 R60 Monogram ΕΥΡ r.

a. Silifke Museum: Meydancıkkale, 1980: *CH* VII (1985), 80; *CH* VIII (1994), 308 (Davesne and Le Rider, *Meydancıkkale*, 2588 [Amphipolis]); *CH* X (2010), 269 — 17.12 g - -

b. Peus 324 (1989), 123 — 16.79 g - -

[O(b): more worn than in no. 6; flaw off nose. Cut on space 7, badge r. worn (signs of upright *pedum* beneath curved *pedum*). Flaws on spaces.
R(a): flaw prolonging l. crest; (b): diagonal test cut on figure].

*** *** ***

21. Chr. Habicht, "Epigraphische Zeugnisse zur Geschichte Thessaliens unter den Makedonischen Herrschaft," *Archaia Makedonia* I (Thessaloniki, 1970), 265–279, pl. 75= idem, *HL Monarchies*, 59–73, fig. 1; Helly, *Gonnoi* II, 13–4, no. 12; Liampi, *MS*, 61, pl. 6.1.

22. See n. 4.

O: As above.
R: Similar.

Group 12

Specimens: 7 Obverses: [1-1]
Die Combinations: 3 Reverses: 3

63. O03 R61 O: *Pedum* upright, alongside inner badge circle.

a. CNG Triton 3 (30.11–1.12.1999), 391;Tkalec AG (1998), 31 17.13 g - -
b. Lanz 146 (25.5.2009), 128 17.10 g - -
c. Shore MBS 80 (22.5.1997), 20 17.05 g - -

64. O03 R62

a. N. Syria, 1960: *IGCH* 1533 (Seyrig, *Trésors*, 22–24, no. 68) 16.96 g 1 h -
b. Lanz 38 (1986), 242 17.06 g - -
c. Vecchi 1 (1996), 243 17.14 g - -

[O (a): flaws on spaces 2 and 3 and between badge circles off "unit" 2, on spaces 5 and 6. (b): breaks off spaces 1, 2, 5 and off "unit" 7. Crude.
R (a): l., diagonal flaw from above head to lateral bar of A. (b): l., flaw between legend and l. pleat. Also in exergue, beneath l. foot].

65. O03 R63

a. Rauch 70.1 (14.11.2002), 56 17.12 g - -

*** *** ***

O: Similar.
R: Similar.

Group 13

Specimens: 8 Obverses: [2-2]
Die Combinations: 6 Reverses: [6-2]

66. O04 R60

a. Gorny & Mosch 134 (11–12.10.2004), 1281 17.09 g (b) - -
b. Gorny & Mosch 208 (16.10.2012), 1312 16.66 g - -

67. O04 R63

a. Gorny & Mosch 142 (10–11.10.2005), 1381 16.97 g - -

68. O04 R64

a. MMAG 10 (1938), 221; Wulfing 162 (17.12 g) 17.10 g 12 h -

[O (a): diagonal flaw, from nose to l. outer badge circle; signs of flaw on space 1; also, on "crescents" 6.

R (a): l., diagonal flaw from A to edge. Flaw beneath l. foot].

69. O04 R65

a. BM 1911-4-9-280 (Rollin) 17.04 g 7 h 29.8 mm

70. O04 R66

a. Rauch MBS 7 (23.1.2004), 971 15.74 g - -

[O (a): struck twice. Die flaw on space 5].

71. O10 R67

a. G. Hirsch 135 (1983), 185; Kurpfälzische Münzhandlung 22 (1982), 27
16.62 g - -

b. Pecunem 14 (2.3.2014), 123 16.90 g - 31 mm

[O (a): on badge, horizontal flaw off nose; second, diagonal, flaw from mouth to space 5. Diagonal flaw from tie to "unit" 5.
R (a): flaw on exergue].

All four obverses combined with variations of Monogram [monogram] are linked to the previous varieties of the same period, and their degree of wear generally confirms their production alongside monogram [monogram]. The *terminus ante quem* offered by no. 62b, from Meydancıkkale, 1980, for O02, c. 240–235 BC, and the good condition of the coin, are compatible with the dates suggested for the related issues, 245–239 BC.

A test cut appears on the reverse of tetradrachm 62b.

*** *** ***

Crested Helmet l.—KT *r.*

O: Head large. Hair locks flow towards face; deeply set eye; two wrinkles on neck. *Pedum* large and dotted.
R: Legend characters on the left are smaller than those on the right. Athena crude, holds small thunderbolt and small round shield. Small helmet, with crest ending very close to main figure.

Group 14

Specimens: 17 Obverses: 1
Die Combinations: 7 Reverses: 7

72. O12 R68

a. BM G0514 (Graves); Münzzentrum Lagerkatalog 2 (1995), 25; Münzzentrum 84 (1995), 17 16.40 g - -

b. Hija se Korbit, 1982: *CH* VIII (1994), 299 (Shpresa Gjoncecaj, *Iliria* I (1985), 190, no. 283, pl. XIV) - - -

c. Müller 71 (1992), 111 16.40 g - -

[O (a): flaws: on spaces 1, 2, 5; off nose, off "unit" 6. On badge, breaks off nose and chin.
(b): flaw develops from "unit" 6 through to nose.

R (a): up l., flaws: above shield, beneath NTI, between second N and edge, pleat and figure. In field r., flaws between r. pleat and TI, B and edge. Beginning of flaw between l. leg and Σ. (b): flaw between l. foot and r. helmet crest. (c): r., flaw between Σ and chiton].

73. O12 R69

a. Künker 94 (27–28.9.2004), 716 17.06 g - -
b. Tkalec (2007), 41 16.96 g - -

74. O12 R70

a. ANS 1977.158.168 K 17.07 g 8 h -
b. Vico 106 (4.11.2004), 204 17.00 g - -
c. Raymond (1936), 25 - - -

[O (a): new flaw off "unit" 5].

75. O12 R71

a. NAC A (27–8.2.1991), 1371 17.07 g - -
b. Gorny & Mosch 180 (12.10.2009), 117 17.09 g - -

[O (a): flaw on inner badge circle, off space 2].

76. O12 R72

a. Schulten (1–3.4.1987), 118 16.91 g - -
b. Negrini 18 (28.11.2002), 86 - - -

[O (a): development of old flaws, new flaw on "unit" 5. Horizontal flaw off Σ].

77. O12 R73

a. Athens: *SNG Saroglos* 927 17.15 g 11 h -
b. Gorny 92 (21–22.11.1998), 136 16.85 g - -
c. ANS: *SNG BYB* 356 17.08 g 3 h -
d. Negrini 23 (8.6.2006), 282 16.80 g - -

[O (a): new flaw between "unit" 2 and badge. Flaw in space 3.
R (a): flaws: l., between legend letters and edge; (b): r., legend and foot recut].

78. O12 R74

a. Baldwin 44 (2.5.2006), 51; Mørton & Eden (11.12.2003), 11
17.04 g - -

*** *** ***

O: Similar.
R: Similar.

GROUP 15

Specimens: 21 Obverses: 1
Die Combinations: 5 Reverses: [5-1]

79. O13 R70

a. ANS 1944.100.13853; E. T. N.	17.06 g	3 h	-
b. Gorny & Mosch 125 (13.10.2003), 132	17.02 g	-	-
c. Schulten (24–5.5.1983), 46	16.92 g	-	-

[O (a): angular flaw on space 3. Flaw between badge circles off space 2. (b): flaw on space 6; on badge, between nose and badge circles].

80. O13 R75

a. ANM: Thesprotia, 1992 (Touratsoglou, *DM*, no. 41)	16.965 g	7 h	-
b. ANS: *SNG BYB* 355; MMAG L 510 (1988), 11; Pilartz L 22 (9.1965), 38 (17.15 g); Pilartz 7 (1964), 45	17.14 g	5 h	-
c. Spink Z 20 (6.10.1986), 203	17.08 g	-	-
d. Cahn (6.5.1930), 197	-	-	-
e. Lanz 78 (1996), 234	16.83 g	-	-
f. Helbing 4 (1928), 198	17.10 g	3:30 h	-
g. Glendining (10.3.1965), 244	-	-	-
h. Glendining (5.11.1980), 23	-	-	-
i. Vico 105 (10.6.2004), 110	17.0 g	-	-

[O (a): flaws on spaces 4–5. (f): flaw on space 1, between "unit" 2 and badge circle].

81. O13 R76

a. Leiden, 1946/15	16.86 g	11 h	-
b. Seaby 680 (1975), A239; Waddell L 36 (-), 30	-	-	-
c. Gordion, 1951: *IGCH* 1406 (Cox, Gordion 8, pl. IV.53)	16.62 g	-	30 mm
d. Seaby-Glendining (1–2.12.1927), 295	-	-	-
e. Gemini 11 (12.1.2014), 71	17.05 g	1 h	-

[O (a): development of flaws].

82. O13 R77

a. ANM: Thesprotia, 1992 (Touratsoglou, *DM*, no. 42)	17.03 g	1 h	-
b. Schlessinger (4.2.1935), 777	17.00 g	3 h	-
c. Superior (30.5.1995), 7315B	-	-	-

[O (a): flaw develops off space 2; signs of new flaw on space 6].

83. O13 R78

a. Gorny & Mosch 151 (9.10.2006), 146; Gorny 133 (11.10.2004), 153	17.16 g	-	-

*** *** ***

O: As above.
R: Similar.

Group 16

Specimens: 8	Obverses: 1
Die Combinations: 2	Reverses: [2-1]

84. O14 R75

a. Berlin 7780/1957	17.03 g	12 h	-
b. Cahn 1 (1911), 152	17.30 g	-	-
c. Seaby 732 (9.1979), C890	16.43 g	-	-
d. Künker 182 (14.3.2011), 192	16.39 g	-	-

[R (a): flaw on "units" 1, 3–4, 7].

85. O14 R79

a. S. Asia Minor, 1963: *IGCH* 1426 (Boehringer, *Chronologie* 156, 25, pl. 26.25) - - -
b. Naville I Pozzi 971 = Collection Pozzi 2038 - - -
c. G. Hirsch 14 (1977), 13; Bayerische Vereinsbank 14 (4.1977), 13; Naville 1 (1921) 17.04 g - -
d. N. Syria, 1960: *IGCH* 1533 (Seyrig, *Trésors*, 22–24, no. 59; Müller 34/35 (1981), 60; MMAG L 331 (1972), 6 16.98 g - -

[O (a): countermark on cheek.
R (a): worn; l., flaw beneath letters A–N].

*** *** ***

O: Head cruder, with deeper face lines and with wrinkles on neck.
R: Athena crudely modelled, of moderate size, chiton with elaborate fall in middle. Legend characters small.

Group 17

Specimens: 8	Obverses: 1
Die Combinations: 2	Reverses: [2-1]

86. O15 R79

a. Mey 9 (30.10.1982), 12	-	-	-
b. Künker 59 (26-28.9.2000), 129	17.06 g	-	-
c. Waddell 33 (14.7.1988), 17	16.88 g	-	-

87. O15 R80

a. CGB MBS 51 (17.11.2011), 105	17.13 g	11 h	31.5 mm
b. NFA 33 (1994), 133	17.07 g	11 h	-
c. Superior (7–10.6.1987), 4071	17.00 g	-	-
d. Kölner Münzkabinett 41 (1986), 59; Coin Galleries (1973), 206; Ratto L 4 (1971), 206	16.89 g	-	-

e. Bourgey (21–2.1.1992), 58 - - -

[O (b): worn on spaces 1–3].

*** *** ***

Crested Helmet l.—Monogram ᛗ r.

O: Similar.

R: Similar to no. 63, but shield larger, helmet smaller. Many folds on lower chiton.

Group 18

Specimens: 7 Obverses: [1-1]

Die Combinations: 1 Reverses: 1

88. O13 R81

a. Unknown Findspot ("Seleucus III" Hoard), 2002: *CH* X (2010), 272; A. Houghton—C. Lorber—O. Hoover, *SC* II.2, 142–150, Lot F: "Best Coins," photos 839–840; Gemini LLC 1 (13–16.1.2005), 92 16.88 g 7 h -

b. ANM: Thesprotia, 1992 (Touratsoglou, *DM*, no. 49) 16.385 g - -

c. Berlin Dannenberg 16.96 g 11 h -

d. Unknown Findspot ("Seleucus III" Hoard), 2002: *CH* X (2010), 272; A. Houghton—C. Lorber—O. Hoover, *SC* II.2, 142–150, Lot F: "After Cleaning," 1291–1292, photos 194–195 = 987–988 (before cleaning); Lanz 123 (30.5.2005), 199 (16.82 g) 16.97 g 12 h -

e. Roma 7 (26.4.2014), 415 16.92 g 12 h 30.0 mm

f. Unknown Findspot ("Seleucus III" Hoard), 2002: *CH* X (2010), 272; A. Houghton—C. Lorber—O. Hoover, *SC* II.2, 142–150, Lot F: "Best Coins," photos 1221–1222 = 985.2–986.2; Freeman & Sear MBS 14 (21.6.2007), 150 (16.91 g before cleaning) 16.63 g 6 h -

g. Unknown Findspot ("Seleucus III" Hoard), 2002: *CH* X (2010), 272; A. Houghton—C. Lorber—O. Hoover, *SC* II.2, 142–150, Lot F: "After Cleaning," photos 1223–1224=985.1–986.1, CD 00000124-5 16.97 g 1 h -

[O (b): development of die break off spaces 2 and 3. R (a): die break in field, from up l. edge through to shield border].

*** *** ***

Crested Helmet l.—KT *r.*

O: Semicircular crescents. Horns upright. Lower locks parallel with each other. One curved fold on drapery. *Pedum* constituted by small dots. Horizontal flaw, from nose to l.

R: Helmet larger, shawl pleats thin; helmet short, with small cheek flaps. In exergue, KT—K with short diagonal bars.

GROUP 19

Specimens: 4	Obverses: [1-1]
Die Combinations: 1	Reverses: 1

89. O13 R82

a. Bourgey (13–14.11.1980), 32; Peus 283 (1974), 87			
	16.55 g	-	-
b. MMAG 5 (2–3.12.1975), 77	16.96 g	-	-
c. Unknown Findspot ("Seleucus III" Hoard), 2002: *CH* X (2010), 272; A. Houghton—C. Lorber—O. Hoover, *SC* II.2, 142–150, Lot F: "After cleaning," photos 989.2–990.2			
	16.97 g	5 h	-
d. CNG 87 (18.5.2011), 396	16.96 g	3 h	30.0 mm

[O (a): development of flaw off space 2. New flaws starting from nose].

The obverse die shared by Groups 14, 18, and 19 prompts us to consider Groups 14–19 together. Groups 14–17 and 19 combine a crested helmet symbol with letters KT on the reverse. Even though the first three groups (14–17) occur in much later hoards, their stylistic proximity to the coins of the second period and the similarity of the legend letters to those of the third period might favor a date around the 240s.

The letters K and T on the reverse may stand for a single mint official, or for an "end-user," i.e. the recipient of these coins;[23] or for two independent mint-officials or "end-users"/coin recipients, represented by K and T separately. The countermark on the obverse of specimen 85a, on Pan's cheek, indicates an extended use of this coin.

No. 88 (Group 18) is obverse linked with Group 15; it also carries the crested helmet symbol on the reverse and is represented in hoards best of the other groups with this type of helmet. Its right-hand control mark, ᛗ, is obviously an inversion of one of the mainstream monograms, ᛞ. Of the four coins coming from the Commerce, "Seleucus III" Hoard, 2002, no. 88a is in the best condition. The lighter tetradrachm from Thesprotia, 1992, presumably circulated widely before its deposition.

The crested helmet—KT combination also occurs in Period IV, where KT is also combined with a winged helmet [Chapter 5, Groups 4–5 (crested helmet); Group 1 (winged helmet)].

*** *** ***

Crested Helmet l.—IT *r.*

O: Similar, wrinkle on neck.
R: R. pleat longer.

Group 20

Specimens: 2	Obverses: [1-1]
Die Combinations: 1	Reverses: 1

90. O03 R83

a. Brussels, de Hirsch 116	17.08 g	11 h	31 mm
b. Antiquarius 18 (4.1989), 32	-	-	-

[R: flaw l. of crest].

A distinct series is introduced with Groups 20, 21, and 22, carrying a bulgier, bell-shaped helmet symbol, with a larger crest, on the reverse. In addition to the common obverse O03, which is shared between Groups 20 and 22, they all present similarities in style and in the engraving of the legend letters. Group 20, with letters IT, may precede Groups 21 and 22, with TI. The (die-linked) combinations IT and TI during this period might indicate either a cooperation of mint officials, i.e. I and T, or the independent function of mint officials with similar names, which might have been represented in i.e. IT and TI.

*** *** ***

Crested Helmet l.—IT *r.*

O: *Pedum* curved.
R: Letters not regularly arranged, shield and helmet small. Dots respectively beneath A, N, T, O, Y in the l. legend and beneath B, Σ, Ω in the r. legend.

Group 21

Specimens: 2	Obverses: [1-1]
Die Combinations: 1	Reverses: 1

91. O02 R84

a. Pliego (23.11.2006), 50; Pliego (13.12.2005), 20 (17.20 g); Gorny & Mosch 117 (14.10.2002), 181 (17.12 g)	17.18 g	-	-
b. Gorny & Mosch 122 (10–11.3.2003), 1259	17.08 g	-	-

[O (a): sign of tooling on space 3. (a–b): progressive die wear in the area between the scepter and the pleats, extending upwards to star/crescent 1 on coin (b).
R (a–b): in field l., dots among the letters of the legend. Diagonal die flaw across Y].

*** *** ***

O: Diagonal line on neck, cheekbones prominent.
R: As above.

GROUP 22

Specimens: 13	Obverses: [1-1]
Die Combinations: 5	Reverses: [5-1]

92. O03 R84

a. Berlin: Sperling; Friedl.- v. Sallet, 386	17.09 g	12 h	-
b. Canessa (22.5.1922), 401	14.30 g	-	-
c. N. Syria, 1960: *IGCH* 1533 (Seyrig, *Trésors*, 22–24, 58)	16.72 g	12 h	-
d. Pegasi 12 (3.5.2005), 124	16.92 g	-	-

93. O03 R85

a. Sotheby (9–10.10.1995), 73	17.03 g	-	-
b. Baudin (1920), 69	-	-	-

[O (b): struck twice].

94. O03 R86

a. Burgan (22.12.1990), 25; Burgan (24.5.1986), 312 (17.02 g)	16.98 g	11 h	31 mm
b. Unknown Findspot ("Seleucus III" Hoard), 2002: *CH* X (2010), 272; A. Houghton—C. Lorber—O. Hoover, *SC* II.2, 142–150, lot F "after cleaning," photos 991.2–992.2	16.83 g	11 h	-
c. CNG Triton 17 (7.1.2014), 174	17.07 g	11 h	-

[O (a): l., flaw between edge and star/crescent 7].

95. O03 R87

a. Münzzentrum L II (Summer 1995), 24; Münzzentrum 77 (1994), 78	17.00 g	-	-

96. O03 R88

a. *SNG Blackburn* 517	17.09 g	11 h	-
b. NFA 7 (1979), 109	17.09 g	-	-
c. Pegasi BBS 133 (2.8.2005), 66	16.74 g	-	-

*** *** ***

O: Two wrinkles on nose. *Pedum* decorated by two dots. Two wrinkles on neck.
R: Athena taller and stylized, *aegis*/head on shield discernible.

Group 23

Specimens: 3 Obverses: [1-1]
Die Combinations: 3 Reverses: 5

97. O04 R89

a. BM 1911-4-9-279 (Rollin) 17.15 g 7 h 31.2 mm

98. O04 R90

a. *SNG Newnham Davis* 164 16.90 g 11 h -

[O (a): high degree of wear in space 1 and between star/crescent 2 and badge circles. Flaw between star/crescent 5 and badge circles. In badge area, flaw from nose to badge circles. R (a): l., diagonal flaw between Γ and pleat; r., horizontal flaw from between IΛ and edge and from lower horizontal bar of Σ and main figure. Beginning of flaw between feet].

99. O04 R91

a. Bourgey (4–5.6.1991), 78 16.99 g - -

*** *** ***

O: Similar.
R: Athena figure taller, shield large.

Group 24

Specimens: 10 Obverses: [3-1]
Die Combinations: 4 Reverses: 3

100. O16 R92

a. Cambridge: Grose, *McClean* 3593 17.01 g 11 h 30.5 mm
b. Auch-en-Gascogne (24–26.02.1995), no number
- - -

101. O16 R93

a. Peus 313 (1985), 67 17.06 g - -
b. ANM: Karditsa (Palaiokastro), 1929: *IGCH* 162, 8
16.535 g 11:30 h 31.0 mm
c. Lanz 151 (30.6.2011), 49; NAC A (1991), 1370 (16.965 g); Coin Galleries (14.11.1984), 313; Coin Galleries L 11.3 (1970), B24; J. Hirsch 25 (1909), 546 (17.00 g) (coll. Philipsen); Sotheby (24.4.1907), 99 (Delbeke) [17.042 g]; Florange 6 (1929), 97
17.00 g - 31 mm
d. Ciani-Vinchon MBS (6–8.2.1956. coll. M. Hindamian), 346 (17.08 g); J. Hirsch 33 (1913), 668 (17.05 g) 17.08 g - 26 mm
e. Vico (19.11.1992), 111; Albuquerque MBS 35 (18.6.1992), 44
17.07 g - -

[O (b–c): worn on badge, off "units" 7 and 3.
R (b): signs of dotted border from r. end of exergue upwards. (c): r., two signs of attempted piercing].

102. O17 R94

a. CNG 322 (12.3.2014), 171	16.87 g	11 h	30.0 mm

103. O08 R94

a. Dorotheum (26.5.2014), 60; Grün 55 (24.5.2011), 26 (17.04 g); Grün 53 (20.5.2010), 43 (17.04 g); Meister & Sonntag 8 (13.10.2009), 7 (17.06 g); G. Hirsch 249 (7–10.2.2007), 1326 (17.05 g); G. Hirsch 245 (4–5.5.2006), 108; G. Hirsch 242 (22–24.9.2005), 2003; Gorny & Mosch 114 (4.3.2002), 86 (17.16 g)	17.07 g	11 h	-
b. G. Hirsch 284 (26.9.2012), 2042	16.40 g	-	-

[(a): slightly corroded].

*** *** ***

O: Similar.
R: Similar.

GROUP 25

Specimens: 40	Obverses: [1-1]
Die Combinations: 11	Reverses: 11

104. O10 R95

a. Glasgow: MacDonald, *Hunterian* 5	16.92 g	-	29 mm
b. CNG 302 (8.5.2013), 64	16.65 g	11 h	31 mm

105. O10 R96

a. ANM: Thesprotia, 1992 (Touratsoglou, *DM*, no. 16)	16.745 g	11 h	-
b. Leiden 3152	16.92 g	12 h	-
c. CNA 27 (1993), 454; Burgan (30.6.1987), 276; Burgan (24.5.1986), 311	16.99 g	-	-
d. Elsen 88 (10.6.2006), 75	17.08 g	-	-
e. Pecunem 12 (2.2.2014), 138	17.00 g	-	31 mm
f. Superior 85 (3–6.6.1985), 2106	17.00 g	-	-
g. Gorny 96 (7.6.1999), 116; Sotheby (30.4–1.5.1958); Haughton 106 (17.06 g)	17.10 g	-	-
h. Rauch 72 (20–21.9.2003), 176	17.04 g	-	-
i. Helbing 70 (1932), 594	-	-	-
j. Berk 153 (13.3.2007), 136	16.68 g	-	-
k. Phillips 256 (7.2000), 26; Phillips 253 (4.2000), 30	-	-	-

[O (a): light scrape before chin, corrosion on cheek; (b–c): flaws on spaces 1, 3, 5, 7].

106. O10 R97

a. ANM: Thesprotia, 1992 (Touratsoglou, *DM*, no. 17) 16.955 g 3 h -
b. Ritter 64 (12.2003), 538 - - -
c. Rauch 72 (20–21.9.2003), 177 16.85 g - -
d. Kress 152 (5.7.1971), 105 17.00 g - -
e. Dombrowski L 63 (1975), 106 17.00 g - -

[O (b): worn between badge circles; flaw on chin; (d): countermark on cheek: triskeles].

107. O10 R98

a. Hija se Korbit, 1982: *CH* VIII (1994), 299 (Shpresa Gjongecaj, "Thesari Hijes së Korbit," *Iliria* 1 [1985]: 167–193, esp. 190.281, pl. 24) - - -
b. Baldwin, Markov and M&M 32 (8.1.2014), 136 ("The New York Sale") 17.01 g 11 h -

108. O10 R99

a. Kress 127 (1963), 377 - - -
b. Elsen 65 (17–18.3.2001), 287 17.06 g - -

[R (a): letters more regular. Shield prominent].

O: Different arrangement of "units" and spaces.

109. O10 R100

a. Ponterio 133 (14–15.1.2005), 1368 17.01 g - -
b. Rauch 72 (20–21.9.2003), D177 16.85 g - -
c. Münzzentrum 62 (4–6.11.1987), 117; Münzzentrum 54 (26–28.3.1985), 95; Kress 142 (1968), 92 (17.00 g) 16.95 g - -

[O (a): flaws: in central badge, from end of *pedum* through to internal circle of badge, off "star/crescent 2; between circles of circular badge off "star/crescents" 6 and 7, respectively; on spaces 3 and 4; between "star/crescents" 1 and 6, respectively, and external badge circle].

110. O10 R101

a. BNF 1376 16.77 g 11 h -
b. CNG 229 (10.3.2010), 80 16.93 g 8h 31 mm
c. Spink 15 (1981), 35 17.04 g - -
d. Riechmann 37 (1926), 6; Riechmann 30 (1924), 467 - - -
e. Larissa ("Sitochoro"), 1968: *IGCH* 237 (Price, "The Larissa, 1968 Hoard" (*IGCH* 237), in Le Rider et al., *Kraay-Mørkholm Essays*, 235, pl. 46.15) 17.44 g 11 h -

[O (a): flaw up l., scratch up r., above thunderbolt. (b): development of flaw off units between badge circles off unit 7. (d): worn].

O: Medium-sized, regular legend letters. Oval shield, held upright. Note bar of K, helmet with very short cheek flaps. In exergue.
R: Many folds on chiton. Helmet symbol large. Shield oval, horizontal.

111. O10 R102

a. Unknown Findspot ("Seleucus III" Hoard), 2002: *CH* X (2010), 272; A. Houghton—C. Lorber—O. Hoover, *SC* II.2, 142–150, photos 740–741
17.00 g - -
b. G. Hirsch 247 (21–23.9.2006), 1940 16.75 g - -
c. Sternberg 8 (1978), 60 17.13 g - -

112. O10 R103

a. Henzen L 174 (1.2007), Dellnemer Hollland Coin Fair, 104; Henzen L 170 (8.2006), 113 17.00 g - -
b. Weil (17.6.1998), 39 - - -

113. O10 R104

a. BNF H. S. 1973.75 17.10 g 10 h -
b. UBS 59 (29–30.1.2004), 5447 16.99 g - -
c. Cederlind 139 BBS (29.6.2006), 41; Ritter 72 (3.2005), 482 (16.98 g); Ritter 71 (2.2005), 88; Ritter 68 (8.2004), 526; Gorny & Mosch 117 (14.10.2002), 182 (17.12 g); Pegasi BBS 134 (2.8.2006), 58; Pegasi 6 (8.4.2002), 135; Pegasi 113 (24.5.1999), 85
17.06 g - -

114. O10 R105

a. Pecunem 14 (2.3.2014), 122 16.70 g - 31 mm
b. Gorny & Mosch 142 (10–11.10.2005), 1382 16.98 g - -

*** *** ***

O: Similar.
R: Similar.

GROUP 26

Specimens: 48 Obverses: [1-1]
Die Combinations: 12 Reverses: 12

115. O11 R106

a. Spink 14005 (25.6.2014), 85; Spink Num. Circular 62.2 (4.2004), 1204; G. Hirsch 223 (26–28.9.2002), 1572 17.16 g - -
b. Vico 113 (8.3.2007), 140; Vico 108 (9.6.2005), 87
17.10 g - -
c. Meister & Sonntag 17 (3.6.2013), 40 16.64 g - -
d. G. Hirsch 177 (1993), 214 16.42 g - -
e. Markov MBS 10 (23–24.10.2001), 56 16.49 g - -

116. O11 R107

a. CGB MBS 53 (19.4.2012), 52; Argenor (13.4.2005), 43 (Claude Lainé Collection) 17.05 g - -
b. The Numismatic Auction 3 (1985), 75 17.03 g - -
c. Peus 410–411 (31.10.2013), 169 16.96 g - -
d. Dupriez 110bis (1912), 1357 - - -

[O (a): on badge, flaw between hair locks and upper *pedum*. Flaws on spaces 1–3 and 7].

O: As above.
R: Crude Athena holding shield on level of shoulders, badge prominent. Small, round shield. Helmet with long crests and short cheek pieces, long pleats away from helmet but close to TI, r.

117. O11 R108

a. ANS 1944.100.13850 17.09 g 12 h -
b. Münzzentrum 19 (1974), 21; Numismatica 4 (1974), 97; J. Schulman 256 (28–30.5.1973, Veiling), 1154 (16.99 g) 17.01 g - -
c. Seaby-Glendining (1–2.12.1927), 294 - - -

[O (d–e): flaw on space 5.
R (d–e): flaw between chiton and shield; also, off Y. (e): recut on nose].

118. O11 R109

a. Peus 340 (1994), 321 17.01 g - -
b. Lanz 158 (5.6.2014), 105 17.07 g - -

119. O11 R110

a. Oxford: *SNG Ashmolean* 3260 (Godwyn); Cahn 71 (14.10.1931), 290 17.07 g 11 h 32 mm
b. Private Collection L. C.; H. Saskey 17.07 g - -
c. MMAG 26 (1996), 129 17.15 g - -
d. Stack's (10–11.6.1970), 194 17.00 g - -
e. G. Hirsch 142 (1984), 24 16.50 g - -
f. Saive 1 (2.2005), 3481; Superior (1970), 164; Superior (24–26.9.1970), 1657 17.12 g - -
g. Gorny 102 (24.5.2000), 175 17.12 g - -
h. Feuardent (8–12.7.1919), 299 - - -
i. Freeman & Sear, Manhattan Sale II (4.1.2011), 142 16.99 g - -

120. O11 R111

a. CNG Triton 15 (3.1.2012), 1140; CNG Triton 8 (11–12.01.2005), 187 17.12 g 10 h 30.0 mm
b. Burgan (22.12.1992), 28 17.08 g - -
c. NFA 11 (1992), 95 16.94 g - -

d. Unknown Findspot ("Seleucus III" Hoard), 2002: *CH* X (2010), 272; A. Houghton—C. Lorber—O. Hoover, *SC* II.2, 142–150, cf. notes; Lot F, "Late report of a fragment," photos 882–883, no. 48	-	-	-

[O (a): development of flaw between hair locks and upper *pedum*, and from nose to inner circle. In field, off "units" 1–3, flaws from *nebris* through to inner circle].

121. O11 R112

a. Malter 34 (1986), 24	16.87 g	-	-
b. Müller 71 (1992), 112	16.40 g	-	-
c. Spink-GMG (10.10.1977), 165	16.92 g	-	-
d. Galata L (3.1978), 8	-	-	-
e. Freeman & Sear, Manhattan Sale II (4.1.2011), 142	16.99 g	-	-
f. Lyon	-	-	-

[R (c–d): l., flaw off Υ and r., off ΛΕ].

O: Drapery, *pedum* smaller.
R: Small, round shield. Letters medium-sized. Athena tall.

122. O11 R113

a. Gorny 31 (1985), 89; CNG 10.5 (1985), 413	17.01 g	-	-
b. Berk 152 (19.12.2006), 90	16.88 g	-	-
c. F. Schlessinger (1935), 782	17.00 g	3 h	-

123. O11 R114

a. Peus 282 (1973), 95	16.99 g	-	-

124. O11 R115

a. Leiden 3151	17.08 g	11 h	-
b. Lanz 42 (1987), 186	16.80 g	-	-
c. Spink 25 (1982), 60	-	-	-
d. Elsen 86 (10.12.2005), 74	17.06 g	-	-

[O (b–c): flaw from r. angle of neck through to unit 4 and from unit 1 to badge circle (7 h). Also, from neck through to badge circles. (c): flaw in inner badge circle, off chin].

125. O11 R116

a. Pherai, 1937–1938 (T. R. Martin, "A Third-Century B.C. Hoard from Thessaly at the ANS (*IGCH* 168)," *ANSMN* 26 (1981): 64, pl. 14.538	17.08 g	11 h	-
b. Gorny 46 (1989), 134 (16.76 g); Kricheldorf L 74 (1964), 16; Dupriez 104bis (1912), 48; Dupriez 110bis (4–7.11.1912), 1357	16.76 g	-	-
c. G. Hirsch 97 (1976), 61	16.96 g	-	-
d. Glendining (9.3.1931), 1006	17.06 g	-	-
e. Superior (1969), 133	-	-	-
f. Elsen 110 (10.9.2011), 172	17.05 g	-	-

[O (d): flaw off nose to inner badge circle.

R (a-b): horizontal flaw r. (3 h), through Β–Α to edge. (b): l., worn l. of Ν].

O: Curved wrinkle on neck. Crescents more circular/regular.
R: Legend characters medium-sized. Small helmet with thin crest and short cheek flaps. Shield small.

126. O11 R117

a. Kress 132 (1965), 137 16.85 g - -
b. Unknown Findspot ("Seleucus III" Hoard) 2002: *CH* X (2010), 272; A. Houghton—C. Lorber—O. Hoover, *SC* II.2, 142–150, Lot F, "Late Report of A Fragment," photos 882–3, no. 49 - - -

The parallel existence of two styles is also observed on the tetradrachms signed with ΤΙ r. on the reverse. Of the seven different obverses used with this variety, only O16 and O17 are exclusively combined with the letters ΤΙ. The presence of tetradrachms 101b, in Karditsa, 1929, no. 125a, in Pherai, 1937–1938, nos. 105a, 106a in Thesprotia, 1992 and 107a, in Hija se Korbit, 1980 is compatible with the suggested issue dates of this period. The worn state of no. 92c from Northern Syria, 1960 suggests a long period of circulation before burial in 213–205 BC.

*** *** ***

4.1.2 Athena r.

4.1.2.1 *Desmos* l.

Desmos l.—Monogram [monogram] *r.*

O: Three concentric circles on edge of shield. In middle, head of young horned Pan with diadem, *nebris* (round the neck) and *pedum* at shoulder. Horns lean backwards. Crescents with three elliptic circles. Between the two concentric circles round emblem, ΒΑΣΙΛΕΩΣ ΑΝΤΙΓΟΝΟΥ (in very small characters).
R: ΒΑΣΙΛΕΩΣ l., ΑΝΤΙΓΟΝΟΥ r. Athena r., without *aegis*, brandishing thunderbolt. Oblong shield. Dotted border.

Group 27

Specimens: 2	Obverses: 1
Die Combinations: 1	Reverses: 1

127. O18 R118

a. Berlin; Gaebler, *AMNG* III.2, 185–6.1, pl. 34.1; Tarn, *AG*, front cover; Liampi, *MS*, front cover 16.99 g (p) 11 h -
b. Unknown Findspot ("Seleucus III" Hoard), 2002: *CH* X (2010), 272; A. Houghton—C. Lorber—O. Hoover, *SC* II.2, 142–150, Lot F: "After Cleaning," photos 1205–6 = 995–996 (Lot F: "Before Cleaning") 16.89 g 3 h -

[(b): Off-center. O (a): small flaw on r. end of "unit" 1; also, on spaces 2–3, 7. On badge, horizontal flaws on either side of head.
R (a): r., beginning of flaw off nose and off shield].

*** *** ***

4.1.3 Athena l.

Desmos l.—r.

O: Similar.
R: ΑΝΤΙΓΟΝΟΥ l., ΒΑΣΙΛΕΩΣ r. Athena l. wearing *aegis*, shield with large border decorated with *aegis* and head in center. Dotted border.

Group 28

Specimens: 1	Obverses: [1-1]
Die Combinations: 1	Reverses: 11

128. O18 R119

a. Schulten 26 (7.3.1981), 26; Schulten L (11.1980), 34

16.35 g - -

[O (a): diagonal flaw on spaces 1–4, 6; r., horizontal flaw between Σ and border.
R (a): l., diagonal flaw beneath pleat; r., horizontal break from border to Σ].

*** *** ***

4.1.4 Athena r.

Desmos l.—Monograms [monogram] and [monogram] r.

O: Similar.
R: ΒΑΣΙΛΕΩΣ l., Α–ΝΤΙΓΟΝΟΥ r. Athena r. without *aegis*, brandishing thunderbolt with her uplifted r. hand and holding large shield with her l. hand. Horned head of Pan in center of shield.

Group 29

Specimens: 4	Obverses: 1
Die Combinations: 3	Reverses: 3

129. O19 R120 ΑΝΤΙΓΟΝΟΥ l., ΒΑΣΙΛΕΩΣ r. Monogram [monogram].

a. ANS 1975.212.1	17.08 g	3 h	-
b. Lanz 146 (25.5.2009), 130	16.94 g	-	-

[O (a): diagonal flaw from "unit" 7 to border r.; also, worn between space 1 and border].

130. O19 R121 ΑΝΤΙΓΟΝΟΥ l., ΒΑΣΙΛΕΩΣ r. Monogram [monogram].

a. ANS 1965.77.7	16.92 g	12 h	-

[O (a): poorly preserved. Curved flaw from l. end of "unit" 1 via upper badge end to "unit" 7; diagonal flaw on space 6.
R (a): up r., worn].

131. O19 R122 ΒΑΣΙΛΕΩΣ l., ΑΝΤΙΓΟΝΟΥ r. Monogram [monogram].

a. Elsen L 117 (1989), 16; Superior, *Money Talks* 19.2 (12.1987), G10 (16,81 g)

16.83 g - -

[O (a): on badge l., diagonal flaw between nose and lower l. border; also, diagonal flaw from "unit" 1 through badge to no. 6].

The mature features of the diademed head of Pan on these very well executed specimens, struck on small flans, distinguish them from their counterparts of the *desmos* group, which have been assigned to the first period of Antigonid coin production (cf. Chapter 2.2.3.2.1). These mature Pans are characterized by an elaborate Makedonian shield on the obverse, carrying eight-rayed stars and three elliptic crescents. The "star/crescents" are identical with those on the Makedonian shield from Dodona.[24] The name and royal title of Antigonos (in small characters) that surround the emblem on nos. 127–131 (Groups 27–29) are reminiscent of the legend around the badge of the Makedonian shield from Vegora.[25]

W. W. Tarn saw in the features of Pan the first portrait of king Antigonos, wearing a diadem.[26] Specimen 128 is the only specimen from the *desmos* variety with Athena facing l., carrying an *aegis* across her back and on the shield. A *desmos* on the left is combined with monograms [monogram] and [monogram], not known on the main helmet series. The excellent quality of this group is also confirmed by the consistent alignment of the dies around 12 and 3 h.

*** *** ***

4.1.5 Athena l.

4.1.5.1 X l.

X ***l.—Monogram* [monogram] *r.***

O: Eight-rayed stars. Horned head diademed, with hanging ribbons. *Nebris* ties in front of neck, scepter curved.
R: ΒΑΣΙΛΕΩΣ r., ΑΝΤΙΓΟΝΟΥ l. Shield diameter and legend letters larger.

Group 30

Specimens: 10	Obverses: 1
Die Combinations: 4	Reverses: 4

132. O20 R123 R: Helmet with high crest. Athena tall, thunderbolt elaborate.

a. Munich: *SNG München* 1080 (Acc. 94546); S. Asia Minor, 1963: *IGCH* 1426 (Boehringer, *Chronologie* 156, pl. 25.18) 16.85 g 11 h -
b. Unknown Findspot ("Seleucus III" Hoard), 2002: *CH* X (2010), 272; A. Houghton—C. Lorber—O. Hoover, *SC* II.2, 142–150, Lot B, photos 165B–166B = 145.2, 146.2, 147.2 17.02 g 11 h -
c. Warsaw 56711 17.00 g - -

24. Liampi, *MS*, pl. 1.2 (S 2); cf. Chapter 6.1.
25. Plate 62b; Liampi, *MS*, pl. 1.3 (S 3); cf. Chapter 6.1.
26. *AG*, 174, n. 20; cf. 250, n. 106. C. T. Selman, "A Synopsis of the Coins of Antigonus I and Demetrius Poliorcetes," *NC* (1909), 268; Imhoof-Blumer, *MG*, no. 70. Nachtergael assigns the issues carrying diademed heads of Pan on the obverse to either Gonatas or Doson and considers them contemporary with the introduction of the Delian Paneia and Soteria: *Galates*, 180. On the diadem as one of the royal signs in the Hellenistic period, see Le Bohec, *AD*, 202–203.; cf. B. Virgilio, Lancia, *Diadema e Porpora. Il Re e la regalità ellenistica*, Studi ellenistici 11 (Pisa/Rome: F. Serra, 2003), 87–130; A. Lichtenberger, K. Martin, H.-H. Nieswalt, and D. Salzmann (eds.), *Das Diadem der hellenistischen Herrscher, Überbagnem Transformation oder Neuschöpfnung eines Herrschaftszeichens?, Kolloquium von 30.-31. Januar 2009 in Münster* (Bonn: Habelt, 2012), 163–179, 181–208, 249–278, 293–313, 315–334, 337–383.

d. ANM: Eretria, *1937*: *CH* IX (2002), 194; *IGCH* 175, 18
17.08 g 5:30 h 30.0 mm

e. Unknown Findspot ("Seleucus III" Hoard), 2002: *CH* X (2010), 272; A. Houghton—C. Lorber—O. Hoover, *SC* II.2, 142–150, Lot F: "Before Cleaning?," photos DSCN 993.1–994.1 - - -

[O (a): flaws: on space 5; off "unit" 1, between inner badge circle and crescent; also, between badge circle and "unit" 3; recut on l. end of crescent 4. On badge, two small vertical flaws, off nose and off chin.
R (a): r., beginning of flaw on r. end of pleat].

133. O20 R124 R: X —monogram A, corrected to monogram R. Athena figure taller and thinner, diameter of shield smaller.

a. Berlin; Löbbecke 1905	17.17 g	12 h	-
b. Cambridge: *SNG Fitzwilliam* 2307	17.00 g	11 h	-

[O (a): dot between hair and internal circle, as in previous specimen. Flaw on space 3; die break l. of horns. On space 5, star: overstrike?
R (a): flaws, up r. and r., between Λ and monogram].

134. O20 R125

a. Leiden 3154	17.10 g	12 h	-

135. O20 R126

a. Berlin; Sperling	16.73 g	12 h	-

[O (a): dot on internal badge circle, off hair].

b. Unknown Findspot ("Seleucus III" Hoard), 2002: *CH* X (2010), 272; A. Houghton—C. Lorber—O. Hoover, *SC* II.2, 142–150, Lot F: "Before Cleaning?" photos DSCN 993.2, 994.2 - - -

[O(a): die break on spaces 3 (starting from crescent 3) and 7.
R (a): r., flaws through legend letters ΕΩ.
NB: off-center].

This special issue with a stylized Athena facing left, but with different control marks can be considered in the context of the battle of Andros. Merker's assignation of this issue to the mint of Chalkis because of the letter X on the reverse, is disproved by an obverse link between this group and the helmet series (Group 31). The association of the X variety with a Makedonian mint is further supported by the presence of the letter X on posthumous Alexander issues from Uranopolis.[27] In fact, the small size of this issue, the presence of a diadem and the reversed *pedum* (or scepter) on the badge may indicate its production under circumstances analogous to those that created these changes on the Athena right, *desmos* variety of the first period (see Chapter 2.2.2). The two groups cannot have been contemporary, for they differ stylistically and have different patterns of appearance in hoards. The inclusion of a tetradrachm from this variety in the Eretria, 1937, hoard indicates 245–240 BC as a *terminus ante quem* for its striking.

*** *** ***

27. See also Chapter 6.5.

4.1.6 Crested Helmet l.—No Monogram r.

O: Eight-rayed stars. Horned head, diademed, with hanging ribbons. *Nebris* ties in front of neck, scepter curved.
R: Similar.

Group 31

Specimens: 1	Obverses: [1-1]
Die Combinations: 1	Reverses: 1

136. O20 R127

a. S. Asia Minor ("Pisidia"), 1963: *IGCH* 1411 (Boehringer, *Chronologie*, 177.8, pl. 35)
17.10 g 11:30 h -

[O (a): more worn than nos. 130–133.
R (a): signs of monogram r.]

This specimen is distinguished by an elaborate head wearing a diadem (cf. Groups 27–31) and carrying a curved *pedum* (cf. Groups 2–3).[28] The *nebris* ties three-quarters facing to the front of the neck. The forward-pointing horns differentiate this head from the rest of the coinage struck during this period and foreshadow the heads of period IV. The corpulent head may have been influenced by Ptolemaic heads on contemporary coinages,[29] while Athena is depicted r. She is more stylized and the shield is held in front of her chest.

The obverse link between this specimen and Group 30 with the letter X left on the reverse disproves Merker's assignation of the X group of Pans to a mint different from that of the Helmet group, and suggests that this variety too was stuck at the main Makedonian mint, Amphipolis.[30] The diadem on the head of Pan and the different direction of the scepter place this group among the small celebratory issues of "King Antigonos." These features suggest that this group is later than Boehringer's c. 270 BC, possibly within the context of a naval victory such as Andros. An association of (at least part of) this issue with the departure of the Antigonid garrison from Athens in 229 BC is also possible.

28. Merker, *Silver Coinage*, 39–52, esp. 52. Boehringer, *Chronologie*, 177.8, pl. 35.
29. Hazzard, *Ptolemaic Coins*, 28–33; Mørkholm, *EHC*, 107–109, no. 316.
30. *Contra* Boehringer, *Chronologie*, 177.8, who identifies the main Makedonian mint with Pella (Chapter 6.5).

4.2 Poseidon Head Tetradrachms

Monogram

O: Bearded head of Poseidon r. in wreath of reeds; hair locks flow from crown downwards. Dotted border.

R: ΒΑΣΙΛΕΩΣ up, ΑΝΤΙΓΟΝΟΥ down, on prow facing l. Apollo holding bow, seated on prow.

Group 32

Specimens: 5	Obverses: 1
Die Combinations: 2	Reverses: 2

137. O21 R128

a. Kress 143 (1968), 252a	17.00 g	-	-
b. MMAG L 19 (1959), 403	17.07 g	-	-
c. Sotheby (3–11.7.1911), 140	-	-	-
d. *SNG Cop* 1204; Rollin	16.17 g	12 h	-

[Flan rough, flaw off nose and r., from hair downwards. Also, off l. foot. Diagonal flaw on prow, from O to l., downwards.
O (a): beginning of flaws on level of eye, off nose and mouth. (b): monogram.
R (c): progression of flaw from toes of r. foot downwards. (d): very worn].

138. O21 R129

a. CNG Triton 10 (9–10.1.2007), 169	17.05 g	11 h	-

*** *** ***

Monogram —Monogram

O: Similar.
R: Similar.

Group 33

Specimens: 22	Obverses: [3-1]
Die Combinations: 8	Reverses: 8

139. O21 R130

a. Athens: *SNG Alpha Bank* 1048 (5683)	16.61 g	11 h	30.2 g
b. NumVis 4 (1991), 35; Aes Rude (7–8.4.1978), 95	17.05 g	-	-

[O (a): flan rough. Flaws from nose off eye outwards and from middle of nose outwards; also, from mouth outwards. Flaw off hair.
R (a): flaws: between arm and prow; l. of prow; from r. foot to lower field. In field up r., letters BA/graffito erased. Monogram above monogram . (b): development of flaw beneath l. foot].

140. O21 R131 R: Flan rough.

a. Weil (15–16.11.1994), 11; Spink Zürich 20 (6.10.1986), 204; Sternberg (1976), 38; Hamburger 7 (1933), 524 (16.95 g) 17.11 g - -
b. Numismatic Review & Coin Galleries FPL 5.1 (1964), A 25
14.95 g - -
c. Ball (5.12.1932), 2013 16.60 g - -

141. O21 R132

a. Gorny 40 (1988), 137 - - -

[O (a): development of flaw off eye and nose.
R (a): development of flaw from r. foot downwards.

142. O22 R133

a. SB 28 (1991), 91 16.48 g - -
b. Berlin; Löbbecke (1906), 902 17.11 g 12 h -
c. CNG 208 (8.4.2009), 46 16.89 g 11 h 31 mm
d. Elsen 120 (15.3.2014), 29; Elsen 119 (7.12.2013), 118 (16.90 g); Elsen 72 (14.12.2002), 178 (16.88 g); Peus 334 (1992), 360; Lanz Graz 5 (1975), 145 (16.85 g); Coll. Virzi 467
16.88 g - -
e. Gorny & Mosch 146 (6.3.2006), 179 17.08 g - -
f. CB (1992), 354 16.48 g - -
g. NFA 6 (1979), 155 16.99 g - -

[O (a): flan rough. In field l., flaw near dotted border; horizontal flaw along side locks.
R (a): flaw on edge, beneath l. foot].

143. O22 R134 R: Monogram .

a. ANS 1944.100.13855 (Newell) 17.17 g 11 h -
b. ANM 1610b 17.09 g 11:30 h 32.0 mm

144. O22 R135

a. BM 1947-4-6-192 16.83 g 11 h 32 mm
b. Unknown Findspot ("Achaeus" Hoard), 2002: *CH* 10 (2010), 277; A. R. Meadows and C. C. Lorber, "Commerce ("Achaeus" Hoard), 2002 (*CH* 10.277)," ibid., 115–127, pls. 17–20, esp. p. 116, pl. 17.3; Freeman & Sear FPL 9 (Spring 2004), 23[31]
17.13 g - -
c. CNG 43 (1997), 287 16.56 g - -

[O (a): l. portion of metal flaked off cheek. (b): flaw off nose and behind hair locks.
R (b): flaws r. of prow, horizontal flaw beneath legs].

145. O22 R136

a. Stack's (15–16.3.1979, coll. Dr. J. A. Sawhill), 74; Hess 207 (1.12.1931, Coll. H. Otto, Stuttgart), 368 16.70 g - 31 mm
b. Kurpfälzische Münzhandlung 45 (1993), 45 - - -
c. Gorny & Mosch 117 (14.10.2002), 183 17.12 g - -

31. Note in *CH* 10 (2010), 277, 116: "not certainly from hoard."

[O (a): flaw off nose.
R (a): horizontal flaw from Apollo's head to edge; scratch beneath l. foot].

O: Hair ends in two locks. Wreath similar.
R: Similar. Bow diagonal.

146. O23 R137 R: Monogram [monogram].

a. J. Hirsch 32 (1912), 467 (17 g); MMAG 10 (1938), 222; Wulfing 163
16.98 g 11 h -

*** *** ***

Monogram [monogram]—Monogram [monogram]

O: As above.
R: Similar.

GROUP 34

Specimens: 2	Obverses: [1-1]
Die Combinations: 1	Reverses: 1

147. O21 R138

a. Unknown Findspot, ("Antiochus III" hoard), 2005: *CH* X (2010), 288; A. Houghton—C. Lorber—O. Hoover, *SC* II.2 (Lancaster 2008), p. 150; C. Lorber—A. Houghton, "Antiochus III Hoard," *AJN* 21 (2009), 89–104, pl. 9.15; Gemini II (10.1.2006), 67
17.05 g - -
b. Seaby-Glendining (1–2.12.1927), 291; Hesperia Art 26 (-), 12
\- - -

[O (a–b): flan rough. Progression of flaws on nose and off mouth. Monogram [monogram] corrected to monogram [monogram]].

*** *** ***

Monogram [monogram]—M

O: Similar. Linear border.
R: Similar.

GROUP 35

Specimens: 21	Obverses: [2-1]
Die Combinations: 7	Reverses: 7

148. O23 R139

a. Roma 2 (2.10.2011), 254 17.01 g 12 h 31 mm
b. G. Hirsch 293 (25.9.2013), 2231; G. Hirsch 287 (7.2.2013), 1853
17.08 g - -

149. O23 R140

a. G. Hirsch 281 (2.5.2012), 245; G. Hirsch 272 (4.5.2011), 221; Gemini 7 (9.1.2011), 281 (17.09 g); CNG 213 (1.7.2009), 84 (17.07 g) 17.08 g 12 h 30.0 mm

b. NFA 1 (20–1.3.1975), 94 16.87 g - -

O: Similar. Hair ends in three locks. Linear border.

R: Similar. Apollo archaizing.

150. O24 R141 R: Monogram [monogram].

a. Leiden, von Rede 4755; *Aréthuse* 1 (1929), 198; Florange (1924), 198 17.09 g 12 h -

b. NYS 7 (15.1.2004), 86; Hess-Leu (24.3.1959), Lucerne Sale 174 (17.17 g); Jameson, 1008 (17.15 g) 17.16 g 12 h -

c. Pergamon, 1960: *IGCH* 1303 (Boehringer, *Chronologie*, 163, 10) - - -

d. Schlessinger 13 (4.2.1935), 774 17.10 g - 31 mm

e. H. J. Berk BBS 150 (8.8.2006), 160 17.12 g - -

[O (a–c): flaw on upper lock of hair; also, on cheek.

R (a–d): flaw from l. foot to l. end of prow; also, from r. foot to end of M. Monogram recut. (f): development of flaws on either side of r. foot].

151. O24 R142 R: Monogram [monogram].

a. Madrid, Mus. Arq. Nacional 17.01 g 12 h -

b. Kress 140 (1967), 62 17.00 g - -

[R (a): scratches near head, r. of figure, and near l. foot and at level of prow. Below, r., signs of tooling. (b): flaw from l. foot to the l. end of prow].

152. O24 R143 R: Monogram [monogram].

a. Unknown Findspot, ("Antiochus III" hoard), 2005: *CH* X (2010), 288; A. Houghton—C. Lorber—O. Hoover, *SC* II.2 (Lancaster 2008), 150; C. Lorber—A. Houghton, "Antiochus III Hoard," *AJN* 21 (2009): 89–104, pl. 9.14; Gemini II (10.1.2006), 66 17.12 g - -

b. Vinchon (13–15.11.1986, coll. Armand Trampitsch), 136 16.80 g - -

153. O24 R144 R: Monogram [monogram].

a. BM Payne Knight (1824): RPK, 2, p. 174; Mektepini 1956: *IGCH* 1410 (Olcay and Seyrig, *Mektepini*, 699) 16.67 g 12 h 31 mm

b. Vinchon, Auction, Monte Carlo (7–8.11.1977), 62 16.97 g - -

c. Platt (18–19.11.1935), 43 16.90 g - -

d. CNG 247 (12.1.2011), 66 16.57 g - -

[O (a): worn in field, up r., and on forehead. Flaw on cheek. In field r., curved line off brow. Off-center.

R (a): flaws on top of head; off prow; between l. foot and prow. Alpha without horizontal bar, the r. lateral line shorter than the l.].

154. O24 R145 R: Monogram .

a. BNF AF 1328	17.07 g	12 h	-
b. Sotheby (27–28.10.1993), 446	17.12 g	11 h	-
c. Gemini 7 (9.1.2011), 281	17.09 g	11 h	-
d. G. Hirsch 242 (22–24.9.2005), 2004; G. Hirsch 239 (17–18.2.2005), 1344	15.93 g	-	-

[O (a): development of flaw on cheek].

*** *** ***

Monogram —Monogram

GROUP 36

Specimens: 3	Obverses: [1-1]
Die Combinations: 1	Reverses: 1

155. O24 R146 O: As above. R: Similar. Monogram .

a. NAC 29 (11.5.2005), 161; Numifrance (2.6.1982), 58	17.06 g	-	-
b. CGB MBS 47 (19.3.2011), 67	17.01 g	12 h	30.0 mm
c. Antiqua 11 (8.11.2001), 27	17.01 g	-	-

A number of specimens with an archaizing figure of Apollo on the reverse may tentatively be placed at the beginning of the Poseidon head tetradrachms, on stylistic grounds. The obverse heads are very well executed, despite the small size of the flans. Remains of dotted borders on some specimens indicate care in the execution of this issue. The first specimen of this series, no. 137, is signed with a distinctive monogram; its small flan, similar to those of the last two Pan head special tetradrachm groups from the same period, with the d*esmos* symbol and with the letter X, respectively, might suggest they are all contemporary. The obverses of the next specimens are combined with reverses carrying a second monogram alongside , which runs through most of the series. The secondary monograms, and , establish some connection between the Pan head and the Poseidon head tetradrachms (Chapter 6.2.4, Figs. 6.7–6.9). The correction of monogram to monogram on specimen 147a, in particular, confirms the approximately contemporary operation of these two officials, who are also attested on Pan head tetradrachms. The occurrence of monogram on these specimens and not on the Pan head tetradrachms of this period may indicate either that this experienced official was assigned to the execution of the new type; or that payment to the recipient was made with this new coinage.

The only specimens from securely dated hoards are nos. 150c and 153a, respectively from Pergamon, 1960 and from Mektepini, 1956, but the late burial date of these hoards and the worn state of the two coins provide no clues for the introduction date of this group. Their tentative placement at the beginning of this series has been primarily determined by the archaizing style of the Apollo and by the angular and crudely engraved legend characters (with splayed sigmas) on the reverse.

The series begins with small flans, often too small for the designs. The designs have been struck on rough flans on a number of specimens (i.e. nos. 142a, 147a–b). The monogram has been recut on a number of coins (i.e. nos. 147a–b; 150a).

*** *** ***

Monogram

O: Poseidon in different wreath. Dotted border.
R: Similar.

Group 37

Specimens: 84	Obverses: 1
Die Combinations: 17	Reverses: 17

156. O25 R147 Monogram .

a. BM G10-III-106, G0526	17.08 g	12 h	32 mm
b. Kress 132 (1965), 135	16.805 g	-	-
c. J. Vinchon-Françoise Berthelot-Vinchon & Annette Vinchon-Guyonnet. Collection A.B. (7.11.2001), 38	16.81 g	-	-
d. Sotheby (30.3.1997), 381; Sotheby (4.1992), 59; Glendining (18–20.4.1955), 291	17.17 g	-	-
e. Gorny 46 (1989), 136	17.10 g	-	-
f. Noble 67 (18–19.7.2001), 1651; Baldwin 24 (9–10.10.2000), 592	17.026 g	-	-
g. NFA 28 (1992), 648	16.83 g	-	-
h. Egger (28.11.1904) (Theodor Prowe Collection), 627; Feuardent (17.12.1921), 41	16.47 g	-	30 mm

[(b): bad photograph].

157. O25 R148 Monogram .

a. Bourgey (11.1957), 65; Feuardent (18.6.1924), 80	17.00 g	-	-
b. Peus 288 (1975), 145	17.13 g	-	-
c. Argenor (22.4.2004), 33	17.03 g	11 h	-
d. Müller 60 (1989), 45	17.20 g	-	-
e. MMAG L 320 (1971), 11	17.10 g	-	-
f. Helios 6 (9.3.2011), 462	17.08 g	-	-

[O (a): r., die ready to break between forehead and side lock. Edge slightly deformed (4 h). Beginning of flaw on border (8 h).
R (e): die break from lower edge to legs].

158. O25 R149

a. SKA Bern 3 (1985), 164; MMAG 47 (1972), 458	16.88 g	-	-
b. Münzhlg. Basel 4 (1.10.1935), 649	17.00 g	-	-

c. Coin Galleries (1988), 151 17.04 g - -
d. Peus 305 (1982), 57 16.84 g - -
e. NFA 462 (1989), 463 16.86 g - -

[R (a): flaw on monogram].

159. O25 R150

a. Auctiones 27 (1996), 219 17.12 g - -
b. CNG Triton 17 (7.1.2014), 175; RAJ Collection; CNG Inventory 717992 (12.1999); Spink New York (6.12.1999), 527; Hamburger (29.5.1929), 206
17.10 g 11 h 30.0 mm
c. Gemini 11 (12.1.2014), 72 16.99 g 11 h -
d. Morton & Eden (11.12.2003), 12 17.06 g - -
e. Baldwin's—D. Markov—M&M (11.1.2006), 123
17.16 g - -
f. Gordion. 1951: *IGCH* 1406 (Cox, *Gordion*, 8.54, pl. 4.54)
15.15 g 12 h 32.0 mm
g. T. Høiland Møntauktion 25 (20–23.11.2003), 6043
- - -

[O (a): flaw off eye].

160. O25 R151

a. ANS 1977.158.172; Sotheby (1894), 14 17.06 g - -
b. CNG 96 (14.5.2014), 77 17.12 g 5 h 31 mm
c. Hess-Leu 31 (1966), 265; Frankfurt am Main, 1
17.16 g 11 h 31 mm
d. Private Collection L.C. 8 - (p) - -
e. *SNG Ashmolean* 3266 (ex Robinson) 16.98 g (p) 11 h 31 mm
f. Numismatica Genevensis 7 (27.11.2012), 60 17.01 g - -
g. Burgan MBS 32 (22.12.1992), 29 16.84 g - -
h. NFA (12.10.1989), 463 16.86 g - -
i. Védrines (27.3.1990), 28 17.04 g - -
j. Nomos 8 (22.10.2013), 111; KMK 69 (18–19.11.1998), 71
17.27 g 12 h 28 mm
k. Goldberg 80 (3.6.2014), 3289 17.00 g - -
l. Whitford (30.11.1992), 118; Superior (1–2.12.1990), 1993
16.97 g - -

[O (a): development of flaw in field r., starting from nose, at the level of the eye; also diagonally, from dotted border (6 h) downwards. (d): development of flaw off nose, on dotted border (6 h). Off-center.
R. (a-d): flaw starting from end of flan l. towards prow, from prow's lower end to legs. (e): l., flaw beneath prow.
NB (h): very bad photograph].

161. O25 R152 Monogram .

a. Peus 270 (1969), 65 17.05 g - -

b. CNG MBS 64 (24.9.2003), 123 17.12 g - -
c. G. Hirsch 284 (26.9.2012), 2043 17.12 g - -
d. Spink *NCirc.* 59.2 (4.2001), 150 17.09 g - -
e. Aufhäuser 6 (1989), 76 17.19 g - -
f. Kurpfälzische Münzhandlung 24–25 (9.1971), 48; MMAG L 320 (1971), 11
17.10 g - -
g. MMAG L 294 (1969), 11 17.30 g - -
h. Müller 58 (3–4.6.1988), 38 17.30 g - -
i. Bourgey (17–18.5.1984), 48 - - -

[Flan surface rough.
O (a): flaws on nose and on beard.
R (a): flaw along l. leg; from l. foot to the flan's l. end; from r. foot to monogram. Die breaks on end].

162. O25 R153

a. Müller 62 (1989), 49; Ritter L 27 (1988), 305 17.10 g - -
b. Lanz 155 (10.12.2012), 117 17.02 g - -
c. Künker 248 (14.3.2014), 7189; Künker 89 (8–9.3.2004), 1224; Dieter Braun Collection
16.87 g - -
d. Gemini 11 (12.1.2014), 72 16.99 g 11 h -
e. Gorny & Mosch 191 (11.10.2010), 1320 16.99 g - -
f. Helios 6 (9.3.2011), 47 15.10 g - -

[O (a): development of existing flaws.
R (a): reverse recut bow held horizontally, legend letters recut].

163. O25 R154 Monogram 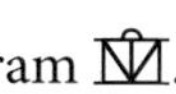.

a. Lanz 26 (1983), 187 17.05 g 11 h -
b. CNG Triton 6 (14–15.1.2003), 190 (17.22 g); Coin Galleries (10.4.1991), 93; Coin Galleries (23.5.1990), 96; Coin Galleries (9.11.1988), 90
17.189 g - -

164. O25 R155

a. G. Hirsch 195 (5–7.5.1997), 153; G. Hirsch 192 (27–29.11.1996), 101; G. Hirsch 190 (1990), 212; G. Hirsch 187 (1995), 312; Peus 340 (1994), 322 (17.05 g); G. Hirsch 185 (1994), 175G; Coin Galleries (9.11.1988), 60 (17.073 g); Sotheby (2.1878), 75
17.01 g - -
b. CNG 265 (5.10.2011), 76 16.98 g 11 h 33 mm
c. HWCA 3032 (10.4.2014), 23140; ex A. C. Dimitriadis Collection; Stack's (18.7.1990), 77
16.95 g 11 h 30.0 mm
d. Feuardent-Leman, Collection Engel-Gross (17.12.1921), 41
- - -

165. O25 R156

a. Noble Numismatics 68 (21–23.11.2001), 1846 16.918 g - -

166. O25 R157

a. Serrure (18.11.1911), 46; Sotheby (13–20.6.1911), 134

	-	-	-
b. Glendining (4.1955), 291	-	-	-
c. Aufleger, Verzeichnis, 4	-	-	-
d. Waddell L 16 (1985), 12	16.88 g	-	-
e. G. Hirsch 161 (1989), 176	17.02 g	-	-
f. Athena 1 (1987), 70	17.07 g	3 h	-
g. Stack's (1–2.12.1999), 92	17.01 g	-	-

[O (a): new flaw off nose. (e): recut off nose; new diagonal flaw from nose to end (3:30 h) and from beard to end (5 h).
R (a): die breaks from end towards main figure (3 h, 6 h 7:30–9:30 h). (f): ΑΝΤΙΓΟΝΟΥΣ].

167. O25 R158

a. Baranowsky (25.2.1931, coll. Valerio Traverso di Genova-Mr. Joseph Martini et al.), 449

	16.57 g	-	-
b. Roma 7 (22.3.2014), 462	17.08 g	12 h	29 mm

168. O25 R159

a. M. Feuardent, Collection Leman (11.6.1925), 60

	-	-	-

169. O25 R160

a. Hamburger (27.5.1929), 206	-	-	-
b. Védrines (25.3.1988), 33	17.27 g	-	-
c. CNG MBS 64 (24.9.2003), 122	17.10 g	-	-
d. Kurpfälzische Münzhandlung 2 (1971), 48	-	-	-

170. O25 R161

a. Athena 2 (1988), 101; SKA Monetarium L 50 (1988), 42 (17.18 g)			
	17.19 g	-	-
b. Elsen 9 (1988), 35	17.09 g	-	-
c. SKA Monetarium L 52 (1989), 51	17.17 g	-	-
d. Ahlström 30 (1984), 1966; Schlessinger 13 (4.2.1935), 775			
	17.00 g	3 h	-
e. Serrure (18.11.1911), 46; Sotheby (13–20.6.1911), 134			
	17.04 g	-	-
f. Aufhäuser 6 (5–6.10.1989), 76; MMAG L 190 (1959), 11			
	17.19 g	-	-
g. Rauch 41 (1988), 147	17.10 g	-	-

171. O25 R162

a. Kassandreia, 1985/7 (*CH* VIII (1994), 322, pl. 39.6)

	-	-	-

[O (a): recut r. of forehead and nose].

172. O25 R163

a. Dorotheum L 285 (1966), 132; G. Hirsch 11 (1956), 130	16.90 g	-	-
b. Coin Galleries (14.4.1993), 224	17.04 g	-	-

[O (a): r., new flaw from middle of nose through to edge].

The monogram has been recut on nos. 166e, 171a. The worn tetradrachm from Kassandreia, 1985–1987, provides a *terminus ante quem* for this group around 225 BC. The archaizing figures of Apollo on the reverse are henceforth combined with a single monogram on the rough flans of this group.

*** *** ***

O: Similar. Dotted border.
R: Similar.

Group 38

Specimens: 1	Obverses: 1
Die Combinations: 1	Reverses: 1

173. O26 R164

a. Berlin (Fox)	16.97 g	12 h	-

*** *** ***

Monogram 

O: Similar. Dotted border.
R: Similar.

Group 39

Specimens: 3	Obverses: [1-1]
Die Combinations: 1	Reverses: 1

174. O26 R165

a. BNF 1697	17.06 g	-	-
b. Berlin (Löbbecke)	16.97 g	12 h	-
c. Gorny & Mosch 122 (10–11.3.2003), 1262; Gorny & Mosch 113 (18.10.2001), 5151	16.97 g	-	-

[O (a–c): diagonal flaws off forehead, off side lock; also, diagonally from eye to cheek. (a–b): developing flaw from cheek through l. eye to *anastole*. On upper end of flan, flaw crossing end of wreath. (b): small breaks on edge (6 h).
R (a–b): flaw on r. foot; also, between l. foot and end of prow flaw on l. heel.
Flan rough].

A distinctive monogram and the tall archaizing Apollo seated on a higher prow characterize this group. The details of the head and the beard locks on the obverse are rendered in lines. A flaw reaches the end of Poseidon's cheek through the eye's edge. The monogram is larger.

*** *** ***

Monogram [monogram]

O: Wreath of different type. Head l.
R: Figure more comfortably seated r. on prow, head leans forward. String close to bow.

GROUP 40

Specimens: 1	Obverses: 1
Die Combinations: 1	Reverses: 1

175. O27 R166

a. Gans 2 (1960), 255	-	-	-

This change in the direction of the designs on both the obverse and the reverse in this group is presumably a mistake of the die-cutter. This is also suggested by the fact that the legend on the existing specimen cannot be read.

*** *** ***

O: Poseidon r.
R: Apollo l.

GROUP 41

Specimens: 89	Obverses: 3
Die Combinations: 15	Reverses: 15

176. O28 R167

a. BNF AF 1065; *SNG Delepierre*, 1065; J. Hirsch 15 (1930), 54	17.02 g	6 h	-
b. Rauch 87 (8.12.2010), 106	16.81 g	-	-
c. Spink *NCirc* 60.2 (4.2002), 525	17.05 g	-	-
d. Roma 7 (26.4.2014), 418 (E-sale)	16.47 g (b)	10 h	30.0 mm
e. Kress 152 (1971), 104	16.90 g	-	-
f. Haughton Collection, 105A	16.99 g	-	-
g. Gorny & Mosch 185 (8.3.2010), 104	17.01 g	-	-
h. Künker 174 (27.9.2010), 231	16.68 g	-	-
i. *SNG Klagenfurt* 579 (1251)	16.822 g	12 h	-

[(c): found in Asia Minor, 1947/8. R (e): off-center].

177. O29 R168

a. G. Hirsch 135 (1983), 184	16.62 g	-	-
b. Gorny & Mosch 134 (11–12.10.2004), 1283	16.79 g	-	-
c. Roma 7 (26.4.2014), 417 (E-sale)	16.98 g	1 h	30.0 mm
d. CNG 244 (10.11.2010), 51	15.59 g	12 h	33.0 mm

178. O29 R169

a. Cambridge: Grose, *McClean* 3591; Sotheby (11–13.12.1894), 127
14.72 g 12 h -
b. Goldberg 72 (5.2.2013), 4323 16.93 g - -
c. *SNG Blackburn* 518 14.97 g 10 h -
d. J. Hirsch 82 (1973), 51 16.74 g - -
e. SKA Monetarium L 57 (Spring 1992), 59 16.99 g - -
f. G. Hirsch 71 (1971), 78 16.98 g - -
g. CNG 246 (15.12.2010), 42 16.20 g 5 h 31 mm

[R (a): upright scratch/flaw at r. end of prow. (a): on string, flaw].

179. O29 R170

a. Leiden 3149 (17.09 g); Kress 127 (1963), 379 (17.00 g); Helbing 31 (31.3.1930), 206 (17.05 g) 17.10 g 11 h 31 mm
b. CNG 87 (18.5.2011), 397 17.04 g 11 h 30.0 mm
c. Roma 7 (26.4.2014), 419 (E-sale) 17.07 g 10 h 31 mm
d. NFA 7 (1979), 110 16.85 g - -
e. Gemini 11 (12.1.2014), 73 17.08 g 12 h -
f. MMAG 85 (1997), 60 17.09 g - -
g. SB 24 (1990), 29 17.08 g - -
h. Spink London Brutus-1297 Sale (11.4.2001), 21
- - -
i. ANM: Karditsa (Palaiokastro), c. 1929: *IGCH* 162, 9
15.99 g (b) 11 h 32 mm
j. X4: Ripollès, "X4 Hoard," 60.6, pl. 3.6; Vico (17.11.1994), 1
15.72 g (b) - -

180. O29 R171

a. ANM: Thesprotia, 1992 (Touratsoglou, *DM*, no. 52)
17.05 g 11 h -
b. Vinchon (2–3.12.1975), 51 16.85 g - -
c. Cederlind L 94 (Fall 1991), 34 - - -
d. Aufhäuser 5 (1990), 80 17.06 g - -
e. TNF (9.1992), 6768 17.06 g - -
f. UBS 57 (15–17.9.2003), 179 16.90 g - -
g. Hirsch 236 (23–25.9.2004), 1722 16.80 g - -
h. CNG MBS (8.6.2005), 197 17.07 g - -
i. CNG Triton 7 (13–14.1.2004), 147; CNG Triton 5.2–4 (14–15.1.2002), 1308 (17.05 g); R. Schonwalter Collection (17.05 g) 17.10 g - -
j. CNG Triton 9 (10–11.1.2006), 833 (17.01 g); G. Hirsch 149 (19.2.1986), 79; John F. Sullivan Collection 17.10 g 12 h -

181. O29 R172

a. Unknown Findspot ("Seleucus III" Hoard), 2002: *CH* X (2010), 272; A. Houghton—C. Lorber—O. Hoover, *SC* II.2, 142–150, Lot F: "After Cleaning," photos 1188–1189 =

DSCN 0997.1, 0998.1 17.01 g 11 h -
b. Pecunem 9 (3.11.2013), 140 17.00 g - 32 mm

182. O29 R173

a. Lanz 125 (18.11.2005), 260 17.03 g - -

183. O29 R174

a. Naville 16 (3.7.1933), 1051; A. Sambon, Collection G. P[icard] (14–16.3.1923), 403; Ratto (26.9.1909), 1965; Rollin-Feuardent (1895), 1131
17.00 g - -

184. O29 R175

a. Schulman Amsterdam 262 (1975), 1049 16.91 g - -
b. Brussels, du Chastel (acq. 1899) 16.90 g 6 h 34 mm
c. New Yoik: ANS 1966.75.27: *SNG BYB* 367 17.08 g 12 h -
d. Gemini 11 (12.1.2014), 73 17.07 g 12 h -
e. Superior (7–10.6.1987, The Edwards Metcalf and Buddy Ebsen Collections), 4072; Peus 332 (23–8.10.1991), 176 17.07 g - -

[R (e): diagonal flaw across prow and bow].

185. O29 R176 Monogram .

a. New York: ANS 1966.75.25: *SNG BYB* 368 17.06 g 12 h -
b. NFA 18 (1987), 125 17.06 g - -

186. O29 R177

a. Syria, 1959: *IGCH* 1535 (Boehringer, *Chronologie*, 159.11, pl. 27.11)
- - -
b. Lanz 76 (18.5.1996), 184; Peus 338 (1994), 433 (17.04 g)
17.01 g 11 h -
c. Roma 7 (26.4.2014), 419 17.07 g 10 h 31.0 mm
d. Unknown Findspot ("Seleucus III" Hoard), 2002: *CH* X (2010), 272 (17.14 g before cleaning); A. Houghton—C. Lorber—O. Hoover, *SC* II.2, 142–150, Lot F: "After Cleaning," photos 1192–1193 17.14 g 11 h -
e. Unknown Findspot ("Seleucus III" Hoard), 2002: *CH* X (2010), 272; A. Houghton—C. Lorber—O. Hoover, *SC* II.2, 142–150, Lot F: "Best Coins," photos 843–844
16.94 g 12 h -
f. Kricheldorf 26 (19–21.2.1973), 57 - - -
g. NFA 22 (1.6.1989), 462 16.97 g - -
h. Sotheby (27–28.10.1993), L 445 (17.11 g); NFA 18 (1987), 125
17.06 g 5 h -
i. G. Hirsch 239 (17–18.2.2005), 1345 16.71 g - -
j. Gorny 130 (8–9.3.2004), 1165 15.99 g - -
k. Hess 236 (3.4.1939), 530 16.81 g - 30.5 mm
l. CGB MBS 57 (20.2.2013), 94; CGF (2000), 54 (17.04 g)
17.12 g 11 h 33.0 mm

[R (g): flaw r. of monogram].

187. O29 R178

a. *SNG Sweden* II, 1143 (F. W. Spiegelthal)[32] 16.27 g 11 h -
b. P. Ciani-J. Vinchon MBS (6–8.2.1956), 344; J. Hirsch 34 (1914), 299 (16.75 g); Merzbacher 15.11.1910 409 16.72 g - 30.0 mm
c. Florange-Ciani (16.10.1923, collection Mr. E. A.), 41; Naville 12 (18.10.1926), 1186 17.10 g - -
d. Roma 7 (26.4.2014), 418 (E-sale) 16.47 g (b) 10 h 30.0 mm
e. Horsky (30.4.1917), 701 - - -
f. Commerce ("Pamphylia or Cilicia" Hoard), 2000: O Hoover, "Commerce ('Pamphylia or Cilicia' Hoard), 2000 (*CH* 10.292)," *CH* X (2010), 292, pp. 129–152, esp. 136, pl. 21.20 - - -

[O (a): flaw r., off nose.
R (a): flaw l., beside upper prow].

O: Similar.
R: Similar.

188. O30 R179

a. Berlin; Ratto (1909), 1965; Gansauge (1873) 16.70 g - -
b. Noble Numismatics 75 (31.3–1.4.2004), 1764 17.002 g - -
c. Roma 7 (26.4.2014), 417 (E-sale) 16.98 g 1 h 30.0 mm
d. Mektepini, 1956: *IGCH* 1410 (Olcay and Seyrig, *Mektepini*, 694) 17.02 g - -
e. Kölner Münzkabinett 48 (1989), 34; Kölner Münzkabinett 42 (1986), 31 17.02 g - -
f. Cahn (27.2.1933), 181 16.66 g - -

189. O30 R180

a. Peus 333 (1992), 240 17.06 g - -
b. *SNG Klagenfurt* 579 16.82 g 12 h -
c. Gorny 100 (20.11.1999), 137 17.04 g - -
d. CNG Triton VII (13–14.1.2004), 147; Gorny & Mosch 121 (10.3.2003), 99 17.10 g - -
e. NAC L (18.5.2001), 1293 16.61 g - -
f. Superior (1985), 2107 17.00 g - -
g. Lee (10–11.5.1954), 156 16.98 g - -

[O (a–b): flaws behind head.
R (a): diagonal flaw from prow through bow. (b): break on edge (1 h)].

190. O30 R181

a. Tradart (18.11.1993), 67 17.10 g 11 h -
b. SB 38 (1995), 115 16.49 g - -
c. Pecunem 9 (3.11.2013), 140 17.00 g - 32 mm

32. The name "Jpiegelthal" in *SNG Sweden* II must be a typographical mistake.

d. Spink *NCirc* 64.2 (4.2006), 1852	17.05 g	-	-
e. Leu 2 (1972), 173	17.06 g	12 h	-
f. J. Hirsch 13 (1905), 1174	17.78 g	-	29.5 mm
g. UBS 49 (2000), 85	16.99 g	11 h	-

[O (a): flaw off nose.
R (f): vertical flaw from elbow to prow. (g): letters IE beneath l. foot?].

*** *** ***

O: Similar, hair locks more dense and regular; r. hair lock shorter than l. Wreath made by a main branch with flowers; side branches twine with the main branch. Dotted border.
R: Prow larger, figure upright.

GROUP 42

Specimens: 35	Obverses: 1
Die Combinations: 5	Reverses: 5

191. O31 R182

a. Kassandreia, 1985/7 (*CH* VIII (1994), 322, pl. XXXIX.7)			
	-	-	-

[R (a): flaw above prow; monogram larger, ΩΣ floating].

192. O31 R183

a. MMAG 54 (1978), 196	17.05 g	-	-
b. Roma 7 (26.4.2014), 416 (E-sale)	17.06 g	12 h	30.0 mm
c. NAC 64 (17.5.2012), 793	15.52 g	-	-
d. Roma 7 (22.3.2014), 458	-	-	-
e. Kölner Münzkabinett 38 (1985), 56; Feuardent (8–12.7.1919), 298			
	17.06 g	-	-
f. Gorny 60 (1992), 131; Gorny 58 (1993), 262			
	-	-	-
g. MMAG 37 (23.11.2012), 22	17.00 g	-	-
h. Gorny 48 (1990), 263	-	-	-

[O (a): beginning of flaw on nose].

193. O31 R184

a. Boston 715, 77; Kricheldorf 17 (1967), 77	-	-	-
b. Kricheldorf 22 (1971), 54	-	-	-
c. Sotheby (3.2.1909), 438	16.98 g	-	-
d. Sambon (1889), 309	-	-	-
e. Superior (30.5.1990), 6800	17.03 g	-	-
f. Chaponnière & Hess-Divo 3 (21.5.2012), 123	17.00 g	-	-
g. Superior (1988), 1484	17.08 g	-	-
h. ANM: Thesprotia, 1992 (Touratsoglou, *DM*, no. 53)			
	17.085 g	11 h	-

i. HWCA. New York Signature Sale 3030 (6.1.2014), 23742
15.76 g 8 h 30.0 mm
j. G. Hirsch (22–24.11.2000), 140 - - -

[Flan rough. O (h): flaw across nose.
R (a): similar. Similarities in engraving of legend. Monogram larger].

194. O31 R185

a. Unknown Findspot ("Seleucus III" Hoard), 2002: *CH* X (2010), 272; A. Houghton—C. Lorber—O. Hoover, *SC* II.2, 142–150, Lot B, photos 168.1–169.1, CD02760148.1, 02760149.1 16.36 g 11 h -
b. Cambridge: *SNG Fitzwilliam* 2309 (Leake 282) (A. Monophthalmus); Babington, p. 9.36; Thomas collection, 1142 16.89 g 12 h -
c. Sotheby Zürich (7.5.1975), 90 17.02 g 11 h -
d. Numismatic Auction Ltd Ancient Coins 1 (13.12.1982), 69
17.03 g - -
e. CNG 67 MBS (22.9.2004), 467 16.95 g - -

[R (a–e): flaw developing above head; small legend letters. Worn].

195. O31 R186

a. Norman Davis 97; NFA 11 (1982), 97; Coin Galleries 2.3 (1961), A570; Sambon (12.3.1883), 309 17.03 g 12 h -
b. Unknown Findspot ("Seleucus III" Hoard), 2002: *CH* X (2010), 272; A. Houghton—C. Lorber—O. Hoover, *SC* II.2, 142–150, Lot F: "Best Coins," photos 1190–1191
17.04 g 5 h 32 mm
c. Unknown Findspot ("Seleucus III" Hoard), 2002: *CH* X (2010), 272; A. Houghton—C. Lorber—O. Hoover, *SC* II.2, 142–150, Lot F: "Best Coins," photos 845–846
16.94 g 5 h 31 mm
d. NFA 38 (1990), 33 17.11 g - -
e. Ahlström 32 (1985), 1972 - - -
f. Syria, 1959: *IGCH* 1535 (Boehringer, *Chronologie*, 159.11, pl. 27.10)
- - -
g. Gorny & Mosch 156 (6.3.2007), 1327 17.01 g - -
h. Roma 4 (28.12.2013), 208 (E-sale) 16.91 g 2 h 31 mm
i. CNG MBS 67 (22.9.2004), 467 16.95 g - -
j. Gorny & Mosch 190 (11.10.2010), 181 16.60 g - -
k. Poindessault-Védrines (15.11.1991), 146 - - -

[R (a): flaw from toes of l. foot downwards. Recut on monogram. (f): die breaks up (12 h), r. (2–4 h)].

The figure of Apollo on the reverse resting on his bent l. elbow is more comfortably rendered than in the previous groups: the god leans on the prow, his head leaning forward. The *embolon* is larger. The border of the upper prow ends before the upper bar of the sigma. No. 191a forms part of the Kassandreia, 1985–1987 hoard, which is approximately dated to 225 BC (see Chapter 6.3, Fig. 6.13, no. 14).

*** *** ***

O: Head with two long hair locks and beard, arranged in two levels. His wreath made of a reed ending in a *thyssanos*; four flowers and side branches attached. Dotted border.
R: Similar.

Group 43

Specimens: 98	Obverses: 1
Die Combinations: 17	Reverses: 17

196. O32 R187 Monogram .

a. Berlin; Rauch	15.53 g (b)	11 h	-
b. MMAG 7 (1948), 434	16.93 g	-	-
c. *SNG Manchester*, 739	17.11 g	11 h	-
d. Vico (21.6.2001), 87	17.20 g	-	-
e. Sotheby (9–10.10.1995), 75	17.12 g	-	-

[O (a): beginning of flaw on nose.
R (a): flaw r., circular, from prow upwards].

197. O32 R188

a. Leiden 3262	16.99 g	11 h	-
b. CGF (22.6.2006), 49; G. Hirsch 175 (23–26.9.1992), 246	16.44 g	11 h	31 mm

[O (a): die ready to break off forehead. Diagonal flaws on lower field.
R (a): flaw diagonally, l. of l. foot. Flaws around monogram; also r., beneath prow].

198. O32 R189

a. Künker 158 (28.9.2009), 187; Künker 94 (27–28.9.2004), 719; P. Ciani-J. Vinchon MBS (6–8.2.1956), 345 (17.02 g); Platt (27.3.1922), 385; coll. Luneau	17.07 g	-	-
b. CNG 248 (26.1.2011), 58	16.90 g	12 h	33 mm
c. Ahlström 28 (22–23.10.1983), 1914	-	-	-
d. Peus 384 (2.11.2005), 265; Spink-GMG (15–16.2.1977), 48; Mc Sorley & Adams FPL (pre-1968), 126	17.11 g	-	-
e. Spink 15 (15.5.1981) 36	17.13 g	-	-
f. Goldberg (15–17.9.2003), 1502	17.10 g	-	-

[O (a): dots behind head and off nose; also, beneath beard. (b): development of flaw behind head.
R (a): flaw on end (12 h); r., sign of tool. Beginning of flaw between uplifted arm and prow. Flaws on both feet. Beginning of flaw (dot) r. of r. foot. (b–c): development of flaw between l. toes and prow. (c): vertical flaws l. and r. of prow].

199. O32 R190

a. Mygind L 6 (3.1992), 54; CNA 16 (16.8.1991), 107; CNA 14 (20.3.1991), 72 (16.96 g); Christie's (13.3.1990), 49 (17,00 g); Christie's (28.2–1.3.1989), 1276	16.97 g	-	-

b. J. Schulman (29–30.6.1922), 25   16.74 g   -   -
c. Seaby 589 (9.1967), A 973   -   -   -

[O (a): development of flaws across neck and along beard; also, development of those off forehead, nose and beard. Flaw on cheek].

200. O32 R191

a. Baldwin-Markov-M&M, The New York Sale 32 (8.1.2014), 137; Künker 89 (8–9.3.2004), 1225 (17.09 g); Auctiones 15 (18–19.9.1985), 83; NFA 11 (8.12.1982), 96
    17.12 g   11 h   -
b. New York: ANS 1966.75.23: *SNG BYB* 369   17.12 g   10 h   -
c. New York: ANS 1966.75.21: *SNG BYB* 370   17.03 g   10 h   -
d. Gorny 44 (1989), 245   17.11 g   -   -
e. Kurpfälzische Münzhandlung 47 (1994), 47   -   -   -
f. Superior, Auction & MBS (1.6.1988, Moreira Collection Sale, Part 1), 1485
    17.10 g   -   -
g. Vinchon (17.11.1990), 19   17.10 g   -   -
h. Gemini 11 (12.1.2014), 74   17.05 g   11 h   -
i. Freeman & Sear, Manhattan Sale I (5.1.2010), 50; Freeman & Sear FPL 11 (Spring/Summer 2006), 37; CNG MBS (21.9.2005), 141 (17.13 g)
    17.18 g   11 h   -
j. Elsen L 116 (1989), 40   17.13 g   -   -

[O (a): new diagonal flaw continuing side lock. (e–f): diagonal flaw across side locks; also, off forehead. Development of diagonal flaw from nose to edge.
R (a): flaw off prow; also, r. of prow upwards. (e): monograms erased beneath l. foot].

201. O32 R192

a. Vinchon (11–13.4.1988), 357; Naville 14 (2.7.1929), 204
    16.84 g   -   -
b. Schulman Amsterdam 254 (1971), 3039   16.06 g   -   -
c. Numismatica 13 (1976), 133   17.00 g   -   -
d. London: BM G0526   17.09 g   12 h   32 mm
e. Albuquerque MBS 36 (23.7.1992), 4; Albuquerque MBS 29 (8.8.1991), 30; Ratto (13.3.1912), 649   16.61 g   -   -
f. Kurpfälzische Münzhandlung 46 (9–10.6.1994), 51
    15.27 g   -   -
g. Dorotheum 244 (24–27.10.1961), 439   17.00 g   -   -
h. Superior (1987), 302   17.01 g   -   -
i. Superior (1990), 6800   17.03 g   -   -
j. Jenkins 739   -   -   -
k. Superior (1–2.10.2001), 1023   17.26 g   -   -
l. CNG Triton 6 (14–15.1.2001), 191; Stack's (2–3.12.1998), 70
    17.14 g   -   -
m. MMAG 25 (17.11.1962), 391; Raymond (1936), 24
    17.02 g   -   -
n. Stack's (2–3.12.1998), 69; Cederlind BBS 115 (14.4.1999), 1207

17.13 g - -

o. Stack's (2–3.12.1998), 70 17.14 g - -

p. Whitford (23–24.11.2001), 17 16.6 g - -

[O (a): l., horizontal flaw off head. Beginning of flaw (dot) on forehead. (b): flaw behind head.
R (b): r., diagonal flaw between l. arm and prow. (c): two diagonal scratches on upper field. Flaws, up and off l. foot diagonal flaw across l. foot. Also, vertical flaw l. of prow].

202. O32 R193

a. Auctiones 23 (1993), 300 (17.08 g); MMAG 47 (6–7.12.1946), 628; MMAG 4 (1.10.1935), 648; Monetarium 3 (19–20.4.1985), 164; Hamburger 98 (3–4.4.1933), 523 (17.05 g)
17.07 g - 32 mm

b. Lanz 151 (30.6.2011), 50 17.05 g - -

c. Coin Galleries MBS (11.1988), 151 17.04 g - -

d. Peus 305 (12–15.10.1982), 57 16.84 g - -

e. NFA 462 (14.12.1989), 463 16.86 g - -

f. Myers 12 (4.12.1975), 128 16.91 g - -

[O (a): flaw behind head. (c): development of existing flaws. Two new flaws, the first off forehead and the second starting from end of neck].
R (a): signs of flaw r. of prow. (c): flaw l., r. of prow upwards].

203. O32 R194

a. Naville 14 (2.7.1929) 203; Sotheby (5–15.7.1909) 61; Sotheby (9.5.1904) 118; Rollin-Feuardent (1-2.5.1903) 114 16.98 g - -

b. J. Vinchon (24.11.1969) 117; Bourgey (11.1909) 117
17.09 g - -

c. CNG 248 (26.1.2011), 58 16.90 g - -

d. A. Page (19–22.6.1933, collection d' un amateur parisien), 174; Bourgey (7–8.6.1909, Bourgerol), 217 - - -

e. Delestre-Sambon (11–12.12.1899), 8 - - -

f. Albuquerque MBS 21 (1990), 59 16.70 g - -

[O (a): flan rough. Development of diagonal flaw on neck and of flaws off nose. New diagonal flaws across neck. Development of curved flaw beside head].

204. O32 R195 Monogram  .

a. Auctiones 22 (16–17.06.1990), 209 16.96 g - -

b. Kress 140 (7–8.8.1967), 61 17.00 g - -

c. Sotheby (9–10.10.1995), 75 17.12 g - -

d. Sotheby (9.1976), 35 16.84 g - -

e. Cayón Numismática (30.11.2013), 262; UBS 61 (14.9.2004), 4289; Pegasi BBS 95 (20.11.1995), 82 (17.02 g); Vigne (25.11.1999), 7 (16.90 g); Kurpfälsische Münzhandlung 42 (2–3.6.1992), 155; NFA (12.10.1988), 209 (G. Brauer coll.); KuMü 26 (13–15.5.1988), 70; MMAG L 315 (8.1970), 20 (17.15 g); Dupriez, 112bis (1913), 70
17.16 g - -

f. Peus 274 (1970), 1577 17.01 g - -

g. Madrid 1972/66 14.64 g (b) 11 h -

[Flan rough. O (a): development of flaw beside head; new flaw from hair locks upwards. Flaw off locks. (e): die break behind forehead.
R (d): flaws around monogram and above head, l. Legend letters ΩΣ floating. (f): flaws from end of prow to edge and from lower arm upwards; below, flaw from dot through monogram; horizontal flaw from l. foot to monogram].

205. O32 R196

a. Pegasi 16 (8.5.2007), 69 16.87 g - -
b. iNumis MBS 9 (23.10.2009), 17 17.07 g 11 h 30.0 mm
c. CNG 94 (18.9.2013), 288 17.05 g 12 h 31 mm
d. X4 Hoard: Ripollès, "X4 Hoard," 60.5, pl. 3.5; Villaronga, *Denario Romano*, 559; Vico (6.6.1991), 89 16.70 g - -
e. MMAG 30 (28.5.2009), 947 16.75 g - -

206. O32 R197

a. Vinchon (22–24.2.1971), 79 - - -

207. O32 R198 R: Monograms larger, legend letters small but regular.

a. Bourgey (4–5.6.1991), 77 17.06 g - -
b. Coin Galleries 3.6 (1962), F54 17.00 g - -
c. Sotheby (4.4.1991), 46 - - -
d. Berlin; Prokesch-Osten 1875 17.18 g 6 h 31 mm
e. Vinchon (14–15.3.1989), 90; Bourgey (21–2.6.1979), 43 17.03 g - -
f. Leiden; van Rede, 4754 17.10 g 5 h -
g. G. Hirsch 159 (9.1988), 221 17.03 g 10 h -
h. J. Hirsch 19 (1907), 182 17.05 g - -
i. Hess-Leu 31 (1966), 265 17.16 g - -
j. Bourgey (11–12.3.1980), 61 16. 95 g - -
k. Myers 13 (1976), 113; Myers L (1972), 21 16.93 g - -
l. Gorny & Mosch 216 (15.10.2013), 2336 17.13 g - -
m. *RN* (12.1994), 24; Mygind L 6 (1992), 54; Mygind L 4 (2.1991), 61 (17.02 g); Mygind L 2 (2.1990), 91 16.97 g - -
n. CNG 96 (14.5.2014), 77 17.12 g 5 h 31 mm
o. NFA (12.10.1988), 209 17.02 g - -

[O (a): signs of flaw behind head. Sign of flaw off end of nose. (b): development of vertical flaw from circular flaw to hair locks.
R (b): l., flaw from l. end of prow to l. foot. Dots in field up r.]

208. O32 R199

a. Oxford: *SNG Ashmolean* 3265 (Bodleian) 16.82 g 12 h 30.5 mm
b. Naville 15 (1930), 526; J. Hirsch 25 (29.11.1909), 545; J. Hirsch 20 (1907), 255 17.00 g - -
c. Ratto (4.4.1927), 728; Egger 13 (1906), 208 17.40 g - -

[O (a): development of flaw beside head. Horizontal scratch off forehead.
R (a): up l., flaw. Letters ΩΣ higher.
NB: flan rough].

209. O32 R200

a. Rosenberg (9.3.1914, coll. Helferich-Eisenach), 90; Kroyer (n.d.), N2
16.90 g - -
b. Oldenburg 26 (1.11.1991), 121 - - -
c. MMAG 17 (7–8.6.1988), 166 17.08 g - -

[O (a): recut in front of forehead and nose. Development of flaw beside head. (b): l., flaw beneath circular flaw.
R (a): flaw between r. foot and monogram. Break on lower edge, l. (c): flaw above string of bow; below, l. and r., circular flaw beneath monogram].

O: Dotted border.

210. O32 R201 R: Figure smaller. Legend letters smaller. Monogram 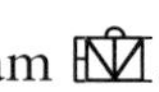.

a. Künker 139 (4.1998), 17; Künker FPL 136 (12.1997), 27; Künker 129 (5.1997), 9
- - -
b. Künker 193 (26.9.2011), 161; Künker 136 (10.3.2008), 566
17.13 g - -
c. Elsen L 182 (1996), 16 17.05 g - -
d. Chapponière & Hess-Divo 1 (18.5.2010), 93 17.33 g - -
e. Braunschweig 3 (1927), 289 - - -
f. Gemini (13–16.1.2005), 93 (Commander D. R. Hinkle Collection); Gorny 22 (1982), 56 (17.17 g); Glendining (7.4.1971), 43 (17.17 g)
17.09 g - -

[O (b): up l., die break (10–12 h). (c): development of flaw beside head.
R (b): l. on edge, signs of tool. R., flaw. (d): very worn. Diagonal flaw.
NB: Surface rough].

211. O32 R202 R: A without horizontal bar, splayed Σ.

a. Elsen 56 (1998), 141; Elsen 47 (1996), 128 17.05 g - -

[O (a): l., new flaw beneath l. hair lock.
R (a): monogram recut; flaws r. and l., off prow and on lower prow.
NB: Surface of flan rough].

212. O32 R203

a. Bourgey (11–12.3.1980), 61 16.95 g - -
b. Plumier (6.1979), 26; Sternberg 8 (16–17.11.1978), 61
16.95 g - -
c. Lanz 32 (29.4.1985), 173 17.05 g 5 h -

[O (a–b): development of existing flaws. (b): new flaw l., from attempted piercing to hair lock. In field r., flaw continuing lock. (c): new flaw from nose downwards.
R (b): flaws starting from feet and monogram].

*** *** ***

O: Similar.
R: Edge of prow higher, more elaborate. Legend characters smaller.

Group 44

Specimens: 69 Obverses: 1
Die Combinations: 12 Reverses: [12-1]

213. O33 R204

a. Athens, ANM: Thesprotia, 1992 (Touratsoglou, *DM*, no. 56) 16.77 g 5 h -
b. New York: ANS 1966.75.24: *SNG BYB* 362 17.06 g 12 h -
c. Coin Galleries (18.7.1995), 2108; NFA 18 (1980), 14 17.06 g 5 h -
d. G. Hirsch 165 (1990), 218 17.00 g - -
e. Munich: *SNG München* 1123 16.52 g (p) 11 h -
f. Leu 53 (1991), 78 17.05 g - -
g. CNG Triton 17 (7.1.2014), 176; Gemini 5 (06.1.2009) 391; Estate of J. D. Leggett, Jr., 1997 16.95 g 6 h 31 mm
h. Leu L 20 (1995), 10 16.85 g - -
i. Gorny 46 (1989), 135 17.10 g - -
j. Waddell L 38 (-), 36; Waddell L 36 (-), 31 17.14 g - -
k. Athens, ANM: Larissa ("Sitochoro"), 1968: *IGCH* 237 (Price, "The Larissa, 1968 Hoard (*IGCH* 237)" in Le Rider et al., *Kraay-Mørkholm Essays*, 235.20) 16.80 g 5 h -

[O (b–c): flaws r. of nose. (b): flaw behind head.
R (b): flaw l. of l. foot and low in field. (b): l., scrape l. of prow; r., vertical flaws].

214. O33 R205

a. Button 101 (28–29.10.1959), 58 17.00 g - -
b. Hariga (8.2.1992), 32 (17.10 g); Sotheby (4–5.10.1990), 85 (17.4 g); Bourgey (17–19.6.1959), 285 17.02 g - -
c. Oylum Höyüğü, 1989: E. Ogzen and A. Davesne, "Le trésor de Oylum Höyüğü," *TCMAA*, 45–49, esp. p. 45, 50, pl. 80 17.00 g 12 h 34 mm

215. O33 R206

a. Poindessault-Védrines (28.12.1999), 40; Elsen L 106 (3.1988), 31 (17.17 g) 17.13 g - -
b. CGB MBS 38 (30.4.2009), 131 17.14 g 12 h -
c. Rauch 86 (12.5.2010), 329 17.09 g - -
d. Leu 91 (10–11.5.2004), 132 16.77 g 11 h -

[O (a): flaw behind head and in front of nose].

216. O33 R207

a. Künker 236 (7.10.2013), 38; Künker 97 (7–8.3.2005), 502; Leu 38 (13.5.1986), 73; Merzbacher 2 (1909), 2800 (17.08 g); Sotheby (24–25.4.1907), 97 (Delbeke); Sotheby (28.5.1900, coll. G. Duruflé or Rothschild?), 216; Rollin
17.09 g 12 h 32 mm
b. Gorny & Mosch 200 (10.10.2011), 1469 16.98 g - -

[O (a): two die breaks, the former on forehead and the latter continuing the side lock].

217. O33 R208

a. Paris: BNF AF 1329A 16.97 g 12 h -
b. Paris: BNF 1973 I.74 17.19 g 12 h -
c. NAC 4 (1974), 96 17.10 g - -
d. Nomos 7 (15.5.2013), 63 17.07 g 12 h -
e. MMAG 73 (1988), 144; MMAG 72 (1987), 579 (17.10 g)
16.94 g - -
f. Stack's (8–10.6.1994), 2104; Stack's (12.1989), lot 3094
17.08 g - -
g. Elsen 32 (1993), 57; Elsen 26 (1992), 188 - - -

[O (a): progressively larger diagonal flaw on forehead. In field l., horizontal flaw off hair].

218. O33 R191

a. NFA Fall MBS (18.10.1990), 626 16.85 g - -
b. Budapest, National Museum (Mayar Nemzeti Mus.), 8
17.02 g 12 h -
c. Kress 91 (1951), 55 17.10 g - -
d. Gorny & Mosch 195 (7.3.2011), 150 16.44 g - -

219. O33 R209

a. NFA Fall MBS (12.10.1988), 208 16.88 g - -
b. Baldwin-Markov—M & M (4.1.2012), 315 (The New York Sale; The Prospero Collection of Ancient Greek Coins) 17.17 g - -
c. HWCA, New York Signature Sale 3021 (6.1.2013), 21168
17.05 g 12 h 29 mm
d. Weil (17.11.1991), 34; Künker 35 (11–14.3.1997), 143; Glendining (6.1992), 57
17.06 g - -
e. Argenor (3.5.2006), 76 16.91 g - -
f. CNG Triton 16 (8–9.1.2013, continental collection, purchased privately in the 1970s), 306 17.07 g 12 h 32 mm
g. Burgan (30.9.1994), 336; NFA MBS (12.10.1990, colls. L. M. Cutler, Al. Suthers, T. Ward, H. St. G. Tucker), 626 (16.85 g); CNA 5.6 (9.12.1988), F 59; MMAG 20 (8–9.11.1988), 272; Seaby-Glendining (1–2.12.1927), 292 16.85 g - -
h. Burgan (22.12.1990), 26; MMAG 18 (21–22.9.1989), 620
17.03 g - -
i. NFA 22 (1989), 269 16.70 g 12 h -
j. Gorny 50 (1990), 265 17.07 g - -

k. NFA 9 (1980), 184 17.09 g - -
l. Gorny 89 (5.5.1998), 127 - - -

[R (d–e): vertical flaw from elbow to prow].

220. O33 R210

a. Roma 6.2 (29.9.2013), 569; Nomos FPL (2009), 42; CNG Triton 9 (10.1.2006), 832; R. Weimer Collection (17.07 g) 17.11 g 12 h 31 mm
b. Rauch 94 (9.4.2014), 256 16.98 g - -

221. O33 R211

a. Spink *NCirc* 43.1 (2.1985), 17 16.51 g - -
b. Gorny & Mosch 195 (7.3.2011), 150 16,44 g - -
c. Malter 47 (4.2.1992), 80; SB 2 (27.10.1977), 305; Coin Galleries (9.3.1956), F 59; Raymond MBS (19.12.1938), 43 16.88 g - -
d. Roma 5 (23.3.2013), 276 16.98 g 6 h 31 mm
e. CNG Triton 16 (8.1.2013), 306 17.07 g 12 h 32 mm
f. Berk BBS 148 (29.3.2006), 111 17.00 g - -
g. Elsen 16 (2.6.1990), 49 - - -
h. Gorny & Mosch 121 (10.3.2003), 100; Gorny & Mosch 117 (14.10.2002), 184 - - -
i. Nomisma (1991), 38 17.14 g - -
j. CNG MBS 75 (23.5.2007), 147 16.85 g 5 h -
k. Waddell 38 (no date), 36 17.14 g - -
l. Berk BBS 146 (29.11.2005), 65 17.00 g - -
m. Frey (15–16.4.1955), 1057; Egger 41 (18.11.1912), 438 17.09 g - 32 mm

222. O33 R212

a. Unknown Findspot, ("Antiochus III" hoard), 2005: *CH* X (2010), 288; A. Houghton—C. Lorber—O. Hoover, *SC* II.2 (Lancaster, 2008), 150; C. Lorber—A. Houghton, "Antiochus III Hoard," *AJN* 21 (2009): 89–104, pl. 8.12 - - -

[R (a): in field below, monogram  erased twice, r. of and beneath l. leg].

223. O33 R213

a. Milan, Gab. Num. B1183 (coll. Brera) 15.30 g 10 h -
b. Cambridge: *SNG Lockett* 1527 16.86 g 9 h -
c. Vinchon (24.11.1969), 117; Glendining (2.1958), 1395 17.09 g - -
d. Lanz 86 (18.5.1998), 135 - - -

224. O33 R214

a. Athens: *SNG Alpha Bank* 1047 (5682) 16.93 g 11 h 34 mm
b. ANS: Norman Davis 96 16.71 g 12 h -

c. Freeman & Sear MBS 17 (15.12.2009), 7 16.91 g - -
d. Gorny 52 (6.11.1990), 204; Athena (15.5.1990), 100
17.09 g - -
e. Gorny 52 (6.11.1990), 203 17.14 g - -

[O (a): vertical break on forehead. Diagonal flaw off nose.
R (a): vertical flaw from upper field to upper prow; scratches up r. In field l., horizontal scratch off *embolon*. (c): slight bend in flan at 1–2 h and tiny metal delamination on edge at 4 h. (d): flan rough].

*** *** ***

O: Similar, wreath different.
R: Similar.

Group 45

Specimens: 77 Obverses: 3
Die Combinations: 15 Reverses: 15

225. O34 R215 Monogram .

a. BNF AF 1327 16.93 g 12 h -
b. CNG MBS 67 (22.9.2004), 466 17.07 g - -
c. HWCA (6.9.2012), 24919 (Long Beach Signature Sale 3020) (ex T. P. McKenna, 25.10.1988) 16.95 g 12 h 30 mm
d. Elsen 76 (13.9.2003), 89 17.05 g - -
e. Stack's (2–3.12.1997), 511 16.99 g - -
f. Glendining 11 (5.11.1980), 24; Santamaria MBS (10.1951), A.442
17.05 g - -
g. Kress 142 (22.1.1968), 91 16.90 g - -
h. Bourgey (20–21.12.1929), 24 - - -
i. Sotheby (4–5.10.1990), 84 17.10 g - -
j. MMAG 76 (19–20.9.1991), 699 17.12 g - -

[R (a): r., splayed Σ. (f–i): flaw behind r. foot. Monogram large].

226. O34 R216 R: vertical line on upper prow.

a. *SNG Alpha Bank*, 1046 (5681) 17.07 g 12 h 31.2 mm
b. HWCA, New York Signature Sale 3021 (6.1.2013), 21169
17.15 g 12 h 33 mm
c. Burgan (5.11.1993), 56; Vico (8.3.1990), 121; Superior (1989), 2534; Bourgey (12.1929), 24
16.93 g - -
d. CNA 36 (5–6.12.1995), 1841 (Jay Dawley Coll.)
17.00 g - -
e. Hess-Leu 49 (27–28.4.1971), 140 17.02 g 12 h -
f. MMAG 8 (22–23.3.1937), 259; H. Weber 2191 16.92 g - -

[R (c–d): vertical flaw r.]

227. O34 R217

a. Glendining (11.12.1974), 31 - - -
b. Cederlind BBS 139 (29.6.2006), 42; J. Elsen 76 (13.12.2003), 89
17.05 g - -
c. Egger 41 (18.11.1912), 439; Feuardent (17–19.12.1919), 207
16.54 g - -

228. O34 R218

a. Feuardent (26–27.5.1914), 195 - - -
b. Leu 83 (6–7.5.2002), 205; Leu 71 (1997) 161 (16.78 g); M & M 76 (19.9.1991) 699
17.07 g 12 h -
c. Glendining (1943), 37 - - -

[O (a): flaw off nose].

229. O34 R219 Monogram .

a. Asia Minor, c. 1947: *IGCH* 1451; Sotheby (30.4.1958), 105A
17.00 g - -
b. Unknown Findspot ("Seleucus III" Hoard), 2002: *CH* X (2010), 272; A. Houghton—C. Lorber—O. Hoover, *SC* II.2, 142–150, photos 168A–169A
- - -
c. Lanz 153 (12.12.2011), 197 (ex PGB Collection; purchased by F. Knobloch)
16.91 g - -
d. Glendining (13.12.1963), 228 - - -
e. ANM: SNG Saroglos 933 17.11 g 12 h -
f. Auktion LHS 95 (25.10.2005), 590 17.01 g 11 h -
g. Nomos 5 (25.10.2011), 149 (F. Knobloch; ex PGB collection, purchased in 1968 in New York) 16.91 g 6 h -
h. Bourgey (20–21.12.1929), 24 - - -

[O (a–c): progression of flaw continuing side lock and behind head].

230. O34 R220

a. Münzzentrum 66 (26–28.4.1989), 150; SKA Bern 7 (27–29.4.1987), 182; Peus 308 (19–21.10.1983), 121; Waddell (11.12.1980), 130; Peus 290 (5–7.10.1976), 94
14.16 g (b) - -

[Test cut on edge (6:30 h). O (a): flaw off nose; also, from upper lock to edge].

O: Similar.
R: Similar.

231. O35 R221

a. Glendining (2.1972), 154; Sotheby (20.7.1914), 69; J. Hirsch 20 (2.1907, coll. H. C. Hoskier), 256 16.912 g - -
b. Ciani-Vinchon (6–8.2.1956, coll. Y. E. Hindamian), 344
16.72 g - -
c. Coin Galleries MBS (16.2.1994), 90; Aufhäuser (1–9.10.1986), 32 (17.00 g)
16.89 g - -

d. A.Weil (24.9.1998), 10 - - -
e. Berlin; Vinchon MBS (20–22.5.1959), 454; Ciani (20–22.2.1935, coll. Grandprey), 101; Feuardent (12–13.12.1919), 207 17.00 g - -
f. Leu 61 (17–18.5.1995), 111; Leu 54 (28.4.1992), 91 17.02 g 12 h -
g. Spink *N.Circ.* 63.4 (8.2005), 1676 16.70 g - -
h. CGB MBS 51 (17.11.2011), 107 17.04 g 11 h 31 mm
i. Sangiorgi Strozzi (1907), 1495 - - -

[O (a–b): r., horizontal flaw.
R (a–c): flaw l., off prow. Monogram corrected; r. of monogram, flaw].

232. O35 R222

a. ANS: Dewing 1206 (Robinson) 16.76 g 11 h -
b. Hess 3 (30.4.1917), 701 17.06 g 10 h -
c. Kricheldorf 26 (19–21.2.1973), 57 - - -
d. SKA Monetarium L 47 (Spring 1987), 27 17.02 g - -
e. Aufhäuser 2 (21–22.10.1986), 32 17.00 g - -
f. MMAG 23 (17–18.6.1993), 78 17.12 g - -
g. Kricheldorf 10 (1962), 77 17.15 g - -
h. Leu 42 (1987), 205 16.97 g - -
i. Kurpfälzische Münzhandlung 51 (12–13.2.1996), 75 17.05 g - -
j. Gorny 60 (5.10.1992), 132 17.05 g - -
k. Lanz 50 (27.11.1989), 168 16.98 g - -
l. NFA 16 (1985), 147 16.23 g - -
m. CNG 318 (15.1.2014), 100 (E-sale); Demetrios Armounta Collection 15.35 g 5 h 31 mm
n. Poinsignon MBS (14.12.1985), 103 - - -

[O (i–l): die break on edge (9 h)].

233. O35 R223

a. Unknown Findspot ("Seleucus III" Hoard), 2002: *CH* X (2010), 272; A. Houghton—C. Lorber—O. Hoover, *SC* II.2, 142–150, Lot F: "Best Coins," photos 843–844 16.94 g 12 h -

234. O35 R224

a. Védrines MBS (4.11.1992), 31; Christie's (16.3.1990), 530; Christie's (28.2.1988–1.3.1989), 1276; Frey, 1057 16.53 g - -
b. Lanz Graz 10 (3.12.1977), 105 15.84 g - -
c. CNG 67 MBS (22.9.2004), 466 17.07 g - -

235. O35 R225

a. Kurpfälzische Münzhandlung 18 (20–22.5.1980), 39 - - -
b. CNG 306 (10.7.2013), 53 (coll. F. Knobloch, 1968) 16.52 g 5 h 32 mm

c. ANM: Thesprotia, 1992 (Touratsoglou, *DM*, no. 54)
16.75 g | 12 h | -
d. NAC P (12.5.2005), 1439 | 16.70 g | - | -

236. O36 R226

a. New York: ANS 1966.75.26: *SNG BYB* 361 | 17.08 g | 10 h | -
b. Sotheby (27–28.10.1993), 444; NFA 25 (29.11.1990), 88
16.99 g | 12 h | -
c. Spink 71 (11.10.1989), 62 | 17.05 g | - | -
d. Aufhäuser 8 (5–6.10.1993), 61 | 17.22 g | - | -
e. Ball 1 (9.2.1932), n.n. | - | - | -

[R (a): monogram farther than foot; in field, flaw].

237. O36 R227

a. Seaby 713 (1978), C16 | - | - | -
b. H. Hoffmann (15.1.1882), 872 | 17.00 g | - | -
c. Ciani—Vinchon. coll. Y. E. Hindamian (6–8.1956), 344
16.72 g | - | -
d. Unknown Findspot (Commerce, "Seleucus III, Hoard, 2002): *CH* X (2010), 272; A. Houghton—C. Lorber—O. Hoover, *SC* II.2, 142–150, photos DSCN 0997.2, DSCN 0998.2 | - | - | -

[R (d): photo before cleaning].

238. O36 R228

a. Munich, 42 (Acc. 22677): *SNG München* 1122 | 15.96 g (b) | 6 h | -
b. Kurpfälzische Münzhandlung 51 (12–13.12.1996), 75
17.05 g | - | -

239. O36 R229

a. *SNG Ashmolean*, 3263 (Christ Church, 310) | 15.63 g[33] (b, p) | 11 h | 30 mm
b. New York: ANS 1966.75.19: *SNG BYB* 364 | 17.06 g | 10 h | -
c. CNG 66 MBS (19.5.2004), 264; BPN-CB (10.1986), 669; BPN (6.1984), 66
16.84 g | - | -
d. Aufhäuser 5 (9–10.10.1990), 80 | 17.06 g | - | -

*** *** ***

33. Not 15.03 g. as in *SNG Ashmolean*.

O: Similar, the wreath wider, the knobs on wreath larger; a thinner branch discernible further up in wreath. The distance between the outer l. lock and the circumscribing lines larger. The third row of beard smaller, made by elliptic circles. Direction of locks in last row different. Neck ends in curve. Dotted border.
R: Legend characters smaller.

Group 46

Specimens: 32	Obverses: 1
Die Combinations: 5	Reverses: [5-1]

240. O37 R194

a. ANM: *Thesprotia, 1992* (Touratsoglou, *DM*, no. 55)	16.89 g	5 h	-
b. BM T. C., p. 106. No. 1	-	-	-
c. Leiden 3148	17.13 g	12 h	-
d. Lanz 158 (5.6.2014), 106	17.08 g	-	-
e. New York: ANS 1966.75.22: *SNG BYB* 365	16.98 g	12 h	-
f. New York: ANS 1966.75.18: *SNG BYB* 366	17.02 g	12 h	-
g. MMAG 37 (5.12.1968), 621; MMAG 22 (16–17.6.1992), 210; Blançon L 14 (1986), 405	16.92 g	-	-
h. Berk 40 (10.12.1985), 53	-	-	-
i. Hess 257.1 (2.11.1986), 94	16.90 g	-	-
j. CNG 67 MBS (22.9.2004), 468	17.06 g	-	-
k. Pegasi 10 (5.5.2004), 133	17.03 g	-	-

[O (a–c): l., flaw behind head and r., as extension to side hair lock; also, from nose. Cut up r.
R.(a): l., below, badly cleaned].

241. O37 R230

a. SKA Monetarium L 61 (Spring 1994), 37	17.16 g	-	
b. Malter 51 (2.6.1993), 46; Lepczyk 50 (26–27.11.1982), 920	17.02 g	-	-
c. Gorny 55 (14.5.1991), 178; Gorny 50 (24.9.1990), 266; Gorny 62 (20.4.1990), 144; SB 21 (24.6.1989), 50	17.09 g	-	-
d. Lanz 158 (5.6.2014), 106	17.08 g	-	-
e. Leu 79 (31.10.2000), 525; Pilartz 7 (1–3.10.1964), 44 (17.17 g)	17.07 g	12 h	-
f. Argenor (13.4.2005), 45	16.92 g	12 h	-

[O (a): flaw behind head; r., development of flaw from side lock onwards. (c): r., curved flaw from side lock to dotted border; also, behind head.
R (a–b): r., horizontal flaw off head. Also, flaws beneath feet. Monogram erased and engraved r. of l. foot. (c): monogram beneath l. foot. Flaw up, l. of head r.; also, l. of prow; also below, l. of l. foot and r. of monogram].

242. O37 R231 R: Similar. Prow wider. Monogram larger.

a. Munich, 22 (Acc. 22677): *SNG München* 1121	17.03 g	12 h	-
b. Gorny 64 (11.10.1993), 93	-	-	-
c. Spink NY (7.2.1995), 2052	17.00 g	-	-
d. Berk 41 (11.2.1986), 102	17.15 g	-	-
e. Elsen 111 (10.12.2011), 90	17.06 g	-	-
f. CNG 320 (12.2.2014), 65 (E-sale); Demetrios Armounta Collection	16.15 g	12 h	31 mm
g. CNA 14 (20.3.1991), 73; Leu-Spink 187 (26.9.1987), 95 (17.05 g)	17.01 g	-	-
h. NAC 23 (19.3.2002), 1197	16.99 g	-	-
i. Kritt FPL 26 (11.1994), 9	16.99 g	-	-
j. Vigne (17.1.1996), n.n.; Vigne (11.1993), n.n.	17.00 g	-	-

[O (a): development of flaw starting from r. hair lock. Also r., off nose, and up, from side lock to coin edge. Badly cleaned].
R (a): monogram larger, flaw off l. toes and heel and on r. edge of monogram. Badly cleaned].

243. O37 R232

a. PMV FPL 34 (12.1987), 4	-	-	-

244. O37 R233

a. *SNG Lewis*, 541; *ANSMN* (1960), 39 ff.; ex Subhi (1978), 1139	17.06 g	12 h	-
b. Leu 79 (2000), 524	17.07 g	12 h	-
c. Leu 74 (1998), 154	16.10 g	12 h	-
d. CNG 67 MBS (22.9.2004), 468	17.06 g	-	-

*** *** ***

O: Wreath interrupted by two flower branches.
R: Bow small. Monogram smaller, legend characters more elaborate, with ΩΣ floating, and with an open Ω.

Group 47

Specimens: 38	Obverses: [4-1]
Die Combinations: 8	Reverses: 8

245. O37 R234

a. Stageira excavation, 16.07.1996 (ΣΤΑΓ749 / AEN1847): Gatzolis, *Κυκλοφορία*, vol. 1, p. 453, 606.348	9.60 g (b)	6 h	30 mm

246. O38 R235 Monogram 28d.

a. Cahn 84 (17.11.1933), 260; Hirsch 14 (1905), 310	16.23 g	-	31.5 mm
b. Cahn 61 (1928), 80	16.22 g	-	-

c. Gorny & Mosch 196 (7.3.2011), 1428	16.95 g	-	-

[O (a): flaw r. of nose and mouth; also, behind head. Beside Poseidon's head, signs of overstrike (?).
R (a): in field up r., circular object (?): metal flaw between Apollo's l. foot and lower r. edge; on various parts of field, on obverse and reverse. Also, beside Apollo, circular badge: countermark (removed later?). Die repaired along horizontal lines that form the *embolon* of the ship. Two scratches cross Apollo's r. arm diagonally, like a different type of bow].

247. O39 R236

a. Oxford: *SNG Ashmolean* 3264 (Bodleian)	17.20 g	12 h	30.5 mm
b. Lanz 62 (26.11.1992), 222	17.13 g	12 h	-
c. Münzzentrum 66 (26–28.4.1989), 151	16.91 g	-	-
d. Lanz 68 (6.6.1994), 125	-	-	-
e. Roma 7 (22.3.2014), 461	17.07 g	12 h	29 mm
f. Hess-Divo 321 (25.10.2012), 102	17.00 g	-	-
g. Spink 87 (9.10.1991), 44	16.73 g	-	-
h. Burgan (18.7.1995), 18	-	-	-

[O (a): flaw between eye and brow].

248. O40 R237

a. Rollin-Feuardent (9–11.05.1910), 343; Bunbury sale, 820	-	-	-
b. Kress 120 (30.11.1961), 163a	-	-	-
c. Ratto (4.4.1927), 729	16.96 g	-	-
d. Münzzentrum 84 (29–30.11.1995), 18	16.90 g	-	-
e. CNG Triton 5.2–4 (14–15.1.2002), 1309; NFA 32 (10.6.1993), 46	17.07 g	-	-
f. SKA Monetarium 49 (Spring 1988), 33	17.14 g	-	-
g. Hesperia Art 12 (1960), 17	-	-	-
h. Hesperia Art 28 (1963), 61	-	-	-
i. Dewing 1207; Baranowsky 1931	16.49 g	12 h	-
j. Vigne (21.3.1997), 18; Vigne (9.1987), 350	16.99 g	-	-

[R (b): r., flaw from end of prow towards monogram].

249. O40 R238

a. Münzzentrum 53 (13–15.11.1984), 1529	16.94 g	-	-
b. CGB MBS 53 (19.3.2012), 53	17.16 g	11 h	29 mm
c. Stack's (11.1.2010), 104 (Vermeule, Ward, and Mexico Maxico Collections)	16.96 g	-	-

250. O40 R239

a. Gans 16 (1960), 259	16.95 g	-	-
b. NFA 29 (13.8.1992), 92; NFA 32 (8.12.1993), 46	17.05 g	-	-
c. Egger 40 (2.5.1912), 770	16.50 g	-	31 mm

251. O40 R240

a. Poinsignon (4.12.1985), 104	-	-	-
b. Kölner Münzkabinett 85 (9–10.5.2006), 22	16.97 g	-	-
c. Dorotheum 498 (18.11.2003), 48	16.99 g	-	-
d. Védrines MBS (23.6.1993), 30	17.12 g	-	-
e. Weil (1.1987), 8; Parsy (18.11.1999), 9q	17.04 g	-	-

252. O40 R241

a. NAC A (27–28.2.1991), 1372	17.02 g	-	-
b. Künker 216 (8.10.2012), 296	16.92 g	-	-
c. CNG MBS 81 (20.5.2009), 372; UBS/BAM (29–31.1.2002), 47 (17.03 g); Waddell 50 (12.3.2002), 32	17.04 g	12 h	-
d. Roma 7 (22.3.2014), 460	17.00 g	12 h	30 mm
e. Lanz 38 (24.11.1986), 244	17.13 g	-	-

*** *** ***

O: Wreath with a single reed, ending in a *thyssanos*. The wreath is decorated by two flowers in the middle; a side branch rises in its upper part. Hair ends in two side locks and a third, shorter, one hangs r. Dotted border.
R: Apollo seated comfortably, cross-legged, on prow whose upper part is shown by a straight line. Hair locks on either side of face, rest of hair at the back. Legend letters regular, close but on lower border; splayed Σ. Horizontal bars of monogram prominent.

Group 48

Specimens: 50	Obverses: 1
Die Combinations: 9	Reverses: 9

253. O41 R242

a. ANS 1977.158.172 (Kelley)	17.06 g	12 h	-
b. CNG 247 (12.1.2011), 66	16.57 g	12 h	-
c. Gorny & Mosch 196 (7.3.2011), 1428	16.95 g	-	-
d. Weil (27.5.1983), 141	-	-	-

[O (a): flaws right beside upper head.
R (a): flaw off l. foot; above r. arm; on upper prow].

254. O41 R243 O: Dimple on cheek.

a. Warsaw 106553	17.10 g	-	-
b. SKA Monetarium 63 (1995), 69; Sotheby (18–19.4.1994), 491	17.01 g	-	-
c. Superior (30.5.1995, Lewis Egnew Collection), 7314	-	-	-
d. MMAG L 510 (5.1988), 12	17.13 g	-	-
e. Elsen 15 (3.2.1990), 36	17.13 g	-	-
f. NAC 2 (21.2.1990), 149	17.16 g	-	-
g. Bourgey (4.1934), 18	-	-	-

h. BPN-CB (1987), 111 - - -
i. Coin Galleries FPL 62 (6.2.1965), B58 - - -
j. ANA 63 (17–21.8.1954), 2334 17.05 g - -
k. Cederlind L 90 (Autumn 1990), 19 - - -
l. Superior (10–11.12.1993), 1675 16.60 g - -

[O (a–d): flaw behind head. (g): r., diagonal flaw from nose to edge.
R (a–d): flaw at end of prow, dots on r. foot. (g): flaw behind head; also, flaws above and on r. end of prow, between r. arm and main figure; below, l. and r., beneath foot. Bow larger].

255. O41 R244

a. Sotheby (20.5.1986), 53; Hamburger (21.11.1910), 140
- - -
b. MMAG L 309 (1970), 160; Kricheldorf 4 (7.10.1957), 160
16.71 g - -
c. Gorny & Mosch 216 (15.10.2013), 2337 16.96 g - -
d. Shore FPL 100 (15.3.2002), 33; Shore FPL 96 (Spring 2001), 34
17.03 g - -
e. Coin Galleries MBS (10.4.1991), 94 16.99 g - -
f. Cederlind BBS 142 (5.4.2007), 54 17.05 g - -
g. Rauch MBS 7 (23.1.2004), 972; Rauch MBS 6 (4.10.2002), 61
17.19 g - -
h. CNG 90 (23.5.2012), 489 16.80 g 12 h 31 mm
i. D. Miller (no date), L 18, 8 - - -
j. Gorny 90 (12-13.10.1998), 214 16.82 g - -

[O (a): flaw beside head, a little higher than wreath. (a-b): flaws off nose.
R (a): flaw l. of end of prow].

256. O41 R245

a. Glendining (2.1983), 39 - - -
b. CNG Triton 8 (11–22.1.2005), 189; Antiqua 13 (6.2005), 26
16.90 g - -
c. Gorny & Mosch 199 (10.10.2011), 224 16.96 g - -
d. NAC A (27–28.2.1991), 1373 17.06 g - -

257. O41 R246

a. Royal Ontario Museum, 5 16.26 g 12 h 31.2 mm
b. Aufhäuser 8 (5-6.10.1993), 61; Aufhäuser 7 (7–9.10.1992), 44
17.22 g - -
c. MMAG 66 (22–23.10.1984), 80 17.03 g - -
d. G. Hirsch 162 (8-10.5.1991), 180; NFA 20 (1988), 683
16.83 g - -
e. NFA 5 (23–24.2.1978), 88 17.13 g - -
f. NFA 25 (29.11.1990), 192 16.80 g - -
g. CNA 26 (11.6.1993), 256 17.06 g - -

[O (a): flaw on neck.

R (a): flaw on r. foot. ΩΣ floating].

258. O41 R247

a. G. Hirsch 166 (16–19.5.1990), 232; Schulten L (8.1989), 22
15.93 g - -
b. NFA 35 (1988), 33; NFA 30 (1992), 59 (16.99 g)
16.93 g 12 h -

O: Similar.
R: Prow and Apollo figure larger. Apollo archaizing.

259. O41 R248

a. Gans (1960), 259; Kress 96 (21.6.1957), 158; Kricheldorf 2 (28–29.5.1956), 993
17.00 g - -
b. CNG 249 (9.2.2011), 58 16.64 g 11 h 31 mm
c. Vico 109 (10.11.2005), 1228; Argenor (13.4.2005), 44 (17.10 g); Morton & Eden (25–26.5.2004), 328 (17.05 g); Glendining (6.12.1978), 189 (17.05 g)
17.06 g 12 h -
d. CNG 249 (9.2.2011), 58 16.64 g 11 h 31 mm
e. Cahn (26.11.1930), 1246 17.10 g - -
f. NFA 25 (29.11.1990), 193; Superior (27–30.9.1980), 12 (16.76 g)
16.74 g - -
g. Gorny 118 (14–15.10.2002), 1290 17.18 g - -

[O (a): flaw behind head and in front of nose.
R (a): monogram recut].

260. O41 R249

a. Künker FPL, Spezialangebot Weihnachten 2005, 11; Künker 97 (7–8.3.2005), 503
16.82 g - -
b. CGF (1998), 41 16.86 g 12 h 33 mm

261. O41 R250

a. Münzzentrum 47 (10–12.11.1982), 44 16.27 g - -
b. Sotheby (20.12.1920), 98 16.84 g - -

[O (a): l., scratches along hair. Flaw off nose].

The bulk of the Poseidon head tetradrachms from this period are signed with monogram , which runs throughout this series. Particular groups may be distinguished through the different types of wreaths that occur on the obverses, the posture of Apollo, and the type of the prow on the reverse. Thus a reed with five side branches on Group 41 is combined with smaller figures of Apollo, leaning on the small prow. This wreath type gives way to that with side branches twining around the main branch, which ends in a *thyssanos* in the next group and with taller Apollos on the reverses, leaning on larger ships. Group 43 is characterized by larger flans, decorated by dotted borders on the obverse, and a circular die break beside the head of Poseidon on the only obverse die used facilitates the arrangement of the specimens. A different wreath type, a reed twining around the main branch, which ends in a *thyssanos*, is introduced with Group 44. Taller Apollo figures are depicted on larger prows in Groups 45–48; a reed with five side branches in Group 45 is replaced by one with floral decoration on Obverses 38 and 39 of Group 46, giving way to one with short side branches on O40. Finally, of the three side branches on the reed in Group 48, the upper one is protruding. Only a vague *terminus ante quem* c. 225 BC is broadly established through the occurrences of specimens from these groups in hoards.

5.0
Period IV: Antigonos Doson (229–221/0 BC)

"Expressive Style"

New financial requirements emerged from the military threats from North and South, provoked by the unexpected death of Demetrios II. While the Dardanians invaded from the North, the Aitolians temporarily annexed areas of Thessaly to the Aitolian League,[1] and the Boiotians, who had already shown signs of independence from Makedonia,[2] and the Phokians made an alliance with the Achaian League in Central Greece, at a time when the Cleomenean War (late 229/8 BC) between Sparta and the Achaian League was raging in the Peloponnese.[3] The infant Philip (V), the legitimate heir to the Makedonian throne, was therefore temporarily replaced by the nephew of Gonatas, Antigonos Doson or Physcus, who was appointed ἐπίτροπος of the young king and στρατηγός, in order to tackle these various challenges.[4]

The new Makedonian ἐπίτροπος is credited with the first significant naval enterprise in the East undertaken by the Antigonids after Gonatas, the Karian expedition (227–225 BC), which presumably took place after he had established his position in Makedonia and despite the newly established Roman protectorate on the Adriatic coast.[5] Even though the itinerary of this trip is well documented,[6] its motives are obscure. Countering Ptolemy III in the Aegean, an agreement

1. Just. 28.3.14. F. W. Walbank, "Antigonus Doson (229–221 B.C.)," in Hammond and Walbank, *Macedonia* III, 338–40, with earlier bibliography; Scholten, *Politics of Plunder*, 164–70; J. B. Scholten, "Macedon and the Mainland," in Erskine, *Companion*, 153–6; Shipley, *HWA*, 151–2.

2. Thespiae and Thebes had already given loans to Athens, for her liberation: *IG* VIII. 1737–8, 2405–6: F. W. Walbank, "Antigonus Doson (229–221 B.C.)," in Hammond and Walbank, *Macedonia* III, 341, n. 4.

3. Plb. 1.13.5, 2.46.1–7, 2.56.2.

4. Liv. 40.54.5; Athen. 6.251 d; Paus. 2.8.4, 6.16.3, 7.7.4, 8.8.11; Plb. 20.5.7. Plut. *Aem.* 8.3: ἐπίτροπον καὶ στρατηγόν.

5. Plb. 20.5.11: τὸν προκείμενον ἐτέλει πλοῦν ἐπὶ τὴν Ἀσίαν. P. Trog. *Prol.* 28: ...*in Asia Cariam subjecit.*

6. On Doson's itinerary, see F. Walbank, "Antigonus Doson (229–221 B.C.)," in Hammond and Walbank, *Macedonia* III, 343–344; Le Bohec, *AD*, 327–335.

between Attalos and Doson for the division of Seleukid possessions in Asia Minor, a *coup d' arrêt* to the expansion of the kingdom of Pergamon and the creation of bases in Karia have all been considered, but none is firmly supported by the surviving documentation.[7] This was the last ambitious Makedonian maritime enterprise in the East.

When this expedition was completed, Antigonos was able to turn to the Peloponnese, in order to organize an alliance between Makedonia and the Achaian, Epeirote, Phokian, Boiotian, Akarnanian and Thessalian Leagues (224 or 223/2 BC). This was a new version of the Hellenic League set up by Antigonos I and Demetrios I in 302 BC to serve as the basis for Makedonian control of Greece.[8] It was this alliance, along with the military defeat of Kleomenes of Sparta at Sellasia (222 BC), that consolidated the realm bequeathed to Doson's successor, Philip V.[9]

*** *** ***

Financing the military operations of Doson's short reign presumably required the use of old and the minting of new coinage. To the old individual tetradrachm types in the name of Antigonos are now added fractional denominations, drachmae of Attic weight and a single silver tetrobol, which is obverse linked to the Attic drachmae. The introduction of fractions has been related above with the financial requirements of the Karian expedition in Asia Minor, where silver drachmae were extensively used in everyday transactions (see Chapter 6.4.4).

The distinction of these tetradrachm groups from those of the third period of Antigonid coinage remains tentative, because it is primarily based on stylistic criteria and on hoard evidence, and because some groups of the third period may perhaps be assigned to Doson. The winged helmet symbol, linking the silver drachmae with the first three groups of Pan tetradrachms, favours the assignation of these two groups to the time of the Karian expedition; payments related to the withdrawal of the Makedonian garrison from Attika in 229 BC may also have prompted their minting. The stylistic similarity of the obverses of these groups to the following eleven groups suggest chronological proximity, which we have been tempted to date to the time of Antigonos Doson. A late date for these groups is confirmed by their presence in hoards from the 220s BC: the earliest hoard with this variety is Thesprotia, 1992, which is dated to 227–225 BC. Sophikon, 1893, with Antigonid silver drachmae carrying a winged helmet symbol left on the reverse, is also late (Table 5.1; cf. Chapter 6.3, Fig. 6.13).

7. A more detailed discussion in Le Bohec, *AD*, 336–342, with earlier bibliography.

8. Plb. 2.54.4, 4.9.4.

9. On the battle at Sellasia, see Plb. 2.54.5–71; 2.22.5; 20.5.12; Plut. *Cleom.* 23–32.1; *Arat.* 45–56; *Philop.* 6; Tacit., *Ann.* 4.43.4. For a detailed account of this period, see, for instance, J. Briscoe, "The Antigonids and the Greek States, 276–196 BC," in Garnsey and Whittaker, *Imperialism*, 145–157; J. B. Scholten, "Macedon and the Mainland," in Erskine, *Companion*, 153–156; Shipley, *HWA*, 120–152; W. L. Adams, "Alexander's Successors to 221 BC," in Roisman and Worthington, *CAM*, 208–224; R. Lane Fox, "Philip of Macedon: Accession, Ambitions and Self-Presentation," in Lane Fox (ed.), *CAM*, 335–366, esp. 339–340; M. B. Hatzopoulos, "Macedonians and other Greeks," in Lane Fox (ed.), *CAM*, 51–78, esp. 74.

Table 5.1. Period IV: Silver specimens in hoards

No.	Hoard	Catalogue No.	Group	Obverse	Monogram/Letters
		Pan Tetradrachms			
1a	Thesprotia, 1992	2b	1	01	KT
1b	Thesprotia, 1992	7c	1	03	KT
1c	Thesprotia, 1992	11d	1	04	KT
1d	Thesprotia, 1992	33a	7	11	TI
1e	Thesprotia, 1992	38a	7	11	TI
1f	Thesprotia, 1992	39a	7	11	TI
1g	Thesprotia, 1992	47a	11	14	[monogram]
1h	Thesprotia, 1992	55b	13	12	[monogram]
2a	Unknown Findspot ("Seleucus III"), 2002	4b	1	01	KT
2b	Unknown Findspot ("Seleucus III"), 2002	11a	1	04	KT
2c	Unknown Findspot ("Seleucus III"), 2002	15a	1	06	KT
2d	Unknown Findspot ("Seleucus III"), 2002	17a	2	04	TI
2e	Unknown Findspot ("Seleucus III"), 2002	22b	4	07	KT
3a	Kassandreia, 1985/7	6a	1	02	KT
3b	Kassandreia, 1985/7	12a	1	04	KT
4	Hija se Korbit, 1982	52b	12	11	[monogram]
5	Unknown Findspot, "X4"	52d	12	11	[monogram]
6	S. Asia Minor ("Pisidia"), 1963	61a	14	15	[monogram]
		Zeus Tetradrachm			
7	Unknown Findspot ("Antiochus III"), 2005	63a	15	16	TI
		Poseidon Tetradrachms			
6	Syria, 1959	64b	16	17	[monogram]
7	Syria?, 1962	78a	21	21	Trident—[monogram]
8	Oylum Höyüğü, 1989	80a	21	21	Trident—[monogram]
9	Unknown Findspot ("Seleucus III"), 2002	81b	21	21	Trident—[monogram]
		Zeus Drachms			
10a	Sophikon, 1893	84a	23	23	TI
10b	Sophikon, 1893	86g	23	23	TI
10c	Sophikon, 1893	90a	23	23	TI
11	Drama, 1989	84d	23	23	TI
12	Korinth environs, 1938	85b	23	23	TI

Table 5.2a. Period IV: Weights of silver tetradrachms

Weight (g)	1	2	3	4	5	6	7	8	9	10	11	12	13	14	15	16	17	18	19	20	21	22	23	24	All Tetradrachms
17.80–17.76																									
17.44–17.41																									
17.40–17.36																									
17.35–17.31																									
17.3–17.26	1																								1
17.25–17.21																									
17.2–17.16							1									1	1								3
17.15–17.11	1		1				5				1	1	1			3					1				14
17.1–17.06	7			5	3	6	1		1			1	2			7		1		1	1	1			37
17.05–17.01	6			3	3	2	2	1		2		2	3			4	3	1	1		2	1			36
17.0–16.96	6	1		1	1		3			1		1		1		4	1				1				21
16.95–16.91	2		1	1		1				2	1		1	1		2						1			13
16.9–16.86	6	1		1	1	2					1														12
16.85–16.81	2										3	1													6
16.8–16.76	3						1					1			1		1								7
16.75–16.71	2						2				1														5
16.7–16.66	2						2																		4
16.65–16.61					1		1						1								1				4
16.6–16.56	1																								1
16.55–16.51							1																		1
16.50–16.46	1											1													2
16.45–16.41																									0
16.40–16.36																1									1
16.35–16.31				1							1														2
16.3–16.26												1													1
16.25–16.21																									
16.2–16.16																									

Table 5.2a (continued). Period IV: Weights of silver tetradrachms

Weight (g)	1	2	3	4	5	6	7	8	9	10	11	12	13	14	15	16	17	18	19	20	21	22	23	24	All Tetradrachms
16.15–16.11																					1				1
16.10–16.06					1																				1
16.05–16.01																									
16.0–15.96										1															1
15.95–15.91													1												1
15.90–15.86																									
15.85–15.81																									
15.80–15.76																									
15.75–15.71																									
15.70–15.66																									
15.60–15.56																									
15.55–15.51																									
15.35–15.31																									
15.30–15.26																									
15.1–15.06																									
15.05–15.01																									
15.0–14.96																									
14.95–14.91																									
14.75–14.71																									
14.3–14.26																									
14.25–14.21					1																				1
14.20–14.16																									
13.80–13.76																									
Unknown Weight	10			1	1	2	2	1		1	1	7	1	3			1				1		5		37
Broken/Pierced	1											1									1				3
Total	51	2	2	13	12	13	21	2	1	7	9	17	10	5	1	22	7	2	1	1	9	3	5	0	211

Table 5.2b. Period IV: Weights of silver fractional denominations

Weight (g)	23	24	All Drachms	All Tetrobols
4.3–4.26	1		1	
4.25–4.21	1		1	
4.2–4.16	1		1	
4.15–4.11	3		3	
4.1–4.06				
4.05–4.01				
4.0–3.96				
3.95–3.91	5		5	
3.90–3.86	5		5	
3.85–3.81	12		12	
3.80–3.76	4		4	
3.75–3.71	4		4	
3.70–3.66	1		1	
3.65–3.61	3		3	
3.60–3.56	5		5	
3.45–3.41	1		1	
3.40–3.36	1		1	
3.30–3.26	1		1	
2.95–2.91	2		2	
2.90–2.85				
2.5–2.46		1	1	
Unknown Weight	5		5	
Broken/Pierced				
Total	55	1	55	1

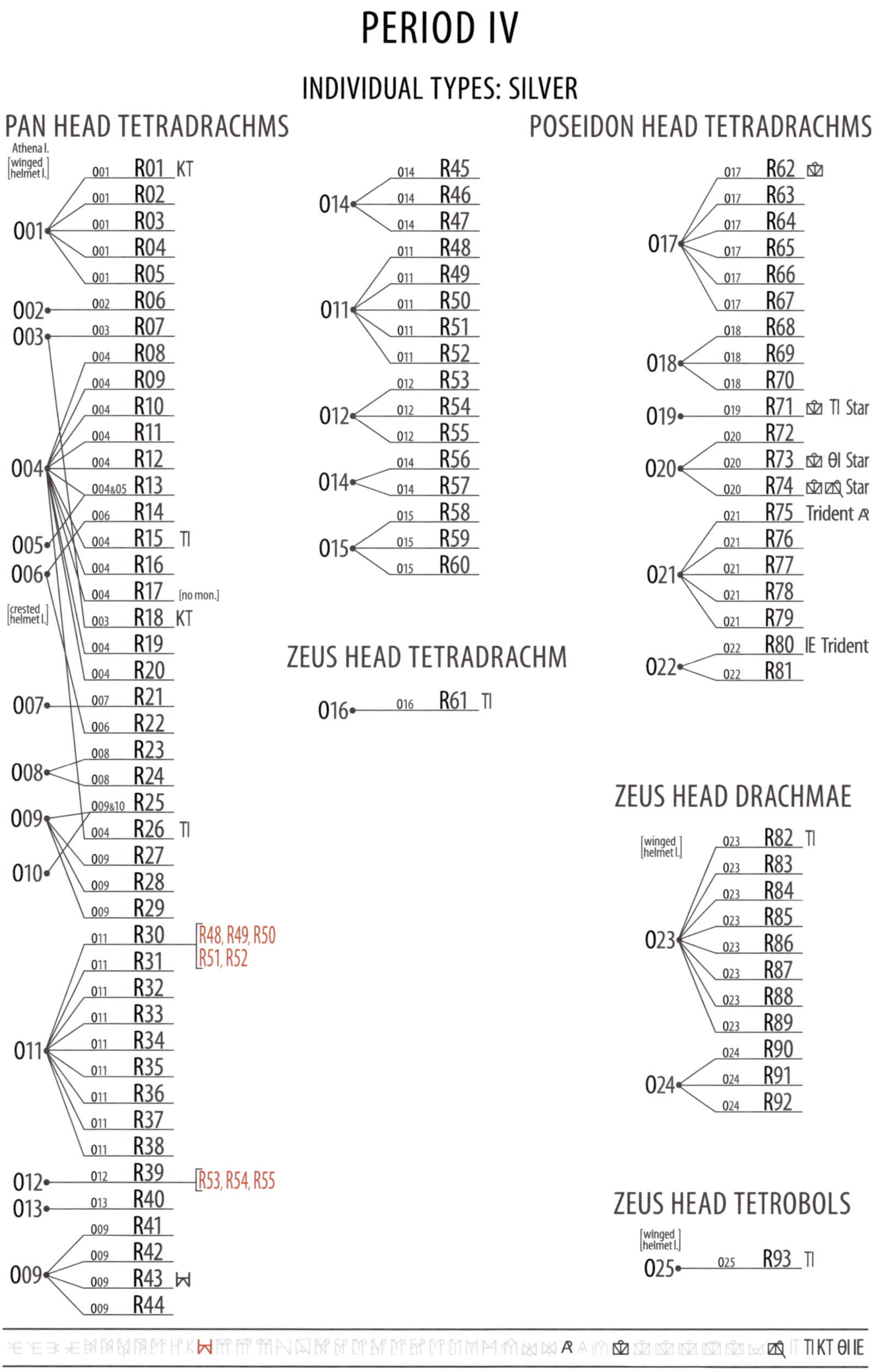

Figure 5.3. Period IV: Silver die links.

5.1 Pan Head Tetradrachms

Mint A

5.1.1 Winged Helmet l.

Winged Helmet l.*—KT *r.

O: Star/crescents nearly semicircular. Hair locks more curved. *Nebris* ties in front of neck, no wrinkles on neck.
R: Legend letters medium-sized. Athena with elaborate fall in middle of hem and with dove-tail pleat edges; rich folds. Shield smaller, upright.

Group 1

Specimens: 51 Obverses: 6
Die Combinations: 15 Reverses: 14

1. O01 R01

a. ANS 1977.158.169 17.09 g 12 h -
b. Peus 265 (1963), 272; Cahn 65 (15.10.1929), 129; Cahn 60 (2.7.1929), 460
17.30 g - -
c. Superior (1987), 300 16.81 g - -

2. O01 R02

a. BerLMC 9 (29–30.11.1979), 27; Coin Galleries MBS (19.11.1973), 187 (16.96 g)
16.88 g - -
b. ANM: Thesprotia, 1992 (Touratsoglou, *DM*, no. 44)
16.73 g 11 h -
c. Künker 23 (30.9–2.10.1992), 43 16.88 g - -

[O (a): countermarked: caduceus].

3. O01 R03 R: Helmet with long and thin crest ends, very short cheek flaps. Letters regular and small.

a. New York: ANS 1944.100.13852 17.11 g 11 h
-
b. Künker 97 (7–8.2005), 501; Button 111 (27–28.09.1965), 359 (17.00 g)
16.97 g - -
c. Gorny 101 (6.3.2000), 204 16.93 g - -
d. CNG 264 (21.9.2011), 35 17.03 g - -

[O (a): flaws on badge, under drapery and between *pedum* and inner badge circle, between badge circles].

4. O01 R04

a. Morton & Eden (25–26.5.2004), 327; Lanz 14 (18.4.1978), 60 (17.01 g)
17.02 g - -

b. Unknown Findspot ("Seleucus III" Hoard), 2002: *CH* X (2010), 272; A. Houghton—C. Lorber—O. Hoover, *SC* II.2, 142–150, Lot B, photos 165.3, 166.3, 167.3, CD 0276145.3, 02760146.3, 02760147.3 17.05 g 11 h -
c. *SNG Lockett* 1525 17.00 g 12 h -
d. Gorny 78 (13.6.1996), 111 16.89 g - -

5. O01 R05

a. Lanz 38 (24.11.1986), 243 17.06 g - -
b. Schulten (27–29.3.1990), 79; Schulten (20–21.10.1988), 126
16.87 g - -
c. Elsen L 232 (4–6.2005), 15 17.09 g - -

6. O02 R06

a. Kassandreia, 1985/7: *CH* VIII (1994), 322, pl. 39.4
- - -
b. Oxford: *SNG Ashmolean* 3261 17.06 g 12 h 30.5 mm
c. BM R.P.K., A 16.72 g (p) 4 h -
d. Ljubljana 3 (1995), 59 16.97 g - -

[O (a–c): die break on edge between badge and "unit" 2. Start of flaw on badge, r.].

7. O03 R07

a. CNG 265 (5.10.2011), 75; Bartholt-Baudey (22–23.6.1983), 76 (16.84 g); SKA FPL Monetarium 38 (4.1982), 60 (16,93 g); CNA Num. Rev. FPL 3.3 (1962), C31 (16.93 g)
16.91 g 11h 30.0 mm.
b. Raymond MBS, Rare Coins (12.9.1944), 34 - - -
c. ANM: Thesprotia, 1992 (Touratsoglou, *DM* , no. 43)
16.68 g 11 h -
d. Dorotheum (22.5.2013), 66 16.57 g - -

8. O04 R08

a. Copenhagen: *SNG Cop* 1201 (ex Reutze 274); Rooke (16.2.1994), 77
16.82 g 12 h -
b. Christie's (20.9.1988), 37); CNA MBS (19.11.1973), 187 (16.96 g)
17.00 g - -

[O (a): countermark on face: caduceus.
R (a): flaw from upper end of coin towards head].

9. O04 R09

a. Rauch 76 (17–18.10.2005), 275; Dorotheum 500 (29–30.11.2004), 60 (17.09 g); Dorotheum 339 (12–15.12.1972), 100 (17.02 g) 17.10 g - -
b. Leu 79 (31.10.2000), 523 17.02 g 12 h -
c. Elsen 119 (7.12.2013), 117 16.72 g - -

10. O04 R10

a. Münzzentrum 67 (7–9.11.1989), 1339; Müller 58 (3–4.6.1988), 37
16.90 g - -

b. Oldenburg 23 (11.03.1989), 32 - - -

11. O04 R11

a. Unknown Findspot ("Seleucus III" Hoard, 2002): *CH* X (2010), 272; A. Houghton—C. Lorber—O. Hoover, *SC* II.2, 142–150, Lot F: "After Cleaning," photos 991.1-992.1=1219–1220; Freeman & Sear 12 (28.10.2005), 88 (16.63 g)
16.68 g 11 h -

b. Grunow L 8 (2.1986), 1519; Poinsignon MBS (04.12.1985), 102
- - -

c. Kricheldorf 5 (20–21.10.1958), 66; Glendining (12.02.1958), 1393
- - -

d. ANM: Thesprotia, 1992 (Touratsoglou, *DM*, no. 45)
16.475 g 12 h -

e. Sincona AG 4 (25.10.2011), 4015 16.80 g - -

12. O04 R12

a. Kassandreia, 1985/7: *CH* VIII (1994), 322, pl. 39.3
- - -

b. UBS 59 (29–30.1.2004), 5446 17.07 g - -

c. G. Hirsch 203 (24–26.02.1999), 189 16.88 g - -

d. Dorau 17 (12–13.12.1983), 23 - - -

13. O04 R13

a. G. Hirsch 176 (19–20.11.1992), 168 16.76 g - -

b. Münzzentrum 67 (7–9.11.1989), 1340; Schlessinger (4.2.1935), 778 (17.00 g)
16.97 g - -

c. Karametrou-Menteside, *Βήιον*, pl. 34 - - -

d. CNG 306 (10.7.2013), 52 17.01 g 11 h -

e. Sincona 10 (27.5.2013), 86 16.80 g - -

f. Numismatica Genevensis SA 7 (27.11.2012), 59
17.02 g - -

[O (a): flaw on lower badge, off "unit" 5.
R (a-b): flaw from field (5 h) to center of chiton; worn r. Horizontal breaks from l. to neck and to l. badge accordingly; (a-b): flaw from below (7 h) to lower badge].

14. O05 R13 O: Differences in *nebris* binding, upper hair locks, *pedum* shape, dot on edge of *nebris*.

a. Berlin (ex Knobelsdorf) 16.99 g 12 h -

b. New York: ANS 1948.78.1 17.07 g 12 h -

c. Grunow L 23 (4.1992), 36; Grunow L 17 (-), 4414; Grunow L 13 (12.1987), 2768
- - -

15. O06 R14

a. Unknown Findspot ("Seleucus III" Hoard), 2002: *CH* X (2010), 272; A. Houghton—C. Lorber—O. Hoover, *SC* II.2, 142–150, Lot B, photos 163–164
- - -

*** *** ***

Winged Helmet l.—*TI *r.

O: "Star/crescents" nearly semicircular. *Nebris* ties in front of neck.
R: Legend letters moderate, regular. Athena with elaborate fall in middle of hem. Shield smaller, upright.

Group 2

Specimens: 2	Obverses: [1-1]
Die Combinations: 2	Reverses: 2

16. O04 R15

a. Kritt FPL 37 (1.1999), 8	16.90 g	-	-

[R (a): In field r., letters TI overwritten on KT].

17. O04 R16

a. Unknown Findspot ("Seleucus III" Hoard), 2002: *CH* X (2010), 272; A. Houghton—C. Lorber—O. Hoover, *SC* II.2, 142–150, Lot F, photos 989.2–990.2
16.97 g 5 h -

*** *** ***

Winged Helmet l.

O: "Star/crescents" nearly semicircular. *Nebris* ties in front of neck.
R: Legend letters moderate, regular. Athena with elaborate fall in middle of hem. Shield smaller, upright.

Group 3

Specimens: 2	Obverses: [1-1]
Die Combinations: 1	Reverses: 1

18. O04 R17

a. Berlin, Staatliche Museen, Imhoof-Blumer	17.11 g	12 h	-
b. CNG 227 (10.2.2010), 77	16.94 g	1 h	-

[R (a): r., traces of letters erased].

The winged helmet, with which the first three groups are stamped, also occurs on the silver fractional denominations of this period and on bronze specimens of types Athena/Pan with trophy and shield/helmet. The letters KT to right on the reverse also occur on four groups (14–17, 19) from the third period. The order of the letters, as opposed to the letters TI, might either represent a single official or the cooperation of two different officials signing with these initials, K and T. It is remarkable that specimens from this variety are absent from earlier hoards. Specimen 16 is most significant: the overwritting of letters TI on KT in the right reverse field area confirms the transition from KT to TI.

The presence of the winged helmet—KT variety in Kassandreia, 1985/7 and in Thesprotia, 1992, both dated around 225 BC, indicates that these coins were issued before that date.

*** *** ***

5.1.2 Crested Helmet l.

Crested Helmet l.—KT *r.*

O: Similar.
R: Similar; shield larger.

Group 4

Specimens: 13	Obverses: [3-2]
Die Combinations: 4	Reverses: 4

19. O03 R18

a. Vigne (12.1981), 14	16.88 g	-	-
b. Lanz 156 (2.6.2013), 111	17.00 g	-	-
c. G. Hirsch 287 (7.2.2013), 1852	17.01 g	-	-
d. Rauch (20.9.2012), 261	17.08 g	-	-
e. Helios 3 (29.4.2009), 44	17.10 g	-	-

20. O04 R19 R: legend characters larger.

a. ANM: *SNG Saroglos* 926	17.08 g	3 h	-
b. Jenkins 734; *SNG Manchester* 734	17.04 g	5 h	-
c. Gorny & Mosch 129 (8.2.2004), 94	17.10 g	-	-
d. JNFA 1.2 (2–3.1971), 274	17.01 g	-	-

[O (c): development of flaw from upper badge, r., and on spaces 2, 4, 6].

O: Spaces tend to become semicircular. Eight-rayed, relief stars.
R: Similar.

21. O04 R20

a. New York: ANS 1967.152.210	16.92 g	12 h	-
b. CNG 213 (1.7.2009), 83	16.3 g	3 h	-

22. O07 R21

a. Elsen L 173 (7.1995), 37; Elsen 32 (11.12.1993), 54; Elsen L 138 (12.1991), 49; Elsen L 129 (1.1991), 21; Elsen L 134 (7.1991), 46; Seaby (4.1964), A218
17.09 g - -

b. Unknown Findspot ("Seleucus III" Hoard), 2002: *CH* X (2010), 272; A. Houghton—C. Lorber—O. Hoover, *SC* II.2, 142–150, Lot F, "Late Report of a Fragment," photos 882–883, no. 45 - - -

*** *** ***

O: Similar, "star/crescents" nearly semicircular.
R: Similar.

Group 5

Specimens: 12	Obverses: [4-1]
Die Combinations: 5	Reverses: 4

23.O06 R22

a. Gorny & Mosch 212 (05.03.2013), 1417	17.08 g	-	-

24 O08 R23

a. Aurea 53 (7.12.2013), 2620); Gorny 204 (5.3.2012), 1308 (16.65 g); Grün 42 (9–10.11.2004), 76	16.64 g	-	-
b. Münzzentrum 47 (10–12.11.1982), 43	17.06 g	-	-
c. Gemini 11 (12.01.2014), 70	17.04 g	10 h	-
d. Vico 109 (10.11.2005), 1227	17.02 g	-	-
e. Ratto (4.4.1927), 731; Seaby-Glendining (1–2.12.1927), 296	17.10 g	-	-

[O (b): horizontal flaw from tie to "unit" 6].

25. O08 R24 R: Helmet with one cheek flap in middle of bowl.

a. Gorny & Mosch 156 (6.3.2007), 1326	16.97 g	-	-
b. Pecunem 11 (29.12.2013), 146	16.90 g	-	30.0 mm
c. Cahn 68 (26.11.1930), 1247; Glendining (15–17.7.1929), 296	14.23 g	-	

[O (a–c): flaws off "unit" 2 and off nose].

O: Head smaller, not carefully/hastily engraved.
R: Heavy fall in middle. Medium-sized, regular legend characters. Oval shield, held upright, helmet with very short cheek flaps. In exergue.

26. O09 R25

a. New York: ANS: *SNG BYB* 357	17.05 g	3 h	-

[Overstrike, undertype uncertain].

27. O10 R25

a. Parsy (7.4.1998), 10	16.06 g	-	-
b. G. Hirsch 33 (10.1.1963), 1183	-	-	-

Seven obverse dies are combined with various reverses, yielding twenty-five specimens signed with a crested helmet and with the letters KT. The single specimen from a known hoard, 22b, indicates a date earlier than c. 225–224 BC for this variety. No. 26a is an overstrike, but the undertype is uncertain. The combination of a crested helmet symbol with KT on the reverse is also found on five groups from Period III (see Chapter 4.1, Groups 14–17, 19).

*** *** ***

Crested Helmet l.—*Tl *r.

O: As above.
R: Athena tall, shield large. Helmet with very short cheek flaps. Medium legend characters.

GROUP 6

Specimens: 13	Obverses: [2-2]
Die Combinations: 4	Reverses: 8

28. O04 R26

a. Myers 1 (18–19.11.1971), 89; Coin Galleries MBS (25.11.1969), 1036	17.02 g	-	-
b. CNG FPL (named Classical Numismatic Review), 19.3 (1994), 51	17.07 g	-	-
c. G. Hirsch 198 (11–13.02.1998), 143	16.87 g	-	-
d. Phillips 318 (9.2005), 24	-	-	-

[O (a): flaws on spaces 4–7].

29. O09 R27 R: Figure and legend letters elaborate.

a. Athens: *SNG Alpha Bank* 983 (5680)	17.09 g	11:30 h	30.8 mm
b. New York: ANS: *SNG BYB* 358	17.05 g	11 h	-
c. InAsta 11 (23–24.4.2005), 115; G. Hirsch 233 (12–14.2.2004), 1364 (16.94 g)	16.90 g	-	-
d. Hess-Divo 317 (27.10.2010), 156	17.08 g	-	-

[O (a): more worn than no. 40. Development of flaws on spaces 1 and 3. Flaw off nose. Scratch on face].

30. O09 R28

a. MMAG 54 (26.10.1978), 195	17.08 g	-	-
b. Nummus et Ars Asta 56 (3.12.2005), 26	-	-	-
c. Münzzentrum 121 (12–14.5.2004), 143	17.10 g	-	-
d. Ponterio 149 (24.4.2009), 2030	16.92 g	-	-

[O (a): development of flaw off nose. Also, on spaces 1–3 and 5.
R (a): signs of flaw from upper end towards face].

31. O09 R29

a. Spink New York 4 (10–11.11.1983), 534; Phillips (18.6.1981), 53; RCCA-Superior (1980), 2113	17.07 g	-	-

[O (a): on badge, diagonal flaw off *pedum*. Flaw on space 3].

*** *** ***

O: Similar.
R: Similar.

Group 7

Specimens: 21 Obverses: 1
Die Combinations: 9 Reverses: 9

32. O11 R30

a. Berlin (Löbbecke)	17.11 g	1 h	-

33. O11 R31

a. ANM: Thesprotia, 1992 (Touratsoglou, *DM*, no. 10)	17.065 g	11 h	-
b. Freeman & Sear 14 (21.6.2007), 149; Superior (-), 56	17.12 g	-	-
c. New York: ANS: *SNG BYB* 359	17.02 g	11 h	-

[O (b): die break on badge circles, off "unit" 1, on spaces 2 and 3.
R (c): l., flaw beneath A and r., beneath TI].

34. O11 R32

a. Henzen L 177 (05.2007), 93	16.66 g	-	-
b. Roma 4 (28.12.2013), 206 (E-sale)	16.77 g	10 h	32 mm

35. O11 R33 R: Similar, shield upright; pleats longer. Letters small, regular. Middle fall shorter.

a. MMAG L 329 (11–12.1971), 170	17.14 g	-	-
b. Peus 361 (3–6.11.1999), 138; Grunow L 33 (4.1994), 154; Künker 26 (9–11.3.1994), 108 (17.00 g)	17.04 g	-	-

[O (a): flaw on space 5].

36. O11 R34

a. G. Hirsch 242 (22–24.9.2005), 2002	16.64 g	-	-
b. Malter 74 (28.3.1999), 91	16.67 g	-	-

37. O11 R35

a. Aes Rude (3–4.11.1978), 140	-	-	-
b. Superior, Chicago International Coin Fair (5.1980), F61, 150	17.00 g	-	-
c. Freeman & Sear MBS 12 (28.10.2005), 87	17.13 g	-	-
d. Ponterio 61 (26–27.2.1993), 150	17.00 g	-	-
e. Serrure (30–31.3.1914), 62	-	-	-
f. Gorny & Mosch 212 (5.3.2013), 1418	16.52 g	-	-

[O (b): development of existing flaws; horizontal flaw on space 4.
R (b): l., above legend, worn; flaw l. of legend letters. Flaw between l. pleat and chiton].

38. O11 R36

a. ANM: Thesprotia, 1992 (Touratsoglou, *DM*, no. 12)
16.73 g 11 h -
b. Gorny & Mosch 190 (11.10.2010), 180 17.16 g - -

[O (a): diagonal flaw on space 6].

39. O11 R37

a. ANM: Thesprotia, 1992 (Touratsoglou, *DM*, no. 11)
16.75 g 11 h -
b. CNG Triton 13 (5.1.2010), 113 17.15 g 2 h -

[O (a): flaw from space 3 to space 4. Flaw between crescents of "unit" 3].

40. O11 R38

a. Spink Z-Taisei Z 41 (1992), 20 16.96 g - -

[O (a): diagonal flaw across badge circles through "unit" 3].

*** *** ***

O: Similar.
R: Similar.

GROUP 8

Specimens: 2 Obverses: 1
Die Combinations: 1 Reverses: 1

41. O12 R39

a. Leu 91 (10–11.5.2004), 130 (17.04 g); Ciani-Vinchon (6–8.2.1956), 347
17.03 g 11 h -
b. HWCA 3022 (15.1.2013), 26269 (New York Signature Sale)
\- - -

[O (a): flaw on nose.
R (a): between helmet and Athena, vertical flaw on knee].

*** *** ***

O: Similar.
R: Similar.

GROUP 9

Specimens: 1 Obverses: 1
Die Combinations: 1 Reverses: 1

42. O13 R40

a. CGF (26.6.1998), 40 17.07 g - -

To two obverse dies known from the crested helmet left with letters KT right combination are added three new obverses (O11–13). Combined with letters TI, admittedly the most common letter combination in the early Antigonid issues, they yield fifteen die combinations and thirty-seven specimens. The fact that the only hoard in which this variety is represented (with three specimens) is Thesprotia, 1992 prompts us to consider it approximately contemporary with the winged helmet groups.

*** *** ***

Crested Helmet l.—Monogram ⋈ r.

O: As above.
R: Similar.

Group 10

Specimens: 7 Obverses: [1-1]
Die Combinations: 8 Reverses: 4

43. O09 R41

a. NFA 16 (29.3.1985), 146; MMAG 18 (21–2.9.1989), 619 17.03 g - -
b. NAC P (12.5.2005), 1437 17.03 g - -
c. Proschowsky (6–9.3.1970), 571 16.94 g - -

[O (a): signs of flaws on spaces 3–4.
R (c): flaw across B; l. up, scratches; r., erasure].

44. O09 R42

a. G. Hirsch 123 (20–23, 26–28.1.1981), 2065; Kress (11.6.1951), 179 (17.00 g); Rosenberg 64 (19.6.1928), 1426 (17.10 g) 16.95 g - -
b. Oldenburg 24 (3.1988), 33 - - -

[O (a): progression of flaws. (b): badge pierced up l.
R (b): l., flaw].

45. O09 R43

a. Kress 137 (1966), 175 16.00 g - -

46. O09 R44

a. Künker 226 (11.3.2013), 341; Gorny & Mosch 104 (9–10.10.2000), 287 (17.07 g) 17.00 g - -

[O (a): in field l., horizontal die break from nose through badge edges to “unit” 6. Progression of flaws].

*** *** ***

R: Shield small, round, held horizontally, with badge prominent. Middle fall starts higher. Helmet elaborate, with thin crest at the same level as cheek flaps, monogram edges not joined. Legend letters small, regular, spread in field.

GROUP 11

Specimens: 9	Obverses: 1
Die Combinations: 3	Reverses: 3

47. O14 R45

a. ANM: Thesprotia, 1992 (Touratsoglou, *DM*, no. 32)
16.32 g 3 h -

b. Auctiones 4 (1.10.1935), Prince W.Coll. and the C. de B. Collections, 651; Feuardent (19.12.1921), 89 17.11 g - -

48. O14 R46

a. Grunow L 23 (4.1992), 3394; G. Hirsch 157 (24–26.2.1988), 90
16.88 g - -

b. J. Elsen 82 (11.12.2004), 140 16.81 g - -

c. Stack's (11.1.2010), 234 (Craig and Ruanne Smith Collection)
16.95 g - -

d. Antiquarius 22 (9.1990), 24 - - -

[O (a): flaws on spaces 4–5, 7].

49. O14 R47

a. Schulten 6 (2–4.6.1982), 109 16.84 g - -

b. Lanz Graz 10 (3.12.1977), 104 16.81 g - -

c. CNG 225 (13.1.2010), 62 16.71 g - -

[O (a): development of existing flaws, new flaw off nose. O (b): worn; test cut on R: 11:30 h, 4 h].

*** *** ***

O: Change in depiction of shield: crescent units tend to become semicircular, spaces and head different.
R: Athena shorter, head smaller, with fulmen more stylized, monogram and helmet smaller and more elaborate. Her middle fold spreads nicely with diagonal, free side folds. Legend letters more elaborate.

GROUP 12

Specimens: 17	Obverses: [1-1]
Die Combinations: 5	Reverses: 5

50. O11 R48

a. Frey (1.1957), 21 - - -

[O (a): curved flaws on spaces 2, 4–6].

51. O11 R49

a. Elsen 41 (16.09.1995), 48; Coin Galleries MBS (19.11.1971), 48
16.85 g - -
b. Ahlström 51 (8–9.4.1955), 1623 - - -
c. Ball 8 (5.12.1932), 2014; Ball 6 (9.2.1931), 210 (16.10 g)
16.30 g - -
d. Kölner 82 (16.11.2004), 33 16.79 g - -

[O (c): die flaw (and repair) beneath chin].

52. O11 R50 R: legend spread. Helmet larger, with short cheek flaps.

a. Elsen 81 (11.9.2004), 90; Elsen 77 (13.12.2003), 81
17.14 g - -
b. Hija se Korbit, 1982: *CH* VIII (1994), 299: p. 190, n. 284; pl. XIV
- - -
c. Münzzentrum 76 (11.1998), 20028 - - -
d. X4 (no date): Ripollès, "X4 Hoard," 60.4, pl. 3.4; Vico (17.11.1994), 1
8.52 g (b) - -

[O (b): flaws: off nose, beneath chin, on spaces 1–2, 5–7, off "unit" 3].

53. O11 R51

a. Berk 40 (10.12.1985), 54 - - -
b. Waddell (12.9.1987), 114 16.47 g - -
c. Gemini 6 (10.2010), 76 16.99 g - -

54. O11 R52 R: Head smaller, legend characters more regular.

a. Lanz 112 (25–26.11.2002), 163 17.09 g - -
b. Coin Galleries Num. Review L 6.4 (1965), D35; Coin Galleries Num. Review, L 5.6 (1964), F58 - - -
c. Ahlström 2 (Hede) (1991), 331 17.05 g - 32 mm
d. Hess (18–19.05.1918), 331; Ratto (4.4.1927), 730 (17.02 g)
17.05 g - -
e. Serrure (18–19.3.1910), 101 - - -
[O (a): new diagonal flaw from badge circles off space 6 through to neck. Flaw on space 5. (b–c): "units" 1–2, 6 worn.
R (c): l., scratches on edge of legend letters: ΑΝΤΙΓ; small scratches on l. and r. edge].

*** *** ***

R: legend letters larger, irregular. Athena small, middle fall starts from high up. The l. pleat slightly longer. Helmet small, with short cheek flaps and long thin crest. Rich folds.

GROUP 13

Specimens: 10 Obverses: [2-2]
Die Combinations: 5 Reverses: 5

55. O12 R53

a. ANS: *SNG BYB* 351 17.06 g 12 h -
b. ANM: Thesprotia, 1992 (Touratsoglou, *DM*, no. 40)
16.925 g 1 h -
c. Peus 409 (25.4.2013), 120 17.14 g - -

[O (a): die ready to break on inner badge circle, off space 2. (b): flaw on spaces 2–3; also, off nose and off chin.
R (b): flaws: between legends and edges, under exergue. NB (b): module larger].

56. O12 R54

a. Freeman-Sear MBS 12 (28.10.2005), 86; Mc Sorley & Adams FPL (-, prob. pre-1968), 15 17.05 g - -

57. O12 R55

a. Münzzentrum 53 (13–15.11.1984), 1527 17.02 g - -
b. Stack's (17–18.9.1980), 83 17.04 g - -

[R (a): flaw between A and l. edge].

58. O14 R56

a. Peus 292 (25.10–16.11.1977), 5046 15.94 g - -
b. Hamburger 5 (29.5.1929), 242 16.65 g - 28.5 mm

[O (a): diagonal flaw from space 2 through "unit" 1 to "unit" 7; also on spaces 2–3, 5–7.
R (a): very slight difference from previous die combination in the position of the monogram, as opposed to the legend in field, r.].

59. O14 R57

a. Superior (1–2.12.1990), 1992 17.08 g - -
b. Platt-Kampman 4 (1970), 84; Feuardent (19.12.1921), 89
- - -

[O (a): development of flaw off nose; also, from tie to "unit" 5. Diagonal flaw on space 4, off "unit" 5.
R (a): l., flaw from l. crest to Y].

*** *** ***

O: Similar.
R: Similar.

Group 14

Specimens: 5	Obverses: 1
Die Combinations: 3	Reverses: 3

60. O15 R58

a. SKA Bern FPL 39 (12.1982), 64 - - -
b. Antiquarius 6 (10.1983), 20 - - -
c. Rauch Summer Auction 2012 (20.9.2012), 262
16.92 g - -

[O (a): horizontal flaw on space 6; diagonal flaw on space 7; flaw on nose].

61. O15 R59

a. S. Asia Minor, 1963: *IGCH* 1426 (Boehringer, *Chronologie*, pl. 26.24)
- - -

[O (a): development of flaws on and off nose, on space 7].

62. O15 R60

a. Kurpfälsische 42 (2–3.6.1992), 154; Kress 132 (8.2.1965) 138
17.00 g - -

[NB: very worn].

Heads of Pan with mature features, carrying small, dotted *pedum*s occupy the central badge of the obverses. Stars in relief decorate the shield, the legend letters on the reverse are large and spread over the flan. The head of Pan is more elaborate than in the previous groups, with very small horns, and the *pedum* is reminiscent of a scepter.

The shield "units" tend to become semicircular and the distance between the two badge circles is larger than in the previous groups. The head of Pan is considerably small and elaborate, with very small horns, and the *pedum* is reminiscent of a scepter. The arrangement of the hair is such that the main head is separated from its lower right locks.

Athena on the reverse is of moderate size, with a middle fall starting from her chiton and with stylised folds. The thunderbolt is smaller and the round shield is held diagonally in front of her chest. The crested helmet is characterised by a large bowl, short and thin cheek flaps and a thin crest, whose edges hardly reach the level of the cheek pieces. The legend letters are very carefully engraved. The monogram is small and the diagonal bars are not joined with the vertical ones. A specimen from this variety occurs in Hija se Korbit, 1982, dated to 250–225 BC. A second specimen comes from *IGCH* 1426 from Southern Asia Minor, dated to 210–200 BC (cf. Chapter 6.3).

*** *** ***

5.2 Zeus Head Tetradrachm

Letters ΤΙ

O: Bearded male head laureate r.

R: ΒΑΣΙΛΕΩΣ ΑΝΤΙΓΟΝΟΥ (in two rows), on prow looking l. On prow, Apollo seated l. cross-legged (the r. leg backwards), leaning on his l. hand and holding with his protruding r. hand bow (with string up); his hair behind his ears, with two long locks hanging on chest and on the back of his neck. In field, below, letters ΤΙ.

Group 15

Specimens: 1	Obverses: 1
Die Combinations: 1	Reverses: 1

63. O16 R61

a. Unknown Findspot ("Antiochus III" Hoard), 2005: *CH* X (2010), 288; A. Houghton—C. Lorber—O. Hoover, *SC* II.2 (Lancaster, 2008), p. 150; C. Lorber—A. Houghton, "Antiochus III" hoard, *AJN* 21 (2009), 89–104, pl. 9.11; Gemini II (10.1.2006), lot 65; Wartenberg Kagan, forthcoming. 16.78 g - -

*** *** ***

This unique tetradrachm is recognized as the most important Makedonian coin in the Unknown Findspot ("Antiochus III" Hoard), 2005 (see Chapter 6.3, no. 37). The male bearded head right in laurel wreath on the obverse is identified by the hoard's publishers as Zeus; on the reverse, Apollo is leaning left on a prow, with his left elbow bent, and holding a bow with his uplifted right hand.[10]

The bearded laureate head on the obverse is reminiscent of the laureate Zeus head on the silver coins of Philip II and on the early Makedonian tetradrachms of Alexander III, with an eagle, rather than of that on the obverse of the Zeus/Athena silver drachmae ΒΑΣΙΛΕΩΣ ΑΝΤΙΓΟΝΟΥ.[11] The two locks at the back of this head clearly make it comparable with the Poseidon head tetradrachms (5.3);[12] so does the bow-bearing Apollo on prow on the reverse, which is the typical reverse type of the Poseidons.

Control marks on the reverse provide little help towards a more accurate attribution and/or dating. The letters ΤΙ are the most common letter combination in the Pans. They are also combined

10. C. Lorber and A. Houghton, "Antiochus III Hoard," *AJN* 21 (2009), 89–104, pl. 8–13.

11. On the Zeus on the silver tetradrachms of Philip II, see Gaebler, *AMNG* III.1, 165.18–25, pl. 30.37–44; Le Rider, *Philip II*, 363–64; cf. Chapter 06.1. It is worth noting that Zeus had not occurred on Makedonian coinage prior to Philip II. On the head of Zeus on the early silver of Alexander III, see Gaebler, *AMNG* III.1, 1, pl. XXXI.18. On the cult of Zeus and the Antigonids, see S. Le Bohec-Bouhet, "The kings of Macedon and the cult of Zeus in the Hellenistic period," in D. Ogden (ed.), *The Hellenistic World. New Perspectives* (Swansea 2002), 41–57. On a bronze specimen ΔΙΟΣ ΕΛΕΥΘΕΡΙΟΥ dated to c. 168 BC, found in a hoard at Serres, see K.Liampi, "Die Einführung des Kultes des Zeus Eleutherios in Makedonien. Die numismatischen Zeugnisse aus dem Hortfund von Serres," *MDAI(A)* 117 (2002), 202–220 and pl. 40. Cf. Serres, Greece, 1998: *CH* X (2010), 123.

12. Similar proportions and the short nose prompt Houghton and Lorber to associate the head of Zeus on the tetradrachms with the Zeus head in wreath of marine plants on the obverse of the Zeus / Athena silver drachmae of our period IV as "an especially intriguing comparison, not an exact parallel" ("Antiochus III Hoard," *AJN* Second Series 21 (2009), 89–104). However, this association remains highly speculative. Similarly, there are no explicit parallels confirming that the wreath on the Zeus head of the silver drachmae was made of oak, as the authors suggest, rather than of marine plants: the oak depicted in H.Baumann, *Pflanzen auf griechischen Münzen* (München: Hirmer, 2000), 24–25, for one thing, is clearly different from the plants on othe Zeus wreath of our drachmae (marine plants are missing from this volume).

with monogram  and with a star to the right on the Poseidons and with a winged helmet on the Zeus drachmae (see Chapter 6.2.4). It is worth noting that this is the only specimen in which letters (as control marks) occur on their own and are not combined with a monogram. As TI appears in the last three periods of Antigonid tetradrachms and on both tetradrachm types, Pans and Poseidons, this specimen may be assigned to one of the three Antigonids, Gonatas, Demetrios II, or Doson. Lorber and Houghton assign this issue to either of the last two kings. They base the assignation to Demetrios II on the stylistic similarity of the Zeus on this tetradrachm variety to that on the Zeus/Athena drachmae, which they interpret as a "posthumous coinage" issued by Demetrios II: they mention a suggestion by Ute Wartenberg Kagan, but fail to refer to any published corroborative argument; nor do they quote their own criteria in support of this thesis.[13]

It is the absence of any Pan head tetradrachms from this hoard that prompts its publishers to abandon their initial attribution of this isolated special issue to after Gonatas' naval victory over the Ptolemaic fleet at the battle of Kos, which they date between 262 and 255 BC, and the dedication of his flagship to Apollo. They believe, however, that this *unicum* coin is clearly earlier than the Poseidon varieties contained in this hoard, which are dated to our Period III (246/5–229 BC). The authors recognize the relative value of wear comparison in dating, when based on a single coin; and underrate the early date for this *unicum* tetradrachm.

The argument that the Zeus tetradrachm is the only hoard specimen dated to Gonatas' reign is weakened by the fact that at least some of the four Poseidons from this hoard may belong to the last phase of Gonatas' reign, i.e. after 246/5 BC. As for the absence of Pans from this hoard from Asia Minor, Touratsoglou and I have already pointed out the general absence of the Pan head tetradrachm type from hoards from Asia Minor, the Near East, and Egypt before the 220s and its rare presence beyond the Balkans.[14] The assignation of this unique type to Gonatas need therefore not be discarded *a priori*, especially if the Pans spread between Gonatas and Doson.

The selection of Zeus laureate for the obverse of these coins after the battle of Kos calls for an explanation: the reasons that led Lorber and Houghton initially to prefer this naval victory at Kos to Gonatas' equally important, second major naval victory over the Ptolemies at Andros (246/5 BC) for the minting of this exceptional issue (they completely omit this second naval battle from the discussion) ought to be stated clearly.[15] The fact that Gonatas is compared with Poseidon (rather than Zeus) by Sextus Empiricus after the battle of Kos might favor his association with Zeus after the latter naval victory:[16] an explicit challenge to the established parallelism of Ptolemy with Zeus and of Gonatas with Poseidon might have been more appropriate in the context of his second, conclusive naval victory at Andros over Ptolemy's omnipotent fleet. At the same time, Zeus on the obverse of a celebratory special issue might have been meant to recall the principal obverse type of the silver tetradrachms of Philip II and the early Makedonian issues of Alexander III: underlining that the restoration of the Makedonian kingdom under Gonatas largely followed the lines of the policy established by Philip II would have been more appropriate around 245 BC, after the suppression of upheavals in the Peloponnese, including the revolt of tyrant Alexander at Korinth c. 250 BC.[17]

13.C. Lorber—A. Houghton, "Antiochus III Hoard," *AJN* 21 (2009), 89–104, esp. 93–94 (they provide, though, no photographs of the Zeus drachmae).

14. Touratsoglou, DM, 76; K. Panagopoulou, "The Antigonids, Patterns of a Royal Economy," in Z. Archibald, J.Davies, V.Gabrielsen and G. J.Oliver (eds.), *Hellenistic Economies* (London: Routledge, 2001), 336, 344–346. See also Chapter 7.

15. C. Lorber—A. Houghton, "Antiochus III Hoard," *AJN* 21 (2009), 89–104, esp. 93–95.

16. Sextus Empiricus, *Adversus Mathematicos* I, 276. Buraselis, *HM*, 163, n. 182; 165–166. See Chapter 6.1.

17. Cf. Kralli's suggestion regarding the offering of divine honours to Gonatas around this date: I. Kralli, "The Date and

Demetrios II and Antigonos Doson may also be credited with this special issue. The military campaigns of the former in mainland Greece might have prompted his association with the main thread of the mainland Greek policy of Philip II, adopting Zeus laureate on the obverse of his tetradrachm type; but the innovatory depiction of a naval scene, an Apollo on prow, on the reverse is hard to fit in with the rest of the information on Demetrios' reign, even if he is taken to be replicating a reverse design introduced by Gonatas. Lorber and Houghton leave unexplained whether, in addition to this special issue, the minting by Demetrios II of "posthumous" drachmae with Zeus "with an oak wreath" on the obverse and Athena on the reverse, as was allegedly once suggested by Wartenberg Kagan and adopted by them, was accompanied by any Pan head tetradrachms or not.[18] Demetrios' constant engagement, for one thing, in military campaigns in the Peloponnese and elsewhere would have required large quantities of coinage for military and other payments.

Antigonos Doson also emerges as an equally plausible candidate for this special issue and is, in fact, the option ultimately promoted by Lorber and Houghton. Yet the selection by Doson of a Zeus laureate for the obverse of this special issue remains unexplained, as an allusion to the policy of Philip II is underrated in this context. An association with Zeus venerated in Karia (i.e. Labraundeus) may have been justified in view of Doson's Karian expedition, but remains for the moment unsupported, stylistically.

This unique tetradrachm with its hybrid combination of Zeus laureate on the obverse with Apollo on prow on the reverse, from a hoard identified in commerce, calls for more careful consideration.[19] It is taken by the hoard's publishers to antedate the four Poseidon specimens in the Antiochus III hoard, on the basis of style (of the head on the obverse) and of wear. All the Poseidons in this hoard belong to our Period III (245–229 BC); hence, at least some may have been lifetime issues of Gonatas. On the other hand, it is indeed puzzling that the style of the Apollo on the reverse of this *unicum* tetradrachm approximates to that of the Poseidon head reverse types of our Period IV. As I have been unable to examine this specimen personally, I inevitably rest on the word of the publishers that this tetradrachm is genuine and that it forms part of this hoard, found in commerce. If that is ultimately confirmed, certain Poseidon head tetradrachm groups may need to be downdated from Period III to Period IV.

The stylistic proximity of the Apollo on the reverse to that on the Poseidon head tetradrachms of our Period IV prompts us to date this tetradrachm provisionally to the time of Doson. This is not incompatible with the suggested burial date of this hoard in c. 197 BC. It is worth noting that the addition of a second control mark alongside the main monogram, [monogram], on the Poseidon tetradrachms is not rare:[20] the letter M on specimen 14, for example, occurs on the Poseidon head Group 35 of our Period III. It is the combination of monogram [monogram] (correcting an earlier monogram, possibly [monogram] or [monogram]) with monogram [monogram] on specimen no. 15 of this hoard that occurs for the first time. At any rate, monogram [monogram] is combined with monograms [monogram], [monogram], [monogram] on a number of specimens, respectively in Groups 33, 34 and 36 of Period III and with N, TI, ΘI, along with a

Context of Divine Honours by Antigonos Gonatas—A Suggestion," in S. Tracy and O. Palagia (eds.), *The Macedonians in Athens, 322-229 BC, Proceedings of an International Conference held at the University of Athens, May 24–26, 2001* (Oxford: Oxbow, 2003), 61-66

18. C. Lorber—A. Houghton, "Antiochus III Hoard," *AJN* 21 (2009), 89–104, esp. 94: "Another possibility, once suggested by U. Wartenberg Kagan, is that the Zeus drachms might represent a posthumous coinage issued by Demetrius II, in which case the Zeus/Apollo tetradrachm itself could also be an issue of Demetrius II" (sic).

19.The term "hybrid," which Lorber and Houghton use for this tetradrachm, is inappropriate, since there are no other early Antigonid coins in any metal with a head of Zeus.

20. *Contra* C. Lorber—A. Houghton, "Antiochus III Hoard," *AJN* 21 (1909), 89–104, esp.95.

star in Groups 18–20. It is combined with monogram [monogram] only on the specimen in the Unknown Findspot ("Antiochus III" Hoard) (Period III, Group 34).

*** *** ***

5.3 Poseidon Head Tetradrachms

Monogram [monogram]

O: Poseidon head r., in wreath of marine plants, side branches with buds spring heraldically from main branch. Neck ends in curve. Dotted border.

R: ΒΑΣΙΛΕΩΣ ΑΝΤΙΓΟΝΟΥ (in two rows), on prow looking l. On prow, Apollo seated l. cross-legged (the r. leg backwards), leaning on his l. hand and holding with his protruding r. hand bow (with string up); his hair behind his ears, with two long locks hanging on chest and on the back of his neck. In field, below l., trident.

Group 16

Specimens: 22 Obverses: 1
Die Combinations: 6 Reverses: 6

64. O17 R62

a. BNF Armand Valton 324 17.15 g 6 h -
b. Védrines MBS (29.12.1990), 10; Gadoury, Monte-Carlo (13–15.10.1980), 193; Syria, 1959: *IGCH* 1535 (Boehringer, *Chronologie*, 158–61, pl. 17.9); MMAG 52 (19–20.6.1975), 132; Kricheldorf 8 (2.11.1959), 82 17.01 g - -
c. Roma 7 (22.3.2014), 459 17.14 g 11 h 32 mm
d. Parsy (7.6.2000), 19; Tkalec-Rauch (11.1987), 72; Egger 40 (1912), 771 17.05 g - -
e. Hess-Leu 28 (5–6.5.1965), 161 16.97 g 11 h -
f. Marseille 1 (coll. Vermi, 391) 17.09 g - -
g. NFA 22 (1.6.1989), 462 16.97 g - -
h. CNG Triton 16 (8–9.1.2013), 305; Gorny 48 (2.4.1990), 262 (17,06 g); RCM Collection 17.05 g 11 h 31 mm
i. Gorny & Mosch 133 (11.10.2004), 154 17.08 g - -

[O (a): r., flaw.
R (a–d): l., flaw through to foot; also, up l. (h): l., monogram erased beneath feet; flaws beneath monogram].

65. O17 R63

a. MMAG L 496 (2.1987), 9; Bourgey (13–14.11.1980), 31; NAC 21 (1978), 46; NAC 13 (9–11.11.1976), 132; NAC 7 (1975, Wendt), 59 16.91 g 11 h 31 mm
b. CNA 9 (7.12.1989), 50; Christie's (7.9.1989), 26 (ex Garrett Collection), (17.10 g); NFA & Bank Leu 85 (29.3.1985), 47 16.94 g - -
c. Hess-Divo AG 307 (8.6.2007, P.A. Collection), 1147; MMAG 61 (1982), 103 17.08 g - -
d. Rauch 41 (5–8.6.1988), 146 17.10 g - -

66. O17 R64

a. Elsen 24 (14.3.1992), 94	17.07 g	-	-
b. Tkalec (26.3.1991), 89	17.17 g	-	-
c. Bloesch, *Winterthur*, pl. 72.1624 (ex O. van Lennep; Imhoof, Bernhard)	17.06 g	7 h	31.9 mm

67. O17 R65

a. Glasgow: MacDonald, *Hunterian* 340, no. 2	17.08 g	11 h	-
b. CNG 229 (10.03.2010), 81	16.38 g	11 h	33 mm

68. O17 R66

a. Hess-Leu 28 (5–6.5.1965), 161	16.97 g	11 h	-
b. Gorny 44 (3.4.1989), 246	17.11 g	-	-
c. Tkalec-Rauch (4.1989), 73	16.98 g	-	-

69. O17 R67

a. Spink-Taisei 7 (2.7.1989), 173	17.05 g	-	-

*** *** ***

O: Similar.
R: Similar.

GROUP 17

Specimens: 7 Obverses: 1
Die Combinations: 3 Reverses: 3

70. O18 R68

a. New York: ANS 1966.75.20: *SNG BYB* 363	17.02 g	11 h	-
b. G. Hirsch 198 (11–13.2.1998), 144	16.79 g	-	-
c. CNG Triton XVI (8.1.2013), 305	17.05 g	11 h	31 mm
d. Tkalec-Rauch 1987, 72	17.05 g	-	-

[O (a): flaws off nose].

71. O18 R69

a. Henzen L 175 (3.2007), 115; Henzen L 171 (7.2006), 111; Henzen L 167 (3.2006), 115	16.97 g	-	-

72. O18 R70

a. ANS 1948.78.2	17.17 g	12 h	-
b. Westfälische 64 (13.12.2012), 26	-	-	-

*** *** ***

Monogram [monogram]—*TI *underneath—Star r.

O: Similar. Hair locks shorter, beard constituted by irregular locks. Wreath composed of five branches, ending in flowers, which are formed by dots. The whole ends in a flower made by many dots. Dotted border.

R: Similar. No star r. Dot/flaw on upper flan; surface of coin uneven. Die break on r. upper edge of coin. Stuck twice. Prow smaller. Flan larger.

Group 18

Specimens: 2	Obverses: 2
Die Combinations: 2	Reverses: 2

73. O19 R71

a. Leiden 3150 17.08 g 2 h -

[O (a): flaw off head, l. Flaw (or worn) on nose].

O: Similar. Hair locks flow downwards. Two little edges on upper lock. Dotted border. Small flaws on forehead. Five wreath branches, with two intermediate flowers on middle and on upper wreath. Locks shorter than neck.

R: ΒΑΣΙΛΕΩΣ ΑΝΤΙΓΟΝΟΥ (in two rows), on prow looking l. Prow more elaborate. Apollo more elaborate, leaning to front, head to front. Legend letters smaller and more regular; floating *omega*, splayed *sigma*.

74. O20 R72

a. BM 1896-7-3-193 (Bunbury) 17.04 g 12 h -

*** *** ***

Monogram [monogram]—*ΘI *underneath—Star upper r.

Group 19

Specimens: 1	Obverses: [1-1]
Die Combinations: 1	Reverses: 1

75. O20 R73

a. Sotheby Zürich (4–5.4.1973), 344 17.03 g 3 h 32 mm

*** *** ***

Monogram [monogram]— [monogram] underneath—Star upper r.

Group 20

Specimens: 1	Obverses: [1-1]
Die Combinations: 1	Reverses: 1

76. O20 R74

a. Gemini 11 (12.1.2014), 75; Sotheby (04–5.4.1973), 344; John Ward Collection
17.07 g 9 h -

This is a *unicum* specimen with a star above the prow and with a second monogram,, under monogram . The diagonal right hasta of monogram  is extended beyond the right corner.

Trident—Monogram 

O: Poseidon head r., in wreath of marine plants. Dotted border.
R: ΒΑΣΙΛΕΩΣ ΑΝΤΙΓΟΝΟΥ (in two rows), on prow looking l. On prow, Apollo seated l. cross-legged (the r. leg backwards), leaning on his l. hand and holding with his protruding r. hand bow (with string up); his hair behind his ears, with two long locks hanging on chest and on the back of his neck. In field, below l., trident.

GROUP 21

Specimens: 9 Obverses: 1
Die Combinations: 5 Reverses: 5

77. O21 R75

a. Glasgow: MacDonald, *Hunterian* 340, no. 1 17.07 g 8 h -

78. O21 R76

a. NFA 41 (6.1992), 77; ex Syria? 1962, 3: *IGCH* 1531; MMAG 25 (1962), 443
16.96 g - -
b. Coll. Comte de D. (1889), 55; Brussels; Rollin-Feuardent (27–28.05.1889, C. de D.), 55
16.61 g - -

[O (a): flaw off nose, between the two lower hair locks.
R (a): flaws l. and r., respectively off prow and on prow's edge.]

79. O21 R77

a. Leu 91 (10–11.5.2004), 131[21] 17.02 g 4 h -
b. Gorny & Mosch (13.10.2003), 133 16.15 g - -

80. O21 R78

a. Oylum Höyüğü, 1989: *TCMAA*, 45–49, 81 17.05 g 9 h 29 mm

81. O21 R79

a. BNF: Luynes, 1696 17.05 g (p) 6 h -
b. Unknown Findspot ("Seleucus III" Hoard), 2002: *CH* X (2010), 272; A. Houghton—C. Lorber—O. Hoover, *SC* II.2, 142–150, Lot F: "After Cleaning," photos 1194–5 = 999–1000 (before cleaning) 16.63 g 11 h -
c. Weber 2190 17.14 g - -

[O (a): flaw between r. hair lock and end of neck].

*** *** ***

Letters* ΙΕ—*Trident l. (horizontally)

O: Similar, but the distance between the two side locks is different and the wreath branches are shorter.

R: ΒΑΣΙΛΕΩΣ ΑΝΤΙΓΟΝΟΥ (in two rows), on prow looking l. On prow, Apollo seated l. cross-legged (the r. leg backwards), leaning on his l. arm and holding with his outstretched r. hand bow (with string up); hair behind ears, with long lock hanging on chest. In field, below, letters ΙΕ in middle, under l. foot; trident l. (horizontally).

Group 22

Specimens: 3	Obverses: 1
Die Combinations: 2	Reverses: 2

O: Poseidon head r. in wreath of marine plants with many branches.

R: Similar, letters ΙΕ l. beneath prow.

82. O22 R80

a. Berlin (Imhoof); Imhoof-Blumer, *MG*, 123.64, pl. D.9; Gaebler, *AMNG* III.2, 187.4, pl. 33.25	17.07 g	-	-
b. Brussels	17.02 g	4 h	-

83. O22 R81

a. Leu 72 (1998), 191; Leu 13 (29–30.4.1975), 141	16.93 g	12 h	-

[O (a): flaw off nose].

Certain groups of Poseidons, having elaborate bearded heads with rich hair locks on the obverses, may tentatively be placed in the fourth period of Antigonid coin production. The heads are crowned with wreaths with a main branch ending in a *thyssanos*. A number of side branches ending in flowers spring from the main branch, and these side branches become progressively more prominent in Groups 16–19.

The taller figures of Apollo leaning forward are combined with long and elaborate prows on the reverses of Groups 19–22. The legend letters are regular, they do not occupy all the space available for the legend in the first dies but they tend to become larger in the last groups. Groups 18–20 are characterized by the addition of a star symbol at upper r. in the reverse field, and of letters, ΤΙ in Group 18 and ΘΙ in group 19, beneath the main monogram on the reverse.

The very carefully engraved Groups 21–22, characterized by small flans and with a trident symbol on the reverse, deserve particular attention. The designs are in high relief and they may be assigned through the rendering of the hair and beard to a later date. The obverse of specimens 82 and 83 (O22) is stylistically similar to that of silver autonomous Rhodian-weight drachmae of Kos, dated to the early second century BC (Pl. 61, nos. 9–11).[22] The striking resemblance of Poseidon (not least, of his wreath) on O22 to the Zeus head on the Tauropolos tetradrachms of the

22. J. Kroll, "The late Hellenistic tetrobols of Kos," *ANSMN* 11 (1984), 81–117, esp. 83–84. H. Ingvaldsen, *Cos—Coinage and Society, The Chronology and Function of a City-State Coinage in the Classical and Hellenistic Period, c. 390–c. 170 BC* (PhD Thesis, Oslo: Unipub AS, 2002), 44–45. See also R. Ashton, "The Pseudo-Rhodian Drachms of Kos," *NC* 158 (1998), 223–228; V. Stefanaki, *Κως* I (Athens: Tameio Archaiologikon Poron kai Apallotrioseon & Archaeologiko Institouto Aigaiakon Spoudwn, 2012), 107–108, n. 770.

first Makedonian *meris*, i.e. Kremydi-Sicilianou's O03 (specimens 4–9) is also striking, and has been taken to suggest that Poseidon served as the prototype for the Zeus on the later First Meris issue.[23] Apollo on the reverse is shorter than in the previous groups, leaning forward and holding a curved bow. The sea waves depicted on the prow indicate care in the execution of the reverses. The legend letters are progressively larger and angular, with a "splayed" *sigma*. The letters IE on these specimens may be taken to represent initials of mint officials, or eponymous archons.

Merker's tentative attribution of the Poseidon head groups with the trident symbol to the mint of Korinth is rejected by Boehringer and Touratsoglou, who reassign them to Makedonia. Touratsoglou, in particular, associates Group 21 through its control marks with the Pan head tetradrachms carrying a trident and monogram ΑΡ on the reverse.[24] Moreover, he considers the obverse of the same group to be the iconographic prototype for the Poseidon on the Makedonian silver tetradrachms of the first μερίς (Poseidon r./Artemis Tauropolos).[25] Merker's tentative date of c. 224 BC is adopted by Touratsoglou and is not incompatible with the *terminus ante quem* provided by the Syria?, 1962 hoard, dated by Boehringer c. 225–220 BC (Chapter 6.3).

*** *** ***

23. Kremydi-Sicilianou, *Tauropolos*, 195, n. 13–14; 200, nos. 4–9; the obverse of our specimens, nos. 82–83, is stylistically very close to her O03. But, unlike her p. 194, n. 14, the wreaths on the Poseidon tetradrachms are very different than the ones in her O01–O02. The stylistic proximity between the specific Antigonid Poseidon heads and the Zeus on the First Meris Tetradrachms was first noted by Imhoof-Blumer, *MG*, 124–127; see also Touratsoglou, *DM*, 81.

24. Boehringer, *Chronologie*, 99–100, 153; Touratsoglou, *DM*, 81–2.

25. Touratsoglou, ibid. On the Tauropolos tetradrachms, see also Kremydi-Sicilianou, *Tauropolos*.

5.4 Fractional Denominations

5.4.1 Silver Drachmae

Winged Helmet l.—*ΤΙ *r.

O: Bearded head of god r., in wreath. The neck ends in a curve. The beard locks arranged in four rows.

R: ΒΑΣΙΛΕΩΣ r., ΑΝΤΙΓΟΝΟΥ l. of Athena brandishing winged thunderbolt with r. hand and a shield held horizontally with l. hand. In field l., winged helmet; r., letters: ΤΙ.

Group 23

Specimens: 55 Obverses: 2
Die Combinations: 11 Reverses: 11

84. O23 R82

a. ANM: Sophikon, 1893: *IGCH* 179 (Svoronos, *JIAN* 2 (1899), 289–96, no. 774) 3.85 g 11 h 17 mm
b. Kress 159 (3.4.1974), 397; Kress 154 (21.3.1972), 158; Kress 147 (5.5.1969), 125 3.80 g - -
c. Gorny & Mosch 142 (10–11.10.2005), 1383 3.81 g - -
d. *Drama, 1989: CH* VIII (1994), 403 - - -

[R (b): two cuts on *chiton* and on horizontal bar of Τ].

85. O23 R83

a. Cambridge: *SNG Fitzwilliam* 2308 (Leake, *Kings*, 13.2); ex Till Sale 655 3.70 g 11 h -
b. ANM: Korinth environs, 1938: *IGCH* 187: S. Noe, "The Corinth Hoard of 1938," *ANSMN* 10 (1962), 9–41, esp. 19, no. 250 3.92 g 12 h -
c. Superior (30.5.1995), 7896 - - -
d. Oxford: *SNG Ashmolean* 3262 (bt. Oman 1947) 3.60 g 11 h -
e. Gorny & Mosch 122 (10–11.03.2003), 1261 3.86 g - -
f. J. Hirsch 25 (29.11.1909), 548; J. Hirsch 13 (15.5.1905), 1177 3.60 g - -
g. Israel, Eretz 2 3.65 g 12 h -
h. Gemini 11 (12.01.2014), 67 3.84 g 10 h -

[R (b): flaw in field l. R (e): Flaw above shield, on end of lower bar of Τ. Worn].

86. O23 R84

a. BM (3,90 g); Spink 71 (11.10.1989), 61 3.84 g 11 h -
b. Aufhäuser 6 (9–10.10.1991), 68 3.56 g - -
c. Gorny 56 (7.10.1992), 261 3.80 g - -
d. Leu 13 (29–30.4.1975), 140 3.84 g 12 h -
e. Waddell L 73, 36 - - -
f. Gorny & Mosch 219 (10.3.2014), 153 3.91 g - -

g. ANM: Sophikon, 1893: *IGCH* 179 (Svoronos, ibid., no. 775)
2.93 g 12 h 15 mm
h. Naville 12 (18.10.1926), 1189; Sambon (26.3.1889), 310; Sambon (12.03.1883, Milan), 310 3.85 g - -

[O (a): diagonal line on hair.
R (a): difference in *chiton*'s central pleat.
NB (f): badly cleaned].

87. O23 R85

a. BNF 1382	3.91 g	12 h	-
b. Künker 89 (8–9.3.2004), 1222; Lanz 123 (2005), 200 (3.81 g)	3.85 g	-	-
c. CNG MBS 67 (22.9.2004), 465	4.15 g	-	-
d. Gorny & Mosch 204 (5.3.2012), 1309	3.87 g	-	-
e. Gemini 11 (12.1.2014), 67	3.84 g	10h	-

88. O23 R86

a. BM 5762 H.M. 22 (Ticanis 15)	3.74 g	12 h	-
b. Berlin (Fox)	4.13 g	12 h	-
c. New York: ANS; MMAG 19 (5–6.6.1959), 402	3.86 g	-	-
d. Gorny 62 (20.4.1993), 143	4.25 g	-	-
e. Berlin; Prokesch-Osten	3.61 g	1 h	-
f. Madrid DNM XXII/42/41	3.91 g	11 h	-
g. CNG Triton 8 (11–12.1.2005), 188	3.80 g	11 h	-
h. Hirsch 17 (2.1907), 1207	3.93 g	-	-
i. Gemini 11 (12.1.2014), 66	4.17 g	-	-

[O (a–f): flaw on top of wreath. O (a): cut between hair and back of neck; also, on hair and on wreath (roughly in middle).
R (a–e): flaw l. of l. foot; also, r. of r. leg].

89. O23 R87

a. Berlin; Glendining (12.1981), 35; Löbbecke	3.73 g	12 h	-
b. New York: ANS 1944.100.13854	3.85 g	12 h	-
c. Meister & Sonntag 14 (7.5.2012), 522	3.73 g	-	-

90. O23 R88

a. Sophikon, 1893: *IGCH* 179 (Svoronos, ibid., 776)	2.95 g	6 h	17 mm
b. Rauch 76 (17.10.2005), 276 (Tuck Pittman Collection)	3.82 g	-	-

[O: in center, test cut].

91. O23 R89

a. Athens: *SNG Alpha Bank* 984 (3971)	4.27 g	9:30 h	17 mm
b. Sternberg 27 (11.1994), 145	4.13 g	-	-

c. Cahn 8 (14.10.1931), 291 3.82 g - -
d. Henzen L 176 (4.2007), 111; Henzen L 172 (10.2006), 110; Henzen L 168 (2006), 112; Henzen L 164 (10.2005), 112; Henzen L 160 (21.7.2005), 106
3.87 g - -
e. CNG Triton 9 (10–11.1.2006), 829; R. Weimer Collection
3.58 g 11 h -

O: Bearded head of god r., in wreath from laurel leaves and flowers with three dots. His neck ends in a curve. His nose is curved. The beard locks arranged in four rows. The head spreads beyond the flan.
R: ΒΑΣΙΛΕΩΣ r., ΑΝΤΙΓΟΝΟΥ l. of Athena brandishing winged thunderbolt with r. hand and a semicircular shield held horizontally with l. hand. In field l., winged helmet; r., letters: ΤΙ.

92. O24 R90

a. MMAG L 227 (11.1962), 454 3.71 g - -
b. *SNG Lockett* 3, 1526 3.38 g - -
c. H. Weber, no. 2192 3.43 g - -

[O (b): recut off nose. (c): flaw on nose; below, countermark: caduceus.
R (a): flaw above shield. (b): l., flaw. (c): l., flaw on diagonal bars of Α; badly cleaned; bad photograph].

93. O24 R91

a. *SNG Cop* 1203 3.60 g 9 h -
b. Munich: *SNG München* 1079 3.63 g 11 h -
c. Cahn 4 (1928), 461 3.26 g - -
d. Glendining (2.1958), 1394 - - -

[O (c): diagonal cut across head. Breaks on edge up l. and at lower end.
R (a): dot beneath r. vertical bar of Ν, which is shorter].

94. O24 R92 R: Legend letters crude.

a. Gorny & Mosch 211 (4.3.2013), 201; Gorny & Mosch 199 (10.10.2011), 223; MMAG 19 (1959), 402 3.87 g - -
b. CGB MBS 51 (17.11.2011), 106; Lanz 123 (30.5.2005), 200
3.81 g 10 h 17 mm
c. CNG MBS 84 (5.5.2010), 330; CNG MBS (5.5.2005), 330; Rauch 75 (17.10.2005), 276
3.82 g 11 h 16 mm
d. Helios 8 (13.10.2012), 18 3.79 g - -

*** *** ***

5.4.2 SILVER TETROBOLS

O: Bearded head of god r., in wreath. The neck ends in a curve. The beard locks arranged in four rows.

R: ΒΑΣΙΛΕΩΣ r., ΑΝΤΙΓΟΝΟΥ l. of Athena brandishing winged thunderbolt with r. hand and a shield held horizontally with l. hand. In field l., winged helmet; r., letters: ΤΙ.

GROUP 24

Specimens: 1	Obverses: 1
Die Combinations: 1	Reverses: 1

95. O25 R93

a. Berlin (Fox)	2.46 g	9 h	-

A few silver drachmae in the name of "King Antigonos," with a bearded head on the obverse and Athena looking left on the reverse, are associated through the control marks on the reverse, a winged helmet symbol left and the letters ΤΙ right, with the Pan head tetradrachms of this period. The two specimens from Sophikon, 1893 (*IGCH* 179), that from Drama, 1989 and the one from Korinth environs, 1938 (*IGCH* 187) fix a *terminus ante quem* for these denominations around the 220s BC. For a commentary and for the significance of these drachmae in dating the Pan head tetradrachms, see Chapter 6.4.4. The smallest denomination, the tetrobols, came from the same pair of dies as the drachmae and represented a day's pay for a soldier.[26]

26. Kroll, *Agora*, 22.

6.0
Numismatic Evidence: General Considerations

Current views concerning the division of the precious metal coinages of "King Antigonos" between the two Antigoni of the third century BC, Gonatas and Doson, may be summarized as follows:

1. The posthumous Alexander tetradrachms end with the introduction of the Pan head tetradrachms, i.e., tetradrachms carrying the head of Pan in the center of a Makedonian shield on the obverse, in 271/0 BC.[1]
2. The "transitional Alexander" tetradrachms, that is, tetradrachms retaining the designs of Alexander III, but carrying the legend ΒΑΣΙΛΕΩΣ ΑΝΤΙΓΟΝΟΥ, were struck at the end of the Monogram group of posthumous Alexanders.[2]
3. The Pan tetradrachms were introduced in 271 BC, at Amphipolis. The crested helmet symbol and monograms they share with the Makedonian posthumous Alexander tetradrachms suggest that the two issues were produced at the same mint and that the Pans started at the end of the Alexanders.[3]
4. The Poseidon tetradrachms (i.e., tetradrachms in the name of "King Antigonos" carrying the head of Poseidon on the obverse) are not related to the Makedonian posthumous Alexander tetradrachms.

1. Mathisen, *Silver Coinages*, 85, 110–114; Price, *Alexander*, 141.
2. Mathisen, *Silver Coinages*, 95–96; Price, ibid.
3. Mathisen, *Silver Coinages*, 110–114; idem, *Pan Heads and Poseidon Heads*, 31 *contra* Merker, *Silver Coinage*, 46, who suggests Pella as the mint for the Pan series with the helmet symbol.

5. The relationship between the Pan and the Poseidon tetradrachms has raised most controversy. Current opinions range between the introduction of the Poseidons late under Gonatas, parallel to the Pans, and the assignation of them all to Doson (chapter 6.4.3).[4]

6. The few and rare fractional denominations, with a head of Pan or Zeus on the obverse and with Athena left on the reverse, are related to the Pans rather than the Poseidons. This is determined both by their typology and via their control marks, that is, the winged helmet to the left and the letters TI to the right on the reverse (see chapter 6.4.4).[5]

7. It is unclear whether the king who reigned between the two Antigoni, Demetrios II, should be given any coinage.[6]

8. Common (or similar) monograms on the Pans, the Poseidons and the tetradrachms of Philip V suggest continuity in the production of these issues at the Makedonian mint.[7]

*** *** ***

I shall argue below that both of the individual Antigonid tetradrachm types ("Pans" and "Poseidons") were both struck from Gonatas through to Doson, that the Pan head tetradrachms were introduced by Gonatas during the Chremonidean War (268/7–261/60 BC) and that both his individual tetradrachm types, Pans and Poseidons, were continued posthumously by his successors, at least until Antigonos Doson. Those struck between the 260s and the mid-240s may be ordered with some degree of certainty, but the chronological sequence of those struck between the mid-240s and the end of reign of Antigonos Doson remains unclear. The silver fractional denominations elucidate the chronology of the Pans associated with them. Moreover, the δημητρίειοι δραχμαὶ mentioned on the accounts of the priests of Beroea from the second half of the third century BC, rather than denoting specific coins, have been taken to specify that the weight of these drachmae is Attic (i.e., 4.3 g) rather than Thrako-Makedonian (i.e., 3.7 g); in other words, they represent the unit of weight valid in Antigonid Makedonia under Demetrios II (rather than I).[8] Alongside

4. For a summary of past opinions, see Paschides, *Ποσειδώνες και Αντίγονοι*, 236–240; Mathisen, *Administrative Organisation* III, 46.

5. Paschides, Ποσειδώνες και Αντίγονοι, 245.

6. Boehringer, *Chronologie*, 99; Ehrhardt, *Studies*, 79.

7. Touratsoglou, *DM*, 82.

8. Hatzopoulos, *Institutions* II, no. 82 I, l. 6, II, l. 14, 21, 40 = *SEG* 40 [1990] 530, with earlier bibliography. Hatzopoulos ("Ἀργυρές δραχμές και χρυσοί στατῆρες σὲ ἐπιγραφές τῆς Μακεδονίας," in *Το νόμισμα στο Μακεδονικό χώρο, Πρακτικά Β' Επιστημονικής Συνάντησης*, Οβολός 4 (Thessalonike: University Studio Press, 2000), 79–84, esp. n. 36) explains the term "demetrian drachmai" through the introduction by Demetrios I Poliorketes of the Attic weight standard in Macedonia, arguing that the coinage of Alexander III was used beyond Makedonia, while the "philippoi" were used within the state. Doyen also considers that the Ἀλεξάνδρειον νόμισμα was equivalent to ἀττικόν and to the δημητρίειον in documents from the Aegean islands (*Étalons*, 62–63). The presence of Alexander silver tetradrachms outside Macedonia may be explained through precious metal payments made to foreign agents, but the manager of such payments was certainly the issuing authority of such coins, i.e., the Makedonian state; it would indeed be very hard to assume that Alexander-type coinage was not valid within the country at that time, not least as good portions and diverse denominations of it were struck there: Price, *Alexander*, 85–151; Le Rider, *Alexandre*, 29–63, 335–340. Not least, Attic-weight posthumous Alexander tetradrachms have been found in a good number of hoards within the broader Makedonian realm, such as Verge, (Perge), 1955 (*IGCH* 455), Pontolivado-Kilkis, 1961 (*IGCH* 445), Jabukovac, before 1920 (*IGCH* 447), Zemun, 1924 (*IGCH* 458), Rumania, Căbeşti, 1962 (*IGCH* 817), Mathisen, *Macedonian Silver*, 83, table 2. After all, Poliorketes' reign in Makedonia was so brief that he can hardly be credited with the use of Attic-weight large silver denominations within the country. One also wonders why the Macedonian Attic-weight tetradrachms mentioned outside Macedonia, in the Attic inscriptions from the Athenian Asklepieion, are not mentioned as δημητρίεια but as Ἀντιγόνεια. Cf. V. Allamani-Souri, Ἀπόλλωνι, Ἀσκληπιῷ, Ὑγίειαι. Επιγραφική μαρτυρία για το Ασκληπιείο της Βέροιας', *AD* 39 (1984), Meletai, 205–231, esp. 215–217. Cf. kalyx-cups and kylixes inscribed with their weight in

the τετρᾶχμα ἀντιγόνεια mentioned on the inscriptions from the Athenian Asklepieion from the mid-250s to the last two decades of the third century,[9] these δημητρίειοι δραχμαὶ share the winged helmet symbol with the Pan tetradrachm Groups 1–3 of Period IV and might indicate the continuous production and use of royal Antigonid issues from Gonatas to Doson. Finally, the continuity of the control marks between both the Antigonid silver types and the contemporary Makedonian posthumous Alexanders suggests that the latter may have continued after the introduction of the individual Antigonid silver issues.

Attic drachmae in the "royal" tomb at Vergina: Andronikos, *Vergina*, 157–159; Price, *Alexander*, 39, n. 1. On the names of coinages in inventories, see "Monnaies des inscriptions grecques," *RN* (1962), 7–24 (= *OMS* II 1039–1040); Robert, *Monnaies antiques en Troade* (Geneva: Minard, 1966), 22–46; Doyen, *Étalons*, 62–4.

9. Aleshire, *Asklepieion*, 261–263, 269.

6.1 TYPES AND ICONOGRAPHY

The international political persona promoted by Gonatas for himself and for his kingdom may be recovered through the designs on his gold and silver coinage. Iconographic themes already familiar to the Makedonians were adopted and adapted to produce contemporary nuances.

1. TRANSITIONAL ALEXANDER TYPES, GOLD AND SILVER, WITH THE LEGEND OF KING ANTIGONOS.[10]

Reverting to the coin types of previous kings was not unprecedented in Makedonia. Under the Temenid dynasty, Perdiccas II had struck coins with the types of his predecessor, Alexander I, while the pentedrachm of Archelaos I may be seen as a return to the types of Alexander I.[11] It has also been argued that the Apollo on the silver fractional denominations of Philip II originates in the young diademed head introduced as a coin type by Archelaos.[12] Similarly, bronze coins with the types of Perdiccas III were struck under Philip II,[13] just as bronze issues in the name of the latter were continued in the Makedonian kingdom posthumously, under Alexander III.[14]

It is not therefore surprising that the Alexander coin tradition, which was retained in most Alexander mints long after the death of the conqueror and the division of his empire, lasted in Makedonia and Thrace longer than in other regions. Just as the gold and silver coin types of Philip II were continued posthumously under Alexander,[15] gold staters and silver tetradrachms in the name of Alexander continued under Kassander and his sons, and occasionally until under Philip V.[16] The gold staters and silver tetradrachms in the name of Alexander struck posthumously, prior to and during the reign of Gonatas, form part of this tradition.[17]

Gold Staters:

O: Head of Athena r. in crested Korinthian helmet, decorated with coiled snake.
R: Nike standing to l. holding *aphlaston* in outstretched right hand, and mast (*stylis*) in her left hand.[18] Legend ΒΑΣΙΛΕΩΣ ΑΝΤΙΓΟΝΟΥ.

10. A posthumous gold stater in the name of Philip II, with the same helmet symbol as that on the Pans and on the contemporary Makedonian posthumous Alexanders, may also belong to the reign of Gonatas. But its authenticity requires confirmation: Lanz 68 (1994), 124.

11. M. J. Price, *Coins of the Macedonians* (London: British Museum, 1974), 18–21.

12. U. Westermark, "Remarks on regal Macedonian coinage," in Le Rider et al. (eds.), *Kraay-Mørkholm Essays*, 301–315; eadem, "Apollo in Macedonia," in *Opus mixtum*, 149–154; eadem, "The Staters of Archelaus. A Die Study," in Price et al., *Essays Carson-Jenkins*, 17–30; Le Rider, *Monnayage et finances*, 16.

13. Le Rider, *Philippe II*, 17; C. A. Hersh, "An unpublished coin of Philip II of Macedonia from his first issue of bronzes," *AJN* 1 (1989), 33–36; Le Rider, *Monnayage et finances*, 17, n. 1.

14. Gatzolis, *Κυκλοφορία* II, 538–539, favors the continuation of the striking of posthumous bronze types of Philip II through to 316 BC and of bronzes in the name of Kassander during the reign of Antigonos Gonatas. Cf. Le Rider, *Alexandre*, 55–63, esp. 63: "L' idée qu' Alexandre a continué l' émission des monnaies de son père me paraît s'imposer."

15. M. J. Price, "The coinage of Philip II," *NC*[7] 89 (1979), 234–235; idem, "Alexander's reform of the Macedonian Regal Coinage," *NC* 142 (1982), 180–190, esp. 188, n. 20; idem, *Alexander*, 38–39; Martin, *Sovereignty*, 271–292; Le Rider, *Monnayage et finances*, 53, n. 1, 55.

16. The torch symbol has suggested the assignation of a variety dated to c. 315–294 BC to Amphipolis: Price, *Alexander*, nos. 438–497. A second group is attributed to the reign of Poliorketes: ibid., nos. 498–508. A third group has been assigned to Uranopolis (c. 300–c. 290 BC): ibid., nos. 509–523. The posthumous Alexanders resumed in Pella under Philip V, presumably for a particular payment: H. Seyrig, "Monnaies hellénistiques, 5. Philippe V ou les Bottiéens," *RN*[6] 5 (1963), 14–18; Price, *Alexander*, 150–151.

17. Ibid., 141–149.

18. See chapters 2.2.1, 6.4.1.

Price is reluctant to see in the choice (by Alexander) of Athena, armed goddess of citadel and city, as the obverse type any attempt to appease the Athenians, and one need not consider such an association for the staters struck under Gonatas, either.[19] The symbolic reference to the naval victory of Salamis during the Chremonidean War through the reverse type of Nike with the *aphlaston* might tally with his naval victory over the Ptolemies at Kos. It is also compatible with the incorporation by Gonatas of the Persian Wars in his political discourse vis-à-vis the Greeks of the South (chapter 6.4.2).[20]

Silver Tetradrachms:

O: Beardless head of Herakles r.
R: Zeus Aetophoros seated on stool-throne l., holding eagle on outstretched r. hand and scepter in l. hand.[21] Legend ΒΑΣΙΛΕΩΣ ΑΝΤΙΓΟΝΟΥ.

These types, especially the Herakles on the obverse, in particular, may well have served to emphasise the connection with the Temenid royal line that was always claimed by the Antigonids.[22] This demonstration of respect for the previous Makedonian dynasty (and Alexander, in particular), recalls the covering over of the tombs at Aegae, which had been plundered by the Celtic mercenaries under Pyrrhos, and the construction of the portico to Gonatas' forebears at Delos.[23]

*** *** ***

2. Individual Types: Silver

2.1 Pan Head Tetradrachms, Drachma ("Pans")

Tetradrachms, Drachma:

O: Head of Pan l., in center of Makedonian shield.
R: Archaizing Athena l./r., in high relief, brandishing a thunderbolt; in exergue.[24] Legend ΒΑΣΙΛΕΩΣ ΑΝΤΙΓΟΝΟΥ.

The Makedonian shield with Pan on the obverse of the new coinage became the personal emblem of Antigonos Gonatas. The horned head of Pan is depicted with a three-fold drapery (*nebris*) around the neck and with a *pedum* at his shoulder. Allusions to the warrior god's cult may be observed on

19. Price, *Alexander*, 29.
20. On the *stylis* held by Nike, see E. Babelon, "La stylis, attribut naval sur les monnaies," *RN*[4] 11 (1907), 1–39 = *Mélanges Numismatiques* 4 (1912), 199; J. Svoronos, "Stylides, ancres hierae, acrostolia, embola, proembola et totems marins," *JIAN* 16 (1914), 81–152. Cf. V. Sergueenkova, "The Stylis of the Gold Coins of Alexander the Great," *NAC* 35 (2006), 165–178. Cf. chapter 2.4.1.
21. See n. 18.
22. Le Rider, *Philippe II*, 367; Ch. Edson, "The Antigonids, Heracles, and Beroea," *HSCP* 45 (1934), 213–246, esp. 214–216, 220–223. The star symbol on the Makedonian shield may also have been intended to reinforce the connection between Temenids and Antigonids. For the iconography and symbolism of Herakles in the Makedonian kingdom, see: P. Iliadou, *Herakles in Makedonien* (Hamburg: Kovac, 1998), 108–112; Zimi, *Silver Plate*, 52–53.
23. See chapter 1.2. On the stoa at Delos, see Smith, *HRP*, 24–25; Ameling et al. (eds.), *Schenkungen*, 190–193, with earlier bibliography; B. Schmidt-Dounas, "Der dorische Fries der Stoa des Antigonos Gonatas auf Delos," *MDAI*(A) 109 (1994), 227–242; C. Tarditi, "Architectura come propaganda. Esame dell' attivita edilizia degli Antigonidi in Grecia e nuove proposte di attribuzione," *Aevum antiquum* 3 (1990), 43–74. Cf. chapter 1.2.
24. See chapters 2.2.3, 6.4.2.

bronze coins of Philip V[25] and on bronze coinage struck at Pella under the Romans.[26] They may also be seen in the iconography adopted for the reverse of bronze coins from Amphipolis and Thessalonike of the second century BC, carrying a type identical to that on the middle *akroterion* of the pediment above the entrance to the cave of Pan in Thasos. A rise in the god's popularity in Makedonia during the third century BC, in particular, is suggested by the proliferation of literary references to him: the hymn composed by Aratos in Makedonia, the references to Pan in *Suida* and the analysis of "panic fear" by the Cypriot peripatetic philosopher Klearchos of Soloi relate to this period.[27] To these may be added a dedication of an altar to Pan at Beroia by Hippokles, thanking "Antigonos" for the renewal of the ἀτέλεια granted to his ancestors by Philip II,[28] and the institution by Gonatas of festivals in honor of the god, such as the Basileia at Pella[29] and the Paneia at Delos in 245 BC.[30]

H. Usener, in his commentary on an epigram from Knidos mentioning an "Antigonos, son of Epigonos," was the first to suggest that the head of Pan on the obverse of the Pan tetradrachms refers to an epiphany of the god to help Gonatas against the Celts at Lysimacheia in 277 BC,[31] rejecting Eckhel's earlier association of these coins to the Celtic attack on Delphi.[32] Usener even posited the subsequent introduction of a cult in honour of Pan and suggested that this cult and the above literary references to Pan and to "panic fear" were the result of the victory at Lysimacheia.[33] It is on these grounds that Pan has since been interpreted as the tutelary deity of Antigonos Gonatas,[34] just as the hero Perseus was apparently the protector of Philip V and Perseus.[35]

Even though the "Antigonos, son of Epigonos" mentioned in the epigram from Knidos is no longer identified with Gonatas,[36] the majority of scholars still believe that the Pan on the coins refers to the god's appearance at Delphi, and alleged appearance at Lysimacheia.[37] Yet Pan is ab-

25. *I. Knidos* 157; H. Usener, "Ein Epigramm von Knidos," *Rheinisches Museum N. F.* 29 (1874) 43–47, esp. 43; Gaebler, *AMNG* III.1, 35.34, note, pl. 9.9, with earlier bibliography; 118.3, pl. 22.25, 191.12, note, pl. 35.2.

Doubts may be cast upon the alleged representation of Pan on silver coins of Amyntas II, as these coins do not carry horned heads: Gaebler, *AMNG* III.1, 158.2–3, pl. 29, 28–29; *BMC Macedonia*, 168, no. 2. On the assignation of coins with Pan to Amyntas II, see Head, *HN*², 221–222; Svenson, *Darstellungen*, 48; Nachtergael, *Galates*, 178, n. 231.

26. Gaebler, ibid., 99.30, 33, pl. 19.23, 25; 100.36, pl. 19.24; Head, *HN*², 244; Tarn, *AG*, 174, n, 19.

27. Hymn of Aratos: *Vit. Ar.* 3.19, p. I, 86; *Suida*, s.v. ὕμνους εἰς Πᾶνα; Clearchos of Soli: Athen. 9, p. 389 ff. Usener, ibid., 43–47.

28. Th. Pazaras and M. B. Hatzopoulos, "Ἐπίγραμμα ἀπὸ τὴ Βέροια τῶν Ἀντιγονιδῶν," *Τεκμήρια* 3 (1997), 71–77; L. Gounaropoulou and M. B. Hatzopoulos, *Επιγραφές Κάτω Μακεδονίας*, Τεῦχος Α', *Επιγραφές Βεροίας*, Athens 1998, no. 37. Particular thanks are due to Prof. M. B. Hatzopoulos and to P. Paschides, for information and comments on this document.

29. *IG* II², 1367; Tarn, *AG*, 174, n. 18. Buraselis, *HM*, 145, n. 127.

30. On the Paneia at Delos, see chapter 1.2.

31. H. Usener, "Ein Epigramm von Knidos," *Rheinisches Museum, N. F.* 29 (1874), 43–7; Imhoof-Blumer, *MG*, 219; Tarn, *AG*, 174; H. Gaebler, *AMNG* III.2, 186; Boehringer, *Chronologie*, 99; Mørkholm, *EHC*, 134; Gabbert, *AG*, 68. F. W. Walbank, "The Years of Chaos," in Hammond and Walbank, *Macedonia* III, 255–8; Will, *HPMH* Iᵃ, 105–7, 109–10.

32. J. Eckhel, *Doctrina Nummorum Veterum*, pars 1.2² (Vindobonae, 1794), 124.

33. Usener, "Ein Epigramm," 43–7; certain of Usener's arguments are now outdated, see Habicht, *Gottmenschentum*, 79; Nachtergael, *Galates*, 177–9, n. 231; Blümel, *Knidos*, 157j, no. 301; cf. *IK Knidos* 157.

34. Tarn, *AG*, 174, n. 19; 226; Gabbert, *AG*, 68.

35. P. A. MacKay, "Macedonian Tetradrachms of 148–147 BC," *ANSMN* 14 (1968), 15–40; Boehringer, *Chronologie*, 107–110, 116–118; Mettout, *Persée*, 2; Mørkholm, *EHC*, 135–136.

36. U. von Wilamowitz-Moellendorf, *Hellenistische Dichtung* II (Berlin, 1924), 104–105 identified Antigonos with a rich Knidian, in honour of whom a gymnasium was erected in front of the gates of Knidos after his death. Blümel, *Knidos*, 158, believes that he belonged to the group of rich Knidians who in 282 BC lent to the Milesians large amounts of silver. Cf. W. W. Tarn, "The dedicated ship of Antigonus Gonatas," *JHS* 30 (1910), 209–222, esp. 214–215.

37. Gaebler, *AMNG* III.2, p. 186.2, note; Tarn, *AG*, 174, n. 20; Will, *HPMH* Iᵃ, 101–110. Liampi, *MS*, 108–111, with earlier bibliography. Only Imhoof-Blumer diverges from this general belief, arguing that Gonatas did not issue coins before 265 BC: *MG*, 129. Cf. Pritchett, *Greek State at War* III, 33, n. 93. Gabbert points out the uncertainties in dating

sent from the surviving references to the battle. This omission has generally been explained by the distance in time between the literary sources and the actual events.[38] However, the apparent rise in the popularity of Pan during the third century BC does not prove a particular connection of the god with Lysimacheia or with Gonatas, and the idea remains highly speculative.

By downdating the introduction of the Pan head tetradrachms to 271 BC, R. W. Mathisen dissociated them from Lysimacheia and regarded them as bearers of a particular ideology rather than as evidence for a contemporary military event (see chapter 6.4.2). Moreover, there is no reference to Pan on the bronze coins of the shield/helmet type that were allegedly struck after Lysimacheia: one would expect some allusion to the god, Nachtergael argues, on the coins issued immediately after his *epiphaneia*.[39] It is, after all, worth noting that the projection by Gonatas of Pan as his protector god at so early a stage of his reign would have been incompatible with his conscious efforts to relate himself to the Temenid dynasty, in order to gain the trust and recognition of the Makedonians (see chapter 1.2).

In the absence of evidence to associate the Pan head tetradrachms with Lysimacheia, the participation of Gonatas with five hundred mercenaries at Thermopylai and the suppression of the Celtic mutineers at Megara during the Chremonidean War become alternative occasions for the launching of the new coinage. Pan is not explicitly related to either incident.[40] In fact, the only reference to Panic fear from this period survives in Pausanias' account of the Celtic attack on Delphi under Brennos in 279 BC, after the failure of the allied Greek forces to overcome the Celts at Thermopylai:[41] ἐν δὲ τῇ νυκτὶ φόβος σφίσιν ἐμπίπτει Πανικός˙ τὰ γὰρ ἀπὸ αἰτίας οὐδεμιᾶς δείματα ἐκ τούτου φασὶ γίνεσθαι. ἐνέπεσε μὲν ἐς τὸ στράτευμα ἡ ταραχὴ περὶ βαθεῖαν τὴν ἑσπέραν, καὶ ὀλίγοι τὸ κατ᾽ἀρχὰς ἐγένοντο οἱ παραχθέντες ἐκ τοῦ νοῦ, ἐδόξαζόν τε οὗτοι κτύπου τε ἐπελαυνομένων ἵππων καὶ ἐφόδου πολεμίων αἰσθάνεσθαι, μετὰ δὲ οὐ πολὺ καὶ ἐς ἅπαντας διέδρα ἡ ἄγνοια (Mss., ἄνοια Schubolt)… ἥ τε ἐκ θεοῦ μανία πλεῖστον ἐξειργάσατο ὑπ᾽ ἀλλήλων τοῖς Γαλάταις τὸν φόνον (Paus. 10.23.7–8). οἱ δ᾽ἐν τῇ χειμερίῳ διαφθαρέντες νυκτὶ καὶ ὕστερον οἱ ἐν τῷ Πανικῷ δείματι ἐγένοντο ὑπὲρ τοὺς μυρίους, τοσοῦτοι δὲ ἄλλοι καὶ ὑπὸ τοῦ λιμοῦ (Paus. 10.23.10). It is a large body of Celts briskly retreating from Delphi that was allegedly destroyed by Gonatas at Lysimacheia.[42]

this coinage and considers Gonatas' victory over the Ptolemies off Kos as an equally possible starting point for his allegiance to the god Pan: *AG*, 68.

38. Nachtergael, *Galates*, 82–87, 177–180. A sudden attack of Gonatas' troops is mentioned in Just. 25.2.3 (*in silva taciti se occultarent*), but there is no reference to Pan in the text.

39. See further discussion and bibliography in Nachtergael, *Galates*, 177–179; cf. H. P. Laubscher, "Hellenistische Herrscher und Pan," *MDAI* (Ath) 100 (1985), 340, n. 41.

F. M. Heichelheim, "Numismatic Evidence of the Battle of Lysimacheia," *AJPh* 64 (1943), 332–333, suggests that a Makedonian shield/helmet bronze coin in the Fitzwilliam museum, which was overstruck on a bronze of Lysimacheia (head of Athena r./ΛΥΣΙ ΜΑΧΕΩΝ; lion r.), is evidence for military payments made after the battle. But this is speculation.

40. Just. 26.2.7; P. Trog. *Prol.* 26. Cf. chapter 6.4.2.

41.Paus. 10.20.4: βασιλέων δὲ ξενικὰ πεντακόσιοί τε ἐκ Μακεδονίας καὶ ἐκ τῆς Ἀσίας ἴσοι σφίσιν ἀφίκοντο ἀριθμόν… Usener adds the worship of Pan at the *Korykeion andron*, at Parnassos, to the same context: Paus. 10.32.7; Usener, ibid., 44, n. 2.

42. E. Will, "The formation of the Hellenistic kingdoms," in *CAH* VII.I², 115, considers the tradition relating to the sack of Delphi to be late and false. For more evidence regarding the Celtic invasions into the Makedonian kingdom, see I. Touratsoglou, "Les Galates sur les pentes de l' Olympe: le trésor de Néos Pantéleimon, lieu-dit Krania, 2000," *RN* 162 (2006), 99–116. J. B. Scholten, "Macedon and the Mainland," in Erskine, *Companion*, 134–144.

Evoking the protection of Delphi from the Celts in 279 BC established a link with a major Panhellenic event of the third century, that of the Celtic invasion, whose memory was recalled many times during the third and second centuries.[43] If Pausanias' account of the events is accurate,[44] the emphasis on the divine protection of the sanctuary on the new silver tetradrachms may have been meant to minimise the role of the Aitolians in that battle.[45] The selection of Pan rather than Apollo, whose intervention against the Celts is reported in the most contemporary sources,[46] is justified by the chronological distance of Pausanias from this event. It also suggests the introduction of the new coin types at a time when the legends on the sack of Delphi were under development.[47]

An indirect reference to the personal victory of Gonatas over the Celts may still be seen in the subsidiary projection of the divine protection of Delphi in 279 BC: as the Celts no longer constituted a threat for Greece after Lysimacheia, Gonatas presumably meant to underline that it was he who wrote the epilogue in the chapter of the Celtic threat to mainland Greece.

The allusion to Thermopylai is reinforced by other iconographic themes on the new coinage. A Makedonian shield, with seven embossed crescent and six/seven/eight-rayed star units (henceforth: "star/crescents," "units") arranged around a central emblem and with two or three circles on the edge, frames Pan's *clipeus* on the obverse. This shield type had been adopted at the end of the fifth/beginning of the fourth century BC by the Makedonian army, in particular by the king and his closest attendants, as a defensive military weapon, and it soon became a favorite theme in art. As a multifunctional military symbol, also known from archaeological finds,[48] it had great appeal

43. Plb. 2.35.7 (see chapter 2.4.2); 9.32.3–39.7. Hannestad, *Celts*, 17; on the references to the Celtic attack by Polybios, see C. Champion, "Polybius, Aetolia and the Gallic attack on Delphi (279 BC)," *Historia* 45 (1996), 316–328, esp. 320. On the development of the legends of the battle, see M. Segre, "La più antica tradizione sull' invasione gallica in Macedonia e in Grecia (280/79 a. Chr.)," *Historia* 1.4 (1927), 18–42; R. Flacelière, "La chronologie du IIIe av. J.-Chr. à Delphes," *REA* 35 (1933), 327; Flacelière, *Aitoliens*, 111; Pritchett, *Greek State at War* III, 31, n. 85; Scholten, *Politics of Plunder*, 31–37, cf. 37–37, 41–45 (the world's reaction to that battle). On the presence of Celts as mercenaries in Hellenistic armies, see, for instance, Rostovtzeff, *SEHHW*, III, 1452–1453, n. 342.

44. In 1979 Habicht suggested that Pausanias' sources were pro-Athenian: *Unters.*, 102–107. More recently, he argued that Pausanias does not make serious errors in his historical accounts: *Pausanias*, 84–86, p. xv; 97–98; cf. idem, *Athens*, 132–133. He suggested that Pausanias' source was reliable, presumably Hieronymos: *Pausanias*, 85, n. 72, 86, n. 79, 97. Cf. Hornblower, *Hieronymus*, 72–74.

45. On the other hand, Polybios' recognition of the important role of the Aitolians in that battle, despite his general antipathy to them, confirms his objectivity: C. Champion, ibid.

46. Epiphany of Apollo at Delphi: *Syll*[3] 398, l. 1–6 (decree of Kos). Apollo's epiphany along with Artemis and Athena, Diod. 22.9.5; Just. 24.8.5–12; Suida, s. v. ἐμοὶ μελήσει; Cicero, *De Div.* 1.81; *FD* III.1.483, l. 6. Dedications to Apollo from Delos: Dürrbach, *Délos*, 298A, l. 85–87, 372B; Habicht, *Athens*, 32–33. J. G. Fraser argues that Apollo Belvedere in the Vatican represents the god repelling the Celts: *Pausanias* (London, 1897), 345–346. Apollo's intervention at Delphi inspired Kallimachos's Hymn to Delos: Pritchett, *Greek State at War* III, 30–32. Cf. H. Pomtow, "Delphische Neufunde, Zur Delphischen Archontentafel des III. Jhdts. (Neue Soterien- und Amphictyonen-Texte)," *Klio* 14 (1914/5), 265–320, esp. 278; idem, „Die Kultstätten der anderer Götter von Delphi," *Philologus* 71 (1912), 54; Pfister, *RE* (1927), 1223, s.v. "Soteria"; C. Champion, "Polybius, Aetolia and the Gallic attack on Delphi (279 BC)," *Historia* 45 (1996), 316–328.

47. See note 42.

48. The closest archaeological parallel to this shield is the fragment of one of the shields that Pyrrhos allegedly dedicated at the sanctuary of Zeus at Dodona in 273 BC, after his victory over Gonatas at the gorge of Aoos (Kleisoura). A second shield of this type has been unearthed in Vegora/Florina, in western Makedonia, and a third in Albania: S. Dakaris, "Ἀνασκαφή τοῦ ἱεροῦ τῆς Δωδώνης," *ΠΑΕ* (1968), 58–59; Liampi, *Meletemata*, 160, n. 14; eadem, *MS*, 31, 52–55, pl. 1.2–3, 33.1. A fourth important fragment was reported by D. Pantermalis from the South side of the temenos of Zeus at Dion: it carries a legend ΒΑΣΙΛΕΩΣ ΔΗΜΗΤΡΙΟΥ between the two concentric circles at the central badge. The excavator assigns it to Demetrios Poliorketes, without providing any concrete evidence for favoring him over Demetrios II, but notes that the legend letters on this shield are similar to the find from Vegora: D. Pantermalis, "Δίον: Ιστορικά και λατρευτικά," *AEMTh* (2009), 261–267, esp. 263–264, pl. 3–4; cf. idem, *AEMTh* (1999), 417 ff. from Dion. Fragments of "Macedonian shields" carrying the inscription ΒΑΣΙΛΕΩΣ ΔΗΜΗΤΡΙΟΥ were also found in Staro Bonče in northern Macedonia: P. Juhel and D. Temelkoski, "Fragments de 'boucliers macédoniens' au nom du roi Démétrios trouvés à Staro Bonče (République de Macédoine," *ZPE* 162 (2007), 165–178 (with similar motifs to that of Dion). See the unpublished dissertation by

mainly in the Hellenistic Makedonian and eastern monarchies but also later on in Italy and in Rome.[49] The shield now fully occupies the obverse as the royal emblem of the Antigonid dynasty, in the same way as the anchor and the forepart of an attacking lion had occurred as symbols on the reverse of silver tetradrachms of Seleukos I and Lysimachos respectively.[50] It initially occurs on the reverse of bronze coins of Philip II and Alexander III and this link with the Temenids is corroborated by the six/seven/eight-rayed stars (a dynastic symbol of the Temenids or a symbol of Makedonia at large), which was introduced by Gonatas as a decorative motif for his larger silver denominations.[51] The star symbol finds an exact parallel on the shield unearthed in Vegora/Florina and resembles those on the shields found at Dodona, at Mit Rahinet (Memphis), and most recently at Dion.[52] It also recalls literary similes, comparing the large numbers of the Celtic invaders with stars.[53] H. W. Ritter sees in this symbol echoes of the "anonymous" bronze coinage of Demetrios Poliorketes, carrying a star in the center of a Makedonian shield on the obverse and a Makedonian helmet on the reverse,[54] and a precedent for the coinage of Philip V: a star is the central emblem on the obverse of the latter's tetradrachms and bronze issues and at the center of the shield of Athena on the reverse of his silver tetradrachms.[55] The depiction of Pan among seven stars is regarded by Ritter as a primary projection of Pan as "Allgott," which was to become popular in Roman imperial times.[56]

The frequent occurrence of Makedonian shields in religious contexts, primarily dedicatory or funerary, underlines the votive character of this symbol and echoes the customary dedication at sanctuaries of shields of the conquered or of distinguished warriors.[57] Shields as archaeological *spolia* have been unearthed at the sanctuaries of Olympia, Dodona, Oropos, and Dion,[58] while pictorial or sculptural representations of them occur on the dedication of Aemilius Paullus at Delphi, on the base of a trophy at Delos and on later representations of the altar of Juno.[59] Similarly, the shield from the necropolis at Mit Rahinet (Memphis) may be paralleled with decorative motifs from tombs, inspired by the decoration of the Makedonian shield.[60] The projection of this symbol echoes the multiple dedications of weapons at Delphi after the retreat of the Celts in 279 BC.[61] It may have

P. Juhel, *L'armée du royaume fd Macédoine à l'époque hellénistique (323–148 BC). Les troupes "nationales'. Organisation et analyse de l'iconographie militaire, avec déductions quant à la nature de l'armément* (Diss., La Sorbonne—Université Paris IV, 2007). See also below, n. 52.

49. On the shield and its badge as bearers of political ideology, see Liampi, *Meletemata*, 157–171; eadem, *MS*, 25–41.

50. Mørkholm, *EHC*, 66, 71, 81.

51. Diverging from M. Andronikos' interpretation of the star as a dynastic symbol of the Temenids, H. W. Ritter regards the star as a symbol of Makedonia: *Sternsymbolik*, 181–182, 184–188. Katerini Liampi reverts to Andronikos' suggestion, providing archaeological and numismatic argumentation: *MS*, 54.

52. Liampi, ibid., 32, 35–6, 53–4. D. Pantermalis, "Δῖον: Ιστορικά και λατρευτικά," *AEMTh* (2009), 261–267, esp. 263–264, pl. 3–4; cf. idem, *AEMTh* (1999), 417 ff. Cf. plate 62b.

53. Kallim., 4.171–6 (esp. l. 174–6: ὀψίγονοι Τιτῆνες ἀφ' ἑσπέρου ἐσχατόωντος ῥώσωνται, νιφάδεσσιν ἐοικότες ἢ ἰσάριθμοι τείρεσιν...); Nachtergael, *Galates*, 180–1; for a synopsis of the significance of the stars and for their interpretation, see Ritter, *Sternsymbolik*, 159–205; Hannestad, *Celts*, 19–20, n. 25.

54. Ritter, *Sternsymbolik*, 161, 166.

55. Liampi, ibid., 111 ff., pl. 24.

56. Projection of Pan as "Allgott": n. 34, 165, n. 6.

57. Liampi, ibid., S 3, pl. 1.3; S 4–6, 14–15, 17–18, S 27. The few exceptions are: the shield from Vegora (Liampi, ibid., S 3); the fresco from Boscoreale (ibid., S 7); the relief on the proxeny decree from Gonnoi (ibid., S 11); shields on architectural elements (ibid., S 17, 20–1, 30); miniatures (ibid., S 31–3) and girdles (ibid., S 34–6).

58. On finds at the first three sanctuaries, see Liampi, ibid., S 1–2, pl. 1.1–2, S 10, pl. 5.2, 34.1. On Dion, see above, n. 52.

59. Liampi, ibid., S 22–24, S 25, S 39 a–b respectively.

60. On such parallels, see, for instance, Liampi, *Meletemata*, 165–166; Liampi, *MS*, 59–60.

61. On the dedication of the shield of Kydias to Zeus Eleutherios: Paus. 10.21.5; Habicht, *Pausanias*, 84; Hannestad, *Celts*, 15–38, esp. 15–18; K. Liampi, "Die Einführung des Kultes des Zeus Eleutherios in Makedonien," *MDAI(A)* 117 (2002), 202–220, pl. 40. Cf. chapter 6.4.2.

been meant to offset the dedication by Pyrrhos of Epeiros of Makedonian shields at the sanctuary of Zeus at Dodona, after the defeat of the Makedonians at the gorge of Aoos (273 BC; cf. chapter 1.2).

This Makedonian shield, described by Asklepiodotos (*Takt.* 5.1) and Aelianus (*Takt.* 12) as ἀρίστη, on the obverse of the new tetradrachms and bronzes was emphatically distinguished from the Celtic and Persian shields, which, according to Pausanias, were similar.[62] Thus any tentative parallelism of the Makedonians with barbarians was effectively refuted, and Makedonia's role as a "shield" against the barbarians of the North (an idea which certainly exists in later literature) was internationally advertised instead.[63]

Before Gonatas, Philip II had used references on his coins to major sanctuaries, in order to promote his political claims in Greece. The combination of Apollo with the Nike in *biga* on the gold staters struck between Philip's victory over the Phokaians at Krokion Pedion (352 BC) and his victory at Olynthos (348 BC), for instance, apparently advertises his involvement in Panhellenic religious events and/or festivals.[64] The horseman with *kausia* on the tetradrachms, allegedly the king himself, was introduced in 356/5 BC, the year of the victory of Parmenion over the Illyrians, of the victory of Philip's horse (ἵππος κέλης) at Olympia, and the birth of Alexander.[65] Finally, the palm branch held by the jockey, and the *tainia* on the young head on the obverse of the second tetradrachm type have recently been related to his victory over the Phokaians during the Third Sacred War or to a new victory of Philip II at athletic games.[66] By projecting his participation in the Olympic games and his role in the protection of Delphi from the Phokaians, Philip legitimized his involvement with political affairs in Central Greece. In drawing on themes from the history of Delphi, Gonatas explicitly reverted to the political track beaten by Philip II in order to appeal to the Greeks. The Makedonian international policy of the Antigonids was thus projected as a continuation of that of the Temenids. This is not surprising, as the systematic restoration of the Makedonian kingdom and its rendering into an effective state, capable of expanding into southern Greece and of leading the expedition of the Greek states to Asia Minor, had been Philip II's achievement in the fourth century BC. By ending the instability/interregnum that followed the death of Poliorketes in Makedonia, and by laying the ground for a functional state and for a long-term dynasty, Gonatas in essence followed the policy adopted by Philip II, diverging from that of Alexander and his successors, whose focus had clearly shifted away from the Makedonian state *per se* towards the East.

Military themes are continued on the reverse, where the type is an archaistic warrior Athena, dressed in a high-girdled chiton, falling in fine folds with one heavy fall in the middle and with the hem ending in points. A shawl over her shoulders falls in dovetail pleats with two-pointed ends. She holds a thunderbolt in her left hand, poised to strike. Her pose is stiff, she is striding, usually with her left leg advanced. Seen in partial front or rear view, she sometimes has an *aegis* across her

62. Paus. 10.19.4: Αἰτωλοὶ δὲ (*sc.* ἀνέθεσαν) τά τε ὄπισθεν καὶ τὰ ἐν ἀριστερᾷ Γαλατῶν δὴ ὅπλα· σχῆμα δὲ αὐτῶν ἐστιν ἐγγυτάτω τῶν Περσικῶν γέρρων.

63. Plb. 9.32.3–7; C. Champion, "Polybius, Aetolia and the Gallic attack on Delphi," *Historia* 45 (1996), 316–328, esp. 317.

64. Plut. *Alex.* 4. Le Rider, *Philippe II*, 428; M. J. Price, "The coinage of Philip II," *NC* (1979), 234–235; Price, *Alexander*, 36, 106; Hatzopoulos, *Actes de Vente*, 85–86; G. Le Rider, "La date des premiers statères d' or de Philippe II," in *Χαρακτήρ*, 261–269; Le Rider, *Monnayage et finances*, 55–66, with earlier bibliography.

65. A. B. West, "The early diplomacy of Philip II of Macedon Illustrated by his Coins," *NC*[5] 3 (1923), 169–210, esp. 177–181, 210; Le Rider, *Philippe II*, 366–367; Le Rider, *Monnayage et finances*, 58, 68, with earlier bibliography. On the *kausia*, see A. M. Prestiani-Giallombardo, "Un copricapo dell' equipaggiamento militare macedone: la kausia," *NAC* 22 (1993), 61–90, esp. 67–68.

66. Ellis, *Philip II*, 237; Le Rider, *Monnayage et finances*, 59, 68.

back. She walks on tiptoe with both feet. In the field to her left is a "Makedonian" helmet; to her right, a monogram.[67]

The cult of Athena in Makedonia had a long history and was inextricably bound with the public domain, both civic and royal. In a royal context, she was worshipped as a protector of the army and carrier of victory, and indeed as a protector of Makedonian kings.[68] Gaebler identified the type of warrior goddess on these Antigonid tetradrachms with an Athena termed Ἀλκίδημος (i.e., "protector of the *demos*"), on the basis of Livy and associated her with the statue of Athena worshipped at Pella. However, Em. Voutyras has argued that the epithet Ἀλκίδημος is an error in the manuscript of Livy and believes that the Athena to whom Perseus sacrificed on the eve of the Third Makedonian War was a(n) (inter)national deity, rather than an otherwise unknown Athena Ἀλκίδημος venerated locally at Pella.[69]

Athena was already represented on the armor of the Argead warrior buried in Tomb II of the Grand Tumulus of Vergina and on one of the relief fragments in the "tholos" at Vergina-Aigai. She had been introduced as a symbol on the reverse of the lifetime tetradrachms of Alexander the Great struck in Makedonia and later on posthumous issues struck at Pella. She was used as a reverse type for the tetradrachms of Ptolemy I and later appears, often in variations, on coins of Agathokles, tyrant of Syracuse, of Demetrios Poliorketes, on certain Italian issues of Pyrrhos, on gold and silver coins of the Seleukid usurper Achaios (220–218 BC), on those of Bactrian and Indo-Parthian kings, and on the tetradrachms of Philip V.[70] Her presence on the badge of Akarnanian staters has been attributed to Makedonian influence.[71] Voutyras argues that, through the adoption of a thunderbolt (instead of a spear), she approximated her father Zeus in the tetradrachm issues of Antigonos Gonatas and Philip V, while diverging from the traditional Athena Promachos, brandishing a shield.[72] The thunderbolt symbol has been interpreted by Nollé as an echo of the Gigantomachy, symbolizing the victory of the Greeks against the barbarians.

As the hoard evidence prompts us to place the younger faces prior to their mature counterparts, the Pans reveal a development both in the self-representation of the ruler during his reign and in the royal imagery from father to son, just as in other Hellenistic royal coinages.[73] The development in Pan's features from the beardless young ruler *à la mode de* Alexander III to royal portraits covering the full range from divine through to realistic attributes confirms the role of the new type as a dynastic coinage in Antigonid Makedonia.

*** *** ***

67. Gaebler, *AMNG* III.1, 185.1; Agnes Baldwin-Brett, "Athena Ἀλκίδημος of Pella," *ANSMN* 4 (1950), 57–58.

68. Em. Voutyras, "Athéna dans les cités de Macédoine," *Kernos* 11 (1998), 111–129, esp. 125–128.

69. Liv. 42.51.2: *Ipse* (i.e., king Perseus) *centum hostiis sacrificio regaliter Minervae quam vocant Alcidemon facto.* H. Gaebler, *AMNG* III.2 (1935), 94, note to no. 4; Kalléris, *Macédoniens*, 95, no. 21; D. Papakonstantinou-Diamantourou, *Πέλλα* I, 38, n. 2. Cf. P. Demargne, s. v. "Athena," *LIMC* II.1, 973, no. 164, with bibliography (but the goddess is not recognised as "Alkidemos').

70. Agnes Baldwin-Brett, "Athena Ἀλκίδημος of Pella," *ANSMN* 4 (1950), 57–58.

71. Liampi, *MS*, 34.

72. On tentative interpretations of Athena brandishing a thunderbolt, see, for instance, A. B. Cook, *Zeus* III.1 (Cambridge, 1940), 868–873; J. Nollé, "Athena in der Schmiede des Hephaistos, Militär-, Wirtschafts-und sozialgeschichtliche Implikationen von Münzbildern," *JNG* 45 (1995), 51–77, esp. 56–63, avoids entering the debate whether the Athena brandishing a thunderbolt is to be identified with Athena Alkidemos of Pella; O. Bopearachchi, *Monnaies gréco-bactriennes et indogrecques* (Paris, 1991), 86 ff.; Voutyras, "Athéna dans les cités de Macédoine," 111–129, esp. 127, n. 75.

73. *Contra* R. Fleischer, who excludes the Antigonids from this practice: "Hellenistic royal iconography on coins," in Per Bilde et al., *Aspects of Hellenistic kingship*, 28. On the hoards, see chapter 6.3, fig. 6.13.

2.2 Poseidon Head tetradrachms ("Poseidons")

Mionnet's attribution of these coins to the founder of the Antigonid dynasty, Antigonos Monophthalmos, has been disproved by the fact that all the hoards in which they occur are from the late third century or later,[74] but whether they belong Gonatas or Doson is still a matter of debate. The types adopted for the new coinage may be described thus:

Tetradrachms:

O: Head of Poseidon r., in wreath of marine plants. Dotted border.
R: Apollo holding bow (with string up) with his uplifted r. hand, seated l. with crossed legs on prow.[75] Legend ΒΑΣΙΛΕΩΣ ΑΝΤΙΓΟΝΟΥ.

The identification of the bearded god on the obverse with Poseidon rests primarily on his wreath, although, with the possible exception of reeds on certain obverses, the plants which compose it are not identifiable. The sea god is rare on Makedonian coins before Demetrios Poliorketes, who regarded Poseidon as his patron deity and protector of his fleet.[76] Thus Poseidon, who first appeared on the reverse of the tetradrachms struck in the name of Poliorketes in the east after his defeat at Ipsos in 301 BC,[77] occurs on the reverse of his silver coinage struck at Pella in 292 and in 290 BC and on his bronze issues. On his tetradrachms from Pella, Poseidon is initially seated, holding an *aphlaston* in his right hand, while his left hand rests on a trident. On a later issue, he is standing with his right foot on a rock, leaning on his trident.

The reference to a deity from a previous coin issue may be seen as an expression of dynastic continuity, just as, for instance, Zeus Aetophoros on the reverse of the silver coinage of Alexander III, recalls the head of Zeus on the gold staters of Philip II.[78] Poseidon not only emphasized the naval aspirations of the first two members of the Antigonid dynasty but also created a precedent for the obverse of the bronze coinage struck in Makedonia under Philip V[79] and, between 187 and 31 BC, at Amphipolis, Pella and Thessalonike, presumably in memory of the Antigonid naval achievements of the past.[80]

Touratsoglou argues that the head of Poseidon was copied on the silver tetradrachms of the first Makedonian region, with Poseidon/Artemis Tauropolos, which he dates to the early second century BC.[81] It has been argued that the type was copied on the coinage of Abdera.[82] A particular version with a wreath composed of many branches may have been copied on the Zeus head on the Tauropolos tetradrachms of the first Makedonian *meris* and on the autonomous Rhodian-weight drachmae struck at Kos in the early second century BC.[83] In addition, the type may reflect Gonatas'

74. Mionnet, *Description* I, 580, 848; Imhoof-Blumer, *MG*, 124, n. 9–10; Merker, *Silver Coinage*, 40–41.
75. See also chapter 2.4.3.
76. Poseidon Hippios only occurs on the silver coinage of Poteidaia, which was a Corinthian colony (end of sixth century–429 BC): Gaebler, *AMNG* III.2, 191.10–11, pl. 34.23–24; E. Simon, "Poseidon," *LIMC* VII.1, 446–479, esp. 455, no. 70 and 479. On Poseidon as protector god of Demetrios, see Mørkholm, *EHC*, 78.
77. Mørkholm, *EHC*, ibid.
78. On Zeus as link between the coinages of Philip II and Alexander III, see, for instance, Price, *Alexander*, 31.
79. Gaebler, ibid., 191.10–11, pl. 34.23–24.
80. Gaebler, ibid., 2, 34.26–7, pl. 9.1–2 (Amphipolis); 94.5, pl. 18.29 (Pella); 121.22, pl. 23.13 (Thessalonike).
81. Touratsoglou, *DM*, 81.
82. H. von Fritze, "Die autonomen Münzen von Abdera," *Nomisma* 3 (1909), 28–9; Strack-Münzer, *Thrakien*, 15, pl. 3, no. 33. R. Ashton, "Hellenistic Bronze Coins of Abdera with a Male Portrait," in R. Ashton and S. Hurter (eds.), *Studies in Greek Numismatics in Memory of Martin Jessop Price* (London, 1998), 17–22.
83. On the similarity of Poseidon with the Zeus on the Tauropolos tetrarachms of the First *Meris*, see chapter 5.2, 207, n. 22. On the Rhodian-weight drachmae of Kos, R. Ashton, "The Pseudo-Rhodian Drachms of Kos," *NC* 158 (1998), 223–228;

claims to international sovereignty, as he was compared by Sextus Empiricus with Poseidon after the battle of Kos (260/255 BC).[84] One might be tempted to speculate that it was this naval victory of Gonatas over the Ptolemies which prompted Poliorketes's descendant to project Poseidon, in order to celebrate the renewal of the Antigonid naval tradition in the Aegean.

This Poseidon head served as the prototype for the obverse of the 20-drachma pieces struck during the so-called First Democracy in Greece in 1924–1935 (see pl. 60, section II).[85]

Poseidon was new to Makedonia, but Apollo, who appears on the reverse of the new tetradrachms, had long formed part of the iconographic repertory of cities, kings and dynasts in the area.[86] He is rendered with long plaits behind his ears falling on his shoulders, with a longer lock falling on his chest. He is seated cross-legged, three-quarters facing left, on a prow. He holds a bow (string upwards) with his outstretched right hand, and his left hand leans on the ship.

The selection of Apollo may have been meant to establish a connection between the new tetradrachms and the coinage of Philip II, Alexander III and Philip III. The god's posture also recalls Seleukid coinage with Apollo seated on an omphalos, holding an arrow in his right hand, while the left rests on his bow.[87] If the Poseidons are to be assigned to Gonatas, one might be tempted to see in them Gonatas' political approximation to the Seleukids, who regarded Apollo as their patron god.[88]

Finally, the prow recalls coins of Poliorketes, both his silver and bronze coins with Nike on prow/Poseidon and with prow/Poseidon respectively and his tetradrachms from an "uncertain" Makedonian mint, possibly Thessalonike or Kassandreia, with a head of Demetrius/Poseidon.[89] The prow has also provoked comparison with the prows on the octobols and tetrobols struck at Histiaia at the end of the fourth century[90] and with those on the coinage of the Akarnanian Confederacy and on Roman *aes grave*.[91] Mathisen suggests that the annual feasts organized in

V. Stefanaki, *Κως* I (Athens, 2012), 107–108, n. 770. See also chapter 5.2, 206, n. 21. Cf. plate 61, 9–11. On Poseidon on other Greek coinages, see Erica Simon, s. v. "Poseidon," *LIMC* VII.1, 446–479.

84. Sextus Empiricus, *Adversus Mathematicos* I, 276. Buraselis, *HM*, 163, n. 182; 165–166; eiusdem, "Μυθική ύλη και ελληνιστική μοναρχία. Το εργαλείο του μύθου στην υπηρεσία της πολιτικής," in Κ. Μπουραζέλης and Μ. Στεφάνου (eds.), *Πρακτικά συμποσίου Μύθος μετά λόγου, Διάλογοι για την ουσία και τη διαχρονική αξία του αρχαίου Ελληνικού μύθου*', Αγ. Κήρυκος, Ικαρία, 17–20 Ιουνίου 2005 (Athens, 2007), 177–197, esp. 179–181. For the date of the battle of Kos, see chapter 3. For the existence of a cult of Poseidon under Doson, see Le Bohec, *AD*, 224.

85. The head in the modern Greek series, whose execution was overseen by the British numismatist Sir G.F. Hill, was engraved by Percy Metcalf, while the prow on the reverse was designed by Langford Jones. This short-lived series was the first to be withdrawn and replaced by paper money put into circulation on 01 June 1940, through law 2153/1939; it circulated as legal tender until the 31 December 1940: An. P. Tzamalis, *Τα νομίσματα της νεώτερης Ελλάδας 1828–1979* (Athens: Νούμμιο, 1980) 163–164, αρ. Ν. 192. Particular thanks are due to Mr. P. Panagakis and to Dr. E. Papaefthymiou for kindly providing me with a photograph of the specimen from the Bank of Greece coin collection.

86. Olga Palagia, "Apollo allein bewaffnet," in *LIMC* II.1, 196-7, pl. 57-66; Ulla Westernark, "Apollo in Macedonia," in *Opus Mixtum*, 149-54; "Remarks on Regal Macedonian Coinage," in Le Rider et al., *Kraay-Mørkholm Essays*, 301-15; "The Staters of Archelaus. A die study," in Price et al., *Essays Carson-Jenkins*, 17-30.

87. E. Babelon, *Les rois de Syrie, d' Arménie et de Commagène*, Paris 1890, p. 43; E. Bikerman, "Sur les batailles navales de Cos et d' Andros," *REA* 40 (1938) 380; L. Lacroix, "Copies des statues sur les monnaies Seleucides," *BCH* 73 (1949), 169–174, pl. III–IV, esp. 158–176; Le Bohec, *AD*, 55, n. 1; Mørkholm, *EHC*, 113. Cf., for instance, Newell, *WSM*, 21, no. 239B.

88. The first group of the Antigonid festivals at Delos, Antigoneia and Stratonikeia, have been dated to 253 BC; the second group, Paneia and Sotereia, took place in 245 BC, presumably after the battle of Andros. Both have been related to the intensified antagonism between the Ptolemies and the Antigonids for sovereignty over the Aegean: Buraselis, *HM*, 142–144. For the association of Gonatas with Apollo, cf. Mathisen, *Pan Heads and Poseidon Heads*, 32.

89. On these last tetradrachms, see Newell, *DP*, 123–124, no. 138, pl. 14.5–8.

90. R. Weil, "Histiaea-Oreos," *ZfN* 1 (1874),189; Picard, *Chalcis*, 176; Le Bohec, *AD*, 55, n. 2.

91. W. Schwabacher, "Some unknown federal coins of the Akarnanians," in Kraay-Jenkins, *Essays Robinson*, 219–221, pl. 62; Crawford, *RRC*, 42, n. 2. Rather than suggesting a late date for the Poseidons, the prow copied on the Akarna-

honour of Apollo at Delos in c. 253 and in c. 245, and Antigonos' dedication to Apollo of his sacred trireme at Delos, in the Neorion or "Hall of Bulls"[92] after his victory over the Ptolemies near the island of Kos, offer the context for this combination of Apollo with a prow on the new coinage.[93] To judge from the two mosaics from Thmuis in Egypt showing a bust of a woman, presumably Berenike II, perhaps as Agathe Tyche, in Hellenistic military attire, crowned with the prow of a ship, this was a theme of contemporary topicality.[94] The strong symbolism of sea power, victory, wealth, and abundance on these mosaics apparently constitutes the respondent in the political "debate" between Ptolemies and Antigonids for control of the Aegean, of which the Poseidons formed an integral part. The prow on this Antigonid tetradrachm reverse type was copied on the 20-drachma pieces of the First Republic (1924–1935), as mentioned above.[95]

*** *** ***

2.3 Zeus Head Tetradrachm ("Zeus")

The so-called Unknown Findspot, "Antiochus III" Hoard, 2005, added a new tetradrachm type to the iconographic repertory of the early Antigonid issues: Catharine Lorber and Arthur Houghton describe a unique tetradrachm combining a head of Zeus laureate on the obverse with a bow-bearing Apollo seated on prow, known from the Poseidon head tetradrachms, with legend ΒΑΣΙΛΕΩΣ ΑΝΤΙΓΟΝΟΥ on the reverse.[96]

The laureate head of Zeus on the obverse of this silver tetradrachm is reminiscent of that on the tetradrachms of the Argead king Philip II: he was the first to adopt the head of Zeus as a type, presumably after his victory over Olynthos, in the summer of 348 BC.[97] The choice of a Zeus head for Philip's silver coins is neither puzzling nor need be tied to a specific event: Zeus, lord of Olympus and father of Makedonia, was particularly popular in Makedonia and beyond.[98] Le Rider suggests that he may have been chosen to act as a parallel for the obverses of the tetradrachms of Chalkidike, which bore a head of Apollo.[99] Alternatively, Zeus may have marked Philip's celebration of the Olympia games in honour of Zeus at Dion, after his victory over Olynthus.

nian coinage of the late third century might reflect the adoption by the Akarnanians of an explicitly pro-Makedonian policy during the last quarter of the third century, to the detriment of the Aitolians: Will, *HPMH* I², 351; F. W. Walbank, "Demetrius II (239–229 B.C.)," in Hammond and Walbank, *Macedonia* III, 333–336. For other parallels, see Le Bohec, *AD*, 225–226.

92. Athen. 5.209e (Moschion): Παρέλιπον δ' ἑκὼν ἐγὼ τὴν Ἀντιγόνου ἱερὰ τριήρη, ᾗ ἐνίκησε τοὺς Πτολεμαίου στρατηγοὺς περὶ Λεύκολλαν τῆς Κῴας, ἐπειδὴ (Mss. ὅπου δὴ Meineke) καὶ τῷ Ἀπόλλωνι αὐτὴν ἀνέθηκεν. W. W. Tarn, "The Dedicated Ship of Antigonus Gonatas," *JHS* 30 (1910), 209; Mathisen, *Pan Heads and Poseidon Heads*, 32, n. 28; J. Tréheux, "Sur le Neorion à Délos," *CRAI* (1987), 168–184.

93. Mathisen, *Pan Heads and Poseidon Heads*, 29–32.

94. On the mosaics, see I. Koenen, "The Ptolemaic King as a Religious Figure," in Bulloch et al., *Images and Ideologies*, 27, figs. 2a–b, with earlier bibliography. On parallel themes in Posidippos of Pella, see S. Stephens, "Posidippus's Poetry Book: Where Macedon meets Egypt," in W. V. Harris and G. Ruffini (eds.), *Ancient Alexandria between Egypt and Greece* (Leiden/Boston, 2004), 63–86, esp. 68–69.

95. See above, n. 85.

96. C. Lorber—A. Houghton, "Antiochus III Hoard," *AJN* 21 (2009), 89–104, esp. 99, 11 and pl. 8, 11.

97. Le Rider, *Philippe II*, 363–364; idem, *Monnayage et finances*, 22; S. Le Bohec, "The Kings of Makedon and the Cult of Zeus in the Hellenistic Period," in D. Ogden (ed.), *The Hellenistic World. New Perspectives* (Swansea, 2002), 41–57. Symbols of Zeus had already been employed by Archelaos I, Amyntas III, and Perdikkas III in Makedonian royal numismatic iconography: Gaebler, *AMNG* III, 1, pl. XXIX, 16, XXX, 1, 7, 17. See also Em. Voutyras, "Le culte de Zeus de Macédoine avant la conquête romaine," in Guimier-Sorbets et al. (eds.), *Rois, cités, nécropoles*, 333–345, esp. 339, n. 56.

98. Ritter, *Bildkontakte*, 134–136; Em. Voutyras, "Le culte de Zeus de Macédoine avant la conquête romaine," in Guimier et al. (eds.), *Rois, cités, nécropoles*, 333–435, esp. 339, n. 57.

99.On Apollo on the coinage of the Chalkidians see Psoma, *Olynthe*, 92–93, 111, 157, 241; Price, *Coins of the Macedonians*, 16–17; on the monetary policy of the Chalkidians of Thrace, Psoma, *Olynthe*, 170–179.

Prior to Philip, the representation of symbols of Zeus on the coinage of Archelaos might reflect his reorganization of the cult of this deity at Dion and his establishment at the end of the fifth century of a *panegyris* termed "Olympia," whose reputation extended beyond local frontiers.[100] Political manipulation of this *panegyris* by Makedonian kings is, it seems, likely: in addition to Philip's grandiose celebration of this festival after his destruction of Olynthos in 348 BC, Alexander's celebration of it in 335 BC, on the eve of his expedition to Asia and after his establishment as *hegemon* in Makedonia and in Greece, may have taken place at Zeus's sanctuary at Dion.[101]

Thus the depiction of a head of Zeus on the obverse of a tetradrachm type is not incompatible with the main threads of Antigonid policy. A sanctuary honouring Zeus Olympios, operating between the third century BC (under Antigonos Gonatas) and the fifth century AD, is now known to have been located on the Agios Antonios summit on mount Olympus:[102] one of the early Antigonids may well have added the Zeus head type to his numismatic iconography on the occasion of festivities in that sanctuary. Certain occasions in Gonatas's reign would have been appropriate for this, but Demetrios II and Antigonos Doson are also plausible candidates. If our tentative attribution of this unique Zeus tetradrachm to Doson is confirmed, its association with a celebration of the Olympia, perhaps on the eve of his Karian expedition, would follow the trend set by his Argead predecessors. Alternatively, a celebration of the vase festival "Soteria" at Delos, honouring Zeus and Athena, which was established by Gonatas after Andros (246/5 BC), could be reflected in the Zeus and Apollo-on-prow types.[103]

2.4 Fractional Denominations

Drachmae, Tetrobols:

O: Head of Zeus r. in wreath.
R: Athena brandishing thunderbolt l., her shield held upright, but without *aegis* and *gorgoneion*. In field l., winged helmet; r., monogram.[104] Legend ΒΑΣΙΛΕΩΣ ΑΝΤΙΓΟΝΟΥ.

The Athena on the reverse of these coins suggests their association with the first type of the individual silver coinage with the name of king Antigonos, the Pan head tetradrachms. The bearded head on the obverse is different in style from that on the Poseidon head tetradrachms, and has a different type of wreath, made from large leaves similar to ivy and berries. F. Imhoof-Blumer believed that the wreath was made from a marine plant and he identified the god with Poseidon rather than Dionysos.[105] Merker adopts Mionnet's description of the wreath as laurel and identi-

100. Em. Voutyras, "Le culte de Zeus de Macédoine avant la conquête romaine," in Guimier et al. (eds.), *Rois, cités, nécropoles*, 333–345, esp. 337, 339, n. 51; M. Mari, "Le olimpie macedoni di Dion tra Archelao e l' età romana," *RFIC* 126 (1998), 137–169, 153–61.

101. On the celebration of the destruction of Olynthos by Philip II, see Dem. 19.192; Diod. 16.55.1. Voutyras notes that Alexander's celebration on the eve of his campaign to Asia Minor may have taken place at Dion or at Aigai: Diod. 17.16.3–4; Arr. *Anab.* 1.11.1. See Em. Voutyras, "Le culte de Zeus de Macédoine avant la conquête romaine," in Guimier et al. (eds.), *Rois, cités, nécropoles*, 333–45, esp. 339–340 (on the celebration of the Olympia by Philip II); on Alexander's possible celebration at Dion, see ibid., 339, n. 53, *contra* M. Mari, "Le olimpie macedoni di Dion tra Archelao e l' età romana," *RFIC* 126 (1998), 137–69, esp. 148–153.

102. Em. Voutyras, "Le culte de Zeus de Macédoine avant la conquête romaine," in Guimier et al. (eds.), *Rois, cités, nécropoles*, 333–345, esp. 340–342. Estimates of the period of function of this sanctuary are based on numismatic evidence.

103. On the Soteria at Delos, see Buraselis, *HM*, 143, 174; C. Champion, "In Defense of Hellas: The Antigonid Soteria and Paneia at Delos and the Aetolian Soteria at Delphi," *AJAH* 3–4 (2004–2005), 72–78. See also chapter 5.2.

104. See also chapters 6.4.4, 5.4.

105. Imhoof-Blumer, *MG*, 124–125; Gaebler, *AMNG* III.2, 187.5, pl. 33.26. Head considers that the head on the silver drachms is of earlier style than that on the Poseidon head tetradrachms: HN^2, 231–232.

fication of the god with Zeus,[106] noting in addition the stylistic similarity of the head with that of Zeus on contemporary coins of Epeiros.[107]

The winged helmet in the reverse field of these drachmae recurs in the left reverse field of the Pan head tetradrachms of Period IV (see chapter 6.4.4).

*** *** ***

To recapitulate, the iconography of the transitional Alexander and the Pan silver issues in the name of Antigonos reflected both the Temenid tradition and the history of Delphi and Delos; and possibly also of two other leading sanctuaries, Eleusis and Dion. The Alexander types established continuity between the Temenid and the new Makedonian dynasty. As for the individual Antigonid silver types, the combination of Pan with the Makedonian shield, with Athena and with the helmet on Gonatas' first tetradrachm type advertised the Makedonian role in the defence of Greece, primarily as part of the Panhellenic resistance to the Celts at Delphi and later at Lysimacheia: unlike the Ptolemies, their military opponents for control over Southern Greece, the Antigonids were active participants in Greek religious and political affairs. It may therefore be argued that the iconography of the Pans was meant to project Makedonian aspirations in mainland Greece. The selection of a Panhellenic event with wide impact explains the continuation of this coin type long after the death of its initiator.

In contrast to his father Demetrios, who placed his own portrait on his coins, adorned with bull horns, bringing him into the sphere of the divine, Gonatas preferred to depict his tutelary deity Pan on his own silver tetradrachms. This may be taken as an indicator of modesty and piety.[108] Some development may be observed in the rendering of the Pans: those of the "plain style' of our Period I, are characterized by shallow curves, by soft forms in the rendering of the face and by natural eyes. The Pans of the next period are large and dynamic, rendered in high relief, with tousled hair locks, fleshy lips and bulging eyes.

It may be argued that certain of the Pan heads of the third period, with mature and individualistic features, represent portraits of members of the Antigonid dynasty: Antigonos Monophthalmos, Demetrios Poliorketes, and Demetrios II become plausible candidates, but Antigonos Gonatas himself need not be excluded, not least as he is now known to have received ἰσοθέους τιμάς during his lifetime.[109] J. Kroll notes that some of the later Pan head coins may be taken as portraits of Gonatas himself, as it was legitimate for the king to present his own portrait without breaking the numismatic tradition.[110] The surviving statues attributed to the early Antigonids are few and their attributions are dubious, hence identifications of portraits may only be tentative, rendering necessary more systematic research on this matter.[111] As the heads of the Pans with

106. Mionnet, I, 581, 583.

107. Merker, *Silver Coinage*, 40, n. 4

108. See, for instance, J. Kroll, "The Emergence of Ruler Portraiture on Early Hellenistic Coins," in P. Schultz (ed.), *Early Hellenistic Portraiture; Image, Style, Context* (New York, 2007), 113–122, esp. 118.

109. C. Habicht, "Divine Honours for King Antigonus Gonatas in Athens," *SCI* 15 (1996), 131–134; I. Kralli, "The Date and Context of Divine Honours for Antigonos Gonatas—A Suggestion," in S. Tracy and O. Palagia (eds.*), The Macedonians in Athens*, 61–66.

110. J. Kroll, "The Emergence of Ruler Portraiture," 113–122, cf. n. 34.

111. Already Tarn, *AG*, 174, n. notes that some of the diademed heads of Pan are not much alike; cf. J. Kroll, "The Emergence of Ruler Portraiture," 113–122, esp. 122. On a surviving (very dubious) bronze statue that has been attributed to the early Antigonids, see Smith, *HRP*, 42, n.; Fröhlich, *Darstellungen*, Kat. Nr. 4; Thomas, *Ptolemaios IV*, 14–15, pl. 6; Himmelmann, *Herrscher und Athlet*, 109–10. The dissertation by Lydia Kappa, entitled "Repräsentation um Macht und Herrschaft. Studien zur Selbstdarstellung und Herrscherrepräsentation der Antigoniden" at the Humboldt Universität in Berlin (2019), under the supervision of Prof. Dr. S. G. Schmidt, is likely to shed light on this issue.

scepter are diverse, they may depict more than one member of the dynasty. One may tentatively conjecture, for instance, that the most elaborate Pan head tetradrachm, no. 127 of our Period III, with the legend ΒΑΣΙΛΕΩΣ ΑΝΤΙΓΟΝΟΥ curved in very small letters between the two concentric circles in the central badge and with a scepter instead of a *pedum*, represents either Antigonos, Monophthalmos or Gonatas. The Pans on the obverses of the tetradrachms of our Period IV are more modestly rendered than those of Period III.

The Poseidon head tetradrachms, on the other hand, were presumably meant to reflect naval ambitions in the Aegean, which had been initiated by the founders of the dynasty, Antigonos Monophthalmos and Demetrios Poliorketes, and were challenged by the Ptolemies. At the same time, the unique Zeus head tetradrachm, projecting a Panhellenic deity, may have been meant to combine a demonstration of piety on a Panhellenic level with a naval theme. Finally, the divergent iconography of the Zeus head silver drachmae, linked through their reverse and symbol (winged helmet) to the main Pan series, suggests the longer-term production of the latter.

6.2 Relative Chronology

6.2.1 Metrology

The Antigonid issues are struck on the Attic weight standard, which had been introduced by Philip II for the Makedonian royal gold coinage and by Alexander III for the silver.[112] Period I has a variety of denominations, comprising gold staters, silver tetradrachms with both Alexander and individual Antigonid (Pan head) types, and a silver Pan head drachma. Periods II and III have tetradrachms only, the former Pans, the latter Pans and Poseidons. A greater diversity in both denominations and types recurs in period IV, comprising Pan and Poseidon tetradrachms, Zeus drachmae and tetrobols, which were struck from dies used for the Zeus drachmae.

The weight standard aimed at seems to have been c. 8.60–8.65 g for the gold staters (the weight-range of 67 % of the specimens) and c. 17.01–17.05 g (for 44.5 %) for the silver tetradrachms with the Alexander types of the first period. The tetradrachms with Antigonos individual types are slightly heavier than their Alexander-type counterparts.

Variations in weights for the individual Antigonid silver issues are shown in Figs. 6.1–6.4. The boxes show the range of weights for 75% of the data in each period: the right and left line of each box represent respectively the first and the third quartiles; the band inside each box is always the second quartile (the median). The ends of the whiskers represent the minimum and maximum weight of all the data in each period.

Peaks for the Pan head tetradrachms range around c. 17.15–17.01 g (41.2%) for Period I, c. 17.15–16.86 g (55.2%) for Period II, c. 17.15–16,81 g (48.99%) for Period III, culminating in 17.06–17.10 g (14.5%); and 17.15–16.86 g (36.32%) for Period IV, where 18.7% of the specimens cluster between 17.01 and 17.10 g.

The Poseidon head tetradrachms vary between 17.20 and 16.66 g (88.2 %) in Period III, 14.5 % weighing 17.06–17.10 g; and between 16.96 and 17.10 g (62.7 %) in Period IV. The slightly heavier weight of the Poseidons may have been intended to encourage the acceptance of the new tetradrachm type.

The silver drachma of the first period weighs 4.02 g; the peak for those of the last period lies between 3.81 and 3.85 g (21.4%) and 3.56–3.60 g. The smallest silver fractions, of c. 2.46–2.50 g (Fig. 6.3), may be identified as tetrobols, i.e., the silver denomination which by the early Hellenistic period represented a soldier's daily wage; similar denominations were struck at Athens during the third century.[113]

The paucity of the fractional denominations may be explained by the continued use of Alexander-type fractions in Makedonia or by the extensive use of bronze coinage.[114]

112. M. J. Price, *Coins of the Macedonians* (London, 1974), 22–23; Le Rider, *Philippe II*, 407; Price, *Alexander*, 41–6; Mørkholm, *EHC*, 41–43. On the Attic weight standard for the silver, see Doyen, *Étalons*, 61–73, esp. 66 (Antigonids).

113. On the Athenian tetrobols of the third century, see Kroll, *Agora*, 11, n. 43; 22, nos. 29a–c.

114. Doyen, *Étalons*, 61–95; P. Baker, "Coût des garnisons et fortifications dans les cités à l' époque hellénistique," in J. Andreau, Briant and R. Descat (eds.), *La guerre dans les économies antiques*, Entretiens d' Archéologie et d' histoire 5 (Saint-Bertrand-des Comminges, 2000), 177–196. On the use of bronze coins for the payment of the military σιτηρέσιον with bronze coins, see S. Psôma, "*Tas sitarchias kai tous misthous* ([Arist.], *Oec.* 1351b), Bronze Currencies and Cash-Allowances in Mainland Greece, Thrace and the Kingdom of Macedonia," *RBN* 45 (2009), 53–38, with earlier bibliography; cf. eadem, "Τὰς παλαιὰς πεντεδραχμίας. Un stratagème de Polyen et le monnayage d' argent des rois de Macédoine de 413 à 360 av. notre ère," *RN* (2000), 123–136.

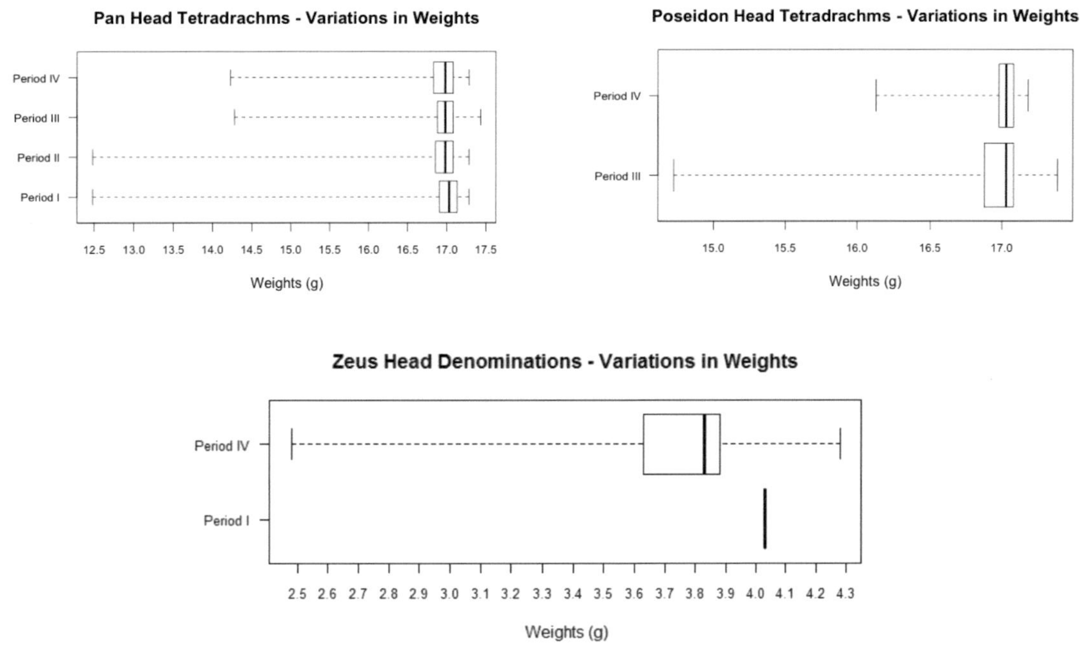

Figures 6.1–6.3. Silver tetradrachm denominations: Box plots per coin type.

6.2.2 Die Axes

The orientation of the dies may help identify the location and chronology of the coinages. The gold staters and silver tetradrachms in the name of Alexander III and the first individual silver issues of "King Antigonos" were struck from loose dies.[115] A general tendency to adjust the dies around 12 h may be observed for Gonatas's individual issues, even if great variety is still preserved in the orientation of the axes of Period I. Unlike Period III, the Pans are aligned around 12 h more consistently than the Poseidons in Period IV. Most of the known silver drachmae also have axes around 12 h.

Different die axes may be observed for different monograms (Chapter 6.2.4). The dies with monogram HP in Period I, for instance, are aligned around 6 h and 12 h. Monogram K is struck by loose dies, and the initial tendency to adjust the dies to 12 h for monogram ⋈ is later abandoned. With the exception of the issues with the letters M and TI, which are consistently adjusted around 12 h, all the other monograms of Period III sign coins with loose dies. In period IV, all mint officials attempt to adjust their dies at 12 h or 3 h for the Pans; many Poseidons and all the silver fractions of the same period are adjusted around 12 h or 3 h or 6 h or 9 h.

Of particular interest is the alignment of the die-axes in certain special groups. Unlike the loose arrangement of the gold stater dies, the *desmos* groups of Periods I (45–49, coin nos. 174–181) and III (27–29, coin nos. 127–135) are consistently aligned around 12 h and 3 h. The alignment of the X group around 12 h and 6 h also suggests a special issue. The assignation of the last two groups to the loosely aligned third period of Pans, suggests their identification as celebratory issues rather than their production at a different mint(s). It is also worth noting that more than half of the Pans, but also nearly two thirds of the Poseidons, of the last two periods are aligned around 12 h. The special care in the alignment of the Poseidons of the third period, in particular, may have

115. See de Callataÿ, *Axes*, 49, n. 181.

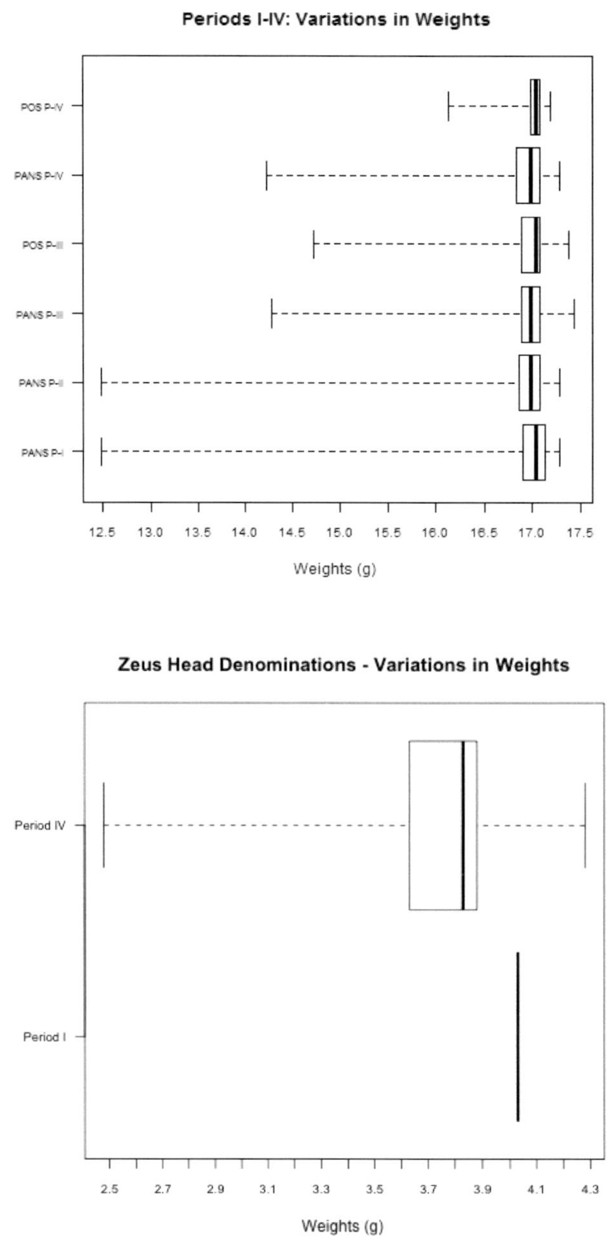

Figure 6.4. Silver specimens, Periods I–IV: Box plots.

been due to the use of thinner flans, which must have required a careful placing of the dies. This further supports the view that the Poseidons were a celebratory issue (chapters 6.4.3, 7.3).[116]

116. On the careful placing of dies on thinner flans, see G. MacDonald, "Fixed and loose dies in ancient coinage," in *Corolla Numismatica*, 178–188, esp. 180.

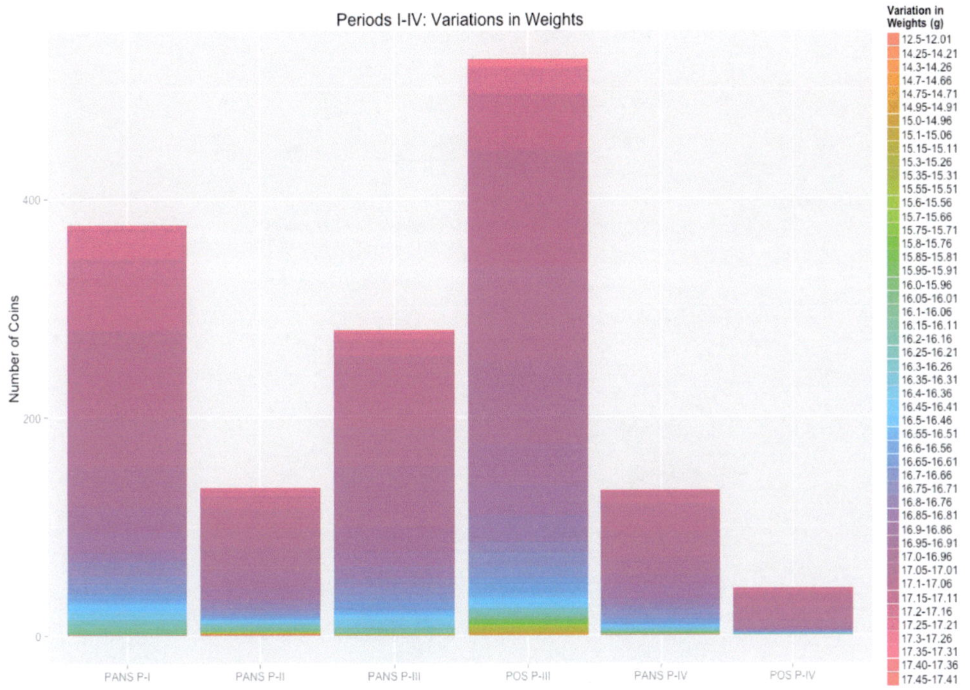

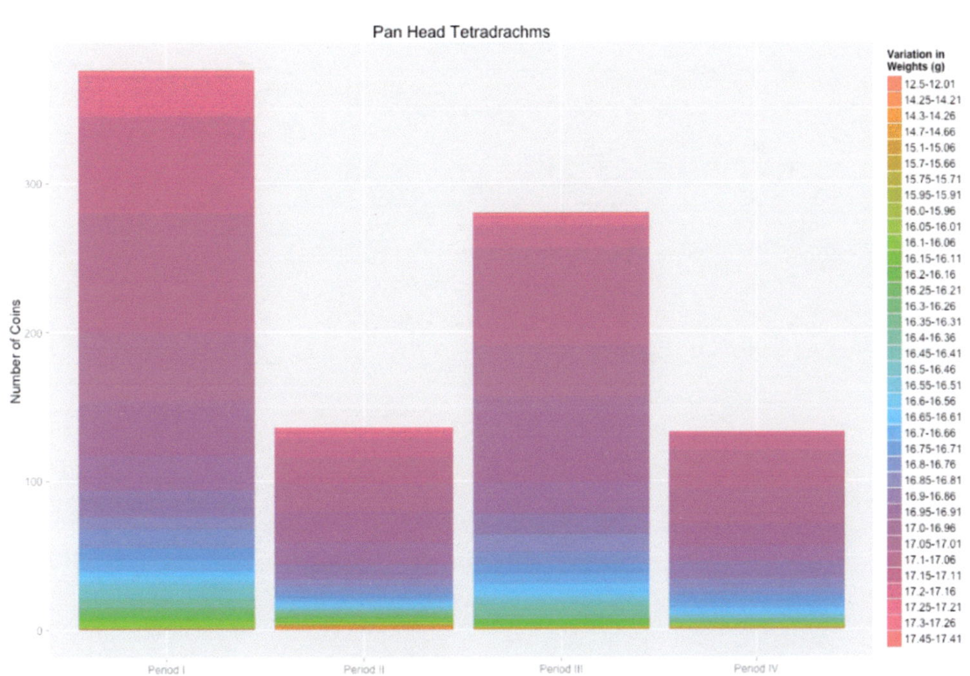

Figure 6.5a. Silver specimens, Periods I–IV: Stacked bar charts.

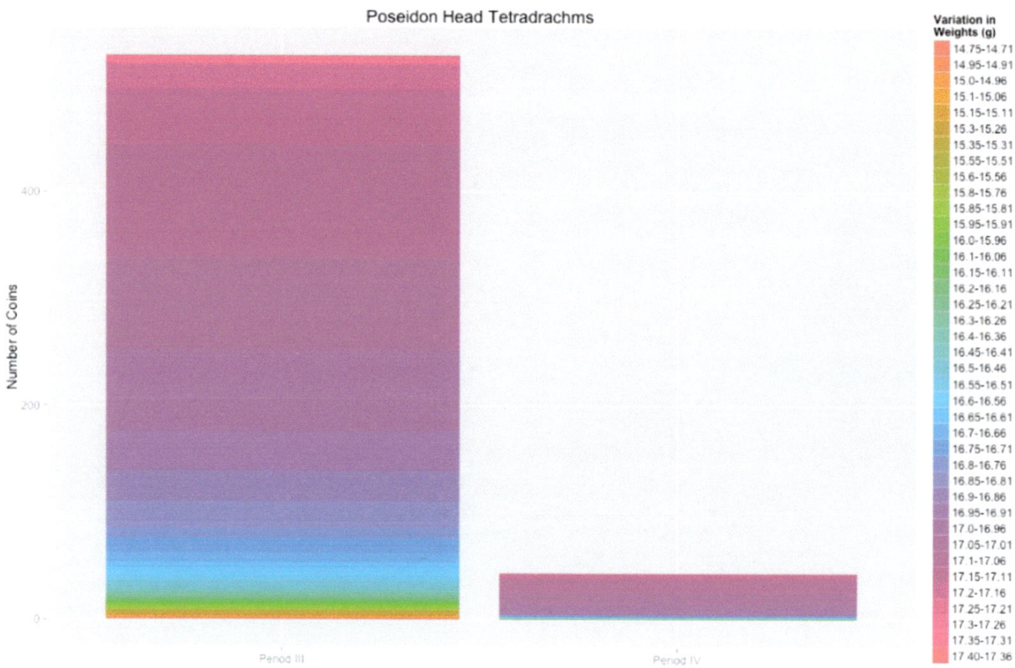

Figure 6.5b. Silver specimens, Periods I–IV: Stacked bar charts.

6.2.3 Style of Lettering

The diverse letter forms on the reverse of the precious metal coinages with the legend ΒΑΣΙΛΕΩΣ ΑΝΤΙΓΟΝΟΥ suggest the parallel long-term employment of various die-cutters in the Makedonian mint. The main features may be outlined as follows: (1) the prevailing *alphas* are those with straight bars (straight *alphas*, i.e., chapter 2.2.1, no. 1), although *alphas* with convex or broken bars occur in Makedonian inscriptions during the second half of the third and the first half of the second century;[117] (2) the horizontal hastae of *sigmas* range from straight (straight *sigmas*, cf. chapter 2.2.1, no. 4), to slightly splayed (slightly splayed *sigmas*, chapter 2.2.1, no. 138) and splayed (splayed *sigmas*, chapter 3.1.1, no. 5); (3) *nus* have vertical bars which are of different (chapter 2.2.1, nos. 1–6) or of the same height (chapter 3.1.1, no. 3); (4) *omegas*, floating (chapter 2.2.1, no. 5) or on the same level as the other letters (chapter 2.2.1, no. 173, are characterized by horizontal hastae which are either "open" (i.e., distant from each other), or "closed."

The gold staters have carefully laid-out legend letters, with an invariably straight *alpha*, a *nu* with even vertical hastae, and with a slightly splayed *sigma*, but, due to the limited space, the last letters tend to be off flan. Their uniform style indicates production within a short period. The different engraving on the silver transitional Alexander tetradrachms, where *nus* with shorter right hastae, splayed *sigmas*, and floating *omegas* are the norm, dissociates them from the gold. The small size of the silver Alexander flans, further limited by the dotted border on the reverse, determines the careful engraving of nos. 1 and 4–6, but some letters are off-flan when the flan is off-center. A more relaxed use of space may be observed on no. 2, with no dotted border and with amply spread legend letters. The great diversity and the hastily engraved, angular characters on most specimens contrast with the generally elaborate figure of Zeus.

The diverse legend letters on the Pans suggest the employment of many artists in the production of a large issue. Period I is characterized by uniform legend letters. Only occasionally does a bowed *alpha* replace that with straight hasta. The right bar of *nu* is generally shorter, with few exceptions, the *sigmas* are straight and the *omegas* are closed.[118] The remarkably uniform engraving of Period II, with large angular and splayed characters, suggests a single engraver for this brief issue: the hastae of *alpha* and sigma are invariably straight, *nu* is characterized by even bars and *omega* is closed. Period III, on the other hand, is characterized by greater variation and by generally large characters. *Alpha* is generally straight, *omikron* is larger and *omega* is invariably closed.[119] The vertical hastae of *nu* are of the same size, while splayed *sigmas* are as frequent as straight ones. On two special groups, characterized by the letter X and by a trident symbol as control marks on the reverse, slightly splayed *sigmas* are the rule. Finally, small and elaborate letters prevail during the fourth period, including the silver drachmae associated with the winged-helmet variation of Pan head tetradrachms. The vertical hasta of *upsilon* tends to be shorter, and *omega* is generally open. The limited space for the legend letters on the Poseidon head tetradrachms results in a general tendency for their letters to be small and elaborate. Groups 32–36 of Period III, some of which share secondary monograms with the Pan head tetradrachm series, are characterized by angular characters, straight alphas, splayed *sigmas*, a *nu* with an occasionally shorter right vertical hasta and by a floating, open *omega*, which significantly improve in the rest of the series. The curved hastae of *lambda* on nos. IV.73–4 (Group 17) may have been due to a mistake of the die cutter. The uniform characters on the rest of the Poseidons, with floating *omegas* and splayed *sigmas*,

117. Hatzopoulos, *Institutions*, 51–54.
118. Except nos. 59–60, 91.
119. Except nos. 52–53, 90–92, 95–96.

show less variation. Finally, the characters on contemporary epigraphic documents reveal that the mainstream epigraphic tendencies are not always followed on contemporary coinage. For example, alphas with convex or broken bars, common in the 250s,[120] are never adopted on Antigonid coinage, whereas the larger *omikrons*, the splayed *sigmas* and the nus with even vertical bars occur on the issues of the 250s.

6.2.4 Control Marks

The organization of the mint(s) in Makedonia early in the reign of Gonatas may be reconstructed from the symbols, monograms and letters on the reverse of the gold and silver issues in the name of "King Antigonos," thus contributing to the debate on the significance of control marks on Hellenistic royal coinages.[121] Mathisen believed that control marks, namely symbols and monograms, were used "for accounting purposes, representing the various officials responsible for the mint operations, the amount or source of metal being minted, the date of issue or a combination of these."[122] He divided those on the contemporary posthumous Alexander tetradrachms into four categories: group identifier (design/letter), on the left and primary/secondary/supplementary control mark (normally monograms), on the right and beneath the throne. According to Mathisen, the secondary control mark represented the turning of the metal into coin, while the primary control mark represented an annual (civic) office. The Group Identifier represented the official responsible for the royal revenues in Hellenistic Makedonia,[123] rather than the mint itself.

In contrast to the transitional Alexanders, the consistent placement of a symbol on the left and of a monogram on the right of the reverse of the new Pan head silver type indicates greater stability in the structure of the mint rather than more rigid control over die engravers (see Chapter 6.4.2).[124] The control marks are reduced to two on the Pans and on the silver drachmae and to one or two on the Poseidons.[125] Obverse links among reverses carrying different monograms show the independent cooperation of those represented by these monograms with the main mint official signing with the main symbol to the left on the reverse. Thus, up to three employees independently cooperated with the main mint official for the Pans, and often one assisted the main official for the Poseidon series.[126] A similar structure on the precious metal coinages of Philip V and Perseus confirms the continuity in mint administration under the last two Antigonids: according to Touratsoglou, three officials almost always cooperated, two of whom were permanent.[127]

The significance of these symbols and monograms is systematically analyzed below.

120. Hatzopoulos, *Institutions*, 51–54.

121. F. de Callataÿ, "Control Marks on Hellenistic Royal Coinages: Use, and Evolution toward Simplification?," *RBN* 48 (2012), 39–62. G. G. Aperghis, "Recipients and End-Users on Seleukid Coins," *BICS* 53.2 (2010), 55–84, assigns the monograms on Seleukid coinage to officials issuing and receiving it, i.e., to financial administrators and to military commanders, respectively; he interprets the symbols with branches of the royal army; idem, "The Armed Forces of Seleukos I, with help from Coins," in *Honorary Volume G. Cohen* (forthcoming).

122. Mathisen, *Administrative Organisation* I, 27.

123. Mathisen, *Administrative Organisation* I, 10–11. No specific term survives for the financial administrator in Makedonia: Hatzopoulos, *Institutions*, 433–434.

124. F. de Callataÿ, "Control Marks on Hellenistic Royal Coinages: Use, and Evolution toward Simplification?," *RBN* 48 (2012), 52–53, 56 argues against assuming efficient monetary control from a large number of control marks, i.e., in the case of the Ptolemies.

125. Mathisen, *Administrative Organisation* III, 44–46.

126. Boehringer, *Chronologie*, 100.

127. Touratsoglou, *Circulation*, 71, "list of monograms on coins of Philip V, Perseus and the Macedonians." Cf. A. Mamroth, "Die Sibermünzen des Königs Philipps V. von Makedonien," *ZfN* 40 (1930), 277–303.

1. Symbols

The transitional Alexander gold and silver types carry a single control mark. The wreath-bearing Nike on the gold staters associated with the Monogram group of posthumous Alexanders now appears in the left field on the reverse and, when taken together with the *aphlaston* in her other hand, suggests a naval victory (Chapter 6.4.1). Its fixed position contrasts with the varied positions of the monograms on the transitional Alexander tetradrachms.

Four different symbols occur on the left reverse of the Pans: the crested ("Makedonian") helmet,[128] which is the most common and is temporarily replaced by a winged helmet, a *desmos*, and a trident. In the first period, the *pilos/konos* on the new Pan head tetradrachms, with a high helmet bowl separated from the *stephane*, with medium cheek flaps and with a long, thin crest, replaced the *pilos/konos* with a lower helmet bowl. A *pilos/konos* with a small bowl and cheek flaps and with a long thin crest, and that with an elaborate crest holder are combined with most monograms of the first period. The various helmet types, alongside the densely obverse linked groups, confirm the operation of several artists during this period. The same *pilos/konos* symbol also occurs on the reverse of the contemporary posthumous silver Alexander tetradrachms.

The second period is characterized by helmets with thin crests and short cheek pieces. The most common variation is that with a smaller but fuller and conical bowl and with a long, richer crest reaching the cheek flaps. A second variety with a smaller bowl and with a long, thin crest developing close to the bowl occurs on a few specimens.

There is greater variation in the helmets during the third period of the Pans. The elaborate crest holder and the type with the small bowl and with a long thin crest developing very close to the bowl, as used in the second period, resume briefly. Also, a bell-shaped medium bowl, with long cheek flaps, with a rich crest and a thick *stephane*, which had occurred once on the second period (Chapter 3, no. 59), now occurs on many specimens. There are also a few examples with a helmet with a round bowl and with the cheek flaps on the edges of the *stephane*; and some with a helmet with a very thin bowl and with a *stephane*, medium cheek flaps and with a thick long crest. Finally, a variation with a round bowl and with the cheek flaps on the edges of the *stephane* also occurs during this period. The *pilos* with a round bowl is characteristic of the silver coins of Antigonos Gonatas with his portrait; it also occurs on coins of Pyrrhos, Philip V, and Perseus.

Finally, the fourth period of the Pans is characterized by more elaborate helmet types, winged (nos. 1–18), or crested (nos. 19–62), with a high bowl, a thin *stephane*, and very short cheek flaps.

Instead of the Makedonian helmet, a few "special" Pans, Groups 45–49 and possibly 27–29 of the first and third periods, respectively, have as symbol a cylindrical object, decorated with two rows of triangles. This is combined with an Athena to the right (rather than left) on the reverse, wearing an Attic helmet, but without an *aegis*, and with a head of Pan badge at the centre of her shield, just as in the mainstream Pan series, with Athena to the left. The only exception is an Athena left with an *aegis*, which appears only on the reverse of Group 28 (specimen 128) in Period III. This cylindrical symbol also occurs on an issue of gold Athenian staters, carrying a head of Athena to the left with an Attic helmet on the obverse and an owl on the reverse, dated to the tyranny of Lachares, in the early third century BC.[129]

128. P. Dintsis, "Über die Bezeichnung ΚΩΝΟΣ im Reglement von Amphipolis," *Archaia Makedonia* IV (Thessaloniki,1986), 171–182.; id., *Helme*, 67–72, pl. 29, Appendix 3, nos. 169, 173, 175, 171. Dintsis (ibid., 76, n. 12), does not consider this type of helmet exclusively Makedonian, unlike I. L. Merker, *Silver Coinage*, 45 ff. Cf. Touratsoglou, *DM*, 80.

129. Kroll, *Agora*, 10; Mørkholm, *EHC*, 86, pl. 13.208.

Reviewing the relevant bibliography, Mitsopoulou showed that a tentative interpretation by Durmesan in 1828 of this symbol as a *calathos,* later corrected into *kalathos,* i.e., "one of the sacred baskets used in the cult of Demeter at Eleusis," has been accepted almost unquestionably. Its reinterpretation (through iconographic parallels) by Beazley as a *bakchos-ring* (ring on a *bakchos,* i.e., a myrtle bundle carried by a *mystes*), renamed by Kroll as an *Eleusis ring,* indicating the same object, though plausible, was not fully adopted in the bibliography in replacement for the *kalathos.*[130] Mitsopoulou provides enough archaeological evidence to corroborate this symbol's association with the metal ring which kept together the *bakchos* of the *mystes* and which was dedicated at the end of the ritual at the sanctuary. In the absence of any specific reference to the ancient term for this object, we follow Mitsopoulou in replacing the tentative terms *bakchos-ring* or *Eleusis ring* with the term *desmos,* proposed by M. Tiverios a little earlier, for this cylindrical symbol on Antigonid coins.[131]

The divergence of these groups from the mainstream helmet symbol may be due to their issue either at a different mint or in association with a special event (see Chapter 6.2.2), not least as the d*esmos* is combined with monograms absent from the mainstream series of the Pan head tetradrachms. The connection of the *desmos* symbol with the *mystes* participating in the Eleusinian Mysteries prompts one to associate the Pan head variations carrying this control mark with this festival: they may have been meant to cover partly the vacuum in Athenian silver coin production between 262 and 215 BC.[132] A first issue of Pan tetradrachms with this symbol may have coincided with the celebration of the Mysteries that followed the end of the siege of Athens during the Chremonidean War (268/7-261 BC). Indeed, Makedonians laying claim to mainland Greece had always respected the Eleusinian Mysteries.[133] It may be argued that, by stressing his respect for the

130. Th. M. Durmesan, *Description des médailles antiques du cabinet de feu M. Allier de Hauteroche* (1829) (calathos); E. Beulé corrects into "kalathos': *Les monnaies d' Athènes* (Paris, 1858). J. D. Beazley reverts to Rubensohn's identification of this symbol as a *bakchos-ring,* pointing out that the *kalathos* apparently played a part in the cult of Demeter at Alexandreia, that the evidence on its use at Eleusis is late, and that its shape was not cylindrical: "Bakchos-rings," *NC* 1 (1941), 1–7; cf. Rubensohn, "Kerchnos," *MDAI(Ath),* 23 (1898), 271–306. Kroll in 1993 proposed the term "Eleusis ring" as an alternative to the *bakchos-ring,* but reverted to Beazley's term in 2003: *Agora,* 28–29, n. 24; cf. J. H. Kroll, "The evidence of the Athenian coins," in S.Tracy and O. Palagia (eds.), *The Macedonians in Athens, 322–229 B.C.* (Oxford: Oxbow, 2003), 206–212, esp. 206.

131.Ch. Mitsopoulou, *Το ιερό της Δήμητρας στην Κύθνο και το αττικό ελευσινιακό σκεύος,* vol. I–III (Athens: ΕΚΠΑ, 2007), 1079–1099, with full bibliography on this symbol. See also ejusdem, "Faisceaux et guirlandes, entre iconographie et réalité: images, gestes, rites et finances éleusiniennes," in F. Jaccotet-Muller (ed.), *Rituels en image—images de rituel: Grèce, Rome, Égypte, Mésopotamie,* Colloque international, Université de Genève, 12–14 mars 2015 (forthcoming). The term *dragma* for the *bakchos,* i.e., the bunch of myrtle branches carried by the *mystes* in the Eleusinian Mysteries, is noted by M. Tiverios, "Αισχύλος και Ελευσίνια Μυστήρια," in D. I. Iakov and E. Papazoglou (eds.), *Θυμέλη. Μελέτες χαρισμένες στον καθηγητή Ν.Χ. Χουρμουζιάδη* (Herakleio 2004), 410–426, esp. 410–412, n. 18. Particular thanks are due to Chr. Mitsopoulou for drawing my attention to the interpretation of this symbol and to most useful discussions on its connotations for the history of Eleusis and for Antigonid history.

132. Kroll adopts G. Oliver's suggestion that the stylistically diverse "heterogeneous" Athenian tetradrachms may have filled in the vacuum in official Athenian silver production between the 280s and 215 BC, and that they were struck intermittently over the middle quarters of the third century: J. Kroll, "The evidence of the Athenian coins," 206–212; cf. G. Oliver, "The Politics of Coinage: Athens and Antigonus Gonatas," in A. Meadows and K. Shipton (eds.), *Money and its uses in the ancient Greek world* (Oxford: University Press, 2001), 35–52. On the production of this coinage, see also C. Flament, *Le monnayage en argent d' Athènes. De l' époque archaique à l' époque hellénistique (c. 550–c. 40 av. J.-C.)* (Louvain-la-Neuve: Association Professeur Marcel Hoc, 2007); eiusdem, *Contribution à l' étude des atélies monétaires grecs, Étude comparée des conditions de fabrication de la monnaie à Athènes, dans le Péloponnèse et dans le royaume de Macédoine à l' époque classique* (Louvain-la-Neuve: Association Professeur Marcel Hoc, 2010).

133. Aelius Aristides, *Eleus. Logos* 22.8; C. Clinton, "Macedonians at Eleusis in the early third century," in S. Tracy and O. Palagia (eds.), *The Macedonians in Athens, 322–229 B.C.* (Oxford: Oxbow, 2003), 76–81, esp. 78, adding that many members of the Makedonian élite are unlikely to have been initiated in the Mysteries.

Eleusinian Festival through this monetary issue, and by adopting the *desmos* symbol, which had first occurred on the gold staters launched by the tyrant Lachares during the siege of Athens by his father in 296/4 BC, Gonatas may have attempted to assuage the Athenians' hostility towards the Macedonians, particularly after his most recent siege of Athens and destruction of the *chora* in Attika in the second half of the 260s. An earlier precedent had been set by Alkibiades, who atoned for his parody of the Eleusis festival prior to the Sicilian Expedition by reestablishing a large procession to Eleusis by land in the autumn of 408/7 BC.[134] Thus this early special series struck under Gonatas may have been meant to celebrate/finance the Mysteries that followed his siege of Athens, as a means of winning the approval of Greek states. Not least, in evoking the Eleusinian Mysteries through the *desmos* symbol, Gonatas may have meant not only to demonstrate his piety and respect for Athens, but also to remind people of his father's initiation into (and high regard for) them. There is no evidence that Gonatas himself was an initiate, but the possibility cannot be excluded. At the same time, he may have taken this opportunity in order to reconnect officially with (and pay tribute to) his father, Poliorketes, restoring him thus as part of the Antigonid dynasty.

In similar vein, it is worth noting that the particularly elaborate *Athena to the right* Pan head tetradrachms that have been assigned to the third period, i.e., the varieties with an elaborate head (possibly a portrait), carrying a scepter instead of a *pedum*, and signed between the two concentric circles surrounding the central badge, with the legend ΒΑΣΙΛΕΩΣ ΑΝΤΙΓΟΝΟΥ, form part of this special *desmos* series (see Chapter 4.1.2).[135] They may have been issued between 255 and 246/5 BC, i.e., between the withdrawal of the Makedonian garrison from the Mouseion and Gonatas' naval victory at Andros: the *desmos* symbol might prompt us to associate their minting with the occasion of an Eleusinian Festival.

A second variant occurs on a small group from the third period of Pans, with a trident-head left: the head of Pan is stylistically different from all others, and resembles a Celtic head.[136] The trident is also similar to that on the Poseidons, which is larger and with a longer handle. Finally, the eight-rayed star on the reverse of the Poseidons has been related by Mathisen to the stars decorating the Makedonian shield on the obverse of the Pans, establishing a connection between the two types.[137]

134. Ch. Mitsopoulou, "Ο Αλκιβιάδης και η πομπή των μεγάλων Ελευσινίων του 408/7 π.Χ.," in Ch. Varalis (ed.), *The World as a Stage: The Spectacle in Antiquity*, Volos 2007 (Athens 2011), see above, n. 20.

135. A more systematic treatment of the association of the *desmos* symbol with these Antigonid tetradrachms will appear in Ch. Mitsopoulou and K. Panagopoulou, "Family Bonds and Religious Rings: The Antigonids and Eleusis," forthcoming.

136. On the significance of the trident symbol and on its occurrence on coins from Karia, Syria and Crete, see Mathisen, *Pan Heads and Poseidon Heads*, 34, n. 35. On the Phoenician origin of the trident symbol, which also appears on late Hellenistic Syrian mosaics of Delos and on some later mosaics of Pompeii and Hadrumentum, see Rostovtzeff, *SEHHRW* III, 1540, n. 150.

137. Mathisen, *Pan Heads and Poseidon Heads*, 33.

2. *Monograms*

The Group Identifiers of the silver transitional Alexanders ("Alex"), Pans ("Pan"), and Poseidons ("Pos"), are combined with one (or more) of the following monograms:

Table. 6.6. Concordance of monograms on the tetradrachm types of "King Antigonos"

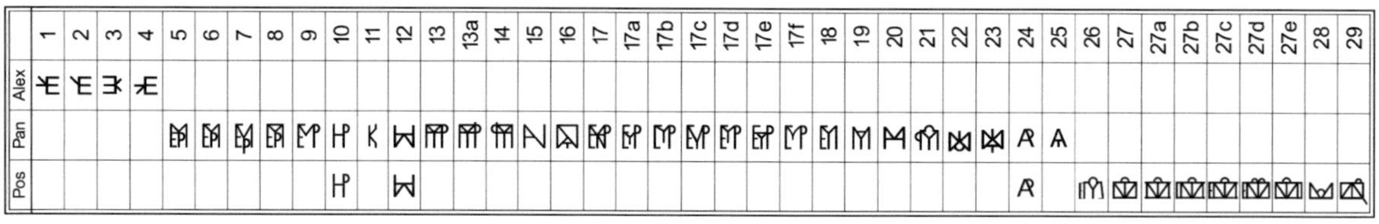

The transitional Alexander tetradrachms, carrying monograms 1–4 in various positions on the reverse, have been placed by Mathisen at the end of the Monogram group of posthumous Alexanders from Pella, to which they are die-linked.[138] They are different in style and in the control marks, there is no symbol and no second monogram, and the legend letters are hastily engraved. The monogram shifts from beneath the throne on the first two specimens to the left of the throne on the remaining four: the first position echoes Mathisen's Helmet group and the second his Monogram group of posthumous Alexanders (cf. Chapter 2.2.1).

The monograms on the Antigonid issues have been taken to indicate either their parallel or their consecutive production. R. W. Mathisen, for instance, believes that the Pans followed in time the monogrammed Makedonian posthumous Alexanders.[139] Touratsoglou, on the other hand, regards the silver Makedonian "autonomous" civic issues and the royal issues prior to the defeat of Perseus at Pydna (168 BC) as contemporary.[140]

138. Mathisen, *Silver Coinages*, 103–108; Price, *Alexander*, 141.
139. Mathisen, *Silver Coinages*, 98–99, table 12; 110–14; *Administrative Organisation* III, 44–46.
140. Touratsoglou, *Circulation*, 71–72; Hatzopoulos, *Institutions*, 253–254.

Table 6.7. Monograms on the Pans and Poseidons arranged by periods

Period																		
I	X	X	X	X	X	X	X	X	X	X	X	X						
II					X	X		X				X	X	X	X	X	X	X
III						X		X					X					X
IV								X										

Period																		
I																		
II	X	X	X	X														
III		X			X	X	X	X	X	X	X	X	X	X	X	X	X	
IV									X	X		X						X

Table 6.8. Poseidon head tetradrachms with two monograms

Period	Monogram 1	Monogram 2	Symbol	Specimen Numbers
I				131–46
II				147
III				155
IV			Star	76

The monograms mainly belong to the first and third periods. Ten and five out of the twenty-nine monograms occur in the first and second periods respectively, eighteen in the third and five in the fourth. Combinations among the letters M, E, P, Y, Π, T may be recognized on monograms  —  (Period I),  — 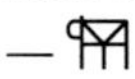 (Periods I–II), 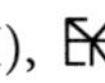 — 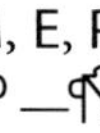 (Periods II–III). The variations of monograms  and  could illustrate certain officials' less successful performances during minting. Similar monograms extend over several periods, and elucidate the relative chronology of the Pans. , for instance, runs through all four periods of the Pans; 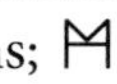 is a reversed version of 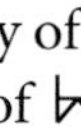. Monograms —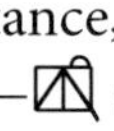 are known only on the Poseidons, but a few specimens carrying the additional monogram 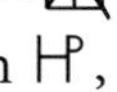, , or , which occur on the Pans, establish a link between the two series (Table 6.8).

The prolonged use of certain monograms, such as , suggests that they stand for permanent mint officials rather than different vein outputs, years of issue, or annual magistrates and establishes firm links among the posthumous Alexander, Pan and Poseidon silver issues.[141] This continuity in the operation of the principal Makedonian mint after the rise of Gonatas to the throne is demonstrated, for instance, by the monograms shared between the Pans and the posthumous Alexanders. In fact, six of the monograms on the Pans occur on the approximately contemporary [Makedonian] posthumous Alexander groups; some also occur on the silver issues of Philip V and Perseus. These monograms have been taken to indicate the consecutive production of these issues, but the uncertain dating of some related hoards alternatively allows for simultaneous production (see Chapters 6.3, 6.4.2–3).[142] Similarly, monogram 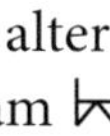 is represented once on the Poseidons, while monogram 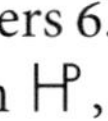, known from the first two periods of the Pans, appears on many Poseidons during the third period. The identification of monograms with names common in Makedonia is deliberately avoided in the present work, as such conjectures can only be subjective.[143]

Certain monograms may refer to the Makedonian administrative divisions: one might be tempted to recognise in the letters M, E, or M, E, and P, which occur on many of the monograms, the first letters of the term: μερίς. M. B. Hatzopoulos has dated the division of Makedonia into μερίδες to as early as the reigns of Philip II and Alexander III. He proposed that the complexity of the Makedonian coinage under the last Antigonids (comprising silver and bronze royal issues; silver and bronze issues labelled ΜΑΚΕΔΟΝΩΝ; silver and bronze issues labelled ΑΜΦΑΞΙΩΝ, ΒΟΤΤΕΑΤΩΝ and ΜΑΚΕΔΟΝΩΝ ΠΡΩΤΗΣ; bronze issues of the capitals of the districts, Pella, Thessalonike and Amphipolis) reflected the composite and variegated nature of the Makedonian state before the Roman conquest.[144] However, he dates this multiplicity after the loss of Makedonia's non-European possessions, that is, after the expedition of Doson to Karia (227 BC).[145] The division of Makedonia into four districts during the Antigonid (rather than in the Roman) period was recently supported by Kremydi-Sicilianou, on the basis of rare didrachms dated to the last Antigonids with the legends ΜΑΚΕΔΟΝΩΝ on the obverse and ΠΡΩΤΗΣ ΜΕΡΙΔΟΣ on the reverse.[146] The presence of the first two or three letters of the term μερίς on the Antigonid silver coinage (see,

141. Mathisen, *Administrative Organisation* I, 10–11, 44–46.

142. On the dating of the hoards of posthumous Alexanders and Pan head tetradrachms, see Mathisen, *Silver Coinages*, 82–85; Mathisen, *Pan Heads and Poseidon Heads*, 29–31; Price, *Alexander*, 141–142; cf. Chapter 6.4.1–2.

143. Identifications of monograms with names have been proposed by Mathisen, *Administrative Organisation* III, 46. Cf. F. de Callataÿ, "Control Marks on Hellenistic Royal Coinages: Use, and Evolution toward Simplification?," *RBN* 48 (2012), 39–62, esp. 51.

144. Touratsoglou, *Circulation*, 71–72.

145. Hatzopoulos, *Institutions*, 248–260; 432–433.

146. S. Kremydi-Sicilianou, "ΜΑΚΕΔΟΝΩΝ ΠΡΩΤΗΣ ΜΕΡΙΔΟΣ: Evidence for a Coinage under the Antigonids," *RN* 163 (2007), 91–99, pl. XIII–XIV.

for instance, monograms [monogram] — [monogram], [monogram], [monogram] — [monogram]), could suggest the division of Makedonia into districts since Gonatas and perhaps indicate the involvement of the administration of the districts in the striking of new coinage or in the supply of silver. For lack of other evidence, though, this suggestion remains conjectural.

The study of the monograms is also detrimental to the integration of the Poseidons in the Antigonid numismatic production. Since the principal monograms, [monogram] — [monogram] and variations thereof, do not occur on the contemporary posthumous Alexanders or Pan head tetradrachms or on any of the local Makedonian or Thessalian bronze coins, they have been assigned to a separate mint. In fact, all the characters of the name ΜΑΓΝΗΤΩΝ have been recognized in it by F. Imhoof-Blumer, who suggests the issue of this type at the Makedonian residence in Thessaly, at Demetrias.[147] Epigraphic and other doubts have also been cast on Mathisen's alternative resolution of this monogram as Demetrios (II) (Chapter 6.4.3).[148]

I suggest that there is no need to exclude the Poseidon head tetradrachms from the main Antigonid mint, given that they share monograms with the posthumous Alexander and Pan series (Table 6.9). The absence of the crested helmet from this series need not indicate a separate mint and the transfer of experienced mint officials to it, for various group identifiers had been simultaneously used both for posthumous Alexanders and for some Pan varieties. Monogram [monogram] may be taken instead to indicate a special issue rather than a different mint (Chapters 6.4.3, 6.5). This is further favored by the supplement of the main monogram with the letters ΤΙ and ΘΙ (on one example accompanied by a star), or by its temporary replacement by a trident (accompanied by [monogram] or by ΙΕ), on a very small issue which is represented by twelve specimens in our catalogue (Period IV, Group 21: trident, [monogram]; Group 22: trident, ΙΕ).

It is also worth noting that monogram [monogram] on the Poseidons is reminiscent of monogram [monogram] of Pan Group 27 from Period III.

The concordance of monograms on these Antigonid silver (posthumous Alexander and individual), tetradrachm types and on those of Philip V and Perseus is outlined in Table 6.9. It is remarkable that monograms [monogram], [monogram], and [monogram] link the Poseidons not only with the Pans but also with the posthumous Alexander tetradrachms. This not only confirms continuity in the administration of the main Makedonian mint but also calls for a revision of Mathisen's *a priori* conviction that the posthumous Alexander tetradrachms ceased with the introduction of the Pan head tetradrachms. Similarly, monogram [monogram] links the Pan head and Poseidon head tetradrachms with the silver coinage of Philip V. The late style of the obverse, though, favors the dissociation of the Poseidon head tetradrachms from the Pan head series and their assignation to a later date.

The correction by the die cutter of monogram [monogram] (or [monogram]) to [monogram] on a Poseidon tetradrachm (Chapter 4.2, no. 147), suggests that the former was only temporary.

147. Imhoof-Blumer, *Akarnanien*, 39, n. 47; idem, *MG*, 127.
148. Mathisen, *Pan Heads and Poseidon Heads*, 34. Touratsoglou, *DM*, 80–81. Cf. Ashton, Review, 10.

Table 6.9. Makedonian royal silver:
Monograms shared by the tetradrachms of "Alexander," "King Antigonos," Philip V, and Perseus

Group Identifier	[monogram]	[monogram]	[monogram]	[monogram]	[monogram]
Posthumous Alexanders					
Omikron-Kappa	X			X	
Triton					X
Grape				X	X
Helmet		X			X
Monogram			X		
ΒΑΣΙΛΕΩΣ ΑΝΤΙΓΟΝΟΥ Pans					
Period I	X	X	X		
Period II	X	X			
Period III		X		X	X
Period IV		X			
Poseidons					
Period III	X	X			X
Period IV					
Philip V					
				X	X
Perseus					
	X		X		

3. Letters

The monograms on the right of the reverse of the individual types of Antigonos Gonatas are occasionally substituted by letters, as shown in fig. 6.10. Leaving X aside, which occurs as group identifier on the reverse of a small Pan group from the third period, the most common letter combination is TI. The reversal of these letters on two reverse dies in Period III shows that they stand for two different names, rather than the same name. The association of TI and KT with a winged helmet for respectively the Zeus drachmae and the Pan tetradrachms reveals the transition process to a different group identifier.

In contrast to the Pans, the presence of certain letters on the Poseidons suggests their identification with annual magistrates rather than with long-term mint officials during the fourth period. The letters TI beneath the monogram of a few Poseidon head tetradrachms, for instance, link the Pan head and the Poseidon head tetradrachms (i.e., Period IV, nos. 63, 73–74). A star symbol occurs on the right reverse of these coins and of that signed with ΘI beneath the main monogram (Period IV, no. 75).[149] Finally, the letters IE occur beneath the prow on a small issue, with a trident on the reverse (Period IV, no. 83).

149. Mathisen, *Pan Heads and Poseidon Heads*, 33.0

Table 6.10. Concordance of letters on the individual silver tetradrachms of "King Antigonos"

Period	X	TI	KT	IT	M	ΘI	IE
			Pans				
II		X					
III	X	X	X	X			
IV		X	X				
IV		X		X			
III					X		
IV		X	X			X	X

By and large, the control marks establish not only the internal structure of the gold and silver issues under Gonatas, but also links among them. Parallel to the Pans with the helmet symbol, which met the bulk of the financial requirements of the state, some small groups with unusual control marks may be interpreted as celebratory issues rather than as products of a different mint. The complex structure of the main mint enables the production also of these special issues, or of the Poseidon tetradrachms, at the same location. This is further supported by the subsidiary monograms that link the Poseidons with the Pans (see Chapter 6.5). Alternative readings of control marks, i.e. as indicators of the recipients of payment lots, offer a different frame of interpretation for the existing evidence; but the outcome of this discussion is not yet conclusive.[150]

150. See n. 10.

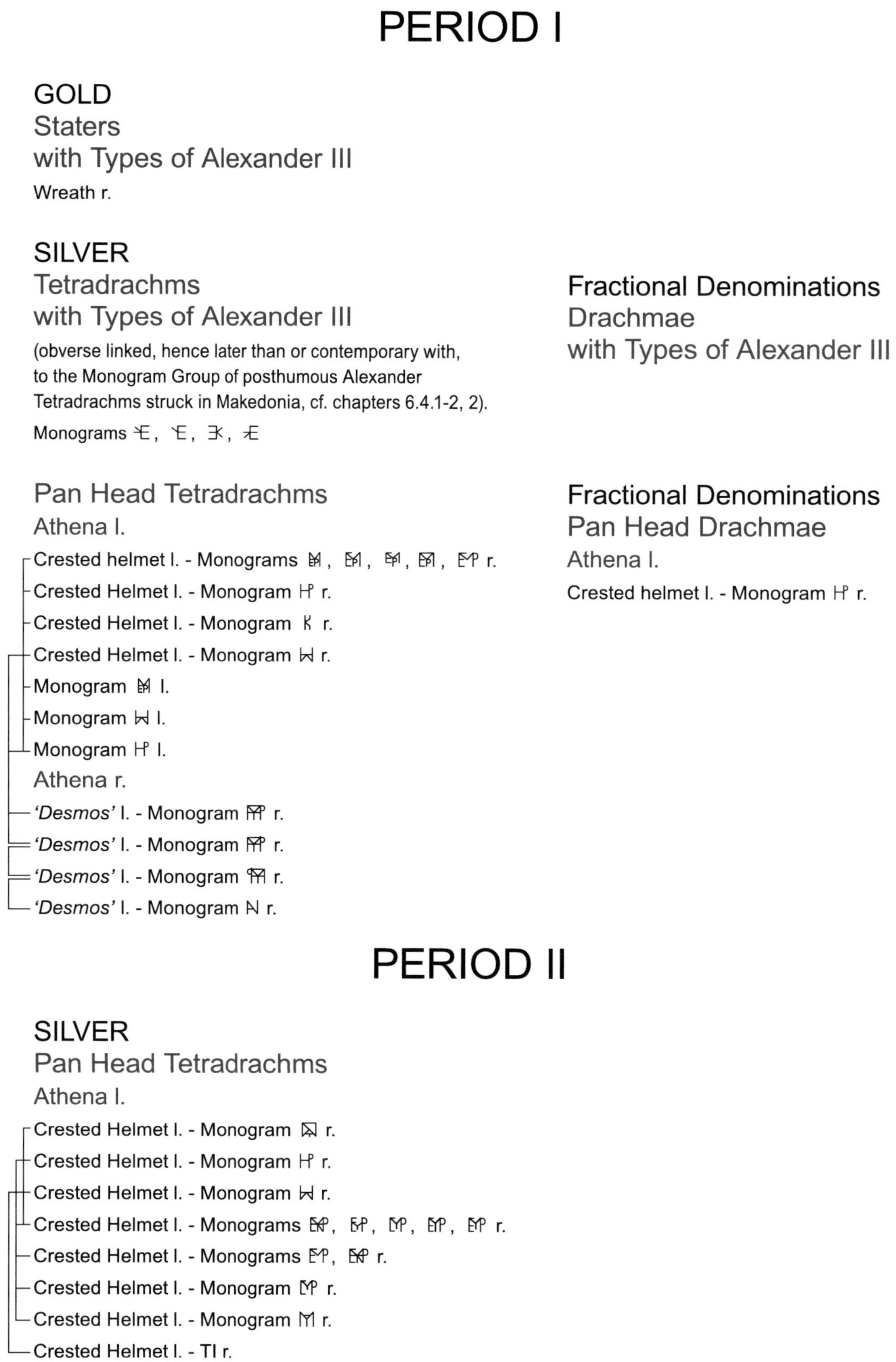

Figure 6.11. Summary of control marks.

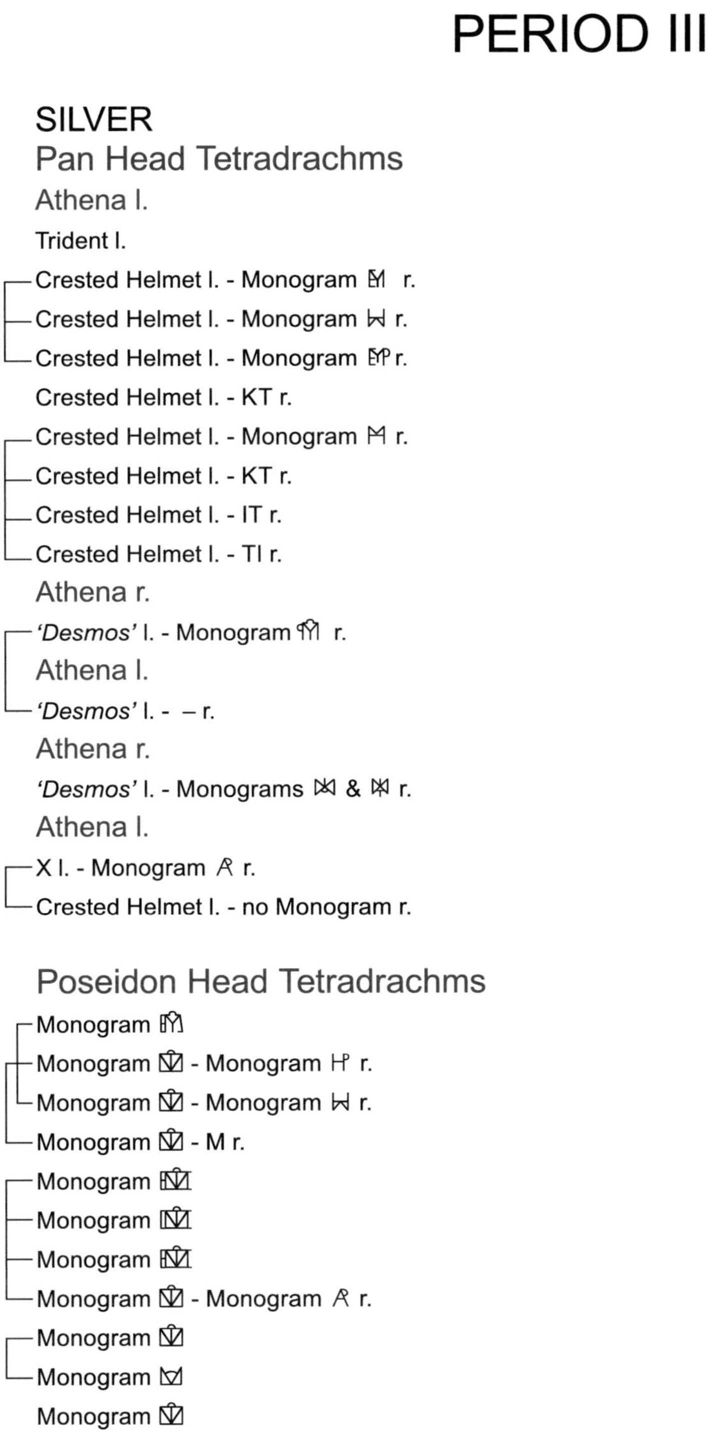

Figure 6.11 (continued). Summary of control marks.

PERIOD IV

SILVER

Pan Head Tetradrachms

Athena l.

- Winged helmet l. - KT r.
- Winged helmet l. - TI r.
- Winged Helmet l.
- Crested Helmet l. - KT r.
- Crested Helmet l. - TI r.
- Crested Helmet l. - Monogram r.

Zeus Head Tetradrachm

TI

Poseidon Head Tetradrachms

Monogram

- Monogram - TI underneath - Star r.
- Monogram - ΘI underneath - Star up r.

Monogram - Monogram underneath - Star up r.

Trident - Monogram

Letters IE - Trident l. (horizontally)

Fractional Denominations

Athena l.

Zeus Head Drachmae

Winged helmet l. - TI r.

Zeus Head Tetrobols

Winged Helmet l. - TI r.

Figure 6.11 (continued). Summary of control marks.

6.3 Coin Hoards

Fifty-five hoards have so far come to light with precious metal coins in the name of king Antigonos, one with a gold specimen, the rest with silver. They have been listed here in the approximate chronological and geographical order proposed by Touratsoglou.[151] Reasons for any divergences from his catalogue are given in the discussion of the hoards whose detailed contents are available. The dating of recent die studies of silver issues occurring in the same hoards has also been considered. The dates for these hoards have been determined by the latest coins included in them and a further definition of their nature as "savings" or "circulation" hoards is also attempted, whenever possible. "Circulation" hoards comprise coins withdrawn on a single occasion, or on several chronologically close occasions, from coins circulating at the time. "Savings" hoards are accumulated over a longer period and comprise coins deliberately selected from circulation on various criteria. "Savings" hoards, being deliberately selective, are not representative of contemporary issues in the same way as "circulation" hoards. A hoard summary, including the proposed dates, appears at the end of this Chapter (Table 6.13). The transitional silver Alexander tetradrachms and drachma do not occur in any known hoards.[152]

(i) Gold

1. Poteidaia/Kassandreia, 1984: *CH* VIII (1994) 276.

c. 240–180 BC

Price, *Alexander* , vol. I, 58.

This hoard, now dispersed in trade, comprised approximately 150 gold coins of Philip II, Alexander III and Philip III, Antigonos Gonatas and Lysimachos.[153] The latest staters are those of Alexander III and Antigonos Gonatas; fifty-six staters belong to the latter, according to *CH* VIII (1994) 276. Most of the above posthumous Alexanders (which are from the mint of Amphipolis), fifty-four out of fifty-six, were struck from the same obverse and possibly from the same reverse die. They belong to a rare issue of gold staters, associated with silver tetradrachms of the group termed by Mathisen the Mu group, from early in the reign of Gonatas.[154] The remaining two coins come from the same pair of dies and may be related to silver tetradrachms of Mathisen's Monogram group, from the same period (cf. Chapters 6.4, 6.4.2). Equally remarkable is the gold Alexander stater, whose control marks, a star and a dog on the reverse, link it with a silver tetradrachm from the Meydancıkkale, 1980 hoard. This tetradrachm is assigned by Price to a group struck at an uncertain mint between 240 and 180 BC.[155]

The star-and-dog Alexander stater gives a *terminus post quem* of 240 BC for the burial of this hoard (see Chapter 6.4).[156] The Antigonid specimens identified from this hoard are nos. 3a and 5a

151. *DM*, 75–107.

152. "Circulation" hoards comprise both "emergency hoards" and "currency deposits", as, for example, in Duyrat, *WAW*, 296–267. On "savings" hoards, see Duyrat, *WAW*, 297.

153. To the 147 coins, photographs of which were sent by M. J. Price to G. Le Rider, the latter added one more specimen: Le Rider, *Potidée*, 89–96, pl. VIII; cf. Price, *Alexander*, 58. To these one might add a distater of Alexander III, recorded in *CH* VIII (1994), 276, and the gold stater with the name and royal title of Antigonos, mentioned in Price, *Alexander*, 142, pl. CLVIII, D, but not in *CH* VIII (1994) 276.

154. On Mathisen's definition of the posthumous Alexander groups, see Mathisen, *Silver Coinages*, esp. 81; also see Price, *Alexander*, vol. 1, 141–142.

155. On the gold stater, see Le Rider, *Potidée*, 93.140; on the silver tetradrachm, see Davesne and Le Rider, *Meydancıkkale*, 2496; Price, *Alexander*, 345, no. 2821A.

156. Le Rider, *Potidée*, 94; cf. Chapters 6.4, 6.4.1.

of Period I. The very good condition of all the specimens and the exclusive presence of gold coins may identify this find as a "savings" hoard.

(ii) Silver

The following are the fifty-four hoards known to have contained Antigonid silver coins. Of these, the chronological sequence of the hoards established by Touratsoglou is retained in the index,[157] and the various burial dates that have so far been proposed for each hoard are recorded. Seven more hoards have been added, which were identified in trade or were fully published recently. All dates are BC.

Table 6.12. Index of hoards

Hoard	Burial	AR coins	Pan tetradrachms	Poseidon tetradrachms	Zeus drachmae
Phayttos, c. 1956	c. 264; 260–240; 250	61	2		
Scotussa area, (pre-)1989	c. 260; 250–230	25	25		
Verge ("Perge"), 1955[a]	c. 250–230	386	1		
Hija së Korbit, 1982	250–225; 227–225	618	18		
Karditsa (Palaiokastro), 1929	c. 250	30	5		
Pherai, 1937–1938	250	591+	7		
Eretria, 1937	245; c. 235	572+	5		
S. Asia Minor, 1976	246	235+			
Meydancıkkale, 1980	240–235	5215	3		
Tell Sukas (Gabala), 1958	c. 240	10	1		
Sophikon, 1893	c. 230–220; 225–200	c. 950			3
"Thessalonike," 1978	230	70	50		
Unknown Findspot "Seleucus III," 2002	225–224	6500	c. 21	7	
Makedonia, 1960s	225–200	16+	12		
Kassandreia, 1985/7	c. 225; 227–225	12	3		
Thesprotia, 1992	225–200	86	45	5	
Troas/Mysia, (pre-)1947	c. 220–210	220+	c. 100	c. 50	
Sardeis, 1911	c. 220–214	55	1		
Syria?, 1962	c. 220	15+		1	
Syracuse, Achradina, 1899	215–212	300–400	11+		
Korinth, environs, 1938	c. 215	c. 400	1		
Enna, environs, 1966	c. 212	c. 100	1(EF)		
S. Asia Minor, 1963	c. 210–200	120+	9		
N. Syria, 1960	c. 210	18	1		
Edremit (Adramytteion), 1954	c. 210	19+	1		
Morgantina, 1982	c. (?)210	280+/294+?	2		
Gordion, 1961	c. 205	100	1		c. 20

157. See n. 40.

Hoard	Burial	AR coins	Pan tetradrachms	Poseidon tetradrachms	Zeus drachmae
Gordion, 1951	c. 205–200 /later	114	1	2	
Unknown Findspot ("Achaeus"), 2002	c. 203/197	87		1	
Pergamon, 1960	c. 201	22		1	
Unknown Findspot ("Antiochus III"), 2005	196	61+		4+1	
Oylum Höyüğü, 1989	205–200	134		2	
Syria, 1971	195/4 or 190	90		1	
"X4" (no date)	c. 210–190	406+	1(b)	2 (1 b)	
Nile Delta, 1927–1928 = Makedonia?, 1927–1928	c. 200–180	24=23+	10=23+		
Asia Minor, 1972	c. 235–230	100+	1		
S. Asia Minor, 1970	c. 210	148	12		
Aleppo environs (Beroia), 1896	c. 190	150+	?		
"Pisidia," 1963	c.190	400, c.	1	1	
Ayaz-In, Phrygia, c.1953	c. 190–188	170+		2 (b)	
Mektepini, 1956	c.190	752+	8		
Thessaly, 1977	190	254+	1		
Unknown Findspot, 2000 ("Pamphylia or Cilicia" hoard)	190–189	750		1	
Drama, 1989	187–168	1	1		
Asia Minor, c. 1947	c. 187	11+		1	
Urfa (Edessa), 1924	185–160	c. 200	5	1	
SW Thessaly, 1977	175	450+	4		
Larissa, 1968	c. 165	2500–3000	3	6	
Asia Minor, 1947/8	160	?			
Balkh, 1974?	150	150+			
Aleppo environs, c. 1930	c. 138	35+	5		
North of Larissa, 1985	75	1260+	11	4	

a. The findspot of this hoard, Verge (near Serres), has been recorded as "Perge" in *IGCH*.

1. *Verge ("Perge"), 1955: *IGCH* 455.

c. 260–230 BC

I. Varoucha, "Chronique des fouilles et découvertes archéologiques en Grèce en 1956," *BCH* 81 (1957), 497, pl. IX, 13; R. Bauslaugh, "The Posthumous Alexander Coinage of Chios," *ANSMN* 24 (1979), 6; *IGCH* 455; Price, *Alexander* I, 59; Touratsoglou, *DM*, table III; Duyrat, *Arados*, 139; Flament, *Athènes*,134, 263.

The tetradrachm of Antiochos I (280–260 BC), from Hecatompylos of Artacoana, determines the date of this hoard, which also comprises posthumous issues of Lysimachos, Makedonian posthumous Alexander tetradrachms and a Pan tetradrachm. Through a Chian drachma of uncertain date, Bauslaugh revised Varoucha's date of 250–230 BC and suggested 260 BC as a *terminus ante quem.*[158] There is no need, however, to accept Mathisen's redating to 275–270 BC. He was led to do so by his conviction that the posthumous Alexander tetradrachms ceased on the introduction of the Pan head tetradrachms in the late 270s (cf. Chapter 6.4.2). Most recently, Touratsoglou reverted to Varoucha's date, between 250 and 230 BC, with no further argumentation.[159]

The Pan tetradrachm (no. 14a) belongs to Group 3 of the first period of Pans, i.e., to their earliest issues. As the posthumous Alexander tetradrachms may have continued under Gonatas (see Chapters 6.4.2, 6.5), the poor condition of the Pan tetradrachm, in contrast with that of the posthumous Alexanders, shifts the hoard date away from the introduction of the new Antigonid type.

2. *Phayttos, c. 1956: *IGCH* 159.

260–230 BC

T. R. Martin, "A third-century BC hoard from Thessaly at the ANS (*IGCH* 168)," *ANSMN* 26 (1981), 54; Heinen, *Unters.*, 177; P. R. Franke, "Zur Geschichte des Antigonos Gonatas und der Oitaioi," *Jahrbuch des deutschen Archäologischen Instituts mit dem Beiblatt Archaeologischer Anzeiger* 72 (1958 [1959]), 38–62; Price, *Alexander* I, 59; Duyrat, *Arados*, 139; Flament, *Athènes*, 244.

The "heterogeneous" Athenian tetradrachm (Style C),[160] and the posthumous Alexanders are the latest in the hoard. The coins of Seleukos I and Antiochos I distinguish this find from *IGCH* 162, 168, *CH* III (1977) 43, whose content is similar in terms of the Alexanders and the Lysimachi.[161]

This hoard need not be considered in the context of the revolt of Alexander of Epeiros in 264 BC, as has been suggested.[162] Varoucha's dating to c. 260 BC was accepted by Nicolet-Pierre and Kroll but was lowered by Touratsoglou to between c. 250 and 230 BC.[163] The large and fractional, silver and bronze, royal and civic, denominations included in it (not least, the four Antigonid bronze coins) presumably represent the circulation pool at the time of burial.

Phayttos, c. 1956 contains two fresh Pan tetradrachms, struck from the same dies: Period I, nos. 47a–b. They belong to Group 13 of the first period, with a crested helmet on the left and with the monogram ΗΡ on the right of the reverse. The earlier state of O17 on the Pans from Phayttos compared with those from the same obverse die in the Scotussa area, (pre-)1989 hoard (no. 5 below), may indicate that Phayttos, c. 1956 was slightly earlier than, or roughly contemporary with, Scotussa area, (pre-)1989.

158. I. Varoucha, "Chronique des fouilles et découvertes archéologiques en Grèce en 1956," *BCH* 81 (1957), 497, pl. IX, 13; R. Bauslaugh, "The Posthumous Alexander Coinage of Chios," *ANSMN* 24 (1979), 6; *IGCH* 455. There is no explanation for the date suggested in Varoucha's list of the specimens in the hoard in *BCH*.

159. Touratsoglou, *DM*, table III.

160. Nicolet-Pierre and Kroll, *Athenian Tetradrachm Coinage*, 26; Flament, *Athènes*, 244.

161. T. R. Martin, "A Third-century BC Hoard from Thessaly at the ANS (*IGCH* 168)," *ANSMN* 26 (1981), 54–57.

162. Heinen, *Unters.*, 177 *contra* P. R. Franke, "Zur Geschichte des Antigonos Gonatas und der Oitaioi," *Jahrbuch des deutschen Archäologischen Instituts mit dem Beiblatt Archaeologischer Anzeiger* 72 (1958 [1959]), 38–62.

163. I. Varoucha, "Chronique des fouilles et découvertes archéologiques en Grèce en 1956," *BCH* 81 (1957), 497–498, pl. IX–X; Nicolet-Pierre and Kroll, *Athenian Tetradrachm Coinage*, 26; Touratsoglou, *DM*, table III.

3. *Pherai, 1937–1938: *CH* IX (2002) 172, cf. 193; *CH* VII (1985) 75; *IGCH* 168 ("Larissa environs") (& 141).[164]

c. 250–240 BC

Varoucha, *BCH* (1938), 446; Bellinger, *CIN 1961. Atti* (1965), 57–60; Nicolet-Pierre and Kroll, *Athenian Tetradrachm Coinage*, 25–26; Merker, *ANSMN* 9 (1960), 41–42; T. R. Martin, "A Third Century Hoard from Thessaly at the ANS (*IGCH* 0168)," *ANSMN* 26 (1981), 73; T. R. Martin, "The Chronology of the Fourth-century BC Facing-head Silver Coinage of Larissa," *ANSMN* 28 (1983), 1–34; Martin, *Sovereignty*, 50; Davesne and Le Rider, *Meydancıkkale*, 338; Price, *Alexander* I, 60; Marinescu, *Lysimachi*, 256–257; Flament, *Athènes*, 128, 245–246.

The latest tetradrachms—"heterogeneous" Athenian (c. 250–220 BC), posthumous Lysimachi from Kyzikos (no. 562), and Eumenes I—support Martin's date of c. 250–245 BC for this important find from "between Pherai and Ag. Gedeon," which has been reconstructed from trade and, although probably incomplete, illustrates the contemporary circulation pool.[165] A slightly earlier date of c. 260 BC was proposed by H. Nicolet-Pierre and J. Kroll, who consider the coin of Eumenes to be earlier, but Price dates the hoard after 250 BC.[166] There is no need to follow Marinescu in considering the one of the three Lysimachi issued at Byzantium (issue 39, cat. No. 93) an intrusion to the hoard, if a date c. 250–240 BC is retained.[167]

Nor is there any reason to accept Martin's alternative date of c. 220 BC, which stems from the existence of later hoards with similar content (tetradrachms of Eumenes and Aitolia). Secondly, Eretria, 1937, with which the present hoard has been compared, is to be dated to c. 245 BC (see below). Finally, the hoard has no drachmae; the silver drachmae of "King Antigonos" appear to be associated with later Pan head tetradrachms than with those from our hoard.

The Pan tetradrachms in the hoard extend through Periods I and III (Period I: Nos. 31a, 70c, 122b; Period II: Nos. 26a, 58a; Period III: No. 125a).

4.* Karditsa (Palaiokastro), c. 1929: *CH* IX (2002) 180;[168] *IGCH* 162.

c. 245–240 BC

K. M. Constantopoulos, 'Προσκτήματα του Εθνικού Νομισματικού Μουσείου κατά τα έτη 1930 και 1931, *ΑΔ* (1930/1) 36, fig. 8; Nicolet-Pierre and Kroll, *Athenian Tetradrachm Coinage*, 29, no. 17; Paschidis, *Ποσειδώνες και Αντίγονοι*, 241; Touratsoglou, *DM*, 79; Marinescu, *Lysimachi*, 258–259; *SC* I.2, 126; Flament, *Athènes*, 134, 245.

The burial of this hoard has been emended from c. 250 BC (*IGCH*) to c. 245–240 BC, as its two tetradrachms of Antiochos II belong to the second half of his reign and are in excellent condi-

164. *Sic* Nicolet-Pierre and Kroll, *Athenian Tetradrachm Coinage*, 25. Cf. T. R. Martin, "The Chronology of the Fourth-century BC Facing-head Silver Coinage of Larissa," *ANSMN* 28 (1983), 1–34.

165. The exact *locus* of this find appears in a handwritten note at the Athens Numismatic Museum coin trays. The absence of foreign civic coins other than Athenian silver has raised suspicions that the hoard is incomplete. T. R. Martin discards the tetradrachm from the Aitolian League as intrusive: ibid., 54–57; *Sovereignty*, 50.

166. Nicolet-Pierre and Kroll, *Athenian Tetradrachm Coinage*, 26. On the coin of Eumenes I, see Westermark, *Philetairos*, 21. Price, *Alexander* I, 60 takes this hoard to confirm the continuing circulation of Alexander coinage in the late third century BC.

167. Marinescu, *Lysimachi*, 257.

168. The bibliographic reference for the Karditsa (Palaiokastro), 1929 hoard in *CH* IX (2002) 180, should be emended to *AJN* 2 (1990), 29, no. 17. *AJN* 2 (1990), 27, no. 14 actually refers to Eretria, 1937 (*IGCH* 175; *CH* IX (2002) 194); cf. *supra* in this chapter, hoard no. 6.

tion.[169] The hoard is the earliest to contain a Poseidon tetradrachm.[170] On the assumption that the Poseidons were struck under Doson, Touratsoglou dates this hoard to c. 227–225 BC,[171] but the inclusion of tetradrachms from the last Pan group of our Period II suggests an earlier date. There is, however, no need to revert to the *IGCH* date, c. 250 BC, as does *CH* IX (2002) 180.

The Byzantine Lysimachos is Marinescu's issue 41, cat. no. 111.1 (based on a cast of a worn Lysimachos tetradrachm reported at the ANS as coming from the "Palaiokastro hoard"), but the ANS notes may be in error or the coin may be an intrusion. All three lifetime Lysimachi at the Numismatic Museum in Athens are quite worn. The Athenian tetradrachms are four examples of *Pi* style and three of the *quadrigité* style, all quite worn.[172]

Finally, the presence of bronze coins (including an Antigonid specimen, with Pan erecting a trophy on the reverse) alongside the silver suggests that this was a circulation hoard.[173]

The four Pan tetradrachms belong to Periods I, II, and III (nos. I.58b, II.38c, II.73b and III.101b). The first Poseidon tetradrachm from a known hoard, no. III.179i, comes from this lot and does not appear to be in greatly better condition than the Pans.

5. Scotussa area, (pre-)1989: *CH* VIII (1994) 283.

c. 245–240 BC

CH VIII (1994) 283, pl. 34, 1–9; Touratsoglou, *DM*, tables III, VI.

As this hoard, dispersed in trade, consists exclusively of Pans from the first period, it cannot determine the introduction of the first type of Antigonid tetradrachms. The date of c. 260 BC, suggested by the editors, may be emended because similar Pans occur in the Eretria, 1937 hoard of c. 245 BC (Chapter 2.2.3). The Pan tetradrachms are nos. I.21b–c, 26a, 31c, 50c, 72d, 81c, 122c, 127a.

6. *Eretria, 1937: *CH* IX (2002)194; *IGCH* 175.

c. 245 BC

Ashton, *Rhodes*, 86; Ashton, *Colossus*, 83–84; Varoucha, *Epitymbion*, 670–2; Wallace, *Euboian League*, 47–49; Picard, *Chalcis*, 153–163, pl. 27–29; Merker, *Silver Coinage*, 43–4; Nicolet-Pierre and Kroll, *Athenian Tetradrachm Coinage*, 1–35, esp. 24; Touratsoglou, *DM*, tables III, VI; *SC* 1.2, 126; Marcellesi, *Pergame*, 220; Lorber, *CPE*, 505–506.

The fractional denominations of the Euboian Confederacy in this hoard suggest burial in c. 245 BC or thereafter.[174] This date is further supported by the Ptolemaic coins carrying no date (dated by Davesne between 249/8 and 247/6 BC),[175] and by the very worn *Pi* style Athenian tetradrachms.[176] Touratsoglou reverts to Wallace's date of c. 235 BC, without argumentation.[177]

169. K. M. Constantopoulos, "Προσκτήματα του Εθνικού Νομισματικού Μουσείου κατά τα έτη 1930 και 1931," *ΑΔ* (1930/1) 36, fig. 8; but a date around 250 BC is maintained in *SC* I.2, 126.

170.Nicolet-Pierre and Kroll, *Athenian Tetradrachm Coinage*, 29; Paschidis, *Ποσειδώνες και Αντίγονοι*, 241.

171. Touratsoglou, *DM*, 79.

172. Nicolet-Pierre and Kroll, *Athenian Tetradrachm Coinage*, 29; Flament, *Athènes*, 245.

173. T. R. Martin, "A Third-century BC Hoard from Thessaly at the ANS (*IGCH* 168)," *ANSMN* 26 (1981), 54.

174. Picard, *Chalcis*, 153–163, pl. 27–29. Alternative dates for this hoard c. of 220–210 BC and c. of 235 BC had been suggested respectively by I. Varoucha and by W. P. Wallace: Varoucha, *Epitymbion*, 670–172; W. P. Wallace, *The Euboian League and its Coinage*, ANS NNM 134 (1956) 47–49.

175. Davesne and Le Rider, *Meydancıkkale*, 298.

176. Nicolet-Pierre and Kroll, *Athenian Tetradrachm Coinage*, 1–35, esp. 24.

177. Touratsoglou, *DM*, tables III, VI.

A burial date of c. 245 BC is confirmed by the large proportion of silver Ptolemaic tetradrachms and by the excellent condition of the Rhodian didrachms. In the first place, the impressive number of Ptolemaic coins, which constitute one quarter of the hoard, may tentatively be assigned to the conscious withdrawal of these (lighter) coins from circulation, as they became unpopular subsequent to the retreat of the Ptolemies from the Aegean after the battle of Andros.[178] Of the seven Rhodian didrachms, the latest three belong to Ashton's series 3, with unradiate head of Helios and a magistrate's name above the rose. The magistrates [ΑΝ]ΤΙΠΑΤ[ΡΟΣ] on nos. 367–368 and ΑΡΙΣΤΟΝΟΜΟΣ on no. 369 (with prow) have been dated by R. Ashton to c. 265–250 BC.[179] The last coin is in particularly good condition.

The Antigonid content comprises exclusively Pan head tetradrachms, from Periods I, II and III: I.2a, 160a; II.5b; III.39b, 42a, 52a, 53a, 54a, 132d.[180] None is in mint condition, and those of Period I are more worn than the later ones.

8. Sardeis, 1911: *CH* IX (2002) 499 (Sardes, Lydia, 1911), also known as "Sardes Basis Hoard"; *IGCH* 1299.

c. 245 BC

H.W. Bell, *Sardis XI. Coins*, Leyden 1916, v–vi; P. R. Franke, "Inschriftliche und Numismatische Zeugnisse für die Chronologie des Artemis-Tempels zu Sardis," *MDAI* (Ath) 76 (1961), 203–7; H. Seyrig, "Monnaies Hellénistiques," *RN*[6] (1963), 23, n. 1, 42 = *Scripta Numismatica* (1986), 27, 46 (220–214 BC); Boehringer, *Chronologie*, 68, Beilage 2 (c. 220 BC); G. Le Rider, "Les trouvailles monétaires dans le temple d'Artemis à Sardes (*IGCH* 1299 et 1300)," *RN* 33 (1991), 71–88, pl. VII (= Le Rider, *Écrits* 1958–1988, II.821–832, 839); A. Houghton, "The Early Seleucid Mint of Laodicea ad Mare (c. 300–246 B.C.)," in *Travaux Le Rider*, 169–184; Marinescu, *Lysimachi*, 267; *SC* I.2, 78; Marcellesi, *Pergame*, 223.

This "savings" hoard, from the base of the cult statue of Artemis at Sardeis, comprised 55 silver coins, of which 46 were tetradrachms and the rest were drachmae.[181] Their deposit date in *IGCH*, 220–214 BC, partly rested upon the assumption that the silver and bronze coins were contemporary and partly on Newell's dating of an Alexander tetradrachm from the Laodicea mint to c. 230–220 BC. The dating of the latter has now been revised to the late reign of Antiochus II.[182] The mint condition of the seven silver tetradrachms of Antiochus I, reassigned by Houghton and Lorber from "Apamea" to an Uncertain Mint 28, western, probably in Syria or Mesopotamia (*SC* 577.1 [2], 577.2 [5]), and the similarity in content with Meydancıkkale, 1980 suggest burial soon after 246 BC.[183] A rather worn specimen among the ten Lysimachus tetradrachms was

178. See Chapters 1.2, 6.0.

179. Ashton, *Colossus*, 83–84; Ashton, *Rhodes*, 105.

180. The specimens observed are kept at the Athens Numismatic Museum.

181. Bell, *Sardis*, v–vii; A. Johnston, "The Greek Coins," in T. V. Buttrey et al., *Greek, Roman and Islamic Coins from Sardis* (Cambridge, Mass., 1981), 2–4. On the site, see Butler, *Sardis*, vol. I.1 (1910–1914) (Leyden, 1922), 76. On the "savings" nature of temple hoards, see Tullia Linders, "Fallen Money and Broken Crowns—or When is a Coin not a Coin?," in *Florilegium Numismaticum*, 255–258. Newell notes (on file at the ANS) that the silver coins of this hoard were found in one part of the basis, while the bronze coins came from another part.

182. A. Houghton, "The early Seleucid Mint of Laodicea ad Mare (c. 300–246 B.C.), in *Travaux Le Rider*, 169–184. Le Rider, *Potidée* had already back-dated the coin to the reign of Seleucus II, *contra* Newell, *WSM*, 184 (230–223 BC).

183. Newell's tetradrachms of "Apameia" have been reassigned by Houghton and Lorber to an Uncertain Mint 28, western, probably in Syria or in Mesopotamia: *SC* I.2, 78; cf. Houghton, *Seleucid Empire*, nos. 415–443. On the Seleukid content of this hoard, see *SC* I.2, 78.

minted in Byzantium (Marinescu's group 1, issue 9, no. 22).[184] Le Rider argued that the Philetairos tetradrachm, Marcellesi's group VI A, no. 30, fixed the closure of the hoard to immediately after the accession of Attalos I.

I have been unable to examine the single Antigonid silver coin (a Pan tetradrachm) from this hoard, which is kept at the Istanbul museum. There is no photograph in Le Rider's publication, but the control marks, crested helmet and , indicate a Pan head tetradrachm of Period I.[185] The hoard does not have a significant impact on the internal sequence of the Pan tetradrachms.

9. Tell Sukas (Gabala), 1958: *IGCH* 1528.

Before 243/2 BC

P. J. Riis, "L' activité de la Mission Archéologique Danoise sur la côte phénicienne en 1958," *AnnArch de Syrie* VIII–IX (1958–1959), 125–126, fig. 7, A–B; Price, *Alexander* I, 414–416; A. Meadows, "Arados," *NC* 158 (1998), 49–51, esp. 50; Duyrat, *Arados*, esp. 38–43, 149; F. Duyrat, "La politique monétaire d' Arados," in *La Syrie Hellénistique*, Topoi Suppl. 4 (2003), 25–52, esp. 39; Duyrat, *WAW*, 97-8, no. 45..

The undated posthumous Alexanders of Arados, struck between 259 and 243/2 BC, encouraged H. Seyrig to suggest a *terminus ante quem* of c. 243 BC for this circulation hoard.[186] The redating by Duyrat of these Aradian coins to c. 246/5 BC has shifted the date for this hoard to c. 240 BC.[187] The absence of Poseidons might indicate burial before the circulation of the second Antigonid tetradrachm type in this area.

The Antigonid Pan tetradrachm in the hoard is no. 130b of Period I.

10. *Meydancıkkale, 1980: *CH* X (2010) 269, *CH* VIII (1994) 308; *CH* VII (1985) 80.

c. 240–235 BC

Davesne and Le Rider, *Meydancıkkale*, 221–30 (reviews: U. Westermark, *RSN* 70 (1991), 97–101; M. Price, *NC* (1991), 97–101); Price, *Alexander* I, 60; C. Arnold-Biucchi, *AJN* 3–4 (1992), 207–214; F. de Callataÿ, "L' instauration par Ptolemée I Sôter d' une économie monétaire fermée," in F. Duyrat and O. Picard (eds.), *L' Exception Égyptienne? Production et Échanges Monétaires en Égypte Hellénistique et Romaine. Actes du Colloque d' Alexandrie, 13–15 Avril 2002* (Cairo, 2005), 117–133 (Ptolemaic); *SC* I.2, 79–80; Marinescu, *Lysimachi*, 261–263; Marcellesi, *Pergame*, 214–215; Duyrat, *Arados*, 145 ; Lorber, *CPE*, 496.

Davesne and Le Rider's dating of this most important hoard to c. 240–235 BC is based on its Aradian Alexander, Ptolemaic, Seleukid, and Attalid content. The presence of only royal issues, and the mixture of coins on both the Ptolemaic and the Attic weight standards may have been due to the burial of the hoard in Kilikia Tracheia, an area disputed by Seleukids and Ptolemies alike, or suggest its depositional nature.[188]

184. Marinescu, *Lysimachi*, 267.

185. Le Rider, "Les trouvailles monétaires dans le temple d' Artemis à Sardes (*IGCH* 1299 et 1300)," *RN* 33 (1991), 71–88, esp. 78 (= Le Rider, *Écrits*, 821–832, esp. 828) assigns this specimen, weighing 17.05 g, to Gonatas (as in Mathisen, *Administrative Organisation*, 111).

186. P. J. Riis, "L' activité de la Mission Archéologique Danoise sur la côte phénicienne en 1958," *AnnArch de Syrie* VIII–IX (1958–1959) 125–126, fig. 7, A–B. On the pseudo-Alexanders from Arados, see Price, *Alexander*, 414–416.

187. Duyrat, *Arados*, esp. 38–43.

188. Davesne and Le Rider, *Meydancıkkale*, 221–230. The Ptolemaic specimens of this hoard have been revised by F. de Callataÿ, "L' instauration par Ptolemée I Sôter d' une économie monétaire fermée," in F. Duyrat and O. Picard (eds.), *L' Exception Égyptienne? Production et Échanges Monétaires en Égypte Hellénistique et Romaine. Actes du Colloque d'*

Davesne and Le Rider treat this hoard as if it illustrated the circulation pattern, despite the presence of coins on both the Attic and the Ptolemaic weight standards. This is justified by the findspot of this hoard in Kilikia Tracheia, on the border between the Seleukid and the Ptolemaic realms.[189]

The relatively limited Antigonid content of Meydancıkkale, 1980 comprised exclusively Pan head tetradrachms, two of Period I (42b, 96a), and one of Period III (62a), and no Poseidons. The specimens of Period I, both with a crested helmet and ЊР, are less well preserved than no. III.62a of Group 11, which is in mint condition; it belongs to the very rare variety with a curved *pedum* or scepter behind Pan's head. This spectacular hoard shows that by 240–235 BC the minting of the (most recent) Group 11 of Period III of the Pans was under way.

13. Asia Minor, 1972: *CH* I (1975) 73.

c. 235–230; 200 BC

Touratsoglou, *DM*, table III; Marcellesi, *Pergame*, 210–11.

The burial date of around the end of the third century suggested in *CH* I (1975), 73 and adopted by Touratsoglou for this hoard, now dispersed in trade, was presumably based on the Attalid issues and was confirmed by the tetradrachms of Attalos I, which are included in the photographs on file at the British Museum.[190] Le Rider's redating of certain Attalid series, i.e., Westermark Group VIA to 241 BC, i.e., at the beginning of the reign of Attalus I, and of her Group VIB to earlier than 220–215 BC,[191] combined with recent analysis of the Seleukid issues,[192] shifts the closure date of this hoard to the period of Antiochos Hierax. The Seleukid issues are listed in *SC* 1.2, 83–84. As for Pergamon, Marcellesi notes an Alexander in the name of Seleukos I (Marcellesi, *Pergame*, no. 11) and 20 Philetairoi (without any detailed description) and opts for a lower date, c. 200 BC.

I have been unable to find any information on the single Antigonid silver coin reported in this hoard.

14. *Kassandreia, 1985/7: *CH* VIII (1994) 322.

c. 225 BC

CH VIII (1994) 322, pl. 38.13–17, pl. 39.1–7; Touratsoglou, *DM*, Tables III, VI; *SC I.2*, 129.

The tetradrachms of Antiochos Hierax in this hoard point to a date of c. 225 BC. The hoard includes three Pans (of periods II and IV) and two Poseidon tetradrachms of the third period. The Pan specimens are II.27a; IV.6a, 12a. The Poseidons are III.171a and 191a.

Alexandrie, 13–15 Avril 2002 (Cairo, 2005), 117–133. An analysis of the Seleukid content appears in *SC* I.2, 79–80. For the Lysimachi, Marinescu, *Lysimachi*, 261–263.

189. Ibid., 225–226, 239–240.

190. Touratsoglou, *DM*, table III.

191. Davesne and Le Rider, *Meydancıkkale*, 334–339; G. Le Rider, "Les tétradrachmes attalides au portrait de Philétaire," in *Florilegium Numismaticum*, 236–240.

192. *SC* I.2, 83–84.

15. Unknown Findspot ("Seleucus III" Hoard), 2002: *CH* X (2010), 272.

225–224 BC

A. Houghton, C. Lorber and O. Hoover, *Seleucid Coins: A Comprehensive Catalogue*, II.2 (Lancaster, 2008), 142–150; Marcellesi, *Pergame*, 228.

This hoard appeared in commerce in 2002, in at least seven lots. It contained Antigonid, Seleukid, and Attalid coins and coins in the name of Lyimachos, in lot B and in lots E and F, which were recorded from commerce in November 2003 and in March 2004, respectively.

Photographs of approximately 38 Pans and Poseidons from this hoard have been kindly placed at my disposal by C. Lorber. With the exception of one specimen from Period I, the vast majority are from the last three periods of Antigonid coinage production, comprising rare groups. It is unusual that three Pan head tetradrachms from this hoard belong to the Athena to the right issue. The first is the Pan head from Period I, which has on the reverse a *desmos* in field left combined with monogram . The other two (from Period III) have on the obverse a mature male portrait with a scepter and a diadem: on the reverse of one the *desmos* left is combined with monogram , while on the other the letter X is combined with monogram (see figures with the presence of Pans and Poseidons in hoards in Chapters 2 and 4). The hoard is also exceptional in that Pans tend not to be hoarded in the East until the 220s. Of the Poseidon head specimens, of particular interest is that with a trident and monogram on the reverse, which belongs to our Period IV (see Chapter 5.3).

The Pans are: I.7b, 70a, 80a, 91a, 180a; II.6b, 22b, 60a, 68e, 71c, 77a; III.7b, 14a, 40a, 53b, 61b, 88a, 88d, f–g, 89c, 94b, 111a, 120d, 126b, 127b, 132b, 132e,135b. The vast majority of the Poseidons come from Period III: III.181a, 186d–e, 194a, 195b–c, 229, 233, 237. Period IV: IV.81b.

16. Hija së Korbit, 1982: *CH* VIII (1994) 299.

c. 225 BC

N. Ceka, "Der Münzschatz von Hija e Korbit," in Eggebrecht et al. (eds.), *Albanien*, 261; S. Gjongecaj, "Thesari Hijes së Korbit," *Iliria* 1 (1985), 167–209; S. Gjongecaj-Vangjeli, *Trésors de monnaies antiques trouvées en Albanie (V–I siècles av. J.-C.)* (Tirana, 2014), 85–118; C. Boehringer, "Fragen zum Münzumlauf in Illyrien in hellenistischer Zeit," *Iliria* 19 (1989), 185–195; Nicolet-Pierre and Kroll, *Athenian Tetradrachm Coinage*, 30–31; Davesne and Le Rider, *Meydancıkkale*, 335–336; Marinescu, *Lysimachi*, 265–267; *SC* I.2, 129; Marcellesi, *Pergame*, 214.

The tetradrachms of Eumenes and Hierax are the latest in this very important hoard of 618 silver coins, whose burial has been lowered from c. 250–225 to c. 227–225 BC.[193] Paschidis, however, is not convinced by Davesne and Le Rider's date of 225 (rather than 235 BC),[194] stressing that the worn coins of Hierax come, in fact, from the king's earliest issues from Lampsakos. Boehringer dates the hoard to c. 230 BC.[195] It is worth noting that most of the coins are of Eastern origin,[196] including three Philetairoi from Pergamon, belonging to groups VI B, V, VI A (nos. 29, 30).[197] The presence of specimens on both the Attic and the Ptolemaic weight standard in this hoard from

193. On past suggestions, see Touratsoglou, *DM*, table V.

194. Davesne and Le Rider, *Meydancıkkale*, 336, n. 279. Paschidis, *Ποσειδώνες και Αντίγονοι*, 243, n. 30.

195. Boehringer, *Hierax*, 43, table 2.

196. N. Ceka, "Der Münzschatz von Hija e Korbit," in Eggebrecht et al. (eds.), *Albanien*, 261, but the alleged formation of the hoard during the war of 280–274 between Pyrrhos and Gonatas has no basis. Cf. Shpresa Gjongecaj, "Thesari Hijes së Korbit," *Iliria* 1 (1985), 167–209.

197. Marcellesi, *Pergame*, 214.

the Western Balkans might be taken to indicate the hoard's depositional nature. The Antigonid content of the hoard comprises only Pans, nos. II.6c; III.107a; IV.52b.

17. Thesprotia, 1992: *CH* IX (2002) 200; Touratsoglou, *DM*, 75–86.

225 BC

Touratsoglou, *DM*, 55–107 (reviews: Ashton, *Review*, 9–10; Callataÿ, *Review*, 296–299); Marcellesi, *Pergame*, 221; Lorber, *CPE*, 509 ("Macedonia/Thessaly, 1992").

This confiscated hoard is dated by Touratsoglou to c. 227–225 BC. The exclusive presence of royal tetradrachms on various weight standards might imply its depositional nature: apart from the Antigonid coins, there are posthumous tetradrachms of Alexander III, and tetradrachms of Demetrios Poliorketes, Eumenes I, Attalos I, Antiochos II, Seleukos II, Antiochos Hierax and Ptolemy II.[198] The hoard contains forty-five Pan tetradrachms from all four periods, and five Poseidon tetradrachms from Period III. The Pans are: Period I, 30a, 31b, 32b, 57a, 69a, 86a, 89a, 95e, 114a, 123a, 140a, 156a, 157a, 170a; Period II, 4a, 7a, 32a, 34b, 39a, 51a, 64a, 65c–d, 67a, 71a, 74a; Period III, 10c, 15c, 18a, 30a, 31a, 32b, 80a, 82a, 88b, 105a, 106a; Period IV, 2b, 7c, 11d, 33a, 38a, 39a, 47a, 55b. The Poseidons are: Period III, 180a, 193h, 213, 235, 240.

18. Sophikon, 1893: *CH* VIII (1994) 316; *IGCH* 179.

c. 230–220 BC

N. Svoronos, "Εὕρημα Σοφικοῦ Ἐπιδαυρίας," *JIAN* 2 (1899), 289–296, pl. I; idem, *JIAN* 10 (1907), 35–46, illus.; idem, *Athènes*, pl. 28; Regling, *Priene*, 39 (no. 41), 43; K. Regling, "Hellenistischer Münzschatz," *ZfN* (1928), 97–98; Newell, *WSM*, index VI: Hoards; Newell, *ESM*, 25, 51, 76, 131; S. P. Noe, "The Corinth Hoard of 1938," *ANSMN* 10 (1962), 34; Hackens, *Antidorum Peremans*, 71–72; Hazzard, *Ptolemaic Coins*, 32–33; Grunauer-von Hoerschelmann, *Lakedaimonier*, 30; S. Grunauer-von Hoerschelmann, "Lacedaemonian Tetradrachms in Peloponnesian Coin Hoards," *Proceedings of the Eighth International Congress of Numismatics* (Paris/Basel, 1976), 79–81; Nicolet-Pierre and Kroll, *Athenian Tetradrachm Coinage*, 31; Price, *Alexander* I, 61; K. Chryssanthaki, "Les monnaies lagides en Égée," in F. Duyrat and O. Picard (eds.), *L' exception égyptienne? Production et échanges monétaires en Égypte hellénistique et romaine, Actes du colloque d' Alexandrie, 13–15 avril 2002*, Études alexandrines, 10 (Cairo: IFPO, 2005), 174, no. 17; Tsangari, *Confédération Étolienne*, 214–215; Marcellesi, *Pergame*, 215; *SC* I.2, 127; Duyrat, *Arados*, 138, 305.

The coin of Ptolemy III of year Β (= 245/4 BC) and the very fresh Aitolian tetradrachm (now Tsangari, *Confédération Étolienne*, III series, 17, D1) led Nicolet-Pierre and Kroll to accept a date of c. 230–220 for this severely corroded underwater find, which has been taken to illustrate the circulation pattern at that period.[199] Tsangari notes that the last coin reported in the hoard is the Lakedaimonian tetradrachm, dated by Grunauer-von Hoerschelmann to the reign of Nabis, 209–

198. See also, Ashton, *Review*, 9–10; Callataÿ, *Review*, 296–299. The reference in *CH* IX to "forty-five silver coins of Antigonos Gonatas from the mint of Amphipolis" and to "Antigonos Doson" (denoting the Poseidon type) is quite confusing.

199. Nicolet-Pierre and Kroll, *Athenian Tetradrachm Coinage*, 31; *CH* VIII (1994), 316 (suggested date: 225–200 BC; according to a note on file at the ANS, it was buried not earlier than 240 and possibly around 230 BC). For a catalogue of the known coins, see J. N. Svoronos, "Εὕρημα Σοφικοῦ Ἐπιδαυρίας," *JIAN* 2 (1899), 289–296, pl. I; idem, *JIAN* 10 (1907), 35–46, illus.; idem, *Athènes*, pl. 28. See also, Newell, *WSM*, index VI: Hoards; Newell, *ESM*, 25, 51, 76, 131; S. P. Noe, "The Corinth Hoard of 1938," *ANSMN* 10 (1962), 34; Hackens, *Antidorum Peremans*, 71–72. Cf. Hazzard, *Ptolemaic Coins*, 32–33.

197 BC (Grunauer-von Hoerschelmann, *Lakedaimonier*, group 9, no. 9, O6/R9) but she doubts that this specimen belonged to the hoard.

The hoard contains three Zeus drachmae of period IV, all from the same obverse (O23), 84a, 86g, 90a. As all these specimens are quite worn (and there is a test punch on 90a), this hoard cannot elucidate the introduction date of Antigonid smaller denominations.

19. Korinth, environs, 1938: *IGCH* 187.

220–215 BC

P. Lemerle, "Chroniques de fouilles et découvertes archéologiques en Grèce en 1938," *BCH* 62 (1938), 446; I. Varoucha, "Πτολεμαϊκά νομίσματα στην κυρίως Ελλάδα," *Επιτύμβιον Χρήστου Τσούντα* (Athens, 1941), 668–79; S. Noe, "The Corinth Hoard of 1938," *ANSMN* 10 (1962), 9–41, pl. II–XII; T.Hackens, "La circulation monétaire dans la Béotie hellénistique: Trésors de Thèbes 1935 et 1965," *BCH* 93 (1969), 705, n. 3; H.Troxell, "The Peloponnesian Alexanders," *ANSMN* 17 (1971), 83, 87–88; Ashton, *Colossus*, 83–86; Nicolet-Pierre and Kroll, *Athenian Tetradrachm Coinage*, 32; Price, *Alexander* I, 61; Hackens, *Antidorum Peremans*, 73; Ashton, *Rhodes*, 85–87; Tsangari, *Confédération Étolienne*, 212–214; *SC* I, 127; Duyrat, *Arados*, 138.

The deposition of this pot hoard c. 220–215 BC is determined by the tetradrachm of Seleukos III,[200] and is not contradicted by the rest of its content: seven fresh Aitolian tetradrachms [c. 220 BC: Tsangari series III.16, 18c, 19a, 20a, 20b (3 specimens)], 18 moderately worn Rhodian didrachms of Ashton's series 3, and Athenian Pi style tetradrachms. It may be argued, as in the Eretria, 1937 hoard, that the absence of Ptolemaic coins later than Ptolemy II, noted by Davesne,[201] need not indicate an earlier burial date but, rather, the new post-Ptolemy II policy to increase the use of bronze coinage and decrease that of silver.[202] The slight wear of the Zeus drachma of this hoard, no. 56b (O23, crested helmet—TI), is not incompatible with a date around the 220s.

22. Enna, 1966: *CH* IX (2002) 670; *IGCH* 2232; *EH* I, 269.

211 BC

A. Burnett, "The Enna Hoard and Silver Coinage of the Syracusan Democracy," *SNR* 62 (1983) 5–26, pls. 1–10; Marcellesi, *Pergame*, 226, cf. 103–5; Lorber, *CPE*, 511.

This hoard, comprising 177 silver coins, is the one of two known Sicilian coin hoards with Antigonid coins, the other being *IGCH* 2230. The rather poor condition of the single Pan head tetradrachm of Period I, group 11 (no. 45a) suggests a date late in the Antigonid period.[203] The hoard also contains a silver tetradrachm in the name of Philetairos (Marcellesi's group IV A).[204]

200. S. P. Noe, "The Corinth Hoard of 1938," *ANSMN* 10 (1962), 32.

201. A. Davesne, "Les Ptolemées," in Davesne and Le Rider, *Meydancıkkale*, 298.

202. Pointing out the presence of bronze coins of Ptolemy III around the Peloponnese, K. Chryssanthaki-Nagle argues against the withdrawal of Ptolemy III from the Aegean: "Les monnaies lagides en Égée," in F. Duyrat and O.Picard (eds.), *L' exception égyptienne? Production et échanges en Égypte hellénistique et romaine, Actes du colloque d' Alexandrie, 13–15 avril 2002*, 159–173, esp. 162–166; G. Reger, "The Date of the Battle of Kos," *AJAH* 10 (1985 [1993]), 155–177, esp. 169–170; idem, "The Political History of the Kyklades, 260–200 BC," *Historia* 43 (1994), 32–69; K. Sheedy, "The Origins of the Second Nesiotic League and the Defence of Kythnos," *Historia* 45 (1996), 423–499. Ashton, *Review*, 5–7 notes that most Ptolemaic specimens found in mainland Greece (including the Peloponnese) come from non-Alexandreian mints and regards the disappearance of silver Ptolemaic coins from the Peloponnese from Ptolemy III onwards as reflecting the closure of these mints under Ptolemy III.

203. A.Burnett, "The Enna Hoard and Silver Coinage of the Syracusan Democracy," *SNR* 62 (1983), 5–26, pls. 1–10.

204. Marcellesi, *Pergame*, 226, cf. 103–105.

24. Edremit (Adramytteion), 1954: *IGCH* 1302.

c. 210 BC

H. Seyrig, "Monnaies Hellénistiques," *RN*[6] V (1963), 26, n. 1; Marcellesi, *Pergame*, 196.

H. Seyrig dates to around 210 BC this unpublished hoard of coins on the Attic weight standard.[205] The Pergamon specimens comprise one or two late Alexanders (Marcellesi, *Pergame*, no. 32) and two Philetairoi (Marcellesi, *Pergame*, nos. 26–31). The other coins are eight or nine Alexanders, four Lysimachi, two of Antiochos II, and a single tetradrachm of Antigonos Gonatas.

25. Gordion, 1951: *IGCH* 1406.

c. 210–200 BC

Cox, *Gordion*, 1–19, pl. I–VIII; H.Seyrig, "Monnaies Hellénistiques,» *RN*[6] 5 (1963) 42, 59; Kleiner, "The Alexander Tetradrachms of Pergamum and Rhodes," *ANSMN* 17 (1971) 116; Boehringer, *Chronologie*, 69; Ehrhardt, *Studies*, 77; Price, *Alexander*, I, 61; Marinescu, *Lysimachi*, 275–277; Duyrat, *Arados*, 142; *SC* I.2, 87–88.

Two tetradrachms of Antiochos III, dated c. 215–205 BC, an Alexander tetradrachm from Arados in good condition, dated 218/7 BC, and the many (18) Lysimachi point to the burial of this "savings" hoard in c. 210 BC.[206] The Lysimachi include two specimens from Byzantium (Marinescu's issue 15, no. 40, with a small test cut, and Issue 65, no. 151, the freshest Lysimachus coin in this group) and one specimen countermarked by Chalcedon. The good condition of the second Lysimachus specimen from Byzantium and that of the Alexander specimen from Arados favor the above dating. Houghton and Lorber consider this find to be slightly later: the two tetradrachms of Antiochos III have their "Type B" portrait of Antiochos III, which they date to 211/0 BC.[207]

The test punches and gashes on most of these heavily corroded coins indicate that the hoard includes coins which had spent some time in circulation. This weakens the degree to which this hoard can shed light on the introduction of the Poseidons: contrary to Chr. Ehrhardt, who reports that the two Poseidons of this hoard are in excellent condition, my observation of Cox's photographs in the ANS file shows that the reverse flan of no. 159f is worn and somewhat curved, while trimmed edges and flaws are also visible (cf. Chapter 6.4.3).[208] As for the only Pan in the hoard, no. 81c from Period III, Group 15, it is also worn.

26. Gordion, 1961: *IGCH* 1405 ("Gordion Hoard V").

c. 205 BC

D. H. Cox, "Gordion Hoards III, V and VII," *ANSMN* 12 (1966), 33–55, pl. III–XXI; Boehringer, *Chronologie*, 60–61 (210–205 BC); Price, *Alexander* I, 61; Touratsoglou, *DM*, pl. III (210–200 BC); Marinescu, *Lysimachi*, 276–277; *SC* I.2, 87; Duyrat, *Arados*, 143; Lorber, *CPE*, 498.

205. H. Seyrig, "Monnaies Hellénistiques," *RN*[6] V (1963), 26, n. 1. Cf. H. Seyrig's list of varieties at the ANS. Seyrig's date for this hoard is followed in *SC* I.2, 85.

206. Cox, *Gordion*, 1–19, pl. I–VIII. Boehringer opts for a slightly later date, c. 200 BC: *Chronologie*, 69.

207. *SC* I.2, 87–88.

208. Ehrhardt, *Studies*, 77. The second Poseidon head tetradrachm is reported by Cox as "similar" to the previous one, but is not illustrated (Cox, *Gordion*, 8, no. 54: 14.69 g, 12 h, 30 mm). I take this opportunity to thank P. van Alfen for allowing me access to Cox's photographs of the entire material.

The tetradrachms of Arados from c. 217–216 BC, the dated Pamphylian Alexanders of years 13 and 14 of the local era (209/8 and 208/7 BC), and the tetradrachm of Antiochos III from Laodikeia point to a date c. 205 BC for this "savings" hoard of c. 100 tetradrachms.[209] All specimens are heavily corroded, including the Pan tetradrachm of Period I, 25a (O09, crested helmet—[monogram]).

27. S. Asia Minor, 1963: *IGCH* 1426.

c. 210–200 BC

Boehringer, *Chronologie*, 69, 155–7, pl. 25–26; *SC* I.2, 86–87; Marcellesi, *Pergame*, 202; Price, *Alexander* I, 61; Duyrat, *Arados*, 147.

With the exception of a coin from Side, this hoard, which was dispersed in trade, consists exclusively of royal issues. The Alexander tetradrachms of Aspendos year 2, Perge year 13, and Arados year 44, suggest a date of c. 210–200 BC. Two Pan tetradrachms from the first period and a tetradrachm of Lysimachos are the earliest in the hoard. Unless they form part of the earlier hoard with which they were found mixed, their inclusion in this find may reflect demonetization.

Marinescu identifies the three Lysimachi of Byzantium and one of Chalkedon as the least worn of the nine specimens in the name of Lysimachos and assigns them to the end of his anonymous Group III.[210]

The Antigonid content of this hoard comprises exclusively Pan and no Poseidon tetradrachms. The nine specimens are: Period I, nos.130a, 132a, 151b (crested helmet—[monogram]); Period II, nos. 42b (crested helmet—[monogram]), 59a (crested helmet—[monogram]); Period III, nos. 3a (trident l.), 60b (crested helmet—[monogram]), 85a (crested helmet—KT), 132a (X—Ȓ).

28. N. Syria, 1960: *CH* I (1975) 75; *IGCH* 1533.

213–205 BC

Seyrig, *Trésors*, 22–24, pl. 9; *SC* I.2, 87, cf. 100; Marcellesi, *Pergame*, 206–207.

The tetradrachm of Antiochos III from Tarsos and the pseudo-Lysimachos struck at Byzantion indicate burial of this hoard between 213 and 205 BC, that is, in the early reign of Antiochos III. Lorber and Houghton opt for c. 210 BC and allow for the possibility that this might be the same lot as *IGCH* 1535 (no. 29 in our catalogue).[211] Two late Alexanders in this hoard may have been struck at Pergamon (Marcellesi, *Pergame*, no. 32; Price, *Alexander,* 1473 and 1483).

Despite the initial reference to a "Gonatas" and a "Doson" tetradrachm in the *IGCH* record, the specimens recorded by Seyrig are exclusively Pan tetradrachms of Periods I–III, as follows: Period I, no. 152b (Group 38, O10, crested helmet—[monogram]); Period II, no. 62a (Group 17, O10, crested helmet—[monogram]); Period III, nos. 64a (Group 12, O03, crested helmet—[monogram]), 85c (Group 16, O14, crested helmet—KT), 92c (Group 22, O03, crested helmet—TI).

209. D. H. Cox, "Gordion Hoards III, V and VII," *ANSMN* 12 (1966), 33–55, pl. III–XXI. Boehringer, *Chronologie*, 69 prefers a date between 210 and 205 BC. Cf. Touratsoglou, *DM*, pl. III (210–200 BC); *SC* I.2, 87.

210. Marinescu, *Lysimachi*, 66–87.

211. *SC* I.2, 87, 100.

29. Syria, 1959: *IGCH* 1535.

213–205 BC?

Boehringer, *Chronologie*, 158–61, esp. 159, 9–11, pl. 27–29; *SC* I.2, 100–101; Marcellesi, *Pergame*, 207; Price, *Alexander* I, 61; A. Meadows, "The Eras of Pamphylia," *AJN* 21 (2009), 51–88, esp. 39; Duyrat, *WAW*, 105, no. 162.

This hoard of exclusively royal issues, which is now dispersed, may form part of N. Syria, 1960 (no. 28 above). Only 35 out of the approximately 250 specimens have been published. Boehringer's closure date, based on the portrait types of Antiochos III, is adopted by Lorber and Houghton, who consider it to be no later than c. 210 BC. The Pergamon issues comprise four Philetairoi, Marcellesi's groups III, IV.A, IV.B, VI.B (nos. 27, 29, 30, 31).

The Poseidons come from the last two production periods (III.186a, 195f; IV.64b). The first coin is quite worn, whereas the last one is in mint-state condition.

30. Syria?, 1962: *IGCH* 1531.

c. 220 BC

Boehringer, *Chronologie*, 153–154, pl. 23–24; id., *Hierax*, 43, table 2 (c. 220 BC); *SC* I.2, 99; Marcellesi, *Pergame*, 206; Duyrat, *WAW*, 99, no. 149.

Boehringer, *Chronologie*, 153–154, pl. 23–24 uses the fresh Poseidon head tetradrachm and that of Antiochos Hierax from Alexandreia Troas to suggest a burial date c. 225–220 for this hoard of more than 16 royal silver coins. Lorber and Houghton opt for c. 220 BC.[212] The Pergamon coins are three *Philetairoi*, Marcellesi's groups IV.A, IV.B, VI.A (nos. 29–30). The Poseidon tetradrachm is Period IV.78a and carries a trident and ℞ on the reverse. Duyrat, *WAW*, 99, no. 149, notes that *IGCH* mistakenly adds a drachm of Seleukos II. Her attribution of the "'Antigonus Doson" tetradrachm to Korinth is not based on any evidence.

31. S. Asia Minor, 1970: *CH* I (1975) 74.

c. 210 BC

Seyrig, *Trésors*, 13–20, pls. 1–8; Davesne and Le Rider, *Meydancıkkale*, 335; G. Le Rider, "Les tétradrachmes attalides au portrait de Philétaire," in *Florilegium Numismaticum*, 239; Marcellesi, *Pergame*, 211; Duyrat, *WAW*, 100–101, no. 152; Houghton and Lorber 2002, 85–86.

The latest coins are an imitation tetradrachm of Antiochos III, copying a coin of Antioch (c. 208 BC), a tetradrachm of Byzantium with no acrophonic letter of the city (c. 205 BC), and a posthumous Alexander from Pergamon (c. 212–200 BC).[213] The presence of four specimens of Antiochos III, and of coins of Seleukos II and III but of no Pamphylian Alexanders, led Seyrig to suggest that the hoard was initially formed c. 220–215 BC, but was supplemented by later additions.[214] Lorber and Houghton date the hoard's closure to c. 210 BC. They tentatively locate its formation in Kilikia Pedias, as two of the three specimens of Antiochos III are scarce issues of Kilikia.[215] Duyrat (*WAW*, 100–101, no. 152) notes that Seyrig failed to identify 25 specimens, most

212. *SC* I.2, 99.

213. Price, *Alexander*, 222–225; Boehringer, *Chronologie*, 42; Le Rider, *Tétradrachmes attalides*; R. Ashton, "Opuscula Anatolica III iii. Redating the Earliest Alexander Tetradrachms of Rhodes," *NC* 164 (2004), 93–102, pl. 8.

214. Seyrig, *Trésors*, 13–20, pl. 1–8. Marcellesi, *Pergame*, 211, follows Le Rider in dating this hoard.

215. *SC* I.1, 86.

of which belonged to Seleucus II. Houghton and Lorber's 2002 list of 114 Seleucid coins does not correspond to Seyrig's catalogue of 105 such tetradrachms. Forty specimens are at the BNF.

The Pan specimen (of the 17 tetradrachms of Demetrius Poliorketes and Antigonos Gonatas) belongs to Period I (I.39b).[216]

32. Oylum Höyüğü, 1989: *CH* IX (2002) 501.

205–200 BC

E. Ögzen and A. Davesne, "Le trésor de Oylum Hüyüğü," in *TCMAA*, 45–49, pl. iii–viii. P. Kinns, "The Attic Weight Drachms of Ephesus: A Preliminary Study in the Light of Recent Hoards," *NC* 159 (1999), 47–97, at 50–51; G. Le Rider, *Antioche de Syrie sous les Séleucides. Corpus des monnaies d' or et d' argent I. De Séleucos I à Antiochos V (c. 301–161)* (Paris: Institut de France, 1999), 157–158; *SC* I.2, 101–102; Marcellesi, *Pergame*, 224; Duyrat, *WAW*, 107, no. 166.

The dated Alexander tetradrachms of Aspendos and Perge (Aspendos years 1–2, Perge year 19) and the drachma from Marathos (year 35) point to the burial of this circulation hoard (of 134 silver coins) between 200 and 195 BC. This is backdated by Meadows to 205–200 BC. Lorber and Houghton retain Seyrig and Price's chronology for this hoard, leaving open a possible redating of the tetradrachms of Perge.[217] Of the other specimens, the Pergamon coins are represented by one Lysimachus (Marcellesi no. 9) and by two Philetairoi, groups V and VIA (nos. 29–30).

The two Poseidon tetradrachms come respectively from Periods III (215c) and IV (80a). No. 215c of Period III is quite worn, while no. 80a is in fresh condition. The hoard may be found at the Gaziantep Archaeological Museum.

33. Unknown Findspot ("Achaeus" Hoard), 2002: *CH* X (2010) 277.

204–199 BC

A. R. Meadows and C. C. Lorber, "Commerce ("Achaeus" Hoard), 2002 (*CH* 10.277)," *CH* X (2010), 115–127, pl. 17–20; *SC* II.2, 150–1.

Between 77 and 81 tetradrachms from this hoard were identified in trade from October to November 2002, dispersed in four lots. The hoard contained Seleukid tetradrachms from Antiochos II to Antiochos III, but its dating was determined by Meadows and Lorber from its non-Seleukid contents, i.e., tetradrachms of Alexander III, Lysimachus, the Aitolian League, Prusias I, Side, Northeastern Arabia, Philip V, and Marathos, and perhaps also an Antigonid Poseidon head tetradrachm.[218] The Poseidon head tetradrachm (which is assigned by the authors to Antigonos Doson) forms part of lot D, which was identified in November 2003 and comprised mostly non-Seleukid specimens. It may not belong to this hoard, as the only specimen that clearly belongs to this lot is the coin of Achaeus.

The non-Seleukid content led Meadows and Lorber to emend the concealment date of c. 197 BC, proposed by Houghton, Lorber, and Hoover to between 204 and 199 BC. The latest coin is a tetradrachm of Antiochos III from uncertain mint 68, with an elderly portrait of Antiochos III and with the control marks of *SC* 1133.4a. Meadows uses the Poseidon tetradrachm and other

216. According to a note in the records of the British Museum, this coin belongs to the lot which was entered at the BM as *CH* I (1975), 74, but may actually be *IGCH* I (1975) 73. See also Chapter 2.2.3.1.1, 38, no. 39b.

217. *SC* I.2, 101–102. Cf. Le Rider, *Antioche de Syrie*, 157–158.

218. Meadows and Lorber comment that this coin is "not certainly from hoard": A. R. Meadows and C. C. Lorber, "Commerce ("Achaeus" hoard), 2002 (*CH* 10.277)," *CH* X (2010), 116, no. 3.

non-Seleukid issues to locate the formation of this hoard within the Antigonid possessions in southern Asia Minor; he suggests that its findspot was west of the Taurus, and links the hoard to the crossing of the Taurus mountains by Antiochos III in late 204 or 203 BC, in his attempt to extend his realm into southern Ionia and Karia.[219]

The (rather worn) Poseidon tetradrachm in this hoard is no. 144b of Period III.

34. Unknown Findspot, "X4" (no date)

210–190 BC

P. P. Ripollès, "The X4 Hoard (Spain), Unveiling the Presence of Greek Coinages during the Second Punic War," *INR* 3 (2008), 51–64, pl. 3–4; L. Villaronga, "El denario romano pesado en los tesoros de la península Ibérica," *Scienze dell' Antichità, Storia—Archeologia—Antropologia* 11 (2001–2003), 557–565; J. Sills, *Gaulish and Early British Gold Coinage* (London, 2003), no. 12; J.-C. Hébert, "La datation haute des monnaies aux types de Béziers, Moussan et Bridiers, d' après les monnaies de ces types trouvés dans quatre trésors éspagnols," *Acta Numismatica* 28 (1998), 79–126.

In addition to being crucial to the study and the chronology of monetary series such as the African, Aquitanian, and Iberian imitations of Emporitan drachms, this important hoard, buried in the Ciudad Real-Cuenca area of Spain during the Second Punic War or shortly thereafter, is regarded by Ripollès as a valuable record of the diffusion and use of Greek coinages in the Iberian peninsula during that period, and as a significant marker of the diffusion of Antigonid tetradrachms to the West in this context.

The occurrence of many pre-250 BC coins in this find indicates that they had been long in circulation before hoarding, hence this context may not help to date them accurately. Two of the three Antigonid tetradrachms in this hoard, a Pan (no. 52d of group 12) of Period IV and the one of Period III (no. 179i of Group 41), are fragmentary, but this is not surprising, given the high number of fragmentary pieces in it. The practice of fragmenting indicates a moderately monetized economy in the Western Mediterranean during this period. The third Antigonid coin, a Poseidon tetradrachm of Group 43, no. 205d, is in good condition.

35. Nile Delta, 1927–1928: *IGCH* 1701 = Makedonia, 1927–1928: *CH* VIII (1994) 356, *IGCH* 469.

200–180 BC

SAN 16.2 (1985) p. 30, note; ; Lorber, *CPE*, 471.

Only indirect information survives from this hoard, which was dispersed in trade. Ten Pans were recorded in *IGCH* 1701, while *IGCH* 469 reports 16 "tetradrachms of Antigonos Gonatas." Two of these belong to Period II (2a, 3a) and one to Period III (1a—with trident symbol).[220]

219. Cf. Ma, *Antiochus III*, 63–73.
220. I have been unable to check C. T. Seltman's partial list for this study.

36. Pergamon (Asklepieion), Mysia, 1960: *IGCH* 1303.

c. 201 BC

Boehringer, in *AvP* 11.1, 132–134; Boehringer, *Chronologie*, 69, 162–171; id., *Hierax*, 43, table 2 (201 BC); Marcellesi, *Pergame*, 196.

Considering this lot to represent a dedication at the Asklepieion, Boehringer uses the Alexander tetradrachms from Pergamon (before 200 BC), the Alexander from Perge (year 15, 205–204 BC), and the tetradrachm of Antiochos III (c. 215 BC) to suggest burial of this pot hoard in c. 200 BC.[221] All coins are severely corroded. The Poseidon tetradrachm, no. III.150c, a photograph of which may be found on file at the ANS, appears to be in relatively good condition (a horizontal die flaw may be observed along the god's cheek).

37. Unknown Findspot ("Antiochus III" Hoard), 2005: *CH* X (2010) 288.

c. 197 BC

A. Houghton, C. Lorber and O. Hoover, *SC* II.2, 150; C. Lorber and A. Houghton, "Antiochus III Hoard," *AJN* 21 (2009), 89–104, pl. 9.11; Wartenberg, forthcoming; *CH* X (2010) 288; Marcellesi, *Pergame*, 228.

Recently C. Lorber and A. Houghton brought to light this important hoard of 77 silver tetradrachms, recorded from commerce in 2005. In addition to the 5 Antigonid tetradrachms, which will be discussed below, the hoard comprised 10 tetradrachms of Alexander III, 14 of Lysimachus, 8 Attalid, 1 from Perge, and 40 Seleukid tetradrachms, ranging from Antiochus I to Antiochus III. The closing coin is probably a mint-state silver tetradrachm of Antiochus III of the Lysimacheia mint, one of four known specimens from the same die pair, which is datable to (or shortly after) 196 BC. The date of this coin is emended to 197 BC in *CH* X (2010) 288. The formation of this hoard must have taken place in Northwestern Asia Minor.

Although the proposed burial date does not elucidate the date of introduction of the Poseidons, the importance of this hoard lies in that it included a *unicum* hybrid tetradrachm carrying the obverse bearded male head right in laurel wreath, and Apollo seated comfortably left on a prow, holding a bow on the reverse (see Chapter 5.2). This unique specimen was found together with four more Poseidon tetradrachms, all of our Period III (246/5–229 BC). The hoard data fail to determine conclusively its minting date independently or in relation to the Poseidon head specimens in the hoard. On the basis of style and wear, Lorber and Houghton consider it to be "clearly earlier" than the Poseidons (p. 94); but, a few lines down, they admit that, on the basis of wear, "the coin does not give an impression of being thirty or more years older than the Poseidon/Apollo tetradrachms in the hoard. Yet its wear may be excessive for an issue of Antigonos Doson that can be no more than nine years older than the Poseidon tetradrachms." They then underplay the dubious validity of wear comparison in dating, when based on a single specimen.

Certain points in Lorber and Houghton's analysis of the *unicum* tetradrachm risk creating unnecessary confusion. In the first place, their main argument for not assigning this coin to Gonatas, i.e., that this would then be the only specimen in the hoard dated to his reign, contrasts with the fact that at least some of the four Poseidons may have come from the last phase of Gonatas' reign,

221. Boehringer, *Chronologie*, 69, 162–171. On the withdrawal of coins from circulation for temple hoards see n. 31. See also *SC* I.2, 88–89.

i.e., between 246/5 and 239 BC, as they all fall into our Period III (246/5–229 BC). It is clear that behind the statement that "it would be highly unusual if the only issue of Gonatas in our hoard should be a unique variety never seen before" lies their conviction that all the Poseidon issues belong to Doson. Secondly, regarding the absence of Pan head specimens from this hoard as an indicator that all Antigonid coins in the hoard, i.e., the Poseidon heads and the hybrid tetradrachm, belong to Antigonos Doson, they fall back on the theory that Pan head coins were not minted under Doson. However, the absence of Pan head tetradrachms from Asia Minor hoards has already been explained by Touratsoglou, followed by myself, as forming part of a general pattern: the Pan head tetradrachms are generally absent from Asia Minor, the Near East, and Egypt between the 240s and 220 and are rare in the Balkans.[222] Thus it need not challenge my proposed classification of the Pan head tetradrachms, as Lorber and Houghton seem to suggest, without explaining their point further. Moreover, as the absence of Pans from the hoard need not suggest a late date for this *unicum* Zeus head tetradrachm, its attribution to Gonatas cannot be excluded.

Finally, the denial that the Pans continued after Gonatas through to Doson is in sharp contrast with a possibility that Lorber and Houghton do leave open, i.e., that the Zeus tetradrachm would match the Zeus drachmae issued by Demetrios II in the name of "King Antigonos," which they term "posthumous coinage." In the first place, as the types of the Zeus drachmae differ from the (Pan head) small denomination matching Gonatas's Pan tetradrachms, the term "posthumous" cannot apply to the former. One might find contradictory, if not confusing, that, latent in the suggested existence of such drachmae of Demetrios II is the acceptance of the idea of the continuation of Antigonid individual types by Gonatas' successors.[223] As it would be hard to assume that Demetrios II minted only few and rare drachmae in the name of "King Antigonos," not pairing them with any large silver denominations in order to meet his military and other commitments, one would be inclined to favor, in the first place, the continuation of individual Antigonid tetradrachm types under Demetrios II and to investigate the possibility that they may have been extended to the other members of the Antigonid dynasty.

Reasons for dating the Zeus Head coin provisionally to the reign of Doson have been given above (see Chapter 5.2). That all four Poseidon head tetradrachms in this hoard belong to our Period III may indeed be pure coincidence. Yet their dating to Period III, covering Gonatas' reign between 246/5 and 239 BC, may offset the absence from this hoard of Pan head tetradrachms struck by Gonatas. It may still be possible that certain Period III Poseidon head groups may need to be downdated to Period IV. Lastly, there appears to be no reason for one to link the introduction of the Poseidon issues exclusively with the Karian expedition: Doson, like his predecessors, had to meet other state expenses throughout his reign, possibly using Poseidon head tetradrachms alongside other mainstream issues.

The Poseidon tetradrachms come from Period III (147a, 152a, 223a).[224] The Zeus tetradrachm is no. IV.63a.

222. Touratsoglou, *DM*, 76; Panagopoulou, *Antigonids*, 336, 344–346. See also Chapter 5.2.

223. The hoard publishers credit Ute Wartenberg with this suggestion, but provide no specific reference: C. Lorber and A. Houghton, "Antiochus III Hoard," *AJN* 21 (2009), 89–104, esp. 94.

224. No photograph is provided of no. 13 (as no. 12), C. Lorber—A. Houghton, "Antiochus III Hoard," *AJN* 21 (2009), 99, no. 13.

38. Syria (perhaps Aradian Peraea), 1971: *CH* II (1976), 81; *CH* X (2010), 289.

195/4 or 190 BC

G. Le Rider, "Les ressources financières de Séleukos IV (187–185) et le paiement de l' indemnité aux Romains," in Price et al., *Essays Carson-Jenkins*, 52; G.Le Rider, "Un trésor hellénistique de monnaies d' argent trouvé en Syrie en 1971 (*CH* II, 81)," *Syria* 75 (1998), 89–96; A. Meadows, "The Eras of Pamphylia," *AJN* 21 (2009), 53–55; Marcellesi, *Pergame*, 211; Duyrat, *WAW*, 112, n. 174.

This (or a portion of this) hoard, comprising 90 specimens, most of which are on the Attic weight standard, was identified by P. Girardi in 1971 and was fully published in 1998 by G. Le Rider. The most important coins are the 40 posthumous Alexander tetradrachms struck between 225 and 190 BC, not least of which are those of Arados, alongside the tetradrachms of Side, Philip V and the Ptolemies, and the drachmae of Ephesos. As the Seleukid tetradrachms do not postdate the reign of Antiochos III, and as the tetradrachm of Philip V is dated before the end of the Second Makedonian War, Le Rider dates the hoard around 190 BC or slightly later: he adds it to a cluster of nine known hoards from Syria and Asia Minor, which were buried in the 190s, presumably reflecting the upheaval caused by Antiochos III in Greece and in Asia between 191 and 189 BC. His proposed date is emended by Meadows to 195/4 BC:[225] the presence of five Ptolemaic tetradrachms alongside coins of Attic weight, and the presence of five Alexanders of Arados (nos. 49–53), prompt him to locate the formation of this hoard on the frontier of Koile Syria and Phoenicia, presumably around the Aradian *peraia*.

As the posthumous Alexanders are of eastern origin, the Poseidon head tetradrachm emerges as the one of the two Macedonian issues in the hoard (the other being the tetradrachm of Philip V). Its photograph is omitted from the hoard publication, but, according to the file at the ANS, it carries a test cut on the reverse, on Apollo's body; the obverse is relatively well preserved. The absence of Pan head tetradrachms from this hoard is not surprising: they are absent from other eastern hoards of the third quarter of the third century BC.[226]

39. S. Asia Minor ("Pisidia"), 1963: *IGCH* 1411.

190–189 BC

Boehringer, *Chronologie*, 70; 172–5; *SC* I.2, 91–92; Duyrat, *Arados*, 146–147.

This hoard of approximately 400 coins came to light in 1963, in three separate lots. Accepting a burial date c. 190–189 BC for the first two (he did not know about the third), Boehringer placed them in the context of the Antiochic War (192–189 BC).[227]

The hoard contained a single Pan head tetradrachm of Period III, no. 136a.

225. Cf. A. Meadows, "The Eras of Pamphylia and the Seleukid invations of Asia Minor," *AJN* 21 (2009), 51–88, esp. 53–56. The 195/4 date is retained in *CH* X (2010) 289.

226. See above, no. 37; see also chapter 7.2–3.

227. On the first two lots, see Boehringer, *Chronologie*, 70; 172–175 ("Pisidia, 1963," last coins: Aspendos year 18 [193/2 BC], Perge year 29 [191–190 BC], Antiochos III at Tarsos and Nisibis [c. 195 BC]); ibid., 176–179 ("Asia Minor, 1963," last coins: Pergamon after 200 BC, Side c. 200 BC, Antiochos III at Antiocheia/Orontes, c. 197 BC); information on the third lot has been drawn from A. Spaer. Cf. *SC* I.2, 91–92.

40. Unknown Findspot ("Pamphylia or Cilicia" Hoard), 2000: *CH* X (2010) 292.

190/89 BC

SC I.2, 94–95; O. Hoover, "Unknown Findspot ('Pamphylia or Cilicia' Hoard), 2000 (*CH* 10, 292)," *CH* X (2010), 129–152, pl. 21–36.

This hoard of 545 tetradrachms and 205 drachmae was identified in commerce in 2000, in three lots. It is assumed to have been formed in the area of Pamphylia or Cilicia, on the basis of its large quantities of Pamphylian Alexanders and of an early tetradrachm of Seleukos IV.[228] O. Hoover, following Meadows' high chronology for the Pamphylian eras regarding the issues of Phaselis, Perge and Aspendos, emends the dating of this hoard from 188/7 BC to 190/89 BC. He is tempted to locate its burial somewhere in Phrygia, after the Seleukid defeat at Magnesia ad Sipylum in 190 BC and the removal of the Seleukid garrison commander in Perge.

The single Poseidon head tetradrachm is the only non-posthumous Alexander specimen with attested Makedonian origin in this lot. Hoover assigns it to Antigonos Doson and associates it with the Antigonid conquest and administration of Karia between 227 and 210 BC. However, if the Poseidons were associated with a more permanent Antigonid presence in Karia in the 220s, one would expect them to occur in greater numbers in contemporary hoards, especially if the mainstream view associating the minting of the Poseidon type with the Karian expedition is taken as valid (I have given reasons against this above). In any case, Antigonid claims to Karia have recently been attested in the time of Gonatas, as has been noted above.

The single Poseidon head tetradrachm from this hoard belongs to Period III (no. 187f) and is relatively worn.

41. Ayaz-In (near ancient Prymnessus), Phrygia, c. 1453: *IGCH* 1413.

190–188 BC

Seyrig, *Trésors*, 36–46, hoard 8, 36–46, pl. 12–18; *SC* I.2, 91–92; Price, *Alexander* I, 62; Marcellesi, *Pergame*, 201; Duyrat, *Arados*, 144–145.

This hoard, dispersed in trade except for an important lot kept in Paris, comprises more than 170 tetradrachms: coins of Alexander III and one imitation, tetradrachms of Alabanda and Side, Seleukid, and two Poseidon tetradrachms (with monogram [monogram], broken, not weighed). Seyrig notes that the composition of this hoard is strongly reminiscent of Mektepini, 1956 (no. 42 below). The Pergamon issues comprise exclusively "international" coinage (late Alexanders, i.e., Marcellesi, *Pergame*, no. 32; Price, *Alexander*, 1473, 1488, 1490). The latest Alexander tetradrachm of Arados (the palm tree series) is dated year 63, i.e., 197/6 BC (Duyrat, *Arados*, 144). There are no photographs of the two Poseidon specimens recorded by Seyrig.

42. Mektepini, 1956: *IGCH* 1410; Lorber, *CPE*, 498.

196/5 or 190–188 BC

Olçay and Seyrig, *Mektepini*, 3–4; Boehringer, *Chronologie*, 69–70; id., *Hierax*, 43, table 2 (190–188 BC); Price, *Alexander* I, 62; *SC* I.2, 89–90; A. R. Meadows, "The Eras of Pamphylia," *AJN* 21 (2009), 66–68; Marcellesi, *Pergame*, 200; Duyrat, *Arados*, 141–142.

228. *SC* I.2, 94–95; O. Hoover, "Unknown Findspot ('Pamphylia or Cilicia' Hoard), 2000 (*CH* 10, 292)," *CH* X (2010), 129–152, pl. 21–36.

This pot hoard was originally dated c. 190 BC, but an earlier date, c. 196 / 5 BC, has been suggested by Meadows.

The three Pan tetradrachms in the hoard represent the first three periods of Pan tetradrachm production (I.72f; II.65b; III.11a) while the two Poseidon tetradrachms belong to Period III (153a, 188d).

43. Aleppo area (ancient Beroia), 1896: *IGCH* 1539, which makes no mention of Antigonid coins.

c. 190 BC

J. Rouvier, "Le monnayage alexandrin d' Arados," *RNum* (1900), 42–43; K. Regling, Hellenistischer Münzschatz aus Babylon," *ZfN* (1928), 94; Westermark, *Philetairos*, 15–16; Marcellesi, *Pergame*, 207; Duyrat, *WAW*, 109–10, no. 170.

This hoard of more than 150 tetradrachms, found in a military camp, is only partially known. The Philetairoi belong to Marcellesi's Groups VI.A, VI.B (nos. 30–31). In addition to the Antigonid coins (of Poliorketes and Gonatas), the hoard comprised coins of Side and in the names of Alexander, Lysimachos, Prusias I, and the Seleukids (Antiochos I to III).

44. Latakia (ancient Laodicea by the sea), Seleucis, 1946: *IGCH* 1536.

Seyrig, *Trésors*, hoard 6; Price, *Alexander* I, 62; *SC* I.2, 102; Duyrat, *WAW*, 110–111, no. 172.

This "savings" hoard was found during an excavation work, but has been dispersed.

45. Drama, 1989: *CH* VIII (1994) 403.

187–68 BC

Touratsoglou, *Circulation*, no. 34.

This tomb hoard, comprising a single Antigonid silver drachma alongside a tetradrachm from Thasos and 30 bronze coins, has been dated by Touratsoglou to 187–168 BC. The Antigonid Zeus drachma from this hoard belongs to Period IV (84d) and is rather worn.

47. Asia Minor, c. 1947: *IGCH* 1451.

c. 187 BC

O. Mørkholm's date c. 187 BC for this hoard, now dispersed in trade, was presumably based on the tetradrachms of Antiochos III. The hoard contains one "Antigonos Doson" tetradrachm.

48. Urfa (ancient Edessa), Mesopotamia, 1924: *IGCH* 1772.

c. 185–160 BC

Jenkins, *ANSMN* 13 (1967), 56; M. J. Price, "Greek Coin Hoards in the British Museum, v. The Urfa Hoard of 1924," *NC* (1969), 10–14; Price, *Alexander* , vol. I, 64; *SC* I.2, 111–112; Marcellesi, *Pergame*, 209.

We owe the detailed catalogue of the Seleukid issues in this hoard to Houghton and Lorber.[229] Jenkins dated this hoard to c. 190 BC, on the basis of a posthumous Alexander tetradrachm from

229. *SC* I.2, 111–112.

Perge dated to year 32 (190/89 BC). This was emended by Price to c. 185 BC and later to c. 165–150 BC.[230]

The presence of both Pans and Poseidons in the heart of the Seleukid Empire at so late a date may indicate the late circulation of both Antigonid tetradrachm types in the Seleukid realm.

50. Larissa ("Sitochoro," near Pharsalos), 1968: *CH* IX (2002) 247 (Larissa ("Sitochoro"), 1968); *IGCH* 237.

c. 165 BC

M. J. Price, "The Larissa, 1968 Hoard (*IGCH* 237)," in Le Rider et al., *Kraay-Mørkholm Essays*, 2; M. Karamessini-Oikonomidou, "Θησαυρός νομισμάτων ἐκ Θεσσαλίας 1968," *AE* (1970 [1971]), 13–26; "Νομισματικό Μουσεῖο Ἀθηνῶν," *ΑΔ* 31 (1976) Chronicle: 4–5; *SC* I, 155; Crawford, *Coinage and Money*, 121–122; Price, *Alexander* I, 63; Touratsoglou, *Circulation*, 36, n. 12; Hatzopoulos, *Institutions*, 250–255; H. Mattingly, "Some Numismatic Puzzles," *NC* (2002), 464; Marcellesi, *Pergame*, 222; ; Lorber, *CPE*, 510.

This hoard is crucial for determining the introduction dates of the Athenian New Style and First Meris coinages. It comprises a wide range of coins, including a full record of tetradrachms of Perseus later than 172 BC, tetradrachms of the First Meris, tetradrachm varieties of Lysimachos issued after 168 BC and imitations of Rhodian drachmae probably struck in Thessaly. The contents of this clearly "savings" hoard and the absence of Athenian New Style tetradrachms or of Seleukid issues later than Seleukos IV led Price to suggest c. 165 BC for its burial. Touratsoglou generally accepts this date, but he distinguishes two lots for this hoard, the former dated to c. 187 BC and the latter to c. 168/7 BC. The late burial date means that the hoard is of little help in determining the date of the rather worn Pans and Poseidons of the third period, which it contained.

I have been able to trace only two of the nine Antigonid specimens, three Pans and six Poseidons, recorded in this hoard. Both the Pan and the Poseidon specimen which I have studied come from Period III, nos. 110f (with a crested helmet and TI) and 214l (⊠)], respectively.

51. Asia Minor, 1947/8: *CH* VII (1985) 99.

c. 160 BC

NCirc. (1949), 176–179; Marinescu, *Lysimachi*, 291, no. 38.

A date of c. 160 BC has been proposed for this hoard, which included coins of Amyntas III, Philip II, Alexander III (Mesembria, Aspendos, Rhodes, Karia, Temnos), Philip III, Demetrios Poliorketes and Antigonos Gonatas, Lysimachus (11—including later Byzantium) and Karia. The Poseidon tetradrachm, from Period III, is no. 230a.

53. Aleppo environs, c. 1930: *IGCH* 1562.

133/130 BC

Seyrig, *Trésors*, 87–88, pl. 32; Duyrat, *WAW*, 141–142, no. 235, with further bibliography.

The very fresh tetradrachms of cities of the East place the deposition of this hoard, which was dispersed in trade, soon after 133/0 BC.[231]

230. Jenkins, *ANSMN* 13, 56; Price, *NC* (1969), 15 (c. 185 BC); Price, *Alexander* I, 64 (c. 165–150 BC).
231. Seyrig, *Trésors*, 87–88, pl. 32.

54. North of Larissa, 1985: *CH* VIII (1994) 517.

c. 75 BC

Touratsoglou, *DM*, pl. VI, note 1; Paschidis, *Ποσειδώνες και Αντίγονοι*, 241.

This hoard with civic and royal, large and smaller denominations including a Pan tetradrachm with Athena right, has been dated to c. 75 BC and has been dispersed in trade. Touratsoglou identified two lots, formed respectively in c. 270 and c. 75 BC, on the basis of the hoard content, and, in particular, on the good state of the Pan tetradrachm.[232] This may, however, simply reflect the gradual accumulation of a "savings" hoard. The Pan tetradrachm in this hoard is I.181e (*desmos*—AN).

*** *** ***

The Poteidaia/Kassandreia, 1984 find establishes a *terminus ante quem* of 240 BC for the introduction of the gold Alexander specimens inscribed ΒΑΣΙΛΕΩΣ ΑΝΤΙΓΟΝΟΥ. The hoards establish *termini ante quos* of c. 260 BC for introduction of the Pans and c. 245 BC for the Poseidons. These dates derive from the Phayttos, 1956 hoard, for the Pans, and from the absence of Poseidons from Eretria, 1937, despite the presence of Pan specimens of Period III, but their presence in Karditsa, (Palaiokastro), 1929, with Pans of the second period. It must be admitted, however, that the exact introduction date of the Poseidons is not conclusively established by the hoard evidence.[233]

The dates of the hoards are largely determined by external evidence, from contemporary royal and civic coinages. I have tentatively taken the accumulation in hoards of coins of the first two Ptolemies in peninsular Greece and in the Aegean after the Ptolemaic defeat off Andros as a criterion for identifying a "savings" hoard; I have thus been able to make a distinction between "savings" and "circulation" hoards (cf. Chapter 7.3). At the same time, the Pans and the Poseidons determine the chronological arrangement of certain hoards: the dating of the most significant, Eretria, 1937 hoard, with Pans but no Poseidons, to c. 245 BC, for instance, inevitably downdates Scotussa, (pre-)1989, which is similar in content. The internal sequence of Period IV is established with less certainty, as most of the hoards with the related varieties are "savings" hoards. It is worth noting that it is specimens of the first period that occur, severely corroded, in hoards of the late third century in the East. Finally, drachmae are present in few hoards, such as in the underwater find at Sophikon (*IGCH* 179/*CH* VIII [1994], 316), and in the Drama, 1989 and Korinth, 1938 hoards.

232. Touratsoglou, *DM*, pl. VI, note 1; Paschidis, *Ποσειδώνες και Αντίγονοι*, 241.
233. See Chapter 6.4.3.

Table 6.13. Antigonid silver: Hoard summary[234]

No.	Hoard	*IGCH*, *CH* etc.	Proposed burial	Pan: LG (CM)	Poseidon: LG (CM)	Zeus: LG (CM)	Zeus: LG (CM)	C/S
1	Verge ("Perge"), 1955	455	-260 (c.)	I.3 ([monogram])				
2	Phayttos, 1956 (c.)	159	260–230 (c.)	I.12 ([monogram])				C
3	"Pherai," 1937-8	*CH* IX (2002) 172 and 193; *CH* VII (1985) 75; 168 (and 141)	250–240 (c.)	III.26 (TI)				C
4	Karditsa (Palaiokastro), c. 1929	*CH* IX (2002) 180; 162	245–240	III.24 (TI)	III.41 ([monogram])			C
5	Scotussa area, (pre-) 1989	*CH* VIII (1994) 283	245–240 (c.)	I.32 ([monogram])				C?
6	Eretria, 1937	*CH* IX (2002) 194; 175	245 (c.)	III.30 ([monogram])				S
7	S. Asia Minor, 1976	*CH* III (1977) 41	246					
8	Sardeis, 1911	*CH* IX (2002) 499; 1299	240 (c.)	I ([monogram])?				S
9	Tell Sukas (Gabala), 1958	1528	Before 243/2 (c.)					
10	Meydancıkkale, 1980	*CH* X (2010) 269; *CH* VIII (1994) 308; *CH* VII (1985) 80	240–235	III.11 ([monogram])				C/S?
11	Thessalonike, 1978	*CH* V (1979) 36	230					
12	Makedonia, 1960s	*CH* I (1975) 72	225–200					
13	Asia Minor, 1972	*CH* I (1975) 73	235–230 (c.); 200					
14	Kassandreia, 1985/7	*CH* VIII (1994) 322	225 (c.)	IV.1 (wh—KT)	III.37 ([monogram])			S
15	Unknown Findspot ("Seleucus III"), 2002	*CH* X (2010) 272	225–224	IV.4 (KT)	IV.21 ([monogram])			
16	Hija së Korbit, 1982	*CH* VIII (1994) 299	225 (c.)	IV.12 ([monogram])				S
17	Thesprotia, 1992	*CH* IX (2002), 200	225 (c.)	IV.13 (wh—KT), IV.10 ([monogram])	III.46 ([monogram])			S
18	Sophikon, 1893	*CH* VIII (1994) 316; 179	230–220 (c.)				IV.23 (TI)	C
19	Korinth environs, 1938	187	220–215 (c.)					
20	Troas/Mysia, (pre-)1947	1301	220–210 (c.)					

234. The numbers in Latin characters represent the period of issue, Arabic numbers represent group numbers. The monograms on the reverse are mentioned in brackets, and the symbol is only mentioned when it is different from the crested helmet symbol. The winged helmet is the left reverse symbol of the drachmae and of some of the latest Pan tetradrachms. LG = latest group; CM = control marks. C = "circulation" hoard; S = "savings" hoard.

Table 6.13 (continued). Antigonid silver: Hoard summary

No.	Hoard	*IGCH*, *CH* etc.	Proposed burial	Pan: LG (CM)	Poseidon: LG (CM)	Zeus: LG (CM)	Zeus: LG (CM)	C/S
21	Syracuse, Achradina, 1899	2230	215–212					
22	Enna environs, 1966	*CH* IX (2002) 670; 2232	211 (c.)	I.11 HP				S
23	Morgantina, 1982	*CH* VIII (1994) 329	210 (c.?)					
24	Edremit (Adramytteion), 1954	1302	210 (c.)					
25	Gordion, 1951	1406	210 (c.)	III.15 (KT)				S
26	Gordion, 1961	1405	205 (c.)	I.5 ([monogram])				S
27	S. Asia Minor, 1963	1426	210–00	IV.14 ([monogram])				S
28	N. Syria, 1960	1533	210 (c.)	III.22 (TI)				S
29	Syria, 1959	1535	213–205 (c.)		IV.16 ([monogram])			S
30	Syria?, 1962	1531	225–220		IV.21 (trident—[monogram])			?
31	S. Asia Minor, 1970	*CH* I (1975) 74	200 (c.)	IV.9 (I)				
32	Oylum Höyüğü, 1989	*CH* IX (2002) 501	205–200		IV.21 (trident—[monogram])			?
33	Unknown Findspot ("Achaeus" Hoard), 2002	*CH* X (2010) 277	c. 204–199		III.33 ([monogram] HP)			
34	"X4"		210–190	IV.12 ([monogram])	III.43 ([monogram])			
35	Nile Delta, 1927–8 = Makedonia?, 1927	*CH* VIII (1994) 356; 469; 1701	200–180 (c.)	III.1 (trident)				
36	Pergamon, 1960	1303	200 (c.)		III.35 ([monogram] M)			S
37	Unknown Findspot ("Antiochus III" Hoard), 2005	*CH* X (2010), 288	196 (c.)		III.35 ([monogram])	IV.15 (TI)		
38	Syria, 1971	*CH* X (2010) 289; *CH* II (1976) 81	195/4 or 190					
39	"Pisidia," 1963	1411	190/89 (c.)	III.31				
40	Unknown Findspot, 2000 ("Pamphylia or Cilicia" Hoard)	*CH* X (2010) 292	190–89		III.41 ([monogram])			
41	Ayaz-In, Phrygia, c. 1953	1413	190–188 (c.)		Pos ([monogram])			
42	Mektepini, 1956	1410	196/5 or 190–188 (c.)	III.4 ([monogram])	III.41 ([monogram])			?

Table 6.13 (continued). Antigonid silver: Hoard summary

No.	Hoard	*IGCH, CH* etc.	Proposed burial	Pan: LG (CM)	Poseidon: LG (CM)	Zeus: LG (CM)	Zeus: LG (CM)	C/S
43	Aleppo environs (Beroia), 1896	1539	190 (c.)					
44	Latakia	1536	190 (c.)					
45	Drama, 1989	*CH* VIII (1994) 403	187–168			IV.23 (TI)		
46	Thessaly, 1977	*CH* VI (1981) 35; *CH* V(1979) 42	190					
47	Asia Minor, c. 1947	1451	187 (c.)			III.45 ([monogram])		
48	Urfa (Edessa), 1924	1772	185–160					
49	SW Thessaly, 1977	*CH* VI (1981) 35	175					
50	Larissa ("Sitochoro," near Pharsalos), 1968	*CH* IX (2002) 247; 237	168–167	III.25 (TI)	III.44 ([monogram])		IV.23 (TI)	S
51	Asia Minor, 1947/8	*CH* VII (1985) 99	160		III.45 ([monogram])			
52	Balkh, 1974?	*CH* II (1976) 88	150					
53	Aleppo environs, c. 1930	1562	133/0 (c.)					
54	North of Larissa, 1985	*CH* VIII (1994) 517	75 (c.)	I.49 ([monogram])				S

6.4 Absolute Chronology

Posthumous Alexander gold staters and silver tetradrachms are currently believed to have been minted between the death of Poliorketes in 283 BC and the introduction by Gonatas of issues in his own name to meet his financial needs in Makedonia (Chapter 6.1). The silver tetradrachms with the legend ΑΛΕΞΑΝΔΡΟΥ on the reverse produced within this period[235] are characterized by large flans, very large and well-proportioned portraits, in high relief, which tend to fill the flans; and by the progression from a double row of short, downward-pointing spikes towards that with looser, downward-hanging locks on the lion's mane. Mathisen's tentative arrangement of these Makedonian posthumous Alexanders on the basis of hoards, style and monograms[236] has been updated by M. J. Price, who takes the control mark patterns of these coins to reflect the political instability during the *interregnum* after Poliorketes' death. Eleven varieties have been distinguished altogether; six of them are currently dated to the reign of Antigonos Gonatas, as follows:[237]

1. *Omikron-Kappa* [532-545], named after the monogram beneath the throne; 281/0 (M); c. 285 (P).
2. Triton [524–530], with a triton blowing a trumpet and holding a scepter in the left reverse field; 279/8 (M).
3. Mu [604–619], with a monogram behind the throne and monogram combinations in the left field; 276/5 (M).
4. Grape [574–603], with a bunch of grapes in the left reverse field; 275/4 (M).
5. X [572–573]; 274/3 (M).
6. Helmet [621–632], the largest group, named after the Makedonian helmet it bears on the reverse l. field; 273/1, Amphipolis (M); 275–270, Pella (P).
7. Bipennis [569–570], 288/83, Pella (M, P).
8. Monogram [550–653], with several monograms, die-linked to a reverse inscribed ΒΑΣΙΛΕΩΣ ΑΝΤΙΓΟΝΟΥ. 274/3, Pella (M).
9. Var. [867–8]: "uncertain" but possibly of North Greek origin in style and provenance (P).
10. Group [564–568], present in the Armenak hoard, with Makedonian traits of style (P).
11. Var. [809], regarded by M. J. Price as probably Makedonian in origin, with parallel gold issues ([808]—from the Skione, Greece, 1985/6 hoard -, [807]).

A few gold staters can be associated by their control marks with two varieties of these posthumous Alexander tetradrachms (Pl. 54.2). To the five gold staters listed by Mathisen Price adds one specimen, related to a silver tetradrachm from the Monogram group.[238] The number of staters has been significantly increased by the Poteidaia/Kassandreia, 1984 hoard, which has been dispersed in trade (Chapters 6.3, 6.4.1): nos. 17 and 18 of this hoard correspond to silver Alexander tetradrachms from the Monogram group, while nos. 19–72 may be related to the Mu group of posthumous Alexander tetradrachms struck during the early reign of Gonatas. Accepting Mathisen's interpretation of the Makedonian gold staters as payment by Gonatas to Celtic mercenaries, Price attributes the stylistic differences between the two issues to the simultaneous functioning of two

235. On the occurrence of the royal title on the reverse of gold and silver posthumous Alexanders, see Price, *Alexander*, 32–3.

236. Mathisen, *Silver Coinages*, 79–123, pl. 17-22.

237. The numbers in square brackets are those of Price, *Alexander*, 141-2. Mathisen's suggestions are indicated by "(M)," Price's by "(P)." For a list of the new hoards since Mathisen's publication, see Price, *Alexander*, 141-2.

238. Mathisen, *Silver Coinages*, 89–90, 95–96, pl. 18.11–12, 21.32–33, 21.5; Price, *Alexander*, 141, 145.562.

mints in ca. 276/5 BC and adopts Mathisen's assignation of the former group to Pella and of the latter to Amphipolis. It may be argued that the more elaborate transitional staters with the legend of king Antigonos were also struck at Amphipolis, presumably after the staters attached to the Mu group.

*** *** ***

The attempts of Mathisen and Price to date these posthumous Alexander issues were based on the following three assumptions:

1) that Gonatas used the staters to pay Celtic mercenaries;
2) that Gonatas' individual coinage was introduced in 272/1 BC, after the death of Pyrrhos, which left Gonatas the only claimant to the Makedonian throne, and prior to the Chremonidean War;
3) that Gonatas' introduction of his personal issues put an end to the posthumous gold and silver Alexander coinage.

1. Gold staters and Celtic mercenaries

Mathisen relies primarily on Polyaenos' account for the initial agreement of Gonatas to pay each of his Celtic mercenaries for the battle against Antipater Etesias χρυσοῦν μακεδονικόν (Polyaen. *Strat.* 4.6.17 ff.), and notes further the presents in gold which, according to Polybios, the citizens of Byzantion gave to the Celts in order to prevent them plundering their land,[239] and the gift of gold by the people of Herakleia to the Byzantines in the same context.[240] He is also tempted to relate the Poteidaia, 1984 hoard to Gonatas' ten-month siege of the city, known as Kassandreia in the Hellenistic period, immediately after the battle of Lysimacheia and to its final capture with the aid of 2,000 mercenaries by the pirate Ameinias (Polyaen. *Strat.* 4.6.18).[241]

Attractive though this explanation may seem, it is far from conclusive. These gold staters are not found in hoards of the early third century from Asia Minor, where the Celts migrated in the first half of the 270s.[242] Furthermore, the number of gold staters issued in this period would probably not have sufficed for the payment of the Celtic mercenaries employed by Gonatas early in his reign. To the three military occasions pointed out by Mathisen, in which Celtic mercenaries served under Gonatas, that is, the campaign against Antipater Etesias, the siege of Kassandreia after Lysimacheia in 276 BC, and the rivalry between Gonatas and Pyrrhos for the Makedonian throne in 274 BC, one may also add the Chremonidean War, given the mutiny of Celtic mercenaries at Megara during the siege of Athens by Gonatas.[243] According to Polyaenos, the overall amount owed by Gonatas to the Celtic mercenaries for the battle against Antipater Etesias was thirty talents. Given that each soldier was initially to receive one gold stater after the battle, with a

239. Plb. 4.46: κατὰ μὲν οὖν τὰς ἀρχὰς ἐν ταῖς ἐφόδοις αὐτῶν τὰς κατὰ Κομοντόριον τὸν πρῶτον βασιλεύσαντα δῶρα διετέλουν οἱ Βυζάντιοι διδόντες ἀνὰ τρισχιλίους καὶ πεντακισχιλίους, ποτέ δὲ καὶ μυρίους χρυσοῦς, ἐφ᾽ ᾧ μὴ καταφθείρειν τὴν χώραν αὐτῶν.

240. Memnon of Herakleia, *FGH* IIIb, F 434 Nr. 297–607, 11 (19).

241. Mathisen, *Silver Coinages*, 102–103, n. 29; 118; Price, *Alexander*, 142; Le Rider, *Potidée*, 94. On the participation of Celts in the Makedonian army, see C. B. Welles, "Gallic Mercenaries in the Chremonidean War," *Klio* 52 (1970), 477–490; Hannestad, *Celts*, 15–38, esp. 16–20; Cunliffe, *Celts*, 81–82. On the Celts' appreciation of gold, see Chr. Goudineau, "Les Celtes, les Gaulois et l'or d'apres les auteurs anciens," in B. Cauuet et al. (eds.), *L'or dans l'antiquité: de la mine à l'objêt*, Aquitania Supplément 9 (Bordeaux: Aquitania 1999), 331–336; cf. M. Szabo, *Les Celtes de l'Est* (1992).

242. On the absence of these staters from hoards, see Price, *Alexander*, 141.

243. P. Trog. *Prol.* 26; Just. 26.2; C. B. Welles, "Gallic mercenaries in the Chremonidean War," *Klio* 52 (1970), 477–90; Heinen, *Unters.*, 170–172.

gold : silver *ratio* of c. 1:10, the 9,000 staters which would come from the thirty talents would pay off approximately 9,000 soldiers.

Each gold stater is believed to have represented the wages of a soldier for a minimum period of one month.[244] However, the financial needs raised by the continuous enlistment of Celts for a full ten-month war period would have required the issue of a considerably higher number of gold staters. In fact, it is highly dubious whether the amount of gold which could potentially be coined from the known obverse dies would have sufficed for the payment of the Celts in gold for relatively long periods. The six posthumous gold staters so far known come from five different obverse dies. Assuming the potential production of approximately 10,000 to 30,000 coins from each obverse die, one is left with a speculative number of 50,000 to 150,000 gold staters struck from the five Makedonian posthumous Alexander obverse dies. This amounts to 166.6 to 500 talents of gold. These would have sufficed for approximately eleven monthly payments of 9,000 mercenaries, that is, for only one ten-month war period. Increased demand for gold staters would partly have been met with already existing coinage, such as gold Philippi, Alexanders, Demetrii or Lysimachi, as only one third of the known needs for gold coins could have been covered by the posthumous Alexander staters struck during this period.[245] If the Celtic mercenaries demanded payment in gold, one might speculate that they may not have been employed continuously in the Makedonian army.

On the other hand, there is admittedly no reason to discard Justin's reference to the Celts' appreciation of other forms of wealth beyond gold.[246] In fact, rather than a response to a request by mercenaries, the gold issues of this period may relate to local preferences. The presents of the Byzantines to the Celts, for instance, may simply indicate that transactions in this metal were the general rule in the Black Sea area, rather than any exclusive preference of the Celts for gold.[247] It is also worth noting that the prolific Alexander tetradrachm issues in the Black Sea region and in Asia Minor in the 270s and the popularity of posthumous Alexanders in the fourth-century BC Northern Balkan area have been taken to indicate that payments to the invading Celtic tribes were demanded in Alexander gold staters and silver tetradrachms.[248] Nor is the issue of gold staters incompatible with earlier royal practices in Makedonia, whose abundant resources justified the production of coins in this metal.[249] Suffice it to note the large numbers of lifetime and posthumous gold staters in the name of Philip II and Alexander III,[250] and the epigraphic evidence showing the

244. Griffith, *Mercenaries,* 293; Launey, *Armées* I, 495–496; *Armées* II, 759–760. G. Le Rider points out that the Celts were not unfamiliar with the level of wages in the Greek world: Le Rider, *Potidée*, 94, n. 7. Chr. Goudineau, "Les Celtes, les Gaulois et l'or," 331–336.

245. Mathisen, *Silver Coinages*, 102–103. G. Le Rider, in particular, is tempted to see in the content of the Poteidaia, 1984 hoard an illustrative sample of the gold coins in which Celtic mercenaries were paid in the 270s: Le Rider, *Potidée,* 84.

246. Just. 25.1.5: *Sed Galli expositum grande auri argentique pondus admirantes atque praedae ubertate sollicitati infestiores quam venerant revertuntur...*; Diod. 22.9.4.

247. O. Mørkholm, "Some reflections on the production and use of coinage in Ancient Greece," *Historia* 31 (1982), 297, 299 notes that gold was preferred in trade around the Black Sea. Cf. Ed. Schönert-Geiß, "Die Wirtschafts- und Handelsbeziehungen zwischen Griechenland und der nördlichen Schwarzmeerküste im Spiegel der Münzfunde (6.–1. Jh. v. u. Z.)," *Klio* 53 (1971), 105–117.

248. Price, *Alexander,* 75–76.

249. E. N. Borza, "The natural resources of early Macedonia," in Adams and Borza, *Macedonian Heritage* (Washington 1982), 1–20, esp. 8–10; idem, *In the Shadow of Olympus*, 53–55; Billows, *Kings and Colonists*, 7, n. 23; Hammond, *Macedonia* I, 12–18; Hammond and Griffith, *Macedonia* II, 69–91.

250. Le Rider, *Philippe II*, 129–198 (Pella), 202–252 (Amphipolis); 255–284; 401–434 (discussion); id., "The Coinage of Philip II and the Pangaion Mines," in Hatzopoulos and Loukopoulou, *Philip of Macedon*, 48–57; id., *Monnayage et finances*, 49–66; for Alexander's Makedonian gold, see Price, *Alexander*, 144–145, 148 For Alexander's lifetime gold coinage from Makedonia, cf. Troxell, *Studies*, 65, 100–128, pl. 20–25.

use of gold at Amphipolis for purchases of houses and land until the mid-third century BC,[251] and at Beroia for the manumission of slaves in 239–229 BC.[252] There is therefore no need to see in these gold posthumous Alexander staters in the name of king Antigonos a connection with Celtic mercenaries (cf. Chapters 7.0, 7.3). This is supported by the gold stater with the star-and-dog symbols from the Poteidaia, 1984 hoard, for the same control marks appear on an Alexander tetradrachm from Meydancıkkale, 1980. This tetradrachm belongs to a group assigned by Price to an uncertain mint and dated to 240–180 BC.[253] The gold stater may allow for a later burial date for the Poteidaia, 1984 hoard, with 240–180 BC serving as a plausible *terminus ante quem* for the posthumous Alexander gold staters and for the transitional issue of king Antigonos.

The introduction of the personal issues of the king Antigonos has recently been dated to 272/1 BC.[254] The new legend both on the transitional Alexanders and on Gonatas' individual types, ΒΑΣΙΛΕΩΣ ΑΝΤΙΓΟΝΟΥ, constitutes an ideological turning point for the king, who now explicitly declares his royal authority.

If the gold staters belong to the period after 276/5 BC, the Mu and Monogram group of Alexander tetradrachms will belong between 276/5 and 272/1 BC, on the assumption that the posthumous Alexander varieties ceased after the introduction by Gonatas of his personal types in 272/1 BC.[255]

Within this period Mathisen, followed by Price, assigns the Mu, Grape, Xi and Helmet groups to Amphipolis, after the *Omikron-Kappa* and Triton groups. He is tempted to interpret the triton on the reverse of the last as a reference to a naval victory before 276/5 BC. Mathisen's Bipennis and Monogram groups are assigned to a different mint, Pella, when it was under Gonatas' control during his confrontation with Pyrrhos in 274–272 BC. However, we have seen that the dating of the gold staters is now open to question, and that the order of the posthumous Alexander tetradrachms is in many cases not firmly corroborated by the hoard evidence. In fact, one may wonder why they occurred in Makedonia but only in one hoard and not in hoards from Asia Minor dated to the 270s, such as the Armenak, 1927 hoard,[256] if they were issued in a period of large movements of Celtic mercenaries to the East.

That the Alexander silver types were replaced by those of Antigonos Gonatas in 272/1 BC is not supported by any evidence, and there is no reason why both series should not have been issued more or less in parallel. This practice is testified, for instance, in Pergamon as late as c. 210/190 BC, and on the gold staters of Alexander type but with the legend of Mithridates II from Bithynia (c. 255–220 BC). The absence of the posthumous Makedonian Alexanders from hoards from Asia Minor dated to the 270s is particularly remarkable, given the possible presence of Antigonid troops in Karia, as attested from a document as early as 268 BC (cf. Chapter 6.4.2). Finally, the presence of single coins of Antiochos I in the Kilkis, 1961, the Jabukovac, (pre-), 1920 and the Verge ("Perge"), 1955 hoards (*IGCH* 445, 447 and 455), may attest not only a later date for the hoards *per se.* It may also indicate that the posthumous Alexander tetradrachms were in use (if not production), within the 260s, that is, during the Chremonidean War.

251. Hatzopoulos, *Actes de Vente*, 38–54, 75–86; idem, *Institutions* II, 102–5, nos. 88–91.
252. Hatzopoulos, *Institutions* II, 108–110, no. 93, l. 9–10, 21–22.
253. Cf. Chapter 2.3.
254. Mathisen, *Silver Coinages*, 110–118.
255. Mathisen, *Silver Coinages*, 107–108; Price, *Alexander*, 141.
256. Price, ibid.

The internal structure of the Makedonian posthumous silver Alexander tetradrachms cannot be firmly determined by the hoard evidence. The criteria on which Mathisen's reconstruction is based, such as the progression in the size of the flans or the stylistic development of the lion mane, as opposed to the stylistically divergent reverses of the transitional Alexander tetradrachms, leave room for alternative arrangements.[257] Symbols such as the triton, which is regarded by Mathisen as an allusion to a naval victory, may alternatively, for instance, indicate naval activity before or during the Chremonidean War. The Triton specimen from Thessaly, 1983 might thus indicate a date later than the pre-271 BC suggested by Price,[258] not least as Demetrias, the Makedonian royal residence in Thessaly, might have served as a dockyard for the Makedonian navy during the 260s BC. Moreover, similarities in symbols and monograms between the posthumous Alexanders and the Pan head tetradrachms may be taken to suggest parallel production, for example, the helmet in the reverse field of both series. Similarly, the monogram of the Bipennis group is similar to that of the *Athena right* Pan head variety and also occurs on bronze coinage with the monogram of Pyrrhos on the obverse, dated by Price to 273/2 BC:[259] the mint official who signed the posthumous Alexander group presumably continued to hold his office after the departure of Pyrrhos from Makedonia.

The prolific production of posthumous Alexander coinage may plausibly be associated, at least in part, with the preparations for the war against the Greek cities of the south in the 260s. The international acceptance of the posthumous Alexander tetradrachms may in fact have provided a very good reason for their continued issue during the Chremonidean War, perhaps parallel to the Pan head tetradrachms.

Particularly remarkable in the flow of gold and silver tetradrachms with the types of Alexander III is the introduction of coins with the personal name of Antigonos and his royal title. The circumstances of this change are worthy of a further investigation.

6.4.1 Gold staters and silver tetradrachms with the types of Alexander III in the name of Antigonos

The rarity of both the gold and the silver posthumous Alexanders in the name of Antigonos has been taken by Mathisen to indicate their short duration and their status as transitional issues between the posthumous Alexander tetradrachms, struck by Antigonos Gonatas in the name of Alexander, and the introduction by Gonatas of his own types.

In the first place, six gold Alexander staters with the name and the royal title of Antigonos on the reverse survive from five different obverse dies. They are currently assigned to Antigonos Gonatas rather than Monophthalmos, who is now left without coins in his name.[260] Their initial attribution by Mionnet to Monophthalmos[261] was challenged by E. T. Newell, who favored their assignation to Gonatas: "Their comparatively late style, their monograms, and their symbols occur on the contemporaneous Makedonian issues of Gonatas."[262] Without arguing against Mionnet,

257. Mathisen, *Silver Coinages*, 80; cf. chapter 6.4.
258. Price, *Alexander*, 58, 141.
259. Price, *Alexander*, 141.
260. Mørkholm, *EHC*, 59, 77. The reluctance of Monophthalmos to strike coins in his name has been interpreted as a deliberate policy, in view of the international popularity of the Alexander coinage and secondly because much of the treasure he got hold of must have been in Alexander coins already: Billows, *Antigonus*, 218, n. 82, 259, 292.
261. Mionnet, *Description*, Suppl. 3, 244, 587, XI, 1, followed by Head, *HN*², 229; Gaebler, *AMNG* III.2, 179, n.
262. *DP*, 14, n. 1.

and despite some scholars' reservations about Newell's arguments,[263] Mathisen, followed by Price, regards them as issues of Gonatas struck to supplement the Philip and Alexander staters already in circulation, for the payment of Celtic mercenaries.[264]

A reappraisal of the evidence is clearly desirable. Since the surviving Antigonid gold staters come from the same number of obverses as the contemporary posthumous Alexander staters, the amount of gold Antigonid staters which could potentially be produced by five obverse dies is analogous to those in the name of Alexander (Chapters 6.4, 7). The absence of obverse links between the two categories has led to the belief that they are not contemporary and/or come from two separate mints, the wreath on the reverse field left representing the second Makedonian mint for the gold staters under Antigonos.[265]

The elaborate style, the high relief and the careful and regular engraving of the legend letters on the Antigonid gold are in accordance with the general care in the production of gold coins. Rather than limiting this gold issue to the payment of Celtic mercenaries (Chapter 6.4.1), these features indicate that these staters could have been a response to increased military needs or even a commemoration of an outstanding event. This suggestion is further supported by the divergence of the control marks of these staters from those on their posthumous Alexander counterparts. In fact, the substitution of the *aphlaston* for the wreath, which is normally held by Nike on the reverse, is a significant iconographic divergence of these specimens from the traditional Alexander gold staters. The *aphlaston*, which has been interpreted as the *semaphoros* (σηματοθέσιον), of the largest and most ornate ships (στρατηγίδες),[266] may allude to the striking of these coins on the occasion of a naval victory and the wreath symbol left on the reverse is better as reinforcing this rather than as a symbol of a different mint.

The royal title on the reverse points to one of the three kings called Antigonos, namely Monophthalmos, Gonatas, or Doson. If Monophthalmos, then the coins belong to the period between 305 and 301 BC, that is, after the official assumption of the royal title by Monophthalmos after his son's victory over the fleet of Ptolemy I at Salamis and before his death at the battle of Ipsos.[267] If Gonatas, then the possible span is between 283 and 239, i.e., after the assumption of the royal title by Gonatas until the end his reign. Finally, if Doson, the Karian expedition (227–225 BC), offers a possible context for this issue.

Two arguments tell against attribution to Antigonos Monophthalmos. Firstly, the coins are stylistically more elaborate and distant not only from those gold staters produced at the main mints in Asia Minor during the reign of Monophthalmos, but also from those struck in the name of Poliorketes.[268] The helmet type, Athena's features in high relief, the hairstyle, the neck curve

263. Gaebler, ibid.

264. Mathisen, *Silver Coinages*, 103, n. 29–30; Price, *Alexander*, 141–142. Cf. Griffith, *Mercenaries*, 68–79.

265. R. W. Mathisen relates the posthumous Alexander staters of the Mu and Monogram group to the silver in the name of Alexander struck in Pella in 274 BC and those in the name of Antigonos to the transitional silver tetradrachms in the name of Antigonos. Price favors the issue of the respective series in two different mints: *Alexander*, 141; cf. Chapter 6.5.

266. E. Babelon, "La stylis, attribut naval sur les monnaies," *RN*[4] 11 (1907), 1–39 = *Mélanges Numismatiques*, 199; J. Svoronos, "Stylides, ancres hierae, aphlasta, stoloi, akrostolia, embola, proembola et totems marins," *JIAN* 16 (1914), 81–152, esp. 120–130; V. Sergueenkova, "The Stylis of the Gold Coins of Alexander the Great," *NAC* 35 (2006), 165–178; Casson, *Ships and seamanship*, 110–111. Cf. Chapter 6.1.

267. A more detailed analysis on the political significance of the assumption of the kingship by Monophthalmos and Poliorketes in E. Gruen, "Coronation of the Diadochoi," in Eadie and Ober (eds.), *Essays Starr*, 259–260; Billows, *Antigonus*, 155–159.

268. Cf., for instance, Price, *Alexander*, 225–234, pl. VI.1527A, 1536, 1552, 1556–9, 1561–1563, 1568–1574 (Abydos); 271, pl. XVII.L30 (Magnesia ad Maeandrum); 424–425, pl. XII.3340 (Arados); 436, pl. XII.3456 (Sidon); 409, pl. XI, 3257–3258 (Ake). For the gold staters under Poliorketes, cf. Newell, *DP*, 19–20, pl. I.3, 7–10.

and the horizontal wrinkles on her neck produce a more natural portrait, more akin to the gold Alexander staters issued in Amphipolis in the early third century and during the early reign of Antigonos Gonatas.[269] The style of Athena's locks on the obverse is also more elaborate than that of their contemporary posthumous Alexander staters, which are related to the Mu and Monogram group of silver tetradrachms.

Secondly, a stater with the legend ΒΑΣΙΛΕΩΣ ΑΝΤΙΓΟΝΟΥ forms part of the Poteidaia, 1984 hoard (Chapter 6.3). Its occurrence in Makedonia and its absence from hoards found in Asia Minor favor a Makedonian provenance, even if the circulation of gold and silver coins in antiquity was not as limited as that of the bronzes. Moreover, the stater's uncirculated condition and remarkably high relief may indicate the chronological and topographical proximity of its production to the date and place of burial of the hoard. Given the latter's *terminus post quem* of 281 BC,[270] the gold stater in the name of king Antigonos cannot have been struck much earlier, and attribution to Monophthalmos is unlikely.

It is more difficult to decide between Gonatas and Doson. Three weak arguments tend to support the former. Firstly, there is a gradual tendency in the Balkans towards a monometallic currency based on silver during the third century BC,[271] and the last recorded transaction in gold from Makedonia is dated to 239–229 BC.[272] Secondly, the allusion to the god Pan through the replacement of the *aphlaston* by Pan's *syrinx* in specimen 5, from the British Museum, marginally favors assignation to Gonatas, during whose reign Pan's cult flourished in Makedonia (Chapter 6.1). Following Newell, one may regard the gold staters in the name of king Antigonos as a continuation of the gold posthumous Alexander staters struck in Makedonia during the reign of Gonatas. Thirdly, the order of the legend on the gold staters, ΒΑΣΙΛΕΩΣ l.—ΑΝΤΙΓΟΝΟΥ r., may have influenced the arrangement of the legend on two tetradrachms with Alexander types (Chapter 2.2.1, Group 1, nos. 1–2), and on certain Pan head tetradrachms, no. 181 from period I and nos. 127 and 131 from period III, with Athena r. and a *desmos* left on the reverse (Chapter 2.2.3, Group 49, and Chapter 4.3, Groups 27 and 129, respectively). The haste in the engraving of the legends of the transitional Alexander tetradrachms in the name of Antigonos may differentiate the circumstances of their issue from the introduction of the gold staters and of the Pan head tetradrachms; the last two may be regarded as contemporary.

The possibility that the *aphlaston* and the wreath indicate a naval victory might give a clue. The battle of Lysimacheia took place on the coast and close to Gonatas' fleet, but no naval activities are mentioned in relation to it.[273] This limits our choice to the two known major naval conflicts during the reign of Gonatas, that off Kos (dated between 262/1 and 255 BC) and that off Andros (246/5 BC).[274] The association of Pans with a reversed legend order to both naval battles, of no. 181 to the first period of issue and of nos. 127 and 131 to the third period of Antigonid tetradrachms, fails to relate the striking of the Antigonid gold staters to either event. It could be argued that the

269. The Makedonian fabric of the coins is suggested by their stylistic similarity to the Alexander staters issued towards the end of the fourth century BC; see Troxell, *Studies*, 100–106, pl. 20–25. For the gold staters of Gonatas' early reign: Mathisen, *Silver Coinages*, 89, 95, pl. XVIII, 11–12, XXI, 31, 33, 35; Price, *Alexander*, 141–142.

270. Le Rider, *Potidée*, 94; cf. Chapter 6.3.

271.Mørkholm, *EHC*, 4–6. It is worth noting, for instance, that three of the forty-five hoards from the third century that are recorded at *IGCH*, 865–866 and 1369 (= *CH* VIII, 324), and two of the fourteen recorded at *CH* VIII, nos. 300 and 312, are securely dated to the second half of the third century BC.

272. Hatzopoulos, *Institutions* II, 108–110, no. 93.

273. Justin 25.2.6: ...*ad litus conuertuntur (sc. Galli). Ibi dum naves incautius diripiunt, a remigibus et ea exercitus parte, quae eo cum conjugibus et liberis confugerant, nihil tale metuentes trucidantur*. Cf. Nachtergael, *Galates*, 179, n. 231.

274. Cf. Chapters 1.2, 2.0, 4.0.

battle off Kos is only vaguely supported by the dedication at Athens in c. 250 BC to Athena Nike of stelai in memory of the Celtic attack on Delphi by Herakleitos, from the deme of Athmonai. This dedication may have been preceded by the gold staters in the name of Antigonos, carrying Athena on the obverse and Nike on the reverse (Chapter 6.1).[275]

The same occasion may have accounted for the rearrangement of the legend on the Pan head tetradrachms. In fact, the outstandingly good quality of the engraving both on the gold staters and on the Pan head/Athena right, *desmos* tetradrachms[276] and the similarity of the carefully and regularly engraved legend letters suggest that the gold staters and the Pan head/Athena right, *desmos* tetradrachms were made by the same hand.

*** *** ***

Even though the date of introduction of the Alexander-type silver tetradrachms in the name of king Antigonos cannot be determined from hoards (no hoard contains any), it is certainly not unrelated to the structure of the main Makedonian mints during the issue of the posthumous Alexander tetradrachms. Their initial allocation to Antigonos Monophthalmos[277] was challenged by E. T. Newell, who favored their assignation to Antigonos Gonatas, on the grounds of their typically Makedonian fabric and of the fact that Monophthalmos never gained control of Makedonia.[278]

Although certain of Newell's observations are not confirmed by examination of the coinage in the name of Gonatas,[279] nevertheless, his association of these transitional silver specimens to the Makedonian posthumous Alexanders struck during the reign of Gonatas is confirmed by their obverse link with the Monogram variety of the latter;[280] the latter has been taken by Lee Avdoyan, a student in Margaret Thompson's Columbia seminar of Spring 1971, as the last of a series issued in Makedonia under Pyrrhos. The transitional Alexanders have been taken to represent the first issue of Antigonos on regaining Makedonia from Pyrrhos in 272 BC, by Newell and, more recently, by Lee Avdoyan.[281] This suggestion is followed by Mathisen in his systematic die study of the Makedonian posthumous Alexander tetradrachms. On the other hand, I. L. Merker assigns this coinage "very early in the reign of Antigonos Gonatas," that is, according to Hyla A. Troxell, shortly after 276 BC.[282]

275. *IG* II^2 774 = *Syll*^{3} 401; S. Tracy, "Two Attic letter cutters of the third century, 286/5–235/4 B.C.," *Hesperia* 57 (1988), 303–322, esp. 304, pl. 85–87; Habicht, *Unters.*, 71, n. 18. Dinsmoor favored a date long after the victory over the Celts for this decree; Nachtergael suggests a date during the period of Athenian independence, see Nachtergael, *Galates,* 180–181, n. 237; Mikalson, *Religion*, 164, with earlier bibliography.

276. Chapter 2.2.2.

277. Mionnet, *Description,* Suppl. III, 244. Following Mionnet, Head assigns these coins to a Peloponnesian mint, struck under Demetrius Poliorketes in the name of his father Antigonos in c. 303 BC: Head, *HN*, 229, fig. 140.

278. *DP*, 14, n. 1.

279. Monogram [monogram] on these coins, for instance, which Newell believed to also occur on the coins of Antigonos Gonatas with his personal types and on Alexanders in Alexander's name, and which he assigned to Pella, is in fact absent from the silver coinage with Antigonos' personal types.

280. Hyla A. Troxell, "The Peloponnesian Alexanders," *ANSMN* 17 (1971), 41–94, esp. 75, n. 68, pl. XIX.2; Mathisen, *Silver Coinages*, 95–96, pl. XX.27; Price, *Alexander*, 141, 145.563, pl. CLVIII.E). H. Gaebler prefers their assignation to Monophthalmos rather than Gonatas (*AMNG* III.2, 179.3). Troxell (ibid.) reports three posthumous Alexander tetradrachms from the same obverse die as the transitional Alexanders in the name of Antigonos, with the same reverse markings, but coming from different reverse dies. On the coin from London, see Price, *Alexander*, 144, no. 553, pl. XXXIII.

281. These suggestions are reported in Hyla A. Troxell, "The Peloponnesian Alexanders," *ANSMN* 17 (1971), 41–94, esp. 76, n. 68, pl. XIX, 2; Mathisen, *Silver Coinages*, 104–105, n. 32.

282. Merker, *Silver Coinage*, 39; Hyla A. Troxell, "The Peloponnesian Alexanders," *ANSMN* 17 (1971), 75, n. 47.

Particular features of these transitional silver Alexanders suggest that they were struck in the first period of coin production in Makedonia under Gonatas, raising the probability that they constituted the inaugural silver issue in the name of Antigonos Gonatas after the death of Pyrrhos, which left him as the undisputed heir to the Makedonian throne. The progression of wear on their obverse die, in the first place, with a developing die break off Pan's nose which is repaired in the last two specimens, and the monogram they share with the Alexander variety, place them towards the end of the posthumous Alexander varieties of the Monogram group. Mathisen dates them to a late stage in the production of the Makedonian posthumous Alexanders and assigns them to Pella, but the remaining uncertainties regarding the sequence of the latter render their attribution to a specific mint difficult.[283]

The divergences in the depiction of Zeus on the reverse are not incompatible with the posthumous Alexander tetradrachms issued in Amphipolis; they may be taken to suggest the issue of certain posthumous Alexander varieties within a shorter period.[284] The scepter of Zeus is always carefully rendered, with a lotus-tipped ending similar to that on the silver tetradrachms of Poliorketes from Pella (cf. Chapters 2.2.1, 6.1).[285]

Despite the good quality of the Zeus on most of these coins, the irregular and rapidly engraved legend letters indicate their hasty production; the title ΒΑΣΙΛΕΩΣ in the legend gives a *terminus post quem* of 283/2 BC for their introduction, the date when Gonatas acquired of the royal title (but not yet the kingdom), on the death of his father.[286] The order of the legend is reversed in the third die combination: the name of the king is transferred from the right to the left and his title is on the left rather than on the right. There is a tendency towards a more careful engraving of the legends, with smaller characters fitting into the small flans.

Finally, the various combinations of the letters Ε and Κ, which constitute the monograms on the reverse of these coins, relate them to the *Omikron-Kappa* and to the Monogram groups of the Makedonian posthumous Alexanders.

The dotted border on the obverse and reverse (except the reverse of the second die combination, which is without a dotted border), also indicates care in the engraving, echoing perhaps that on two specimens of the Athena right, *desmos* variety with the legend ΒΑΣΙΛΕΩΣ on the left and ΑΝΤΙΓΟΝΟΥ on the right on the reverse, but the fact that the Alexander tetradrachms are off-center differentiates them from the carefully centered Pan head issues, possibly as a result of the smaller flans used for these posthumous Alexander tetradrachms or of a less advanced minting technique, presumably at an earlier stage of the functioning of the mint.

A date early in the reign of Gonatas for the transitional Alexander tetradrachms is confirmed by the parallel of early issues of other Successors with Alexander types but in their own names. The early silver issues of Lysimachos, Demetrios Poliorketes, and King Areus of Sparta,[287] for instance,

283. Mathisen, *Silver Coinages*, 95–96, pl. 20, 27–28, 21, 29 (judging by the looser locks of the mane on the lion's scalp on the obverse).

284. The figure on the first reverse is stylistically reminiscent of the Helmet group (Price, *Alexander*, nos. 625; 629a–b, 521–522 [legs of stool]); the second, of the Uranopolis, the Triton and the Monogram group (Price, ibid., nos. 522, 531, 546, 553, 606, 620, 625); the third and fourth, of the *Omikron-Kappa*, Monogram, and Grape group (Price, ibid., nos. 532a–b, 534; 572, 578, 617, 622 (figure and legs of stool), 629b; 637, 639); the fifth resembles earlier issues from Amphipolis, dated between the 290s and the 270s.

285. Newell, *DP*, 83.74–75, pl. VII, 5–6.

286. They need not have been introduced after 277 BC, as is suggested by Mathisen and Price, for Antigonos had already acquired the title of king after the death of his father in 283 BC, prior to his official rise to the Makedonian throne; see chapter 1.2. Cf. M. B. Chambers, "The first regnal year of Antigonos Gonatas," *AJPh* 75 (1954), 392 ff.

287. Lysimachos: M. Thompson, "The Mints of Lysimachus," in *Essays Robinson*, 163–182; Mørkholm, *EHC*, 81, nos. 176–177. Poliorketes: Newell, *DP*, 18–19, 22–23, 60–61, 70–75, 80, 101–103; Mørkholm, *EHC*, 778. Areus of Sparta: Grunauer and von Hoerschelmann, *Lakedaemonier*, 2.

and those in the name of Antiochos I (281–261), from Antioch and the Alexander silver coinage in the name of Seleukos I, struck at Pergamon between 279 and 271 BC.[288]

Tentative changes in the order of the legend may have taken place in Gonatas' inaugural issues. The legend initially echoes that on the silver tetradrachms of his father, with his name on the right and with his royal title on the left, but it conforms on the last three specimens to the contemporary posthumous Alexander tetradrachms, with the name of Alexander on the left. The last form of the legend is not only retained in the personal issues of Gonatas, but it also may have functioned as a prototype for the rare silver tetradrachms with Alexander types but in the name of King Areus (plate 61.4).[289] The inaugural silver coinage in the name of Antigonos cannot have been struck any earlier than the period between Gonatas' recovery of Pella from Pyrrhos in 272 BC and the demise of Areus on the battlefield in 265 BC.

The notion that these tetradrachms should be associated with the transitional gold staters and with the Pan/Athena right, *desmos,* tetradrachms, is however, very unlikely, despite the name "Antigonos" on the reverse of all these coins. This association has been put forward by Newell, Gaebler and Mathisen,[290] on the analogy of the association of the posthumous Alexander gold staters to the Monogram group of Alexander tetradrachms. It is weakened by the absence of common control marks between the Antigonid transitional gold staters and tetradrachms and the posthumous Alexanders and, secondly, by the contrast between the hasty legends on the transitional tetradrachms and the elaborate characters on the transitional staters. Moreover, the naval allusion in the *aphlaston* on the reverse of the gold specimens does not have any parallel in the tetradrachms in the name of Antigonos. Similarly, although there is a dotted border on both the Alexanders and the Athena right, *desmos* Pans, they diverge markedly in control marks, in their striking technique and in the quality of their engraving. The Alexander tetradrachms in the name of Antigonos may therefore be dissociated from the gold staters and from the Athena right, *desmos* Pans. The Alexanders in the name of Antigonos may mark an earlier incident, such as Gonatas' undisputed recovery of the Makedonian throne after the death of Pyrrhos, whereas the gold staters and *desmos* Pans may celebrate a naval victory or other major event.

6.4.2 The Introduction of the Pan Head Tetradrachms

The Pan head tetradrachms constitute the principal coinage struck under Gonatas, but attempts to establish a firm date for their introduction have only recently progressed from remarks on the iconographic allusions on the coinage to tentative observations of its internal structure and to the evidence of the hoards. The first epiphany of Pan at Delphi against the Celts[291] and the reference to τετρᾶχμα Ἀντιγόνεια in the inscriptions from the Athenian Asklepieion[292] mark 279 and 256/5 BC as the respective *termini, post* and *ante quem,* for the launching of the new silver coinage.

Mathisen suggested that the introduction date of the Pan head tetradrachms be shifted from its traditional date after the battle of Lysimacheia (277 BC) to after the death of Pyrrhos and the

288. Alexanders in the name of Antiochos I from Antioch: Newell, *WSM,* nos. 931–932. Alexanders in the name of Seleukos I at Pergamon: ibid., nos. 1531–1536.

289. Troxell, "The Peloponnesian Alexanders," ANSMN 17 (1971), 41–94, esp. 75–76, n. 68, pl. XIX, 2; Grunauer and von Hoerschelmann, *Lakedaemonier,* 2.

290. Newell, *DP,* 14–15, n. 1; Gaebler, *AMNG* III.1, 17.1–3, pl. XXXII, 21–22; Mathisen, *Silver Coinages,* 94–96, pl. 20, 27–28; 21.29.

291. Chapter 6.1.

292. *IG* II^2, 1534B, l. 231, 266, 272, 279; S. V. Tracy, "Five letter-cutters of Hellenistic Athens (230–130 B.C.)," *Hesperia* 47 (1978) 267, l. 5, 11, 15–16: ca. 215 BC; cf. Habicht, *Studien,* 34 ff.; Aleshire, *Asklepieion,* 250–305, 325.

widespread recognition of Gonatas as king of Makedonia, and linked to expenditure on the Chremonidean war.[293]

Archaeological evidence, the hoards, other coinages, the bronze coins and literary, epigraphic and other references will all help to give a clearer picture.

Internal Structure

The Pan tetradrachms fall stylistically into four main periods. The first period has obverses of a "plain style," with a schematic and flat depiction of the young head of Pan, presumably all coming from one engraver. The obverses of the next two periods become more personified: Pan's features and the "star/crescents" are rendered in relief in Period II and his features become more mature in the third period (Chapters 3.1, 4.1). Finally, to a fourth period may be dated some elegant Pans in relief with projecting chin and eyebrows, and deeply set eyes, which fit in with the "expressive" style of the last quarter of the third century (Chapter 5).

The bulk of these tetradrachms carry Athena left, with the crested helmet symbol left on the reverse. The first period ends with four die combinations of poor quality, with a monogram left on the reverse instead of the helmet (Chapter 2.2.3, A.2, nos. 167–73). The only small denomination coinage from this period is a silver drachma with the same types as the tetradrachms and with monogram ҤР. Finally, the small series of the fourth period with a winged instead of a crested helmet is associated with a few drachmae with a winged helmet left and with the letters TI right on the reverse (Chapter 5.2).

The Pan tetradrachms with the helmet symbol were presumably meant to finance military enterprises, as this was the function of the bulk of precious metal coinage in the Hellenistic period.[294] However, certain small issues of high artistic quality have been identified as "special" because of their distinct control marks. In the first place, a few tetradrachms with Athena right on the reverse have been assigned to the first period, presumably celebrating a major event (Chapter 2, nos. 174–81).[295] A second, particularly elaborate group, with a Makedonian shield decorated by "units" with three concentric "crescents" and with the legend ΒΑΣΙΛΕΩΣ ΑΝΤΙΓΟΝΟΥ around the badge, has been assigned to the third period (Chapter 4.3, nos. 127–131). The change in the direction of the *pedum* on the obverse of this group, as well as on a Pan group with a trident symbol and on that with the letter X left on the reverse (ibid., nos. 132–135), may coincide with military achievements of the king during the third period, such as the recapture of Korinth or the battle of Andros.

Assigning this coinage to its appropriate historical context involves a closer examination of the first period of the Pan head tetradrachms. Their stylistic divergence from the "dramatic style" of the 270s and their good quality suggest the introduction of the new coinage within the context of the Chremonidean War.[296] As shown elsewhere (Chapters 2.2.2, 6.2.4), 36 obverse dies were in use during this period, all combined with 12 monograms.

293. Mathisen, *Silver Coinages*, 110–114. Mathisen's suggestion is a development of Lee Avdoyan's dating of the Helmet group and of the Pan head tetradrachms to after 272 BC, in Margaret Thompson's Columbia Seminar of Spring 1971: Hyla A. Troxell, "The Peloponnesian Alexanders," *ANSMN* 17 (1971) 75, n. 68. Price has reservations in accepting the striking of the new coinage as late as 272/1 BC: *Alexander*, 141. For a summary of past views, see Paschidis, *Ποσειδῶνες και Αντίγονοι*, 236, n. 5, 238, n. 6.

294. Mathisen, *Silver Coinages*, 114–118; F. de Callataÿ, "A Quantitative Survey on Hellenistic Coinages: Recent Achievements," in Archibald et al., *MMM*, 73–91.

295. Touratsoglou assumes from their absence from hoards their early issue and short duration: *DM*, 71.

296. On the "dramatic style," see B.R.Brown, *Royal Portraits*, 11–40. Lysimachos' and Ptolemy I's coins with Alexander heads, and the portrait coins struck by Poliorketes are representative examples of the "dramatic style," which may also be observed on certain groups of the so-called later Makedonian posthumous Alexander tetradrachms.

(a) Archaeological evidence

The absence of isolated specimens from systematic excavations of sites is not puzzling, for few silver tetradrachms are found in excavations.[297]

A dating for this coinage in the late 270s BC might be supported archaeologically by the strikingly similar decoration on the known fragments of the Makedonian shields belonging to this period, i.e., from Dodona, from Vegora, from Mit Rahineh and the more recent ones from Dion and from Staro Bonče (North Makedonia), with the decoration on the obverse of the Pan head tetradrachms (Chapter 6.1; Pl. 62.a–b).[298] But they cannot be dated precisely, nor can one determine how old or current their models were, in order to achieve a closer dating for the Pans. As for the Pan heads, there is a striking stylistic similarity between Pan's bust (three-quarters facing) in the medallion in the interior omphalos of a mesomphalos cup found in the Great Tumulus at Vergina (Tomb III) and the profile heads in our Period I, Groups 1 and 2.[299] The cup's dating to the last quarter of the fourth century BC prompts us to place the first two tetradrachm groups with a young profile head of Pan at the beginning of our catalogue, but cannot fix any more accurately their exact production date (see also Chapter 2.2.3.1, Groups 1–2 (O01–O05).

(b) Hoards

The earliest hoards with Pan head tetradrachms in Makedonia and Thessaly, Verge ("Perge"), 1955 and Phayttos, 1956, are respectively dated to c. 260 and c. 260–230 BC (Chapter 6.3, Fig. 6.11; Chapter 2, Fig. 2.3b). The early date suggested by Mathisen for the Verge ("Perge"), 1955 hoard, does not stand on firm ground: Mathisen initially accepted that the Pan head tetradrachms were issued at the beginning of Gonatas' reign, in order to update this hoard from the 260s to 275–270 BC.[300] He shifted upwards the dates of the two coins which might have been issued after the 270s, that of Antiochos I and the Pan head tetradrachm. He then used the same hoard to redate the Pan head tetradrachms to the late 270s. Their introduction in the 270s is therefore based on a circular argument. Finally, a Pan head tetradrachm with Athena right included in the first lot of Thessaly, 1994 (*CH* VIII [1994], 517) has led Touratsoglou to date this lot to c. 270 BC, presumably echoing Imhoof-Blumer's conviction that the rare variation with Athena right on the reverse preceded in style the varieties with Athena left, but with no firmer supporting evidence.[301] A lower date for the Athena right variety inevitably undermines the high date for this lot (Chapter 6.3, Fig. 6.11).

The testimony of the hoards is therefore not conclusive. Their reappraisal points to a tentative *terminus ante quem* of approximately 260 BC.

297. Remarkable is the absence of Makedonian silver coins from the excavations at Athens between 264 and 261, i.e., during the siege of Athens by Gonatas, despite the presence there of the Makedonian army: K. Lönnqvist, "Studies on the Hellenistic coinage of Athens: the impact of Makedonia on the Athenian money market in the 3rd century BC," *Papers and Monographs of the Finnish Institute at Athens*, vol. VI (1997) 119–212, but the general rarity of silver tetradrachms in securely dated archaeological contexts weakens the lowering of the date of the inscription of the Inventory V of the Asklepieion at Athens from 261/0 BC (Ferguson) to the 250s. J. Kroll suggests that "most of the war currency in Athens was Macedonian" after 261 BC in and around Athens. On the circulation of Antigonid bronzes in Athens, see the present chapter, below.

298. Liampi. *MS*, 4–5, 52–55, S 2–3. Dion: D. Pantermalis, "Δίον: Ιστορικά και λατρευτικά," *AEMTh* (2009), 261–267, esp. 263–264, pl. 3–4; idem, *AEMTh* (1999), 417 ff.; Staro Bonče, Skopje: P. Juhel and D. Temelkoski, "Fragments de 'boucliers macédoniens' au nom du roi Démétrios trouvés à Staro Bonče (République de Macédoine)," *ZPE* 162 (2007), 165–178. Cf. Chapter 6.1.2.1.

299. Zimi, *Silver Plate*, 217, no. 71, cf. H. Zimi, *Macedonian Silver Plate Fourth to Second Centuries BC* (DPhil thesis, Oxford) 80, no. 44; Andronikos, *Vergina*, 212, fig. 180.

300. Chapter 6.3.

301. Touratsoglou, *DM*, pl. VI, n. 1.

(c) Other silver coinages

The difference between the monograms of the transitional Alexander tetradrachms in the name of king Antigonos and his personal issues weakens their direct association. However, the former are obverse linked to the Monogram variety of posthumous Alexander tetradrachms, with which they share a monogram, and monograms of Pans also occur on the Helmet and *Omikron-Kappa* variety of posthumous Alexander tetradrachms.

A corpus of the posthumous Alexander tetradrachms is still needed, but the systematic reconstruction of the silver issues of Antigonos Gonatas calls for a revision of Mathisen. Mathisen's remarks on the structure of the Pan head tetradrachms derive from his study of the posthumous Alexander tetradrachms struck in Makedonia in the 270s. He argues that the end of the posthumous Alexanders and the inauguration of Gonatas' personal issues in Amphipolis in approximately 271 BC is supported by the common monograms on the Helmet group of both the posthumous Alexanders and of the Pan head variety, which are thus taken as consecutive issues. Finally, the omission of the helmet, which regularly occurs as a symbol left on the reverse of the vast majority, and the transfer of monograms [monogram], [monogram], and [monogram] from the right to the left is assigned to the mint official represented by the crested helmet of the Helmet group of the posthumous Alexander tetradrachms. It is on these grounds that Mathisen places those tetradrachms at the beginning of the Pan head issues.

There appears to be some inconsistency in Mathisen's explanation of the absence of the helmet on a small number of Pan head tetradrachms. This he does by positing the engagement of the main mint official in minting the Helmet Alexander group at the time of the issue of the Pan head tetradrachms and also by assigning two specimens of poor quality to the beginning of the new types. However, the ideological burden of the new coinage introduced allegedly after the death of Pyrrhos would have required tetradrachms of a generally good quality. In fact, it may be argued that, rather than suggesting continuity between the two series, the monograms shared by the Makedonian posthumous Alexanders and by the Pan head tetradrachms may just as well imply their parallel issue, particularly as certain of the hoards discussed by Mathisen in his study of the posthumous Alexander tetradrachms are not incompatible with a later date (cf. Chapters 6.2.4, 6.3, 6.4).

Finally, the Chremonidean War need not be considered the only occasion appropriate for the introduction by Gonatas of his royal types. Financing the army and the fleet in view of the battle at Lysimacheia, and later the naval conflicts off Kos and Andros against the Ptolemies, also caused an increased need for currency.

(c) Bronze coins

Although the study of the bronze coins in the name of Antigonos Gonatas is beyond the scope of this monograph, it may be said, provisionally, that, unlike the *desmos* or the letter X of the Athena right variety, which are not attested on the bronzes, the Makedonian helmet of the Athena left variety occurs as a symbol on the reverse of many bronzes struck under Gonatas. A more detailed typological study of the Makedonian helmet on the silver and the bronze is likely to enhance our knowledge of their chronology.

(d) Literary, epigraphic and other testimonia

Further indications may be provided by literary and epigraphic *testimonia*. An argument *ex silentio* for the date of introduction of the Pan head tetradrachms is the philosopher Zeno's comparison of Attic and Alexandrine tetradrachms, dated c. 265 BC: Zeno concludes that they both have the same value, even though the former are roughly and carelessly cut, whereas the latter are more attractive and well centred.

> Ἔφασκε μὲν (sc. Ζήνων) τοὺς μὲν τῶν ἀσολοίκων λόγους καὶ ἀπηρτισμένους ὁμοίους εἶναι τῷ ἀργυρίῳ τῷ Ἀλεξανδρινῷ· εὐοφθάλμους μὲν καὶ περιγεγραμμένους καθὰ καὶ τὸ νόμισμα, οὐδὲν δὲ διὰ ταῦτα βελτίονας. τοὺς δὲ τοὐναντίον ἀφωμοίου τοῖς Ἀττικοῖς τετραδράχμοις εἰκῇ μὲν κεκομμένους καὶ σολοίκως, καθέλκειν μέντοι πολλάκις τὰς κεκαλλιγραφημένας λέξεις (Diog. Laert. 7.18 = v. Arnim., *SVF* I 81 = Wilamowitz, Antigonos 119).

Knoepfler identifies the ἀργύριον Ἀλεξανδρινὸν with the coinage with the types (generally) of Alexander, irrespective of mints. The comparison between the Attic tetradrachms and their Alexander counterparts in this passage, dated to c. 265 BC, has been justified by Knoepfler by the fact that the posthumous Alexanders, both municipal and royal, had reached the peak of their reputation by 270–265, even though they showed signs of wear.[302]

Notable is the absence of reference to the Pan tetradrachms, as representing the new valid Makedonian coinage. Knoepfler considers that the Alexander tetradrachms would have been more appropriate for comparison than the new royal issue, but it may be argued that the better quality and presumably the higher value of the fresh coinage would have rendered it equally suitable for a comparison with the Athenian tetradrachms, particularly as they also followed the Attic weight standard. The omission of the Pans may be random or to an extent justified by the more limited circulation of the newly introduced royal issues, compared to the Alexander and the Attic tetradrachms; it might, however, raise the suspicion that the Pans had not been introduced, or, at least, were not widely in use in the Athenian market by 265 BC.

In fact, the specific references to τετρᾶχμα Ἀντιγόνεια in the inventories from the Athenian Asklepieion, in 256/5 BC, 251/0, 250/49, 249/8, and 215 BC, constitute the earliest firm epigraphic testimony for Gonatas' personal types.[303] That the inventory of 256/5 BC is the first surviving record from the Asklepieion after the Chremonidean War deprives this reference to the τετρᾶχμα Ἀντιγόνεια of any value in determining the chronology of the individual Antigonid issues. These must be tetradrachms from Antigonos' main series. For one thing, the continuing references to τετρᾶχμα Ἀντιγόνεια as late as 215 BC are incompatible with the short duration of the very rare transitional issue with the Alexander types and the legend of king Antigonos on the reverse. They are presumably the same coins repeated year after year (as happens in the Delian inventories), rather than evidence that the coins were being struck as late as 215 BC.[304] Furthermore, the earliest date for the Poseidon head tetradrachms, which were also possibly struck under Gonatas, is 246 BC (Chapter 6.4.3). It is also worth noting that the types selected for the typical bronze issue of Gonatas, with the head of Athena/Pan with trophy, are variations of those on his tetradrachms.[305] The only other candidates for the issues mentioned in the inscriptions from the Asklepieion are the Pan head tetradrachms, which had therefore been introduced by 256/5 BC.

With these limitations in mind, we are left to consider three possible occasions for the introduction of the Pans between 278 BC and 256 BC, that is, 272/1, 268/7, and 265/4 BC. The rise of

302. D. Knoepfler, "Tétradrachmes attiques et argent "alexandrin' chez Diogène Laërce, première partie," *Museum Helveticum* 44.4 (1987), 241 (text); idem, "Tétradrachmes attiques et argent "alexandrin' chez Diogène Laërce, deuxième partie," *Museum Helveticum* 46 (1989) 193–230. On the Athenian context, see also Erskine, *Hellenistic Stoa*, 90.

303. See above, n. 2.

304. Particular thanks are due to Prof. Gary Reger for this remark.

305. *SNG Cop*, 1205–1213; Gaebler, *AMNG* III.2, 187.6–188.11, pl. XXXIV.4 (obv.)–XXXIV.6 (rev).

Gonatas to the Makedonian throne after the death of Pyrrhos and his preparations for the Chremonidean War have so far been taken (by Mathisen and Price) to justify the inauguration of the new coinage in 272/1 BC; on the other hand, their absence from important numismatic contexts of the early 260s and the low dates of the earliest hoards with Pan head tetradrachms allow for their introduction even during the Chremonidean War.

*** *** ***

The Historical Context

The foreign policy of Gonatas was dominated by his rivalry with Ptolemy II and III. The conflicting interests of Gonatas and Egypt in the Aegean made a clash inevitable. Ptolemaic strategy had two main strands: on the one hand, the Ptolemies instigated and supported revolts of the Greeks on the mainland against Gonatas, in order to distract the Makedonian king from the Aegean; the Chremonidean War was an outcome of this policy. At the same time, official demonstrations of wealth and power emphatically underlined the Ptolemies' attachment to thalassocracy: penteteric processions were organized in Alexandreia from 280–275 onwards[306] and silver decadrachms were struck in honor of Arsinoe Philadelphos posthumously (268 BC),[307] followed by gold octodrachms and silver tetradrachms in her name in c. 261/0 and by gold octodrachms and tetradrachms glorifying the dynasty a little earlier in the 260s.[308] Finally, the dispatch to Gonatas of a large fish and green figs by Patroklos, Ptolemy's admiral during the Chremonidean war, presumably in the context of the naval battle between Gonatas and the Ptolemies off Kos, revealed the importance that both the Antigonids and the Ptolemies attached to thalassocracy: ἢ γὰρ θαλασσοκρατεῖν ἡμᾶς φησι Πάτροκλος ἢ τῶν σύκων τρώγειν.[309]

In peninsular Greece, the wide impact of the Celtic invasion in 279 BC is demonstrated by the many manifestations of gratitude on behalf of many Greek political organizations and by the introduction at Delphi of a special celebration in memory of that event, the Soteria.[310] The "rescue

306. P. Fraser saw in these processions successive penteteric celebrations which continued into the reign of Philadelphos, the one described by Kallixenos, dating from c. 280–275 BC, being the first of the series: Fraser, *Ptol. Alex.*, I, 231–232; id., "Two Hellenistic Inscriptions from Delphi," *BCH* 78 (1954), 49–67, esp. 57–58, n. 3; Rice, *Procession*, 107 (interpretation of grand procession of 280–275 BC as a veiled warning to Gonatas of the importance of Greece and of the revitalized Korinthian League to Ptolemy, presented as liberator of the Greek cities), 186, 190–191; Will, *HPMH* I², 197 ff. Cf. Charlotte Wikander, "Pomp and Circumstance, The Procession of Ptolemaios II," *OAth* 19 (1992), 143–150; Gehrke, *GH*, 200. On the date of the first Ptolemaieia, see Hazzard, *Imagination*, 31–36, 48–49, 57–79, 109–110; eiusdem, "The Use of the Macedonian Calendar under Ptolemies V and VI," in M. Amandry and S. Hurter (eds.), *Travaux de numismatique grecque offerts à Georges Le Rider* (London, 1999), 147–159; cf. G. Hölbl, *A History of the Ptolemaic Empire,* trans. Tina Saavedra (London/New York: Routledge, 2001), 94–98; eiusdem, "Bemerkungen zur frühptolemâischen Chronologie," *Tyche* 7 (1992), 117–122.

307. On Arsinoe's death in 268 BC, cf. E. Grzybek, *Du calendrier macédonien au calendrier ptolemaique, problèmes de chronologie hellénistique*, Heft 20, Basel: F. Reinhardt, 1990, 103–112; Hazzard, *Ptolemaic Coins*, 4.

308. Mørkholm, *EHC*, 102–103; Hazzard, *Ptolemaic Coins*, 4–7, 29–33, 75–81; Hyla A. Troxell, "Arsinoe's Non-Era," *ANSMN* 28 (1983), 35–70; J. N. Svoronos, *Τά νομίσματα τοῦ κράτους τῶν Πτολεμαίων* (Athens, 1904–8), vol. I, 64–74, nos. 408–485.

309. The anecdote is recorded by Phylarchos: Athen. 8.334a = *FGH* 81 F 1. Buraselis, *HM*, 159 ff. Cf. F. W. Walbank, "Sea-power and the Antigonids," in Adams and Borza, *Macedonian Heritage*, 213–215; F. W. Walbank, "Antigonus Gonatas: The Naval Situation," in Hammond and Walbank, *Macedonia* III, 291, n. 6.

310. Kos: decree ordering special offerings at Delphi and in Kos (April/July 278): *Syll*³ 398. Aitolians: dedications at Delphi, of a) enemy arms: Paus. 10.19.4; b) trophy and image of armed Aitolia: Paus. 10.18.8; c) statues of most of their generals, images of Artemis and Athena, two images of Apollo: Paus. 10.15.2; d) erection of monument at Thermon. Athens: painted portrait: Paus. 1.3.5; dedication of shield of Athenian Kydias to Zeus Eleutherios: Paus. 10.21.5. Patrae: statue of Apollo from the spoils taken from the Celts: Paus. 7.20.6. Delphi: Introduction of Soteria. Lise Hannestad, "Greeks and the Celts: The Creation of a Myth," in Per Bilde et al.,*Centre and Periphery*, 15–38, esp. 15–18; *Scholten,*

of the Greeks" from the Celts in 279 BC recalled similar themes from the Persian Wars, and an analogy developed between the Celts of the third century BC and the Persians of the fifth. Pausanias, for instance, claims that the Celts at Delphi imitated Persian military tactics (10.19.11). He also argues that the number of Greeks who fought against Xerxes at Thermopylai was comparable to those who opposed the Celts (10.20.2–5). Finally, Polybios recognizes the combination of these two events in Greek history as contributing to the idea of the common cause of the "freedom of the Greeks": καὶ γὰρ τοὺς τὴν Περσῶν ἔφοδον ἐπὶ τὴν Ἑλλάδα καὶ Γαλατῶν ἐπὶ Δελφοὺς εἰς μνήμην καὶ παράδοσιν ἡμῖν ἀγαγόντας οὐ μικρὰ μεγάλα δ' οἴομαι συμβεβλῆσθαι πρὸς τοὺς ὑπὲρ τῆς κοινῆς τῶν Ἑλλήνων ἐλευθερίας ἀγῶνας (2.35.7).

That the Persian legend served as a prototype for the development of the Delphic legend is shown by the fact that many of the victors' acts imitated previous acts performed during the Persian Wars: the dedication at the Delphic sanctuary of enemy arms by the Aitolians, for instance, echoes that of the Athenians after Marathon.[311] Moreover, the conclusion of the defensive treaty among the Lakedaimonians, the Athenians, and their respective allies in 268/7 BC was legitimized through appeal to similar coalitions of the Greeks in the past, presumably those during the Persian and the Lamian Wars.[312] A return to the themes of the political discourse after the Persian Wars may also be seen in the revived efforts of the allied Greeks to preserve the κοινὴν τ[ῶν] Ἑλλήνων ἐλευθερίαν and ὁμόνοιαν on the eve of the Chremonidean War.[313]

It may be argued that the memory of the Persian Wars was further revived and transformed in relation to the growing opposition of the Greeks to Gonatas in the early 260s. The allusions to τοὺς καταλύειν ἐπιχειροῦντας τούς τε νόμους καὶ τὰς πατρίους ἑκάστοις πολιτείας and to τοὺς νῦν ἠδικηκότας καὶ παρεσπονδηκότας τὰς πόλεις in the Chremonidean Decree of 268/7 BC presumably refer to the Makedonian king, whereas Ptolemy II is presented as σπουδάζων ὑπὲρ τῆς κοινῆς τ[ῶν] Ἑλλήνων ἐλευθερίας.[314]

This turning of the Greek cities to the Ptolemies against Gonatas had been anticipated by honors paid to pro-Ptolemaic citizens in the 270s and early 260s. With regard to Athens, in particular, for which most evidence survives, the decree in honour of Laches' father Demochares (271/0), who had played a leading role in the revolt against Demetrios Poliorketes in 287/6,[315] and the dedication in the Stoa of Zeus Eleutherios at Athens of the shield of Leokritos, one of the liberators of Athens from the Antigonid garrison at the Mouseion in 287 BC,[316] may be regarded as parts of the anti-Makedonian atmosphere of the 270s. Finally, the tribute paid by the Athenians to Kallias, son of Thymochares, of Sphettos, a "democrat" who had consistently favored Ptolemy II, had been in

Politics of Plunder, 33–34. The head of Apollo on the obverse of silver coins struck in Rome between 275 and 270 BC might also illustrate the wide impact of the Celtic attack on Delphi on the western Mediterranean; on the coins, see Crawford, *RRC*, table V, nos. 18, 19. Development of the myth of sack of Delphi in Italy during the second century BC: Flacelière, *Aitoliens*, 102. See also chapter 6.1.

311. Paus. 10.19.4: ὅπλα δὲ τῶν ἐπιστυλίων χρυσᾶ, Ἀθηναῖοι μὲν τὰς ἀσπίδας ἀπὸ τοῦ ἔργου τοῦ ἔργου τοῦ Μαραθῶνι ἀνέθεσαν. Αἰτωλοὶ δὲ τὰ τε ὄπισθεν καὶ τὰ ἐν ἀριστερᾷ Γαλατῶν δὴ ὅπλα... Cf. Habicht, *Athens*, 143–144.

312. *IG* II², 687 = *Staatsvertr.* III.476 = *Syll*³ 434/5, l. 9–16: ἐπειδὴ πρότερον... καὶ τὰς πατρίους ἑκάστοις πολιτείας. Cf. Habicht, *Athens*, 144.

313. Ibid.: ὑπὲρ τῆς κοινῆς τ[ῶν] Ἑλλήνων ἐλευθερίας; l. 33: ὅπως οὖν κοινῆς ὁμονοίας γενομένης τοῖς Ἕλλησι.

314. *IG* II², 687 = *Staatsvertr.* III.476 = Dittenberger, ibid., l. 15–16, 33; 19. Cf. Habicht, *Athens*, 143–144. See also Erskine, *Hellenistic Stoa*, 90–95.

315. Plut., *Mor.* 850f–851f.

316. Paus. 1.26.2; Jessen, s. v. "Eleutherios," *RE* V 2 (1905) 2348–2349; K. Buraselis, "Γλαύκων Ἐτεοκλέους μετηλλαχώς, Παρατηρήσεις στην επιγραφή,"*BCH* (1975), 53–53," *AE* 1982 (1983), 158, n. 5. The exact date of the dedication is not known.

his service in 270/69 BC and provided the Athenians with military aid, money and corn from the Ptolemies,[317] fits the same pattern.

The enmity towards the Antigonids found eloquent ways of expression in themes drawn from the Persian Wars. The fish and green figs sent by Patroklos to Gonatas, for instance, recall that the Skythians had sent to Dareios during the Skythian expedition a bird, an arrow and a frog.[318] After the end of the Chremonidean War, the Athenian Glaukon, explicitly a supporter of Ptolemy II, received honours both from the Koinon of the Hellenes at Plataiai as "champion of Greek independence and unity,"[319] and from Ptolemy III at Olympia.[320] Finally, the Troizenian version of the Themistokles Decree may also be a product of the same historical context.[321] All these incidents, together with the dedication of an armed Aitolia on Celtic and Makedonian shields at Delphi in commemoration of Athenian resistance to the Celts,[322] may be taken to suggest that the Makedonians, as well as the Celts, now tended to be identified with the Persians.

The growing opposition of the Greeks to the Makedonians culminated in the Chremonidean War (268/7–262/1 BC) and in the final capitulation of Athens to Gonatas. The retreat of Lakedaimonian troops to the Peloponnese after the unsuccessful mutiny of Celtic mercenaries against Gonatas at Megara (Just. 26.2.7), then the retreat of the Ptolemaic fleet, and finally the death of King Areus I at Korinth in 265/4 BC were major turning points in the war.[323] During the second phase, the Ptolemies systematically avoided direct military confrontation with the Antigonids on land; Sparta's severely reduced support for the besieged Athens was offset by the orchestration of minor revolts and mutinies, in order to distract Gonatas from the destruction of the Attic *chora*. The temporary treaty of Gonatas with Athens ended with a second invasion of Attika and the final capitulation of the city (Paus. 3.6.6; Polyaen. 4.6.20).

Central Greece plays a major role during the Chremonidean War: revolts and general reaction to Gonatas effectively distracted the Makedonian king from the siege of Athens. The increased prestige and dramatic expansion of the influence of the Aitolians (from the Ionian Sea to the Malian Gulf and to Euripos) after their opposition to the Celts at Delphi entitled them to control the

317. Kallias had led the revolt against Poliorketes in 287/6 BC: T. L. Shear, *Kallias of Sphettos and the Revolt in Athens in 286 BC*, Hesperia, Supplement 17 (1978), 3–4, l. 40–78 = *SEG* 28 (1978), 60, 11.19 ff., 40 ff., 49 ff., 66 ff.; Habicht, *Unters.*, 48, 85; Gabbert, *Greek Hegemony*, 146–147; K. Buraselis, "Ambivalent Roles of Centre and Periphery: Remarks on the Relation of the Cities of Greece with the Ptolemies until the end of Philometor's Age," in Per Bilde et al., *Centre and Periphery*, 252–253. This decree is comparable to that in honor of Phaidros, Kallias' brother, who was on good terms with Poliorketes but at least neutral towards Gonatas in 255 BC (*IG* II^2 682=*Syll*^{3}, 409).

318. Cf. n. 196.

319. Cf. n. 314.

320. *Syll*^{3} 462; K. Buraselis, "Γλαύκων Ἐτεοκλέους μετηλλαχώς," *BCH* (1975), 52–53, *AE* 1982 (1983), 136–9; Habicht, *Athens*, 155–156, n. 122.

321. The appropriation of the "freedom of the Greeks" by the Ptolemies in the third century BC is suggested by a number of inscriptions, see Meiggs and Lewis, *GHI*^{2}, 23, l. 14–16, *BCH* 99 (1975), 53, 22–24; *Syll*^{3} 390 = *Staatsvertr.* 476, l. 81; N. Robertson, "The Decree of Themistokles in its Contemporary Setting," *Phoenix* 36 (1982), 31–32. A. Erskine sees the influence of the Stoic School in the concepts of *homonoia*, *eleutheria* and *douleia* in the Chremonidean Decree and in the inscription honouring Glaukon, but he does not ignore their origin in ideas of the fourth century BC: *Hellenistic Stoa*, 94–95.

322. Paus. 10.18.7; A. J. Reinach, "Un monument delphien. L' Étolie sur les trophées gaulois de Kallion," *JIAN* 13 (1911), 177–240; Liampi, *MS*, 139–140, n. 392 (M 90–91).

323. On the death of Areus, see P. Trog. *Prol.* 26: *Ut defectores Gallos Megaris (sc. Antigonus) delevit regemque Lacedaemonium Area Corinthi interfecit*; Plut. *Agis*, 3.4; Diod. 20.29.1. W. W. Tarn dates the event to 265 BC ("Telokles and the Athenian archons of 288/7–262/1 BC," *JHS* 40 (1920), 150–159), whereas the next year is favored by P. Cloché ("La politique extérieure de Lacédémoine depuis la mort d' Agis III jusqu'à celle d' Acrotatos, fils d' Areus Ier,"*REA* 48 (1946), 29–61, esp. 52 ff.). A critical presentation of the sources and bibliography appears in Heinen, *Unters.*, 170, 174–175. Cf. Chr. Ehrenberg, s. v. "Sparta," *RE* III.A (1929), col. 1423 ff.

Delphic Amphictyony between 280 and 190 BC.[324] They may have opposed the Makedonian king partly, at least, because their interests as pirates conflicted with his naval activities and because of his cooperation, at least before he gained the throne, with pirates from the Black Sea.[325] However, they generally avoided direct opposition to the Makedonians.[326] They do not figure among the supporters of the Chremonidean Decree, although they did conclude a defensive treaty with the Athenians, presumably during the first phase of the war.[327]

This hostility between Aitolians and Makedonians is illustrated in the participation of the Aitolian allies in, and in the absence of the Makedonian allies from, the *pylaiai* of the Delphic Amphictyony at least during the first part of the third century.[328] The disappearance of the Thessalians from the Amphictyonic records, for instance, is attributed to the reconquest of Thessaly by Gonatas, in approximately 278/7 or 277/6 BC.[329] The opposition of the Aitolians to the Makedonian king possibly accelerated in the mid-260s, after the probable destruction of Eretria by Gonatas in 265 BC, when the Aitolians honored an Eretrian, possibly Menedemos.[330] Finally, in 264/3 BC, three Aitolians, Nikophon, Euryos and Theodoros, are mentioned as *proxenoi* at Histiaia.[331]

*** *** ***

The shifts in the balance of power among the Antigonids, the Ptolemies, and the Central Greeks help determine the date of the introduction of Gonatas's personal coin types. A date of c. 271 BC may lead one to interpret the Pan head tetradrachms as part of the preparations for the Chremonidean War. This date is not incompatible with the later dates of the hoards, but is perhaps weakened by the paucity of obverse dies used during the first period of issue, assuming that no other silver

324. On the effective Aitolian resistance to the Celts at Delphi, see Flacelière, *Aitoliens*, 93, 104–107; Scholten, *Politics of Plunder*, 33–34; J. B. Scholten, "Macedon and the Mainland, 280–221," in Erskine, *Companion*, 137–144. Expansion of Aitolians: Flacelière, *Aitoliens*, 191 ff.; institutional aspects of expansion: Larsen, *GFS*, 202. Aitolian version of Celtic attack at Delphi: C. Champion, "Polybius, Aetolia and the Gallic attack on Delphi (279 BC)," *Historia* 45 (1996), 316–318; Scholten, *Politics of Plunder*, 31–37. 94.

325. On the cooperation of Antigonos with pirates, see, for instance, Polyaen. 4.16.18; P. Trog. *Prol.* 25; cf. *SEG* 24 (1969), 154, the decree for the strategos Epichares. Cf. Hammond and Walbank, *Macedonia* III, 259, 279, n. 3, 283–389; Gabbert, *Greek Hegemony*, 240–244; Heinen, *Unters.*, 157 ff.

326. Flacelière, *Aitoliens*, 180.

327. *IG* IX², part 1, no. 176. D. Knoepfler dates the treaty between 268 and 266 BC. He assigns the absence of evidence regarding any active participation of the Aitolians during the first phase of the war to the paucity of sources from the first half of the third century: "Les relations des cités Eubéennes avec Antigone Gonatas et la chronologie delphique au début de l' époque Étolienne," *BCH* 119.1 (1995), 137–156, esp. 150–152.

Before the conclusion of the treaty, an Athenian embassy was sent to the Aitolians: *Staatsvertr.*, 470 a 4. D. Knoepfler dates it to the beginning of the Chremonidean war, pointing out that the Athenians would have had difficulty in sending the embassy after the beginning of their siege by Gonatas: ibid., esp. 151, n. 83. It may be argued, however, that the various distractions Antigonos had to tackle during the siege of Athens and the concomitant retirement of Makedonian troops would have allowed time for the dispatch of an Athenian embassy to the Aitolians even during the Chremonidean War.

328. F. Lefèvre, "La chronologie du IIIe siècle à Delphes d' après les actes amphictyoniques (280–200)," *BCH* 119.1 (1995), 161–208, esp. 166, n. 16, *contra* the assumed friendship between the Aitolians and the Makedonians proposed by Flacelière, *Aitoliens*, 180–191.

329. D. Knoepfler, ibid., 170, no. 14.

330. F. Lefèvre, ibid., 171, nos. 18–19. Habicht, *Athens*, 143, n. 80 considers the siege of Eretria to have been earlier. On the destruction of Eretria by Gonatas, see S. Schmidt, "A group or Early Hellenistic Pottery from a Well in Eretria," *Ε' Επιστημονική Συνάντηση για την Ελληνιστική κεραμεική*, Χανιά, 6–13 Απριλίου 1997, 82; P. Ducrey and S. Schmidt, "Les activités de l' École Suisse d' archéologie en Grèce 1996," *Antike Kunst* (1997), Heft 2, 103–107, with further bibliography on the at least partial destruction of Eretria by Gonatas around 265 BC. On the two hoards with similar content, see P. G. Kalligas, "Ἀνασκαφή στην Ερέτρια 1981," *AE* 122 (1983[1985]), 113–116; Mando Karamessini-Oikonomidou, "Δύο νομισματικοί θησαυροί ἀπό τήν ἀνασκαφή στην Ἐρέτρια," *AE* 122 (1983 [1985]), 137–147.

331. *Syll*³ 492; F. Lefèvre, ibid., 177, n. 64.

coins accompanied the Pan head tetradrachms after their introduction. In other words, if the Pan head tetradrachms started in c. 272/1 BC to replace the Makedonian posthumous Alexander tetradrachms, as argued by Mathisen, the thirty-six obverse dies of the first period would have had to finance the eight years of the war. The average annual production of 4.33 obverse dies during the Chremonidean War would be lower than the annual use of 20 or 25 obverse dies of posthumous Alexander tetradrachms in the preceding period,[332] whereas the financial requirements of the Chremonidean War would have been no smaller than those of Gonatas' struggle to establish himself on the Makedonian throne.

The single issue of drachmae associated with the early Pans carrying monogram ΗΡ on their reverse might tempt one to relate the introduction of the Pans to a time when Gonatas laid claim to Asia Minor, where drachmae were a popular denomination. His early presence in Karia is suggested by an inscription from Kaunos, the only known decree of a city in Asia Minor mentioning a regnal date of an Antigonos; it is dated to "the fifteenth regnal year of king Antigonos" (βασιλεύοντος Ἀντιγόν[ου ἔτει πεντεκαιδεκά[τ]ω[ι]), that is, according to P. Frei and C. Marek, to 268/7 BC.[333] It is confirmed in the final publication of the inscription that it refers to Gonatas, one might regard the Pans as contemporary with this early presence of Gonatas in Karia; the single surviving drachma from this period, however, does not lend much support to this association.

The beginning of the new silver coinage during the Chremonidean War in 268/7 BC, is indeed justified by the increased financial needs of the Antigonids in view of the siege of Athens and of the naval preparations against the Ptolemies. Whether Gonatas built a fleet in order to challenge Egypt or whether, forced by the opposition of the Greeks, he built a fleet during the war in order to restore the *status quo* in the Aegean,[334] he is known to have invaded Attika with a military force, followed by ships (στρατιᾶ-ναυσίν, Paus. 1.1.1; πεζῷ-ναυσίν, Paus. 3.6.4).[335]

The importance of this war could lead one to assume that some at least of the expenditure on it by the Antigonid side was made with posthumous Alexander tetradrachms (cf. chapters 6.4.1, 7); the introduction of new silver coin types and the abundant production of silver and gold coins by Gonatas' rival, Ptolemy II, in the 260s might provide a useful yardstick for the higher financial needs during their military conflict.[336] The Pans would have thus functioned as a supplement to the existing silver coinage. Might one lower their beginning even further?

The outbreak of the second phase of the war in approximately 265/4 BC is worth considering: the siege of Athens was still under way and the Spartan front was significantly weakened after the death of King Areus, but the Ptolemaic fleet under Patroklos was still in the Aegean. A demonstration of power in a presumably contemporary procession in honor of Ptolemy in

332. Mathisen, *Silver Coinages*, 116–117, table 16.

333. P. Frei and C. Marek, "Die karisch-griechische Bilingue von Kaunos: eine zweisprachige Staatsurkunde des 4. Jahrhunderts v. Chr.," *Kadmos* 36.1 (1997), 1–89; Ivo Kajnal, "Die karisch-griechische Bilingue 44* aus Kaunos: Ein erster Augenschein," *Kadmos* 37 (1998), 141–166; P. Frei and C. Marek, „Die karisch-griechische Bilingue von Kaunos. Ein neues Textfragment," *Kadmos* 37 (1998), 1–18. The dating of the first fragment is based on (a) the similarity of the letter forms to a decree of Stratonikeia, dated after 268 BC, that is, according to the Seleukid Era; (b) the fact that Monophthalmos dated his years from the death of Philip Arrhidaios in November 317 BC.

334. H. Heinen and Ed. Will see in the construction of an Antigonid fleet the cause of the Chremonidean war (Heinen, *Unters.*, 100; Will, *HPMH* I², 219–121), whereas Chr. Habicht interprets it as a result of the outbreak of the war (*Unters.*, 62–63, n. 79.); F. W. Walbank, "Sea-power and the Antigonids," in Adams and Borza, *Macedonian Heritage*, 219–220. The ships, however, with which Gonatas sailed in order to receive his father's urn in the Kyklades (Plut. *Dem.* 55) and his aid to Pyrrhos (Just. 17.2.13) suggest that Gonatas apparently had at least a small fleet in Greece after 288/7 BC: Buraselis, *HM*, 152 ff. Cf. Chapter 2.0.

335. Heinen, *Unters.*, 167–169.

336. See n. 18.

Alexandreia in c. 265/4 may have influenced the Greek cities in favor of Ptolemy.[337] Finally, the revolt of the Celtic mercenaries at Megara during the siege of Athens in 265 BC could have offered Gonatas the opportunity to recall his role in countering the Celts both during their invasion of Delphi and later, in his personal victory at Lysimacheia, by introducing Pan on his coinage.[338]

Gonatas' authority in Southern Greece was rendered precarious by revolts in Central Greece during the second phase of the Chremonidean War. The growing hostility of the Aitolians to Gonatas, in addition to the revolt of Alexander the Molossian and his invasion of Makedonia apparently dictated the temporary treaty between the Makedonian king and Athens. Presumably this is the context of Patroklos' arrogant remark to Gonatas about the importance of thalassocracy and of the major victory of the Makedonian king over the Ptolemaic fleet off Kos.

*** *** ***

Iconography and policy

Was the selection of the Pan/Athena types significant? Which occasion would have been most appropriate for Gonatas to introduce his personal types, and so replace the existing coin tradition? It has already been shown that there is no contemporary evidence for the introduction of the Pan head tetradrachms immediately after the accession of Gonatas (Chapter 6.1). Whether Gonatas was then in control of the Makedonian mines and forests, or whether he was in a position to issue coinage in the city soon after his recovery of Makedonia, remains uncertain.[339]

The combination of Pan with the stars on the obverse of the Pan head tetradrachms and the star units on the Makedonian shield recall comparisons made in literature between the large numbers of the Celtic invaders and stars, as in Kallimachos' *Hymn to Delos*.[340] Pan, worshipped by Athenians and later by Antigonids and Ptolemies alike,[341] recalls both the warrior god's *epiphaneia* recorded by Pausanias in the Celtic attack on Delphi under Brennos, in 279 BC (Chapter 6.1), and his intervention in the battle of Marathon in 490 BC, after which Pan had received great honors in Athens. Herodotos 6.105, copied by Pausanias 1.28.4 and 8.54.6, records Pan's *epiphaneia* to the ἡμεροδρόμος Pheidippides and his promise to come and fight with the Athenians at Marathon. Pan is also mentioned in Herodotos' introduction to his account of the Persian defeat at Salamis and at Psyttaleia.[342]

The divergences in the literary accounts of the resistance to the Celtic attack at Delphi presumably result from their chronological distance from the event and illustrate the manipulation of the retreat of the Celts by diverse political entities.[343] The emphasis attached to the divine protection of the sanctuary from the Celtic threat was presumably meant to downplay the role of the Aitolians

337. See n. 16.

338. On the Celtic mutiny at Megara, see Paus. 3.6.5. On Gonatas' role countering the Celts at Delphi and at Lysimacheia, see Chapter 2.1.

339. Cf. Chapters 1.2, 7.

340. Kallim. 4.171–6, esp. l. 174–176; see Chapter 2.1.

341. Dedications to Pan: Fraser, *Ptol. Alex.*, 562, 586. Terracotta heads present Ptolemies (I [posthumous], II and IV) as Pan: Svenson, *Darstellungen*, 47–48, Kat. Nr. 57, pl. 22; Kat. Nr. 59, pl. 22; Kat. Nr. 87, pl. 54. A Paneion was also constructed at Alexandreia probably by Ptolemy II: Fraser, *Ptol. Alex.*, 26; 29–30, n. 209.

342. Str. 9.21 (p. 398); *AJA* 7 (1903), 286; A. J. Reinach, "Un monument delphien. L'Étolie sur les trophées gaulois de Kallion," *JIAN* 13 (1911), 177–240, pl. 5; Borgeaud, *The Cult of Pan*, 286. On parallels between the epiphanies during the battle of 480 BC with that of the sack of Delphi: P. Roussel, *BCH* (1931), 100–103; Nachtergael, *Galates*, 82–292; Scholten, *Politics of Plunder*, 40.

343. On the surviving tradition and on the historicity of the literary accounts of the sack of Delphi, see Flacelière, *Aitoliens*, 93–106; Nachtergael, *Galates*, 82–106, 175–205.

in countering the Celts, as was recognized by Polybios. The placing of Pan, rather than Apollo, on the obverse of the silver coins suggests a chronological distance from the Celtic invasion and shows that it was the Athenian version of the battle, as preserved by Pausanias, that Gonatas tried to appropriate.[344] The fact that the account of Herodotos of Pan's *epiphaneia* to Pheidippides during the Persian Wars served as a prototype for Pausanias suggests that by the time of Pausanias the parallelism between the Celtic wars and the Persian wars was a commonplace.

In view of the rising Greek opposition to Makedonian rule, the Delphic legend was dynamically rephrased, though potentially not in favor of Gonatas. Parallels with the Persian Wars were thus manipulated in the 260s in order to legitimize Makedonian claims to mainland Greece and to the Aegean. By emphasizing the critical role of Makedonia in the Gallic invasions, Gonatas legitimized his claim to parts of mainland Greece and the Aegean against the Ptolemies, just as Athens in the fifth century BC had projected her contribution to the defeat of the Persians.

The ideological references latent in the new coin types, the Pan head tetradrachms, thus accord with the revival of the Persian Wars in the historical memory of the Greeks during the Celtic wars of the 270s and 260s.[345] They constitute Gonatas' eloquent reply to the attempts of the Greeks to draw a parallel between the Makedonians and the Persians, by showing the Celts as parallel to the Persians.

The appropriation of the Delphic and Persian legends by the Makedonians on these coins and the projection of a recent major chapter of Greek history from which the Ptolemies were absent confirmed the Makedonians' Greek identity in opposition to their Egyptian rivals. Moreover, the Makedonian shield framing the obverse of the coins may have been meant to stress that the epilogue in this chapter was written by Gonatas at Lysimacheia: the end to the Celtic invasions in Greece was marked by his personal victory over the Celts, subsequent to which Gonatas' royalty was recognized in Makedonia, his "spear-won land."[346]

*** *** ***

Concluding remarks

To recapitulate, the outer limits of the date-span for the introduction by Gonatas of his new coin types, 279–256/5 BC, may be refined to between 268/7 and 265/4 BC. It has been shown that the introduction of the coins in 277 BC, after the battle of Lysimacheia and Gonatas' elevation to the throne, has no firm basis. The ideological burden of the coinage and particularly the allusions to the Persian and the Celtic wars suggest its introduction at a time of a lively interaction between the two legends, in response to an implicit identification of the Makedonians with the Celts by the Greeks of the South: the appropriation and adaptation of the Delphic legend to that of the Persian Wars, implicit in the image of Pan on the obverse of the new Makedonian coins, legitimized the participation of the Makedonians in the Greek world and countered any attempt to compare them with barbarians, Persians or Celts.

344. See Chapter 2.1.

345. Paus. 10.19.11: Ταῦτα ἐμοὶ δοκεῖν ἐνομίσθη τοῖς Γαλάταις ἐς μίμησιν τοῦ ἐν Πέρσαις ἀριθμοῦ τῶν μυρίων, οἵ ἐκαλοῦντο Ἀθάνατοι; 10.20.2–5: Πάρεστιν δὲ, ὅστις ἐθέλει καὶ ἀνταριθμῆσαι τοὺς ἐπὶ βασιλέα Ξέρξην ἐς Πύλας καὶ τοὺς τότε ἐναντία Γαλατῶν ἀθροισθέντας.

346. For the theory of "spear-won land" in the Hellenistic period and for further examples of the development of such theories from the Seleukid Empire, cf., for instance, A. Mehl, "Δορίκτητος χώρα. Kritiscche Bemerkungen zum "Speerwerb' in Politik und Völkerrecht der Hellenistischen Epoche," *Ancient Society* 11–12 (1981), 183–212; F. W. Walbank, "Monarchies and Monarchic Ideas," in *CAH* VII .1², 66; E. G. Turner, "Ptolemaic Egypt," ibid., 122; n. 5; J. K. Davies, "Cultural, Social and Economic Features of the Hellenistic World," ibid., 296, n. 238.

This leads one to associate the introduction of individual types by Antigonos Gonatas with his political activities *vis-à-vis* the Greeks of the South. The inauguration of the Pan head tetradrachms was an essential part of the political discourse developed in view of or during the Chremonidean War. The Pan head tetradrachms may be regarded as generally contemporary with the Chremonidean Decree, in which the latent enmity to Gonatas is defined through support of Ptolemy II, who is now presented as "protector of the common freedom of the Greeks," and possibly in some relation to the treaty between the (anti-Makedonian) Aitolians and the Athenians. It is at that moment that the absence of the Ptolemies from the defence of Greece against the Celts in the early 270s would have been worth pointing out.

The significance of the iconography of the coinage thus shifts: rather than in direct relation to contemporary events, it acquires a special ideological burden later.[347] One may, in fact, be tempted to date the new coinage during the first phase of the war, between 268/7 and 265/4 BC; a revival of the Celtic legend on the eve of the new war and particularly on the occasion of the revolt of the Celtic mercenaries at Megara may have inspired the issue of the new coinage. This date agrees with the clues provided by the numismatic, archaeological, literary and epigraphical evidence and is justified by the increased financial needs of the Makedonian state for the military operations both in mainland Greece and against the Ptolemies for control over the Aegean. This high demand for cash at this stage would imply that some at least of the initial expenditure on the Chremonidean War was made with other coinage, presumably posthumous Alexander coins struck in Makedonia.

The Delphic allusions on the Pan head tetradrachms and the wide impact of the Celtic invasions in the Greek world justified the continuation of these types after the death of Gonatas, throughout the entire confrontation between the Ptolemies and Antigonids in the Aegean. The defensive character of both the Makedonian shield on the obverse and of the Makedonian helmet on the reverse of these coins is reminiscent of later literary identifications of Makedonia as a "shield" of Greece from barbaric invasions from the North.[348] It was only the redistribution of the political cards at the time of Philip V, and the emergence of Rome as the new threat to the Antigonid kingdom, that prompted a change and the replacement of Pan by Perseus, the protector hero of Philip V and his son, as the badge of the Makedonian shield on the last tetradrachms of the Makedonian kings.[349]

347. The developing analogy between the Persian/Celtic legend of "barbaric invasions" in the Greek world may also explain the crescent, which occurs as a symbol left on the reverse of the Mu variety of Makedonian silver posthumous Alexander tetradrachms. The crescent occurs as a symbol on silver drachmae of Philip II, from Amphipolis, c. 355–349/8: Le Rider, *Philippe II*, 380, no. 110. This may be taken as an echo of that on the silver Athenian owls subsequent to their victory over the Persians: Starr, *Athenian Coinage*, 10–12; Kraay, *Archaic and Classical Greek Coins*, 64–65, pl. 11.187; Wartenberg, *After Marathon*, 6; N. Moutsopoulos and G. Dimitrokallis, *Η Ελληνική ημισέληνος / Le croissant grec* (Athens, 1988), 73–81, 111–115. Crescent as symbol of Marathon or Salamis: Seltman, *Athens*, 102–104; J. P. Six, "Monnaies grecques, inédites et incertaines," *NC*[3] 15 (1895), 176 (Marathon); H. Sorge, "Der Mond auf den Münzen von Athen," *JNG* 2 (1950/1), 7–13 (Salamis). One might therefore be tempted to date the Mu group to the time when the parallelism of the Chremonidean with the Persian wars was well under way. *Contra* Starr, ib., Franke and Hirmer, *GM*, 89 (crescent as ornament).

348. Plb. 9.35.3: ὅτι γὰρ αἰεί ποτ᾽ἄν ἐν μεγάλοις κινδύνοις τὰ κατὰ τοὺς Ἕλληνας, εἰ μὴ Μακεδόνας εἴχομεν πρόφραγμα καὶ τὰς (τῶν) παρὰ τούτοις βασιλέων φιλοτιμίας, τίς οὐ γιγνώσκει; C. Champion, "Polybius, Aetolia and the Gallic attack on Delphi," *Historia* 45 (1996), 316–328, esp. 323–324.

349. For bibliography on the coinage of Philip V and Perseus, see chapter 6.5.

6.4.3 The Introduction of the Poseidon head Tetradrachms

Much ink has been spilt in determining when the Poseidon head tetradrachms were introduced. Leaving aside Mionnet's attribution of this coinage to Antigonos Monophthalmos, which has been made unlikely by the presence of these coins in hoards of the 240s or 220s, our choice is confined to the two kings named Antigonos, Gonatas and Doson (cf. Chapter 6.1). Until 1960, Imhoof-Blumer's attribution of both Pans and Poseidons to Gonatas was universally accepted. His suggested sequence was as follows: Pan/Athena right, after Lysimacheia (277 BC)—Poseidon/Apollo on prow, trident, immediately after Kos (then dated to 265 BC)—Pan/Athena left, Poseidon/Apollo on prow, later issues under Gonatas.[350] Head, who had initially related the Poseidon head coins to Doson's Karian expedition (227 BC), accepted Imhoof-Blumer's dating of this coinage to the reign of Antigonos Gonatas, and Gaebler, following Tarn, suggested that both series continued down to Doson.[351] In 1960, Merker reverted to Head's original assignation of the Poseidon head tetradrachms to the Karian expedition of Antigonos Doson, but doubts were cast on his argumentation by Ehrhardt, Buraselis, and later by Mathisen.[352] Mathisen, in particular, reassigns the Poseidons to Gonatas and argues that one or other of these tetradrachm types may have continued under Demetrios II and Doson. A little earlier, Boehringer had suggested that the Poseidons were struck by Doson, but he implied that the Pans were continued under Demetrios II.[353]

The debate was renewed in the 1990s. In 1994, the chronological and geographic arrangement of all the known hoards with Pan head and Poseidon head tetradrachms led Touratsoglou to relate the introduction of the Poseidons to Doson's expenditure subsequent to the Karian expedition.[354] Recently, Paschidis proposed that the Poseidon head tetradrachms began immediately after Gonatas' naval victory over the Ptolemies near Andros, in 245 BC.[355]

Past chronologies have been based on one or more of the following criteria: (i) the evidence of the hoards; (ii) the style of the coins and the internal numismatic evidence; (iii) the iconography. Underlying all reconstructions has been the uncertainty in the chronology of the two naval conflicts between the Antigonid and the Ptolemaic fleets, off Kos and Andros respectively, for control of the Aegean. The need for a corpus of the respective issues, however, has been widely recognized as a prerequisite for a definitive discussion.[356]

(1) The evidence of the hoards

The first to consider the hoard evidence was Dorothy M. Cox. In her discussion of the Gordion, 1951 hoard (cf. Chapter 6.3), she accepts that both Pan heads and Poseidon heads in the name of "king Antigonos" were inaugurated under Gonatas and continued down to Doson. She dates accordingly the worn Pan tetradrachm of this hoard to the late reign of Gonatas and the two Poseidons, both in excellent condition, to the time of Doson.[357] A consideration of three hoards, Larissa

350. Imhoof-Blumer, *Akarnanien*, 39, n. 17; *MG*, 123–131.

351. Head, *HN*², 231–232; Gaebler, *AMNG* III.2, 187; Tarn, *AG*, 463–464.

352. Ehrhardt, *Studies*, 75–81; Buraselis, *HM*, 163, n. 182, 164; Mathisen, *Pan Heads and Poseidon Heads*, 29–35, who leaves it open whether the Pans continued after Gonatas.

353. *Chronologie*, 99, 153.

354. Touratsoglou, *DM*, 59–65.

355. Paschidis, *Ποσειδώνες και Αντίγονοι*, 235–258.

356. Boehringer, *Chronologie*, 99: "Noch immer sind eine Anzahl weiterer Fragen zu den Münzserien der beiden Antigoniden unbeantwortet geblieben, Fragen, die erst durch ein Corpus der Makedonischen Prägungen von Gonatas bis Doson gelöst werden können"; Picard, *Chalcis*, 66, n. 5; Mathisen, *Administrative Organisation* III, 46; Le Bohec, *AD*, 53, n. 1; Paschidis, *Ποσειδώνες και Αντίγονοι*, 250; Liampi, *MS*, 110.

357. Cox, *Gordion*, 1–19, esp. 8.

environs, 1937–1938, Eretria, 1937 and Gordion, 1951, led Merker in 1960 to conclude that the Poseidons not only postdate the Pans, but also that they must belong to Doson. He uses the introduction of the Poseidon tetradrachm type as an argument for dating the battle of Andros to the period of the Karian expedition (227–225 BC).[358] Ehrhardt pointed out that the excellent condition of the Poseidon head tetradrachms from the Gordion, 1951 hoard, dated to c. 205–200 BC, would have entailed their immediate withdrawal from circulation.[359] Mathisen's study of thirty-three hoards suggested c. 250 and 220 BC as respective *termini ante quos* for the Pans and for the Poseidons. Mathisen regarded the twenty-year gap (on his chronology) between the introduction of the new coinage and its occurrence in hoards as analogous to the presence of the Pans in hoards later than their issue. He fails, however, to determine conclusively the start-date of the Poseidons.

Through a study of all the known hoards, Touratsoglou reassigned the Poseidons to Antigonos Doson. He suggested that the Pans were hoarded between 260 and 200 BC in the Balkans and between 220 and 200 BC in Asia Minor and the Middle and Near East, whereas the Poseidons appear in hoards of the East after 220 BC but rarely occur in the Balkans, and then only after 227–225 BC. He thus related the Poseidons to Doson's military expenditure for the Karian expedition. Doubts about this raised most recently by Ashton and by Paschidis, who attributes the absence of Poseidons from hoards of the East before the 220s to the lack of large military enterprises before the Karian expedition. Paschidis redates the earliest hoard with Poseidon head tetradrachms, Karditsa 1929, to c. 245–240 BC, on the basis of its tetradrachms of Antiochos II. He also considers an earlier date for a few other hoards, but admits that the hoard evidence cannot determine the introduction date of the Poseidon head tetradrachms.[360]

The hoards allow us to conclude only that the Poseidon heads were in circulation by c. 245–240 BC. A *terminus post quem* may be regarded as c. 246/5 BC, for the chronology of the latest hoard with Pans and without Poseidons from the Balkans, Eretria, 1937, has now been backdated on the basis of new evidence to c. 245–240 BC, within the context of the battle of Andros (cf. Chapter 6.3). The introduction of the Poseidons can therefore be placed between c. 246/5 and 240 BC.

Finally, the geographic distribution of the Poseidons reveals that neither the Poseidons nor the Pans are represented in Eastern hoards dated between 240 and 220 BC. The only exception is Meydancıkkale, 1980 (c. 240–235 BC), the only hoard of the East with Pans (and no Poseidons) from this period,[361] which does not affect the introduction date of either variety (see Chapter 6.3). The introduction of the Poseidon head tetradrachms in the 240s would therefore not have been reflected in the hoard patterns of the East (see Chapter 7.2).

(ii) Style and internal numismatic evidence

The first attributions of the Poseidons focused on their style and relation to the Pans. Imhoof-Blumer accepted Head's remarks on the similarity in style and fabric between the Poseidons and the coins struck by Philip V and by the first μερίς of the Makedonians, but he preferred to date the Apollo on the prow on the reverse to the time of Demetrios Poliorketes rather than to Philip V. Also on stylistic grounds, he dated the Poseidons before the Pans with Athena left and he suggested the naval victory of Gonatas off Kos, then dated to c. 265 BC, as an appropriate context for

358. Merker, *Studies*, 70–143; Merker, *Silver Coinage*, 32–52. Ehrhardt, *Studies*, 76–78.

359. *Studies*, 76–78. See Chapter 6.3.

360. R. Ashton, Review of Y. Touratsogou, *Disjecta Membra, NCirc.* 2 (1996) 9–10. Paschidis, *Ποσειδώνες και Αντίγονοι*. An earlier date is suggested, for instance, for *Hija së Korbit, 1982* (see Chapter 6.3), but the nature of this "savings" hoard limits its usefulness in determining the introduction date of the Poseidons.

361. Cf. Chapter 6.3.

this issue. He took the iconography of the silver drachmae, with the bearded head r. on the obverse and with Athena (then termed "Alkidemos") left on the reverse, as marking the transition from the Poseidons to the Pans under Gonatas. Although the futility of the stylistic arguments to date these coins has been pointed out by Merker,[362] Touratsoglou reverts to Head's stylistic comparison of the Poseidons to the tetradrachms of ΜΑΚΕΔΟΝΩΝ ΠΡΩΤΗΣ, in order to support the late introduction of the former.[363]

More important for the introduction date of this coinage is the internal numismatic evidence, from which some relationship between the Pan head and the Poseidon head series may be detected. A trident symbol occurs, for instance, on the reverse of certain Pan and some Poseidon varieties (Chapter 4.1, nos. 1–3 and Chapter 5.3, nos. 77–83, respectively). Moreover, monograms HP, ⋈, AP and the letters TI are engraved right on the reverse of some Pan tetradrachms and right of the main monogram on certain Poseidons. These common control marks, taken as internal links between the two series, are a further reason why Imhoof-Blumer assigned both types to Gonatas. He compared the tetradrachms with the trident symbol on the reverse to the silver coinage of Demetrios Poliorketes, rather than with the Antigonid bronzes carrying on the reverse a Pan erecting trophy.[364] The significance of these common control marks is underplayed by those who assign the Poseidon type to Antigonos Doson, notably Merker and Touratsoglou.[365] It has been argued above, however, that the presence of these varieties in later hoards only provides a *terminus ante quem* for them, rather than conclusively determining their introduction date. Mathisen, on the other hand, takes these common control marks (and the star symbol on the reverse of certain Poseidon head tetradrachms, Chapter 5.1.2, nos. 73–76 in our catalogue) to indicate the rough contemporaneity of both types. Moreover, he suggests that the disparity in the ratios of (a) the duration of the respective issues (Pans : Poseidons, 6+ : 1 years), and of (b) their sizes (Pans : Poseidons, 12–13 : 6 specimens) renders the introduction of the Poseidons under Doson unlikely. He therefore concludes that the Poseidons start under Gonatas and coincide with some Pan head varieties.[366] Paschidis most recently, also allowing for the accidental coincidence of monograms on the two types, considered the numeric analogy of the monograms on the respective series and certain internal monogram and letter links between them, in order to conclude that the Poseidons must have been introduced under Antigonos Gonatas.[367]

The Poseidons form a generally homogeneous issue, struck from twenty-seven obverse dies. Five of the earliest groups, with archaizing figures of Apollo, are signed with a second monogram or letter to the right of the main monogram of the issue: monograms HP, ⋈, AP, and the letter M occur on the first issue of Poseidon heads. A gradual transition from the archaizing figures of Apollo on the reverse of the first groups to the more natural ones on the rest of this first issue may be observed on the tetradrachms with a single monogram. A distinct group, characterized by corpulent heads on the obverse, spreading beyond the flans, and by tall and straight figures of Apollo on the reverse, may belong either to the end of this issue or to the beginning of the next period (IV).

Coins with the beard of Poseidon rendered in curvilinear forms have been tentatively assigned to a different period. The tall and thin figures of Apollo on the reverse harmonize well with the

362. *Silver Coinage*, 40.
363. *DM*, 81.
364. Imhoof-Blumer, *MG*, 127–128.
365. Merker, *Silver Coinage*, 49; Touratsoglou, *DM*, 80.
366. Mathisen, *Pan Heads and Poseidon Heads*, 32–34.
367. See n. 6, esp. 244–250.

elaborate prows and with the small and carefully spaced legend letters. Unlike the secondary letters and monograms assigned to the first issue, which are engraved right of the main monogram, the letters TI and ΘI are placed beneath the main monogram. The star on specimens 73–76 (Period IV) and the trident on the last group of the series may be allusions to the Karian expedition and may thus encourage the association of the second lot with the fourth period of Antigonid issues.[368] Two secondary control marks figure alongside the main symbol on the trident group, monogram [monogram] to the r., and the letters IE to the left of the trident on the last two groups. There seems to be no chronological association between this Poseidon trident symbol group and the Pan-with-trident variety.

Even so, the internal sequence of the two individual silver tetradrachm types struck under Antigonos corroborates some relationship between the Pans and the Poseidons. In the first place, a trident symbol occurs on groups from both series. Secondly, it may be argued that the monograms shared by the Pans and the Poseidons are not due to pure coincidence. I have suggested that the monograms on the Pans represent officials responsible for different branches of the same mint who may have held office for many years rather than annual officials and hence imply no close chronological connection between the Pans and the Poseidons; even if these monograms denoted the recipients of specific payments, payments with a different coin type were also possible (cf. Chapter 6.2.4). Turning to the Poseidons and leaving aside the principal monogram, which is not paralleled by any of the control marks on silver or bronze (Antigonid) coins from within or outside Makedonia (except possibly the symbol on no. 127 of the Pans from Period III), one may focus on the secondary monograms and letters, which occur on the Poseidons alongside the main monogram. Of those, [monogram], [monogram], [monogram] and the letters TI are among the main control marks of the Pans: the first occurs in the first two periods of the Pans, the second runs through the entire series, and the letters TI sign specimens of the last three periods (cf. Chapter 6.2.4). It would be hard to imagine that the occurrence of these particular monograms on the second type with the legend ΒΑΣΙΛΕΩΣ ΑΝΤΙΓΟΝΟΥ, the Poseidons, is fortuitous. Rather this denotes the involvement of some of the principal officials of the main mint, in which the Pans were produced, in the launching, at least, of the new type; or that specific payments were made with the new coin type instead with the Pans.

Paschidis' remarks in regard to these common monograms are now supplemented by internal numismatic evidence. In the first place, monogram [monogram] occurs in the third period of Antigonid issues, both on Group 30 of the Pans (Chapter 4.1.2, nos. 132–135), and on the Poseidons' Group 36 of Period III and Group 21 of Period IV (respectively Chapters 4.1.2, no. 155, and 5.1.2, nos. 77–81). The few coins signed with this monogram, and its alteration to [monogram] on specimen 147 from Period III, suggest that this mint official was involved only briefly in this issue and indirectly confirm that it is the regular officials of the main Makedonian mint who, at least initially, were in charge of the new issue. The occurrence of monogram [monogram] on a single specimen is in marked contrast to the presence of [monogram] on eight die combinations of Poseidons from period III. This is of particular interest if combined with the absence of monogram [monogram] from the third period of Pans. Paschidis argues that the assignation of the Poseidons to Doson would entail the recalling of the official with monogram [monogram] to office 25–35 years after his first employment. He opts instead for the attribution of the Poseidon head tetradrachms with monogram [monogram] to the time of Gonatas.

368. The star symbol might be reminiscent of that on the coinage of Philip II: Le Rider, *Philippe II*, 135, no. 59; idem, *Monnayage et finances*, 50 (first series of gold staters); Le Rider, *Philippe II*, 49, 370–373; idem, *Monnayage et finances*, 33–34 (silver). Ashton is not convinced by Touratsoglou's interpretation of the trident symbol as denoting a naval enterprise: *DM*, 81–82; cf. Ashton, Review of Touratsoglou, *Disjecta Membra*, *NCirc.* 2 (1996), 9–10. Cf. Chapter 6.2.4.

The employment under Doson of a second official using the monogram HP is admittedly possible, but the absence of this monogram from the control marks on the silver tetradrachms of Philip V would then suggest that he was employed only briefly.[369] Moreover, the assignation of the Poseidons with HP to the third period effectively accounts for the discontinuity of this monogram on the Pans after the second period: it is simpler to assume the assignation to this experienced official of the new Poseidon issue before his retirement. The official signing with monogram ⋈ was only briefly diverted to the new issue; he almost immediately returned to the Pans.

Paschidis offers the same interpretation for the letters TI, which occur on the Poseidons, on the Pans, and on the few silver Zeus drachmae. These tetradrachms and drachmae have been related to the Karian expedition of Antigonos Doson (cf. Chapters 5.1.1, 5.3, 6.2.4, 6.4.2–4), and the second issue of the Poseidons may also form part of the same context.

(iii) Iconography and policy

The naval pretensions implied by the combination of the bearded Poseidon head on the obverse with Apollo on the prow on the reverse of the second tetradrachm type in the name of king Antigonos, have been analyzed in relation to the iconography (Chapter 6.1). These point to the association of the new tetradrachm type with one of the following three occasions: the naval victories of Gonatas over the Ptolemies, off Kos (dated between 262/1 and 255 BC) and near Andros (246/5 BC), and Doson's Karian expedition (227–225 BC).

Imhoof-Blumer, who assigned both tetradrachm types to Gonatas, related the Poseidons to the battle of Kos, then dated to 265 BC, and argued that they were earlier than the Pans with Athena left. He thus deprived Demetrios II and Antigonos Doson of silver issues. In his doctoral dissertation, I. L. Merker developed Dorothy B. Cox's remark that the Pans with Athena to the left in fact antedate the Poseidon type. Diverging from Cox, who assigned both types to a period from Gonatas through to Doson, Merker associated the naval connotations in the iconography of the Poseidons with the battle of Andros, which he dated to the period of the Karian expedition (227–225 BC). He thus reverted to Head's initial tentative association of the Poseidons with Doson.[370] Through the study of a small sample of hoards, further developed in an article published in 1960, he expanded Head's argumentation, which was based on fabric and style, in the following respects:

(i) The iconography of the Poseidons relates to the battle of Andros.
(ii) The accepted dates for Eretria, 1937 and for Gordion, 1951 point to the introduction of the Poseidons between c. 235 and c. 210–200 BC.
(iii) Doson's Karian expedition offers an appropriate background for an important naval conflict.
(iv) The Poseidons and the chronological context in Pompeius Trogus are not incompatible with a date of the battle of Andros under Doson. The reference to Andros in relation to Gonatas in Plutarch is a mistake for Kos.
(v) Therefore, the battle of Andros is to be dated to the reign of Antigonos Doson.

369. On the monograms on the silver tetradrachms of Philip V, see A. Mamroth, "Die Silbermünzen des Königs Philippos V. von Makedonien," *ZfN* 40 (1930), 277–303, esp. 277; Touratsoglou, *Circulation*, "list of monograms on coins of Philip, Perseus and in the name of Macedonians". On the monograms on the silver coinage of Perseus, see also Touratsoglou, ibid.; A. Mamroth, "Die Silbermünzen des Königs Perseus," *ZfN* 38 (1928), 1–28, esp. 1; Mettout, *Persée*, pl. II. Cf. Mørkholm, *EHC*, 163–166.

370. See n. 9.

The debate has continued in the 1980s. Redating the battle of Andros to 246/5 BC in the light of new evidence, Buraselis conclusively dissociated this naval conflict from Doson's Karian expedition, and argued that the iconography of the Poseidons is better associated with Gonatas rather than Doson. Firstly, Apollo is not related to Doson but rather to Gonatas, who made various dedications (including the "Monument of his Ancestors" and his sacred trireme) at the god's temple at Delos after his naval victory off Kos. He argued that the Apollo-on-prow was an allusion to the battle of Kos and that Poseidon on the obverse was not only a return to the numismatic tradition of the Antigonids, but also connected with the approximation of Antigonos (probably Gonatas after Kos) to Poseidon in Sextus Empiricus (see Chapter 6.1).[371] In 1985, independently of Buraselis' remarks, Mathisen reappraised the known hoards, the internal numismatic evidence and the iconography, and related the Poseidons to the battle of Andros, which he dated to the late 240s, as indicated by Pompeius Trogus.[372]

Although the battle off Andros (246/5 BC) has now been dissociated from the Karian expedition (227 BC), the alleged earliest presence of the Poseidons in hoards (in the 220s) has prompted Touratsoglou to suggest that the type was introduced in connection with military expenditure for the Karian expedition, and to downdate for this purpose the Karditsa, 1929 hoard to the 220s (Chapter 6.3). Reconstructing this view, Paschidis focuses on the following points:

(i) He repeats Mathisen's methodological reservations in relating the new type with the military expenditure for an imminent expedition and points out that a military enterprise could have been funded with existing currency.

(ii) He argues that the connotations of naval sovereignty on the new coinage do not tally with the motives and results of the naval enterprise to Karia, after which Antigonid sovereignty in the area was neither pursued nor achieved.

(iii) On the other hand, he stresses that the new iconography is compatible with the impact of the Antigonid naval victory off Andros, as put forward by Buraselis. He suggests that the "messages" of the new iconography (that is, the declaration of Gonatas' control of the Aegean and of his recapture of Korinth in 246 BC, as well as some influence on Delos) may have been put out when Gonatas' Aegean policy was at its most successful.[373]

*** *** ***

Our study of the evidence shows that the last Balkan hoard with Pans but with no Poseidons, Eretria, 1937, and the earliest hoard with both tetradrachm types, Karditsa, 1929, limit the date of the introduction of the Poseidons to between c. 246/5 BC and 240 BC. Moreover, the control marks shared between the Pans and the Poseidons may be taken to indicate the introduction of the Poseidons during the third period of issue of the Pans; that is, after the battle of Andros. Even though the inscriptions from Labraunda show unequivocally that first Doson and then Philip V exercised sovereignty in Karia for at least a decade,[374] the iconographic connotations of naval sovereignty on the Poseidons must have acquired particular gravity at the peak of Gonatas' military and political achievements against the Ptolemies. Both tetradrachm types may have continued to be used through to Antigonos Doson.

371. Buraselis, *HM*, 162–163.
372. Mathisen, *Pan Heads and Poseidon Heads*, esp. 33–35.
373. See. n. 6, esp. 250–255.
374. Crampa, *ILabraunda* I, nos. 5–12; G. Reger, "The Koinon of the Laodikeis in Karia," *EA* 30 (1998), 11–17; Dignas, *Economy of the Sacred*, 63–65, 217, n. 507.

The Poseidons may thus be argued to relate to Gonatas' naval achievements over the Ptolemies with the Antigonid Aegean tradition and present Apollo as protector of his flagship and hence of the Antigonid fleet. Thus Apollo, and Poseidon, are presented as having given Gonatas the naval victory at Andros. It has been shown that reference to the Celtic attack at Delphi had been made on the Pans (Chapter 6.4.2). The Poseidons, alongside the new vase festivals introduced by Gonatas at the god's other main sanctuary at Delos after Andros, the *Soteria* and the *Paneia*, were expressions of his piety to Apollo at the god's other major sanctuary. In fact, the unusual names of these two vase festivals, *Soteria* and *Paneia*, were presumably meant to stress Pan's role in the Panhellenic resistance to the Celts at Delphi and indirectly to recall Gonatas' role in this resistance, alongside the Aitolians.[375]

I am inclined to suggest that this renewed emphasis at Delos on the Celtic attack at Delphi and the reestablishment of the links with mainstream Antigonid Aegean policy and Delos were the two sides of the same Antigonid policy *vis-à-vis* mainland Greece and the Aegean. Both the Delian foundations and the Poseidon head tetradrachms, respectively directly and indirectly, formed part of Gonatas' riposte to the potentially anti-Makedonian stance of the Aitolians. The initiative of the latter in transforming the annual Soteria at Delphi into what was effectively a Panhellenic festival was intended to win Panhellenic acknowledgement of their control of Delphi (chapter 6.1). Gonatas' expressions of piety at a different major Greek sanctuary may have been intended not merely to honor the gods who had helped him, but also to prevent possible Aitolian manipulation of his abstention from the Delphic celebrations into a potential identification of the Makedonians with barbarians.

6.4.4 Fractional Denominations

The internal sequence of the tetradrachms of "King Antigonos" may, at least partly, be determined by the few silver fractions issued by the same authority. These include a drachma with the types of the Pan head tetradrachms; thirty-two drachmae with the head of Zeus on the obverse and with Athena to the left on the reverse, with a winged helmet and the letters TI on either side of Athena (chapter 6.1). The smallest denomination is a Zeus tetrobol, struck from a pair of dies used for the drachmae (chapter 5.4, no. 95a).

The Pan drachma, with a crested helmet and monogram HP on the reverse, is stylistically associated with the Pan tetradrachms of the "plain style" (chapters 6.4.2, 2.2.3). As for the Zeus drachmae, Imhoof-Blumer considered them to mark the transition from the Poseidons to the Pans with Athena left, but Mathisen associates them with the Pans. He identifies the bearded head on the obverse as Zeus rather than Poseidon and he relates them via their control marks, the winged helmet symbol left on the reverse and the letters TI on the right, to a small group of Pan tetradrachms instead.[376] He assigns these Pans and the Zeus drachmae to a brief period in the reign of Gonatas, but he is not more precise.

375. The gods honored at the Soteria have been identified with the *Theoi Soteres*, Zeus Soter and Athena Soteira. Tarn identifies the new festivals with "Apollo of Delos and the gods associated with him": *AG*, 380. Ed. Will relates them to Pan's alleged role at Lysimacheia: *HPMH* I², 323, cf. Chapter 6.4.2. Walbank relates these names to Pan's popularity in Makedonia and to his representation on the Pan head tetradrachms (Hammond and Walbank, *Macedonia* III, 592–595). Finally, Buraselis assumes an epiphany of Pan at the battle of Andros, as at Lysimacheia: *HM*, 145. Cf. C. Champion, "In Defense of Hellas: The Antigonid Soteria and Paneia at Delos and the Aetolian Soteria at Delphi," *AJAH* 3–4 (2004–2005), 72–88.

376. Imhoof-Blumer, *MG*, 124, 127; Merker, *Pan Heads and Poseidon Heads*, 40, 44–45.

A *terminus ante quem* for these issues is provided by the Sophikon, 1893 hoard, dated to c. 230–220 BC; two of the three drachmae included in this hoard are in good condition, suggesting that they and the Pan tetradrachms with winged helmet symbol belong not long before that date (chapter 6.1). Their limited numbers, however, suggest that they were not part of a monetary system structured exclusively on individual types of king Antigonos. The specimen weighing 2.46 g is obverse linked to the drachmae of full weight, and may be identified as a silver tetrobol.[377]

Given that the production of silver drachmae was far more common in Asia Minor than in Greece,[378] these fractional denominations may be related to Antigonid naval or other military enterprises in the East. Three occasions spring to mind: an early presence of Gonatas in Karia, implied by an inscription from Kaunos, currently dated to c. 268 BC (see Chapter 6.4.2), a possible involvement of Gonatas in the Third Syrian, or Laodikean, War (246–241 BC)[379] and a naval expedition, such as that of Antigonos Doson to Karia in 227–225 BC. The close association of the Pan drachma with Group 10 of the Pan variety through identical designs, style and control marks could suggest the striking of the Pan drachma on the first occasion, but it is difficult to base such assumptions on a single coin. Moreover, the evidence for Gonatas' involvement in Karia in the early 260s remains uncertain.[380] Gonatas' participation in the Laodikean War is a possible alternative, but it is not firmly supported by the existing evidence. Furthermore, the representation of Zeus on the obverse would seem to be incompatible with Gonatas' identification with Poseidon in later literature. The Karian expedition of 227–225 BC therefore remains at present the only appropriate naval enterprise in the East.

377. Cf. Kroll, *Agora*, 10–11, 22.

378. See, for instance, Thompson, *Drachm Mints* II, 9; Mørkholm, *EHC*, 50, n. 15; Price, *Alexander*, 208–9.

379. Buraselis, *HM*, 119 ff., 172–176.

380. P. Frei and C. Marek, "Die karisch-griechische Bilingue von Kaunos: eine zweisprachige Staatsurkunde des 4. Jahrhunderts v. Chr.," *Kadmos* 36.1 (1997), 1–89; Ivo Kajnal, "Die karisch-griechische Bilingue 44* aus Kaunos: Ein erster Augenschein," *Kadmos* 37 (1998), 141; P. Frei and C. Marek, "Die karisch-griechische Bilingue von Kaunos. Ein neues Textfragment," *Kadmos* 37 (1998), 1–18; Marek, *I. Kaunos*, 4.

6.5 Mints

How many mints may be distinguished for the precious metal coinage in the name of "King Antigonos"? For how long did they operate? Was their operation continuous? Finally, can they be located? Can numismatic evidence shed light upon their internal structure?

Continuity and change in the mint organization in Makedonia under Gonatas can only be properly assessed in the light of earlier practices in the area. The precious metal coinage of Philip II and the lifetime coinage of Alexander III in Makedonia have been assigned to three Makedonian mints,[381] the main one being traditionally identified with Amphipolis.[382] The coinage in the name of Alexander III was continued posthumously under Philip Arrhidaeus and Kassander, presumably at the same mints. The Makedonian silver coinage with the personal types and name of Demetrios Poliorketes presumably comes from two mints, and possibly from a third, labelled by Newell as "uncertain Makedonian."[383] It is the posthumous gold and silver issues in the name of Alexander that set the direct precedent for the coinage struck in Makedonia during the *interregnum* and under Gonatas. Mathisen proposes the production of the gold staters at two mints. He assigns the bulk of the silver coinage to the main Makedonian mint, which he identifies as Amphipolis; a few issues are attributed to a second mint, Pella.[384] Finally, the mint of the silver coinage of the last two Antigonids remains uncertain.[385] The reconstruction of the monograms on the precious-metal coinage of Philip V and Perseus has led Touratsoglou to conclude that three officials almost always cooperated, two of whom were permanent.[386]

The stylistic homogeneity of the transitional gold staters in the name of Antigonos favours their attribution to a mint distinct from that of the posthumous Alexander staters, which are themselves associated with the posthumous Alexander tetradrachms struck under Gonatas (Chapter 6.4.1). I would argue that the wreath on the reverse of the transitional staters points to their striking under particular circumstances (Chapter 6.4.1). The paucity of surviving specimens, and the absence of control marks, suggest that this was a one-off issue, for a particular payment or celebration. As for the transitional silver Alexanders, the obverse link between them and the silver posthumous Alexanders might point to the striking of both at the same mint, although the presence of a single monogram differentiates them from the posthumous Alexanders, which regularly carry three monograms on the reverse.

381. Le Rider, *Philippe II*, 325–332; Price, *Alexander*, 85–89; M. J. Price, "The Coinage of Philip II," *NC* 19 (1979), 234–240; Le Rider, *Monnayage et finances*, 26–31.

382. Newell, *Demanhur*, 67; Bellinger, *Essays*, 44, n. 37; Price, *Alexander*, 86, n. 4; Troxell, *Studies*, 17.

383. Newell, *DP*, passim; Mørkholm, *EHC*, 78–81.

384. Mathisen, *Silver Coinages*, 101–102, 104–110.

385. On attempts to reconstruct the respective coinages, see A. Mamroth, "Die Silbermünzen des Königs Philippos V. von Makedonien," *ZfN* 40 (1930), 277–330; P. A. MacKay, "Macedonian tetradrachms of 148–7 B.C.," *ANSMN* 14 (1968), 5–13; Boehringer, *Chronologie*, 107–110, 116–118. A. Mamroth, "Die Silbermünzen des Königs Perseus," *ZfN* 38 (1928), 1–28; Mettout, *Persée*; P. R. Franke, "Zur Finanzpolitik des makedonischen Königs Perseus während des Krieges mit Rom 171–168 v. Chr.," *JNG* (1957), 31–50, pl. II–IV; Mørkholm, *EHC*, 135–136; S. Kremydi-Sicilianou, "ΜΑΚΕΔΟΝΩΝ ΠΡΩΤΗΣ ΜΕΡΙΔΟΣ: Evidence for a Coinage under the Antigonids," *RN* 163 (2007), 91–99, pl. XIII–XIV; eadem, "The Tauropolos Tetradrachms of the First Macedonian Meris: Provenance, Iconography and Dating," in *Κερμάτια Φιλίας. Τιμητικός Τόμος για τον Ιωάννη Τουράτσογλου*, vol. 1, Athens: Numismatic Museum 2009, 191–201; eadem, "Coinage and Finance," in R. Lane-Fox (ed.), *Brill's Companion to Ancient Macedon*, Studies in the Archaeology and History of Macedon, 650 BC–300 AD (Leiden: Brill, 2011), 159–178; N. G. L. Hammond, "The Defeat of the Macedonian Army and the Roman Settlement (197–196 B.C.)," in Hammond-Walbank, *Macedonia* III, 460–468.

386. Touratsoglou, *Circulation*, 71, "list of monograms on coins of Philip V, Perseus and in the name of the Macedonians."

It is the combination of the Makedonian shield on the obverse with the crested helmet on the reverse on most of the Pans thar has led to the assignation of these issues to the main Makedonian mint.[387] The crested helmet left on the reverse relates this tetradrachm type to the Helmet group of the Makedonian posthumous Alexander tetradrachms and to the shield/helmet Antigonid bronze coins.[388] At the same time, the typological variations of the crested helmet suggest that the Pans were of long duration. The helmet in Groups 41–45 of the first period is replaced by monograms [monogram], [monogram] and [monogram] on the left reverse field, establishing a connection with the Pans. A winged helmet temporarily replaces the crested helmet in period IV. Rather than indicating the striking of these coins at a different Makedonian mint, this replacement may suggest their issue on a particular occasion. In fact, the Karian expedition of Antigonos Doson might have offered him the opportunity to distinguish himself from his predecessor and to adopt temporarily a different symbol on the reverse (Chapters 5.1.2, 6.4.2); the withdrawal of the Makedonian garrison from Attika in 229 BC might have offered an alternative occasion.

Small issues with different symbols on the reverse may equally well have been struck at different mints or at the main Makedonian mint. A variation with Athena facing right and with a *desmos* left on the reverse has been assigned to the mint of Athens by Merker, who interpreted the obverse link of this variety with the Athena left series as a die transfer to the new mint.[389] Boehringer, on the other hand, prefers the attribution of the right-facing Athena to the beginning of the main Makedonian mint, originally proposed by Imhoof-Blumer and Gaebler.[390]

The second Pan group with distinct control marks consists of four die combinations with the letter X on the left and with monogram [monogram], later corrected to [monogram], on the right These have been assigned by Merker to a third Makedonian mint, located at Chalkis. Finally, a third Pan group with a trident symbol l. on the reverse has been assigned by Merker to Korinth.[391] Mathisen's association of this group with the battle of either Kos or Andros is rejected by Touratsoglou. He prefers to associate it with the Poseidons with a trident on the reverse, interpreting the trident as a general symbol of sea power.[392]

The different symbols, however, do not form a sufficient basis for the attribution of these varieties to different mints, given that posthumous Alexander tetradrachms with various group identifiers had already been minted at the main Makedonian mint under Gonatas.[393] The association of the *desmos* with the Eleusinian rituals, for instance, does not justify the hypothesis of a new Antigonid mint at Athens and the transfer to it of an obverse from the main mint, as suggested by Merker. Indeed the small size and high quality of this issue may suggest its production at the main Makedonian mint in commemoration of a particular occasion. Similarly, the occurrence of the letter X among the control marks of the posthumous Alexander tetradrachms struck at Uranopolis, and of monogram [monogram] on the so-called "Xi group" of the posthumous Alexander tetradrachms, need not *a priori* exclude the striking of the corresponding Pans in Makedonia.[394] The occurrence

387. Merker, *Silver Coinage*, 45–46; Ritter, *Sternsymbolik*, 165, n. 7.

388. See pl. 61.2, 14.

389. Merker, *Silver Coinage*, 47–49.

390. *Chronologie*, 100, n. 9.

391. Merker, *Silver Coinage*, 49–50.

392. Mathisen, *CW* (1983), 113; Touratsoglou, *DM*, 80.

393. Mathisen, *Silver Coinages*, 79–123, esp. 86–96, 81 (table 1); *Administrative Organisation* I, 10–1; Price, *Alexander*, 141–142.

394. On the issues of Uranopolis, see Chr. Ehrhardt, "A Catalogue of Issues of Tetradrachms from Amphipolis, 318–294 BC," *JNFA* 4 (1976), 85–89, esp. 87–88; Price, *Alexander*, 139–140, pl. 32.511–514. On the "Xi" group of Makedonian posthumous Alexanders, see Price, *Alexander*, 141, 146.

of monogram ΑΡ with a Poseidon head obverse and a trident on the reverse might suggest the supervision by the same official of both Pans with Athena to the right and Poseidons; or the use of both coinage varieties for a specific payment. Moreover, the small size of the Pan head groups without a helmet symbol does not suggest the parallel operation of two mints. After all, the stylistic similarity of O18–O20 with O02 in the third period shows that these dies were cut by the same die engraver. There is therefore no reason to reject Boehringer's identification of a single Makedonian mint for all the Pans,[395] including the special groups struck for exceptional circumstances.

Merker's belief that mints operated outside Makedonia under Gonatas is thus not supported by the existing evidence.[396] There is no reason to assume that Gonatas or any of his successors in Makedonia exercised such an authority *vis-à-vis* Greek political entities, either. Purchase of silver from the royal mines may simply have been unprofitable for the cities. This may have accounted for their preference for "international" coinages, whether royal Makedonian or others.

Was the second tetradrachm type of Antigonos, the Poseidons, struck at a different mint? The absence of its main monogram from the Pans, from the related posthumous Alexanders, and from the Antigonid bronze coinage, is not sufficient reason to exclude the Poseidons from the main mint. The Makedonian fabric of the Poseidon head tetradrachms points to their production in Makedonia, as suggested by Mathisen, rather than at Thessalian Demetrias (see Chapter 6.2.4).[397] The monograms in common with the Pans, ΗΡ, ΗΜ and ΑΡ, which occur alongside the main monogram, suggest production of the Poseidons at the main Makedonian mint rather than the temporary transfer of some of its officials elsewhere. Moreover, the twenty-seven Poseidon obverse dies suggest a larger issue than the special Pan groups. The periodical issue of this Poseidon head type might thus be confirmed (cf. Chapters 6.4.3, 7.3).

Price and Troxell are sceptical about the possibility of identifying mints in Makedonia. Price uses inverted commas for uncertain earlier attributions to mints, while Troxell deliberately avoids this discussion altogether.[398] The Makedonian posthumous Alexanders that set the direct precedent to the Pans have been assigned by R. W. Mathisen to two mints, Amphipolis and Pella, on the assumption that an official from the main mint oversaw at Pella a small issue with monogram ΥΕ. One must admit that the transfers of dies and officials to different mints are possible, as are "moving mints";[399] but these interpretations rest on the assumption that control marks represent mint officials.

The structure of the Pans suggests their production at the principal Makedonian mint: the crested helmet and common monograms establish continuity with the posthumous Alexanders struck at Amphipolis, according to Mathisen and Price.[400] The same mint may well have occasionally struck special issues, in commemoration of important events. This is suggested by the obverse link between the *desmos* group and the main Helmet group. As for its precise location, Mathisen's suggestion of Amphipolis is supported by its proximity to the mines of Pangaion.[401] This is further

395. Boehringer, *Chronologie*, 100.

396. J. J. Gabbert concludes that Gonatas honoured the tradition of the autonomy of the Greek polis so long as it did not violate his primary goals: Gabbert, *Greek Hegemony*, 251–259. On the impact of sovereignty on royal numismatic policies, see Martin, *Sovereignty*, 5, n. 2, 13, 196–203. Howgego, *Ancient History from Coins*, 39–49, 59–60.

397. Mathisen, *Pan Heads and Poseidon Heads*, 32.

398. Price, *Alexander*, 36, 85–131; Troxell, *Studies*, 17–18.

399. O. Mørkholm, "The 'Behaviour' of Dies in the Hellenistic Period," in *INC Berne Proc.* (1982), 209–14; idem, "Some Reflections on the Production and Use of Coinage in Ancient Greece," *Historia* 31 (1982), 290–305; idem, "The Life of Obverse Dies in the Hellenistic Period," in *Studies Grierson*, 11–21.

400. Mathisen, *Silver Coinages*, 101–110; Price, *Alexander*, 141–142. Cf. Chapter 6.2.4, fig. 6.9.

401. Mathisen, *Macedonian Silver*, 114–118, with earlier bibliography. On the Makedonian mines, see Chapters 1.2, 7.

favored by the occurrence of one of the principal monograms on the Pans, ⋈, on the reverse of silver coins from Thasos.[402] It is not necessary to assign the special Pan groups to a different mint, in order to confirm Mathisen's distinction of two Makedonian mints for the posthumous Alexanders of the 280s and 270s. In fact, Mathisen's consideration of the Pan group with the trident symbol as celebratory may be expanded on all these special issues.[403] The suggested celebratory nature also of the Poseidons might allow for their minting at the principal Makedonian mint (cf. Chapters 6.4.3, 7.3); their alternative production at Pella is a possible, but not necessary, hypothesis.

The operation of a single mint in the eastern half of the Antigonid kingdom is suggested not only by the concentration of mines in the eastern half of Makedonia, but also by Pyrrhos' capture of Pella in 273 BC. This, together with the invasion of Makedonia by Alexander the Molossian during the Chremonidean War, demonstrated that the western part of the realm was vulnerable. Hence the establishment of the royal treasury at Pella is perhaps to be dated after the consolidation of Antigonid control in the area.[404] Some connection between mints and treasuries has been suggested by Hatzopoulos, who favors the existence of a royal treasury at, among other cities, Amphipolis.[405]

To conclude, the internal structure of the Antigonid silver coinage suggests a change in the traditional mint organization in Makedonia after the *interregnum*. The symbols and monograms common to the Pans, the Poseidons, and the Alexander staters and tetradrachms, posthumous and transitional, suggest their consecutive or parallel production over a long period at the same Makedonian mint. Since Gonatas' individual silver issues are normally signed by two control marks, as opposed to the three signing the posthumous Alexanders, one might suggest a loosening of control. If control marks represent mint officials, the independent cooperation of approximately three individuals with the main one, signing with the Makedonian helmet, demonstrates the shift of emphasis to coordinated work among different branches of the same mint under the Antigonids.

402. *SNG Cop.* 1054.

403. *CW* (1983), 113; Touratsoglou, *DM*, 80.

404. The literary sources presented by Hatzopoulos for Pella as the royal treasury date from the period of the Roman conquest: Liv., 44.6.2, 10.1; Plut. *Aem.* 23.6. Cf. Hatzopoulos, *Institutions*, 256, n. 6.

405. *Institutions*, 256, n. 6. On Aemilius Paullus' request to more than one cities for the transport of the royal monies to Amphipolis in 167 BC, see Liv. 45.29.1.

7.0
Coinage, Money, and the Economy

The main Antigonid silver tetradrachm types have been divided into those with Alexander types and those with Gonatas' personal designs, Pan head on shield, Zeus head and Poseidon head." These individual tetradrachm types have been related to financial requirements caused by military enterprises and/or religious celebrations. The exact dating of the transitional Alexander-type tetradrachms "of King Antigonos" during the first period of Antigonid coin production remains uncertain, but the introduction of the Pans relates to Gonatas' financial requirements during the Chremonidean War. The iconography of the Pans refers to the Celtic invasion of the early 270s. It is only during the third period of coin production that the Poseidon head tetradrachms were introduced alongside the Pan heads, presumably in order to celebrate the culmination of Gonatas' naval aspirations in the Aegean after his naval victory over the Ptolemaic fleet off Andros. Both the Pans and the Poseidons continued to be produced until the reign of Antigonos Doson. They are supplemented by very few surviving silver fractional denominations, an early drachma with the same types as the Pan head tetradrachms, fifty-five drachmae and one tetrobol with the head of Zeus on the obverse and Athena to the left on the reverse. A few rare transitional Alexander-type gold staters and certain silver Pan head groups have been defined through their distinct control marks and style as celebratory; that does not mean that this coinage was not used for payments. The Poseidons may also have been introduced on a celebratory occasion.

In contrast to the posthumous Alexander tetradrachms, which have three control marks on the reverse, the number of control marks on the new Antigonid issues is limited to one on the transitional Alexanders and the bulk of the Poseidons, and to two on the Pans and on some Poseidon head varieties. Even so, the helmet symbol and certain monograms which are common to both the posthumous Alexanders and the Antigonid silver suggest their consecutive or contemporary production at the main Makedonian mint. Moreover, the obverse die link and the control marks shared between the transitional Alexander-type tetradrachms in the name of "King Antigonos' and the Makedonian posthumous Alexanders establish a closer connection between the posthumous Alexander tetradrachms and the Antigonid issues struck at the main Makedonian mint. The hoard evidence, vague though it is, would allow for the issue of these Alexanders to be contemporary with the Pan head tetradrachms and reveals that the Antigonid economy was far more complicated than initially thought.

The nature of the royal economy in Hellenistic Makedonia may be better understood in the light of the definition of economy in Pseudo-Aristotle's *Oeconomicus*. Although originally an analysis of the structure of the fourth-century BC Persian economy, the text may be applied on a general level to the Hellenistic kingdoms.[1] The royal economy is described as one of the four main types of economy, δυναμένη τὸ καθόλου, and is divided into the following categories of finance: περὶ <τὸ> νόμισμα, περὶ τὰ ἐξαγώγιμα, περὶ τα εἰσαγώγιμα, περὶ τὰ ἀναλώματα.[2] The policy related to coinage (περὶ <τὸ> νόμισμα) encompasses decisions concerning the type of coinage to be validated at a particular moment and the appropriate time for the confirmation of its validity (ποῖον καὶ πότε [τίμιον ἢ εὔωνον] ποιητέον). The "imports"/"exports" refer to the appropriate timing for the redistribution of the goods received by regional administrators (πότε καὶ τίνα παρὰ τῶν σατραπῶν ἐκλαβόντι αὐτῷ λυσιτελήσει διατίθεσθαι). Finally, decisions on the nature of the expenses at a particular moment and on the form of payment, in coins or goods, are related to royal policy on expenses (περὶ τὰ ἀναλώματα).[3]

Compared to Pseudo-Aristotle's other types of economy, satrapal, civic and private, the royal economy is described as μεγίστη and ἁπλουστάτη. It is the role of the king as regulator of the (re)distribution of goods that accounts for its simplicity. The royal economy has an effect on the function of the other three types and it is in turn affected by their individual functions: in other words, interaction between the four types is inevitable.[4]

The structure of the Antigonid royal economy has been elucidated by Hatzopoulos' discussion of the surviving literary and epigraphic evidence.[5] The Makedonian king is presented in the documentation as an administrator of public property (βασιλικὰ/*patrimonium*), namely of land (agricultural land, forests, groves), harbor dues, and mines.[6] Royal land was often granted to individuals or groups as δωρεά; the mines, the collection of harbor dues and the revenues from the royal land were leased to contractors for a fixed sum.

The bulk of the raw material for the production of the royal precious coinages came from the royal mines,[7] but estimates of the annual income from this are highly speculative. Through a

1. Martin, *Sovereignty*, 266–270.

2. [Arist.] *Oec.* 2.1–2.

3. [Arist.] *Oec.* 2.2: περὶ δὲ τὰ ἀναλώματα τίνα περιαιρετέον καὶ πότε, καὶ πότερον δοτέον νόμισμα εἰς τὰς δαπάνας ἢ ἀντί νομίσματος ὤνια.

4. [Arist.] *Oec.* 2.1: ἐπικοινωνεῖν μὲν τὰ πολλὰ ἀλλήλοις ἀναγκαῖον ἐστιν· ὅσα δὲ μάλιστα δι'αὐτῶν ἑκάστῃ συμβαίνει, ταῦτα ἐπισκεπτέον ἡμῖν ἐστιν.

5. Hatzopoulos, *Institutions*, 431–442; Faranguna, *Aspetti*; M. Faranguna, "L' economia della Macedonia ellenistica: un bilancio," in A. Bresson, P. Briant, F. Burkhalter (eds.), A*pproches de l' économie hellénistique [4e rencontre de l' économie antique, Saint-Bertrand-des-Comminges (6–7 Mai 2004)* (Paris: de Boccard, 2006), 121–146; S. Kremydi-Sicilianou, "Coinage and Finance," in R. Lane Fox (ed.), *Brill's Companion to Ancient Macedon, Studies in the Archaeology and History of Macedon, 650 BC–300 AD* (Leiden: Brill, 2011), 159–161.

6. Hatzopoulos, *Institutions*, 433, who also considers in this context the reference in the Suida: οὐ τὰ δημόσια τῆς βασιλείας κτήματα.

7. On the Makedonian silver mines around Damasteion, Mt. Dysoron, Pangaion and Cholomon, see Billows, *Kings and Colonists*, 7; Borza, *In the Shadow of Olympus*, 53–55; id., "The natural resources of early Macedonia," in Adams and Borza, *Macedonian Heritage*, 10–12. Cf. Mathisen, *Silver Coinages*, 114–118, with earlier bibliography; Tarn, *AG*, 187–188, on the royal sources of income. Le Rider speculates that booty and gold imported from Asia Minor were additional sources of income for Philip II: *Monnayage et finances*, 76.

calculation of the size of the precious coinage in the name of Philip II, G. Le Rider concludes that Diodorus' report (Diod. 16.8.6–7) that the (annual) income of Philip II from Pangaion was 1000 talents of gold is exaggerated. He suggests that the 1,000 talents mentioned by Diodorus were not calculated in gold but in silver and that the sum amounts to approximately a hundred talents in gold.[8] This figure tallies with the general agreement that only half of the reported annual income of the entire Makedonian kingdom under Perseus (which was approximately 200 talents) came from the mines. This confirms Mathisen's assumption that the annual royal income from the mines under Gonatas amounted to 100 talents.[9] Indeed, one might then, with Faranguna, wonder how the indemnity of 1200 talents which Philip V and Perseus had to pay the Romans, had been calculated, when it is compared with the 15,000 talents imposed on Antiochos III in 189 BC.[10]

Later literary references to royal money (Liv. 45.29.1), and to payments to the king (Liv. 45.18.7, 29.4, 29.11; Diod. 31.8.3), which presumably ended up in the βασιλικὸν ταμιεῖον, might also echo earlier economic practices. To the regular royal revenues from taxation, including dues on the transport of goods,[11] may be added casual sources, such as booty shared between the king and his men or taxes on the manumission of slaves.[12] On the other hand, new coinage was required to finance military payments, public works and religious festivals. With the exception of certain groups, whose distinctive features suggest that they were celebratory, the silver posthumous and transitional Alexanders and the Pans must generally have been intended to finance the military needs of Gonatas.[13] The second tetradrachm type, the Poseidons, may have been meant to mark a special, political or other, occasion (cf. Chapters 6.4.3, 7.3).

Admittedly, the use of gold and silver Antigonid issues in transactions within Makedonia is attested by the presence, in generally large proportions, of Pan head tetradrachms in only five hoards, dated between c. 260 and 187–168 BC: Verge ("Perge"), 1955, Thessalonike, 1978, Kassandreia, 1985–1987, Makedonia?, 1927–1928, Drama, 1989. The hoard evidence is not supplemented by any other references to the use of these particular issues within Makedonia. There is no mention of the issuing authority of the gold coins in the purchase of a house and land in the deeds of sale from Amphipolis dated to the mid-third century BC. This contrasts with the explicit use of gold *philippoi* in equivalent transactions of the fourth century BC.[14] As for the silver issues, the

8. *Monnayage et finances*, 75–77. His calculations, however, are based on Carter's equations for estimating ancient coin production, which are not reliable (cf. Chapter 7.1).

9. Plut. *Aem.*, 28.3, cf. Liv. 45.18, 29; Mathisen, *Silver Coinages*, 114–115, n. 62.

10. Plb. 18.39.5–6; 44.1–7; Liv. 33.13.14–15, 30.1–11 (Philip V); Liv. 34.52.4–8, Plut. *Flam.* 14. On the tribute the Romans imposed on Perseus, see Liv. 45.29.4, Diod. 31.8.5, Plut. *Aem.* 28.6. M. Faranguna, "L' economia della Macedonia ellenistica: Un Bilancio," in A. Bresson, P. Briant, and F. Burkhalter (eds.), *Approches de l' économie hellénistique [4e rencontre de l' économie antique, Saint-Bertrand-des-Comminges (6–7 mai 2004)* (Paris: De Boccard, 2006), 121–146, esp. 133–134.

11. Information on taxation on private property under the first Antigonids is drawn from a metric inscription from Beroia, recognising the tax exemption that had been granted on a house since Philip II. A second inscription suggests that the priests of Asklepios were also granted ἀτέλεια, which was extended by the regent Demetrios to the priests of Herakles Kynaigidas in 248 BC: Hatzopoulos, *Institutions*, 433, n. 6, 440.

12. Plunder in the Macedonian economy is explored by P. Millett, "The Political Economy of Macedonia," in Roisman and Worthington, *CAM*, 490–491; cf. J. K. Davies, "Ancient Economies," in A. Erskine (ed.), *A Companion to Ancient History* (Malden Mass./Oxford; Wiley-Blackwell, 2009), 436–446 ; Z. Archibald and J. K.Davies, "Introduction," in Archibald et al., *EHS*, 1–18, esp. 3–11; Archibald, *Northern Aegean*, 77–78. Slave manumissions: Hatzopoulos, *Institutions* II, no. 93.

13. M. Austin, "Hellenistic Kings, War and the Economy," *CQ* 36 (1986), 450–466; cf., however, Chr. Howgego, "Why did ancient states strike coins?," *NC* 150 (1990), 1–25 *contra* M. H. Crawford, "Money and Exchange in the Ancient World," *JRS* 60 (1970), 40–48.

14. Hatzopoulos, *Institutions* II, nos. 91 (Amphipolis, mid-third century), 31 (Beroia, 239–229 BC). Cf. ibid., nos. 88, 90 (Amphipolis, 350–300 BC).

references to δημητρίειοι δραχμαὶ in the accounts of the priests of Beroia from the second half of the third century BC are worthy of particular attention. Rather than denoting specific objects and as there is no need to assume the existence of drachmae with distinct types of Demetrios I, the δημητρίειοι δραχμαὶ have been taken to represent the unit of weight valid in Antigonid Makedonia under Demetrios II and thus to demonstrate the role of the king as regulator of values in Antigonid Makedonia.[15] The reference to "demetrian drachmae" in Makedonian documents is distinguished from the τετρᾶχμα Ἀντιγόνεια mentioned in the inscriptions from the Athenian Asklepieion from the mid-250s.[16] The δημητρίειοι δραχμαί, as a conventional unit of weight in the 230s and 220s, and the variegated content of Makedonian silver hoards from the same period,[17] seem to belie the exclusive use of Antigonid issues within the Makedonian realm. They indicate rather the mixed nature of the circulation pool in Hellenistic Makedonia.

The precious metal Antigonid issues, comprising as they do silver tetradrachms, very few drachmae and a silver tetrobol, along with a few gold staters, illuminate only large-scale transactions, predominantly state payments.

The production rate of the silver issues in the name of "King Antigonos" may now be tentatively recovered by calculating the number of obverse dies used in every period of royal coin production.

15. Hatzopoulos, *Institutions* II, no. 82 I, l. 6, II, l. 14, 21, 40 = *SEG* 40 [1990] 530, with earlier bibliography. Cf. V. Allamani-Souri, *AD* 39 (1984), Meletai, 205–231, esp. 215–217. Cf. calyx-cups and *kylixes* inscribed with their weight in Attic drachmae in the "royal' tomb at Vergina: Andronikos, *Vergina*, 157–159; Price, *Alexander*, 39, n. 1. M. Hatzopoulos, "Αργυρές δραχμές και χρυσοί στατήρες σε επιγραφές της Μακεδονίας," in *Το νόμισμα στο Μακεδονικό χώρο, Πρακτικά Β' Επιστημονικής Συνάντησης, Οβολός 4* (Thessalonike: University Studio Press, 2000), 79–87, n. 36 interprets the "demetrian" drachmae in Makedonian inscriptions as Attic-weight drachmae, which he takes to have been established in Makedonia by Demetrios Poliorketes; S. Kremydi-Sicilianou, "Coinage and Finance," in R. Lane Fox (ed.), *Brill's Companion to Ancient Macedon, Studies in the Archaeology and History of Macedon, 650 BC–300 AD* (Leiden: Brill, 2011), 159–161 also associates them with Poliorketes, with no argumentation.

16. Aleshire, *Asklepieion*, 261–263, 269. Cf. Chapter 2.4.2.

17. Ehrhardt, *Studies*, 79.

Table 7.1. Periods I–IV: Classification of issues (summary)

PERIOD I

Alexander Types

	AV	AR	4D		D
Group	1	1	2	Total	3
Specimens	6	5	6	11	1
Die combinations	5	2	4	6	1
Obverse dies	5	1	[1-1]	1	1
Reverse dies	3	2	4	6	1

Pan Head Tetradrachms

Group	1	2	3	4	5	6	7	8	9	10	11	12	13
Specimens	24	2	6	15	20	2	13	3	17	2	10	18	9
Die combinations	10	1	4	5	9	1	3	1	6	1	4	6	3
Obverse dies	4	1	2	1	1	1	1	1	2	1	1	[3-2]	[2-2]
Reverse dies	10	1	4	5	9	1	3	1	6	1	4	[5-1]	3

PERIOD II

Pan Head Tetradrachms

Group	1	2	3	4	5	6	7	8	9	10	11	12	13
Specimens	6	17	4	13	9	16	9	1	11	2	9	12	3
Die combinations	3	7	3	6	4	5	4	1	7	1	3	7	2
Obverse dies	2	[2-2]	3	[1-1]	1	[2-2]	[2-2]	1	2	1	[1-1]	[3-3]	[2-2]
Reverse dies	3	7	2	6	4	5	4	1	7	1	3	7	2

Group	1	2	3	4	5	6	7	8	9	10	11	12	13
Specimens	3	2	7	8	13	12	21	16	12	30	2	7	8
Die Combinations	3	2	4	5	6	7	9	8	6	11	1	3	6
Obverse dies	1	2	[1-1]	[1-1]	1	[3-1]	2	1	1	1	[1-1]	[1-1]	[2-2]
Reverse dies	3	2	4	5	[6-1]	7	9	8	[6-1]	11	1	3	[6-2]

PERIOD III

Pan Head Tetradrachms

Group	1	2	3	4	5	6	7	8	9	10	11	12	13
Specimens	51	2	2	13	12	13	21	2	1	7	9	17	10
Die combinations	15	2	1	4	5	4	9	1	1	4	3	5	5
Obverse dies	6	[1-1]	[1-1]	[3-2]	[4-1]	[2-2]	1	1	1	[1-1]	1	[1-1]	[2-2]
Reverse dies	14	2	1	4	4	4	9	1	1	4	3	5	5

Table 7.1 (continued). Periods I–IV: Classification of issues (summary)

PERIOD I

Pan Head Tetradrachms

Group	14	15	16	17	18	19	20	21	22	23	24	25
Specimens	27	6	2	20	9	12	36	1	1	3	1	52
Die combinations	8	3	2	5	5	5	14	1	1	2	1	5
Obverse dies	1	[1-1]	[1-1]	2	1	[2-2]	4	1	[1-1]	[1-1]	[1-1]	1
Reverse dies	8	3	2	5	5	[5-1]	[13-1]	1	1	[2-1]	1	5

PERIOD II

Pan Head Tetradrachms

Group	14	15	16	17	18	19	20	21	22	23	Total
Specimens	5	5	1	17	9	5	2	7	8	1	172
Die combinations	3	3	1	4	3	1	2	2	5	1	78
Obverse dies	[2-1]	[1-1]	[1-1]	[2-2]	[1-1]	[1-1]	[2-1]	[1-1]	[2-2]	[1-1]	12
Reverse dies	3	3	1	4	3	1	2	2	5	1	77

PERIOD III

Pan Head Tetradrachms

Group	14	15	16	17	18	19	20	21	22	23	24	25
Specimens	17	21	8	8	7	4	2	2	13	3	10	40
Die combinations	7	5	2	2	1	1	1	1	5	3	4	11
Obverse dies	1	1	1	1	[1-1]	[1-1]	[1-1]	[1-1]	[1-1]	[1-1]	[3-1]	[1-1]
Reverse dies	7	[5-1]	[2-1]	[2-1]	1	1	1	1	[5-1]	5	3	11

PERIOD IV

Pan Head Tetradrachms

Group	1	2	3	4	5	6	7	8	9	10	11	12
Specimens	51	2	2	13	12	13	21	2	1	7	9	17
Die combinations	15	2	1	4	5	4	9	1	1	4	3	5
Obverse dies	6	[1-1]	[1-1]	[3-2]	[4-1]	[2-2]	1	1	1	[1-1]	1	[1-1]
Reverse dies	14	2	1	4	4	4	9	1	1	4	3	5

Table 7.1 (continued). Periods I–IV: Classification of issues (summary)

PERIOD I

Pan Head Tetradrachms

Group	26	27	28	29	30	31	32	33	34	35	36	37	38
Specimens	6	4	8	2	3	11	17	3	8	19	1	2	34
Die combinations	2	2	3	1	2	6	9	2	5	10	1	1	14
Obverse dies	1	[1-1]	1	[1-1]	[2-1]	[1-1]	[1-1]	1	[1-1]	[2-2]	1	[1-1]	[2-2]
Reverse dies	2	[2-2]	3	1	2	6	9	2	[5-1]	10	1	1	14

PERIOD III

	Pan Head Tetradrachms							**Poseidon Head Tetradrachms**					
Group	26	27	28	29	30	31	Total	32	33	34	35	36	37
Specimens	49	2	1	4	10	1	342	5	22	2	21	3	84
Die combinations	12	1	1	3	4	1	136	2	8	1	7	1	17
Obverse dies	[1-1]	1	[1-1]	1	1	[1-1]	20	1	[3-1]	[1-1]	[2-1]	[1-1]	1
Reverse dies	12	1	1	3	4	1	127	2	8	1	7	1	17

PERIOD IV

	Zeus Head Tetradrachm	**Poseidon Head Tetradrachms**					
Group	15	16	17	18	19	20	21
Specimens	1	22	7	2	1	1	9
Die combinations	1	6	3	2	1	1	5
Obverse dies	1	1	1	2	[1-1]	[1-1]	1
Reverse dies	1	6	3	2	1	1	5

Table 7.1 (continued). Periods I–IV: Classification of issues (summary).

PERIOD I

	Pan Head Tetradrachms												D
Group	39	40	41	42	43	44	45	46	47	48	49	Total	50
Specimens	2	2	1	6	3	2	1	4	4	1	8	464	1
Die combinations	1	2	1	2	2	2	1	2	3	1	1	183	1
Obverse dies	[1-1]	[2-2]	[1-1]	[1-1]	[1-1]	[2-1]	[1-1]	[1-1]	3	[1-1]	[1-1]	36	1
Reverse dies	1	2	1	2	2	2	1	2	1	1	1	170	1

PERIOD III

	Poseidon Head Tetradrachms											
Group	38	39	40	41	42	43	44	45	46	47	48	Total
Specimens	1	3	1	89	35	98	68	77	32	38	50	707
Die Combinations	1	1	1	15	5	17	12	15	5	8	9	140
Obverse dies	1	[1-1]	1	3	1	1	1	3	1	[4-1]	1	21
Reverse dies	1	1	1	15	5	17	[12-1]	15	[5-1]	8	9	124

PERIOD IV

	Poseidon Head 4D		D	5O
Group	22	Total	23	24
Specimens	3	45	55	1
Die combinations	2	20	11	1
Obverse dies	1	6	2	1
Reverse dies	2	20	11	1

7.1 The Rate of Production: The Evidence of the Obverse Dies

Even though caution is necessary in calculating ancient coin production,[18] the Antigonid precious metal coinages provide a sample large enough to allow for credible estimations on the basis of probability theory. We will employ the formulae generated by the statisticians Carter, Esty and Good, which have been recognized by S. E. Buttrey and T. V. Buttrey as reliable when applied to large samples.[19] More recently, Esty proposed a further emendation in his formula, favouring the adoption of shape parameter p = 1 instead of p = 2; we may adopt his new type in our calculations.[20]

1. More specifically, with d = the number of different obverse dies observed, n = the number of recorded specimens, Carter calculates the number of dies which were used, k′, with the aid of the following equations:

If $n < 2d$,	$k' = nd / (1.214n - 1.197d)$.
If $2d < n < 3d$,	$k' = nd / (1.124n - 1.016d)$.
If $n > 3d$,	$k' = nd / (1.069n - 0.843d)$.

2. Esty's mathematical revision of the above Carter model has resulted in the following most recent equation, in order to estimate the original number of dies:

(1) $k' = nd / (n - d)$.

(2) The approximate confidence equal-output intervals are obtained from C_2, as follows:

$$C_2 = (d + n / 2) / (k_2 + n/2),$$

where C_2 = output of dies of observed varieties and $k_2' = k' + n\,(k'-d)/(pd)$, with p = 2.

3. Thirdly, Good estimates first the so-called "coverage," i.e., the die varieties of an issue which are observed in a sample, through either of the following equations:

$$(a)\ C' = 1 - (N_1 / n),$$

where C′ = coverage estimator and N_1 = the number of varieties observed exactly once, or, more precisely for smaller samples,

$$(b)\ C' = 1 - (N_1 / n) + 2N_2 / (n\,(n-1)),$$

where C′ = coverage estimator and N_2 = the number of varieties observed exactly twice.

18. The general frame of this debate is exposed in: F. de Callataÿ, "Quantifying Monetary Production in Greco-Roman Times: A General Frame," in idem (ed.), *QMS*, 7–29; idem, "A Quantitative Survey of Hellenistic Coinages: Recent Achievements," in Archibald et al. (eds.), *MMM*, 73–91, with earlier bibliography. More specifically, see T. V. Buttrey, Quantification of Ancient Coin Production: The Third Element," in Callataÿ, *QMS*, 105–112; S. E. Buttrey and T. V. Buttrey, "Calculating Ancient Coin Production, Again," *AJN* (1997), 113–135, *contra* F. de Callataÿ, "Calculating Ancient Coin Production: Seeking a Balance," *NC* 155 (1995), 289–311, and F. de Callataÿ, G. Depeyrot and L. Villaronga, *L'argent monnayé d' Alexandre le Grand à Auguste*, Brussels: Cercle d' Études Numismatiques, Travaux 12 (1993); T. V. Buttrey, Calculating Ancient Coin Production: Facts and Fantasies," *NC* 153 (1993) 335–332; id., "Calculating Ancient Coin Production, II: why it cannot be done," *NC* 154 (1994), 341–352.

19. "We agree that the formulae generated by Carter, Esty, and Good on the basis of probability theory can provide credible solutions under the right circumstances, but they are not fruitful in the case of very small samples": S. E. Buttrey and T. V. Buttrey, "Calculating ancient coin production, again," *AJN Second Series* 9 (1997) 115. Cf. W. S. Esty, "Estimating the Size of a Coinage," *NC* 144 (1984), 180–183; idem, "Estimation of the Size of a Coinage: A Survey and Comparison of Methods," *NC* 146 (1986), 185–215. Cf. Callataÿ, *Recueil*, vi–ix.

20. W. W. Esty, "The Geometric Model for Estimating the Number of Dies," in Callataÿ, *QMS*, 43–58. In order to maintain compatibility between Esty's new type and the respective equations by Carter and Good, we have replaced Esty's "e1" for "estimator" (of the number of dies), with "k," as in *NC* 146 (1986), 185–221.

Table 7.2. Antigonid obverse dies per type per period and their value (in talents)

For 20.000 Specimens Per O Die:

	Alex AV Staters: O Dies	Alex AV Staters: Value (AR Talents)	Alex AR 4Ds: O Dies	Alex AR 4Ds: Value (Talents)	Alex AR Ds: O Dies 1	Alex AR Ds: Value (AR Talents)	Pan AR 4Ds: O Dies	Pan AR 4Ds: Value (AR Talents)	Pan AR Ds: O Dies	Pan AR Ds: Value (AR	Poseidon AR 4Ds: O Dies	Poseidon AR 4Ds: Value (AR Talents)	Zeus AR 4Ds: Dies	Zeus AR 4Ds: Value (AR Talents)	Zeus AR Ds: O Dies	Zeus AR Ds: Value (AR Talents)	Zeus AR 4Os: O Dies	Zeus AR 4Os: Value (AR Talents)	Total Value (AR Talents)
Period I	5	333	1	13,33	1	3,33	36	480	1	3,33									833
Period II							12	160											160
Period III							20	266,66			21	280							546,66
Period IV							15	200			6	80	1	13,33	2	6,66	1	2,22	302,21
																			1841,87

For 30.000 Specimens Per O Die:

	Alex AV Staters: O Dies	Alex AV Staters: Value (AR Talents)	Alex AR 4Ds: O Dies	Alex AR 4Ds: Value (Talents)	Alex AR Ds: O Dies 1	Alex AR Ds: Value (AR Talents)	Pan AR 4Ds: O Dies	Pan AR 4Ds: Value (AR Talents)	Pan AR Ds: O Dies	Pan AR Ds: Value (AR	Poseidon AR 4Ds: O Dies	Poseidon AR 4Ds: Value (AR Talents)	Zeus AR 4Ds: Dies	Zeus AR 4Ds: Value (AR Talents)	Zeus AR Ds: O Dies	Zeus AR Ds: Value (AR Talents)	Zeus AR 4Os: O Dies	Zeus AR 4Os: Value (AR Talents)	Total Value (AR Talents)
Period I	5	500	1	20	1	5	36	720	1	5									1250
Period II							12	240											240
Period III							20	400			21	420							820
Period IV							15	300			6	120	1	20	2	10	1	3,33	453,33
																			2763,33

The coverage estimate is then converted into a die-number estimate (with an assumed shape parameter of the die-output distribution p=1), using type (b) for C′ in the equation:

$$(c)\ k_2' = (d + n / C') - n = (d / C') + n (1 - C') + n (1 - C') / C'.$$ [21]

The application of these three methods to the sample of the Antigonid coinage yields the results shown in Table 7.2. The obverse dies linking two or more groups of the same period are considered with both or all groups, but the accurate number of dies per period for each coin type is quoted in the total number of dies, d. Hence the total number of dies per type per period and the sum of dies of sub-types may sometimes diverge. It is remarkable that the obverse dies observed for the Antigonid types are in full accordance with the statistic estimates. The results from all three methods generally coincide for the larger samples, i.e., the two main tetradrachm types; but none of these may be employed effectively in smaller samples, i.e., in the transitional gold staters or in the Zeus drachmae. Thus Esty's remark that "all the above methods are restricted in practice to samples where N1/n is not greater than about 0.9" is confirmed.[22]

Table 7.3. Antigonid tetradrachms (Pans/Poseidons):
Carter, Esty, Good estimates of numbers of obverse dies

	Carter	Esty	Good
Pan tetradrachm obverses	82.5	89.7	90.5
Poseidon tetradrachm obverses	26.4	28.6	29.2
ALL	108.9	111.4	119.7

The estimated obverse dies, on the basis of the 110 observed for Antigonid silver tetradrachms (83 for the Pans, 27 for the Poseidons) are with Carter's formulae c. 83 obverses for the Pans (with 83 observed) and c. 26.4 obverses for the Poseidons, of which 27 have been traced. The respective numbers for Esty and Good are, c. 90 and c. 91 for the Pan obverses, and c. 29 and c. 29 for their Poseidon counterparts. The figures obtained reveal weaknesses in Carter's method of calculating ancient coin production: apart from its inaccuracy with smaller issues, that his types do not pro-

21. We have modified type K in *NC* 146 (1986), 185–215, p. 219 with the shape parameter of distribution p = 1, following Esty in Callataÿ, *QMS*, 43–58.

22. W. W. Esty, "Estimation of the Size of a Coinage," *NC* 146 (1986), 209.

vide for equality inevitably leaves aside a significant number of specimens (i.e., in Period III, the Athena to the right / to the left, *desmos* Pan variety, the letter X Pan tetradrachms; all categories of Period IV, except Trident—AR). Thus greater faith will be placed in the calculations of the size of the silver tetradrachm issues and, more specifically, in the calculations by Esty and Good based upon the existing sample.

1. Firmly determining the exact duration of the four periods of Antigonid coin production in order to estimate the rate of annual production adds to the conventional nature of these calculations. Bearing this in mind, the 36–39 tetradrachm obverses estimated via the above methods for the first period, ranging from 268/7 or 266/5 to between 261/0 and 255 BC, may have been utilized within an average period of nine years. Approximately 12–14 tetradrachm obverse dies are assigned to the six years between 252 and 246/5 BC of Period II. Finally, c. 63.5 obverse dies of Pans, Zeus, and Poseidons have been assigned to the 25 years between 246/5 and 221 BC (Periods III–IV). The numbers acquired from the estimated annual production for each period are therefore: 4.167 obverses for Period I; 2.17 for Period II; 2.54 for Periods III–IV. By converting all obverse dies known for the gold and silver coinage into tetradrachm equivalents (one gold stater obverse = five silver tetradrachm obverses; one silver tetradrachm obverse = four silver drachma obverses = six silver tetrobol obverses; one silver drachma obverse = 0.25 tetradrachm obverse; one tetrobol obverse = 0.16 tetradrachm obverse), the following average figures of annual consumption of such dies are acquired for each period:[23]

Table 7.4. Variation in die output of Antigonid issues between different periods

Period	Number of tetradrachm-equivalent obverse dies	Average production of obverse dies per year	Average production of obverse dies per year (Carter)	Average production of obverse dies per year (Esty)	Average production of obverse dies per year (Good)
I (271/68–260/55 BC)	62.5	6.94	6.94	7.25	7.91
II (252/1–246 BC)	13	2.17	1.98	2.15	2.36
III (246/5–229)	41	2.91	2.77	2.98	3.07
IV (229–221)	22.70	2.83	3.00	3.06	n/a

2. The number of obverse dies used in every period of coin production may serve as an indicator of the value of the silver coinage minted from them. As the number of coins minted from a die is now agreed to have ranged between 10,000 and 30,000 specimens,[24] and given that one talent equalled 6,000 silver drachmae on the Attic weight standard, the amount of silver (talents) which was minted from the silver tetradrachm obverse dies in each of the four above-mentioned periods may be calculated with some accuracy if we multiply the mean coin output per die, i.e., 20,000 (specimens),[25] by the number of dies per period and then by four and if we then divide the sum by 6000 (the number of drachmae per talent in the Attic weight standard). In regard to the silver

23. Factors such as, differing rates of die survival over the periods or the possibility that dies of different (or of the same) size may have produced quite different numbers of coins would easily have influenced the results. Thus our calculations need not be taken as accurate but rather as offering an approximate overview of the impact of the production of Antigonid coinage in contemporary markets.

24. For a general frame of the debate over the number of coins minted per obverse die see F. de Callataÿ, "Quantifying Monetary Production in Greco-Roman Times: A General Frame," in idem, *QMS*, 7–29, esp. 7–13, who allows for a production up to 40000 specimens per die; but note T. V. Buttrey's strong reservations against such calculations: "Quantification of Ancient Coin Production: The Third Element," in de Callataÿ, *QMS*, 105–112. Cf. W. W. Esty, "Estimation of the Size of a Coinage," *NC* 146 (1986) 185–215, esp. 188–189, n. 9–10.

25. Le Rider, *Alexandre le Grand*, 92, 319 promotes the 20,000 specimens per die.

tetradrachms, the 36 Pan head obverse dies of Period I amounted to 480 talents; the 12 obverse dies of Period II equalled 160 talents, while the 20 and 15 obverses of Periods III and IV amounted to 266.7 and to 200 talents, respectively. Turning to the Poseidon tetradrachms, the 21 and the 6 obverses for Periods III and IV equalled 280 and 80 talents, respectively. To these may be added the coin issues with low die output: the amount of silver coins minted from the single obverse die of the Alexander tetradrachms in the name of King Antigonos from Period I and that of the Zeus tetradrachm of Period IV may have reached 13.33 talents each. It is also remarkable that, with the gold to silver ratio at 1 : 10 in the Hellenistic period, the value of the coinage minted from the five dies of gold staters with Alexander III types, multiplied by 20,000 specimens and given that one gold stater amounted to 5 silver tetradrachms, rose to 333 talents in silver: thus the five only gold stater obverse dies introduced to the market a not insignificant amount of precious metal. Antigonid silver drachmae were launched in much lower amounts: the single drachma obverse die with Alexander types but in the name of king Antigonos and its single Pan counterpart from Period I amount to 3.33 talents each. In Period IV, the two obverses of the Zeus drachmae yielded 6,66 talents, while the single obverse tetrobol die may have minted 2,22 talents of silver. Thus the precious metal output in silver talents per coin production period may be sketched as follows: Period I, 832.99; Period II, 160; Period III, 546.66; Period IV, 302.21 talents. Allowing for a maximum production of 30,000 specimens per obverse die, these amounts may be emended to: Period I, 1250; Period II, 240; Period III, 820; Period IV, 453.33 talents (see Fig. 7.5). These sums gain in perspective if assessed against mainstream practical needs of the state, such as soldier payments: the monthly payment of 1,000 soldiers, at 20 silver drachmae per month each, for instance, would have required a sum of either 3.3 or 5 talents per month, allowing for 20,000 and 30,000 specimens per die, respectively. Thus the 832,99 talents of Period I would have covered the monthly payment of 1000 soldiers for c. 28–42 semester periods; the 160 talents of Period II would have financed them for 5.3–8.1 semester periods; in the same vein, the 546.66 and 302.21 talents of Periods III and IV would have sufficed the same group of soldiers for 18.2–29.6 and for 10.1–15.35 semester periods, respectively.

3. The total volume of silver introduced into the circulation pool, on the basis of the estimate of these Antigonid obverse dies, when compared with the average production of ±28 obverses per year estimated with the same method for Philip II,[26] fall far short of the increased financial needs created by the military, religious and other activities undertaken primarily by Gonatas. An annual rate of 2.17–2.36 obverses for period II, for instance, is as inappropriate for a period of intense military preparations as are the 6.94–7.10 obverses per year for period I. These numbers can neither represent the military expenditure in response to the revolt of Alexander of Korinth and the battle of Andros, nor that during the Chremonidean War and the battle off Kos, respectively (see Chapters 3 and 2). Similarly, the continuous engagement of the Antigonids in warfare in Central and Southern Greece, and the Karian expedition undertaken by Antigonos Doson, would have required larger coin issues than those represented by obverses per year during periods III and IV. A comparison with the large amounts of silver required under Philip V,[27] for instance, reveals that the silver required for large enterprises in the late third century BC by far outnumbered the total estimates for the individual silver issues in the name of "King Antigonos." To the military needs

26. Le Rider, *Monnayage et finances*, 77; Callataÿ, *Recueil*, 96–104.

27. A. Mamroth, "'Die Silbermünzen des Königs Philippos V. von Makedonien," *ZfN* 40 (1930), 277–230. Mørkholm, *EHC*, 135–136; N. G. L. Hammond, "The Defeat of the Macedonian Army and the Roman Settlement (197–196 B.C.)," in Hammond and Walbank, *Macedonia* III, 460–468.

of the Antigonids one may add regular state expenditure, in addition to money spent for religious offerings or for the construction of public buildings, e.g. the construction of the Antigonid portico on Delos.[28]

That new coinage was quite often well below the level of state expenditure is not a novelty in antiquity: it has been argued that a large portion of state expenses was covered by old and "recycled" coin, i.e., coin reentering treasuries through payments.[29] It is also worth stressing that an insufficient production of coinage was not an unusual phenomenon in Hellenistic states, either: F. de Callataÿ, for instance, built upon this type of argument in his discussion of the coinage introduced during the Mithridatic wars, drawing an analogy from similar studies on Roman Provincial issues.[30] Since it is most unlikely that the Antigonids maintained a small standing army and navy or severely restricted state expenditure during this period, alternative sources of coin or transaction practices must be considered. Before this, the distribution pattern of the hoards with Antigonid issues is worth investigating.

28. See, for instance, B. Schmidt-Dounas, "Der dorische Fries der Stoa des Antigonos Gonatas auf Delos," *MDAI(A)* 109 (1994), 227–242; C. Tarditi, "Architettura come propaganda. Esame dell' dell'attività edilizia degli Antigonidi in Grecia e nuove proposte di attribuzione," *Aevum Antiquum* 3 (1990), 43–74.

29. Howgego, *Ancient History from Coins*, 35–36; Burnett, *CRW*, 95, based on Carradice, *Domitian*, notes that new coinage rose to 10% of the coinage used at the time of Domitian. Cf. Aperghis, *SRE*, 211, 245; M. Aperghis, "Population—Production—Taxation—Coinage," in Z. Archibald et al., *Hellenistic Economies* (London: Routledge, 2001), 69–102, esp. 92–97.

30. Callataÿ, *Guerres Mithridatiques*, 407–415; Callataÿ, *QMS*, 17–19, with earlier bibliography and comments. F. de Callataÿ, "'Guerres et monnayages à l' époque hellénistique," *Dossiers d' Archéologie* 248, Nov. (1999), 28–35.

7.2 Distribution

The hoards containing precious metal coinage in the name of "King Antigonos" have been mapped by Touratsoglou, who compares the distribution patterns of the silver Pans (assigned to "Gonatas"), the Poseidons ("Doson"), and the silver coins of Antiochos Hierax (see our updated Map). His conclusions may be summarized thus:

(i) The Pans first occur in hoards of 270/60 BC from mainland Greece, where they continue in circulation until the end of the third century. With the exception of two hoards from Southern Turkey, South Asia Minor, 1976 and Meydancıkkale, 1980, they first occur in Asia Minor, in the Middle and Near East and Egypt only during the 220s. They continued sporadically to circulate in Syria, in particular, until at least 138 BC.[31]

(ii) The long circulation of the Pans in Greece contrasts with their rarity outside the Balkans. This is explained by the use of later Makedonian posthumous Alexanders in North and Eastern Makedonia. Touratsoglou suggests that these Alexanders continued in production until Philip V, citing the common or similar monograms among Pans, Poseidons and the issues of Philip V. But he offers no further argumentation.[32]

(iii) In contrast to their rarity in the Balkans, the Poseidons are attested in large numbers in hoards of the 220s from the Eastern Aegean and the Eastern Mediterranean. This is presumably because they were meant to finance Doson's Karian expedition of 227–225 BC.

(iv) The Poseidons are contemporary with issues of Antiochos Hierax from Alexandreia Troas. The concentration of hoards in the Balkans and Asia Minor with the earliest issues of Alexandreia Troas and Lampsakos and of hoards with the latest issues from Asia Minor and Syria is explained by the transfer of these coins to the Balkans by the Makedonians, as booty, after Doson's Karian campaign.[33]

Criticism of these suggestions will be focused on the following points:

In the first place, the use of Alexanders in transactions in Thrace and the Danube is indeed highly likely, particularly as the hoards from Verge, Kilkis and Jabukovac (*IGCH* 455, 445 and 447), containing later Makedonian posthumous Alexanders, are probably of a later date (cf. Chapters 6.3, 6.4). Moreover, continuity among these Alexanders, the Pans and the Poseidons, is suggested by their shared monograms (cf. Chapter 6.2.4). Thus Ehrhardt's assumption, based on the absence of silver issues of "King Antigonos" from Thrace and the Danube, that Gonatas had no influence in this area and that he did not recruit mercenaries from Thrace, should be treated with caution.[34] Similarly, the alleged absence of Pans from the Black Sea area earlier than the 220s is now undermined by an Alexander silver tetradrachm from Mesembria, dated between 250 and 175 B, which was overstruck on a Pan tetradrachm.[35] The absence of Antigonid issues from Thrace and the Danube may be explained by the application of the closed Ptolemaic monetary system in local transactions during the Ptolemaic presence in Thrace from the late 240s on.[36]

31. Touratsoglou, *DM*, 76.
32. Touratsoglou, ibid., 82. See also Chapter 6.5, p. 304, n. 6.
33. Touratsoglou, ibid., 85.
34. Ehrhardt, *Studies*, 79–80, who points out that Athenian silver coins are also rare in this region during this period; cf. F. W. Walbank, "Antigonus Gonatas: The last years (251–39 B.C.)," in Hammond and Walbank, *Macedonia* III, 314.
35. Price, *Alexander*, 183, no. 1005. This coin formed part of the Propontis, 1950 hoard (*IGCH* 888; *CH* 7 (1985), no. 93): see Appendices.
36. Will, *HPMH* I^2, 250–261.

The hoards with Pans postdate 260 BC. The objections to Touratsoglou's dating by of the first lot of the "savings" hoard North of Larissa, 1985 to c. 270 BC and the shift of the date of the Karditsa, 1929 hoard to c. 245–240 BC have been discussed elsewhere (see Chapter 6.3).

It is worth noting that the absence of Pans from hoards from Asia Minor contrasts with the recently published inscription suggesting Gonatas' presence in Karia in 268 BC.[37] Moreover, with the exception of the S. Asia Minor, 1976 and the Meydancıkkale, 1980 hoard, neither the Pans nor the Poseidons are represented in hoards from Asia Minor between 240 and 220 BC. Furthermore, although the return of the Makedonians from Karia may well explain the arrival of the early issues of Hierax in the Balkans as booty, it certainly does not explain the remarkable rarity of the Poseidons in the Balkans. For, had the Poseidons been meant to finance the Karian expedition, as Touratsoglou argues, one would expect their presence alongside the Hierax issues in hoards from the Balkans. This, however, does not occur.

The distinction between "circulation" and "savings" hoards (Chapter 6.3, Table 6.13), allows us to conclude that it is the issues of the first period that circulated widely in Asia Minor, the Middle and Near East and that occur in late, most often "savings," hoards. The introduction of the Poseidons cannot therefore be determined by the relative wear of the Pans and Poseidons in Eastern hoards, for the particular Pan head specimens may antedate the Poseidon series altogether (cf. Chapter 6.3).[38]

The concentration of issues of the first two Ptolemies in hoards from the Peloponnese and (in smaller proportions) from Northern Greece after 246 BC contrasts starkly with the rarity of precious metal issues of Ptolemy III found in these areas.[39] This might be taken to indicate the "recycling," i.e., melting and reuse, of the lighter Ptolemaic tetradrachms in the Peloponese after that date (Chapters 1.2, 5, 6.4.3). The rarity of precious metal coinages of Ptolemy III in the Balkans is thus more convincingly explained than by the alleged arrival of Ptolemaic coins in Greece through commercial transactions, via Karia or through Ptolemaic gifts to the inhabitants of the Peloponnese.[40] Our explanation of the absence of precious metal Ptolemaic issues from mainland Greece through their "recycling" after 246 BC is further supported by the fact that, as the hoards involved comprise silver coins on two different weight standards, Attic and Ptolemaic, they cannot reflect the contemporary circulation pool in the areas concerned unless they come from "peripheral" regions where both standards were in use. Hence the absence of both Pans and Poseidons from hoards from Thrace and Asia Minor between 240 and 220 BC coincides with the general dearth of hoards from these areas with silver coins struck on the Attic standard during this period.[41] This might be interpreted by the expansion of the Ptolemaic practice of "recycling" silver

37. See Chapter 6.4.2.

38. Doubts on this criterion for dating the respective types have already been expressed by Chr. Ehrhardt: *Studies*, 77–78.

39. Ashton notes the presence of tetradrachms of Ptolemy III in *IGCH* 175, 179 and 237 from the Balkans: *Review*, 10. Indeed the presence of bronze coins of Ptolemy III around the Peloponnese refutes the notion of his complete withdrawal from the Aegean: K. Chryssanthaki-Nagle, "Les monnaies lagides en Égée," in F. Duyrat and O. Picard (eds.), *L'exception égyptienne? Production et échanges en Égypte hellénistique et romaine, Actes du colloque d'Alexandrie, 13–15 avril 2002*, 159–173, esp. 162–166; Cf. Chapter 6.3, hoard no. 19 (Korinth, environs, 1938: *IGCH* 187), 252–253, n. 53. But the absence of his, admittedly lighter, silver and gold specimens from the Peloponnese and from Northern Greece after 246 BC calls for explanation. As the constant military tension in the Peloponnese in the second half of the third century BC must have made the need for silver imperative, such silver coins may have been melted and reused.

40. As Touratsoglou, *DM*, 85–86. He invariably identifies all the related hoards as "circulation" hoards. He notes "the individuality of the coinage of the Lagids and their closed economic policy with its well known protectionism of their currency aimed at preventing any mixing of Ptolemaic tetradrachms with others of the Attic standard." Yet he does not distinguish between the hoards with coins on both standards and those with specimens struck on the same weight standard.

41. Except *IGCH* 869–871, including royal silver issues. The absence of Athenian tetradrachms from Makedonian hoards during this period has been noted by Ehrhardt: cf. n. 34.

in Thrace in the late 240s and in the coastal areas of Asia Minor, over which they gained control during the Laodikean War.[42] Hence the absence of the Poseidons from Asia Minor before the 220s has no chronological implications.

The hoard evidence is not sufficient to reconstruct the distribution of the transitional posthumous gold Alexanders, the Zeus tetradrachm, and the silver Zeus fractions. There survives only a single hoard with a transitional gold stater, Poteidaia/Kassandreia, 1984. Two hoards including silver drachmae are also known, Drama, 1989 and Sophikon, 1893 (cf. Chapter 6.3).

By and large, the distribution of the Antigonid silver issues predominantly reflects local preferences in transactions. The extensive use of the posthumous later Alexander silver issues in the North perhaps explains, to an extent, the absence of hoards with Pans from this area. Pans, however, are popular in the direct Antigonid realm, that is, Makedonia, Thessaly, Epeiros and Eretria. They cluster in the period between 250 and 227 BC and they occur more rarely in "savings" hoards between 220 and 190 BC. No hoards are recorded from Southern Greece, despite the Antigonids' engagement in military expeditions in this area throughout this period.

The absence of Antigonid precious metal issues from Egypt is certainly not surprising, as a letter from the Zenon archive reveals that the mint of Alexandreia normally restruck foreign coin into Ptolemaic coin for "foreigners who came here by sea, the merchants, the forwarding agents and others."[43] As for the Eastern Mediterranean, with the exception of a "savings" hoard from the temple of Artemis at Sardeis and of the hoard from Meydancıkkale, which presumably reflect circulation on the frontiers between the Seleukid and the Ptolemaic realms, the Pans are absent from Asia Minor until the 220s. This may have been due to the application of the Ptolemaic practice of "recycling" silver in the regions the Ptolemies occupied during the second half of the third century, as well as in Egypt itself. The Pans are more consistently represented in hoards after 220 BC, presumably due to the Antigonids' emergence in Karia and the Eastern Mediterranean after 227 BC and to the recovery of the area by the Seleukids. Finally, the very worn Pans from the first period in some of these (clearly late) "savings" hoards attest the popularity of this type in Asia Minor,[44] despite the *lacuna* in the hoards between the mid-240s and the mid-220s.

The absence of Poseidons from hoards from Asia Minor between the 240s and the 220s may also have been due to the "recycling" of silver in Asia Minor and the Near East. Their absence from hoards from the Balkans, apart from those from Kassandreia, Karditsa, and Thesprotia, is also noteworthy (cf. Chapter 6.3). Their presence in deposition and circulation hoards from Asia

42. Will, *HPMH* I^2, 251. On the conquest of Thrace during the Laodikean War (246–241 BC), see *OGIS* 54; cf. Bagnall, *Administration*, 159–168. On the administration of Asia Minor in this period, see ibid., 89–116. On the coinage and on its circulation in the Ptolemaic realm, see ibid., 176–212, esp. 210–212. The quasi-absence of Ptolemaic coinage from excavation contexts in Thrace, in the Aegean and in Asia Minor has been interpreted as absence of a uniform Ptolemaic monetary policy for the regions under Ptolemaic control: P. Rodriguez, L'intervention ptolémaique dans la guerre de Chremonidès au vu du monnayage lagide," *RN* 155 (2000), 9–16; K. Chryssanthaki, "Les monnaies lagides en Égee," in Duyrat—Picard, *L'exception égyptienne?*,159–175; A. Davesne, "Les monnaies des premiers Ptolemées en Asie Mineure et à Chypre," in Duyrat—Picard, *L' exception égyptienne?*, 177–185; Psoma, Karadima, and Terzopoulou, *The Coins from Maroneia*, 2221–2223, esp. 222, n. 49, 248; S. Psoma, "Numismatic Evidence on the Ptolemaic Involvement in Thrace during the Second Syrian War," *AJN* 20 (2008), 257–263. But it may be argued that the possibility of melting down and "recycling" this foreign Ptolemaic lighter-weight coinage in precious metal need not be excluded altogether: K. Panagopoulou, "Silver as a Commodity in the Hellenistic Period," *BSA* 102 (2007), 315–343, esp. 333, n. 85.

43. *P. Cairo Zenon* 59021 = *Select Papyri* II, no. 409; cf. W. Schubart, "Die ptolemäische Reichsmünze in den auswärtigen Besitzungen unter Philadelphos," *ZfN* 33 (1922), 74–82; Mørkholm, *EHC*, 104; cf. C. J. Howgego, "Coin Circulation and the Integration of the Roman Economy," *JRA* 7 (1994), 5–21, for Roman examples. The Delta, 1927–1928 hoard, dated to the early second century BC, is the only known hoard with Antigonid silver issues from Egypt: cf. Chapter 6.3.

44. Cf., for instance, the Gordion, 1961 hoard (Chapter 6.3).

Minor, Syria, and the Near East after 220 BC is presumably explained by the recovery of these areas by the Seleukids.[45] Finally, the alleged transport of the issues of Hierax to the Balkans after the Karian expedition does not show that the Poseidons were introduced to finance the Karian expedition, particularly as the Poseidons are not as extensively represented in hoards of the Balkans as the Hierax varieties. Last but not least, the transfer of these issues to the West must be related to the emergence of Rome in the Eastern Mediterranean.[46]

45. Will, *HPMH* I^2, 256–261.
46. Touratsoglou, *DM*, 78.

7.3 Economic Systems at the Time of the Antigonids

Prima facie the low annual consumption of silver Antigonid obverse dies suggests that Antigonos Gonatas, Demetrios II and Antigonos Doson did not aim to provide currency for international or large-scale national commerce. The fact that the Antigonid silver coins are generally outnumbered by foreign coins in Makedonian hoards indicates that there was no attempt to impose a monopoly of Makedonian coinage, as was done from 305 BC in Egypt and in Pergamon, during the second century BC.[47] At the same time, the fact that only six of the fifty-four recorded hoards with Antigonid silver coins come from Makedonia seems to indicate the reverse, i.e., that Antigonid coinage was intended for international use.

Walbank claims that Makedonian coins were outnumbered by foreign coins in Makedonia, Thessaly and Euboia, while they rarely occur outside these areas. Assuming that the minting of an adequate and reliable silver coinage is an indicator of the prosperity of the kingdom, he concludes that Makedonia was not as wealthy under the Antigonids as the other Hellenistic states.[48] Yet the military activity argues against poverty for Makedonia in the Antigonid period.

In order to reconcile the limited Antigonid coin production with the intense financial needs of their military (and other) enterprises, one must ask whether the small size of this coinage is an indicator of poverty in Antigonid Makedonia. How did the Antigonids finance their activities, if their coin output was insufficient for the purpose?

Unless technical difficulties impeded the extraction of silver from the mines, it would be difficult to explain this low level of minting during a period of particularly intense military enterprises as a sign of poverty. The hypothesis is also incompatible with the Antigonids' demonstration of wealth through dedications to Apollo and through the extensive building programmes undertaken by Gonatas both in Makedonia and on Delos.[49] The covering over by Gonatas of the royal tombs at Vergina and the construction of the portico of his ancestors, the dedication of his flagship to Apollo, the foundation of vase festivals on Delos and the celebratory issues introduced after his naval victories at Kos and Andros, are all signs of wealth (see Chapters 1.2, 6.4.3); so is his dispatch to Aratos of Sikyon of twenty five talents, following his predecessors' policy of supporting pro-Makedonian parties in the Greek states.[50] Similarly, the increasing demand for silver plate, for domestic and funerary use, which has been attested archaeologically in Makedonia from the mid-fourth century BC onwards, echoing the legendary donations of gold and silver cups and vases during Makedonian *symposia*, illustrate a quite proliferating noble society.[51]

47. See n. 17. On the presence, for instance, of Athenian tetradrachms alongside Alexander tetradrachms in Macedonia, see Touratsoglou, *Contribution*, 132–133 and 232, with earlier bibliography; Y. Touratsoglou, "Les Galates sous les pentes de l' Olympe: le trésor IV de Néos Pantéléimon, lieu-dit Krania," *RN* 162 (2006), 99–116; F. de Callataÿ, "Athenian 'New Style' Tetradrachms in Macedonian Hoards," *AJN* 3–4 (1992), 11–20.

48. F. W. Walbank, "The End of Antigonus' Reign," in Hammond and Walbank, *Macedonia* III, 314–315.

49. On the practice of constructing buildings as a form of accumulation of surplus at controlling Greco-Makedonian centers, see G. Shipley, "Distance, Development, Decline? World-systems Analysis and the 'Hellenistic World,'" in Per Bilde et al., *Centre and periphery*, 276. Cf. K. Bringman, "The King as Benefactor: Some Remarks on Ideal Kingship in the Age of Hellenism," in Bulloch et al., *Images and Ideologies*, 7–24; Chapter 1.2.

50. Plut. *Arat.* 11.2; Touratsoglou, *Contribution*, 112, 230; F. G. Maier, *Geschichte Mauerbauinschriften*, I, *Texte und Kommentare*. II, *Untersuchungen* (Heidelberg 1961); G. Shipley, "Between Macedonia and Rome: Political Landscapes and Social Change in Southern Greece in the Early Hellenistic Period," *ABSA* 100 (2005), 316–330.

51. On the prolific archaeological evidence for Macedonian silverware, see, for instance, E. Zimi, *Late Classical and Hellenistic Silver Plate from Macedonia* (Oxford: University Press, 2011), with earlier bibliography. On the use of silver plate for Macedonian *symposia*, see Athen. 4.128a–130d; M. Faranguna, "L' economia della Macedonia ellenistica: Un Bilancio," in A. Bresson, P. Briant and F. Burkhalter (eds.), *Approches de l' économie hellénistique [4e rencontre de l' économie antique, Saint-Bertrand-des-Comminges (6–7 mai 2004)* (Paris: De Boccard), 121–146, esp. 129; cf. Touratsoglou, *Contribution*, 86–89, 98–101, 106 and 228–229, 230–231; Archibald, *Northern Aegean*, 271–296.

Indirect ways of meeting military costs, such as booty, taxation from Makedonia and from the Antigonid strongholds in Greece, may have significantly reduced the cost of maintaining the Makedonian army and fleet.[52] It has also been suggested that the cities may have financed military garrisons, recruited citizens, or even billeted soldiers and officers in citizens' households.[53] A clue to the nature of transactions in Makedonia may be seen in Pseudo-Aristotle's *Oeconomicus*, according to which the king is responsible for the approval of a particular type of coinage and for the selection of the appropriate moment to confirm its validity (ποῖον καὶ πότε [τίμιον ἤ εὔωνον] ποιητέον). The fact that the king is reported to regulate the quality (ποῖον) but not the quantity (πόσον) of the coinage struck confirms that he did not monopolise coinage.[54] It also suggests that he not only validated the type of the metal to be minted at a particular moment, but also accepted the use of other, earlier or foreign, coinages within his realm.

It may in fact be argued that the Attic weight standard allowed for considerable flexibility in the acceptance in Makedonia of coinages struck by various issuing authorities from the Greek mainland, the Seleukid empire and the West. This trend, set by Alexander the Great,[55] must have been the norm during the *interregnum* in the third century BC: the "king without a kingdom" must at least until his nomination in Makedonia have used coins in the names of others for the payment of troops. Obviously the most useful coinages for payments in the Antigonid realm, besides the Antigonid personal issues, were the Attic-weight royal coinages which were struck in Makedonia, i.e., Alexanders and others. The transitional posthumous Alexanders indicate the continued production and use of posthumous Alexander tetradrachms at least until the 260s (see Chapter 6.4.1). The stylistically divergent heads of Herakles on these Alexanders, the various sizes of the modules on both the Pans and the Alexanders, and the compatibility of the last hoards with these Alexanders of a later date are remarkable (see Chapters 6.4.1–2). Moreover, the different types of the crested helmet symbol on both issues establish internal links between them and thus suggest their parallel production after the introduction of the Pans.[56] The crested helmet also links

52. For the finance of the army, see Le Bohec, *AD*, 310–321.

53. G. Shipley, ibid., 275; Préaux, *Monde Hellénistique*, 309–310; Callataÿ, *Guerres Mithridatiques*, 400.

54. See the reconstruction of Gröningen's theory regarding the royal monopoly of coinage in Martin, *Sovereignty*, 266–270. Bresson, *Coinage and Money Supply*, 3 argues that a king inevitably determined the size of a new issue, even though this is not explicitly mentioned in Pseudo-Aristotle (*Oec.* 2.1.2); but as, further down, he admits the complexity in defining whether ancient states could estimate the size of the coinage already in circulation (ibid., 57–58), he leaves open the criteria by which the king defined each time the amount of the new coinage. The introduction of new coin issues may not be identified as an essential royal task through *Oec.* 2.1.2, also because new coin issues (or, at least, new coin types) were not introduced by all Hellenistic kings.

55. Le Rider, *Alexandre*, 337–338 points out that Alexander III never imposed the exclusive use of his coinage in his realm and considers the large-scale production of Alexander coinage throughout a process which did not require royal intervention.

56. I have argued this in K. Panagopoulou, "The Antigonids: Patterns of a Royal Economy," in Z. Archibald, J.K.Davies, V. Gabrielsen and G. Oliver (eds.), *Hellenistic Economies* (London: Routledge, 2001), 313–364, esp. 348–349; cf. M. Faranguna, "L'economia della Macedonia ellenistica: un bilancio," in A. Bresson, P. Briant, and F. Burkhalter (eds.), *Approches de l'économie hellénistique [4e rencontre de l' économie antique, Saint-Bertrand-des Comminges (6–7 Mai 2004)* Saint-Bertrand-des Comminges: Musée Archéologique de Saint-Bertrand-des Comminges (Paris: de Boccard, 2006), 121–146, esp. 134 ff. (model B). Kremydi confuses the coexistence of Antigonid with foreign coins in Northern Greek hoards pointed out by Walbank (see above, n. 34) with my point that Antigonid coins could have been exchanged with precious metal coins struck on the same (Attic) weight standard, primarily Alexanders: S. Kremydi, "Coinage and Finance," in R. Lane Fox (ed.), *Brill's Companion to Ancient Macedon: Studies in the Archaeology and History of Macedon, 650 BC–300 AD* (Leiden: Brill, 2011), 172, n. 52 ("Her view that the monetary needs of the Macedonian state could be met with other contemporary Attic-weight currencies—because they circulate together in the hoards—should be regarded with some caution"). Foreign Attic-weight coins could not have been used for official state payments, but the Makedonian state was perfectly entitled to make payments with earlier Makedonian Attic-weight coins, i.e., lifetime and posthumous Alexanders.

these issues with the "anonymous" bronze coins, which have now been dated to approximately the turning point between the fourth and the third century.[57] The numerous bronze coins in the name of "king Antigonos' may have been intended to cover the soldiers' daily maintenance and may thus have helped to reduce the need for precious metal coinage.[58]

The internal structure of the Antigonid personal silver issues elucidates that of the contemporary silver Alexanders, through common control marks.[59] The silver Antigoni may have been struck in parallel with other royal coinages popular in the Balkans and the Black Sea, with which they share control marks. In fact, common monograms among the Antigonid issues, the posthumous Alexanders and those of Demetrios Poliorketes and Lysimachos may be taken to suggest their consecutive or simultaneous production at Amphipolis.[60] Some posthumous Lysimachi, in particular, may have been struck in the context of the vaguely known military activities of Gonatas in Thrace and the Hellespont.[61] Moreover, the monograms that the above four issues (Antigoni, posthumous Alexanders, coins of Demetrios Poliorketes and Lysimachos) share with Antigonid bronze coins might unravel the extremely complicated numismatic pattern in the region. Finally, the paucity of Antigonid silver fractions suggests that it was not Gonatas' intention to construct a completely new numismatic system. Their rarity might imply the use of other coinages, silver and bronze, for smaller scale transactions and possibly their introduction for a particular purpose (see Chapter 6.4.4).

The low production rate of Antigonid coinages cannot have been sufficient for the Antigonids' intense military and other enterprises during the second and the third quarter of the third century BC, which must have been funded by other coinages. Antigonid practice is in stark contrast to the remarkable variety and quantity of the contemporary Ptolemaic issues, military, celebratory and other, in gold and silver. The abundant coinage produced by the Ptolemies results from the limitations of the closed Ptolemaic monetary system. The exclusive use of locally produced coinage ultimately predetermined its brief duration.[62] By contrast this indirectly underlines the benefits from the plurality of the potentially exchangeable coinages in a market based on the Attic weight standard, such as that of Makedonia, mainland Greece and Asia Minor. Thus Antigonid practice obviously reflects attitudes developed within a cosmopolitan Hellenistic environment, rather than an insufficient use of the mines and the lack of other resources in Antigonid Makedonia. After all,

57. Katerini Liampi, "Zur Chronologie der sogennannten 'anonymen' makedonischen Münzen des späten 4. Jhs. v. Chr.," *JNG* 36 (1986), 41–65, pl. 4–6, 2. Price, *Alexander*, pp. 116–130.

58. S. Psôma, "Tas sitarchias kai tous misthous ([Arist.], Oec. 1351b). Bronze Currencies and Cash Allowances in Mainland Greece, Thrace and the Kingdom of Macedonia," *RBN* 45 (2009), 3–38, with earlier bibliography.

59. That common control marks also exist between Makedonian Alexanders and those struck in Asia Minor cannot have been just coincidence: G. Le Rider, "Antiochos II à Mylasa," *BCH* 114 (1990), 543–557.

60. Mathisen, *Silver Coinages*, 98–99, table 12; cf. Chapter 2.2.4. Price assumes (through common monograms) the striking of the silver issues of Kassander and those of Lysimachos at the same mint: *Alexander*, 130–131.

61. The attribution to Ptolemy Keraunos of the silver Lysimachi with elephant scalp and lion head symbols legitimizes Gonatas' continuation of posthumous Lysimachi. The *terminus post quem* for these coins (281 BC) coincides with Gonatas' intensified activities in Thrace and the Hellespont prior to his rise to the Makedonian throne: W. Hollstein, "Münzen des Ptolemaios Keraunos," *SNR* 74 (1995), 13–25. See Mathisen, *Silver Coinages*, 108–109 ("thunderbolt" and "Triton" Alexanders assigned to Keraunos); Price, *Alexander*, 131, no. 503 (Alexander drachma with thunderbolt, from the reign of Poliorketes, assigned to Keraunos). The two rare bronze coins in a hoard of Thracian origin attributed to Ptolemy Keraunos by M. Arslan and A. Özen ("A Hoard of Unpublished Bronze Coins of Ptolemy Ceraunus," *AJN* 12 (2000), 59–66 have been reattributed to the period of the Ptolemies' war against Antiochos II in the 250s: S. Psoma, "Numismatic Evidence on the Ptolemaic Involvement in Thrace during the Second Syrian War," *AJN* 20 (2008), 257–263.

62. Bagnall, *Administration*, 211–212: "The many variants and differences noted, especially the cleavage between the monetary zone and the other possessions, must to a large extent reflect the results of Ptolemaic power and its limits. Two questions surely governed the royal decision about treatment of a subject area or city: was it desirable (that is, profitable to the crown) to impose a monetary zone of isolation; and was it possible to do so."

as coined money has been argued to have met only 20% of the military needs of Hellenistic states, alternative ways of payment, i.e., with raw metal (ἄργυρον, ἀργύριον), may also be considered.[63]

As for the distribution of the Antigonid precious metal coinages, it may be argued that the well established economic, political and military network between Greece and Asia Minor, based on the Attic weight standard, would ultimately seem to contradict the alleged concentration of the Pans in the Balkans and of the Poseidons in Asia Minor and the East. It is true that the concentration of hoards with Antigonid silver issues in the direct Antigonid realm contrasts with their absence from Thrace and Asia Minor between the 240s and the 220s. However, a distinction between "circulation" and "savings" hoards with Antigonid issues reveals that their representation in hoards has been fragmented by the interaction of diverse economic practices in the periphery of the Antigonid realm, such as the apparent expansion of the Ptolemaic practice of "recycling" silver in Thrace, the Danube region and on the coastal areas of Asia Minor after the 240s, as a result of their occupation by the Ptolemies. These more "peripheral" areas show, in this case, what has been termed the "negative effects of imperial dynamics" in the Eastern Mediterranean.[64]

Some final remarks might be added about the nature of the Pans and Poseidons. Both types have been related to increased military expenditure in view of Gonatas' enterprises both in peninsular Greece and in the Aegean. It has also been shown that the Poseidons would not have been superfluous to the existing Antigonid coinage. Their concentration in hoards from Asia Minor, the Middle and Near East might be related to the naval connotations in their iconography.

I have argued that the new type was introduced in order to celebrate Gonatas' naval victory over the Ptolemies at Andros. Renewing the Antigonid naval tradition after Andros meant not only a demonstration of power analogous to the processions, the honorary coin issues, and the festivals at Delos organized by the Ptolemies. It was also part of Gonatas' riposte to the Aitolian policy in the mainland (cf. Chapter 6.4.3).[65] However, this coin issue by far outnumbers the groups denoted as celebratory. Could this have had a particular significance?

It is possible that the Poseidons were minted for the payment of Antigonos' navy after Andros. Given the strong Antigonid naval tradition in Asia Minor stretching back to Monophthalmos and Poliorketes, the distribution of this coinage in the East might be explained by the return of the members of the crews to their homelands. Since Doson and Philip V are now known to have been active in Karia from the early 220s, the distribution of the coins in the East may be explained through the continuing Antigonid involvement in the East since the Karian expedition of 229–227 BC, especially if we should now suppose that the Antigonids maintained an active fleet after 245 BC. The similarity of Apollo to that on contemporary Seleukid tetradrachms is thus comprehensible.

Alternatively, or in addition, one may regard this issue as referring to celebrations that followed this second naval victory. This is suggested by the elaborate features of the Poseidons, by the distinctive monogram and by the naval connotations of the iconography. It is possible that the second tetradrachm type was struck periodically, on the occasion of the celebration of the *Soteria* and the *Paneia* (cf. Chapter 6.4.3).

63. F. de Callataÿ, "Reflexions quantitatives sur l' or et l' argent non monnayés à l' époque Hellénistique (pompes, triomphes, réquisitions, fortunes des temples, orfèvrerue et masses metalliques disponibles)," in A. Bresson, P. Briant and F. Burkhalter (eds.), *Approches de l'économie hellénistique [4e rencontre de l'économie antique, Saint-Bertrand-des-Comminges (6–7 Mai 2004)* (Paris: De Boccard, 2006), 37–84; idem, "A Quantitative Survey of Hellenistic Coinages: Recent Achievements," in Archibald et al., *MMM*, 88. Archibald, *Northern Aegean*, 83–84 adds payment with booty and with precious metal converted into plate; but neither the use of booty nor that of silver plate (rather than coinage) for official military payments can be attested in the ancient sources.

64. G. Shipley, "Distance, Development, Decline? World-systems Analysis and the 'Hellenistic' World," in Per Bilde et al., *Centre and Periphery*, 277. Cf. Bagnall, *Administration*, 211.

65. E. Will, however, relates them to Pan's role at Lysimacheia: *HPMH* I^2, 323.

8.0
Concluding Remarks

The precious-metal coinages in the name of "King Antigonos" add a missing link to our knowledge of the Makedonian macroeconomy and policy between the Temenid dynasty and the last two Antigonids. The introduction of both their personal silver tetradrachm types, Pans and Poseidons, has been assigned to Gonatas. Their continued production through to Doson demonstrates a strong sense of dynastic continuity among Gonatas' successors, similar to that in the other Hellenistic dynasties.[1] The relative paucity of Antigonid silver issues was presumably a result of the limited exercise by the Antigonids of proactive economic and administrative control: in contrast to the Ptolemies, the Antigonids used other precious-metal coinages on the Attic weight standard, in addition to their own.[2] It may therefore be argued that the introduction of the Antigonid personal issues was determined by political rather than by economic forces.

Politics (and religion) largely determined the iconography of the individual Antigonid types. In fact, establishing links with the major Greek sanctuaries at Delphi and Delos, and possibly also with Eleusis and Dion, the Antigonids aimed at the effective manipulation of local mentalities, in order to coordinate the regional diversities in the Makedonian state and mainland Greece. I have argued that the first Antigonid tetradrachm type, the Pan head, echoes the Panhellenic defence of the Delphic sanctuary during the Celtic attack of 279 BC, possibly with particular emphasis on Makedonia's role in this as a "shield" for the Greek peninsula. The participation of Gonatas' troops in the Greeks' resistance to the Celts at Delphi, possibly together with his personal victory over the Celts at Lysimacheia, advertised Makedonia as an integral part of the Greek world. Similarly, the resumption of the naval claims of Monophthalmos and Poliorketes and the protection of the Antigonid fleet by Apollo were advertised on the Poseidons, after Gonatas' naval victory over the Ptolemaic fleet off Andros (246/5 BC) and the concomitant decline of Ptolemaic claims to the Aegean.

1. Cf. chapter 6.1.
2. For the Seleukids and the Ptolemies, cf. G. Shipley, ibid., 283.

The emphasis that the Antigonids attached to their Hellenic identity and their demonstration of piety at the two main sanctuaries of Apollo was aimed at two main audiences: firstly, the Ptolemies, the main rivals of the Antigonids for control of the Aegean until the emergence of Rome; secondly, the Greek states, control over which was a prerequisite for the Antigonids' more active engagement in international affairs. Among the latter the principal audience were the Aitolians, who aimed to control Delphi and played a key role in the formation of political attitudes towards Makedonia in Central Greece throughout the third and the early second centuries BC.

The military themes on the Pans relate the bulk of this coinage to military finance, but special gold and silver issues, possibly also the Poseidons, presumably celebrated particular events in the rivalry between Antigonids and Ptolemies for control over the Aegean. There is no need to assign them to a different mint, as various control marks had signed issues of the main Makedonian mint during the interregnum prior to Gonatas. Amphipolis is perhaps the most plausible candidate.

In terms of chronology, a clearer picture of the coinages minted under Antigonos is obtained until Gonatas' naval victory at Andros (246/5 BC). With the exception of certain issues, presumably meant to celebrate this naval victory, it is more difficult to "render unto Caesar what is Caesar's" between 246/5 and 221 BC, when both types were presumably struck in parallel. With regard to the size of the individual Antigonid issues, the calculations based on the existing sample suggest that the personal issues of "King Antigonos" could not cover all the military activities undertaken by the Antigonids throughout this period. This leads us to speculate that the posthumous Alexander silver tetradrachms continued alongside coins in the name of "King Antigonos," initially with the types of Alexander and later with his personal types;[3] or that the σιτηρέσιον of the Antigonid soldiers was covered by bronze coins; or that metal ingots (rather than coin) may have been used for military payments. The preponderance of foreign currency in hoards from Antigonid Makedonia and mainland Greece presumably indicates easy acceptance of foreign money in transactions following the Attic weight standard. This contrasts with the wide range of the coin issues launched by the Ptolemies during the same period, due to the closed monetary system applied in their realm since 306 BC.

There are many gaps in our knowledge of the history and the economy of Makedonia and Greece during the third century BC, which is a period prolific in coinage but not in other forms of documentation. The size of the later Makedonian posthumous Alexanders, for instance, remains to be calculated, and the processes whereby other coinages were incorporated in the contemporary economic market remain unexplored. At the same time, a systematic die study of the bronze issues in the name of "King Antigonos" is needed. The reconstruction of the Antigonid precious metal coinages from Gonatas through to Doson has shown, however, that stability in Antigonid Makedonia was attained through a return to the political and ideological principles set out by the Temenids and reflected in the numismatic iconography.

Finally, the complex structure of royal finance, making payments through personal Antigonid silver as well as Alexander coinage (and perhaps also through raw (precious) metal and bronze coins), was only possible because the Makedonian state was now fully integrated into the more flexible market of the Eastern Mediterranean, based upon the Attic weight standard. Indeed this radical change of the state's macroeconomic profile, opening up an enormous potential, would not have been achieved without Alexander the Great's inspired globalizing military and monetary endeavors.

3. On the acceptability of Attic-weight coinages in the Greek poleis, see M.-C. Marcellesi, "Commerce, Monnaies locales et monnaies communes dans les états hellénistiques," *REG* 113 (2000), 326–357.

9.0
Appendices

9.1 Counterfeit Antigonid-Type Coins

Pan Head Tetradrachms

Period I

Crested Helmet l.—Monogram* Ꝁ *r.

O: Stars hastily engraved. Head of Pan crude.
R: ΒΑΣΙΛΕΩΣ r., [ΑΝ]ΤΙΓΟΝΟΥ l. downwards. Athena l. In field, Makedonian helmet. In field r., monogram Ꝁ.

1.	Athens: *SNG Alpha Bank* 988 (5712)	15.23 g	1 h	31.5 mm[1]

*** *** ***

Period II

Crested Helmet l.—*ΤΙ *r.

O: Elliptic star/crescents, Pan head crude and very small. Neck ends in curve.
R: Large and irregularly placed legend letters. Athena crude, with diagonal pleats on hem, small figure, letters ΤΙ.

2.	Munich: *SNG München* 1074 (Acc. 22681) [R: struck twice].	14.37 g	8 h	-

1. The specimen in the *SNG* publication is recorded as of 15.72 g, and as "debased," but at my recent enquiry Dr. S. Kremydi agreed that this is a plated coin.

The crude iconographic and epigraphic features of this plated specimen might identify it as an ancient imitation, but they are not incompatible with the general style of Pans of Period II; no more specimens come from this die combination.

*** *** ***

PERIOD III

Crested Helmet l.—Monogram ᛞ r.

O: Similar.
R: Similar.

3.	Munich: *SNG München* 1076 ("anima")	12.64 g	12 h	-
4.	ANM: *SNG Saroglos* 922	17.04 g	12 h	-

*** *** ***

Crested helmet l.—Monogram indiscernible r.

O: Head of Pan in center of Makedonian shield.
R: Athena l., holding shield and brandishing thunderbolt. Athena's figure rough.

5.	ANM (1910 / 11, ΛΑ7, donation K. Karapanos)	10.95 g	8 h	29 mm

[Obverse crude. Disfigured by corrosion on the reverse, so that the monogram cannot be read].

*** *** ***

SILVER DENOMINATIONS

PERIOD IV

ZEUS HEAD DRACHMA

Winged Helmet l.—TI r.

O: Head of Poseidon in wreath of marine plants r.
R: Athena carrying shield and brandishing thunderbolt l. In field l., winged helmet; r., TI.

6.	Berlin: Stattl. Museen, 392/1872	2.27 g (b)	3 h	-

[Fragment].

*** *** ***

ZEUS HEAD TETROBOL

Winged Helmet l.—TI r.

7.	Berlin 392/1872	2.27 g (b)	3 h	15 mm

[*O (a):* worn.
R (a): up r., portion of metal flaked off between helmet and legend].

This (rather worn) plated pentobol comes from the same dies as drachma no. 25.

*** *** ***

Silver-plated specimens survive from most "international" coin series of the Classical and Hellenistic period, and the Antigonid issues are no exception.[2] I have collected seven such specimens: five tetradrachms, from the first three periods of Antigonid coin production, plus a drachma and a tetrobol from Period IV. All tetradrachms belong to the Pan type; no Poseidons are known to have been counterfeited. Apparently all counterfeits were produced through the application of silver foil over a base metal core, which was then heated and struck.[3] The most outstanding example is no. 3, from Period III, of which only the *anima*, the base metal core, survives; its crude iconographic and epigraphic features might even identify it as an ancient imitation. All specimens, with a crested helmet symbol in the reverse field left, carry the legend ΑΝΤΙΓΟΝΟΥ left and ΒΑΣΙΛΕΩΣ right of the standing Athena left figure. The control marks depicted are: monograms Ꝁ (Period I) (no. 1) and Ⱶ (Period III) (no. 3); letters ΤΙ (Period II) (no. 2). The reverse of no. 5 is so corroded that the monogram is indiscernible. Period IV is represented by smaller denominations, a drachma and a tetrobol; the counterfeit tetrobol comes from the same dies as tetrobol no. 95, but the fact that this is a single specimen need not indicate that this was a legitimate Antigonid issue. Even though there is no literary or epigraphic equivalent to the Athenian Nikophon Law of 375/4 BC from Makedonia, the presence of *agoranomoi* in Makedonian markets may suggest that official measures were taken against fraud.[4] No plated Antigonid-type specimens have been found in hoards.

2. On plated coins in the Hellenistic period, see P. van Alfen, "Problems in ancient imitative and counterfeit coinage," in Z. Archibald et al., *MMM*, 322–354. The present section follows the excellent analysis of plated Seleukid-type coins by O. Hoover in *SC* II, vol. 2, 241–263.

3. This method is described by O. Hoover, "Appendix 8: Plated Seleucid-Type Coins," *SC* II, vol. 2, 241–463.

4. Z. Archibald, "*Agoranomoi* in Macedonia," in *Agoranomes et édiles, Institutions des marchés,* ed. L. Capdetrey and C. Hasenohr (Bordeaux: Ausonius, 2012), 109–119.

9.2 Overstruck Antigonid Coins

Overtype O: Beardless head of Herakles r.
Overtype R: Zeus seated on throne l., holding eagle on outstretched r. hand and scepter with his l. hand.

Undertype O: Head of Pan in center of Makedonian shield.
Undertype R: Athena l., holding shield and brandishing thunderbolt.

1. Tucker (1879); Propontis, 1950: N. Waggoner, *RN* 21 (1979): 7–29, p. 11, no. 31; I. Karayotov, "Chronologie des Tetradrachms de Mesambria," *Numismatica* (Sofia) 18.4 (1984), 5–14 (in Bulgarian); Price, *Alexander* I, 183, no. 1005; Karayotov, *Mesembria* I, no. 202 16.72 g[5] 12 h -

Price recorded an Alexander tetradrachm from Mesembria which was "overstruck on a 'shield/ Athena' tetradrachm of Antigonos Gonatas" (see Plate 55). It came from the Propontis, Turkey, 1950 hoard (*IGCH* 888; *CH* VII [1985], no. 93), which comprised 162+ silver coins and is dated (by Houghton and Lorber, followed by Marcellesi) to 180–170 BC.[6] H. Mattingly proposed a later date, around 166 BC.[7] In addition to an Alexander in the name of Seleukos I, minted at Pergamon, the hoard contained an Alexander tetradrachm with a "cistophoric" countermark (i.e., imposed on the Attic-weight tetradrachms which were associated with it). This is the earliest hoard to include such a countermarked tetradrachm.[8]

Rather than determining the hoard's closing date, the overstriking of this specimen by the most active mint of the Black Sea region from the mid-third century through to the demise of Mithridates VI of Pontus forms part of the movement of flans of Macedonian provenance to the Black Sea area by the first half of the second century BC: several Alexander pieces of Mesembia are overstruck on coins of Thasos and of the First Makedonian Meris, the latter now dated to the late Antigonid period.[9]

5. I have not seen this coin. I have retained the weight quoted in the most recent publication, which is identical in Waggoner's original hoard publication: N. Waggoner, *RN* 21 (1979), 7–29; *SC* I, vol. 2, no. 31.

6. N. Waggoner, *RN* 21 (1979), 7–29; *SC* I, vol. 2, 96. Price, *Alexander*, 183, no. 1005; Marcellesi, *Pergame*, 213; *SC* I, vol. 2, 96. The coin is also mentioned in I. Karayotov, "The Chronology of Mesembrian Tetradrachms," *Numismatica* (Sofia) 18.4 (1984), 5–15.

7. H. B. Mattingly, "Some numismatic puzzles," *NC* 162 (2002), 465.

8. Mattingly, "Some numismatic puzzles," 464.

9. On the overstrikes of Mesembria on Makedonian coins, see Price, *Alexander* I, 181. The redating by Kremydi-Sicilianou of the coins of the first Makedonian *meris* to the end of the reign of Philip V may shift upwards the later issues of Mesembria: S. Kremydi-Sicilianou, "ΜΑΚΕΔΟΝΩΝ ΠΡΩΤΗΣ ΜΕΡΙΔΟΣ: Evidence for a Coinage under the Antigonids," *RN* 163 (2007), 91–99. On the significance of overstriking, see G. Le Rider, "Contremarques et surfrappes dans l' antiquité grecque," *Numismatique Antique. Problèmes et Méthodes* (Nancy/Louvain, 1975), 27–56, esp. 46–56 = *Études Le Rider*, I, 230–240; on its functions, see O. Hoover, "Appendix 5: Overstruck Seleucid Coins," in *SC* II, vol. 2, 216–217.

9.3 Countermarks on Antigonid Silver Coins

Pan Head Tetradrachms

AN

Period III

1. *Crested Helmet l.*—KT *r.*
Countermark: Monogram AN.
Position: Obverse, on chin.

S. Asia Minor, 1963: *IGCH* 1426 (Boehringer, *Chronologie,* 156, no 25, pl. 26.25); Pozzi 971 - - -

See Catalogue above, Period III, no. 85a.

Caduceus

Period I

2–3. *Crested Helmet l.*—HP *r.*
Countermark: Caduceus.
Position: Obverse, on Pan's cheek.

a. ANM: Thesprotia, 1992 (*CH* IX [2002], 200; Touratsoglou, *DM*, no. 24)
17.03 g 12 h -

b. Gorny 95 (9.3.1999) 205 17.01 g - -

See Catalogue above, Period I, nos. 95e–f.

4. *Crested Helmet l.*—HA *r.*

Countermark: Caduceus.
Position: Obverse, on face.

a. G. Hirsch 68 (1970), 115; G. Hirsch 27 (1961), 759
16.81 g - -

See Catalogue above, Period I, no. 163a.

Period IV

5–6. *Winged Helmet l.*—KT *r.*
Countermark: Caduceus.
Position: Obverse, at the level of the ear.

a. BerLMC 9 (29–30.11.1979), 27; Coin Galleries MBS (19.11.1973), 187 (16.96 g)
16.88 g - -

b. Künker 23 (30.9–2.10.1992), 43 16.88 g - -

See Catalogue above, Period IV, nos. 2a, c.

7. Countermark: Caduceus.
Position: Obverse, on face, at the level of the ear.

a. Copenhagen: *SNG Cop.* 1201 (ex Reutze 274); Rooke (16.2.1994), 77
16.82 g 12 h -

[O (a): countermark on face: caduceus.
R (a): flaw from upper end of coin towards head].

See Catalogue above, Period IV, no. 8a.

EAGLE

PERIOD I

8. ***Crested Helmet l.*—ΗΡ *r.***
Countermark: Eagle with head l., three-quarters facing.
Position: Obverse, between neck and badge circle.

a. Milano, B1185 (coll. Brera, n. 1185, N. Inv.: M 0.9.36659): *SNG Milano* 375
17.16 g 12 h 31.5 mm

See Catalogue above, Period I, no. 86b.

STAR

PERIOD I

9. ***Crested Helmet l.*— [monogram] *r.***
Countermark: Star.
Position: Obverse, between *pedum* and head.

a. Edinburgh, ED55.1923.819: Rutter, *Edinburgh* 55; FM 132 (30–31.5.1989) 35 (17.08 g); SB 41 (10–12.9.1996) 44 (17.07 g) 17.10 g 4 h 32 mm

See Catalogue above, Period I, no. 7a.

10. ***Crested Helmet l.*— [monogram] *r.***
Countermark: Indiscernible (star?).
Position: Obverse, on *pedum*.

a. Schulman L 204 (12.1973), 28 17.09 g - -

See Catalogue above, Period I, no. 18b.

It is worth noting that this countermark is not similar to the star on reverse of the Poseidon head tetradrachms, nos. 74–76.

TRISKELES

PERIOD III

11. ***Crested Helmet l.*—ΤΙ *r.***
Countermark: *Triskeles* l.
Position: Obverse, between cheek and neck.

a. Kress 152 (5.7.1971), 105 17.00 g - -

See Catalogue above, Period III, no. 106d.

Zeus Head Drachma

Wreath?

Period IV

12. Winged Helmet l.—TI r.
Countermark: Caduceus or wreath?
Position: Obverse, in front of mouth.

a. H. Weber, no. 2192 3.43 g - -

See Catalogue above, Period IV, no. 92c.

As well as the bronze coins, whose extensive countermarking has long been debated, quite a few silver Antigonid tetradrachms were also countermarked, but only Pans, not Poseidons.[10] The most common countermark types are: (a) caduceus, (b) star, (c) eagle with head left, three quarters facing and with open wings, (d) monogram ΑΝ, (e) triskeles, (f) wreath(?). The monogram ΑΝ, the distinctive royal monogram, and possibly also the star, are the only countermarks which may certainly be assigned to the Makedonian state. The eagle with head l. and with open wings, three-quarters facing, recalls the eagle type on the coins of Philip V and Perseus, or that on the Ptolemaic tetradrachms.[11] The most common countermark, the caduceus, also occurs on a bronze coin in the name of Alexander III and later on the coinage of Roman imperial cities in the broader Black Sea area, in the Pontus.[12] Similarly, the eagle with head left, three-quarters facing recalls that on the reverse of Ptolemaic tetradrachms.[13] The *triskeles* also occurs on bronze coins of Alexander III.[14] The countermarks' position is invariably on the obverse, at random places, most often on Pan's cheek, chin, neck or by his ear, but also on the *pedum* or in the field.

Countermarked Antigonid specimens occur in the following two hoards:

1. Thesprotia, 1992 (*CH* IX (2002) 200; Touratsoglou, *DM*, no. 24; date: c. 225 BC)
2. S. Asia Minor, 1963: *IGCH* 1426 (Boehringer, *Chronologie* 156, no 25, pl. 26.25; 210–200 BC).

A caduceus is the countermark on the Pan tetradrachm from the first hoard, while its counterpart on the specimen from S. Asia Minor, 1963 is monogram ΑΝ. It may therefore be deduced that these two countermarks, the caduceus and ΑΝ, had been employed by the last quarter of the third century BC. Other countermarks may have been applied later.

A comparison of these countermarks with those on the bronze Antigonid coins is likely to yield clues to the chronology and distribution of both categories of issues.

10. On countermarked Antigonid bronze coins, see A. Furtwängler, "Beobachtungen zur Chronologie Antigonidischer Kupfermünzen," *Obolos* 7 (2004), 277–290; B. Poulios, "Contribution to the Study of the Bronze Coinage of the Antigonids, from Antigonos Gonatas to the Early Years of Philip V," *ΑΔ Α* 56 (2001 [2006]), 237–295, who argues that the bronzes were countermarked by Gonatas' successors; E. Vlachogianni, "A Hoard of Coins from Thebes. The Problem of Boiotian Overstrikes," *Νομισματικά Χρονικά* 19 (2000), 55–113; Gatzolis, *Κυκλοφορία*, II, 290–292.

11. For the eagle type on coins of Philip V and Perseus, see Gaebler, *AMNG* III.1, pl. 35.3–4 (bronze, Philip V), 23–24 (silver, Perseus) (but the eagle head is right); for the Ptolemaic specimens, see examples in Mørkholm, *EHC*, pl. 17.284–286, 18.291–293, 18.300, 20.309 ff. A quite different eagle left countermark occurs on Alexander tetradrachms: Price, *Alexander*, 67. A countermark with eagle facing, head left and open wings occurs in the Bosporus area in the Roman imperial period: Howgego, *GIC*, no. 322.

12. For the caduceus type, see Waddington, *Recueil*, pl. 8, 14–15. Price, *Alexander* I, 71, no. P2a, records a caduceus countermark on an Alexander III bronze. On the caduceus as a Roman imperial countermark, see Howgego, *GIC*, nos. 388–393.

13. See, for instance, Mørkholm, *EHC*, pl. 17.285.

14. Price, *Alexander* I, 71 and 126, no. 373b.

9.4 Ancient Imitations

Silver

9.4.1 Pan Head Tetradrachms

Crested Helmet l.—⋈ r.

O: Elliptic star/crescents, Pan head barbaric and very small. Neck ends in curve.
R: Large and irregularly placed legend letters. Athena crude, with diagonal pleats on hem, small figure, monogram ⋈.

1.	Spink London, Sale Brutus—1297 (11.4.2001), 22; Spink 71 (1989), 60	14.80 g	-	-
2.	Malloy MBS 24 (18.3.1988) 56	-	-	-
	[O 6–7 h: test cut].			
3.	CNG 265	-	-	-
4.	Hungary, Mayar Nemzeti, Budapest National Museum, no. 14, Inv. Nr. 7A.1917.6	15.95 g	9 h	-
5.	Time Machine L 9 (25.9.1990) 11	-	-	-
	[R: test cut at 11:30 h].			
6.	a. Paris: BNF1381	15.23 g	5:30 h	-
	b. Bucharest, National History Museum, 2191[15]	21.69 g	-	-

*** *** ***

Crested Helmet l.—KT r.

7.	Dupriez 104bis (31.1.1912), Colls. De Feu M. le Prof. Maas d' Ostende et de M. le Baron de Sant' Anna (2me partie), 47	-	-	-
8.	Athens: ANM 6 (94/1620b 1); coll. Otho I	13.80 g	12 h	31.0 mm
	[disfigured by chisel cut through "unit" 7 to nose].			

Crested Helmet l.—TI r.

9.	Munich: *SNG München* 1075	13.16 g	11 h	-

10. O: Head r.
R: [---]ΝΤΙΓΟΥ. Athena r [brandishing thunderbolt with r. hand], holding shield with her l. arm.

Ripollès, X4 Hoard, 60.7, pl. 3.7; Vico (10.3.1994) 5 — 5.55 g — 6 h — -

[Tetradrachm? Fragment. The reverse type imitates the early Antigonid tetradrachm types; Ripollès associates it with the issues of Antigonos III Doson, but dates it to c. 271–239 BC (i.e., during the reign of Gonatas)].

15.Particular thanks are due to Ms. Ana Maria Raducan for notifying me of this quite heavy specimen. This piece was be published in *Cercetări Numismatice* XVII (2015).

9.4.2 Poseidon Head Tetradrachms

O: Similar; wreath (or tainia?) wider, decorated by two knobs of five dots. Head flatter.
R: Prow shorter and flatter. Legend letters elegant and elaborate, the edges of Ω being high up and distant. Larger distance between bow and string. Apollo archaizing.

11. a. Hirsch 33 (17.11.1913, coll. Rhousopoulos, Munich 1905, Nr. 1174), 667
12.66 g - 29.5 mm

R: ΒΙΛΕΩΣ ΑΝΤΙΓ.

12. a. Künker 236 (07.10.2013), 498; Gorny & Mosch 212 (5.3.2013), 1420
16.06 g - -

13. a. Cahn (27.2.1933), 182; Helbing 3, 2860 15.00 g - -

14. a. G. Hirsch 267 (05.05.2010) 214; (Stack's (11.1.2010), 103 (Vermeule, Ward, and Mexico Maxico Collections); Freeman & Sear 10 (2.2004), 144 (from the estate of C. C. Vermeule) (16.90 g) 16.91 g - -
[R (a): die flaw off prow's upper l. end].

15. a. *SNG Manchester*, 738; Jenkins 738; Hirsch 21 (1908), 1261 (17.00 g)
16.98 g 12 h 31 mm

O: Similar, but branches with flowers (knobs and five dots), springing from thinner wreath. Dotted border.
R: Apollo's figure larger, protruding edges in monogram.

16. a. Hirsch 58 (1968), 3095 - (b) - -
[O: die break starting from eye].

17. a. Milan 18 (Gab. Num. B1183, coll. Brera) 15.30 g 10 h -
b. *SNG Lockett*, 1527; Glendining (12.2.1958), 1395
16.86 g 9 h -

By "ancient imitations" are meant the coins whose crude style and legends betray that they were not produced at an official mint of the Antigonid kingdom, and which imitate the types, legends and control marks of "official" Antigonid specimens.[16] There are no ancient imitations of the, admittedly few, gold staters or of the silver denominations. The survival of ancient imitations of both Antigonid tetradrachm types, the Pans and the Poseidons, demonstrates their popularity, even though they are in smaller quantities than the known examples imitating Alexander-type or Seleucid issues; the Pans outnumber the Poseidons.

The prototypes for the Pans come from our first three periods of Antigonid precious metal coin production. The place of their production is hard to locate, as they do not come from secure excavation contexts, but their allocation to the fringes of the Antigonid realm is sensible. Ripollès considers that our fragment no. 10 was probably struck somewhere in the Danubian zone. The wide appeal of Makedonian royal coinages in that region renders the production there of Antigonid

16. On the types of imitation coinages, see P. van Alfen, "Problems in ancient imitative and counterfeit coinage," in Archibald et al., *MMM*, 322–354. Also see O. Hoover, "Appendix 9: Imitations of Seleucid Coinages," in *SC* II.2, 265–73.

imitations most probable.[17] One might thus follow Lukanc in identifying these issues as "Balkan imitations."[18] The locus of production of the Poseidon imitations is also hard to specify.

These issues may be dated to the early second century BC.

17. Le Rider, *Philippe II*, 442–3. On ancient imitations of Alexander-type coins, see Price, *Alexander* I, 506–10, pls. CLI–CLIII. I.Lukanc, *Les imitations des monnaies d' Alexandre le Grand et de Thasos* (Wetteren: Cultura, 1996).

18. I. Lukanc, *Les imitations*, 12: "...au lieu du terme d' imitations 'est-celtiques,' je propose pour la région du Moyen et du Bas Danube le terme d' imitations 'balkaniques.'"

9.5 Modern Imitations

9.5.1 Silver with Types of Alexander III

1. Fitzwilliam: *SNG MacClean* 3573; Hirsch 21 (16.11.1908, Coll. Ed. F. Weber Hamburg, I), 1252; Gaebler, *AMNG* III.2; Seltman, *NC* (1909), 26; ; Seitnds. f. Umn, 3M (1927) and 298[19] 16.81 g 9 h 25 mm

9.5.2 Pan Head Tetradrachms

2. Ashmolean, Forgeries collection, Christ Church 12.59 g 12 h 30 mm

3. R: in field r., monogram K.

   BNF 12.27 g 12 h 29 mm

   [Technique: cast].

4. Ashmolean, Forgeries collection, Christ Church

   12.65 g 12 h 30 mm

5. Ashmolean, Forgeries collection 12.72 g 11 h 31 mm

6. Brussels, Forgeries collection, inv. II 80482 (don Francheschi)

   9.73 g 7 h 25 mm

7. George Hill, part I, p. 66, pl. III, 50; Brussels, Forgeries Collection

   \- - -

   [Forger: Becker].

8. BNF, Forgeries collection 14.21 g 10 h 30 mm

   [Metal: Mus (silver). Technique: cast].

9. Fitzwilliam 14.46 g 11 h 30 mm

   [Technique: cast].

10. Ashmolean, Forgeries collection, Christ Church; Brussels, Forgeries Collection

    13.13 g 10 h 29 mm

    [Obverse linked to nos. 10–11].

11. Ashmolean, Forgeries collection, Christ Church; Brussels, Forgeries Collection

    12.06 g 10 h 29 mm

12. Ashmolean, Forgeries collection, H. de S. Short Bequest, 1975

    13.01 g 10 h 29 mm

R: Legend letters crude.

13. BNF, Forgeries collection (cast trade 1969, Bartin 1) [no number]

    \- - -

19. Gaebler considers this specimen "a certain forgery," ΑΝΓΙΓΟΝΟΥ, having been re-engraved in modern times over the original ΑΛΕΞΑΝΔΡΟΥ. Seltman had suggested its issue at Antioch-on-the-Orontes in 307 BC.

9.5.3 Poseidon Head Tetradrachms

O: Locks of hair.
R: Apollo holding bow on prow.

14. BNF, Forgeries collection - - -

O: Poseidon head r. in wreath.
R: Apollo holding bow on prow.

15. BNF, Forgeries collection (Barthélemy 1755, technique: cast)
13.85 g 12 h 31 mm

16. Brussels, Forgeries collection - - -

17. BNF, Forgeries Collection; Brussels, Forgeries Collection; Pembroke publ. 1738 (technique: struck) [D. Gerin, "La 'seconde main': gravures et faux d' Antigone Doson (fin XVIIe–début XVIIIe s.)," *Bulletin de la société française de numismatique* 7 (1984), 518, fig. 3]
24.84 g 3 h 38 mm

18. BNF, Forgeries collection (17–18th century, technique: cast) [D. Gerin, "La 'seconde main': gravures et faux d' Antigone Doson (fin XVIIe–début XVIIIe s.)," *Bulletin de la société française de numismatique* 7 (1984), 518, fig. 7; Mionnet, *Decription*, vol. 1, 577]
26.08 g 12 h 32 mm

19. BNF, Forgeries collection 24.1 g 12 h 34 mm

20. Ashmolean, Forgeries collection 14.71 g 6 h 29 mm

By "imitations" are meant those coins which were not produced by the official Antigonid mints, but which imitate their types, legends and control marks; and which are betrayed by their crude style and errors in legends and control marks. This category so far comprises exclusively silver tetradrachms; I have been unable to identify imitations in gold, or in smaller denominations. The ancient imitations of Pan tetradrachms imitate the most common monogram, ᛞ, and letters KT and TI. The Poseidons copy the mainstream monogram on this type, [monogram]; only once is this followed by the letters TI below.

9.6 "Tetrachma Antigoneia"

Antigonid coins are epigraphically attested in inventories from the Asklepieion of Athens and possibly from that of Beroea. The best-known ones are three references to such coinages from the Asklepieion in Athens, currently dated to the 250s:[20] first, a dedication of a τέτρᾱχμον Ἀντιγόνειον is recorded during the priesthood of the fifteenth priest of Asklepios; secondly, under Philocrates, in 294, l. 80, are mentioned τέτρᾱχμα Ἀντιγόνεια τέτταρα; third, a mention of the fifteenth priest of Asklepios, l. 45, finally Ktesonides, the twenty second priest, returns to the treasury some τέτρᾱχμα Ἀντιγό[νεια...] from objects sold for the profit of the temple.[21]

It is worth noting that Ἀντιγόνεια are the only coins distinguished from those mentioned at the Asklepieion at Athens. A parallel to this reference may be found in an inscription from the accounts of the priests of Asklepios in Beroea, from the second half of the third century: in the last record of column II, the restored Ἀντιγονί(δα) (δραχμή) is contrasted with the coin of Demetrios [δημητρίειον (νόμισμα)]. The naming of coin types after the ruler who issued them is not unprecedented in the Greek world. The coins of Croesus were called *kroiseioi;*[22] the gold coins of the Persian kings were called *darics.* The gold coins of Philip II were termed *philippoi/ philippeioi*; later in the second century BC the term expanded to include all gold coins, and this meaning was presumably retained until the first century BC.[23] In the Hellenistic period, Alexander coins, for instance, were termed ἀλεξάνδρειον or ἀλεξάνδρειοι δραχμαί.[24] Antigonid *tetrachma* were initially identified with the silver tetradrachms bearing the *desmos* symbol left on the reverse, assigned then to the mint of Athens but now to Makedonia. Lönnqvist associated recently the τέτρᾱχμα Ἀντιγόνεια with the transitional posthumous Alexanders signed ΒΑΣΙΛΕΩΣ ΑΝΤΙΓΟΝΟΥ, but this suggestion is undermined by their rarity and by their absence from excavation contexts.[25] Finally, the *demetrian drachmae* (δημητρίειοι δραχμαί), which also occur on

20. Lönnqvist takes the absence of Macedonian silver coins between 264 and 261 in the main excavations at Athens to confirm the downdating of the inscription in the Inventory V of the Asklepieion at Athens from 261/0 BC (Ferguson) to the 250s; K. Lönnqvist, "Studies on the Hellenistic coinage of Athens: The Impact of Macedonia on the Athenian Money Market in the Third Century BC," *Papers and Monographs of the Finnish Institute at Athens*, vol. VI (1997), 119–212. J. P. Six, "Tetrachma Antigoneia," *Ann. Soc. Franc. Num. et Arch.* 6 (1882): 29–30.

21. J. P. Six, "Tetrachma Antigoneia," *Ann. Soc. Franc. Num. et Arch.* 6 (1882): 29–30.

22. See Poll. III 87, IX 84; Hesych. s.v. Plut. *Praec. Reip.* 31, 6; Hdt. I.54; Head, *HN*² 176–180; Regling, "Κροίσειος στατήρ," *RE* XI.2 (1922), col. 1941–1942.

23. The coins are termed χρυσοῖ φιλίππειοι (*CIA* IV 834b, Col. II, 88, 89; *Bull. Hell.* VI 131; VIII 198); δαρεικοὶ φιλίππειοι (*CIA* IV 845c, 8; *AM* V 274A); φιλίππειοι στατῆρες (Diod. XVI 8 Poll. IX 84); *philippei* (Palut. Liv. s.v.); *philippi* (Horat. *Epist.* I 233); cf. Seltmann, *RE* XIX.2 (1938), col. 2196. For Δαρεικοί, see, for instance, Hdt. VII.28; Thuc. VIII.28.4; Hultz, "Dareikos," *RE* IV.2 (1901), col. 2181–2184. For Ἀλεξάνδρειοι, Pollux IX. 59. 85; cf. Kubitschek, "Ἀλεξάνδρειος," *RE* I.1 (1893), col. 1397–8. See also L. Robert, "Monnaies dans les inscriptions grecques," *RN* (1962), 7–24 (= *OMS* II 1039–1040); S. Psoma, "Profitable Networks: Coinages, Panegyris and Dionysiac Artists," in *Greek and Roman Networks in the Mediterranean*, ed. I. Malkin, C. Constantakopoulou and K. Panagopoulou (London: Routledge, 2009), 240–1.

24. D. Knoepfler, "Tétradrachmes attiques et argent 'alexandrin' chez Diogène Laërce," *Museum Helveticum* 46 (1989), 204–210; idem, "Tétradrachmes attiques et argent 'alexandrin' chez Diogène Laërce, deuxième partie," *Museum Helveticum* 46 (1989), 193–230; idem, "Alexandreion nomisma. L' apparition et la disparition de l' argent d' Alexandre dans les inscriptions grecques. Quelques réflexions complémentaires," *Topoi* 7.1 (1997), 33–50; S. Psoma, "Alexanders after Alexander: The Epigraphic Evidence," in S. Kremydi Sicilianou and M.-C. Marcellesi (eds.), *Alexanders after Alexander*, forthcoming. The adjective Ἀλεξάνδρειον in the reverse legend of a silver tetradrachm type of c. 314 BC (?) in the name of Ptolemy I, signed ΑΛΕΞΑΝΔΡΕΙΟΝ ΠΤΟΛΕΜΑΙΟΥ, is now taken to mean "of Alexander" rather than "of Alexandreia": C. Lorber, "A Revised Chronology for the Coinage of Ptolemy I," *NC* 165 (2005), 275–300; eadem, "The Coinage of the Ptolemies," in *The Oxford Handbook of Greek and Roman Coinage*, ed. W. E. Metcalf (Oxford: University Press, 2012), 212; Mørkholm, *EHC*, 64–65; Le Rider, *Alexandre*, 262–264; Le Rider and de Callataÿ, *Séleucides*, 133–134, n. 1; O. Masson, *RN* 33 (1991), 69–70.

25. K. Lönnqvist, "Studies on the Hellenistic Coinage of Athens: the Impact of Macedonia on the Athenian Money

inscriptions,[26] have been attributed to Demetrios Poliorketes, although the texts from Makedonia mentioning them date to the second half of the third century BC. Hatzopoulos credits Poliorketes with the introduction of the new, Attic-weight drachmae in the Makedonian realm because contemporary Attic-weight Alexander tetradrachms minted in Makedonia are found outside (rather than within) its realm.[27] However, as the transition to Attic-weight silver coins had already been introduced by Alexander III, it would be hard to believe that the new weight standard was attributed by the Makedonians to a king with a very brief period of reign in Makedonia rather than to its original initiator, who minted coins on this standard in Makedonia. That Alexander's silver larger denominations are found outside Makedonia may be explained through payments and surely does not contradict the issuing authority's control of Makedonian finance. There seems no reason not to consider in this context Demetrios II, who is contemporary with the epigraphic evidence, and, as such drachmae may be taken in terms of their nominal value rather than as actual coins, may be considered a plausible alternative.

Market in the 3rd century BC," in *Early Hellenistic Athens: Symptoms of a Change*, ed. J. Frösen, Papers and Monographs of the Finnish Institute at Athens, vol. VI (Helsinki 1997), 119–212.

26. Hatzopoulos, *Institutions* II, no. 82 I, l. 6, II, l. 14, 21, 40 = *SEG* 40 [1990] 530, with earlier bibliography.

27. M. Hatzopoulos, "Αργυρές δραχμές και χρυσοί στατήρες σε επιγραφές της Μακεδονίας," in *Το νόμισμα στο Μακεδονικό χώρο, Πρακτικά Β' Επιστημονικής Συνάντησης, Οβολός 4* (Thessalonica: University Studio Press, 2000), 79–87, n. 36; S. Kremydi-Sicilianou, "Coinage and Finance," in *Brill's Companion to Ancient Macedon, Studies in the Archaeology and History of Macedon, 650 BC–300 AD*, ed. R. Lane Fox (Leiden: Brill, 2011), 159–161. See chapter 7.3.

9.7 Additions to the Catalogue of Silver Antigonid Coins from C. Boehringer's List

Period I

15. b. Frankfurt 796	15.22 g	5 h	-
22. a. Stockholm (provenance unknown)	16. 20 g	-	-
32. f. Claussenburg 3	16.62 g	8 h	-
66. b. Frankfurt 795	16.45 g	-	-
77. c. Naples F 6675	17.06 g	-	-
81. d. Gotha S	-	11 h	-
86. c. Naples F 6673	17.04 g	11 h	-
& move ANS: SNG BYB 354… to: (d).			
129. a. Naples S 10134	16.80 g	12 h	21 mm
& move Peus 313 (1985), 68 to (b) and Rauch 94 (9.4.2014), 254 to (c).			
178. b. St Petersburg	17.12 g	-	-

Period II

17. c. Berkeley 8-4762 (p, test cut)	16.54 g	-	-
44. a. Lonja del Almidon (30.3.1936), 19	-	-	-
74. b. Frankfurt 794	16.22 g	11 h	-

Period III

12. b. Naples F 6674	16.91 g	11 h	-
c. Philadelphia 29-126-72	17.12 g	9 h	-
75. c. Hess (25.3.1929), 235; plaster cast in Berlin "Hirsch Lager 1930, 152"			
	16.50 g	-	-
77. e. Lempetz (23.02.1926), 238	17.00 g	-	-
95. b. Berlin: plaster cast "Egger 86.80 f"	17.10 g	-	-
101. f. Naples 10133	16.95 g	11 h	-
g. Beirut American University 6698	16.95 g	11 h	-
134. b. Plaster Cast in Berlin, Academy: Seyffer 583a	17.17 g	-	-
144. d. Philadelphia 29-126-73	17.05 g	12 h	-
150. c. Pergamon, 1960: *IGCH* 1303	16.38 g	-	-
157 g. Naples F 6666	17.19 g	11 h	-
h. Vernin	17.02 g	-	-
163 c. Naples F 6665	17.03 g	11 h	-
185. f. Naples S 10131	17.09 g	11 h	-
186. a. Syria 1959, 11	16.91 g	-	-
198. g. Hesperia Art (23.4.1953), 79	-	-	-
236. f. Lyon	-	10 h	-

Period IV

51. e. Ball Lagerkatalog (4.1937), 323b	17.05 g	-	-

9.8. Bronze Issues in the Name of "King Antigonos"

Unlike gold and silver coins, bronzes were struck for the internal market of a state. The Antigonid bronzes display remarkable diversity in fabric for the thickness of their flans varies greatly, suggesting the possibility that they were produced at several mints and/or over a long period. Hence they may provide clues to the mints which produced the gold and silver coinage. In addition, they may indicate which of the posthumous Alexanders and Lysimachi were issued by Antigonos Gonatas. Finally, they may elucidate whether there were posthumous issues in the name of Antigonos or not, for stylistic development is more obvious in them than in the silver tetradrachms.

Two of the three types of the bronzes that are described below had already been adopted by at least one other issuing authority. They are hence distinguished from their counterparts primarily via the king's monogram, ΑΝ. More specifically, the types issued in our period of study are the following:

1. ALEXANDER III TYPES:

   O: Head of young Herakles in lion scalp r.
   R: ΒΑΣΙΛΕΩΣ above, ΑΝΤΙΓΟΝΟΥ below, arranged among the legs of a horse.

   And later:

   Β–Α above, ΑΝ between the legs of a horse. Jockey wearing diadem, on horse trotting r. Symbol.

2. O: Decorated Makedonian shield with six embossed crescent and dot units and dotted border on edge. The space between the crescent units is filled with dot decoration. In the center, ΑΝ.
   R: ΒΑ–ΣΙ l. and r. Crested Makedonian helmet. In field above, monograms left and right.

An identical shield with different monograms in the center occurs on the obverse of two other bronze types. One, on the basis of the ligature in the center, is now attributed to Demetrios Poliorketes; the monogram ΠΥΡ on the other suggests its assignation to Pyrrhos, who briefly gained control of western Makedonia twice, during the "interregnum" 287–285 BC and on his return from Italy, 274/3 BC.[28] Finally, the adoption of a Makedonian shield for the obverse of bronze coins (with an anchor in the central badge) attributed to Antiochos I may have been influenced by the corresponding issues of Antigonos Gonatas.[29]

3. O: Head of Athena r. in crested Corinthian helmet.
   R: Β/Α above, left and right. Beardless figure of Pan erecting trophy with right hand; *nebris* around his left arm. Between his legs, monogram ΑΝ. In field, several symbols.

The head of Athena r. in crested Corinthian helmet of the Alexander gold coins was also adopted for bronze issues of other central Greek states, including Hellenistic Athens, Aitolia and Lokris.[30]

28. K. Liampi, "Zur Chronologie der sogenannten 'anonymen' makedonischen Münzen des späten 4. Jhs. v. Chr.," *JNG* 36 (1986) 41–65, pl. iv–vi, esp. p. 49, 54–55; Liampi, *MS*, 107–108 (M18).

29. Liampi, *MS*, 142 (M 94) (Seleukos I Nikator—Antiocheia); 143–145 (M 96-103) (Antiochos I—Karrhae, Antiocheia, Dura Europos), pl. 109; *SC* I.1, 115 (Antioch on the Orontes).

30. Cf., for instance, Athens: *SNG Cop.* 85, 94–102 (Athena wearing Corinthian helmet; but in *SNG Cop.* 83, 295–292 her helmet is Attic); Aitolia: ibid. 35–40 (c. 279–168 BC) Lokris: ibid., 64–71 (338–300 BC.). Also, Locri Epiknemidii (Opuntii): *SNG Cop.* 58 (369–338 BC); 64 (AR); 65–71 (AE). Corinth: a) Athena l. (*SNG Cop.* 63); *SNG Cop.* 166. b) Athena r., *SNG Cop.* 189. The adoption of a common obverse on bronzes was a practice already common in the Greek mainland in the middle Hellenistic period.

Furthermore, Pan erecting/crowning a trophy of Celtic shields, known as "aposkopon" (watching from afar, keeping his distance) is one of the most uncommon but interesting themes in Makedonian coinage and has parallels on scenes in pottery.[31] Like the Pan on the silver tetradrachms, the theme selected for the reverse of the bronzes alludes to the victory of Antigonos over the Celts.

It is worth noting that the monogram ΑΝ on all the bronze issues of Antigonos Gonatas is also attested on a metal object from the excavations in Vergina.[32] However, the distribution of the bronzes bearing this monogram between Antigonos Gonatas or Doson is far from clear. In fact, the coins with Alexander types used to be attributed by archaeologists to Alexander III. Those with the shield and the Makedonian crested helmet have sometimes been recorded as coins "of Makedonian kings." Only those with Athena right and Pan erecting trophy were attributed to Antigonos Gonatas.[33]

Very little may be said at this stage in respect of the mints of the bronzes or of their circulation. Unlike the silver, appropriate to the payment of mercenaries or to major economic transactions, bronze coins were in the main locally produced and distributed in the Balkans. They are known to have been used in Makedonia, in particular, until the middle of the second century BC, on the evidence of hoards and individual finds in excavations.[34] Their circulation elsewhere on the Greek mainland is also shown by their presence in excavations and hoards.[35] The vast majority of the twenty two coin hoards with bronze specimens so far published are of Makedonian origin (thirteen), but three come from central Greece (Thessaly, Phthiotis and Aitolia), two from Attika and five from the Peloponnese.

Clues to the date of manufacture of the bronzes may be gleaned from a small number of overstrikes. A large number of bronzes, notably from the Athena/Pan erecting trophy variety, were

31. Borgeaud, *The Cult of Pan*, 135, n. 24, 26; 136, n. 29, 30.

32. M. Andronikos, "Vergina. The Royal Graves in the Great Tumulus," *AAA* 10 (1977), 1, 1–72. Cf. Gaebler, *AMNG* III.1, 189, 15 f., pl. 34.11 ff; *SNG Cop.* 1222 ff.

33. Liampi, *MS*, 108–111; B. Poulios, "Συμβολή στη μελέτη της χάλκινης νομισματοκοπίας των Αντιγονιδών από τον Αντίγονο Γονατά έως τους πρώτους χρόνους του Φιλίππου Ε΄, Η περίπτωση πέντε 'θησαυρών' από την Ανατολική Μακεδονία," *ΑΔ* Α 56 (2001 [2006]), 237–295; Gatzolis, *Κυκλοφορία*, II, 290–292; see n. 10. Cf. Chapter 6.1.

34. Note, for instance, the five pot hoards unearthed in Eastern Makedonia, reported by B. Poulios, "Χρονολογημένη ελληνιστική κεραμεική από την Ανατολική Μακεδονία," *Γ' Επιστημονική Συνάντηση γιά την ελληνιστική κεραμεική, Χρονολογημένα σύνολα–εργαστήρια, 24–27 Σεπτεμβρίου 1991, Θεσσαλονίκη*, Αριθ. 137 (Αθήναι: Βιβλ. της εν Αθήναις Αρχαιολ. Εταιρείας, 1994), 115–127, pls. 66–71. See also Poulios, "Συμβολή," 237–295 .

35. Makedonia: Grammeni, Drama, 1927 (*IGCH* 473); Drama, 1983 [*CH* X (2010), 76]; Ampelakia, Drama, 1982 [*CH* IX (2002), 175; Ophrynio, 1980 [*CH* X (2010) 77]; Rodolivos, Serres, 1952 (*CH* IX (2002), 186]; Nea Phyle, 1980 [*CH* X (2010), 79]; Tragilos, ? [*CH* VIII (1994), 297]; Vergina Emathias, 1994 [*CH* X (2010), 74; *CH* IX (2002), 162]; Pella, E. Cemetery, 1993 [*CH* IX (2002), 185]; Veroia, Macedonia, before 1994 [*CH* IX (2002), 192; Edessa, 1937 (*CH* IX (2002), 197; Makrygialos Pierias, 1995 [*CH* X (2010), 75; *CH* IX (2002), 151]; Eginio, Pieria, 1995 [*CH* IX (2002), 226]; Nikisiani, Macedonia, Tomb B, 1959 [*CH* IX (2002), 152; Anarrachi, Makedonia [*CH* VIII (1994), 234]; Nea Zichni, Macedonia, 1982 [*CH* X (2002) 98; *CH* IX (2002) 202; *CH* VIII (1994) 571]; Eion, Eastern Makedonia, 1980/1 [*CH* IX (2002), 173]; Amphipolis, E. cemetery tomb 13, 1999–2001 [*CH* X (2010), 105; Amphipolis, E. cemetery tomb 45, Greece, 1999 = 2001 [*CH* X (2010), 63], North Balkans: Kotcherinovo, Kjustendil region, Bulgaria, 1985 [*CH* X (2010), 187]; Central Greece: Makrakomi Lamias, 1932 (*IGCH* 214); Livanates, 1982, Grave Π-55 [*CH* IX (2002) 149; *CH* VIII (1994) 588]; Livanates, 1982 (Grave Π-58) [*CH* IX (2002), 150]; Medeon, Phokis (grave 59), 1962 [CH IX (2002), 183]; Medeon, Phokis (grave 60), 1962 [*CH* IX (2002), 157]; Medeon, Phokis (grave 129B), 1963 [*CH* IX (2002), 167]; Aitolia?, 1957 (*IGCH* 208); Amphissa, Greece, 1984–1985 [*CH* X (2010) 119; Attika: Attika, 1969 [*CH* I (1975) 95]; Athens environs, c. 1920–1939 [*CH* IX (2002), 313]; Piraeus, Greece, 1973 [*CH* III (1977), 73]; Peloponnese: Korinth, 1933 (*IGCH* 263); Korinth, 1973 [*CH* II (1976), 79]; Kato Kleitoria, Argolis, 1976 (*IGCH* 184); Argos, 1924 (*IGCH* 217); Pselalonia (1), Greece, 1990 [*CH* X (2010), 107]. The Makedonian hoards with bronzes of Gonatas, Demetrios II and Doson have been studied by Gatzolis, *Κυκλοφορία*, 289–292, 539 ff., Appendix 4, 605–649. See also C. Gatzolis, "Δύο ελληνιστικοί 'θησαυροί' από τη Μακεδονία," in *Το νόμισμα στο μακεδονικό χώρο*, Οβολός 4 (Θεσσαλονίκη, 2000), 103-126. See also the publications by B. Poulios mentioned above, n. 34.

countermarked. A coin hoard from the region of Amphipolis (Nea Zichne, 1982), comprising twenty fresh Athena/Pan erecting trophy bronzes countermarked with a Pan's head on the obverse suggests that these coins were also countermarked in Makedonia.

The wide spread of the bronze coins of Antigonos Gonatas in Southern Greece, and the particularly interesting pattern of the countermarks, might favour our case regarding Gonatas' long-term aspiration to partially/indirectly control the political life of the Greek poleis and thus to gradually transform them along the principles of Makedonian cities, rather than to rely on their dubious goodwill towards Makedonian sovereignty.[36]

36. Gabbert (*AG*, 33–40, 58 and *Greek Hegemony*, 107–148, 182–202) comments on the role of Antigonid garrisons in mainland Greece. The remarkable abundance of Antigonid bronzes throughout mainland Greek sites may be explained through the need to finance the σιτηρέσιον and daily expenses for these long-lasting garrisons. On short-term military payments through bronze coinage see, for instance, S. Psoma, "*Tas sitarchias kai tous misthous* ([Arist.], *Oec.* 1351b). Bronze Currencies and Cash-Allowances in Mainland Greece, Thrace and the Kingdom of Macedonia," *RBN* 45 (2009), 3–38.

Bibliography

Aleshire, Sara B. *The Athenian Asklepieion: The People, their Dedications and their Inventories.* Amsterdam: Gieben, 1989.

Alfen, P. van, "Problems in Ancient Imitative and Counterfeit Coinage," in *Making, Moving and Managing: The New World of Ancient Economies, 323–31 BC*, edited by Z. Archibald, J. K. Davies, and V. Gabrielsen, 322–354. Oxford: Oxbow, 2005.

Allamani-Souri, Victoria, "Ἀπόλλωνι, Ἀσκληπιῷ, Ὑγίειαι. Επιγραφική μαρτυρία για το Ασκληπιείο της Βέροιας." ΑΔ 39 (1984): 205–231.

Amandry, M. and G. Le Rider. *Trésors et circulation monétaire en Anatolie antique*, Paris: Bibliothèque Nationale, 1994.

Ameling, W., K. Bringman, and H. von Steuben (eds.). *Schenkungen Hellenistischer Herrscher an griechische Städte und Heiligtümer*, Teil I. Berlin: Akademie Verlag, 1995.

Andronikos, M. "Βεργίνα. Οι βασιλικοί τάφοι της Μεγάλης Τούμπας/The Royal Tombs at Vergina. A Brief Account of the Excavations," in *The Search for Alexander, An Exhibition, National Gallery of Art*, 26–38. Washington, 1980.

———. "Ανασκαφή στη Μ. Τούμπα της Βεργίνας." *AAA* 9.2 (1976): 123–129.

———. *Vergina, The Royal Tombs and the Ancient City*. Athens: Ekdotike Athenon, 1984.

———. *The Finds from the Royal Tombs at Vergina,* Proceedings of the British Academy, vol. 65 (1979). Oxford, 1981.

———. "Vergina. The Royal Graves in the Great Tumulus." *AAA* 10 (1977): 1–60.

Aperghis, G. G. *The Seleukid Royal Economy. The Finances and Financial Administration of the Seleukid Empire*. Cambridge: University Press, 2004.

———. "Recipients and End-Users on Seleukid Coins." *BICS* 53.2 (2010): 55–84.

———. "Creating a Long-Term Model for an Ancient Economy," in *Quantifying the Greco-Roman Economy and Beyond*, edited by F. de Callataÿ, 63–78. Pragmateiai 27. Bari: Edipuglia, 2014.

———. "The Armed Forces of Seleukos I, with Help from Coins," in *New Perspectives in Seleucid History, Archaeology and Numismatics: Studies in Honor of Getzel M. Cohen*, edited by Roland Oetjen, 3–30. Berlin/Boston: De Gruyter, 2019.

Archibald, Z. H. "Agoranomoi in Macedonia," in *Agoranomes et édiles, Institutions des marchés, Ouvrage publié avec le concours du GDRI du CNRS, "Les Marchés dans le monde antique: espaces, pratiques, institutions,"* edited by L. Capdetrey and C. Hasenohr, 109–19. Scripta Antiqua 44. Bordeaux: Ausonius, 2012.

———. *Ancient Economies of the Northern Aegean, Fifth to First Centuries BC.* Oxford: Oxford University Press, 2013.

Archibald, Z. H., J. K. Davies, V. Gabrielsen, and G. J. Oliver (eds.). *Hellenistic Economies.* London/New York: Routledge, 2000.

Archibald, Z. H., J. K. Davies, and V. Gabrielsen (eds.). *Making, Moving and Managing, The New World of Ancient Economies, 323–31 BC.* Oxford: Oxbow, 2005.

———. *The Economies of Hellenistic Societies, Third to First Centuries BC.* Oxford: Oxford University Press, 2011.

Arslan, M. and A. Özen. "A Hoard of Unpublished Bronze Coins of Ptolemy Ceraunus." *AJN* 12 (2000): 59–66.

Ashton, R. H. J. "Rhodian Coinage and the Colossus." *RN*[6] 30 (1988): 75–90.

———. "The Pseudo-Rhodian Drachms of Kos." *NC* 158 (1998): 223–228.

———. "The Coinage of Rhodes 408–c. 190 BC." in *Money and Its Uses in the Ancient Greek World*, edited by A. Meadows and K. Shipton, 79–115. Oxford: University Press, 2001.

Austin, M. "Hellenistic Kings, War and the Economy." *CQ* 36 (1986): 450–466.

Babelon, E. *Les rois de Syrie, d' Arménie et de Commagène.* Paris, 1890.

———. "La stylis, attribut naval sur les monnaies." *RN*[4] 11 (1907): 1–39 (=*Mélanges numismatiques*, vol. 4, Paris: A. Dieudonné, 1912).

Bagnall, R. S. *The Administration of the Ptolemaic Possessions outside Egypt.* Leiden: E. J. Brill, 1976.

Baldwin-Brett, A. "Athena Ἀλκίδημος of Pella." *ANSMN* 4 (1950): 55–79.

Baumann, H. *Pflanzenbilder auf griechischen Münzen.* Munich: Hirmer, 2000.

Bauschlaugh, R. "The Posthumous Alexander Coinage of Chios." *ANSMN* 24 (1979): 1–45.

Beazley, J. D. "Bakchos-rings." *NC* 1 (1941): 1–7.

Bell, H. W. *Sardis* XI: *Coins,* Part 1 (1910–1914). Leiden: E. J Brill, 1916.

Bellinger, A. R. *Essays on the Coinage of Alexander the Great.* New York: American Numismatic Society, 1963.

Beloch, K. J. *Griechische Geschichte.* 4 vols. Strasbourg/Berlin, 1912–1927.

Bérend, Denyse, "Réflections sur les fractions du monnayage grec," in *Festschrift für Leo Mildenberg: Numismatik, Kunstgeschichte, Archäologie / Studies in Honor of Leo Mildenberg: Numismatics, Art History, Archeology*, edited by A. Houghton, S. Hurter, P. E. Mottahedeh, and J. A. Scott, 7–30. Wetteren: Editions NR.

Bikerman, E. "Sur les batailles navales de Cos et d' Andros." *REA* (1938): 369–383.

Bilde, Per, et al. (eds.). *Aspects of Hellenistic Kingship, Studies in Hellenistic Civilization.* Aarhus: University Press, 1996.

Billows, R. A. *Antigonus the One-Eyed and the Creation of the Hellenistic State.* Los Angeles/London: University of California Press, 1990.

———. *Kings and Colonists, Aspects of Macedonian Imperialism.* Leiden: E. J. Brill, 1994.

Bloesch, H. *Griechische Münzen im Wintherthur*, 1. *Spanien, Gallien, Italien, Moesien, dacien, sarmatien, Thrakien, Makedonien, Hellas, Inseln*. Wintherhur, 1987.

Blümel, W. *Die Inschriften von Knidos*. Inschriften griechischer Städte aus Kleinasien, Teil I. Bonn: Österreichische Akademie der Wissenschaften, 1992.

Boehringer, Chr. *Zur Chronologie Mittelhellenistischen Münzserien, 220–160 v. Chr.* Berlin: de Gruyter, 1972.

———. "Antiochos Hierax am Hellespont," in *Essays in Honor of Robert Carson and Kenneth Jenkins,* edited by M. Price, A. Burnett, and R. Bland, 37–47. London: Spink, 1993.

Bopearachchi, O. *Monnaies gréco-bactriennes et indo-grecques, Catalogue raisonné.* Paris: Bibliothèque Nationale, 1991.

Borgeaud, P. *The Cult of Pan in Ancient Greece*, translated by Kathleen Atlas and J. Redfield. Chicago: University Press, 1988.

Borza, E. N. "The Natural Resources of Early Macedonia," in *Philip II, Alexander the Great, and the Macedonian Heritage*, edited by W. L. Adams and E. N. Borza, 1–20. Washington, D.C.: University Press of America, 1982.

———. *In the Shadow of Olympus. The Emergence of Macedon*, Princeton, New Jersey 1992.

Bouzek, I., L. Domaradzka, and Z. H. Archibald (eds.). *Pistiros* III, *Excavations and Studies.* Prague: Charles University in Prague, Faculty of Philosophy, 2007.

Bresson, A. "Coinage and Money Supply in the Hellenistic Age," in *Making, Moving and Managing, The New World of Ancient Economies, 323–31 BC*, edited by Z. Archibald, J. K. Davies, and V. Gabrielsen, 44–72. Oxford: Oxbow, 2005.

Briant, P. "L' économie royale entre privé et public," in *Approches de l' économie hellénistique [4e rencontre de l' économie antique,* edited by A. Bresson, P. Briant, F. Burkhalter, 343–358. Entretiens d' archéologie et d' histoire, 7. Paris: De Boccard, 2006.

Bringman, K. "The King as Benefactor: Some Remarks on Ideal Kingship in the Age of Hellenism," in *Images and Ideologies: Self-definition in the Hellenistic World*, edited by A. Bulloch, E. S. Gruen, A. A. Long, and A. Stewart, 7–24. Berkeley: University of California Press, 1993.

Briscoe, J. "The Antigonids and the Greek States, 276–196 BC," in *Imperialism in the Ancient World*, edited by P. Garnsey and C. R. Whittaker, 145–157. Cambridge: University Press, 1978.

Brooke, C. N. L. et al. (eds.). *Studies in Numismatic Method presented to Philip Grierson*. Cambridge/ New York: Cambridge University Press, 1983.

Brown, Blanche R. *Royal Portraits in Sculpture and Coins. Pyrrhos and the Successors of Alexander the Great*. Hermeneutics of Art, vol. 5, New York: P. Lang, 1995.

Brown, Ed. "Antigonos surnamed Gonatas," in *Arktouros. Hellenic Studies presented to B. M. W. Knox on the Occasion of his 65th Birthday*, edited by G. Bowersock, W. Burkert, and M. C. J. Putman, 299–307. Berlin: de Gruyter, 1979.

Bruneau, Ph. *Recherches sur les cultes de Délos à l' époque hellénistique et à l' époque impériale.* BÉFAR 217. Paris 1970.

Buraselis, K. "Παρατηρήσεις στίς συνθῆκες του βασιλιᾶ Ἀντιγόνου μέ τήν Ἐλεύθερνα καί τήν Ἱεράπυτνα (Staatsv. III 501, 502)." *AE* (1981): 114–126.

Buraselis, K. *Das Hellenistische Makedonien und die Ägäis, Forschungen zur Politik des Kassandros und der drei ersten Antigoniden im Ägäischen Meer und im Westkleinasien*. Münchner Beiträge zur Papyrusforschung und Antiken Rechtsgeschichte, Heft 73. Munich: Beck, 1982.

———. "Γλαύκων Ἐτεοκλέους μετηλλαχώς, Παρατηρήσεις στην επιγραφή." *BCH* (1975): 52–3." *AE* (1982 [1983]): 136–139.

———. "Ambivalent Roles of Center and Periphery: Remarks on the Relation of the Cities of Greece with the Ptolemies until the End of Philometor's Age," in *Center and Periphery in the Hellenistic World,* edited by Per Bilde *et al.*, 252–253. Studies in Hellenistic Civilization 4. Aarhus: University Press, 1993.

———. "Μυθική ύλη και ελληνιστική μοναρχία. Το εργαλείο του μύθου στην υπηρεσία της πολιτικής," in *Πρακτικά συμποσίου Μύθος μετά λόγου, Διάλογοι για την ουσία και τη διαχρονική αξία του αρχαίου ελληνικού μύθου, Αγ. Κήρυκος, Ικαρία, 17–20 Ιουνίου 2005,* edited by K. Buraselis and M. Stephanou, 177–97. Athens: Φεστιβάλ Ικαρίας, 2007.

Burkert, W. *Greek Religion.* Oxford: Oxford University Press, 1985.

Burnett, A. "The Enna Hoard and Silver Coinage of the Syracusan Democracy." *SNR* 62 (1983): 5–26.

———. *Coinage in the Roman World.* London: Seaby, 1987.

Butler, H. C. *Sardis,* vol. I.1. Leiden: Brill, 1922.

Buttrey, T. V. "Calculating Ancient Coin Production: Facts and Fantasies." *NC* 153 (1993): 335–352.

———. "Calculating Ancient Coin Production, II: Why It Cannot be Done." *NC* 154 (1994): 341–352.

Buttrey, S. E., and T. V. Buttrey. "Calculating Ancient Coin Production, Again," *AJN* 9 (1997): 113–135.

Callataÿ, F. de. "Athenian 'New Style' Tetradrachms in Macedonian Hoards." *AJN* 3–4 (1992): 11–20.

———. "Calculating Ancient Coin Production: Seeking a Balance." *NC* 155 (1995): 289–311.

———. *Les monnaies grecques et l' orientation des axes.* Glaux 12. Milan 1996.

———. Review of Y. Touratsoglou, *Disjecta Membra. Two New Hellenistic Hoards from Greece, RBN* 142 (1996): 296–299.

———. *L' histoire des guerres Mithridatiques vue par les monnaies.* Louvain: Departement d' Archéologie et d' Histoire de l' Art, Séminaire Numismatique Marcel Hoc, 1997.

———. *Recueil quantitatif sur les émissions monétaires hellénistiques.* Wetteren: Éditions Numismatique Romaine, 1997.

———. "L' instauration par Ptolémée I Sôter d' une économie monétaire fermée," in *L' exception égyptienne? Production et échanges monétaires en Égypte hellénistique et romaine, Actes du colloque d' Alexandrie, 13–15 avril 2002,* edited by F. Duyrat and O. Picard, 117–133. Études Alexandrines 10. Cairo: IFAO, 2005.

———. "Réflexions quantitatives sur l' or et l' argent non monnayés à l' époque hellénistique (pompes, triomphes, réquisitions, fortunes des temples orfèvrerie et masses métalliques disponibles)," in *Approches de l' économie hellénistique [4e rencontre de l' économie antique, Saint-Bertrand-des-Comminges (06-07 Mai 2004),* edited by R. Descat, 37–84. Paris: De Boccard, 2006.

———. *Quantifications et numismatique antique: choix d' articles (1984–2004).* Wetteren: Moneta, 2006.

———. "Les tétradrachmes hellénistiques au nom des Thasiens et la circulation monétaire en Thrace aux IIe et Ier s. av. J.-C." *RBN* 154 (2008): 31–54.

——— (ed.). *Quantifying Monetary Supplies in Greco-Roman Times.* Bari: Edipuglia, 2011.

———. "Control Marks on Hellenistic Royal Coinages: Use, and Evolution toward Simplification?," *RBN* 48 (2012): 39–62.

Callataÿ, F. de, G. Depeyrot, and L. Villaronga. *L' argent monnayé d' Alexandre le Grand à Auguste.* Brussels: Cercle d' Études Numismatiques, 1993.

Carradice, I. *Coinage and Finances in the Reign of Domitian AD 81–96*. Oxford: BAR, 1983.

Casson, L. *Ships and Seamanship in the Ancient World*. Baltimore/London: Johns Hopkins University Press, 1995.

Ceka, N. "Der Münzschatz von Hija e Korbit," in Eggebrecht et al. *Albanien*, 261.

Chambers, M. "The first regnal year of Antigonos Gonatas," *AJPh* 75 (1954): 392 ff.

Champion, C. "Polybius, Aetolia and the Gallic attack on Delphi (279 BC)." *Historia* 45 (1996): 316–328.

_________. "In Defense of Hellas: the Antigonid Soteria and Paneia at Delos and the Aetolian Soteria at Delphi." *AJAH* 3–4 (2004–2005): 72–78.

Chankowski, V. "Délos et les matériaux stratégiques. Une nouvelle lecture de la loi délienne sur la vente du bois et du charbon (*ID*, 509)," in *Stephanèphoros. De l' économie antique à l' Asie Mineure*, edited by K. Konuk, 31–51. Mémoires 28. Bordeaux: Ausonius, 2012.

Chankowski, V., and F. Duyrat (eds). *Le roi et l' économie: autonomies locales et structures royales dans l' économie de l' empire séleucide: actes et rencontres de Lille (23 Juin 2003): et d' Orléans (29–30 janvier 2005)*. Lyon/Paris: Maison de l' orient méditerranéen, 2004.

Chryssanthaki, K. "Les monnaies lagides en Égee," in *L' exception égyptienne? Production et échanges monétaires en Égypte hellénistique et romaine, Actes du colloque d' Alexandrie, 13–15 avril 2002*, edited by F. Duyrat and O. Picard, 159–175. Cairo: IFAO, 2005.

Clinton, C. "Macedonians at Eleusis in the Early Third Century," in *The Macedonians in Athens, 322–229 B.C. Proceedings of an International Conference held at the University of Athens, May 24–26, 2001*, edited by S. V. Tracy and O. Palagia, 76–81. Oxford: Oxbow, 2003.

Cloché, P. "La politique extérieure de Lacédemoine depuis la mort d' Agis III jusqu' à celle d' Acrotatos, fils d' Areus Ier." *REA* 48 (1946): 39–60.

Coulton, Janice J. *The Architectural Development of the Greek Stoa*. Oxford: Clarendon Press, 1976.

Courby, F. *Délos* V, Paris: Fontemoing, 1912.

Cox, Dorothy M. *A Third Century Hoard of Tetradrachms from Gordion*. Philadelphia: University of Pennsylvania, 1953.

———. "Gordion Hoards III, V and VII." *ANSMN* 12 (1966): 33–55.

Crampa, J. *Labraunda: Swiss Excavations and Researches*, vol. III.1–2. *The Greek Inscriptions*. Lund: C. W. K. Gieerup, 1955.

Crawford, M. H. *Roman Republican Coinage*. Cambridge: Cambridge University Press, 1975.

———. *Coinage and Money under the Roman Republic, Italy and the Mediterranean Economy*. London: Methuen, 1985.

Cunliffe, B. *The ancient Celts*. Oxford: Oxford University Press, 1997.

Daehn, W. E. "Contradictory Theories: Making Sense of Greek Coin Weight Standards." *Celator* 5.8 (1991): 28–33.

Dakaris, S. "Ἀνασκαφή τοῦ ἱεροῦ τῆς Δωδώνης," *ΠΑΕ* (1968 [1970]): 58–9.

Davesne, A. "Les monnaies des premiers Ptolemées en Asie Mineure et à Chypre," in *L' exception égyptienne? Production et échanges monétaires en Égypte hellénistique et romaine, Actes du colloque d' Alexandrie, 13–15 avril 2002*, edited by F. Duyrat and O. Picard, 177–185. Cairo: IFAO, 2005.

Davesne, A., and G. Le Rider. *Le trésor de Meydançıkkale (Cilicie Trachée, 1980)*. 2 vols. Paris: Éditions Recherches sur les Civilisations, 1989.

Davies, J. K. "Ancient Economies," in *A Companion to Ancient History*, edited by A. Erskine, 436–46. Malden, Mass./Oxford: Wiley-Blackwell, 2009.

Descat, R. "Qu' est-ce que l' économie royale?" in *L' orient meditérannéen de la mort d' Alexandre aux campagnes de Pompée,"* edited by F. Prost, 149–168. Toulouse: Pallas et Presses Univérsitaires du Mirail, 2002.

Dimitrov, K. "Celts, Greeks and Thracians in Thrace during the Third Century BC. Interactions in History and Culture," in *In Search of Celtic Tylis in Thrace (III c. BC). Proceedings of the Interdisciplinary Colloquium arranged by the National Archaeological Institute and Museum at Sofia and the Welsch Department, Aberystwyth University held at the National Archaeological Institute and Museum, Sofia, 8 May 2010*, edited by L. Vagalinski, 51–66. Sofia: National Archaeological Institute and Museum, 2010.

Dintsis, P. *Hellenistische Helme,* Rome: G. Bretschneider, 1986.

———. "Über die Bezeichnung ΚΩΝΟΣ im Reglement von Amphipolis." *Archaia Makedonia* 4 (1986): 171–82.

Doyen, Ch. *Études de métrologie grecque,* vol. II, *Étalons d' argent et du bronze en Grèce hellénistique.* Louvain: Association Professeur Marcel Hoc, 2012.

Ducrey, P., and S. Schmidt. "Les activités de l' École Suisse d' Archéologie en Grèce 1996." *Antike Kunst* 2 (1997): 103–107.

Duyrat, F. "La politique monétaire d' Arados." *Topoi* 4 (2003): 25–52

———. *Arados hellénistique, Étude historique et monétaire.* Beirut: IFPO, 2005.

Eckhel, J. *Doctrina numorum veterum*, pars 1.2^2. Vindobonae, 1794.

Edson, Ch. "The Antigonids, Heracles, and Beroea." *HSCP* 45 (1934): 213–246.

Eggebrecht, Arne et al. (eds.). *Albanien: Schätze aus dem Land der Skipetaren.* Mainz am Rhein: Philipp von Zabern, 1998.

Ehrenberg, C. *RE* III.A. 1929, col. 1423 ff., s.v. "Sparta."

Ehrhardt, Chr. *Studies in the Reigns of Demetrius II and Antigonus Doson.* 2 vols. PhD diss. Buffalo, New York, 1975.

———. "A Catalogue of Issues of Tetradrachms from Amphipolis, 318–294 BC." *JNFA* 4 (1976): 85–89.

Ellis, J. R. *Philip II and the Macedonian Imperialism.* Princeton: Princeton University Press, 1976.

Errington, R. M. *A History of Macedonia,* translated by Catherine Errington. Berkeley: University of California Press, 1990.

———. "Macedonian 'Royal Style' and its Historical Significance." *JHS* 94 (1974): 20–37.

———. "The Nature of the Macedonian State under the Monarchy." *Chiron* 8 (1978): 77–134.

Erskine, A. *The Hellenistic Stoa. Political Thought and Action.* Ithaca, New York: Cornell University Press, 1990.

Esty, W. S. "Estimating the Size of a Coinage." *NC* 144 (1984): 180–183.

———. "Estimation of the Size of a Coinage: A Survey and Comparison of Methods." *NC* 146 (1986): 185–215.

Faranguna, M. "Aspetti administrativi e finanziari della monarchia macedone tra IVe III secolo a.C." *Athenaeum* 86 (1998): 349–395.

———. "L' economia della Macedonia ellenistica: un bilancio," in *Approches de l' économie hellénistique [4e rencontre de l' économie antique, Saint-Bertrand-des-Comminges (06–07 mai 2004]*, edited by A. Bresson, P. Briant, and F. Burkhalter, 121–146. Paris: De Boccard, 2006.

Fellmann, W. *Antigonos Gonatas, König der Makedonen, und die Griechischen Staaten.* PhD diss. Würzburg, 1930.

Flacelière, R. *Les Aitoliens à Delphes: contribution à l' histoire de la Grèce centrale au IIIe siècle av. J.-C.* Paris: De Boccard, 1937.

———. "La chronologie du IIIe siècle av. J.-C. à Delphes." *REA* 35 (1933): 321–328.

Flament, C. *Le monnayage en argent d' Athènes. De l' époque archaique à l' époque hellénistique (c.550–c. 40 av. J.-C.).* Louvain: Association Professeur Marcel Hoc, 2007.

———. *Contribution à l' étude des atélies monétaires grecs, Étude comparée des conditions de fabrication de la monnaie à Athenes, dans le Péloponnèse et dans le royaume de Macédoine à l' époque classique.* Louvain: Association Professeur Marcel Hoc, 2010.

Fleischer, R. "Hellenistic Royal Iconography on Coins," in *Aspects of Hellenistic Kingship, Studies in Hellenistic Civilization,* edited by Per Bilde et al., 28–39. Aarhus: Aarhus University Press, 1996.

Franke, P. R. "Zur Geschichte des Antigonos Gonatas und der Oitaioi," *JDAI* 72 (1958 [1959]): 38–62.

———. Zur Finanzpolitik des makedonischen Königs Perseus während des Krieges mit Rom 171–168 v. Chr." *JNG* (1957): 31–50.

———. "Inschriftiche und Numismatische Zeugnisse für die Chronologie des Artemis Tempels zu Sardis." *MDAI* (Ath) 76 (1961): 203–207.

Franke, P. R., and M. Hirmer. *Die Griechische Münze.* Munich: Hirmer, 1964.

Fraser, J. G. *Pausanias' Description of Greece* 5. London: MacMillan and Co., 1897.

Fraser, P. "Two Hellenistic Inscriptions from Delphi." *BCH* 78 (1954): 49–67.

———. *Ptolemaic Alexandria.* 3 vols. Oxford: Clarendon Press, 1972.

Frei, P.–Marek, C. "Die karisch-griechische Bilingue von Kaunos: eine zweisprächige Staatsurkunde des 4. Jahrhunderts v. Chr." *Kadmos* 36.1 (1997): 1–89.

Fritze, H. von, "Die autonomen Münzen von Abdera." *Nomisma* 3 (1909): 28–29.

Fröhlich, B. *Die statuarischen Darstellungen hellenistischer Herrscher.* Hamburg: Kovač, 1998.

Gabbert, Janice J. *Antigonus II Gonatas. A Political Biography.* London/New York: Routledge, 1997.

———. *The Greek Hegemony of Antigonos II Gonatas (r. 283–239 B.C.).* PhD diss. University of Cincinnati, 1982.

———. "The Anarchic Dating of the Chremonidean War." *CJ* 82 (1986): 230–235.

———. Response to G. Reger's Review, *BMCR* 11 (1998): 14.

Gaebler, H. *Die Antiken Münzen von Makedonia und Paionia, AMNG,* vol. III.1, Berlin: G. Reimer, 1906.

———. *Die Antiken Münzen von Makedonia und Paionia. AMNG,* vol. III.2. Berlin: de Gruyter, 1935.

Garoufalias, P. *Pyrrhus, King of Epirus.* London: Stacey International, 1979.

Gatzolis, Chr. "Δύο ελληνιστικοί 'θησαυροί' από τη Μακεδονία," in Το νόμισμα στο μακεδονικό χώρο, 103–126 .Ovolos 4. Thessaloniki: University Studio Press, 2000.

———. *Η κυκλοφορία του χάλκινου νομίσματος στη Μακεδονία (5ος–1ος αι. π.Χ.).* PhD diss. Thessaloniki: Aristoteleion University, 2010.

Gehrke, H. J. *Geschichte des Hellenismus,* Oldenbourg Grundriss der Geschichte. Vol. I.A. Munich: Oldenburg, 1990.

Gerin, D. "La 'seconde main': gravures et faux d' Antigone Doson (fin XVIIe–début XVIIIe s.)." *Bulletin de la société française de numismatique* 7 (1984): 517–527.

Giovannini, A. "Le statut des cités de Macédoine sous les Antigonides." *Archaia Makedonia* 2 (1977): 465–479.

Gjongecaj, S. "Thesari i Hijes së Korbit." *Iliria* 1 (1985): 167–209.

Gjogecaj-Vangjeli, S. *Trésors de monnaies antiques trouvées en Albanie (V-I siecles av,J-C)*. Tirana: École françaises d' Athènes, 2014.

Glotz, G. "L' histoire de Délos d' après les prix d' une denrée." *REG* (1916): 281–325.

Goudineau, Chr. "Les Celtes, les Gaulois et l' or d' après les auteurs anciens," in *L' or dans l' antiquité: de la mine à l' objet*, edited by B. Cauuet *et al.*, 331–6. Aquitania Supplement 9. Bordeaux: Aquitania, 1999.

Gounaropoulou, Loukretia, and M. B. Hatzopoulos. *Επιγραφές Κάτω Μακεδονίας*, Τεύχος Α, *Επιγραφές Βεροίας*. Athens, 1998.

Green, P. *From Alexander to Actium: the Hellenistic Age*. London: Thames & Hudson, 1990.

Griffith, G. T. *The Mercenaries of the Hellenistic World*. Chicago: Ares, 1934 (reprint).

Gruen, E. S. "Coronation of the Diadochoi," in *The Craft of the Ancient Historian: Essays in Honour of Chester G. Starr*, edited by J. Eadie, and J. Ober, 259–260. Langham, Maryland: University Press of America, 1985.

———. "Hellenistic Kingship: an Introduction," in *Images and Ideologies: Self-Definition in the Hellenistic World* , edited by A. Bulloch, E. S. Gruen, A. A. Long, and A. Stewart, 3–8. Berkeley: University of California Press, 1993.

Grunauer-von Hoerschelmann, S. *Die Münzprägung der Lakedaemonier*. Berlin: de Gruyter, 1978.

Grzybek, E. *Du Calendrier Macédonien au Calendrier Ptolemaïque. Problèmes de Chronologie Hellénistique*. Heft 20. Basel: F. Reinhardt, 1990.

Habicht, Chr. *Gottmenschentum und griechische Städte*. Zetemata 14. Second Edition. Munich: C. H. Beck, 1970.

———. "Epigraphische Zeugnisse zur Geschichte Thessaliens unter der Makedonischen Herrschaft." *Archaia Makedonia* 1 (1970): 265–79.

———. *Untersuchungen zur politischen Geschichte Athens im 3. Jahrhundert v. Chr.* Munich: C. H. Beck, 1979.

———. "Bemerkungen zum P. Haun." *ZPE* 39 (1980): 1–5.

———. *Studien zur Geschichte Athens in hellenistischer Zeit*, Göttingen: Vanderhoek & Ruprecht, 1982.

———. "Divine Honours for King Antigonus Gonatas in Athens." *SCI* 15 (1986): 131–134.

———. *Athen in hellenistischer Zeit: gesammelte Aufsätze*. Munich: C. H. Beck, 1994.

———. *Athens from Alexander to Antony*, translated by Deborah Lucas Schneider. Cambridge Mass./London: Harvard University Press, 1997.

———. *Pausanias' Guide to Ancient Greece*. Second Edition. Berkeley/London: University of California Press, 1998.

———. *Hellenistic Monarchies: Selected Papers*. Ann Arbor: University of Michigan Press, 2006.

Hackens, T. "À propos de la circulation monétaire dans le Péloponnèse au IIIe s. av. J.-C." in *Antidorum W. Peremans sexagenario ab alumnis oblatum*. Studia Hellenistica 16. Louvain: Publications Universitaires, 1968.

Hammond, N. G. L. *Epirus*. Oxford: University Press, 1967.

———. *The Macedonian State*. Oxford: University Press, 1989.

———. *A History of Macedonia*. Vol. I. Oxford: University Press, 1972.

Hammond, N. G. L., and G. T. Griffith. *A History of Macedonia*. Vol. II. Oxford: University Press, 1979.

Hammond, N. G. L., and F. W. Walbank. *A History of Macedonia*. Vol. III. Oxford: University Press, 1988.
Hannestad, Lise. "Greeks and Celts: The Creation of a Myth," in *Center and Periphery in the Hellenistic World,* edited by Per Bilde *et al.*, 15–38. Studies in Hellenistic Civilization 4. Aarhus: University Press, 1993.
Hatzopoulos, M. B. *Actes de Vente d' Amphipolis*. Meletemata 14. Athens: De Boccard, 1991.
———. *Macedonian Institutions under the Kings*, Vol. I, *A Historical and Epigraphical Study*. Meletemata 22. Athens: De Boccard, 1996.
———. *Macedonian Institutions under the Kings*. Vol. II, *Epigraphic Appendix*. Meletemata 22, Athens: De Boccard, 1996.
Hatzopoulos, M. B. "Ἀργυρές δραχμές και χρυσοῖ στατῆρες σὲ ἐπιγραφὲς τῆς Μακεδονίας," in *Το νόμισμα στο Μακεδονικό χώρο, Πρακτικά Β' Επιστημονικής Συνάντησης*, Οβολός 4, 79–87. Thessaloniki: University Studio Press, 2000.
Hatzopoulos, M. B. "Macedonians and other Greeks," in *Brill's Companion to Ancient Macedon: Studies in the Archaeology and History of Macedon*, 650 BC–300 AD, edited by R. Lane Fox, 51–78. Leiden/Boston: Brill, 2011.
Hazzard, R. A. *Ptolemaic Coins: An Introduction for Collectors*. Toronto: Kirk & Bentley, 1995.
———. "The Use of the Macedonian Calendar under Ptolemies V and VI," in *Travaux de numismatique grecque offerts à Georges Le Rider*, edited by M. Amandry and S. Hurter, 147–159. London: Spink, 1999.
———. *Imagination of a Monarchy. Studies in Ptolemaic Propaganda* (Toronto: University of Toronto Press, 2000).
Head, B. V. *Catalogue of Coins in the British Museum, Macedonia*, London: Trustees of the British Museum, 1879.
———. *Historia Nummorum: A Manual of Greek Numismatics*, Oxford: Oxford University Press, 1911[2].
________. *Coins of the Ancients*, London: No publisher, 1895[4].
Heichelheim, F. M. "Numismatic Evidence of the Battle of Lysimacheia." *AJPh* 64 (1943): 332–333.
Heinen, H. *Untersuchungen zur politischen Geschichte Athens im 3. Jahrhundert v. Chr.* Munich: C. H. Beck, 1979.
———. "The Syrian-Egyptian Kings and the New Kingdoms of Asia Minor," in *The Cambridge Ancient History*, vol. VII.I[2], edited by A. E. Austin, M. W. Fredricksen, and R. M. Ogilvie, 412–445. Cambridge: University Press, 1989.
Helly, B. *Gonnoi* I–II. Amsterdam: Hakkert, 1973.
Hersch, Ch. "An Unpublished Coin of Philip II of Macedonia from his First Issue of Bronzes." *AJN* 1 (1989): 33–36.
Himmelmann, N. *Herrscher und Athlet. Die Bronzen von Quirinal. Katalog zur der Ausstellung im Akademischen Kunstmuseum Bonn vom 20. Juni bis 05. September 1989*. Bonn: Pappbilderbuch, 1989.
Hölbl, G. "Bemerkungen zur frühptolemâischen Chronologie." *Tyche* 7 (1992): 117–122.
———. *A History of the Ptolemaic Empire*, translated by Tina Saavedra. London/New York: Routledge, 2001.
Hollstein, W. "Münzen des Ptolemaios Keraunos." *SNR* 74 (1995): 13–25.
Hornblower, Jane. *Hieronymus of Cardia*, Oxford: Oxford University Press, 1981.
Hoover, O. "Appendix 5: Overstruck Seleucid Coins," in A. Houghton, C. Lorber, and O. Hoover,

Seleucid Coins: A Comprehensive Catalogue, Part II: *Seleucus IV through Antiochus XIII*. Vol 2, 209–217. Lancaster/London: Classical Numismatic Group, 2008.

———. "Unknown Findspot ('Pamphylia or Cilicia' Hoard), 2000 (*CH* 10, 292), in *Coin Hoards* X: *Greek Hoards*, edited by O. Hoover, A. Meadows, and U. Wartenberg, 129–152. New York: American Numismatic Society, 2010.

Houghton, A. *Coins of the Seleucid Empire from the Collection of Arthur Houghton*. New York: American Numismatic Society, 1983.

Houghton, A. "The Early Seleucid Mint of Laodicea ad Mare (c. 300–246 B.C.)," in *Travaux de numismatique grecque offerts à Georges Le Rider*, edited by M. Amandry and S. Hurter, 169–184. London: Spink, 1999.

Houghton, A., and C. Lorber. *Seleucid Coins: A Comprehensive Catalogue*, Part I, *Seleucus I through Antiochus III*. 2 vols. Lancaster/London: Classical Numismatic Group, 2002.

Houghton, A., C. Lorber, and O. Hoover. *Seleucid Coins: A Comprehensive Catalogue*, Part II, *Seleucus IV through Antiochus XIII*. 2 vols. Lancaster/London: Classical Numismatic Group, 2008.

Howgego, C. *Greek Imperial Countermarks: Studies in the Provincial Coinage of the Roman Empire*, London: Royal Numismatic Society, 1985.

———. "Why did ancient states strike coins?" *NC* 150 (1990): 1–25.

———. "Coin Circulation and the Integration of the Roman Economy." *JRA* 7 (1994): 5–21.

———. *Ancient History from Coins*. London/New York: Routledge, 1995.

Iliadou, P. *Herakles in Makedonien*. Hamburg: Kovac, 1998.

Imhoof-Blumer, F. "Die Münzen Akarnaniens." *NZ* 10 (1878): 1–180.

———. *Monnaies Grecques*, Académie Royale Néerlandaise des Sciences, Paris: C. Rollin-Feuardent, 1883.

Imhoof-Blumer, F., and T. Wiegand (eds.). *Die antiken Münzen Nordgriechenlands*. 3 vols. Berlin: Akademie der Wissenschaften, 1898–1935.

Ingvaldsen, H. *Cos—Coinage and Society, The Chronology and Function of a City-State Coinage in the Classical and Hellenistic Period, c. 390–c. 170 BC*. Oslo: Unipub AS, 2002.

Jameson, R. *Monnaies greques antiques*. Vol. Ib, *Macédoine*. Chicago: Ares, 1980.

Jessen, O. *RE* V 2 (1905), 2348–2349, s. v. "Eleutherios."

Johnston, Ann W. "The Greek Coins," in T. V. Buttrey, Ann Johnston, K. M. MacKenzie. M. L. Bates, and J. A. Charles, *Greek, Roman and Islamic Coins from Sardis*, 2–4. Cambridge Mass./ London: Harvard University Press, 1981.

Juhel, P. and D. Temelkoski."Fragments de 'boucliers macédoniens' au nom du roi Démétrios trouvés à Staro Bonče (République de Macédoine). Rapport préliminaire et Présentation épigraphique." *ZPE* 162 (2007): 165–78.

Juhel, P. *L' armée du royaume de Macédoine à l'époque hellénistique (323–148 BC). Les troupes "nationales". Organisation et analyse de l' iconographie militaire, avec déductions quànt à la nature de l' armément*. PhD diss. Sorbonne–Université Paris IV, 2007.

Kalléris, J. N. *Les anciens Macédoniens*. 2 vols. Athens, 1954–67.

Kalligas, P. G. "Ἀνασκαφή στην Ἐρέτρια." *AE* 122 1983 (1985): 113–6.

Karamessini-Oikonomidou, M. "Θησαυρός νομισμάτων ἐκ Θεσσαλίας 1968." *AE* (1970 [1971]): 13–26.

———. "Νομισματικό Μουσεῖο." *ΑΔ* (1976): Chronicle, 4–5.

———. "Δύο νομισματικοί 'θησαυροί' ἀπό τήν ἀνασκαφή στήν Ἐρέτρια." *AE* 122 (1983 [1985]): 137–47.

Kinns, P. "The Attic Weight Drachms of Ephesus: A Preliminary Study in the Light of Recent Hoards." *NC* 159 (1999): 47–49.

Knoepfler, D. "Tétradrachmes attiques et argent 'alexandrin' chez Diogène Laërce, première partie." *Museum Helveticum* 44.4 (1987): 241.

———. "Tétradrachmes attiques et argent 'alexandrin' chez Diogène Laërce, deuxième partie." *Museum Helveticum* 46 (1989): 193–230.

———. "Les relations des cités euboéennes avec Antigone Gonatas et la chronologie delphique au début de l' époque Étolienne." *BCH* 119.1 (1995): 137–156.

———. "Alexandreion nomisma. L' apparition et la disparition de l' argent d' Alexandre dans les inscriptions grecques. Quelques réflexions complémentaires." *Topoi* 7.1 (1997): 33–50.

Koenen, I. "The Ptolemaic King as a Religious Figure," in *Images and Ideologies: Self-Definition in the Hellenistic World* , edited by A. Bulloch, E. S. Gruen, A. A. Long, and A. Stewart, 25–115. Berkeley: University of California Press, 1993.

Kraay, C. M. "Hoards, Small Change and the Origin of Coinage." *JHS* 83 (1963): 76–91.

———. *Archaic and Classical Greek Coins*. London: Methuen, 1976.

Kralli, I. "The Date and Context of Divine Honours for Antigonos Gonatas—A Suggestion," in *The Macedonians in Athens, 322–229 B.C. Proceedings of an International Conference held at the University of Athens, May 24–26, 2001*, edited by S. V. Tracy and O. Palagia, 61–66. Oxford: Oxbow, 2003.

Kremydi-Sicilianou, S. "ΜΑΚΕΔΟΝΩΝ ΠΡΩΤΗΣ ΜΕΡΙΔΟΣ: Evidence for a Coinage under the Antigonids." *RN* 163 (2007): 91–100.

———. "The Tauropolos Tetradrachms of the First Macedonian Meris: Provenance, Iconography and Dating," in *Κερμάτια Φιλίας. Τιμητικός Τόμος για τον Ιωάννη Τουράτσογλου*, vol. 1, edited by S. Drougou, 191–201. Athens: Numismatic Museum, 2009.

———. "Coinage and Finance," in *Brill's Companion to Ancient Macedon: Studies in the Archaeology and History of Macedon*, 650 BC–300 AD, edited by R. Lane Fox, 159–176. Leiden/Boston: Brill, 2011.

Kroll, J. *The Athenian Agora*, XXVI: *The Greek Coins*, Princeton, New Jersey: American School of Classical Studies at Athens, 1993.

———. "The late Hellenistic Tetrobols at Kos." *ANSMN* 11 (1964): 81–117.

———. "The Evidence of the Athenian Coins," in *The Macedonians in Athens, 322–229 B.C. Proceedings of an International Conference held at the University of Athens, May 24–26, 2001*, edited by S. V. Tracy and O. Palagia, 206–212. Oxford: Oxbow, 2003.

———. "The Emergence of Ruler Portraiture on Early Hellenistic Coins," in *Early Hellenistic Portraiture: Image, Style, Context*, edited by P. Schultz and R. von der Hoff, 113–122. New York: Cambridge University Press, 2007.

Lacroix, L. "Copies des statues sur les monnaies Seleucides." *BCH* 73 (1949): 169–174.

Laix, F. A. de. " The Silver Coinage of the Aetolian League." *California Studies in Classical Antiquity* 6 (1973): 47–75.

Lane Fox, R. "Philip of Macedon: Accession, Ambitions and Self-Presentation," in *Brill's Companion to Ancient Macedon: Studies in the Archaeology and History of Macedon*, 650 BC–300 AD, edited by R. Lane Fox, 336–366. Leiden/Boston: Brill, 2011.

Larsen, J. A. O. *Greek Federal States: Their Institutions and History*. Oxford: Clarendon Press, 1968.

Laubscher, H. P. "Hellenistische Herrscher und Pan." *MDAI* (Ath) 100 (1985): 340–350.

Launey, M. *Recherches sur les armées hellénistiques*. 2 vols. Paris: De Boccard, 1949–1950.

Le Bohec, Sylvie. *Antigone Dôsôn, roi de Macédoine*, Nancy: Presses Universitaires, 1993.

———. "The kings of Macedon and the Cult of Zeus in the Hellenistic Period," in *The Hellenistic World. New Perspectives,* edited by D. Ogden, 41–57. Swansea: Classical Press of Wales, 2002.

Lefèvre, F. "La chronologie du IIIe siècle à Delphes d' après les actes amphictioniques (280–200)." *BCH* 119.1 (1995): 161–208.

Le Rider, G. *Monnayage et finances de Philippe II, un état de la question*, Meletemata 23, Athens: Research Center for Greek and Roman Antiquity, National Hellenic Research Foundation, 1996.

Le Rider, G. "Les tétradrachmes attalides au portrait de Philétaire," in H. Nilsson (ed.). *Florilegium Numismaticum, Studia in honorem U. Westermark Edita.* Stockholm: Svenska Numismatiska Föreningen, 1992, 234–45 = *Études Le Rider* II, 627–639.

———. "Trésors de statères d' or trouvés à Potidée en 1984 et à Skioné en 1985." *RN* 33 (1991): 89–96 = *Études Le Rider* II, 751–759.

———. "La date des premiers statères d' or de Philippe II," *Χαρακτήρ*, 261–269 = *Études Le Rider* II, 485–494.

———. *Le monnayage d' argent et d' or de Philippe II frappé en Macédoine de 359 à 94*, Paris: É. Bourgey, 1977.

———. "Les trouvailles monétaires dans le temple d' Artemis à Sardis (*IGCH* 1299 et 1300)." *RN* 33 (1991): 71–88 = *Études Le Rider* II, 821–839.

———. "Antiochos II à Mylasa." *BCH* 114 (1990): 543–551 = *Études Le Rider* II, 553–561.

———. "The Coinage of Philip II and the Pangaion Mines," in *Philip of Macedon*, edited by Hatzopoulos, M. B. and Louiza Loukopoulou, 10–12. Athens: Ekdotike Athenon, 1980.

———. "Contremarques et surfrappes dans l' antiquité grecque," in *Numismatique antique, Problèmes et méthodes. Actes du Colloque organisé à Nancy du 27 septembre au 2 octobre 1971, par l'université de Nancy II et l'université catholique de Louvain*, edited by J. M. Dentzer, Ph. Gautier, and et Hackens, 27–56. Nancy/Louvain: Peeters, 1975 = *Études Le Rider*, I, 211–240.

———. *Alexandre le Grand, Monnaie, Finances et Politique*, Paris: Presses Universitaires de France, 2003.

Le Rider, G., and F. de Callataÿ. *Les Séleucides et les Ptolémées: l' héritage monétaire et financier d' Alexandre le Grand.* Monaco: Rocher, 2006.

Lévêque, P. *Pyrrhos.* Bibliothèque des Écoles françaises d' Athènes et de Rome, fasc. 185. Paris: De Boccard, 1957.

Levy, Ed. "La monarchie macédonienne et le mythe d' une royauté démocratique." *Ktema* 3 (1978): 201–255.

Liampi, Katerini, "Zur Chronologie der sogenannten "anonymen' Makedonischen Münzen des späten 4. Jhs. v. Chr." *JNG* 36 (1986): 41–65.

———. "Der Makedonische Schild als propagandisches Mittel in der hellenistischen Zeit." *Meletemata* 10 (1990): 157–171.

———. *Der Makedonische Schild.* Bonn: Habelt, 1998.

———. "Die Einführung des Kultes des Zeus Eleutherios in Makedonien." *MDAI(A)* 117 (2002): 202–220.

Lichtenberger, A., K. Martin, H.-H. Nieswalt, and D. Salzmann (eds.). *Das Diadem der hellenist-*

ischen Herrscher, Überbagnem Transformation oder Neuschöpfnung eines Herrschaftszeichens?, Kolloquium von 30.–31. Januar 2009 in Münster. Bonn: Habelt, 2012.

Linders, Tullia, "Fallen Money and Broken Coins—Or When is a Coin Not a Coin?," in *Florilegium Numismaticum, Studia in Honorem U. Westermark edita*, Stockholm: Svenska Numismatica Föreningen, 1992, 255–258.

Lönnqvist, K. "Studies on the Hellenistic Coinage of Athens: The Impact of Macedonia on the Athenian Money Market in the 3rd century BC," in *Early Hellenistic Athens: Symptoms of a Change*, edited by J. Frösen, 119–212. Papers and Monographs of the Finnish Institute at Athens VI. Helsinki: Finnish Institute at Athens, 1997.

Lorber, C. *Amphipolis. The Civic Coinage in Silver and Gold.* Los Angeles: Numismatic Fine Arts International, 1990.

Lorber, C., and A. Houghton. "Antiochus III Hoard." *AJN* 21 (2009): 89–104.

Lukanc, I. *Les imitations des monnaies d' Alexandre le Grand et de Thasos*. Wetteren: Cultura, 1996.

Ma, J. *Antiochos III and the Cities of Western Asia Minor.* Oxford: University Press, 2000.

MacCredie, J. *Fortified Military Camps in Attika*, Hesperia Supplement 11. Princeton: ASCSA, 1966.

MacDonald, G. "Fixed and loose dies in ancient coinage," in *Corolla Numismatica: Numismatic Essays in Honour of B. V. Head*, edited by G. F. Hill, 178–188. London, H. Frowde, 1906.

MacKay, P. A. "Macedonian tetradrachms of 148–147 BC." *ANSMN* 14 (1988): 15–40.

Mamroth, A. "Die Silbermünzen des Königs Perseus." *ZfN* 38 (1928): 1–28.

———. "Die Silbermünzen des Königs Philippos V. von Makedonien." *ZfN* 40 (1930): 277–303.

Marcellesi, M.-C. "Commerce, Monnaies locales et monnaies communes dans les états hellénistiques." *REG* 113 (2000): 326–357.

Mari, M. "Le olimpie macedoni di Dion tra Archelao e l' et l' età romana." *RFIC* 126 (1998): 137–9.

Marinescu, C. *Making and Spending Money along the Bosporus: The Lysimachi Coinages minted by Byzantium and Chalcedon and their Socio-Cultural Context*, PhD Diss. New York: Columbia University, 1996.

Martin, T. R. "A Third-Century BC Hoard from Thessaly at the ANS (*IGCH* 168)." *ANSMN* 26 (1981): 51–77.

———. *Sovereignty and Coinage in Classical Greece*, Princeton, N. J.: University Press, 1985.

Masson, O. "Numismatique chypriote." *RN* 33 (1991): 69–70.

Mathisen, R. W. "The Activities of Antigonos Gonatas 280–77 BC and Memnon of Heracleia, *Concerning Heracleia*." *AncW* 1 (1978): 71–74.

———. "Antigonus Gonatas and the Silver Coinages of Macedonia *circa* 280–270 B.C." *ANSMN* 26 (1981): 79–124.

———. "The Administrative organization of Amphipolis in Early Antigonid Macedonia (c. 280–270 B.C.)." *SAN* 14.1 (1983): 10–12.

———. "The Administrative organization of Amphipolis in Early Antigonid Macedonia (c. 280–270 BC)." *SAN* 14.2 (1983): 24–27.

———. "The Administrative organization of Amphipolis in Early Antigonid Macedonia (c. 280–270 BC)." *SAN* 14.3 (1983): 44–46.

———. "Pan Heads and Poseidon Heads: Two Third-Century Macedonian Tetradrachm Types." *SAN* 16 (1985): 29–35.

Meadows, A. "Money, Freedom and Empire in the Hellenistic World," in *Money and Its Uses in the Ancient Greek World*, edited by A. Meadows and K. Shipton, 53–63. Oxford: Oxford University

Press, 2001.
———. "Amyntas, Side, and the Pamphylian Plain," in *Agoranomia: Studies in Money and Exchange Presented to John H. Kroll*, edited by P. van Alfen, 151–175. New York: The American Numismatic Society, 2006.
———. "The Eras of Pamphylia and the Seleucid Invasions of Asia Minor." *AJN* 21 (2009): 51–88.
Meadows, A., and C. Lorber. "Commerce ('Achaeus' Hoard), 2002 (*CH* 10.277)," in *Coin Hoards* X: *Greek Hoards*, edited by O. Hoover, A. Meadows, and U. Wartenberg, 115–151. New York: American Numismatic Society, 2010.
Mehl, A. "Δορίκτητος χώρα. Kritiscche Bemerkungen zum 'Speerwerb' in Politik und Völkerrecht der Hellenistische Epoche." *Ancient Society* 11–12 (1981): 183–212.
Merker, I. L. "The Silver Coinage of Antigonos Gonatas and Antigonos Doson." *ANSMN* 9 (1960): 39–52.
———. *Studies in Sea-Power in the Eastern Mediterranean in the Century following the Death of Alexander*. PhD diss. Princeton University, 1958.
Meritt, B. D. *The Athenian Year*. Sather Classical Lectures. Berkeley: University of California, 1961.
———. "Mid-Third Century Athenian Archons." *Hesperia* 50 (1981): 78–99.
Mettout, S. *Le monnayage de Persée, dernier roi des Macédoniens (179–168 av. J.-C.)*. Mémoire de maitrise préparé sous la direction de A. Laronde. June 1986.
Michailov, G. "La Thrace aux IVe et IIIe siècles avant notre ère." *Athenaeum* (1960): 33–43.
Mikalson, J. D. *Religion in Hellenistic Athens*. Berkeley: University of California Press, 1997.
Millett, P. "The Political Economy of Macedonia," in *A Companion to Ancient Macedonia* , edited by J. Roisman and I. Worthington, 472–504. Chisester/Malden: Wiley-Blackwell, 2010.
Mionnet, T. E. *Description des médailles antiques grecques et romaines*, vol. I, Paris 1806; Supplément, 1-9. Paris: N.P., 1819–37.
Mitsopoulou, Ch. *Το ιερό της Δήμητρας στην Κύθνο και το αττικό ελευσινιακό σκεύος*. 3 vols. (Athens: ΕΚΠΑ, 2007): 1079–99.
———. "Faisceaux et guirlandes, entre iconographie et réalité: images, gestes, rites et finances éleusiniennes," in *Rituels en image—images de rituel, Grèce, Rome, Égypte, Mésopotamie, Colloque international, Université de Genève, 12–14 mars 2015*, edited by F. Jaccotet-Muller. Forthcoming.
Morgan, J. D. "The Calendar and the Chronology of Athens." *AJA* 100 (1996): 395.
Mørkholm, O. *Early Hellenistic Coinage: From the Accession of Alexander to the Peace of Apamea (336–188 B.C.)*, edited by Philip Grierson and Ulla Westermark. Cambridge: Cambridge University Press, 1991.
———. "Some Reflections on the Production and use of Coinage in Ancient Greece." *Historia* 31 (1982): 290–305.
———. "The Behaviour of Dies in the Hellenistic Period," in *Actes du 9e Congrès international de numismatique, Berne, Septembre 1979. 1. Numismatique antique*, edited by T. Hackens and R. Weiller, 209–14. IAPN Special Publication 6. Louvain: IAPN, 1982.
———. "The Life of Obverse Dies in the Hellenistic Period," in *Studies in Numismatic Method presented to Philip Grierson*, edited by Brooke, C. N. L. *et al.*, 11–21. Cambridge/New York: Cambridge University Press, 1983.
Moutsopoulos, N., and N. Dimitrokallis. *Η Ελληνική ημισέληνος / Le croissant grec*. Athens: No Publisher, 1988.
Nachtergael, G. *Les Galates en Grèce et les Sôtéria de Delphes: recherches d' histoire et d' épigraphie*

hellénistiques, Bruxelles: Palais des Académies, 1977.

Newell, E. T. *The Coinages of Demetrius Poliorcetes*. London: Oxford University Press, 1927.

———. *The Coinage of the Eastern Seleucid Mints, from Seleucus I to Antiochus III*, New York: American Numismatic Society, 1977 (reprint).

———. *The Coinage of the Western Seleucid Mints from Seleucus I to Antiochus III*. ANS Numismatic Studies 4. New York: American Numismatic Society, 1978 (reprint).

Nicolet-Pierre, Hélène, and J. Kroll. "Athenian Tetradrachm Coinage of the Third Century B.C." *AJN* 2 (1990): 1–35.

Nilsson, Harald (ed.). *Florilegium Numismaticum. Studia in honorem U. Westermark Edita*. Stockholm: Svenska Numismatika Föreningen, 1992.

Noe, S. P. "The Corinth Hoard of 1938." *ANSMN* 10 (1962): 9–41.

Nollé, J. "Athena in der Schmiede des Hephaistos, Militär-. Wirtschafts-und sozialgeschichtliche Implikationen von Münzbildern." *JNG* 45 (1995): 51–77.

Olçay, N., and H. Seyrig. *Le trésor de Mektepini en Phrygie*. Paris: P. Geuthner, 1965.

Oliver, G. J. "The Politics of Coinage: Athens and Antigonus Gonatas," in *Money and its Uses in the Ancient Greek World*, edited by A. Meadows and K. Shipton, 35–52. Oxford: University Press, 2001.

Osborne, M. J. *Naturalisation in Athens*. Vol. II. Brussels: Paleis der Academiën, 1981–1983.

Özgen, E. and A. Davesne. "Le trésor d' Oylum Höyügü." *TCMAA*, 45–52.

Palagia, Olga, "Apollo allein bewaffnet," *LIMC* II.1, 196–7.

Panagopoulou, K. "Cross-Reading Images: Iconographic "Debates' between Antigonids and Ptolemies During the Third and Second Centuries BC." *Eulimene* 6–7 (2005–2006): 163–181.

———. "Silver as a Commodity in the Hellenistic Period." *BSA* 102 (2007): 315–343.

Papakontantinou-Diamantourou, Despoina, *Πέλλα* I, Athens 1971.

Paschides, P. "Ποσειδώνες και Αντίγονοι, Παρατηρήσεις στη νομισματική μαρτυρία για τη ναυτική δύναμη του Αντιγόνου Γονατά και του Αντιγόνου Δώσωνα." *Αρχαιογνωσία* 9 (1998): 233–257.

Pazaras, Th., and M. B. Hatzopoulos. "'Επίγραμμα ἀπό τή Βέροια τῶν Ἀντιγονιδῶν." *Τεκμήρια* 3 (1997): 71–77.

Petrakos, B. "Ἀνασκαφή Ραμνοῦντος." *ΠΑΕ* 1989 (1992): 31–34.

Picard, Ch. "Remarques sur les sculptures monumentales du sanctuaire d' Aléa Athéna à Tegée: II. Le côté oriental du temple." *REG* (1934): 385–420.

Picard, O. *Chalcis et la confédération eubéenne: étude de numismatique et d' histoire*, IVe–Ier siècle, Athènes: École française d' Athènes, Paris: De Boccard, 1979.

Pomtow, H. "Delphische Neufunde, Zur delphischen Archontentafel des III. Jhdts. (Neue Soterien- und Amphictyonen-Texte)." *Klio* 14 (1914/5): 265–320.

_________. "Die Kultstätten der 'anderer Götter' von Delphi." *Philologus* 71 (1912): 54.

Poulios, B. "Χρονολογημένη ελληνιστική κεραμεική από την Ανατολική Μακεδονία," in *Γ' Επιστημονική Συνάντηση γιά την ελληνιστική κεραμεική, Χρονολογημένα σύνολα—εργαστήρια, 24–27 Σεπτεμβρίου 1991, Θεσσαλονίκη*, 115–127. Athens: Βιβλ. της εν Αθήναις Αρχαιολ. Εταιρείας.

———. "Συμβολή στη μελέτη της χάλκινης νομισματοκοπίας των Αντιγονιδών από τον Αντίγονο Γονατά έως τους πρώτους χρόνους του Φιλίππου Ε΄." *ΑΔ* Α 56 (2001 [2006]): 237–295.

Préaux, Claire, *Le monde hellénistique: la Grèce et l' Orient (323–146 av. J.-C.)*. Paris 1978.
Price, M. J. "The Coinage of Philip II." *NC*[7] 89 (1979): 234–235.
———. *Coins of the Macedonians*. London: British Museum, 1974.
———. "Alexander's Reform of the Macedonian Regal Coinage." *NC* 142 (1982): 189–190.
———. "The Larissa, 1968 Hoard (*IGCH* 237)," in *Kraay-Mørkholm Essays: Numismatic Studies in Memory of C. M. Kraay and O. Mørkholm*, edited by G. Le Rider et al., 233–43. Louvain: Institut Supérieur d' Archéologie et d' Histoire de l' Art, Séminaire de Numismatique Marcel Hoc, 1989.
———. *The Coinage in the Name of Alexander the Great and Philip Arrhidaeus*. London/Zurich: British Museum/Swiss Numismatic Society, 1991.
Pritchett, W. K. *The Greek State at War* III, Berkeley, London: University of California Press, 1971.
Psôma, S. "Τὰς παλαιὰς πεντεδραχμίας: Un stratagème de Polyen et le monnayage d' argent des rois de Macédoine de 413 à 360 av. J.-C." *RN* 155 (2000): 123–36.
———. *Olynthe et les Chalcidiens de Thrace, Études de Numismatique et d' Histoire*, Stuttgart: Steiner, 2001.
Psôma, S., Ch. Karadima, and D. Terzopoulou. *The Coins from Maroneia and the Classical City at Molyvoti, A Contribution to the History of Aegean Thrace*. Meletemata 62. Athens: De Boccard, 2008.
———. "Numismatic Evidence on the Ptolemaic Involvement in Thrace during the Second Syrian War." *AJN* 20 (2008): 257–63.
———. "*Tas sitarchias kai tous misthous* ([Arist.], *Oec.* 1351b). Bronze Currencies and Cash-Allowances in Mainland Greece, Thrace and the Kingdom of Macedonia." *RBN* 45 (2009): 3–38.
———. "Profitable Networks: Coinages, Panegyris and Dionysiac Artists," in *Greek and Roman Networks in the Mediterranean*, edited by I. Malkin, C. Constantakopoulou, and K. Panagopoulou, 230–48. London: Routledge, 2009.
Reger, G. "The Date of the Battle of Kos." *AJAH* 10 (1985): [1993] 155–177.
———. "The Political History of the Kyklades, 260–200 BC." *Historia* 43 (1994): 32–69.
———. Review of J. J. Gabbert, *Antigonus II Gonatas*. *BMCR* (1988): 17 ff.
———. *Regionalism and Change in the Economy of Independent Delos*, 314–167 B.C. Berkeley: University of California Press, 1994.
———. "The Koinon of the Laodikeis in Karia." *EA* 30 (1998): 11–17.
———. "The Price Histories of Some Imported Goods on Independent Delos," in *Économie antique: Prix et formation des prix dans les économies antiques*, edited by J. Andreau, P. Briant, and R. Descat, 53–72. Entretiens d' archéologie et d' histoire. Saint-Bertrand-de-Comminges: Musée archéologique départemental, 1997.
Regling, K. *Die Münzen von Priene*. Berlin: H. Schoetz, 1927.
———. "Hellenistischer Münzschatz." *ZfN* (1928): 97–98.
Reinach, A. J. "Un monument delphien. L' Étolie sur les trophées gaulois de Kallion." *JIAN* 13 (1911): 177–240.
Rice, Elen E. *The Grand Procession of Ptolemy Philadelphus*. Oxford: University Press, 1983.
Riis, P. J. "L' activité de la Mission Archéologique Danoise sur la côté phénicienne en 1958." *AnnArch de Syrie* 8–9 (1958–9): 125–126.
Ripollès, P. P. "The X4 Hoard (Spain): Unveiling the Presence of Greek Coinages during the Second Punic War." *Israel Numismatic Research* 3 (2008): 51–64.
Ritter, H. W. "Zum Schild auf den Münzen des Ptolemaios Philadelphos und vervandten Denkmälern." *SM* 30 (1980): 33–39.

———. "Zur Sternsymbolik im Antigonidischen und Argeadischen Makedonien." *Archaiognosia* 2 (1981): 159–205.

Ritter, S. *Bildkontakte. Götter und Heroen in der Bildsprache griechischer Münzen des 4. Jahrhunderts v. Chr.* Berlin: Reimer, 2002.

Robertson, N. "The Decree of Themistokles in its Contemporary Setting." *Phoenix* 36 (1982): 1–44.

Rodriguez, P. "L' intervention ptolémaique dans la guerre de Chrémonidès au vu du monnayage lagide." *RN* 155 (2000): 9–16.

Roussel, P. "La fondation des Sôtéria de Delphes." *REA* 26 (1924): 97–111.

Sallet, A. von, "Erwerbungen des Königlichen Münzkabinets in den Jahren 1890–1897." *ZfN* 21 (1898): 202.

Salzmann, D. "Überlegungen zum Schild auf den Münzen des Ptolemaios Philadelphos und verwandten Denkmälern." *SM* 30 (1980): 33–9.

Scheu, F. "Coinage Systems of Aitolia." *NC*[6] 20 (1960): 37–52.

Schmidt, S. "A Group of Early Hellenistic Pottery from a Well in Eretria," in *Ε΄ Επιστημονική Συνάντηση για την Ελληνιστική Κεραμική*: Χρονολογικά προβλήματα—κλειστά σύνολα—εργαστήρια: Πρακτικά,*Chania, 6–13 April 1997*, 82. Athens, 2000.

Scholten, J. B. *The Politics of Plunder, The Aitolians and their Koinon in the Early Hellenistic Era, 279–217 BC.* Berkeley: University of California Press, 2000.

Schönert-Geiβ, E. "Die Wirtschafts- und Handelsbeziehungen zwischen Griechenland und der nördlichen Schwarzmeerküste im Spiegel der Münzfunde (6.–1. Jh. V. u. Z.)." *Klio* 53 (1971): 105–117.

Schmidt-Dounas, B. "Der dorische Fries der Stoa des Antigonos Gonatas auf Delos." *MDAI(A)* 109 (1994): 227–242.

Schubart, W. "Die ptolemäische Reichsmünze in den auswärtigen Besitzungen unter Philadelphos." *ZfN* 33 (1922): 74–82.

Schwabacher, W. "Some Unknown Federal Coins of the Akarnanians," in *Essays in Greek Coinage presented to Stanley Robinson*, edited by C. M. Kraay and G. K. Jenkins, 219–221. Oxford: Oxford University Press, 1968.

Sear, T. L. *Kallias of Sphettos and the Revolt in Athens in 286 BC.* Hesperia Supplement 17. Princeton, N. J.: American School of Classical Studies at Athens, 1978.

Segré, M. "La più antica tradizione sull' invasione gallica in Macedonia e in Grecia (280/79 a. Chr.)." *Historia* 1.4 (1927): 18–42.

Sergueenkova, V. "The Stylis of the Gold Coins of Alexander the Great." *NAC* 35 (2006): 165–178.

Seltman, C. T. *Athens: Its History and Coinage before the Persian Invasion.* Cambridge: Cambridge University Press, 1924.

———. "A Synopsis of the Coins of Antigonus I and Demetrius Poliorcetes." *NC* 9 (1909): 264–273.

Seyrig, H. *Trésors du Levant anciens et nouveaux.* Bibliothèque archéologique et historique 94, Trésors monétaires séleucides 2. Paris: P. Geuthner, 1973.

__________. "Monnaies Hellénistiques, 5, Philippe II ou les Bottiéens." *RN*[6] 5 (1963): 14–18.

Shear, T. L. *Kallias of Sphettos and the Revolt in Athens in 286 BC.* Hesperia, Supplement 17. Princeton, NJ: Princeton University Press, 1978.

Sheedy, K. "The Origins of the Second Nesiotic League and the Defence of Kythnos." *Historia* 45 (1996): 423–499.

Shipley, G. "Distance, Development, Decline? World-Systems Analysis and the 'Hellenistic' World," in *Center and Periphery in the Hellenistic World*, edited by Per Bilde, *et al.*, 276. Studies in Hellenistic Civilization 4. Aarhus: University Press, 1993.

———. *The Greek World after Alexander, 323–30 B.C.* London/New York: Routledge, 2000.

———. "Between Macedonia and Rome: Political Landscapes and Social Change in Southern Greece in the Early Hellenistic Period." *ABSA* 100 (2005): 316–330.

Simon, Erica, *LIMC* VII.1, s.v. "Poseidon."446–9.

Six, J. P. "Tetrachma Antigoneia." *Annuaire de numismatique* 6 (1882): 29–30.

———. "Monnaies grecques, inédites et incertaines." *NC*[3] 15 (1895): 176.

Smith, R. R. R. *Hellenistic Royal Portraits.* Oxford/New York: Clarendon Press/Oxford University Press, 1988.

Sorge, H. "Der Mond auf den Münzen von Athen." *JNG* 2 (1950/1): 7–13.

Starr, C. G. *Athenian Coinage 480–449 BC*, Oxford: Oxford University Press, 1970.

Stefanaki, V. *Κως* I. Athens: Archaiologiko Institouto Aigaiakon Spoudon/Tameio Arxaiologikon Poron kai Apallotrioseon, 2012.

Stephens, S. "Posidippus's Poetry Book: Where Macedon meets Egypt," in *Ancient Alexandria between Egypt and Greece*, edited by W. V. Harris and G. Ruffini, 63–86. Leiden/Boston: Brill, 2004.

Strack, M. L. and F. Münzer. *Die antiken Münzen von Thrakien.* Berlin: K. Reimer, 1912.

Svenson, Dominique, *Darstellungen hellenistischer Könige mit Götterattributen.* Archäologische Studien, vol. 10. Frankfurt: P. Lang, 1995.

Svoronos, J. "Εὕρημα Σοφικοῦ Ἐπιδαυρίας." *JIAN* 2 (1899): 289–96.

———. "Εὕρημα Σοφικοῦ Ἐπιδαυρίας." *JIAN* 10 (1907): 35–46.

———. *Trésor de la numismatique grecque ancienne, les monnaies d' Athènes.* Munich: F. Bruckmann, 1923–6.

———. *Τά νομίσματα τοῦ Κράτους τῶν Πτολεμαίων.* Athens: P. D. Sakellariou, 1904–1908.

———. "Stylides, ancres hierae, aphlasta, stoloi, akrostolia, embola, proembola et totems marins." *JIAN* (1914): 81–151.

Szabo, M. *Les Celtes de l' Est.* Paris: Errance, 1992.

Tarditi, C. "Archittettura come propaganda. Esame dell' attività edilizia degli Antigonidi in Grecia e nuove proposte di attribuzione." *Aevum Antiquum* 3 (1990): 43–74.

Tarn, W. W. "The Dedicated Ship of Antigonus Gonatas." *JHS* 30 (1910): 209–22.

———. *Antigonus Gonatas.* Oxford: Clarendon Press, 1913.

———. "Telokles and the Athenian Archons of 288/7–262/1 BC." *JHS* 40 (1920): 143–59.

Thomas, R. *Eine Postume Statuette Ptolemaios' IV. und ihr historischer Kontext.* Trierer Winckelmannsprogramme, Heft 18. Mainz: Philipp von Zabern, 2002.

Thompson, M. J. "The Mints of Lysimachos," in *Essays in Greek Coinage presented to Stanley Robinson*, edited by C. M. Kraay and G. K. Jenkins, 163–82. Oxford: Oxford University Press, 1968.

———. *Alexander's Drachm Mints* I. *Sardes and Miletus.* ANS NS 16. New York: American Numismatic Society, 1983.

———. *Alexander's Drachm Mints* II. *Lampsacus and Abydus.* ANS NS 19. New York: American Numismatic Society, 1991.

Thompson, M., O. Mørkholm, and C. M. Kraay. *An Inventory of Greek Coin Hoards.* New York: American Numismatic Society, 1973.

Tiverios, M. "Αισχύλος και Ελευσίνια Μυστήρια," in *Θυμέλη. Μελέτες χαρισμένες στον καθηγητή Ν.Χ. Χουρμουζιάδη*, edited by D. I. Jacob and E. Papazoglou, 410–26. Herakleio, 2004.

Touratsoglou, Y. *The Coin Circulation in Ancient Macedonia (ca. 200 B.C.–268 A.D.). The Hoard Evidence*. Athens: Hellenic Numismatic Society, 1993.

———. *Disjecta Membra. Two New Hellenistic Hoards from Greece*, (tr. Marion Tzamali). Athens: Hellenic Numismatic Society, 1996.

———. "Les Galates sous les pentes de l' Olympe: le trésor IV de Néo Pantéléimon, lieu-dit Krania." *RN* 162 (2006): 99–116.

Touratsoglou, Y. *A Contribution to the Economic History of Ancient Macedonia (6th–3rd Century BC)*. ΚΕΡΜΑ 2. Athens: Λυδία Λίθος, Society for the Study of Numismatics and Economic History, 2010.

Tracy, S. "A Fragmentary Inscription from the Agora Praising Ephebes." *Hesperia* 59 (1990): 543–547.

———. "Five Letter-Cutters of Hellenistic Athens (230–130 B.C.)." *Hesperia* 47 (1978): 244–268.

———. *Athens and Macedon: Attic Letter-Cutters of 300 to 229 BC*. Berkeley: University of California Press, 2003.

Troxell, Hyla A. *Studies in the Macedonian Coinage of Alexander the Great*. Numismatic Studies 21. New York: American Numismatic Society, 1997.

———. "The Peloponnesian Alexanders." *ANSMN* 17 (1971): 41–94.

———. "Arsinoe's Non-Era." *ANSMN* 28 (1983): 35–70.

Tsangari, Dimitra, *Corpus des monnaies d' or, d' argent et de bronze de la confédération Étolienne* Athens: Helicon, 2007.

Tzamalis, An. P. *Τα νομίσματα της νεώτερης Ελλάδας 1828–1979*. Athens: Νούμμιο, 1980.

Urban, R. *Wachstum und Krise des Achäischen Bundes: Quellenstudien zur Entwicklung des Bundes von 280 bis 222 v. Chr*. Wiesbaden: F. Steiner, 1979.

Usener, H. "Ein Epigramm von Knidos." *Rheinisches Museum N. F.* 29 (1874): 43–47.

Varoucha, I. "Chronique des fouilles et découvertes archéologiques en Grèce en 1956." *BCH* 81 (1957): 497.

———. *Epitymbion Christou Tsounta*. Athens: N.P., 1941.

Villaronga, L. "El denario roman pesado en los tesoros de la península Ibérica." *Scienze dell' Antichità, Storia—Archeologia—Antropologia* 11 (2001–2003): 557–565.

Virgilio, B. *Lancia, Diadema e Porpora. Il Re e la regalità ellenistica*. Studi ellenistici 11. Pisa/Rome: F. Serra, 2003.

Voegtli, H. "Der Schild des Philadelphos." *SM* 25.97 (1975): 2–3.

Voutyras, Em. "Le Culte de Zeus en Macédoine avant la conquête romaine," in *Rois, cités, nécropoles, Institutions, rites et monuments en Macédoine, Actes des Colloques de Nanterre (Décembre 2002): et d' Athènes (Janvier 2004)*, edited by A. M. Guimier-Sorbets, M. Hatzopoulos, and Y. Morizot, 333–345. Meletemata 45. Athens: De Boccard, 2006.

———. "Athéna dans les cités de Macédoine." *Kernos* 11 (1998): 111–129.

Waddington, W., E. Babelon, and Th. Reinach. *Recueil général des monnaies grecques d' Asie Mineure*. Paris: E. Leroux, 1904–1912.

Walbank, F. W. "Sea Power and the Antigonids," in *Philip II, Alexander the Great and the Macedonian Heritage*, edited by W. L. Adams, and E. N. Borza, 213–5. Washington, D.C.: University Press of America, 1982.

Wallace, W. P. *The Euboian League and its Coinage*. ANS NNM 134. New York: American Numismatic Society, 1956.

Wartenberg, U.. *After Marathon: War, Society and Money in Fifth-Century Greece*. London: British Museum Press, 1995.

Weil, R. "Histiaea-Oropos." *ZfN* 1 (1874): 189.

Weller, C. H. "The Cave at Vari, I, Description, Account of Excavation,and History." *AJA* 7 (1903): 263–288.

Welles, C. B. "Gallic Mercenaries in the Chremonidean War." *Klio* 52 (1970): 477–490.

West, A. B. The Early Diplomacy of Philip II of Macedon Illustrated by his Coins." *NC*[3] 3 (1923): 169–210.

Westermark, U. "Remarks on Regal Macedonian Coinage," in *Kraay-Mørkholm Essays: Numismatic Studies in Memory of C. M. Kraay and O. Mørkholm*, edited by G. Le Rider *et al.*, 301–315. Louvain: Institut Supérieur d' Archéologie et d' Histoire de l' Art, Séminaire de Numismatique Marcel Hoc, 1989.

———. "Apollo in Macedonia," in *Opus Mixtum: Essays in Ancient Art and Society*, edited by E. Rystedt, Ch. Scheffer, and Ch. Wikander, 149–54. Acta Instituti Romani Regni Sueciae, Stockholm: Paul Åström, 1994.

———. "The Staters of Archelaus. A Die Study," in *Essays in Honour of Robert Carson and Kenneth Jenkins,* edited by M. Price, A. Burnett, and R. Bland, 30–35. London: Spink, 1993.

———. *Das Bildnis des Philetairos von Pergamon: Corpus der Münzprägung*. Acta Universitatis Stockholmiensis, Stockholm Studies in Classical Archaeology 1. Stockholm: Almquist and Wiksell, 1961.

Wikander, C. "Pomp and Circumstance, The Procession of Ptolemaios II." *OAth* 19 (1992): 143–150.

Wilamowitz, U. von-Moellendorf. *Hellenistische Dichtung in der Zeit des Kallimachus*. Vol. II. Berlin: Weidmann, 1924.

Will, E. *Histoire Politique du Monde Hellénistique (323 av. J.-C.)*. 2 vols. Nancy: Presses Universitaires, 1979–1982.

Yakountchikoff, B. M. *Rare and Unpublished Greek Coins*. St. Petersburg, 1908.

Zimi, E., *Late Classical and Hellenistic Macedonian Silver Plate from Macedonia*. Oxford: Oxford University Press, 2011.

Indices

Coin Types

Control Marks

Symbols

Monograms

Letters

COIN LEGENDS

COUNTERMARKS AND OVERSTRIKES

Countermarks

Overstrikes

Hoards

HOARDS NOT IN *CH* OR *IGCH*

ANCIENT LITERARY SOURCES

Greek

INSCRIPTIONS AND PAPYRI

Personal Names

Toponyms and Ethnics

General

Plates

Period I: Gold with Types of Alexander III

Period I: Silver with Types of Alexander III

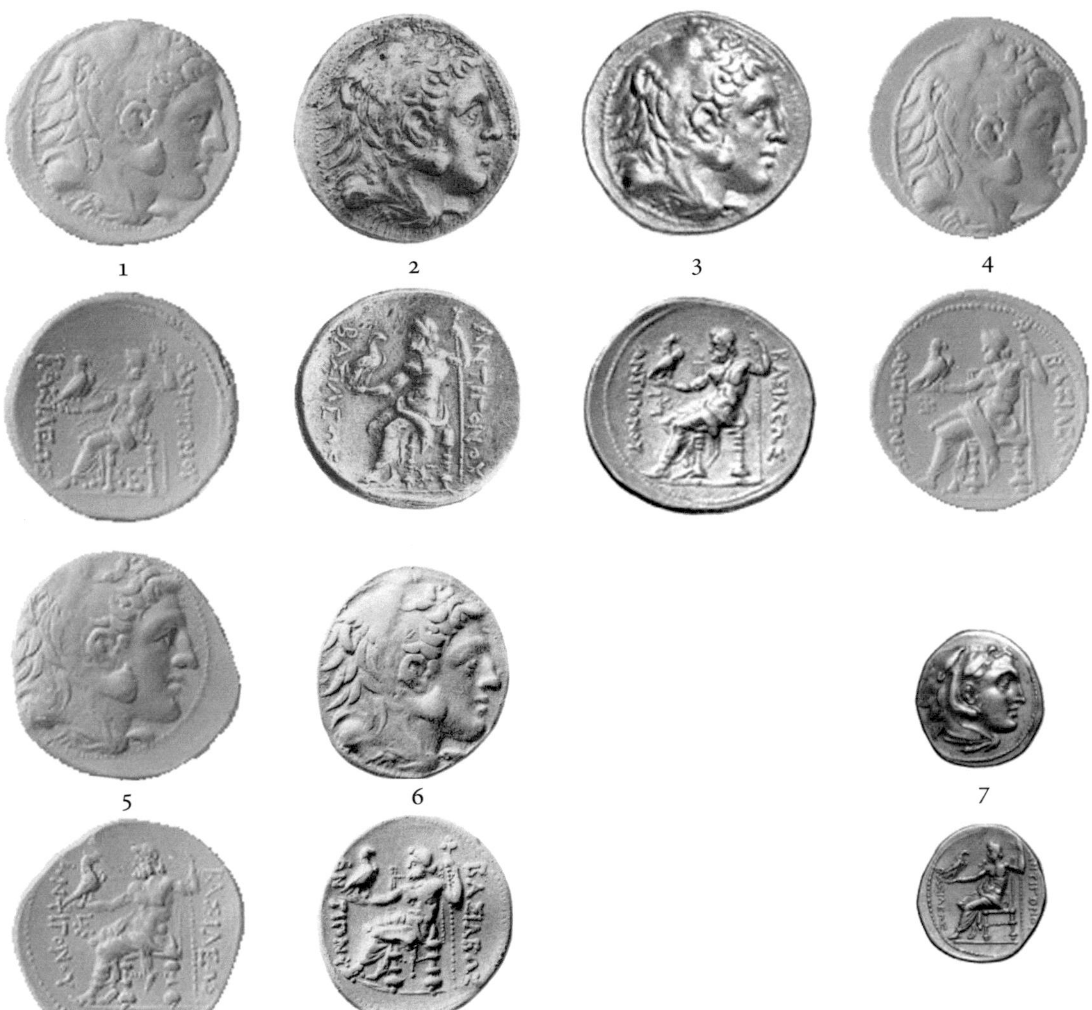

Period I: Silver with Individual Types

13

14

15

16

17

18

19

20

21

22

23

24

25 26 27 28

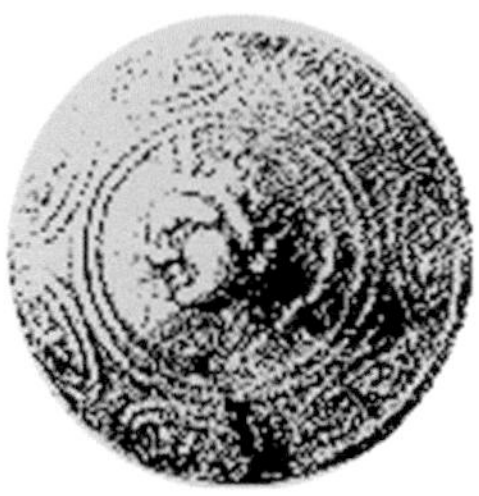

29 30 31 32

33 34 35 36

37 38 39 40

41 42 43 44

45 46 47 48

49

50

51

52

53

54

55

56

57

58

59

60

61 62 63 64

65 66 67 68

69 70 71 72

73 74 75 76

77 78 79 80

81 82 83 84

85 86 87 88

89 90 91 92

93 94 95 96

97

98

99

100

101

102

103

104

105

106

107

108

109 110 111 112

113 114 115 116

117 118 119 120

121 122 123 124

125 126 127 128

129 130 131 132

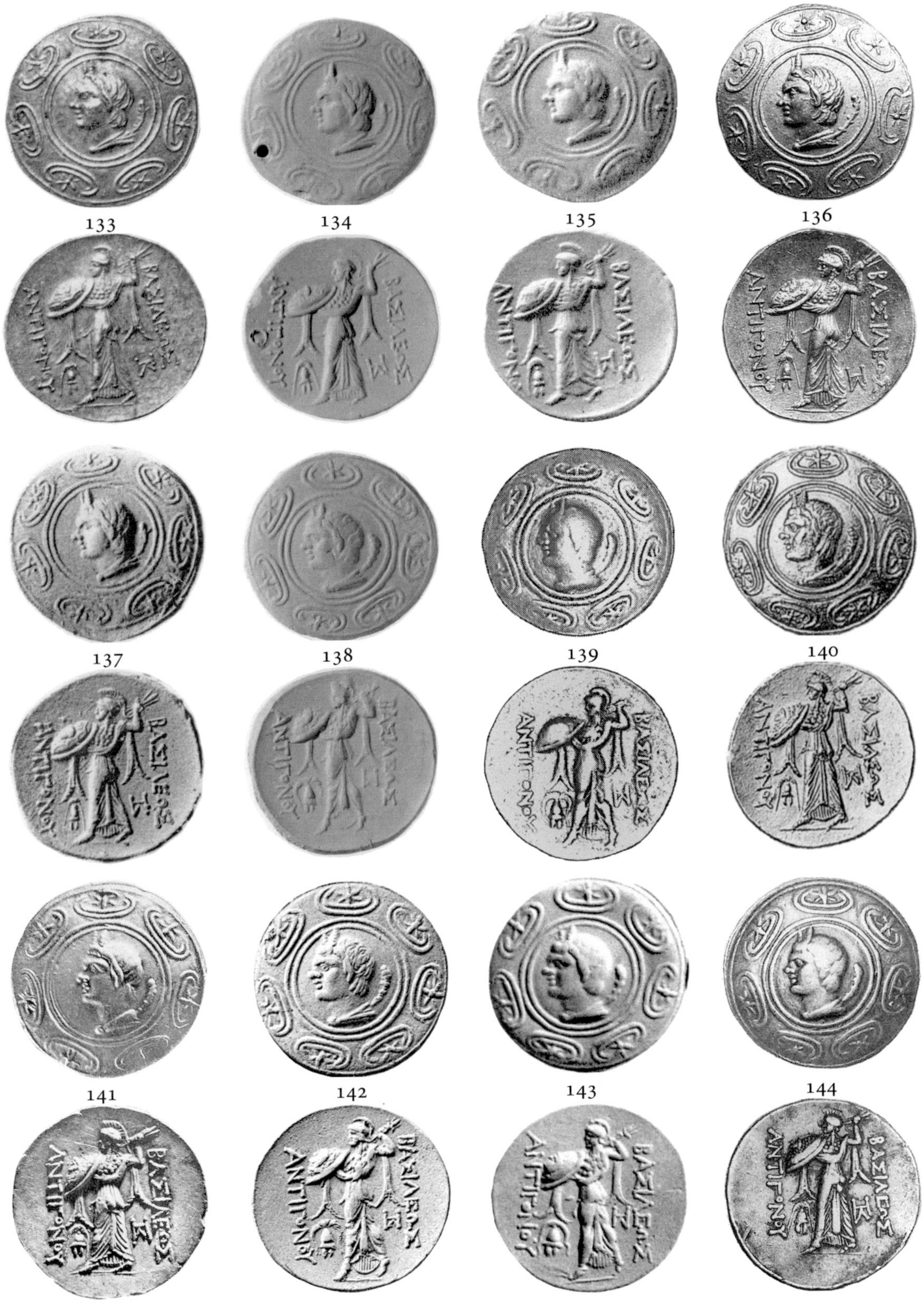

133 134 135 136

137 138 139 140

141 142 143 144

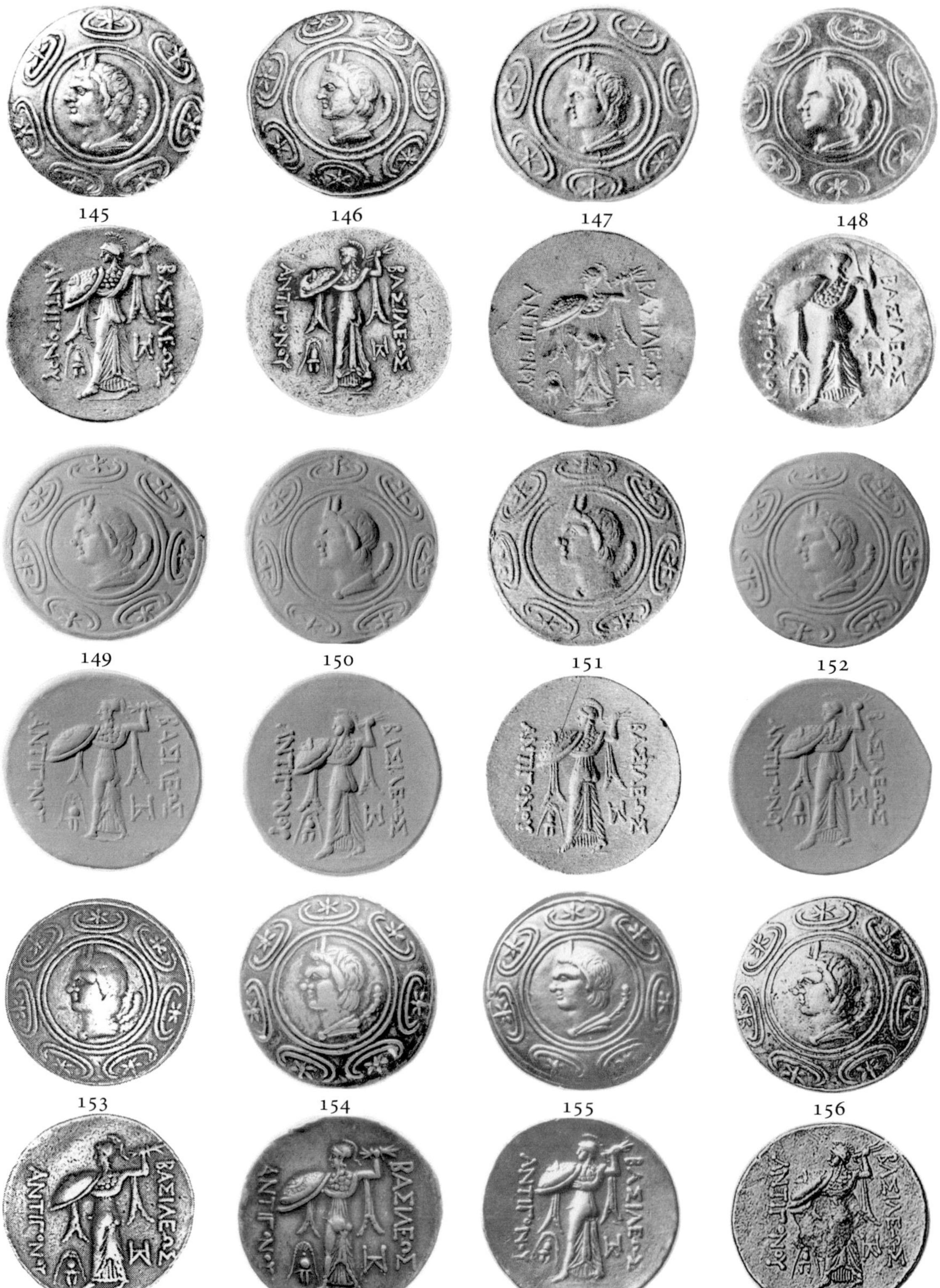

145 146 147 148

149 150 151 152

153 154 155 156

157 158 159 160

161 162 163 164

165 166 167 168

169 170 171 172

173 174 175 176

177 178 179 180

181

182

Period II: Silver with Individual Types

1 2 3 4

5 6 7 8

9 10 11 12

13 14 15 16

17 18 19 20

21 22 23 24

25 26 27 28

29 30 31 32

33 34 35 36

37

38

39

40

41

42

43

44

45

46

47

48

49 50 51 52

53 54 55 56

57 58 59 60

61 62 63 64

65 66 67 68

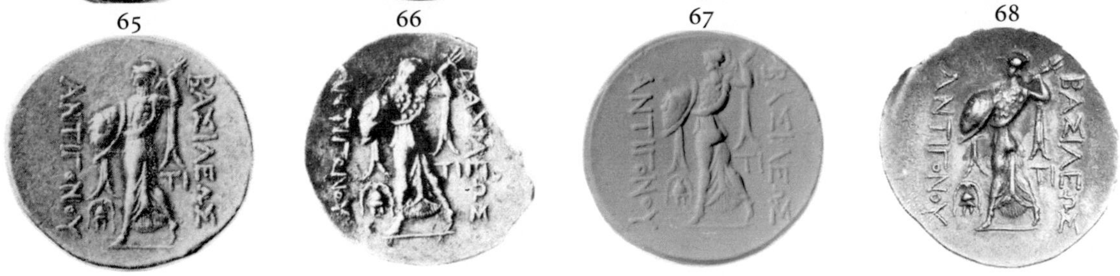

69 70 71 72

73 74 75 76

77 78

Period III: Silver with Individual Types

13 14 15 16

17 18 19 20

21 22 23 24

25

26

27

28

29

30

31

32

33

34

35

36

37 38 39 40

41 42 43 44

45 46 47 48

49 50 51 52

53 54 55 56

57 58 59 60

61 62 63 64

65 66 67 68

69 70 71 72

73

74

75

76

77

78

79

80

81

82

83

84

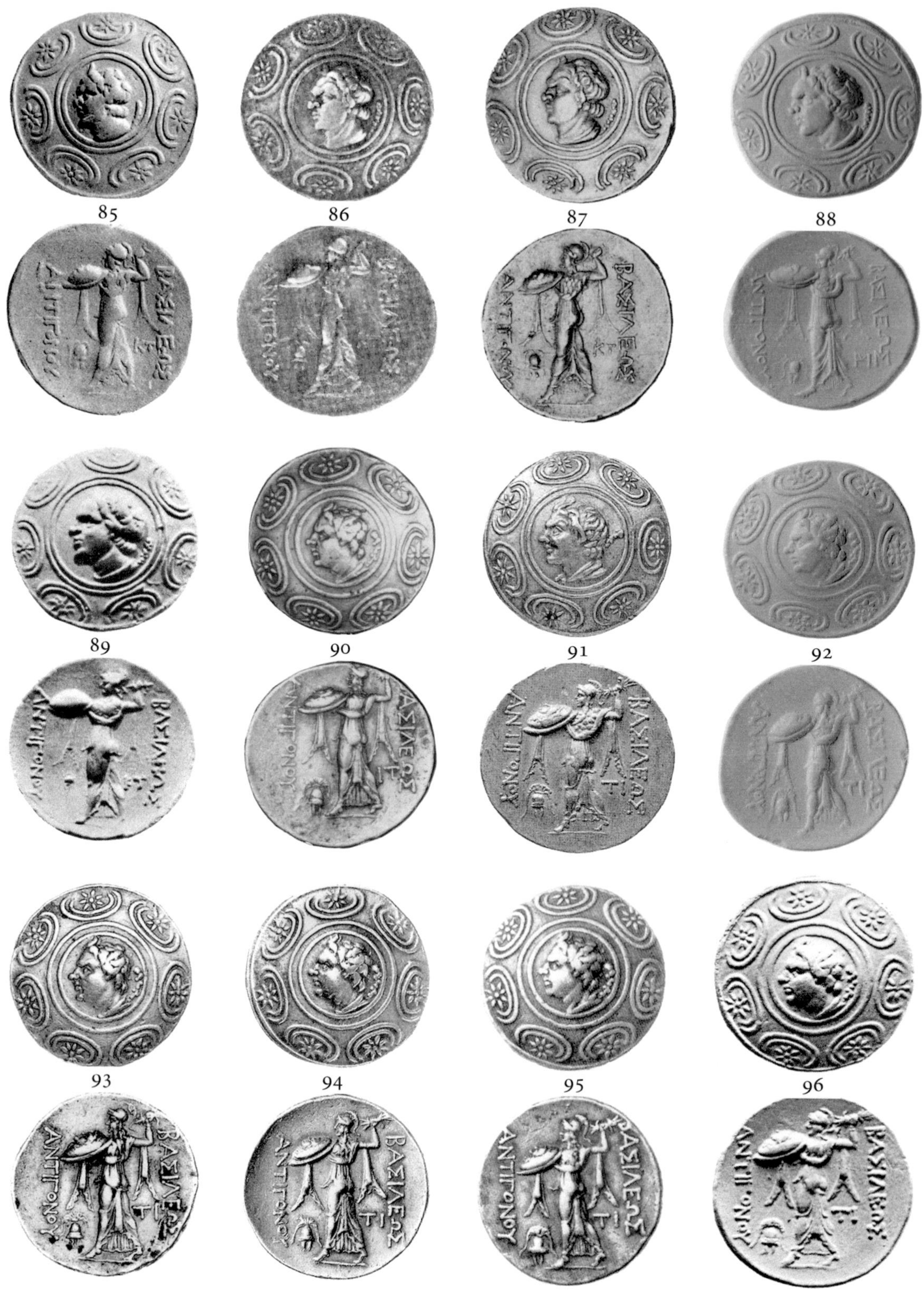
85
86
87
88
89
90
91
92
93
94
95
96

97

98

99

100

101

102

103

104

105

106

107

108

109 110 111 112

113 114 115 116

117 118 119 120

121 122 123 124

125 126 127 128

129 130 131 132

133 134 135 136

137 138 139 140

141 142 143 144

145 146 147 148

149 150 151 152

153 154 155 156

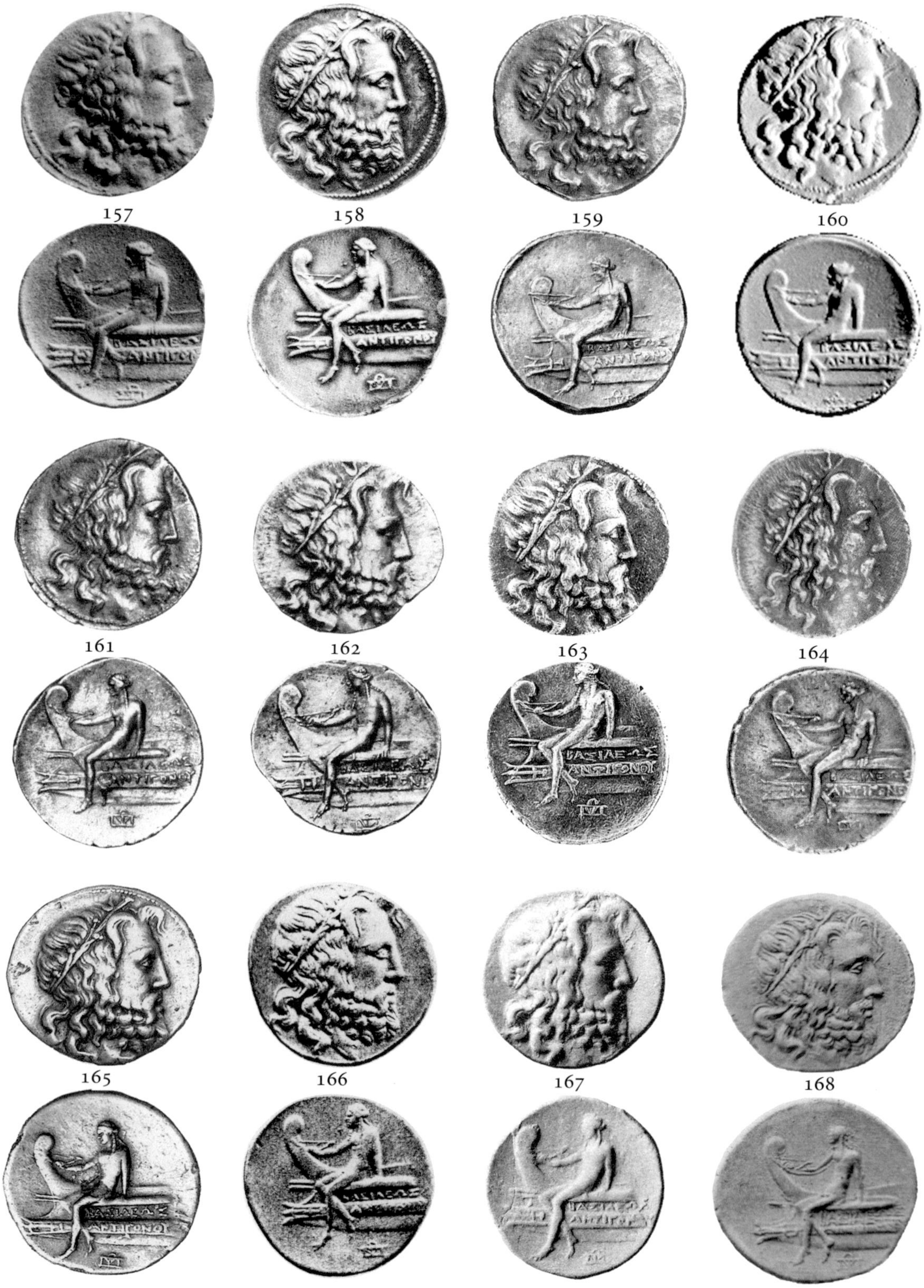

157 158 159 160

161 162 163 164

165 166 167 168

169

170

171

172

173

174

175

176

177

178

179

180

181 182 183 184

185 186 187 188

189 190 191 192

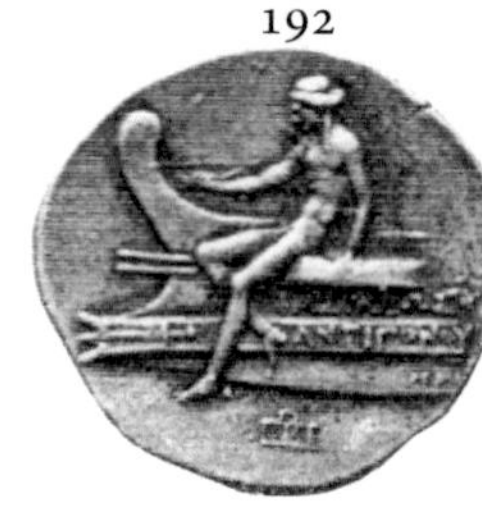

193

194

195

196

197

198

199

200

201

202

203

204

205

206

207

208

209

210

211

212

213

214

215

216

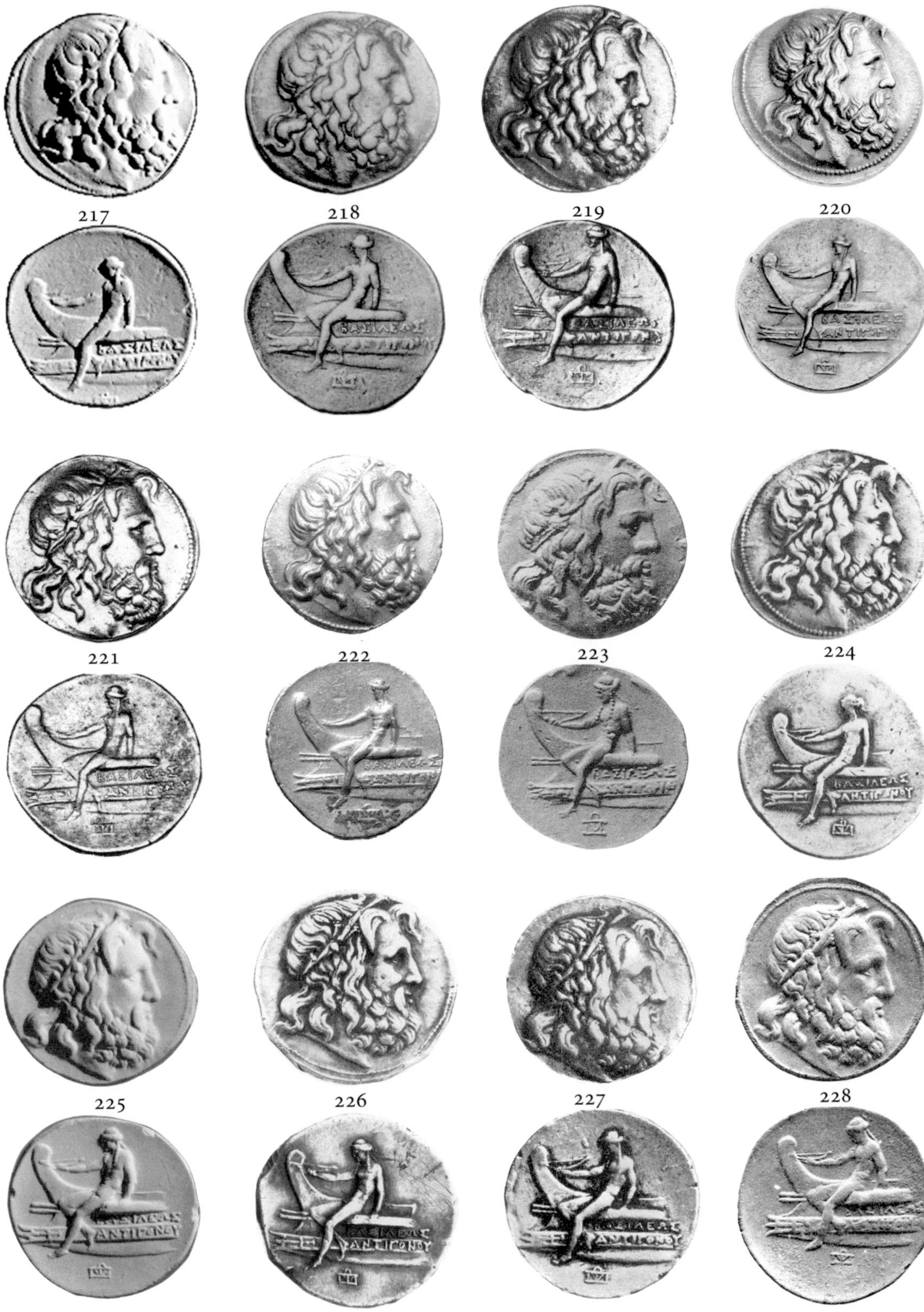

217 218 219 220

221 222 223 224

225 226 227 228

229

230

231

232

233

234

235

236

237

238

239

240

241 242 243 244

245 246 247 248

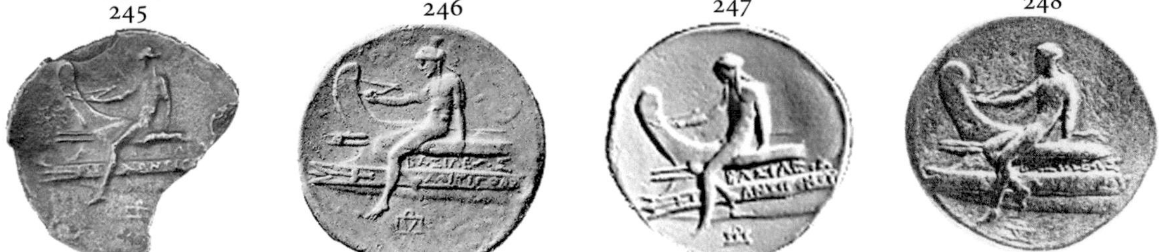

249 250 251 252

253

254

255

256

257

258

259

260

261

Period IV: Silver with Individual Types

1 2 3 4 5 6 7 8 9 10 11 12

13
14
15
16
17
18
19
20
21
22
23
24

25

26

27

28

29

30

31

32

33

34

35

36

37

38

39

40

41

42

43

44

45

46

47

48

49 50 51 52 53 54 55 56 57 58 59 60

61

62

63

64

65

66

67

68

69

70

71

72

73

74

75

76

77

78

79

80

81

82

83

Smaller Denominations

84

85

86

87

88

89

90

91

92

93

94

95

Ancient Counterfeits

1 2 3 4

5

Overstrike

1

Countermarks

Ancient Imitations

1

2

3

4

5

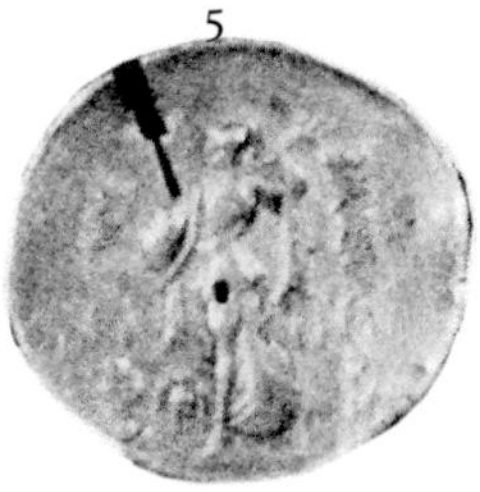

6

7

8

9

10

11

12

Imitations

13

14

15

16

17

Modern Imitations

13 14 15 16

17 18 19 20

II. Modern 20-drachma coin of the Democracy Series
(1930s, Bank of Greece Numismatic Collection)

Comparanda

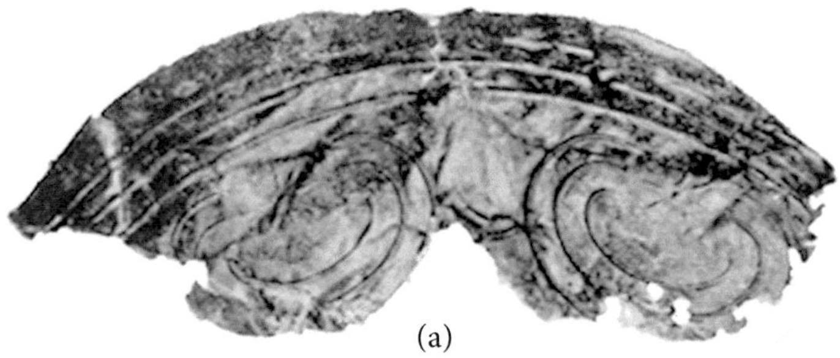

(a)

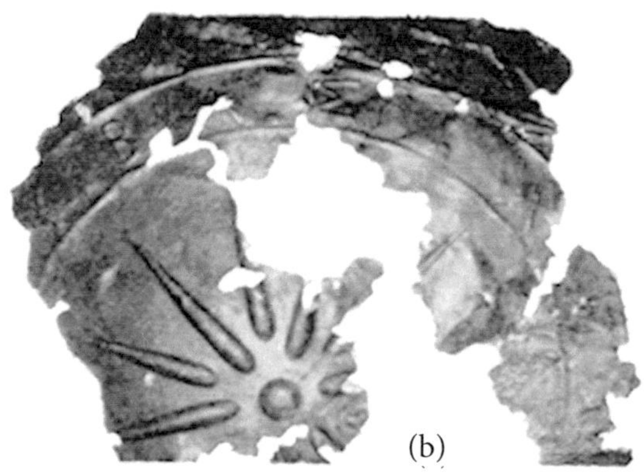

(b)

(c)

Map. Hoard Distribution: Hoards with Pan Head and Poseidon Head Specimens (3^{d} - 2nd centuries B.C.)